Research Instruments in Social Gerontology

Volume 1

Clinical and Social Psychology

Research Instruments in Social Gerontology

Edited by David J. Mangen and Warren A. Peterson

The editors and the University of Minnesota Press gratefully acknowledge the assistance of the U.S. Administration on Aging through contract number HEW 105-76-3107 and grant number HEW AoA 90-A-1370 to the Institute for Community Studies at the University of Missouri—Kansas City and grant number 90-AR-0024-01 to the Minnesota Family Study Center at the University of Minnesota. Without the assistance of the Administration on Aging, this project would not have been possible.

Research Instruments
in Social Gerontology

Volume 1

Clinical
and Social
Psychology

Editors
David J. Mangen
Warren A. Peterson

With the assistance of
Toshi Kii and Robert Sanders

UNIVERSITY OF MINNESOTA PRESS

MINNEAPOLIS

Library of Congress Cataloging in Publication Data (Revised)
Main entry under title:

Research instruments in social gerontology.

Includes index.
Contents: —v. 1. Clinical and social psychology—v. 2. Social roles and
social participation.
1. Gerontology—Research—Addresses, essays, lectures—Collected works.
2. Aging—Psychological aspects—Research—Addresses, essays, lectures—
Collected works. 3. Aged—Socioeconomic status—Research—Addresses,
essays, lectures—Collected works. I. Mangen, David J. II. Peterson,
Warren A., 1922-   . [DNLM: 1. Aged. 2. Social welfare—United States.
3. Sociology. 4. Health services research—United States. WT 30 R433]
HQ1061.R44   305.2′6   81-16449
ISBN 0-8166-0991-8 (v.1)   AACR2
ISBN 0-8166-1096-7 (v.2)
ISBN 0-8166-1112-2 (v.3)

HQ1061
.R44
1982
v.1

Contents

Preface

Research Instruments in Social Gerontology: Clinical and Social Psychology is the first volume in a three-volume series designed to serve the needs of researchers, evaluators, and clinicians in assessing the instruments used in the field of aging. The length of this series and the amount of work involved in preparing the manuscript have greatly exceeded our original estimates. Over 400 measures are reviewed in the three volumes, with topics ranging from formal demography to intelligence and personality. The measures reviewed in volume 1, *Clinical and Social Psychology*, focus on the cognitive reactions to aging of older people and on the assessments of their own and other persons' aging made by people who are not yet old. This volume also contains the series introduction (Chapter 1), which explains the methods we used for evaluating the instruments; Chapter 1 also includes our overall assessment of the status of gerontological measurement today.

The increasing size of the aging population in the United States has brought a corresponding increase in interest about the processes of aging and the effectiveness of social programs for the elderly. Now more than ever before, researchers require conceptually explicit instruments designed to assess individual and social behaviors, attitudes, and traits in the aging population. Measures are needed to help construct effective programs of social assistance and to evaluate those programs. It was in this spirit that we undertook this project, and, on the whole, we feel that our efforts have been successful. To be sure, not every researcher will be able to find in this collection instruments ideal for his or her purposes. Indeed, such uncritical adoption of existent measures would reflect an intellectual stagnation that would endanger the growth of aging as a field of inquiry. We hope that *Research Instruments in Social Gerontology* will serve as a benchmark, helping the researcher who is developing measures to avoid reinventing the wheel. We also hope that our efforts will alert researchers to the necessity of clearly specifying their constructs and the differences between those constructs and other related measures. In short, we hope that our efforts will encourage researchers to use a theoretical basis—either deductively, inductively, or retroductively derived—in developing new measures.

However, many researchers may find useful measures through the reviews in these volumes. This collection of information about the instruments appropriate for work in aging should alleviate the burden of making a literature search. Still, the user of existing measures must recognize the implicit and explicit theoretical bases of an existing measure and contribute to knowledge about that measure. He or she should examine its reliability and validity and report those data in published accounts of the project. Each use of a measure constitutes only one case in the scientific development of a measure, and the importance of developing a cumulative body of knowledge about the use of measures in diverse populations and environments cannot be overstated. Responsibility for the scientific development of a measure lies not only with the original authors, but also with those who choose to use it.

In the interest of promoting the continued development of existing measures, the precise development of new ones, and the ready dissemination of all measures, one of us (the senior editor, David Mangen) will continue compiling and evaluating measures. We also hope to update *Research Instruments in Social Gerontology* sometime in the future, a task that the community of scholars involved in aging can ease through correspondence about their development and use of instruments. Undoubtedly, some instruments have escaped our attention. We intended to exclude no instrument, and we apologize for any oversights that may have occurred. Correspondence with the senior editor will ensure that these omissions will be rectified in the second edition, and his effort will be assisted if such correspondence includes the sorts of information contained within the instrument reviews, together with copies of reprints, complete bibliographies, and research instruments.

We have been blessed with a high degree of cooperation from many persons throughout the life of this project. First, we thank the authors of the instruments who graciously provided us with information about their work and who allowed us to reproduce their materials. The journals and publishers who gave us permission to quote extensively from their publications have acted as true partners in the scientific process by recognizing both the utility of our work and the limitations of our budget. We thank them for their assistance.

A special note of thanks is due the members of the administrative committee for the project; they helped us develop the outline for the volumes and the methods for evaluating the instruments. We are further indebted to these esteemed colleagues—Donald McTavish of the University of Minnesota, Harold Orbach of Kansas State University, Edward Powers of Iowa State University, and Ethel Shanas of the University of Illinois, Chicago Circle—for their assistance in finding appropriate contributing authors for the chapters. Furthermore, they used their own professional contacts to alert the discipline about the existence and importance of this project.

The individual chapter authors undertook a task that seemed to grow and expand every day. Their efforts at searching the literature were monumental; indeed, some of their original contributions could almost qualify as books on their own. An enormous amount of editing was required to produce a manageable manuscript. We hope that we have not distorted their conclusions in the editorial process. Many of the contributors have pointed out that additional instruments have already emerged while we were editing. Unfortunately, we had to close off substantive revisions in order to finish the manuscript. To the chapter authors, therefore, we extend a hearty thank you. Your long efforts and devotion to detail were impressive, and the collegial bonds that developed remain a source of pleasure for us.

As is always the case with a massive undertaking such as this one, a number of people have provided vital assistance. Toshi Kii, now of Georgia State University, was one of the original research associates for the project, as well as a chapter author. His assistance in developing the topical outline for the books and the format for evaluation must be acknowledged. After the initial chapter contributions were received and while the three-part editorial process was underway, Robert Sanders was in charge of disseminating information about our work on research instruments to scholars who wanted information prior to this publication. He, together with Julie Edgerton, was responsible for most of the work involved in securing permissions to use copyrighted materials. These were no small tasks in a project of this magnitude. Sanders and Edgerton were ably assisted by Nellie Lynde, the project secretary during the Kansas City phase of the project.

After the project was transferred to the University of Minnesota, two persons provided a good deal of assistance. Robert Leik, director of the Minnesota Family Study Center, arranged for clerical and secretarial support for preparing the final proposal to the Administration on Aging. After that proposal was approved, Pamela Adelmann joined the project staff. Nominally she was the project's secretary, but functionally she was a research associate who helped document sources, obtain copyrights, and conduct literature searches; she also prepared much of the final manuscript. To all of these people we extend our thanks.

The Administration on Aging of the U.S. Department of Health and Human Services has provided financial assistance through contract number HEW 105-76-3107 and grant number HEW AoA 90-A-1370 to the Institute for Community Studies of the University of Missouri—Kansas City and grant number 90-AR-0024-01 to the Minnesota Family Study Center of the University of Minnesota. A special note of thanks is due to David Dowd, the project officer throughout the life of the project.

Research Instruments in Social Gerontology is a product of the Midwest Council for Social Research on Aging, an interuniversity group of scholars devoted to increasing knowledge about aging. We would like to dedicate our efforts to the memory of two colleagues on the Midwest Council, Arnold Rose and Leonard Breen.

David J. Mangen
Los Angeles, California
Warren A. Peterson
Kansas City, Missouri

How to Use These Volumes

Almost every chapter in these books is composed of three parts. The first part is a concise narrative review of the major theoretical concerns and measurement strategies within that research domain. The second part of each chapter is a collection of abstracts. Each abstract presents a conceptual definition and a description of a specific instrument, together with data about samples, reliability, validity, scaling properties, and correlations with age. Each abstract concludes with a list of references and, when the instrument is reproduced, a code number referring the reader to the instrument itself. The instruments themselves constitute the third part of each chapter. For a variety of reasons, not every abstract includes a separate instrument. At times, we were unable to secure permission to reproduce a copyrighted instrument. Other times, the length of an instrument precluded its publication. This was a difficult editorial decision to make, but it was one that was necessary in order to limit this work to three volumes.

The code numbers on the instruments reproduced in the section at the end of each chapter consist of four parts. The first part refers the reader to the volume in the three-volume series; the three volumes are represented by V1, V2, and V3. The second part of the code number refers to the chapter that reviews the instrument. Usually, the instrument is presented within the same chapter and volume. Occasionally, however, instruments are conceptually relevant to several chapters, and cross-referring is necessary. The third part of each code number is a roman numeral that refers to a subtopic of the general concept reviewed in the chapter. The final part of each code number is a letter code that is sequential after each roman numeral. The roman numerals and letter codes correspond to the codes listed in the tables at the ends of the narrative reviews. The coding system is strictly hierarchical; for example, the code number V1.4.II.b refers to the first volume, the fourth chapter (by Kahana, Fairchild, and Kahana), subtopic II on hypothetical problems in measurement techniques. Instrument b is the ECRC Coping Scale. (See Table 4-1.)

Some research instruments are missing from the instrument sections. This may be due to problems with copyrights or length or the necessity of using cross-references. Often, however, the simplest way to describe a very brief research instrument was to include the instrument in the abstract. When this is the case, a reference is usually made to the appropriate section of the abstract.

We recommend that readers review chapter narratives first and then go on to the abstracts. Only after the first two parts of the chapters have been read will the contents of the instruments sections be meaningful.

Contributors to Volume 1

Linda M. Breytspraak
Department of Sociology
University of Missouri — Kansas City
Kansas City, Missouri

Neal E. Cutler
Andrus Gerontology Center
University of Southern California
Los Angeles, California

Carol J. Dye
Veterans' Administration Hospital
St. Louis, Missouri

Thomas Fairchild
Center for Studies in Aging
North Texas State University
Denton, Texas

Linda K. George
Center for the Study of
  Aging and Human Development
Duke University
Durham, North Carolina

Gunhild O. Hagestad
Individual and Family Studies
Pennsylvania State University
University Park, Pennsylvania

Boaz Kahana
Department of Psychology
Oakland University
Rochester, Michigan

Eva Kahana
Department of Sociology
Wayne State University
Detroit, Michigan

Donald G. McTavish
Department of Sociology
University of Minnesota
Minneapolis, Minnesota

David J. Mangen
Andrus Gerontology Center
University of Southern California
Los Angeles, California

Ron Manuel
Department of Sociology
Howard University
Washington, D.C.

Victor W. Marshall
Department of Behavioural Science
University of Toronto
Toronto, Ontario

Warren A. Peterson
Institute for Community Studies
University of Missouri — Kansas City
Kansas City, Missouri

Robert Sanders
University of Missouri — Kansas City
Kansas City, Missouri

William J. Sauer
Graduate School of Business
University of Pittsburgh
Pittsburgh, Pennsylvania

Rex Warland
Department of Agricultural Economics
and Rural Sociology
Pennsylvania State University
University Park, Pennsylvania

Paul G. Windley
Department of Architecture
Kansas State University
Manhattan, Kansas

Research Instruments in Social Gerontology

Volume 1

Clinical and Social Psychology

Chapter 1

Introduction

David J. Mangen, Warren A. Peterson, and Robert Sanders

In 1976 the Midwest Council for Social Research in Aging (MCSRA) was awarded a contract from the U.S. Administration on Aging "to gather and analyze research protocols, instruments, and measurement scales used in the field of aging" (AoA, 1976). The functions of this project were to compile and evaluate instruments and to establish a handbook of measurement.

The need for such a handbook arises from the recent increase in research and the proliferation of measurement devices in the field of aging. This increase in information has made it difficult for people working in the field to keep up with current developments; moreover, research projects tend to have limited time schedules that can preclude the exchange of information necessary for developing cumulative research strategies. As a result, researchers often devise their own instruments, and general knowledge in the field becomes fragmented. Even when a researcher does want to use previously developed instruments, it is difficult to unearth all of the relevant theoretical and empirical evidence needed for judging their appropriateness to the research being planned. The MCSRA was commissioned to develop this handbook in order to meet the needs of researchers in aging.

For us to accomplish this mission, it became necessary to direct our efforts toward two fundamental goals. First the compilation of research instruments had to be undertaken. In this the principal question was one of developing an overall conceptual structure to guide the collection of instruments. Second, it was necessary to define a rigorous and relevant set of criteria against which instruments could be evaluated and to organize these criteria into a consistent framework for the evaluation of instruments.

The Conceptual Structure of the Field of Aging

Social gerontology exhibits a very complex conceptual structure, which reflects the interdisciplinary nature of gerontology, the levels of analysis implied by the different disciplines, and the policies of government on all levels concerning the delivery of services and the administration of programs. Our initial efforts at developing an appropriate conceptual structure involved a review of previously published compendiums on aging research (e.g., Binstock and Shanas, 1976; Riley et al., 1968, 1969, 1972; Tibbetts and Donahue, 1962). After our review, we formulated one basic level of differentiation within which further subdivision would be possible. This basic differentiation reflected a macroscopic-microscopic continuum ranging from the demography of aging (on the macro end of the continuum) to personal adjustment and psychological characteristics (on the micro end of the continuum), with analyses of social roles, perceptions of aging, and policy research in the middle.

We have retained this differentiation as an organizing vehicle for this three-volume series. Volume 1 is, in general, concerned with the microscopic issues of clinical and social psychology; volume 2 addresses the measurement of role participation and role structure; and volume 3 reviews instrumentation in the areas of demography, social policy, and health.

Previous Inventories of Instruments

In undertaking this inventory of research instruments, our primary goal was to establish a reference source that would summarize the characteristics of instruments in a succinct manner. Which characteristics to include, and in how much detail presented another issue of concern. In attempting to resolve this issue, we reviewed several other compilations of research instruments.

Other areas of social science have found that compendiums of research instruments can help researchers. Psychology (McReynolds, 1968, 1971, 1975; Chun, Cobb, and French, 1975), family sociology (Straus, 1969; Straus and Brown, 1978), child development (Johnson and Bommarito, 1971), mental health (Comrey, Backer, and Glaser,

1973), and attitude researchers (Shaw and Wright, 1967) have profited from the easy availability of measurement handbooks. The hand books vary in the extent of the summaries they provide and the detail to which they report psychometric properties.

More sociologically oriented research instruments have been compiled by Miller (1970) and Bonjean, Hill, and McLemore (1967). Miller's compendium of research instruments and research design emphasizes using research instruments within the context of a good research design. Bonjean and associates have organized over 2,000 scales and indexes into 78 categories of research interest and presented detailed descriptions of 50 frequently used scales.

Robinson and associates (Robinson, Rusk, and Head, 1968; Robinson, Athanasiou, and Head, 1969; Robinson and Shaver, 1973) have assessed attitude measurement in the areas of politics, occupations, and social psychology. Their three volumes represent perhaps the most extensive effort at compiling research instruments, especially insofar as these volumes include an evaluative component. Their reviews include detailed descriptions of the instruments, a summary of the measurement properties of the instruments, the conceptual framework used in the development of the instruments, and the actual measurement devices.

Since we wanted both to compile and to evaluate research instruments in aging, we decided to follow a relatively structured review form. This provided a uniform outline for the reviews and allowed for the explicit delineation of conceptual, descriptive, psychometric, and general evaluative information. The form we developed borrows heavily from the work of Robinson and associates (1968, 1969, 1973), but it was modified to include additional data relevant to our specific concern with aging.

The Criteria for Instrument Assessment

Measurement Theory

Measurement theorists invariably stress the importance of using properly specified theoretical constructs. Torgerson (1958), following the lead of Margenau (1950), suggested that "all constructs must possess constitutive meaning" (1958, p. 5). This is to say that a construct must be located within a theoretical domain. Measurement then becomes the process of assigning epistemic definitions, or rules of correspondence, between constructs and empirical indicators. Given the primacy of conceptualization within this process, the necessity of locating a research instrument within a theoretical, conceptual, and research domain is obvious.

The implications of theory for the process of measurement extend, as a result, to the specific form and content of empirical indicators as well. Nunnally (1967, pp. 31-32) has presented a typical three dimensional data matrix in which objects (or subjects, persons) are arranged on one dimension, stimuli (or questions) are arranged on a second dimension, and responses are arranged on a third dimension. This relatively simple data matrix constitutes a very difficult scaling problem, one that is simplified when only two dimensions are in the matrix. Thus, much research constrains the response dimension so that each individual can give only one response to each stimulus. The resultant two-dimensional matrix is much more amenable to a variety of scaling models. If, however, the theoretical concerns of the researcher are such that additional dimensions of the data matrix are needed, and constraining dimensions to being equal is not a viable strategy, then the scaling model becomes much more difficult. Among the plausible dimensions of theoretical interest to researchers on aging are the following.

1. Stimulus Targets: Researchers may be interested in varying the target to which a given stimulus is applicable. For example, researchers interested in friendship networks might want information concerning the age, sex, and marital status of the respondents' friends. Each friend then constitutes a target to which the stimulus "what is your friend's age" is applied.

2. Research Context: If the theoretical concerns dictate the examination of markedly different social and environmental contexts, then stimuli that are influenced or determined by the context may be inappropriate for part of the measurement model. As an example of this factor, consider the question of rural-urban differences in the utilization of medical care facilities. Though such facilities are geographically proximal in urban areas, they may be quite distant in the rural environment. However, an equal geographic distance in the two contexts may be interpreted differently. Five miles in the urban setting might be cognitively "more distant" than twenty rural miles.

3. Age, Period, and Cohort: In theory, researchers on aging are sensitive to the complexities that time interjects into conceptual analyses of phenonema. Though researchers are aware of the theoretical issues in the study of aging, the nuances inherent in measurement are only now being explored. For example, if research hypothesized the existence of a unidimensional construct called marital satisfaction, of which child socialization is seen as one component, one would expect that the indicator of child socialization would load on a single factor with other indicators of marital satisfaction. If, however, the research is longitudinal, it becomes feasible to ask whether child socialization activities continue to be a component of marital satisfaction at later stages of life. An attempt to replicate the original scaling model later could reveal significant changes in the phenomenon of marital satisfaction, in that child socialization may not load on the factor. This would suggest that the nature of the construct has changed while leaving unanswered the question of the couple's level of satisfaction. In a different but related vein, the cross-sectional relationship of age cohort with education may be such that complex stimuli could be inappropriate for use with some older populations.

What the preceding examples illustrate is that the nature of the stimuli should remain invariant in meaning across members of the research population. In addition, that invariance should extend to additional elements of the research context but especially across those elements of context that are to be analyzed in the research. Furthermore, this discussion suggests that the "normal" three-dimensional property space can be expanded according to theoretical concerns, and yet typical scaling models employ a two-dimensional array. Under these circumstances, scaling often proceeds "to simplify the problem by making the elements in one dimension 'replicates' of one another, or at least assuming them to be so" (Nunnally, 1967, p. 32). Do we wish to make such assumptions?

In attempting to resolve the problems posed by a complex measurement property space, several methodolgical strategies are relevant. First, multidimensional scaling procedures (Kruskal and Wish, 1978; Shepard, Romney, and Nerlove, 1972; Torgerson, 1958), especially three-way multidimensional scaling, are relevant for deriving scales from complex property spaces, provided that an adequate theory concerning the dimensionality of the space and the relationships between points in the space is developed. Second, the multifacet approach to the conceptualization of measurement (Cronbach et al., 1972), with the explicit delineation of sources of measurement error, may be useful in understanding complex measurement property spaces. Finally, one might simply conduct a more traditional analysis of a two-dimensional array but examine the model spearately for relevant (theoretically specified) population subgroups. For example, one might conduct a factor analysis of a measure of functional ability for a sample of "young-old" and "old-old" subjects to ensure that the factor structure remains the same. Coefficients for assessing the similarity of factor structures appear in Harman (1976, pp. 341-47), with additional work on factor invariance presented in Meredith (1964a and b) and Mulaik (1972, pp. 337-60).

Each of these strategies has both payoffs and limitations. Multidimensional scaling and multifacet approaches are mathematically elegant and very complex. Though these procedures produce a significant increase in knowledge about true scores, one might question the usefulness of rushing toward these techniques. Simply put, mathematical elegance *is not* a substitute for a substantive theory of measurement structure. These techniques are applicable only when precise conceptualization precedes data collections. Subsample scaling using more traditional analytic models is more readily understood, but it can become very costly, both in terms of data collection and data analysis. Moreover, this technique is less applicable when the multidimensional property space is not fully crossed. For example, when a different number of stimulus targets are presented to each subject, the property space contains some elements of nesting, making analysis more difficult. Finally, this technique also requires substantive theory concerning measurement structure, as well as theoretical delineation of relevant population subgroups within which the measurement model is examined.

Clearly, researchers in aging need to be aware of the issues surrounding measurement property space and the assumptions that are made when applying scaling models to data. Some solutions and strategies for handling these issues are available; still, none offers a panacea for the problems involved in making successful measurements. What they do succeed in doing, however, is illustrating that measurement models rely upon theoretical models of the substantive problem at hand and that only then can psychometrics assist the researcher.

What the preceding discussion of measurement theory illustrates, therefore, is the primacy of conceptualization in the development of measures. As Blalock (1979) has pointed out, human behavior is so diverse and complex that failure to conceptualize adequately renders problematic the integration of substantive research with general theory. Given the crucial nature of conceptual explication for measurement, a basic part of our evaluation of instruments is a statement of the conceptual definition of the measure and the context of research within which the instrument has been developed and used.

Validity

Insofar as validity refers to the extent to which the measurement instrument measures what is intended and insofar as the additional dimensions of the measurement property space are included for conceptual utility, the issues just discussed are relevant to validity assessment. Indeed, validity is inherently a theoretical, not a mathematical, property. Before turning to a more detailed discussion of specific questions in validity (i.e., convergent, discriminant, and predictive validity), several more general issues must be raised. Robinson, Rusk and Head (1968) have detailed some of these considerations: (1) proper sampling of content, (2) simplicity of item wording, and (3) item analysis.

A proper sampling of content is important in order to ensure that the range of relevant items or behaviors has been incorporated into an instrument in such a way that a person's true position is known. We recognize that the population of items relevant to a construct is almost certainly unknown. Despite this obvious difficulty, procedures for developing item pools exist, among them the use of open-ended questions in the preliminary and pretest phases of the research process. Similarly, item development can proceed through the juxtaposition of general dimensions of interest with areas of specific reference (Straus, 1964; Stephenson, 1953). For example, the researcher interested in family power may, theoretically, define the power domain as consisting of three general domains (e.g., bases of power, techniques of interpersonal influence, and power outcomes [Olson and Cromwell, 1975]), two specific familial referents (e.g., husband-wife system and parent-child system), and four areas of family functioning (e.g., family economics, child socialization practices, couple social activities, and household task performance). Such a researcher may wish to generate a three-by-two-by-four matrix of theoretically possible combinations. (Of course, this is only one plausible conceptualization of family power. It is not intended to be a complete delineation of the conceptual issues.) Several items could be rationally developed to fill each cell of this matrix of theoretical concerns; empirical validation of this theoretical structure would constitute the next step in the measurement process.

Using simply worded items is essential in the measurement process to ensure stimulus clarity for all respondents in a study group. Moreover, given the relationship of age cohort to education, the gerontological researcher must take steps to make sure that items are easily understandable and to preserve meaning across age and education groups within a study. In a similar vein, attention to issues of item wording can help ensure that double-barreled stimuli are eliminated from research instruments, thus making interpretation of measurement models easier.

Item analysis is relevant to the assessment of construct validity.

Simply put, when items correlate strongly with the theoretically designated construct, the correlation provides some evidence as to the appropriateness of the hypothesized structure of the theoretical construct. These data are also relevant to the internal homogeneity or reliability of the construct. Similarly, factor analysis or multidimensional scaling procedures can be used to assess construct validity when the hypothesized dimensional structure empirically emerges.

Whereas the broad, general issues just outlined address the issues of content and construct validity, other, more specialized validity concerns exist. Nunnally (1967, p. 76) has referred to these issues as predictive validity, or validity with reference to an outside criterion. We, however, differentiate these concerns into the following categories.

1. **Convergent or Concurrent Validity:** To what extent are different measures of the same concept related to, or correlated with, one another? High correlations are expected in this context.

2. **Discriminant Validity:** To what extent are the measure and construct different from other (perhaps closely related) constructs and measures? Quite often, the low correlation of an indicator with measures of response bias (such as social desirability, yea-saying, and acquiescence) is taken as an indicator of discriminant validity.

3. **Predictive Validity:** To what extent does the measure correlate as expected with other theoretically relevant variables? Most often, this is used in the sense of an instrument's ability to discriminate known groups, but the concept is also applicable to an analysis of the nomological net of hypothesized relationships of a construct with other variables.

The assessment of validity is highly dependent upon theoretical, as opposed to mathematical or statistical, concerns. The selection of criterion measures or groups for use in validity studies inherently involves conceptual decisions; careful attention must be given to this process. However, once these decisions have been made, validity assessments can be handled within a correlational framework. In this regard, multitrait-multimethod analysis is a powerful procedure for assessing validity (Campbell and Fiske, 1959; Alwin, 1974; Althauser, 1974; Althauser et al., 1971). Other procedures are also available, including multimethod factors (Jackson, 1969), consistency criteria (Althauser and Heberlein, 1970), and confirmatory factor analysis (Werts, Linn, and Jöreskog, 1971). All of these are valuable aids in assessing validity and can be constructively used to enhance our knowledge of instrumentation in the field of aging.

Response Set

Related to concerns about measurement validity is the issue of response set in the items. Response set refers to the tendency of some subjects to respond to items not entirely on the basis of their content; rather, the subject might be trying to project an "agreeable" or "nice person" image and as a result avoid disagreement with items. Similarly, the respondent might assess characteristics of the interview or testing environment and attempt to respond in a manner designed to maximize the respondent's benefit. For example, an older worker who wants to continue working but perceives that his or her employer would prefer that he or she retire might try to exhibit a high degree of job commitment, job satisfaction, and approval of the procedures of superiors. The aged person who wishes to avoid institutionalization might attempt to project the image of a healthy, independent older person when in fact his or her disability levels are high.

Response set is a consequence of three broad factors: (1) structural factors, or characteristics of the testing environment, such as centralized versus diffuse institutional structures or organizational climate; (2) process factors, or the characteristics of the test itself, the person(s) administering the test, as well as subject-rater, subject-instrument, and rater-instrument interactions; and (3) individual factors, such as the respondent's desire to project a good impression. All of these factors potentially affect the measurements that will be obtained; the bulk of the research has, however, been concerned with two sources of response bias.

1. Social Desirability: Edwards (1957) has proposed that some people want to make a good impression and respond accordingly. Age is positively correlated with social desirability (Mutran and Burke, 1979). Techniques for minimizing desirability response include the use of forced-choice items and/or response alternatives are pretested and equated on social desirability ratings. The use of social desirability ratings like the Crowne-Marlowe Social Desirability Scale as a correction factor is another approach to understanding and controlling for response bias (Smith, 1967). Similarly, social desirability ratings can be used with partial correlation and analysis of covariance techniques to remove the effects of social desirability.

2. Acquiescence: The basic proposition behind this aspect of response bias is that an individual's attitude may change in accordance with the situation. Yea-saying, or the tendency to agree with anything that sounds good, is the primary concern here. Strategies for examining and/or reducing acquiescent response set include several strategies, all of which involve using more complex or otherwise different item formats.

The first strategy involves the shifting of response alternatives between positive and negative modes. Simple yes-no response options can be inserted as no-yes sometimes. The Likert response format may also be reversed. This procedure is designed to identify persons who may select alternatives on the basis of the order in which the response alternatives are presented. A related strategy is attempting to vary the item's content from positive to negative. This, however, can be difficult insofar as the basic content of the item, regardless of its positive or negative direction, must remain the same. Too often, the insertion or deletion of a simple negative can produce awkward sounding items; on the other hand, rewriting items to reflect a negative orientation can change both the logic and the substance of the item. Consequently, ths use of the item-reversal technique requires a sensitivity to the theoretical nuances of the concept being measured, as well as a concern for the principles of language. A final strategy uses forced-choice items in which two or more replies to a question are presented and the individual must choose only one of the options. Since the nature of the response options significantly changes the content of what is endorsed, the respondent is forced to make a comparative evaluation as opposed to a decision on the degree of endorsement; this serves to reduce acquiescent response bias. By equating the social desirability of each of the forced choice response options, the researcher can also attempt to control for those effects.

These two concerns do not, however, encompass the total range of possible issues in response bias. The primary thrust of these approaches tends to attribute responsibility for response bias issues to the individual level of analysis and neglects—to some extent—the contribution of structural and process factors. This conceptualization of response bias ignores the plausible argument that the definition of the content of the items varies according to social group, or health status, or some other variables of interest to the researchers and that this systematic variation in the meaning of the stimuli may result in very different response distributions (Mangen, 1977). The researcher might examine these distributions and determine a yea-saying score for respondents, thus attributing the responsibility for "deceiving" the researcher to the subject when in fact the real issue may be one of construct validity.

In summary, the issues of validity and response set are intimately intertwined. Determination of the validity of a research tool involves a research process (i.e., an attempt to disprove the null hypothesis of no validity) that is long-term and cumulative. A range of plausible questions regarding validity and response set must be addressed in order to produce a well-documented research instrument.

Reliability/Homogeneity

Though validity inherently involves a range of conceptual decisions regarding the nature of the construct and the expected patterns of relationships among constructs, questions of reliability and measurement error can be clearly expressed in mathematical terms. Reliability is concerned with the extent to which a given measurement device exhibits repeatable characteristics. The characteristics across which repetition is assessed can be time bound, as in the case of test-retest reliability; individual bound, as in the case of interrater reliability; or item bound, as in parallel-forms or split-half techniques; or they can be grounded in the domain sampling model (i.e., estimates of internal consistency such as coefficient alpha [Cronbach, 1951] or theta [Armor, 1974]). Homogeneity of tests can also be assessed by a variety of techniques, such as indexes of scaleability for Guttman scales, or factor analytic results. However, as Robinson, Rusk, and Head (1968) have pointed out, the interitem correlation matrix combines simplicity of presentation with just as much information regarding homogeneity and should certainly be examined by all developers and users of scales. At the same time, however, the explicit use of scaling models not only provides information regarding the homogeneity of tests, it also allows researchers to test empirically for the emergence of their theoretical constructs.

Though reliability/homogeneity is indeed an important property to assess, such figures should be viewed critically. First, internal consistency (alpha) reliability is a function not only of the correlations among items, but also of test length. A 10-item scale with an average correlation of only .25 yields an alpha reliability of .77, while a 30-item test with the same average correlation exhibits an alpha reliability of .91. Similarly, an item with a factor loading of .50 is equivalent to a correlation of only .25. Test-retest reliabilities are quite often lower than other reliability estimates, but the Guttman coefficient of reproducibility could exceed .90 and still not indicate a unidimensional construct (Schooler, 1968). In short, the researcher must be aware of the relative nature of summary statistics on reliability and critically evaluate instruments in light of the varying distributions of those statistics.

Another word of caution regarding the use of test-retest reliability is in order. Since the field of aging is inherently concerned with the question of change over time, what meaning can be ascribed to a low test-retest correlation? Does it have low reliability, or is the instrument sensitive to change? Recent work in the causal modeling of measurement constructs suggests that reliability can be differentiated from stability when three or more time points are available to the researcher. The interested reader is referred to several treatments of this issue in the methodological literature on assessing change (Bohrnstedt, 1969; Coleman, 1968; Hannan, Robinson, and Warren, 1974; Heise, 1969; Wheaton et al., 1977; Wiley and Wiley, 1970). These researchers have been interested in assessing change in the level or quantity of a construct. Nesselroade and associates have been addressing changes in the quality or structure of a construct over time (Nesselroade, 1977). Nesselroade's strategy is quite relevant to the development of aging-related instruments insofar as different facets of social life may emerge and/or gain prominence with the passage of time, thus leading to the expectation that factoral structure may change. Confirmatory factor analysis is one means by which researchers interested in the changes in the operation of a research instrument can test their suppositions.

Though the theory of measurement error is mathematically elegant, the reader should not infer that reliability is a more important psychometric property than validity. To be sure, an instrument cannot have validity when it has no reliability; reliability places an upper limit upon validity and "is a necessary but not sufficient condition for validity" (Nunnally, 1967, p. 173).

Normative Information

Research inherently involves a process of comparison, and so knowledge can be cumulative only insofar as the results of one research effort can be compared to another. The most basic requirement for comparisons is that the overall central tendency and dispersion of the scale be available, together with basic descriptive information regarding sample characteristics. Population subgroups that are well defined and theoretically relevant can also be separately normed, thus allowing further comparative analysis. This also bears upon the predictive validity of the scale in that research would expect to find discrimination of theoretically known groups.

The preceding paragraph details only the real basics of norming data. A great deal of additional data are relevant to the norming process: (1) central tendencies and dispersion of items, (2) item (and scale) measures of skewness and kurtosis, and (3) statistics about the psychometric properties of the instrument. These additional data allow the researcher who is using a previously developed instrument in a different context to ascertain subtle shifts in scale operation.

The criteria of instrument evaluation outlined in this section apply to all measures, regardless of the substantive domain of the research. Some special concerns especially germane to the field of aging are also included in our evaluations. Specifically, we are concerned with the magnitude of age (or age-proxy) correlations with the substantive concept measures. We have included such correlations in our reviews when such data are available. Furthermore, the usability of the instrument with older populations, as well as general impressions regarding the efficacy of the measurement strategy, are included in the instrument reviews.

Evaluation of Research Instruments and General Recommendations

Each chapter in these three volumes addresses measurement problems in a distinct manner. However, two critical themes emerge so frequently that they can be fairly taken as judgments of social gerontological measurement as a whole.

Psychometric Development

The first general criticism of social gerontological measurement is that relatively few instruments in the field have used the available measurement technology to an adequate degree. Making well-established quantitative assessments of internal consistency, stability, dimensionality, and external correlation patterns is not standard practice in research in social gerontology; in fact, such assessments are rare.

Indeed, the prevalence in many domains of very short instruments and single-item indicators excludes many of these techniques outright or makes their application problematic. Batteries of single items are far more popular than scales and indexes in many research areas.

Systematic replication of measures on significantly diverse or broadly representative samples is uncommon. More than one contributor to this effort has decried a widespread tendency to alter instruments between applications. Not only is replication with constant instruments essential to proper psychometric development, its absence drastically impairs the comparability of measures within a domain and weakens the cumulative impact of multiple researches. When instruments are changed, those who did so ought to assume responsibility for systematically demonstrating that the change is for the better.

Moreover, the social aspects of social gerontology often make regional, environmental, and demographic contexts crucially important to the interpretation of measurements. The scarcity of replications with constant instruments means a scarcity of large-scale norms for many of the very measures that require them most urgently. Many researchers recommend that such norms be developed or that there be better sampling of the elderly in establishing norms.

When we encourage more replication of measures with constant instruments or the establishment of broader norms for existing measures, we do so with the understanding that "replication" does not mean "indiscriminate use." For every instrument there are populations and contexts in which its use would be inappropriate. Responsible replication involves an awareness of the contingent variables that affect both the reliability and the validity of an instrument as it is transferred from context to context. Responsible norm establishment involves the recognition of populations in which use of the instrument would be bound to produce distorted or unstable results. Reliability and validity are only ideal properties of instruments in themselves. One should not assume that a given measure will maintain the same internal consistency and bias from age-group to age-group. This is the case because numerous potent contingent variables are age-related. Because of this, we emphasize that assessing the psychometric quality of an instrument is not the responsibility of its developers alone. Subsequent users of the instrument ought to contribute to the continual improvement of the assessment of the instrument's properties.

Conceptual Grounding

The second general criticism of social gerontological measurement is that few efforts at measurement have adequately reflected the conceptual structure of their field of study. Though almost every variable of interest to social gerontology is in fact a complex of processes and contents, there has been relatively little effort to raise instrumentation above the level of the diffuse, global indicator. Even the lengthier instruments often seem to be unsystematic collections of items selected with little or no concern about representing either multidimensionality or interactions among variables. When psychometric methods are used at all, they are most often applied mechanically, as if by afterthought, to data generated by grabbags of items in the apparent hope that better instruments could be extracted from mediocre ones.

We stress that the most thoroughgoing psychometric development can make little use of a set of items that has failed from the beginning to capture the structural complexity of the concept to be measured. Hence, we have made the call, repeated in various forms from chapter to chapter in these volumes, for extensive conceptual analyses prior to measurement and for instruments designed for multidimensional measurement.

One aspect of this criticism calls attention to unexamined assumptions about what we want to measure, assumptions with grave consequences for how we actually proceed in making measurements. Assumptions affect not only the interpretation of results but instrument development itself, from the construction of items to the selection of validation measures. For example, an instrument developer who assumes that fear of death is an inseparable part of the concept of one's own death is hardly likely to construct items that represent a range of contexts in which the emotional reaction to death is expected to vary. In short, assumptions are empirically testable within the confines of normal meanings—provided that we take the trouble to examine our concepts closely. Careful efforts to frame theories of what we seek to measure, or to deploy theories already current, can help to put otherwise unnoticed assumptions into clearer perspective.

Each of the criticisms just discussed is based on the principle that measurement is actually a theoretical enterprise. There is no such thing as an excellent measurement of ill-conceived variables. The idea of a freestanding measurement technology, applicable without scrupulous regard to the nature of what is to be measured, is a positivist myth. Insofar as the contributors to these volumes make up a fair sample of practicing gerontologists, we can conclude that gerontologists are aware of the problems this myth has raised. However, as their surveys of gerontological research practice reveal, this awareness has yet to immunize social gerontology against the myth at a practical level.

We criticize most of the research instruments used today in social gerontology for their poor psychometric development and fault them as well for their inadequate conceptual grounding. We go so far as to say that only insofar as an instrument has some adequacy of conceptual grounding does it merit any psychometic development at all. Are these criticisms, and particularly their implied remedies, altogether consistent? Though there is no logical incompatibility between nomological and psychometric excellence, there might be a practical conflict between efforts to attain them. There is only so much time, talent, energy, and money at the disposal of social gerontology as an institutional enterprise. How much of its resources should be used for the psychometric improvement of a relatively small number of promising instruments—at the risk of widespread theoretical stagnation? How much should be used for the betterment of our conceptual grasp of aging as a social process—at the risk of even greater disregard of psychometric quality? We suggest that both risks are very real. If it were to become generally understood that research opportunities, the likelihood of publication, and the esteem of colleagues are more available in one of these enterprises than in the other, the other would soon wither. But, if either failed, the scientific value of the other, no matter how great its prestige, would collapse. If social research in aging lost the intellectual ferment that produces new measures and challenges to established ones, it would no longer be a confluence of sciences but a social ritual, and its "theories," minor variants on political dogma. If, on the other hand, all interest were lost in the psychometric properties of measures, what impartial ground would there be for judging the replicability and accuracy of all the factual claims of various theories? For this is what psychometrics is really about: the independent estimation of how close observations come to theoretically defined truth (validity) and of how much variability there is among observations that are supposed to be of the same theoretically defined thing (reliability). Those with no use for mathematics in the social sciences should note that the metrical aspects of psychometrics are not its true gift to social science; rather, the explicit delineation of reliability and validity as properties affecting the comparability of researches constitutes the true contribution of psychometrics to social science research.

If favoring psychometric quality by institutional policy disinherited conceptual excellence and vice versa, what case would there be for favoring either? Why indeed should the institutional rewards and punishments in social gerontology be distributed under any definite policy at all? It is only because of such tacit but nonetheless definite policies that dilemmas of emphasis even occur in science. In their absence, scientists just go ahead with the whole scientific enterprise: thinking about the world, observing it according to their ideas, and striving to ensure the accuracy and repeatability of their observations. Of course, the preceding sentence is an idealistic fiction, for institutional policies have never been absent from the conduct of any science. Even Newton had to feign a doctrinaire empiricism to get into the Royal Society, but he did not have to do it to keep his job, publish his researches, or obtain the respect of his colleagues. Obviously, institutional sanctions have been weaker and stronger in other sciences and eras, and they are today strong in the social sciences. However, power and ubiquity do not make them good.

Summary

The extensive review and assessment procedure that we have conducted has led to a compliation of over 400 instruments that have been used in the field of aging. These instruments have been assessed by leading scholars in the field; their individual chapters form our three-volume work. We would like to summarize our introductory chapter with the following statements.

1. There is a gross lack of attention to the relevance of substantive theory for measurement issues. Theoretical assumptions, as well as conceptions about the connection of empirical indicators with theoretical constructs, are most relevant to the measurement process. Greater attention to this basic research issue is the most pressing need in measurement.

2. Assuming that there is an adequate theoretical framework, greater attention to measurement models is needed. This exists at two levels:

   a. Use of more recent ideas to assess measurement, including the use of nonlinear and/or nonadditive measurement models.

   b. The development of explicit techniques for handling K-dimensional measurement property spaces is necessary. Such techniques should be capable of working with nested data. Some plausible starting points include multidimensional scaling and multifacet approaches.

3. Assuming that there is an adequate theoretical framework, greater use of existing well-established measurement tools is needed. When the researcher feels that a set of items possesses constitutive meaning, then application of factor analysis, cluster analysis, and small-space techniques to these data can be useful in forming more compact psychometric structures.

4. Existing instruments can also benefit from the application of measurement models to these data, assuming that an adequate theoretical framework exists or is developed. We urge researchers to reopen their long-closed data files, to assess these data conceptually, and to reanalyze these data (when justified), using the more powerful statistical tools.

5. Researchers should pay greater attention to measurement error—its sources, the biases it introduces, and the structural and interpersonal factors that are associated with it (Mangen, 1977).

6. Finally, we recommend that no instruments be uncritically borrowed and used in all research contexts. Conceptual concerns must dictate the use of instruments.

REFERENCES

Administration on Aging, request for proposal number 105-76-3107, *Development of an Instrument Bank: Assessment of Available Research Instrument and Measurement Scales for the Study of Aging and the Elderly*. Washington, D.C., 1976.

Althauser, R. "Inferring Validity from the Multitrait-Multimethod Matrix: Another Assessment." In *Sociological Methodology, 1973–1974*, H. L. Costner (ed.), pp. 106–27. San Francisco: Jossey-Bass, 1974.

Althauser, R. P., and T. A. Heberlein. "A Causal Assessment of Validity and the Multitrait-Multimethod Matrix." In *Sociological Methodology, 1970*, E. F. Borgatta and G. W. Bohrnstedt (eds.), pp. 151–69. San Francisco: Jossey-Bass, 1970.

Althauser, R. P., T. A. Heberlein, and R. A. Scott. "A Causal Assessment of Validity: The Augmented Multitrait-Multimethod Matrix." In *Causal Models in the Social Sciences*, H. M. Blalock, Jr. (ed.), pp. 374–99. Chicago: Aldine-Atherton, 1971.

Alwin, D. "Approaches to the Interpretation of Relationships in the Multitrait-Multimethod Matrix." In *Sociological Methodology, 1973–1974*, H. L. Costner (ed.), pp. 79–105. San Francisco: Jossey-Bass, 1974.

American Psychological Association. *Technical Recommendations for Psychological Tests and Diagnostic Methods.* Washington, D.C.: American Psychological Association, 1966.

Armor, D. "Theta Reliability and Factor Scaling." In *Sociological Methodology, 1973–1974*, H. L. Costner (ed.), pp. 17–50. San Francisco: Jossey-Bass, 1974.

Binstock, A., and E. Shanas (eds.). *Handbook of Aging and the Social Sciences.* New York: Van Nostrand Reinhold, 1976.

Blalock, H. M., Jr. "The Presidential Address: Measurement and Conceptualization Problems: The Major Obstacle to Integrating Theory and Research." *American Sociological Review*, 1979, 44: 881–94.

Bohrnstedt, G. "Observations on the Measurement of Change." In *Sociological Methodology, 1969*, E. F. Borgatta (ed.), pp. 113–33. San Francisco: Jossey-Bass, 1969.

Bonjean, C. M., R. J. Hill, and S. D. McLemore, *Sociological Measurement: An Inventory of Scales and Indices.* San Francisco: Chandler, 1967.

Branch, L. G., and F. J. Fowler, Jr. *The Health Care Needs of the Elderly and Chronically Disabled in Massachusetts.* Boston: Massachusetts Department of Public Health, 1975.

Burkhardt, J. E., and J. C. Lewis (Administration on Aging from RMC Corporation). *Assessing the Status and Needs of Older Americans: Questionnaire.* Washington, D.C.: U.S. Department of Health, Education and Welfare, 1975.

Campbell, D., and D. Fiske. "Convergent and Discrimination Validation by the Multitrait-Multimethod Matrix." *Psychological Bulletin*, 1959, 56: 81–105.

Chun, K., S. Cobb, and J. French. *Measures for Psychological Assessment.* Ann Arbor, Mich.: Institute for Social Research, University of Michigan, 1975.

Coleman, J. S. "The Mathematical Study of Change." In *Methodology in Social Research*, H. M. Blalock, Jr., and A. B. Blalock (eds.), pp. 428–78. New York: McGraw-Hill, 1968.

Comrey, A. L., T. E. Backer, and E. M. Glaser. *A Sourcebook of Mental Health Measures.* Los Angeles: Human Interaction Research Institute, 1973.

Cronbach, L. J. "Coefficient Alpha and the Internal Structure of Tests." *Psychometrika*, 1951, 16: 297–334.

Cronbach, L. J., G. C. Gleser, H. Nanda, and N. Rajaratnam. *The Dependability of Behavioral Measurements.* New York: John Wiley and Sons, 1972.

Cumming, E., and W. E. Henry. *Growing Old.* New York: Basic Books, 1961.

Edwards, A. *The Social Desirability Variable in Personality Assessment and Research.* New York: Dryden Press, 1957.

Fitts, W. *Manual: Tennessee Self-Concept Scale.* Nashville, Tenn.: Counselor Recordings and Tests, 1965.

Gilford, R., and V. Bengtson. "Marital Satisfaction in Three Generations: Positive and Negative Dimensions." Paper presented to the 29th Annual Meeting of the Gerontological Society, New York, October 13-17, 1976.

Hannan, M. T., R. Robinson, and J. T. Warren. "The Causal Approach to Measurement Error in Panel Analysis: Some Further Contingencies." In *Measurement in the Social Sciences*, H. M. Blalock, Jr. (ed.), pp. 293–323. Chicago: Aldine, 1974.

Harman, H. *Modern Factor Analysis*. Chicago: University of Chicago Press, 1976.

Havens, B., and E. Thompson. "Differentiation of Unmet Needs Using Analysis by Age/Sex Cohorts of an Elderly Population: Aging in Manitoba." Paper presented to the 39th Annual Meeting of the Midwest Sociological Society, Chicago, April 11, 1975.

Heise, D. R. "Separating Reliability and Stability in Test-Retest Correlation." *American Sociological Review*, 1969, 34: 93–101.

Hoge, D. R. "A Validated Intrinsic Religious Motivation Scale." *Journal for the Scientific Study of Religion*, 1972, 11(4): 369–76.

Jackson, D. "Multimethod Factor Analysis in the Evaluation of Convergent and Discriminant Validity." *Psychological Bulletin*, 1969, 72: 30–49.

Johnson, O. G., and J. W. Bommarito. *Tests and Measurements in Child Development: A Handbook*. San Francisco: Jossey-Bass, 1971.

Kahana, E. *Role of Homes for the Aged in Meeting Community Needs, Final Report*. Detroit: Elderly Care Research Center, Wayne State University, 1974.

Kalish, R. A., and D. K. Reynolds. *Death and Ethnicity: A Psychological Study*. Los Angeles, University of Southern California Press, 1976.

Kruskal, J., and M. Wish. "Multidimensional Scaling." Sage University Paper Series on Quantitative Applications in the Social Sciences, number 07-011. Beverly Hills, Calif.: Sage, 1978.

Laumann, E. O. *Bonds of Pluralism: The Form and Substance of Urban Social Networks*. New York: John Wiley and Sons, 1973.

Lawton, M. P. "The Dimensions of Morale." In *Research Planning and Action for the Elderly*, D. Kent, R. Kastenbaum, and S. Sherwood (eds.), pp. 144–65. New York: Behavioral Publications, 1972.

McReynolds, P. (ed.). *Advances in Psychological Assessment* (vols. 1 and 2). Palo Alto, Calif.: Science and Behavior Books, 1968, 1971.

McReynolds, P. (ed.). *Advances in Psychological Assessment* (vol. 3). San Francisco: Jossey-Bass, 1975.

Mangen, D. "Non-random Measurement Error in the Bradburn Affect-Balance Scale: Toward the Development of a Social and Historical Theory of Measurement Error." Paper presented to the 30th Annual Meeting of the Gerontological Society, San Francisco, November 18–22, 1977.

Margenau, H. *The Nature of Physical Reality*. New York: McGraw-Hill, 1950.

Meredith, W. "Notes on Factorial Invariance." *Psychometrika*, 1964a, 29: 177–85.

———. "Rotation to Achieve Factorial Invariance." *Psychometrika*, 1964b, 29: 187–206.

Miller, D. C. *Handbook of Research Design and Social Measurement* (2nd ed.). New York: David McKay, 1970.

Morgan, L. A., and V. L. Bengtson. "Measuring Perceptions of Aging Across Social Strata." Paper presented to the 29th Annual Meeting of the Gerontological Society, New York, October 13–17, 1976.

Morris, J. N., and S. Sherwood. "A Retesting and Modification of the Philadelphia Geriatric Center Morale Scale." *Journal of Gerontology*, 1975, 30: 77–84.

Mulaik, S. *The Foundations of Factor Analysis*. New York: McGraw-Hill, 1972.

Mutran, E., and P. J. Burke. "Personalism as a Component of Old Age Identity." *Research on Aging*, 1979, 1: 37–63.

Nelson, L. D., and C. C. Nelson. "A Factor Analytic Inquiry into the Multidimensionality of Death Anxiety." *Omega*, 1975, 6 (2): 171–78.

Nesselroade, J. R. "Issues in Studying Developmental Change in Adults from a Multivariate

Perspective." In *Handbook of the Psychology of Aging,* J. E. Birren and K. W. Schaie (eds.), pp. 59–69. New York: Van Nostrand Reinhold, 1977.

Nunnally, J. *Psychometric Theory.* New York: McGraw-Hill, 1967.

Olson, D. H., and R. Cromwell. "Power in Families." In *Power in Families,* R. Cromwell and D. H. Olson (eds.), pp. 3–11. New York: Halstead Press, 1975.

Pfeiffer, E. (ed.). *Multidimensional Functional Assessment: The O.A.R.S. Methodology.* Durham, N.C.: Duke University Center for Study of Aging, 1975.

Ray, J. J., and J. Najman. "Death Anxiety and Death Acceptance: A Preliminary Approach." *Omega,* 1974, 5 (4): 311–15.

Riley, J. W., Jr. "What People Think about Death." In *The Dying Patient,* O. Brim, Jr., et al. (eds.), pp. 30–41. New York: Russell Sage Foundation, 1970.

Riley, M., A. Foner, M. Moore, B. Hess, and B. Roth (eds.). *Aging and Society: An Inventory of Research Findings* (vol. 1). New York: Russell Sage Foundation, 1968.

Riley, M., J. Riley, Jr., and M. Johnson (eds.). *Aging and Society: Aging and the Professions* (vol. 2). New York: Russell Sage Foundation, 1969.

Riley, M., M. Johnson, and A. Foner (eds.). *Aging and Society: A Sociology of Age Stratification* (vol. 3). New York: Russell Sage Foundation, 1972.

Robinson, J. P., R. Athanasiou, and K. B. Head. *Measures of Occupational Attitudes and Occupational Characteristics.* Ann Arbor, Mich.: Institute for Social Research, University of Michigan, 1969.

Robinson, J. P., J. G. Rusk, and K. B. Head. *Measures of Political Attitudes.* Ann Arbor, Mich.: Institute for Social Research, University of Michigan, 1968.

Robinson, J. P., and P. R. Shaver. *Measures of Social Psychological Attitudes* (rev. ed.). Ann Arbor, Mich.: Institute for Social Research, University of Michigan, 1973.

Rosenberg, M. *Society and the Adolescent Self-Image.* Princeton, N.J.: Princeton University Press, 1965.

Sandberg, N. C. *Ethnic Identity and Assimilation: The Polish American Community: Case Study of Metropolitan Los Angeles.* New York: Praeger Publishers, 1972.

Schooler, C. "A Note of Extreme Caution on the Use of Guttman Scales." *American Journal of Sociology,* 1968, 74 (3): 296–301.

Shaw, M. E., and J. M. Wright. *Scales for the Measurement of Attitudes.* New York: McGraw-Hill, 1967.

Shepard, R. N., A. K. Romney, and S. B. Nerlove. *Multidimensional Scaling: Theory* (vol. 1). New York: Seminar, 1972.

Smith, D. "Correcting for Social Desirability Response Sets in Opinion-Attitude Survey Research." *Public Opinion Quarterly,* 1967, 31: 87–94.

Stephenson, W. *The Study of Behavior: Q-Technique and Its Methodology.* Chicago: University of Chicago Press, 1953.

Straus, M. "Measuring Families." In *Handbook of Marriage and the Family,* H. T. Christiansen (ed.), pp. 335–400. Chicago: Rand McNally, 1964.

Straus, M. A. *Family Measurement Techniques: Abstracts of Published Instruments, 1935–1965.* Minneapolis: University of Minnesota Press, 1969.

Straus, M. A., and B. W. Brown. *Family Measurement Techniques* (rev. ed.). Minneapolis: University of Minnesota Press, 1978.

Tibbetts, C., and W. Donahue (eds.). *Social and Psychological Aspects of Aging.* New York: Columbia University Press, 1962.

Torgerson, W. *Theory and Methods of Scaling.* New York: John Wiley and Sons, 1958.

Werts, C. E., R. L. Linn, and K. G. Jöreskog. "Estimating the Parameters of Path Models Involving Unmeasured Variables." In *Causal Models in the Social Sciences,* H. M. Blalock, Jr. (ed.), pp. 400–9. Chicago: Aldine-Atherton, 1971.

Wheaton, B., B. Muthén, D. Alwin, and G. Summers. "Assessing Reliability and Stability in Panel Models." In *Sociological Methodology, 1977,* D. Heise (ed.), pp. 84–136. San Francisco: Jossey-Bass, 1977.

Wiley, D. E., and J. E. Wiley. "The Estimation of Measurement Error in Panel Data." *American Sociological Review,* 1970, 35: 112–17.

Chapter 2

Intellectual Functioning

Carol J. Dye

As early as the 1920s, studies comparing the intellectual performance of older adults to younger adults were written. One of these first reports, that of Foster and Taylor (1920), anticipated later developments in the assessment of intellectual functioning within elderly populations. Foster and Taylor compared the performance of a group of normal older adults (50 to 89 years old), a group of young adults, and a group of school-age children on the Yerkes-Bridges Point Scale. This intelligence scale was derived from the Binet and differed from that test mainly in the method of administration. Foster and Taylor's data indicated a decline in overall performance with increasing age. They hypothesized that this decline did not reflect reduced ability among the aged but a lack of practice in activities related to the tasks on the test and less interest or reduced alertness on the part of the elderly subjects compared to younger individuals. In addition, interesting patterns in the scores of individuals from the three age-groups were found. Comparing individuals from three age-groups matched for overall score, the authors found marked decreases with age in a timed test of free association of words, a test of drawing from memory, and two tests requiring verbal problem solving, i.e., putting three words into one sentence and rearranging dissected sentences. Increases in scores with age were found on a test of vocabulary, a test requiring criticisms of absurd statements, and a test of judgment. Later studies of elderly individuals have confirmed and supported these early results. In addition, Foster and Taylor's 1920 study raised an issue of continuing concern, i.e., whether psychological tests developed for younger age-groups can be used effectively in assessing intelligence in old age.

Despite the concerns Foster and Taylor expressed, other tests of intelligence standardized only on younger populations are still being used to compare the intellectual functioning of the aged to younger age-groups. An apparent decline in an individual's functioning over the years has generally been found, although there have been some exceptions. First, this decline is certainly not uniform from study to study. For example, longitudinal assessments of intellectual performance tend to indicate less decline than do cross-sectional studies, and the point at which the decline begins tends to be later in data from longitudinal studies. In fact, in at least one study of a group of older adults tested over a period of 20 years, no decline in functioning was noted (Blum, Jarvik, and Clark, 1970). Data from studies using different types of tests, while indicating decline in old age, show different points at which the decline begins and different rates for that decline. For a more extensive discussion of the results of these studies, the reader is referred to Botwinick (1977).

The issue at hand in this chapter is the extent to which the instruments currently being used to assess intelligence in old age distort age comparisons by building cohort differences into the results. The question is whether the presently used tests of intelligence reflect environmental differences to which the groups have been subjected, rather than valid declines in ability over the life span. Generally, older people have far less education than younger people (U.S. Department of Health, Education and Welfare, 1972) and a greater percentage are foreign-born (Riley, Johnson, and Foner, 1972). These and other such characteristics of the contemporary group of elderly could cause them to experience difficulty with tests standardized on younger groups. The older adult may find the test-taking situation itself strange and the vocabulary and arithmetic unfamiliar.

Though these are acknowledged objections to using standard tests of intelligence with elderly populations, little has been done to adapt the existing instruments for use with these populations. In addition, little has been done to go beyond present methods of assessing intelligence to investigate how intellectual performance develops over the life span.

Factor analyses of the present tests of intelligence shed some light on which factors assessed by these tests change in importance with age. For example, Cohen (1957) factor analyzed performance on the Wechsler Adult Intelligence Scale (WAIS) for four age-groups within the age span 18 to 75 years. He found a shift in emphasis in performance with increased age toward dependence on verbal comprehension, verbal retention, and ability to form conceptual relationships. Later, Maxwell (1961) in another independent factor analysis of WAIS performance supported these results. He found that the contributions to performance made by inductive and deductive reasoning, perceptual speed, fluency, visualization, and numerical facility gradually declined into old age, with a shift toward other factors, such as those described by Cohen.

Although factor analytic studies of existing tests are important contributions to the understanding of intellectual functioning over the life span, they are limited by the items included in the factor analysis. A wider sample of behaviors considered to be measures of intellectual ability needs to be included in such factor analyses. One approach that has gone beyond those functions assessed by contemporary intelligence tests, and one that may lead to the construction of a special test for the elderly, is the work of Vanderplas and Vanderplas (personal communication with J. Vanderplas and J. Vanderplas from Washington University, St. Louis, in April 1977), who are currently working toward the identification of those factors of intellectual functioning that shift in importance as individuals age. Their work concentrates on the differentiation of those factors in intellectual behavior that improve and do not decline, those that emerge, and those that disappear in old age. Until such approaches come to fruition, the assessment of the mental ability of the aged must proceed with currently existing tests, used with special norms for various age-groups or other adjustments of performance data. For example, data were gathered by Doppelt and Wallace (1955) on the WAIS performance of a group of individuals over 60 years of age. They found that the *mean raw score* of the aged group was lower than the mean raw score of the younger standardization groups. However, since the WAIS measures deviation IQs, the average raw score of the Doppelt and Wallace group became the average IQ score (100 points) for the older adult group. Therefore, the average older person is assigned an IQ of 100 as is the younger person, even though the older person's raw scores are lower than the younger person's.

Tests of Intelligence

Six tests of intelligence that have been used with aged populations are reviewed here. These, of course, do not include all of the instruments that have been used with the elderly. Considerations of space forbid the inclusion of every such instrument, if the more specialized neuropsychological instruments are to be sampled here as well. The intelligence tests included are among the most widely used and psychometrically best developed. They are the Wechsler Adult Intelligence Scale (WAIS), the Full-Range Picture Vocabulary Test (FRPV), the Draw-a-Person Test (DAP), the Kent EGY, the Primary Mental Abilities Test, and the Progressive Matrices Test. The Mill Hill Vocabulary Test is discussed here also, since it is usually used with the Progressive Matrices test. Of these tests the WAIS, the FRPV, and the DAP must be administered individually. Though this tends to be costly and time-consuming for researchers, individual administration has some advantages. It allows the subject to express problems in understanding directions on test items, and the examiner can be alert for signs of fatigue and other factors that can influence the subject's score. The other three instruments reviewed are paper-and-pencil tests that can be administered to groups. Though data for research purposes can be gathered quickly on large groups of individuals by this method, scores on these tests can be influenced by many factors besides intellectual ability.

Tests of Organic Brain Damage

A number of tests have been used to assess the deterioration in psychological functioning that is a result of organic brain damage. Ten of these tests have been used with elderly populations. All of the tests used to diagnose brain damage must be administered individually. The Wechsler Memory Scale, the Shipley-Hartford, and the Halstead Battery take the longest to administer. The first two of these take up to 30 minutes to complete, so they may contribute measurably to a subject's fatigue when they are administered with other performance tests. The Halstead Battery takes two days to complete.

There are three important issues in the use of these tests on elderly populations. Two of the issues involve the validity of the tests: first, the extent to which scores differentiate brain-damaged and non-brain-damaged persons; and, second, the extent to which they can differentiate brain-damaged persons from those who are functionally disordered. The third issue is the ability of the tests to differentiate normal aged persons from brain-damaged aged persons. The status of each of the tests reviewed for this chapter on these issues will be indicated, with relevant studies cited. However, methodological differences make comparisons of the results of these studies difficult. One of the most important differences is in the nature of the groups that have been used in the studies. The composition of the various groups of organically brain-damaged, functionally disordered, and aged individuals vary widely. Groups of organically impaired individuals can be composed of individuals from many diagnostic categories, e.g., chronic brain syndrome, acute brain syndrome, epilepsy, head trauma, and others. Usually, there is a predominance of one type of brain damage within any one study, but there is little uniformity in this factor across studies. The functionally disordered groups are also frequently made up of individuals from several diagnostic categories. Some individuals may be schizophrenic, some may have been diagnosed as psychoneurotic, some may have personality disorders, and so forth. Further descriptions of these groups, as well as the groups of elderly persons, usually include the mean age and sometimes the educational level of the subjects. In some cases, the members of the organically impaired groups are older than those in the groups of functionally disordered or "healthy" individuals. Other relevant characteristics—duration of disability, number and length of hospitalizations, level of medication, socioeconomic status, and other such variables—that are likely to affect scores on the tests are not reported.

There is also variability in the manner with which individuals were classified into organically damaged and functionally disordered groups. In some cases, information regarding the criteria used for classification may have been omitted; in others, supporting evidence may have been insufficiently reported. There is also the possibility that classification was influenced by scores on the test.

Individuals in the non-brain-damaged or non-functionally disordered comparison groups may not have been examined to determine their freedom from organic and functional disorders. "Community-dwelling" aged individuals are sometimes used in comparison groups under the assumption that they are free from organic brain damage; but close examinations of these aged individuals are necessary before they are assigned to comparison groups. It may be that some of the "age-related" differences in performance are due more to the presence of subtle levels of organic damage than to the changes that come with age.

Obviously, there is a need for more study on the validation of these tests, with the factors that influence performance controlled, with criterion populations clearly specified, and with comparison populations clearly differentiated.

Tests Differentiating Brain-Damaged Individuals

The efficiency with which the tests reviewed here are able to identify organically impaired individuals varies. When the cutoff points recognized by the authors of the tests or by others who have worked with the tests are used, the percentages of correct identifications can be predicted (see Table 2-1).

TABLE 2-1
Correct Differentiations of Brain Damage

Test	Correctly Identified Organics	Correct Identifications from Both Groups	Correctly Identified Nonorganics
Trailmaking Test (Reitan, 1955c)	—	84%	—
Halstead Battery (Reitan, 1955a)	96%	—	86%
Hooper (1958)	79%	—	100%
Benton (1974)	57%	—	96%
Graham-Kendall (1960)	50%	—	96%
Bender Gestalt (1946)	—	74%	—

The results of testing with the Shipley Institute of Living Scale indicate no overlap in scores between a group of organics and a group of normals (Shipley and Burlingame, 1941). No statistical analysis was performed on the scores, however, so it is not certain that the scores of these groups were actually statistically different. There were no data regarding this issue available for the Guild Memory Test (Gilbert, no date) or the Wechsler Memory Scale (Wechsler, 1945).

These tests are somewhat similar in their ability to identify nonorganic individuals. However, they vary much more widely in their ability to identify organically impaired persons. At levels of moderate or severe impairment, there is generally little difficulty identifying organic impairment on these tests. For tests with lower identification rates, the problem lies in conclusively identifying organic impairment in its mild forms or early stages. This is an important consideration in using a test, however, since it is in the early stages of impairment that such tests should be of most use.

Differentiating Brain-Damaged from Functionally Impaired Persons

An equally important issue is the effectiveness of tests in differentiating brain-damaged individuals from those who are functionally disordered. On this issue the effectiveness of the reviewed instruments again varies widely. Confusion of these two groups can occur with scores on the Wechsler Memory Scale (Cohen, 1950). There are conflicting results with the Benton Visual Retention Test. In his revised manual, Benton (1974) indicated that depressed patients may appear organically impaired on his Visual Retention Test. Yet, a year earlier in a rather comprehensive study, Watson (1973) had found that the Benton significantly discriminated between organics and groups of nonpsychotic functionally disordered persons, groups of individuals with affective disorders, and a group of acute/reactive schizophrenics.

The ability of the other tests reviewed here to differentiate these two groups is somewhat better. Using the Bender Gestalt, Korman and Blumberg (1963) were able to identify correctly 74% of the group of organic patients from a group of patients with mixed psychiatric diagnoses. Pascal and Suttell (1957) found that their recommended cutoff score screened out 96% of a group of psychotics, 91% of a group of neurotics, and 50% of a nonpatient population. Rosencrans and Schaffer (1969) found that performance on the Bender was better among psychiatric groups than organic groups. After using the background-interference procedure with the Bender Gestalt, Canter (1966) indicated that discrimination between groups of nonpsychotic functionally disordered individuals and organics was significantly improved. In another study, Canter (1971) indicated that more than half of the schizophrenic patients included in his study significantly improved their behavior with this procedure and organic patients did significantly less well.

Hooper (1958) found a 23% overlap in the scores of a group of brain-damaged persons and a group of psychoneurotic and schizophrenic individuals on the Hooper Visual Organization Test. Ascough, Strouf, Cohen, and Smith (1971) indicated a 71% rate of correct identification within a group of 20 organically damaged individuals and 20 schizophrenic patients on the Graham-Kendall Memory-for-Designs Test. Shearn, Berry, and Fitzgibbons (1974) found the MFD scores of groups of organics to be significantly poorer than scores of a mixed psychiatric group.

On the Trailmaking Test, one study by Orgel and McDonald (1967) indicated that there was no significant difference in scores between a group of individuals with mixed psychiatric diagnoses and a group of organics. However, it is possible that the former group may have included some individuals with subtle organic problems. No studies are available for the Halstead Battery regarding discrimination between organically impaired and functionally disordered groups. However, Small, Small, Milstein, and Moore (1972) assessed the same group of functionally disordered individuals (schizophrenics, manic depressives, and others) two to three times during the course of their hospitalization. Scores for this group generally did not fall into the brain-damaged range.

Heaton, Baade, and Johnson (1978) recently reviewed a large

number of articles that dealt with the effectiveness of psychological tests in discriminating between functionally and organically disordered individuals. Their conclusion was that the tests do discriminate between the two groups effectively, except with groups of chronic or process schizophrenics. They cited an overall success rate of 75%, with the schizophrenic groups excluded. They also cited a study by Boll (1974) that had implications for differential diagnoses within groups of elderly individuals. Boll found that psychological tests discriminated between functionally and organically impaired groups better when the organics were of the type that could be treated than when they were of the chronic/static type. Since it is possible that most of the organic conditions affecting the aged are of this latter type, this result suggests that there is greater difficulty in making differential diagnoses among the elderly.

Tests Differentiating Normal Aged from Organically Impaired Individuals

Yet another issue, one of special importance in this chapter, is the ability of the tests to differentiate normal aged individuals from brain-damaged aged individuals. Almost all of the tests reviewed for this chapter show a correlation with age. The exception is the Wechsler Memory Scale (Wechsler, 1945). Scores on the WMS are adjusted for older adult groups to make them unresponsive to the effects of normal aging processes. Instead, it is expected that scores are likely to be affected by the pathological processes that accompany age, such as senile dementia and the various physical disabilities affecting the oxygen supply to the brain.

The correlation with age of the scores on the other tests reviewed here seems to indicate that a significant number of normal older adults would be classified as brain-damaged with these tests. For example, on the Halstead Battery, the mean score of a group of normal aged individuals fell well within the range of scores that indicated impairment. This tendency began in the 45- to 50-year-old group, and the number of older adults included within this range increased regularly through 65 years (Reitan, 1955b).

On the Trailmaking Test, Davies (1968) found that the scores of 76% to 92% of groups of 60- to 70-year-old non-brain-damaged individuals fell within the brain-damaged range according to Reitan's (1955c) cutoff scores. This is similar to what can be found on the Hooper Visual Organization Test. According to the recommended cutoff, 69% of normal aged persons would be diagnosed as moderately impaired, 15% as mildly impaired, and 18% as unimpaired (Hooper,

1958). However, Mason and Ganzler (1964) have developed regression formulas for the Hooper VOT and the Shipley-Hartford that take into account the age and education of the subjects so that, when the adjustments on the two tests are used, there should be no age bias.

One factor that may explain the correlations of these tests with age may be that most of the tests are timed. It is well known that speed of response, motor coordination, and steadiness declines with age (Botwinick, 1973), and these factors could explain the decline with age in scores on the tests.

It is obvious that tests need to be developed that are able to differentiate reliably normal aged and brain-damaged aged. The ramifications will be great if this issue is not addressed. Currently, there is concern that older adults are given diagnoses of organic conditions too readily. There is also concern that functional depression is diagnosed as organic impairment in the elderly. Without adequate differential diagnostic techniques, this situation is likely to continue, which would mean that treatable conditions might be neglected or that inappropriate treatments might be used. Those who work with elderly persons, especially those in clinical settings, need to concern themselves with this important issue.

Summary

Table 2-2 lists the 17 measures of intellectual functioning that have been used in studies of older adults. All of these instruments are copyrighted and so cannot be reproduced in this volume. They are, however, available from their publishers.

TABLE 2-2
Instruments Reviewed in Chapter 2

Instrument	Author (date)	Code Number
I. Tests of Intellectual Function		
a. Draw-a-Person Test	Goodenough (1926)	Copyrighted
b. Full-Range Picture Vocabulary Test	Ammons and Ammons (1948)	Copyrighted
c. Kent Series of Emergency Scales	Kent (1946)	Copyrighted
d. Primary Mental Abilities Test	Thurstone and Thurstone (1947)	Copyrighted
e. Progressive Matrices Test	Raven (1960)	Copyrighted
f. Mill Hill Vocabulary Test	Raven (1943)	Copyrighted
g. Wechsler Adult Intelligence Scale	Wechsler (1955)	Copyrighted

TABLE 2-2—*Continued*

Instrument	Author (date)	Code Number
II. Tests of Organic Brain Damage		
a. Bender Visual Motor Gestalt Test	Bender (1938)	Copyrighted
b. Benton Visual Retention Test	Benton (1974)	Copyrighted
c. Graham-Kendall Memory-for-Designs Test	Graham and Kendall (1960)	Copyrighted
d. Guild Memory Test	Gilbert (1968)	Copyrighted
e. The Halstead Battery	Halstead (1947)	Copyrighted
f. Hooper Visual Organization Test	Hooper (1952)	Copyrighted
g. The Shipley-Hartford	Shipley (1940)	Copyrighted
h. Trailmaking Tests	Armitage (1946)	Copyrighted
i. Wechsler Memory Scale	Wechsler (1945)	Copyrighted
j. Crossing-Off Test	Botwinick and Storandt (1973)	No Special Material

REFERENCES

Ascough, J. C., M. J. Strouf, C. S. Cohen, and R. E. Smith. "Differential Diagnosis of Brain Damage and Schizophrenia by the Memory-for-Designs Test." *Journal of Clinical Psychology*, 1971, 27: 471-72.

Bender, L. *Bender Visual Motor Gestalt Test.* New York: American Orthopsychiatric Association, 1946.

Benton, A. L. *Revised Visual Retention Test.* New York: Psychological Corporation, 1974.

Blum, J. E., L. F. Jarvik, and E. T. Clark. "Rate of Change on Selected Tests of Intelligence: A 20 Year Long Study of Aging." *Journal of Gerontology*, 1970, 25: 171-76.

Boll, T. J. "Psychological Differentiation of Patients with Schizophrenia Versus Lateralized Cerebrovascular, Neoplastic, or Traumatic Brain Damage." *Journal of Abnormal Psychology*, 1974, 83: 456-58.

Botwinick, J. *Aging and Behavior: A Comprehensive Integration of Research Findings*, pp. 154-80. New York: Springer, 1973.

———. "Intellectual Abilities." In *Handbook of the Psychology of Aging*, J. E. Birren and K. W. Schaie (eds.), pp. 580-605.

Canter, A. "A Background Interference Procedure to Increase Sensitivity of the Bender Gestalt Test to Organic Brain Disorder." *Journal of Consulting Clinical Psychology*, 1966, 30: 91-97.

———. "A Comparison of the Background Interference Procedure Effect in Schizophrenic, Nonschizophrenic and Organic Patients." *Journal of Clinical Psychology*, 1971, 27: 473-74.

Cohen, J. "Wechsler Memory Scale Performance of Psychoneurotic, Organic and Schizophrenic Groups." *Journal of Consulting Psychology*, 1950, 414: 371-75.

———. "The Factorial Structure of the WAIS between Early Adulthood and Old Age." *Journal of Consulting Psychology*, 1957, 21: 283-90.

Davies, A. "The Influence of Age on Trailmaking Test Performance." *Journal of Clinical Psychology*, 1968, 24: 96-98.

Doppelt, J. E., and W. L. Wallace. "Standardization of WAIS for Older Persons." *Journal of Abnormal and Social Psychology*, 1955, 51: 312-30.

Foster, J. C., and G. A. Taylor. "The Applicability of Mental Tests to Persons Over 50 Years of Age." *Journal of Applied Psychology*, 1920, 4: 39–58.

Gilbert, J. G. *Guild Memory Test Manual.* Newark, N.J.: Unico National Mental Health Research Center (no date).

Graham, F. K., and B. S. Kendall. "Memory-for-Designs Test: Revised General Manual." *Perception Motor Skills* (monograph supplement number 2-VII), 1960, 11: 147–88.

Heaton, R. K., L. E. Baade, and K. L. Johnson. "Neuropsychological Test Results Associated with Psychiatric Disorders in Adults." *Psychological Bulletin*, 1978, 85: 141–62.

Hooper, H. E. *The Hooper Visual Organization Test: Manual.* Beverly Hills, Calif.: Western Psychological Services, 1958.

Irving, G., R. A. Robinson, and W. McAdam. "The Validity of Some Cognitive Tests in the Diagnosis of Dementia." *British Journal of Psychiatry*, 1970, 117: 149–56.

Kahn, R. L., A. I. Goldfarb, M. Pollack, and A. Peck. "Brief Objective Measures for the Determination of Mental Status in the Aged." *American Journal of Psychiatry*, 1960, 117: 326–28.

Korman, M., and S. Blumberg. "Comparative Efficiency of Some Tests of Cerebral Damage." *Journal of Consulting Clinical Psychology*, 1963, 27: 303–9.

Mason, C. F., and H. Ganzler. "Adult Norms for the Shipley Institute of Living Scale and Hooper Visual Organization Test Based on Age and Education." *Journal of Gerontology*, 1964, 19: 419–24.

Maxwell, A. E. "Trends in Cognitive Ability in Older Age Ranges." *Journal of Abnormal and Social Psychology*, 1961, 63: 449–52.

Orgel, S. A., and R. D. McDonald. "An Evaluation of the Trailmaking Test." *Journal of Consulting Clinical Psychology*, 1967, 31: 77–79.

Pascal, G. R., and B. J. Suttell. *Scoring System, the Bender-Gestalt Test: Quantification and Validity for Adults.* New York: Grune and Stratton, 1957.

Reitan, R. M. "Investigation of the Validity of Halstead's Measure of Biological Intelligence." *A.M.A. Archives of Neurology and Psychiatry*, 1955a, 73: 28–35.

———. "The Distribution According to Age of a Psychologic Measure Dependent upon Organic Brain Function." *Journal of Gerontology*, 1955b, 10: 338–40.

———. "The Relation of the Trailmaking Test to Organic Brain Damage." *Journal of Consulting Psychology*, 1955c, 19: 393–94.

Riley, M. W., J. Johnson, and A. Foner. *Aging and Society* (vol. 3). New York: Russell Sage Foundation, 1972.

Rosencrans, C. J., and H. G. Schaffer. "Bender Gestalt Time and Score Differences between Matched Groups of Hospitalized Psychiatric and Brain-Damaged Patients." *Journal of Clinical Psychology*, 1969, 25: 409–10.

Shearn, C. R., D. F. Berry, and D. J. Fitzgibbons. "Usefulness of the Memory-for-Designs Test in Assessing Mild Organic Complications in Psychiatric Patients." *Perceptual and Motor Skills*, 1974, 38: 1099–1104.

Shipley, W. C., and C. C. Burlingame. "A Convenient Self-Administering Scale for Measuring Intellectual Impairment in Psychotics." *American Journal of Psychiatry*, 1941, 97: 1313–25.

Small, I. F., J. G. Small, V. Milstein, and J. E. Moore. "Neuropsychological Observations with Psychosis and Somatic Treatment." *Journal of Nervous Mental Disorders*, 1972, 55: 6–13.

U.S. Department of Health, Education and Welfare. *Epidemiology of Aging.* Bethesda, Md.: National Institutes of Health, 1972.

Watson, C. G. "A Simple Bivariate Screening Technique to Separate Neuropsychology Hospital Organics from Other Psychiatric Groups." *Journal of Clinical Psychology*, 1973, 29: 448–50.

Wechsler, D. "A Standardized Memory Scale for Clinical Use." *Journal of Psychology*, 1945, 19: 87–95.

Abstracts

DRAW-A-PERSON TEST (DAP)
F. L. Goodenough, 1926

Definition of Variable

The test was originally intended as a test of intelligence for children (Goodenough, 1926).

Description of Instrument

There is no special test material. The subject is supplied with an 8½-by-11-inch sheet of paper and a pencil.

Method of Administration

The subject is instructed to draw a person and to make the drawing as complete as possible. Protests about lack of artistic ability must be met with encouragement and assurance that this does not matter. There is no time limit to the test. It usually takes no more than 15 minutes to complete.

Context of Development and Subsequent Use

The test developed by Goodenough has remained essentially the same. In its original scoring, 73 items were rated. With the 1961 Harris-Goodenough Test of Psychological Maturity revision, instructions were modified so that the subject is asked to draw both a man and a woman and there are 71 criterion items for scoring. The DAP has been used as a test of intelligence and as a projective test of personality (Machover, 1948). It is reviewed here chiefly as a test of intelligence and performance.

Sample

This test was originally used with children. Data were originally gathered from a group of 50 boys and 50 girls, stratified according to their fathers' occupations, from each grade level from kindergarten through ninth grade in urban and rural areas of Minnesota and Wisconsin.

Norms for the reviewed Harris-Goodenough edition (Harris, 1961) were derived from 300 children at each yearly level from age 5 to 15. This sample was selected as one representative of the U.S. population with regard to fathers' occupations and geographical regions.

Scoring, Scale Norms, and Distribution

Seventy-one items are scored. The raw score from these items can be converted into an intelligence quotient. As in the WAIS, the IQs are deviation based, with a mean of 100 and a standard deviation of 15.

Formal Tests of Reliability/Homogeneity

In a study of 386 third- and fourth-grade children, the test-retest correlation was .68 (at a one-week interval). Split-half reliability was .89 (McCarthy, 1944). Harris (1961) reported similar results with the revised form of the test. Kleemeier, Rich, and Justiss (1956) found test-retest reliability for height of drawing to be over .80 for a two-week interval with a group of older adults.

Interrater reliability was .84 in a study of 40 aged males (Jones and Rich, 1957).

Formal Tests of Validity

For the earlier form, correlations with the Stanford-Binet ranged from .41 to .80 (Ansbacher, 1952). The test correlated best with tests of reasoning, perceptual accuracy, and spatial aptitude in a group of 100 fourth-grade children.

Jones and Rich (1957) reported significant correlations of .47 to .65 (significant at the .01 level) between Wechsler-Bellevue full-scale scores and two Goodenough scores, obtained by Goodenough's method (Goodenough, 1926), and a measure of the height of the drawing. Correlations between the various subtests and Goodenough scores ranged from .34 to .65.

Usability on Older Populations

This is a quick test to administer, but it involves a psychomotor component that may handicap older adults.

Sensitivity to Age Differences

This technique has been used with a wide variety of aged subjects. The drawings made by aged subjects have been compared to those made by children (Lakin, 1956) and younger adults (Lorge, Tuckman, and Dunn, 1954). Institutionalized elderly individuals have been compared to noninstitutionalized elderly individuals (Lakin, 1960). The DAP has been used as a measure of intelligence with the Harris-Goodenough scoring system, and other uses have been made of this technique (Tuckman, Lorge, and Zeman, 1961; Gilbert and Hall, 1962). The results of studies with normal elderly subjects reflect deterioration and withdrawal as individuals age. Results of studies with institutionalized aged subjects show this tendency more strongly.

In one study (Lieberman, 1965), the DAP was found to be useful in making predictions of death in a group of elderly people. In the Jones and Rich (1957) study of 40 male residents (average age 78.5 years) of a fraternal home for the aged, the Goodenough scores of the aged sample were found to be similar to scores of 8-year-olds, though the adult group had a greater standard deviation. The Goodenough IQ score correlated significantly (.65) with the Wechsler-Bellevue Intelligence Scale score.

General Comments and Recommendations

Personality assessment using this test has usually been based on dynamic theory. Often, this has resulted in contradictions and overlapping between signs and indicators of certain traits. Very few data exist regarding the validity of the interpretations of personality from the Draw-a-Person Test.

As a test of intelligence, this technique seems to have greater validity; though, as the studies have indicated, validity in a group of older adults is not always high. Also, this test requires fine motor coordination. Artistic ability and previous training do make a difference, regardless of the administrator's assurances to the subject to the contrary. These considerations need to be kept in mind when testing older adults.

References

Ansbacher, H. L. "The Goodenough Draw-a-Man Test and Primary Mental Abilities." *Journal of Consulting Psychology*, 1952, 15: 176–80.

Gilbert, J. G., and M. R. Hall. "Changes with Age in Human Figure Drawing." *Journal of Gerontology*, 1962, 17: 397–404.

Goodenough, F. L. *Measurement of Intelligence by Drawings.* Yonkers, N.Y.: World Book Company, 1926.

Gravitz, M. A. "Marital Status and Figure Drawing Choice in Normal Older Americans." *Journal of Social Psychology*, 1969, 77: 143–44.

Harris, D. R. *Measuring the Psychological Maturity of Children: A Revision and Extension of the Goodenough Draw-a-Man Test.* Tarrytown-on-Hudson, N.Y.: World Book Company, 1961.

Jones, A. W., and T. A. Rich. "The Goodenough Draw-a-Man Test as a Measure of Intelligence in Aged Adults." *Journal of Consulting Psychology,* 1957, 21: 235–38.

Kleemeier, R. W., R. A. Rich, and W. A. Justiss. "The Effects of Alpha- (2 piperidyl) Benzhydral Hydrochloride (Meratran) on Psychomotor Performance in a Group of Aged Males." *Journal of Gerontology,* 1956, 11: 165–70.

Lakin, M. "Certain Formal Characteristics of Human Figure Drawings by Institutionalized Aged and by Normal Children." *Journal of Consulting Psychology,* 1956, 20: 471–74.

———. "Formal Characteristics of Human Figure Drawings by Institutionalized and Noninstitutionalized Aged." *Journal of Gerontology,* 1960, 15: 76–78.

Lieberman, M. A. "Psychological Correlates of Impending Death." *Journal of Gerontology,* 1965, 20: 181–90.

Lorge, I., J. Tuckman, and M. B. Dunn. "Human Figure Drawing by Younger and Older Adults." *American Psychologist,* 1954, 9: 420–21.

McCarthy, D. "A Study of Reliability of the Goodenough Test of Intelligence." *Journal of Psychology,* 1944, 18: 201–16.

Machover, K. *Personality Projections in the Drawing of the Human Figure.* Springfield, Ill.: Charles C. Thomas, 1948.

Tuckman, J., I. Lorge, and F. D. Zeman. "The Self-image in Aging." *Journal of Genetic Psychology,* 1961, 99: 317–21.

Instrument

This copyrighted instrument is available from Harcourt Brace Jovanovich, New York.

FULL-RANGE PICTURE VOCABULARY TEST (FRPV)
R. B. Ammons and H. S. Ammons, 1948

Definition of Variable

The test measures verbal comprehension.

Description of Instrument

The test consists of 16 cards with four line drawings on each and a list of 80 words.

Method of Administration

The subject is shown each of the 16 cards separately, and he or she must indicate which of the drawings corresponds to a word given by the examiner. The subject may point to the picture, or he or she may be requested to answer yes or no in some manner as the examiner points to each picture. The examiner starts with the most difficult word that can apply to the pictures and works down a list to the most simple words until the words that the subject can use and work with are identified. Time required for administration is approximately 15 minutes. Some skill is necessary for administering and scoring this test.

Context of Development and Subsequent Use

The FRPV was originally designed to be an alternate to the vocabulary subtest of the Stanford-Binet. Since its development, it has been used as a measure of verbal intelligence, especially in situations in which a subject's verbal communication skills were a potential problem.

Sample

Standardization was carried out on a population of 589 children and adults in and around Denver, Colorado, and in Nebraska. An additional sample was tested in order to provide information for an adult population. This group was composed of 120 individuals 18 to 34 years old, with equal numbers of males and females, from the Denver, Colorado, area. The occupational status of the group's members was similar to the distribution shown in the 1940 census.

Scoring, Scale Norms, and Distribution

IQs can be estimated from scores and adjusted for age. Additional information on scoring and norms is in the test manual (Ammons and Ammons, 1948). Separate norms are available for Hispanic children, black children, and black adults.

Formal Tests of Reliability

Scores have shown an odd-even reliability of .95 for 52 children (Ammons and Huth, 1949), a correlation between forms A and B of .99 for 360 school children (Ammons, Arnold, and Herrmann, 1950), and a correlation between forms A and B of .93 for a population of 120 adults (Ammons, Larson, and Shearn, 1950).

Sterne (1960) found a correlation of .94 between form A and form B, with one day to three weeks intervening between tests, in a group of 60 general medical and surgical patients ranging in age from 36 to 86 years.

Formal Tests of Validity

Convergent and Discriminant Validity: The FRPV correlated .76 with the Stanford-Binet in a group of 60 male mental defectives (Sloan and Bensberg, 1954), .91 and .82 with the VIBS (vocabulary, information, block design, and similarities) subtests of the WAIS for 102 black adults (Tucker, 1951), .82 with the Wechsler Intelligence Scale for Children (WISC) for 90 children who had reading problems (Sloan and Bensberg, 1954), and .84 with the Ravens for a group of cerebral palsied children (Hudson, 1952). Ammons, Larson, and Shearn (1950) found correlations of .86 for form A and .85 for form B with the Wechsler-Bellevue vocabulary scores in a group of 120 individuals 18 to 34 years of age. In a study of long-term chronically ill individuals aged 36 to 84 years (the median was 65.7 years), Sterne (1960) found the FRPV correlated .84 with the WAIS full-scale scores. The FRPV did not discriminate a group of memory-disordered individuals from the members of a control group (Inglis, 1959).

Usability on Older Populations

This is a simple test easily administered to aged individuals. It does not require a verbal or written response, and it is untimed.

Sensitivity to Age Differences

In a group of memory-disordered aged compared to non–memory-disordered controls, Inglis (1959) found that the correlation of the FRPV with the WAIS verbal subtest in the memory-disordered group was not significant but that it was significant in the control group.

General Comments and Recommendations

The FRPV provides a quick estimate of intelligence as defined by verbal ability. It has good reliability and validity, although there is some variability in the data available. Since it takes about 15 minutes to administer, it is not seen as a substitute for the vocabulary subtests on the WAIS or the WISC, which are shorter tests. It seems to be a good estimate of the total IQ scores on these other tests. The FRPV would be a handy test for use with subjects who have difficulty making verbal responses.

References

Ammons, R. B., and H. S. Ammons. *Full-Range Picture Vocabulary Test, Brochure.* Missoula, Mont.: Psychological Test Specialists, 1948.

Ammons, R. B., P. R. Arnold, and R. S. Herrmann. "The Full-Range Picture Vocabulary Test:

IV. Results for White School Population." *Journal of Clinical Psychology*, 1950, 6: 164–69.

Ammons, R. B., and R. W. Huth. "The Full-Range Picture Vocabulary Test: I. Preliminary Scale." *Journal of Psychology*, 1949, 28: 51–64.

Ammons, R. B., W. L. Larson, and C. R. Shearn. "The Full-Range Picture Vocabulary Test: V. Results for an Adult Population." *Journal of Consulting Psychology*, 1950, 14: 150–55.

Ankus, M., and B. Quarrington. "Operant Behavior in Memory Disordered." *Journal of Gerontology*, 1972, 27: 500–510.

Hudson, A. "A Comparative Study of the Test Responses of Two Groups of Cerebral Palsied Children: Athetoid and Spastic." Ph.D. dissertation, University of Wisconsin, 1952.

Inglis, J. "Learning Retention and Conceptual Usage in Elderly Patients with Memory Disorder." *Journal of Abnormal and Social Psychology*, 1959, 59: 210–15.

Sloan, W., and G. J. Bensberg. "An Exploratory Study of the Full-Range Picture Vocabulary Test with Mental Defectives." *American Journal of Mental Deficiency*, 1954, 58: 481–85.

Smith, L. M., and A. R. Fillmore. "The Ammons FRPV Test and the WISC for Remedial Reading Cases." *Journal of Consulting Psychology*, 1954, 18: 332.

Sterne, D. M. "Use of Ammons FRPVT with Long-Term Chronically Ill." *Journal of Clinical Psychology*, 1960, 16: 192–93.

Tucker, D. A. "A Study of Adult Male Negroes with the Full-Range Picture Vocabulary Test." M.A. thesis, University of Louisville, 1951.

Instrument

This copyrighted instrument is available from Psychological Test Specialists, Missoula, Mont.

KENT SERIES OF EMERGENCY SCALES (EGY)
G. A. Kent, 1946

Definition of Variable

The test measures general intelligence.

Description of Instrument

The EGY is a 10-item test. There are four forms (scales A, B, C, D) for children aged 5 to 14. Apparently, scale D is the form used to assess the intelligence of adults.

Method of Administration

The test is administered individually and orally. It takes about four or five minutes to complete.

Context of Development and Subsequent Use

The EGY was developed as a quick screening device for the measurement of intelligence in children. However, it was used widely during World War II as a quick screening assessment of intelligence for large numbers of recruits being inducted into the army. As a result, it has been frequently used to estimate the intelligence of adults in clinical and research settings.

Sample

Norms for the EGY were originally established only for children (Kent, 1946), but *T* scores and deciles were subsequently established for the aged with a group of 253 individuals 60 years old or older in San Francisco (Katz and Crook, 1962). This group was composed of 151 males and 102 females and was approximately proportional to the national distribution of education and employment status.

Scoring, Scale Norms, and Distribution

Scoring is accomplished as the test is administered. The possible range of scores on this test is 0–36. These scores can be converted to IQs. Within the population of aged persons described above, separate norms are available for men and women since men scored significantly higher than women ($p < .05$) on almost every item and on overall scores. The overall score for men was 25.4 points, versus 19.4 points for women ($\sigma = 6.2$ and 7.1, respectively). The distribution of scores for women was essentially normal. However, the scores for men were negatively skewed, suggesting the need for a few more items in the difficult range.

Formal Tests of Reliability

The test-retest correlation (after a 24-hour interval) in a group of 77 geriatric patients was .84 (Meer and Baker, 1965), and in a group of psychiatric patients it was .82 (after a one-year interval) (Katz and Crook, 1962).

Formal Tests of Validity

Convergent Validity: This test correlated .64 with a composite score from four verbal subtests of the WAIS in an unrepresentative sample of 94 older adults drawn from a sample of 229 individuals admitted to psychiatric wards in San Francisco (Katz and Crook, 1962). The EGY correlated .50 to .70 with the Wechsler-Bellevue for various groups of young adults (Delp, 1953; Lowinski, 1943; Wright, McPhee, and Cummings, 1949).

Predictive Validity: The EGY has not been shown to differentiate individuals with chronic brain syndrome from individuals without this condition (Katz and Crook, 1962).

Usability on Older Populations

Katz and Crook (1962) have established norms for aged subjects, though the items remain the same for both children and older adults. The correlation between age and the EGY score in this population was only −.09. The EGY might be a good screening technique to use with the aged when it is necessary to gather subjects within a certain intellectual range or to make some determination of a lower limit of intelligence. This test would not, however, be usable as a precise measure of intelligence.

Sensitivity to Age Differences

The range of raw scores in the older samples included in the Katz and Crook study (1962) was 6–35. Though in that older population men scored significantly higher than women, no sex difference has been indicated in younger populations. In a group of 229 aged (60 years old and older) psychiatric patients, a significant difference in the scores of men and women again appeared (mean scores 17.3 versus 12.1). There was a small negative correlation with age (−.18) in this population.

General Comments and Recommendations

This is a short, easily administered test of intelligence that could be used with aged subjects as a screening device in clinical and research situations. It has reasonable reliability and validity. As a research tool, however, the investigator could wish a better measurement when precise differentiation in the intelligence of groups is necessary.

References

Delp, H. A. "Correlations between Kent EGY and the Wechsler Battery." *Journal of Clinical Psychology,* 1953, 9: 73–75.

Katz, L., and G. H. Crook. "The Use of the Kent EGY with Aged Population." *Journal of Gerontology,* 1962, 17: 186–89.

Kent, G. A. *A Series of Emergency Scales Manual.* New York: Psychological Corporation, 1946.

Lowenthal, M. R., and P. L. Berkman. *Aging and Mental Disorders in San Francisco.* San Francisco: Jossey-Bass, 1967.

Lowinski, R. J. "Performance of Naval Recruits on the Kent Oral Emergency Test and the Verbal Battery of the Wechsler-Bellevue Adult Intelligence Scale." *American Journal of Orthopsychiatry*, 1943, 13: 138-40.

Meer, B., and J. A. Baker. "Reliability of Measurements of Intellectual Functioning of Geriatric Patients." *Journal of Gerontology*, 1965, 20: 410-14.

Wright, H. F., H. M. McPhee, and S. B. Cummings. "The Relationship between the Kent KGY and the Bellevue Verbal Scale." *Journal of Abnormal and Social Psychology*, 1949, 44: 223-30.

Instrument

This copyrighted instrument is available from the Psychological Corporation, New York.

PRIMARY MENTAL ABILITIES TEST (PMA)
L. L. Thurstone and T. G. Thurstone, 1947

Definition of Variable

The instrument measures four aspects of intelligence: verbal comprehension, perceptual speed, numerical facility, and grasp of spatial relations.

Description of Instrument

This is a factor analytically based test of intelligence generally assessing four or five factors, depending on the form used. There are six forms—grades K-1, 2-4, 4-6, 6-9, 9-12 and adult. On the form for grades K-1, there are four factor scores (verbal meaning, perceptual speed, numerical facility, and spatial relations) and a total score. These same factor scores are on the form for grades 2-4. On the form for grades 4-6, the total score is dropped and reasoning is added as the fifth score. On the form for grades 6-9, the perceptual speed factor is not assessed and the total score is added. These same factors are found on the forms for grades 9-12 and adult. The adult form is the same as that for grades 9-12, except that the name is changed. The PMA is a paper-and-pencil test, so it can be administered to individuals or groups.

Method of Administration

The separate subtests are timed; therefore, the test must be administered by someone familiar with these limits and the test. A high level of skill is not needed for this, however. The test manual supplies all the information needed. The test takes approximately 15 minutes to administer.

Context of Development and Subsequent Use

The PMA was developed by factor analytic procedures, at the time an important advance in the field of intelligence testing. Forms for more advanced grades were added as time passed, with the final form for adults. The PMA has been frequently used with elderly subjects in research settings.

Sample

This test was standardized on a population of 32,393 individuals between 4 and 20 years old. This population was drawn from five different regions, but mostly from the northeast section of the United States. No information is available on the representativeness of this sample in terms of socioeconomic groups, ethnic minorities, and sex.

Scoring, Scale Norms, and Distribution

Raw scores for the separate subtests and total scores are converted to percentiles according to conversion tables available in the manual. Estimated deviation IQs for forms above grade 4 can be obtained from these percentile ranks by using another conversion table. No data were given about the development of this latter conversion table. Below grade 4, ratio IQs are used.

Formal Tests of Reliability

The test manual (Thurstone and Thurstone, 1947) reported reliabilities computed on 500 students in grade 10B of .92 for verbal, .96 for spatial, .93 for reasoning, .89 for numerical, .90 for word fluency, and .93 for the total (there was no indication of the type of reliability). Other data are available for the original sample. Split-half reliabilities were computed by Schaie, Rosenthal, and Perlman (1953) for a sample of 61 persons between the ages of 53 and 78 years. The coefficients ranged from .92 to .96.

Schaie and Strother (1968b) did a test-retest study of the PMA in a population of individuals 20 to 70 years old. Correlations ranged from .75 (spatial subtest) to .94 (total score).

Quereshi (1972) indicated test-retest reliability coefficients of .83 to .95 over a period of one to four weeks (the group was unspecified). Individual factor scores were more unstable.

Formal Tests of Validity

Intercorrelation among the five scores on an earlier form for subjects 5 to 7 years old ranged from .51 to .73. On an earlier form for children 7 to 11 years old, the intercorrelations were lower, ranging from .10 to .63 (Frederiksen, 1959).

Usability on Older Populations

This test has been used with the aged in numerous studies. However, there are no norms for groups above 17.5 years of age, nor are there data on the effects on performance of socioeconomic status, educational level, and other variables. In addition, the entire test is timed. Since it is well known that timing affects the scores of elderly individuals more than those of younger persons, the use of this test with the elderly would seem to be limited.

Sensitivity to Age Differences

Generally, it has been found that performance on the factors of speed, reasoning, and mental ability declines and performance on word fluency, verbal understanding, and numerical ability holds during later life.

General Comments and Recommendations

Few data on the validity of this test with younger versus older subjects are available. The standardization sample is biased. Timed administration of the test seems to dictate against its use with elderly subjects. Though the PMA has been used with elderly subjects in the past, it would seem best to select another test for future use.

References

Baltes, R. B., K. W. Schaie, and A. H. Nardi. "Age and Expected Mortality in a Seven-Year Long Study of Cognitive Behavior." *Developmental Psychology*, 1971, 5: 18–26.

Frederiksen, N. Review. In *The Fifth Mental Measurement Yearbook*, O. K. Buros (ed.), pp. 709–14. Highland Park, N. J.: Gryphon Press, 1959.

Furry, C. A., and P. B. Baltes. "The Effect of Age Differences in Ability, Extraneous Performance Variables on Assessment of Intelligence in Children, Adults and Elderly." *Journal of Gerontology*, 1973, 28: 73–80.

Kamin, L. "Differential Changes in M-Abilities in Old Age." *Journal of Gerontology*, 1957, 12: 66–70.

Nesselroade, J. R., K. W. Schaie, and P. B. Baltes. "Ontogenetic and Generational Components of Structural and Quantitative Change in Adult Behavior." *Journal of Gerontology*, 1972, 27: 222–28.

Quereshi, M. Y. "Review." In *The Seventh Mental Measurements Yearbook*, O. K. Buros (ed.), pp. 1064–66. Highland Park, N.J.: Gryphon Press, 1972.

Schaie, K. W. "Rigidity, Flexibility and Intelligence." *Psychological Monographs*, 1958, 72 (9): 1–6.

Schaie, K. W., F. Rosenthal, and R. M. Perlman. "Differential Mental Deterioration of Factorially 'Pure' Functions in Later Maturity." *Journal of Gerontology*, 1953, 8: 191–96.

Schaie, K. W., and C. R. Strother. " The Effect of Time and Cohort Differences on the Interpretation of Age Changes in Cognitive Behavior." *Multivariate Behavioral Research*, 1968a, 3: 259–93.

———. "A Cross-Sequential Study of Age Changes in Cognitive Behavior." *Psychological Bulletin*, 1968b, 70: 671–80.

Strother, C. R., K. W. Schaie, and P. Horst. "The Relationship between Advanced Age and Mental Abilities." *Journal of Abnormal and Social Psychology*, 1957, 55: 166–70.

Thurstone, L. L. *Multiple Factor Analysis*. Chicago: University of Chicago Press, 1947.

Thurstone, L. L., and T. G. Thurstone. *Primary Mental Abilities*. Chicago: Science Research Associates, 1947.

Instrument

This copyrighted instrument is available from Science Research Associates, Inc., Chicago.

PROGRESSIVE MATRICES TEST (PMT)
J. C. Raven, 1960

Definition of Variable

The capacity to form comparisons between meaningless figures and to develop from them a logical method of reasoning by analogy is tested.

Description of Instrument

The instrument is a timed paper-and-pencil test. The test booklet is arranged so that each page contains one problem. A patterned grid is presented with a part missing. The subject must choose the one correct missing part from those that might fit into the space on the grid.

The standard Progressive Matrices Test for children (under 11 years old) consists of 60 problems divided into sets of 12 each (sets A, B, C, D, and E). Within each set, problems become progressively more difficult. The Colored Progressive Matrices Test (sets A, Ab, and B) is a variation on the standard sets A and B that was developed especially for use with young children and older people. This form can be presented in booklet form or as board with movable pieces.

Method of Administration

Though the test is usually given in individual sessions, there is a special group form. The score is the number correct. It takes 30 to 45 minutes to complete the test. Administration can be timed or untimed. The Colored Progressive Matrices Test is always given without time limits.

Context of Development and Subsequent Use

This test was developed as a nonverbal test of intelligence based on the individual's innate capacity for observation and clear thinking. It was developed for use with the Mill Hill Vocabulary Test to measure the recall of acquired information. Though this test has been used frequently with the Mill Hill, it also has been frequently used alone in clinical and research settings. In research with the elderly, the Progressive Matrices Test has been used as a covariate control measure for performance of other abilities, as well as a dependent measure. The Colored Matrices Test was designed for use with young children and older people in clinical and research work.

Sample

Percentile norms for the standard test were based on the scores of 735 and 1,407 children and on the scores of about 5,000 adults, 6 to 65 years of age. These were British samples. Percentile norms for the aged on the Colored Matrices Test were based on 271 British subjects.

Scoring, Scale Norms, and Distribution

Norms for individual and group standard forms are given in terms of percentile points, through age 65 years. For the advanced test, percentile norms are supplied to age 40 (individual or group test). Norms for the Colored Matrices Test include percentile points for aged persons aged 65 to 85 years. The manual also contains norms for elderly depressives and elderly subjects with senile dementia.

Formal Tests of Reliability

This test was reported by the author to have test-retest reliability of .83 to .93, depending on the age-group tested (Raven, 1960).

Formal Tests of Validity

Convergent Validity: The Progressive Matrices was reported by Raven (1960) to correlate with the Terman-Merrill scale (.86) and to have a *g* saturation of .82 within a group of 1,000 seamen. The Colored Matrices Test has had a correlation of .66 with the Terman-Merrill for a group of children 9 years of age.

Foulds (1949) reported a correlation of .93 with the Terman-Binet.

Usability of Older Populations

This is an easily administered and understood test for use with the aged. It would be especially useful with subjects suffering from communication disorders. Though the Progressive Matrices has been used to explore age relationships in IQ scores, it has also been used frequently as a covariate control measure.

Sensitivity to Age Differences

Scores on the Matrices Test tend to reach their maximum with subjects about 14 years old and remain relatively constant for about 10 years and then uniformly decline after that time (Raven, 1960).

The correlation of the Raven with age have been reported to be $-.59$ ($p < .01$, two tailed test; Storch, Looft, and Hooper, 1972) with a group of 12 males and 12 females ranging in age from 55 to 79 years. The mean age of the males was 67.3 years and of the females, 64.3 years. The mean educational level of the males and females was 10 years. In this study, it appears that the Colored Progressive Matrices was given. In a cross-sectional study of approximately 3,000 males in various occupational groups, Progressive Matrices Test scores declined from about age 30 years and beyond. Those individuals who scored lower percentile rankings within their respective age-groups showed declines increasingly greater than those scoring higher percentile rankings (Foulds, 1949).

General Comments and Recommendations

The Raven has been a useful alternative nonverbal test of intelligence for illiterate and non–English-speaking populations from childhood through young adulthood. Norms are not available for groups beyond age 65, however, and further work needs to be done to determine the factors that produce the negative correlation with age.

References

Chown, S. M. "Age and Rigidities." *Journal of Gerontology*, 1961, 16: 353–62.

Cunningham, W. R., V. Clayton, and W. Overton. "Fluid and Crystallized Intelligence in Young Adulthood and Old Age." *Journal of Gerontology*, 1975, 30: 53–55.

Edwards, A., and D. Wine. "Personality Changes with Age: Their Dependency on Concomitant Intellectual Decline." *Journal of Gerontology*, 1963, 18: 182–84.

Foulds, G. A. "Variations in the Intellectual Activities of Adults." *American Journal of Psychology*, 1949, 62: 238-46.

Orme, J. E. "Nonverbal and Verbal Performance in Normal Old Age, Senile Dementia and Elderly Depression." *Journal of Gerontology*, 1957, 12: 408-13.

Powell, R. "Psychological Effects of Exercise Therapy upon Institutionalized Geriatric Mental Patients." *Journal of Gerontology*, 1974, 29: 157-61.

Raven, J. C. *Guide to the Standard Progressive Matrices.* New York: Psychological Corporation, 1960.

Storch, P. A., W. R. Looft, and F. H. Hooper. "Interrelationship among Piagetian Tasks and Traditional Measures of Cognitive in Mature and Aged Adults." *Journal of Gerontology*, 1972, 27: 461-65.

Young, M. L. "Problem Solving Performance in Two Age Groups." *Journal of Gerontology*, 1966, 21: 505-9.

Instrument

This copyrighted instrument is available from the Psychological Corporation, New York.

MILL HILL VOCABULARY TEST
J. C. Raven, 1943

Definition of Variable

The level of verbal information a person has acquired as a result of intellectual activity in the past is measured.

Description of Instrument

The test consists of two parallel series of 44 words each, arranged in order according to difficulty (sets A and B). Every word on one list is a synonym for a word on the other list. There is a junior form from which the 10 most difficult words in each set were omitted. The senior form includes all but the 10 simplest words.

Method of Administration

There are three administrative procedures possible: (1) oral definition, in which the examiner reads the words and records the definitions given by the subject; (2) written definition, in which the subject is asked to write the meanings of words from one of the lists on the form given with the test; and (3) definition by selection of synonyms, in which the subject defines the words on one of the lists by choosing a synonym for it from the alternate list.

This test takes about 15 minutes to complete, with the more extensive administrations requiring more time.

Context of Development and Subsequent Use

The Mill Hill Vocabulary Test was developed in order to provide a score for comparison to scores on the Progressive Matrices Test. The Mill Hill Vocabulary score was thought to reflect acquired levels of functioning, and the Progressive Matrices was thought to reflect more innate intelligence. Differences in scores on these two tests were intended to be used as an indication of psychological deterioration as a result of organic or functional disability. The score on the Mill Hill was intended to be used as an indication of a subject's present capacity for intellectual activity. In later use, however, the Mill Hill has not been a constant companion to the Progressive Matrices and actually has been used infrequently.

Sample

This test was standardized on a British population of 823 children, 4.5 to 14 years of age, and 1,419 children and 2,300 men, 11.5 to 70 years of age.

Scoring, Scale Norms, and Distribution

Criteria for scoring can be found in the test manual (Raven, 1943). Percentile norms based on the standardization populations indicated above are available for oral and written administrations. With written administration, performance on the oral definitions, written definitions, and synonyms selection apparently have been combined in one score.

Formal Tests of Reliability/Homogeneity

The test has a test-retest reliability of .87 to .98. The correlation of the set A list with the set B list ranged from .86 for a group of 12-year-olds to .88 for adults. The correlation between set A and set B for oral definitions increased from .65 to .95 as the age of the subjects increased; for synonym selection, it increases from .80 for children to .88 for adults (Raven, 1954).

Formal Tests of Validity

The author (Raven, 1954) has stated that a person's percentile grade on the Mill Hill Vocabulary Test usually agrees with his or her percentile grade on the Progressive Matrices Test. However, certain factors such as age, education, interests, physical abnormalities, and mental illness have been recognized as factors in this relationship, although this moderating effect has not been quantified.

Convergent Validity: Correlation between the Mill Hill and the Terman-Merrill mental age was .93 (Raven, 1954).

Usability on Older Populations

This is an easily administered vocabulary test. The alternate administrative procedures might be suited to individuals who are hard of hearing or who have difficulty in coordination and cannot write. However, norms are not available for older adults on the oral administration alone.

Sensitivity to Age Differences

Orme (1957) used the Mill Hill Vocabulary Test (oral definitions form) with two groups of elderly patients (one group of 25 with a diagnosis of senile dementia and a group of 24 depressives) and a group of healthy old people. The means differed significantly between the depressives and the normals. In a study of approximately 3,000 men between the ages of 16 and 65, scores on this test tended to show an increase until about age 30 and then they remained relatively constant, with those scoring lower percentile rankings within their groups showing some decline (Foulds, 1949). Foulds did not report the administrative procedure used in his study. It would appear to have been some combination of scores, since in one graph scores as high as 80 points were reported.

The correlation between the Mill Hill Vocabulary Test and the Progressive Matrices Test generally declined from .57 for 12-year-olds to .44 in the group aged 50 and over.

General Comments and Recommendations

This is an easily administered test of verbal activity that has built-in flexibility for use with special populations in the different methods of administration. However, this test was developed on a British population, so the words on the list may not be useful with an American group. This test was developed for use with, and as a complement to, the Raven Progressive Matrices Test. One study (Raven, 1954), however, indicated that there were low correlations in scores between the two tests and that this correlation declined with increased age. Further validity studies need be done with this test if it is to be used in the future.

References

Foulds, G. A. "Variations in the Intellectual Activities of Adults." *American Journal of Psychology*, 1949, 62: 238–46.

Orme, J. E. "Nonverbal and Verbal Performance in Normal Old Age, Senile Dementia and Elderly Depression." *Journal of Gerontology*, 1957, 12: 408–13.

Raven, J. C. *The Mill Hill Vocabulary Scale*. London: H. K. Lewis, 1943.

_____. *Guide to Using the Mill Hill Vocabulary Scale with Progressive Matrices (1938)*. Beverly Hills, Calif.: Western Psychological Services, 1954.

Instrument

This copyrighted instrument is available from Western Psychological Services, Beverly Hills, Calif.

WECHSLER ADULT INTELLIGENCE SCALE (WAIS)
D. Wechsler, 1955

Definition of Variable

The scale measures general intelligence.

Description of Instrument

The scale consists of questions, problems, and tasks constituting six verbal and five performance subtests.

Method of Administration

The test is individually administered. Skill and training are needed to administer, score, and interpret this test. It takes approximately 60 minutes to administer, with more or less time required depending on the age and ability of the subject.

Context of Development and Subsequent Use

The WAIS was developed in order to provide a comprehensive test of intelligence for adults in clinical and research settings. The WAIS is widely used, in whole and in part, in both of these contexts.

Sample

Following a stratified sampling plan with quotas of cases based on data from the 1950 U.S. census, 1,720 subjects were selected. Norms were developed for each of seven age-groups, ranging from 16 to 64 years. The number of persons in the age-groups were not proportional to U.S. population figures. Equal numbers of men and women were chosen. Additional information regarding the geographical, racial, occupational, and educational characteristics of the sample can be found in Wechsler (1955).

Doppelt and Wallace (1955) supplied standardization data for the WAIS on 352 older subjects, aged 60 years and above. These older subjects were taken from the University of Chicago–Kansas City study of the middle aged and aging. Table 2-3 breaks down the composition of that sample by age and sex.

TABLE 2-3
Number of Cases in Old Age Sample

Age-group	Male	Female	Total
60–64	44	57	101
65–69	42	44	86
70–74	38	42	80
75+	36	49	85

Scoring, Scale Norms, and Distribution

Standard scores can be obtained for the individual subtests as well as for the combined verbal and performance subtests. Deviation IQs can be obtained for the verbal, performance and full-scale scores. The tables listing the verbal, performance, and full-scale deviation IQs for the age-groups tested by Doppelt and Wallace (1955) were developed through the same procedure used for the IQ tables of the national sample (Wechsler, 1944). For each age-group, the mean of the sum of scaled scores was set equal to 100 and the standard deviation was set equal to 15.

Formal Tests of Reliability/Homogeneity

Reliability coefficients (type unknown) for the main standardization sample full-scale scores and IQs ranged from .90 to .97 and for performance and verbal parts from .84 to .96. Split-half reliability for all subtests, main scales, and full scale scores ranged from .60 to .96, depending on the age-group tested. The reliability of verbal and performance scales and the full-scale is better than for individual subtests (Wechsler, 1958).

Formal Tests of Validity

Construct Validity: Cohen (1957) factor analyzed the WAIS, using the standardization data provided by Wechsler (1955) and Doppelt and Wallace (1958). Four age-groups were formed: 18 through 19, 25 through 34, 45 through 54, and 60 through 75 and over. Three correlated primary factors (verbal comprehension, perceptual organization, and memory) were detected in all age-groups, and two unidentified specific factors did not appear in the age-group 60–75 and over. A g factor with high loadings in every subtest appeared and accounted for about half of the subtest variance. Factorial invariance over the age range studied was noted. In the age-group 60–75 years, the memory factor attracted a larger amount of the variance because of the g factor. This revealed a dependency of achievement on retention and memory in old age. Raw scores on the subtests and scales changed with age, as did factor loadings. With increased age, performance depended increasingly on verbal comprehension, retention, and ability to form conceptual relationships. Contribution to performance made by inductive and deductive reasoning, perceptual speed, fluency, visualization, and numerical facility gradually declined (Maxwell, 1961). Median intercorrelations between subtests of the scale were similar between older groups and younger groups. The range of correlations has been found to be greater with elderly groups (Doppelt and Wallace, 1955).

Convergent Validity: Correlations with the Raven Progressive Matrices Test in a group of 82 brain-damaged adult males were .72 for full-scale scores, .58 for verbal scores, and .70 for performance scores.

Correlations with the Stanford-Binet (form L) on 52 reformatory inmates, aged 16 to 26, were .85 for full-scale scores, .80 for verbal scores, and .60 for performance scores (Wechsler, 1958).

Usability on Older Populations

The WAIS has been widely used in studies with the aged. In addition to investigations of the changes or differences in scores with increased age, the WAIS has often been used as a control measure in studies with the aged. Performance, in terms of the magnitude of scores and the patterns of scores, changes when groups of increasing ages are tested. Consequently, the use of raw scores or standard scores to compare age-groups will almost certainly reflect declines in tested intelligence as age increases. However, since the deviation IQ scores are derived within a particular age-group, comparisons between age-groups can be accomplished with these scores.

Sensitivity to Age Differences

The WAIS has been used in so many studies that not all of them can be reviewed here, nor will the readers find a complete bibliography of studies in which the WAIS has been used. An excellent detailed review of significant studies can be found in Botwinick (1977).

Briefly, the studies have indicated the following tendencies. (1) WAIS scores decline with age in cross-sectional as well as longitudinal studies. The decline in scores tends to occur at later ages and is less dramatic in longitudinal studies than in cross-sectional studies. (2) A classic and reliable pattern of stability in scores on the verbal scale and a drop in the scores on the performance scales of the WAIS can be seen over the subjects' life span. (3) The pattern of decline in scores is modified by the initial level of ability of the individual, though the classic pattern applies to all groups. (4) In longitudinal studies, the amount of decline can be influenced by the length of the intervals between testings.

General Comments and Recommendations.

This is a test with known factors and properties that has been widely used in total and as separate subtests with the elderly. The test has not been adapted to the aged so as to overcome cohort problems, but this particular objection is common for measures of intelligence. The use of deviation IQs allows for comparison of age-groups, although an older person may achieve an average IQ score by doing less well than a younger individual. The elderly standardization group was not truly representative or stratified, though the main standardization (and younger) group was.

References

Botwinick, J. "Intellectual Abilities." In *Handbook of the Psychology of Aging*, J. E. Birren and K. W. Schaie (eds.), pp. 580–605. New York: Van Nostrand Reinhold, 1977.

Cohen, J. "The Factorial Structure of the WAIS between Early Adulthood and Old Age." *Journal of Consulting Psychology*, 1957, 21: 283–90.

Doppelt, J. E., and W. L. Wallace. "Standardization of WAIS for Older Persons." *Journal of Abnormal and Social Psychology*, 1955, 51: 312-30.

Eisdorfer, C., E. Busse, and L. D. Cohen. "The WAIS Performance of an Aged Sample." *Journal of Gerontology*, 1959, 14: 197–201.

Hall, E. H., R. D. Savage, N. Bolton, D. Pidwell, and G. Blessed. "Intellect, Mental Illness, and Survival in the Aged: A Longitudinal Investigation." *Journal of Gerontology*, 1972, 27: 237–44.

Inglis, J. "Learning, Retention and Conceptual Usage in Elderly Patients with Memory Disorder." *Journal of Abnormal and Social Psychology*, 1959, 59: 210–15.

Levinson, B. M. " A Research Note on Subcultural Differences in WAIS between Aged Italians and Jews." *Journal of Gerontology*, 1960, 15: 197–98.

Maxwell, A. E. "Trends in Cognitive Ability in Older Age Ranges." *Journal of Abnormal and Social Psychology*, 1961, 63: 449–52.

Meer, B., and J. A. Baker. "Reliability of Measurement of Intellectual Functioning of Geriatric Patients." *Journal of Gerontology*, 1965, 20: 410–14.

Riegel, K. F., R. M. Riegel, and G. Meyer. "A Study of the Dropout Rates in Longitudinal Research on Aging and the Prediction of Death." *Journal of Personality and Social Psychology*, 1967, 5: 342–48.

Riegel, R. M., and K. F. Riegel. "A Comparison and Interpretation of Factorial Structures of the W-B, the WAIS and HAWIE on Aged Persons." *Journal of Consulting Psychology*, 1962, 26: 31–37;

Savage, R. D., and P. G. Britton. "The Factorial Structure of the WAIS in an Aged Sample." *Journal of Gerontology*, 1968, 23: 183–86.

Wechsler, D. *The Measurement of Adult Intelligence*. Baltimore: Williams and Wilkins, 1944.

——. *WAIS Manual*, New York: Psychological Corporation, 1955.

——. *The Measurement and Appraisal of Adult Intelligence* (4th ed.). Baltimore: Williams and Wilkins, 1958.

Instrument

This copyrighted instrument is available from the Psychological Corporation, New York.

BENDER VISUAL MOTOR GESTALT TEST
L. Bender, 1938

Definition of Variable

The test assesses various aspects of functional or organic psychological disturbance as well as some aspects of normal functioning, such as level of maturation and intelligence.

Description of Instrument

This test consists of a set of eight geometric figures of varying complexity, printed on small, separate cards. The subject's task is to reproduce the figures while viewing each of the cards.

Method of Administration

There is no one standard method of administration for this test. Usually, however, an 8½-by-11-inch piece of paper and a pencil are given to the subject. The cards are then presented to the subject separately and in a specified order. The subject must reproduce the design (draw it on the paper) while it is within view. This usually takes only a few minutes to accomplish.

Context of Development and Subsequent Use

This test was based upon the perceptual work of Wertheimer (1923). Bender (1938) selected nine of Wertheimer's figures and studied the performance of children in drawing these. Hutt (1945) noted the diagnostic usefulness of the test with adults. The test has been used in clinical and research settings for exploring aspects of normal functioning, such as maturation, and as a diagnostic tool for differentiating the performance of brain-damaged, functionally disordered, and normal individuals.

Sample

The original sample used by Bender (1938) was 800 children, 3 to 11 years old.

Scoring, Scale Norms, and Distribution

A scoring system developed by Pascal and Suttell (1957) is one of two objective methods of assessing performance. This system involves scoring 105 details. Hutt and Briskin (1960) developed an easily applied scoring system based on 12 errors, in which a subject would be diagnosed as organic when five or more errors were made. The 12 errors are: (1) rotation, (2) overlapping difficulty, (3) closure difficulty, (4) cohesion, (5) perseveration, (6) retrogression, (7) angulation difficulty, (8) fragmentation, (9) collusion, (10) simplification, (11) impotence, and (12) motor uncoordination. Hutt and Briskin presented scores that they had obtained from a group of subjects one or more years out of high school, aged 15 to 50, and of a group, aged 15 to 50, with a year or more of college. Often, in research with the aged, scoring for the Bender Gestalt drawings is developed specifically for the study at hand.

Formal Tests of Reliability/Homogeneity

Pascal and Suttell (1957) reported a test-retest (at a 24-hour interval) correlation of .71 in a group of 44 subjects ranging in education from the first year in high school to graduate school. The reliability correlation of a normal group retested after 18 months was .63. These low reliabilities are partly due to interrater reliability problems, though Pascal and Suttell reported an intrarater reliability of about .90 when the raters had been trained (i.e., after they had scored 25 tests successfully).

Since the method of administration is not standard, scores can vary when the paper is positioned differently from administration to administration (Weiss, 1971) or when other aspects of the mode of administration vary (Hasazi, Allen, and Wohlford, 1971).

Formal Tests of Validity

Convergent Validity: A correlation of .37 between verbal and performance IQ differences on the Wechsler-Bellvue and the Bender Gestalt scores was obtained for a group of 25 psychotics (Pascal and Suttell, 1957).

Shanan, Cohen, and Adler (1966) found a correlation of .74 between performance on the Bender (by Pascal and Suttell scoring system) and the Benton Visual Retention Test in a group of 40 hemiplegic patients.

Predictive Validity: A comparison of the scores of 43 hospitalized psychiatric patients discharged as improved and the scores of 22 discharged as unimproved showed significant (p < .01) differences in favor of the improved diagnostic group (Pascal and Suttell, 1957).

Pascal and Suttell (1957) also indicated that a cutoff score at the mean of the groups cited in the manual would screen out 96% of the psychotics and 91% of the neurotics while also including 50% of the nonpatient population.

Brilliant and Gynther (1963) found that the Hutt-Briskin scoring system significantly differentiated normal from brain-damaged subjects. However, Johnson, Hellkamp, and Lottman (1971) found that the Hutt-Briskin system was effective for diagnosis only when used with patients in the borderline or dull-normal range of intellectual functioning. These authors cautioned against the use of this indicator with patients outside of that IQ range.

Korman and Blumberg (1963) reported that the Bender correctly identified 75% of a group of 40 brain-damaged patients and a group of 40 patients with mixed psychiatric diagnoses.

Riklan, Levita, and Cooper (1965) reported a study of patients who underwent bilateral brain surgery. The Bender Gestalt was one of the instruments used in this study to assess change in functioning after the surgery. There was no significant difference between patients who had undergone surgery and patients who had not. The scores on the Bender used in this study were developed especially for the study.

Shanan, Cohen, and Adler (1966) reported a significant difference in scores on the Bender (obtained by the Pascal and Suttell scoring system) between a group of 40 patients with cerebrovascular disease and 30 healthy controls.

Usability on Older Populations

This is an easily administered test. However, the motor coordination it requires may make it difficult for older people to perform adequately. Indeed, Pascal and Suttell (1957) have recognized that a subject's tremor is likely to result in a poorer score. Scores are also likely to be affected by intelligence and age (Pascal and Suttell, 1957). Though correlations are available between age and performance at early ages, none is available for older adults.

Education was found to correlate significantly — 38 (biserial) — with performance in a group 15 to 50 years of age. This factor would skew the results with the aged, also (Pascal and Suttell, 1957).

In a study of individuals approaching death, Lieberman (1965) found that the Pascal and Suttell score on the Bender Gestalt declined as individuals approached death. Gilbert and Levee (1965) found statistically reliable differences in scores (obtained by the Pascal and Suttell method) in favor of the young subjects in a study of 29 males and 26 females aged 20 to 35 years and 22 males and 28 women aged 60 to 80 years.

Klonoff and Kennedy (1965) worked with veterans 80 to 92 years old. Within this age-group, these investigators found no relationships between age and performance on the Bender (scored by the Pascal and Suttell method); but they did find that the scores were influenced by the subjects' health status. In another study, Klonoff and Kennedy (1966) confirmed these results regarding health status and found a significant difference between mean scores when comparing groups of hospitalized aged subjects and nonhospitalized aged subjects.

General Comments and Recommendations

Though the reliability of performance on the Bender Gestalt test using the detailed Pascal-Suttell scoring system has been reported as good, the validity of this test apparently remains to be established, and the factors determining performance have not yet been isolated. Signs usually taken as indicative of brain damage have been found to be due to stimulus variables, as well as to physiological change (Blakemore, 1965). Adequate norms are not available for populations of various ages. Since the administration of this test is not standardized, variation in performance due to variation in method of administration is likely to occur, further confusing the interpretation of results. The studies now available in this area indicate that scores on the Bender Gestalt may be affected by a host of factors, such as socioeconomic status, fatigue, and the way the piece of paper is presented to the subject (Weiss, 1971).

It would seem that the Bender Gestalt is not an adequate test for use with the elderly.

References

Bender, L. *A Visual Motor Gestalt Test and Its Clinical Use*. Research Monograph number 3. New York: American Orthopsychiatric Association, 1938.

Blakemore, C. B. "Review." In *The Sixth Mental Measurements Yearbook*, O. K. Buros (ed.), pp. 414–15. Highland Park, N.J.: Gryphon Press, 1965.

Brilliant, P. J., and M. D. Gynther. "Relationships between Performance on Three Tests for Organicity and Selected Patient Variables." *Journal of Consulting Psychology*, 1963, 27: 474–75.

Gilbert, J. G., and R. F. Levee. "Age Differences on the Bender Visual Motor Gestalt Test and the Archimedes Spiral Test." *Journal of Gerontology*, 1965, 20: 196–200.

Hasazi, J. E., R. M. Allen, and P. Wohlford. "Effects of Mode of Administration on Bender-Gestalt Test Performance of Familiar Retardates." *Journal of Clinical Psychology*, 1971, 27: 360–62.

Hutt, M. *A Tentative Guide in the Administration and Interpretation of the Bender-Gestalt Test*. U.S. Army, Adjutant General's School, 1945.

Hutt, M., and G. Briskin. "The Clinical Use of the Revised Bender-Gestalt Test." New York: Grune and Stratton, 1960.

Jacobs, E. A., H. J. Alvis, and S. M. Small. "Hyperoxygenation: A Central Nervous System Activator?" *Journal of Geriatric Psychiatry*, 1972, 5: 107–21.

———. "Persistence Effects of Intermittent Hyperoxygenation in the Elderly." In *Fifth International Hyperbaric Conference* (vol. 1), W. G. Trapp, E. W. Bannister, A. J. Davison, and P. A. Trapp (eds.), pp. 439–45. Burnaby, Canada: Simon Frazer University, 1974.

Jacobs, E. A., S. M. Small, P. M. Winter, and H. Alvis. "Hyperbaric Oxygen Effect on Cognition and Behavior in the Aged." *Current Psychiatric Therapies*, 1971, 11: 100–106.

Jacobs, E. A., P. M. Winter, H. J. Alvis, and S. M. Small. "Hyperoxygenation Effect on Cognitive Functioning in the Aged." *New England Journal of Medicine*, 1969, 281: 753–57.

Johnson, J. E., D. T. Hellkamp, and T. J. Lottman. "The Relationship between Intelligence, Brain Damage, and Hutt-Briskin Errors on the Bender-Gestalt." *Journal of Clinical Psychology*, 1971, 27: 84–85.

Klonoff, H., and M. Kennedy. "Memory and Perceptual Functioning in Octogenarians and Nonoctogenarians in the Community." *Journal of Gerontology*, 1965, 20: 328–33.

———. "A Comprehensive Study of Cognitive Functioning in Old Age." *Journal of Gerontology*, 1966, 21: 239–43.

Korman, M., and S. Blumberg. "Comparative Efficiency of Some Tests of Cerebral Damage." *Journal of Consulting Psychology*, 1963, 27: 303–9.

Lieberman, M. A. "Psychological Correlates of Impending Death." *Journal of Gerontology*, 1965, 20: 181–90.

Pascal, G. R., and B. J. Suttell. *Scoring System, the Bender-Gestalt Test: Quantification and Validity for Adults.* New York: Grune and Stratton, 1957.

Riklan, M., E. Levita, and I. S. Cooper. "Psychological Effects of Bilateral Subcortical Surgery for Parkinson's Disease." *Journal of Nervous and Mental Disease,* 1965, 41: 403–9.

Shanan, J., M. Cohen, and E. Adler. "Intellectual Functioning in Hemiplegic Patients after Cerebrovascular Accidents." *Journal of Nervous and Mental Disease,* 1966, 143: 181–89.

Storandt, M., and I. Wittels. "Maintenance of Function in Relocation of Community-Dwelling Older Adults." *Journal of Gerontology,* 1975, 30: 608–12.

Weiss, A. D. "The Influence of Sheet Position on Placement of Bender-Gestalt Figures." *Israeli Annals of Psychiatry,* 1971, 9: 63–67.

Wertheimer, M. "Studies in the Theory of Gestalt Psychology." *Psychologische Forschung,* 1923, 4: 300.

Instrument

This copyrighted instrument is available from Grune and Stratton, New York.

BENTON VISUAL RETENTION TEST (VRT)
A. L. Benton, 1974

Definition of Variable

The presence or absence of brain damage as indicated by visual memory is assessed by this measure.

Description of Instrument

This is a perceptual-motor test consisting of 10 geometric designs. There are three forms of the test provided (C, D, and E). All three are bound together in a spiral binding that makes for easy administration. These forms may be used with any or all of four administrative procedures (administration A, B, C, or D). The first two cards of each series present one simple geometric design, with the last eight cards containing two designs each. The complexity of the designs increases with the order of cards in the set.

Method of Administration

The test is individually administered. In all four administrations, the subject is required to draw each design on a separate piece of paper (approximately 8½ by 5½ inches) that matches the size of the cards. In administration A, the subject is shown the cards for 10 seconds, during which time he or she must look at the design. Then, the card is withdrawn and the subject is required to draw the design. Succeeding designs are presented in the same way. In administration B, the subject is shown each card for 5 seconds and then is required to draw the design after the card is withdrawn. In administration C, the subject is allowed to draw the designs while they remain in view. Administration D requires that the subject study the card for 10 seconds before the card is removed. The subject then must wait 15 seconds before drawing the design. The time required for any of these administrations is about 5 minutes.

Context of Development and Subsequent Use

This is a performance test designed to assess "memory, perception, and visuomotor functions" and then use these variables to differentiate individuals with and without brain damage. It has been used in studies of memory and brain damage and also in clinical work.

Sample

Norms for adults on administration A are based on a group of 600 individuals using inpatient and outpatient services of hospitals in Iowa City and Des Moines, Iowa. This group ranged in age from 15 to 44 years. The norms for children were established by using a group of children in Iowa schools. In addition, a group of mentally defective subjects, who were patients at the Woodward State Hospital and School in Woodward, Iowa, was tested.

Administration B was used for a group of 103 essentially normal adults aged 16 to 60 years. A further comparison was made of a group of 76 patients below the age of 50 years and 27 patients aged 50 to 60 years.

Scoring, Scale Norms, and Distribution

The scores on the test are the number of correct designs produced and the number of errors made. Standards for scoring designs are presented in the manual. There are different types of errors. Scoring requires the determination of the type of error and whether it was in the right or left field of the drawing. This qualitative information is not part of the score, but it indicates the locus of the brain damage.

Norms are presented for the number correct and the error scores for adults and children with administrations A, B, and C and for forms C, D, and E. There have been no norms established for administration D as yet. Cutoff points for grouping individuals according to the degree of their brain damage are furnished. Distributions for number correct scores and for error scores with administration C are given for a group of 100 brain-damaged subjects and 100 control subjects. Benton (1974) presented the results of a French study by Pointrenaud and Clement (1965). This was a study of normal adults divided into six groups ranging in age from under 45 years to over 84 years. Tested were 504 individuals (290 men, 214 women). Intellectual level was estimated by a vocabulary test, and subjects were also divided into three groups (IQs 105–114, 115–124, and 125–134), for a total of 18 groups of subjects. The mean number of correct reproductions was reported for each of these groups.

Formal Tests of Reliability

Benton indicated test-retest reliability for administration A to be approximately .85. No indication was given for population or interval here. Zwann (1967, in Benton, 1974) reported reliability correlations between forms C, D, and E ranging from .79 to .84. (The forms vary in difficulty according to the administration procedure used.)

Formal Tests of Validity

Convergent Validity: Benton (1974) reported a correlation of .70 between the scores on the test and "standard intelligence scales." No indication of the population or the particular intelligence tests correlated was given.

Predictive Validity: Wahler (1956) reported no significant difference for many of the types of errors between a group of normal and a group of brain-damaged individuals. Benton (1974), however, indicated that, when the appropriate cutoff was used, the test picked out 57% of the brain-damage cases and included only about 4% of the normals with administration A (number correct used as the score).

Breidt (1969, in Benton, 1974) found highly significant differences in mean error scores ($p < .001$) between groups of brain-damaged subjects and control subjects.

Sterne (1969) found that the VRT significantly discriminated ($p < .01$) between a group of 49 patients with brain damage and a group without brain damage. Von Kerekjartol (1961, in Benton, 1974) compared the performances of 20 normal subjects on administrations A and B. He found a mean number correct score of 8.5 for administration A and 7.6 for administration B. There was no indication of whether this difference was significant or not. Other specific studies can be found in the test manual (Benton, 1974).

Usability on Older Populations

The fact that the VRT involves motor coordination and that it is timed may contraindicate its use with the aged. Also, performance on this test correlates with age. There are no age norms supplied with this test.

Sensitivity to Age Differences

Benton (1974) reported a progressive rise in scores from subjects 8 years old up to a plateau with 14- or 15-year-olds. This is maintained through the 30s. A decline in efficiency occurs in the 40s and continues on from that time through the group over age 84 years.

Klonoff and Kennedy (1965; 1966) used the VRT with elderly subjects and found that age alone did not produce lowered performance; rather it was hospitalization and level of activity that influenced scores significantly.

A study of the number of correct reproductions made by 504 French subjects, divided into six age-groups ranging from under 45 years to over 84 years, and data for three intellectual groups (estimated IQs 105–114, 115–124, and 125–134) is presented in Benton (1974). Results indicate that more designs are correctly produced as intellectual level increases. Fewer correct productions are made as age increases within each intellectual level (Poitrenaud and Clement, 1965).

General Comments and Recommendations

The Benton VRT has not been used extensively with the aged. There are no norms for the performance of aged individuals. The Klonoff and Kennedy studies (1965; 1966) indicate that there is a need to differentiate the variables that determine performance within aged groups so that unwarranted generalizations are not made about memory, perception, and visuomotor functions in the elderly.

References

Benton, A. L. *Revised Visual Retention Test.* New York: Psychological Corporation, 1974.

Klonoff, H., and M. Kennedy. "Memory and Perceptual Functioning in Octogenarians and Nonoctogenarians in the Community." *Journal of Gerontology,* 1965, 20: 328–33.

———. "A Comprehensive Study of Cognitive Functioning in Old Age." *Journal of Gerontology,* 1966, 21: 239–42.

Poitrenaud, J., and F. Clement. "La Détérioration physiologique dans le Test de Retention Visuelle de Benton." *Psychologie Francaise,* 1965, 10: 359–68.

Sterne, D. M. "The Benton, Porteus and WAIS Digiy Span Tests with Normal and Brain-Injured Subjects." *Journal of Clinical Psychology,* 1969, 25: 173–75.

Wahler, H. J. "A Comparison of Reproductive Errors Made by Brain-Damaged and Control Patients on a Memory-for-Designs Test." *Journal of Abnormal and Social Psychology,* 1956, 52: 251–55.

Instrument

This copyrighted instrument is available from the Psychological Corporation, New York.

GRAHAM-KENDALL MEMORY-FOR-DESIGNS TEST (MFD)
F. K. Graham and B. S. Kendall, 1960

Definition of Variable

Brain damage versus functional disorder versus normality, as indicated by visual recall, is measured.

Description of Instrument

A series of 15 geometric designs of increasing complexity are presented on separate cards. All the designs are made with straight lines to avoid difficulties in scoring curved lines.

Method of Administration

The test is individually administered. Each design is shown to the subject separately and in a prescribed sequence. The subject must view the design for 5 seconds, after which it is withdrawn. The design is drawn on an 8½-by-11-inch piece of paper, with all designs drawn on the same piece of paper. It takes 5 to 10 minutes to complete the test.

Context of Development and Subsequent Use

This test was developed to differentiate organically impaired individuals from functionally disordered individuals. The assumption is that the inability to reproduce geometric designs from immediate memory is related to organic impairment. During the early stages of the test's development, 40 designs were prepared and administered to a small group of brain-damaged subjects and control subjects. Those designs that proved to be easiest to score and to discriminate best between groups were kept for the final set. This test has been used clinically and in research with all age-groups. It has been used with aged groups clinically as well as in research.

Sample

A number of samples were indicated in Graham and Kendall (1960), including the original validation group, a cross-validation group, and others. Originally, a group of 70 brain-disordered patients with mixed diagnoses and a group of 70 controls were matched for age, education, and occupational status. About equal numbers of males and females were included; a small number of blacks were included. The mean age for the sample was 41 to 42 years, with the range being from 8.5 to 70 years. The mean educational level was within the eighth grade. The cross-validation group consisted of 33 brain-disordered patients and 168 controls. This group had approximately one-third more men in it than women. The mean age of the controls was about 28 years, and that of the brain-disordered subjects was about 37 years. The mean education was within the ninth grade for both groups.

Scoring, Scale Norms, and Distribution

The criteria for assigning scores are given in Graham and Kendall (1960). A score of 0–3 is given for each reproduction, with the highest score indicating the poorest performance. No penalty is given for incomplete or forgotten designs, since these variables were not found to differentiate brain-damaged subjects from control subjects (Graham and Kendall, 1947). For cutoff points, see the discussion of the predictive validity of the MFD.

Formal Tests of Reliability

Split-half reliability was .92 for 140 brain-damaged patients. Immediate (same session or within 24 hours) test-retest correlations for other groups ranged between .81 and .90 (Graham and Kendall, 1960).

Formal Tests of Validity

With a sample of 100 people between 16 and 17 years of age, Aftanas and Royce (1969) factor analyzed a large number of tests typically used to diagnose brain damage. In this analysis, the MFD loaded +.597 on the first factor, interpreted as perceptual organization, i.e., the ability to organize or to integrate the relevant aspects of the perceptual field. Judging from the tests that loaded on this perceptual organization factor, the authors indicated that a memory component seemed to be apparent. This suggested to them that perceptual organization would facilitate performance when memory was involved.

Predictive Validity: The mean score difference between a group of brain-damaged and normal individuals was significant at the .01 level ($\bar{X} = 11.54$ and $SD = 7.3$, $\bar{X} = 3.47$ and $SD = 4.62$, respectively). These and other data presented in the test manual (Graham and Kendall, 1960) indicate some overlap in the scores of the non–brain-damaged and brain-damaged groups that may make it difficult to make a judgment about the performance of borderline individuals. For example, at a cutoff point at which 4% of the controls was diagnosed as brain-damaged, 50% in one group and 48% in another group of brain-damaged subjects would be designated with brain damage. Other cutoff points make for different combinations of correct identifications, errors, and false positives.

Convergent Validity: Scores on the MFD correlated .85 (Quattlebaum, 1968) and .81 (Anglin, Pullen, and Games, 1965) with scores on the Bender Gestalt test.

Usability on Older Populations

This test requires manual coordination, and it is timed. With these factors involved, the aged may be handicapped.

Sensitivity to Age Differences

Graham and Kendall (1960) reported a significant correlation of .27 between performance and age, i.e., as the age of the subject increases, the subject's performance becomes poorer. The MFD Test scores also have shown a correlation of $-.31$ with intelligence and a significant multiple correlation of .44 with age and intelligence as assessed by vocabulary score on the Wechsler-Bellevue.

In a study of 36 brain-damaged subjects and 36 controls (who were psychiatric patients) over age 60 years, Kendall (1962) found a significant difference in mean scores; however, the difference was not as great as the difference between brain-damaged and standardization groups of younger ages. The mean score of the controls was 8.44 ($SD = 6.33$), and the mean score of the brain-damaged group was 13.89 ($SD = 5.81$). The scores for this control group differed significantly from those of all younger control groups, but the scores of adults 20 to 60 years old did not differ significantly when compared by decade groups. A confounding factor here, however, was that the controls over age 60 showed a decline in vocabulary scores similar to the brain-damaged group's, whereas this was not true at younger ages. For the older-age group, then, using psychiatric controls may be inappropriate.

In a study of 540 subjects, with 50 men and 40 women in each of the six age decades between 20 and 80, Davies (1968) indicated that the performances of older age groups on the MFD showed no decline until the 50s, after which time rapid decline and increased variability in subjects' performances occurred.

General Comments and Recommendations

This test has good reliability and validity. It discriminates reasonably well between brain-damaged and normal groups. Its drawbacks for use with the aged are that it involves manual coordination and that it is timed and that performance correlates with age and intelligence. More information is necessary on normal aged subjects.

References

Aftanas, M. S., and J. R. Royce. "A Factor Analysis of Brain Damage Tests Administered to Normal Subjects with Factor Score Comparisons Across Age." *Multivariate Behavior Research,* 1969, 4: 459–81.

Anglin, R., M. Pullen, and P. Games. "Comparison of Two Tests of Brain Damage." *Perceptual and Motor Skills,* 1965, 20: 977–80.

Davies, A. "Measures of Mental Deterioration in Aging and Brain Damage." In *Psychological Functioning in the Normal Aging and Senile Aging,* S. M. Chown and K. Riegel (eds.), pp. 78–90. Basel: Karger, 1968.

Graham, F. K., and B. S. Kendall. "Note on Scoring the Memory-for-Designs Test." *Journal of Abnormal and Social Psychology,* 1947, 42: 253.

———. "Memory-for-Designs Test: Revised General Manual." *Perceptual and Motor Skills* (monograph supplement number 2-VII), 1960, 11: 147–88.

Kendall, B. S. "Memory-for-Designs Performances in the Seventh and Eighth Decades of Life." *Perceptual and Motor Skills*, 1962, 14: 399–405.

Powell, R. R. "Psychological Effects of Exercise Therapy upon Institutionalized Mental Patients." *Journal of Gerontology*, 1974, 29: 157–61.

Quattlebaum, L. F. "A Brief Note on the Relationship between Two Psychomotor Tests." *Journal of Clinical Psychology*, 1968, 24: 198–99.

Instrument

This copyrighted instrument is available from Psychological Test Specialists, Missoula, Mont.

GUILD MEMORY TEST
J. G. Gilbert, 1968

Definition of Variable

The test measures the level of deterioration in many types of memory due to mental illness and/or aging.

Description of Instrument

The test consists of several types of subtests (paragraphs, paired associates, digits forward and backward, and designs) administered for immediate and delayed recall and yielding six scores. The six scores are: (1) initial recall of meaningful verbal material, (2) delayed recall of meaningful verbal material, (3) initial associative memory, (4) retention of newly formed associates, (5) immediate rote memory, and (6) nonverbal memory.

Method of Administration

This test can be used in conjunction with the full WAIS, and it can also be used alone. Administered alone, the test requires the use of the WAIS vocabulary test for comparison of data on previous levels of functioning.

The administration of the test must be accomplished in a one-to-one session. Familiarity with the test is necessary to administer it successfully. Testing takes approximately 30 minutes.

Context of Development and Subsequent Use

This test was developed as an alternative to the Wechsler Memory Scale. On the WMS, the separate subtest scores are not converted to scaled scores but must be added together for a total score. On this test, scaled scores are available for each subtest.

Sample

The test was standardized for form A on a group of 400 subjects from the ages of 29 to 34 years. This group consisted of 189 males and 211 females. For form B, a group of 116 individuals between the ages of 20 and 34 years was tested.

Scoring, Scale Norms, and Distribution

Raw scores are converted to scaled scores, as indicated in the test manual. The scores obtained on this test can be compared to the means and standard deviations of the 20- to 34-year-old group. There are no standards for other age-groups.

Formal Test of Reliability

A group of 40 subjects of various ages were split, with half being administered form A and half being administered form B. Correlations between the scores of the various subtests ranged between .84 and .97 (*Guild Memory Test Manual*).

Split-half reliability for a sample of 100 subjects in the basic standardization group was .87 (*Guild Memory Test Manual*).

Correlations between the subjects ranged from .27 to .51 (median .36) in a group of 300 subjects 20 to 34 years old (Gilbert, Levee, and Catalano, 1968).

Usability on Older Populations

This test yields scale scores on various areas of memory. As such, it should be quite useful to gerontologists. However, few data are available on the relationship of scores to education and other factors that typically influence the scores of elderly persons.

Sensitivity to Age Differences

In a study of 316 subjects, Gilbert and Levee (1971) compared the scores of a group aged 35 to 75 years to the standardization group for the Guild Memory Test. All of the results showed a statistically reliable decline in scores in the group 34 years and older, except for the memory-span test. The scores on this test declined after the 50s, with a slight increase in the 60s.

General Comments and Recommendations

This memory test is an alternative to the Wechsler Memory Scale and includes aspects of various tests assumed to measure memory functions. Gilbert provided scaled scores for the various subjects so that comparisons can be made between the various tests. However, these scores were based on a standardization group 20 to 34 years of age. Norms for aged individuals are needed. In addition, the author based the validity of this test on the fact that it borrows from other widely used memory tests. This is no substitute for direct validity data, especially when the other tests have not been very well validated.

References

Gilbert, J. C. *Guild Memory Test Manual.* Newark, N.J.: Unico National Mental Health Research Center (no date).

Gilbert, J. C., K. J. Donnelly, L. E. Zimmer, and J. F. Kubis. "Effect of Magnesium Pemoline and Methylphenidate on Memory Improvement and Mood in Normal Aging Subjects." *International Journal of Aging and Human Development*, 1973, 4: 35–51.

Gilbert, J. G., and R. F. Levee. "Patterns of Declining Memory." *Journal of Gerontology*, 1971, 26: 70–75.

Gilbert, J. C., R. F. Levee, and F. L. Catalano. "A Preliminary Report on a New Memory Scale." *Perceptual and Motor Skills*, 1968, 27: 277–78.

Instrument

Although this copyrighted instrument has not been published, it is available from the Unico National Mental Health Research Center, Newark, N.J.

THE HALSTEAD BATTERY
W. C. Halstead, 1947

Definition of Variable

The presence and location of brain damage is assessed by this measure.

Description of Instrument

Out of an original set of 10 tests, the following 5, which yield 7 scores, are now used as the standard. (1) The category test uses a projection apparatus to present stimulus material. The subject must decide which categories best classify the presented stimuli, such as size, shape, number, position, brightness, and color. (2) The tactual performance test (TPT) has three scores—time, memory, and localization. It is a modification of the Seguin-Goddard form board test. Blindfolded, the subject must fit blocks into the proper spaces with the preferred hand, then with the nonpreferred hand, and then with both hands together. The subject must also draw the board from memory after the blindfold has been removed. (3) The rhythm test is based on one of the subtests of the Seashore Test of Musical Talent. The subject must differentiate between pairs of rhythmic beats that are sometimes the same and sometimes different. (4) In the speech sounds perception test, a standard tape recording presents 60 spoken nonsense words, with the intensity of sound adjusted to the subject's preference. The subject is to select those words spoken from the alternatives printed on the test form. (5) In the finger oscillation test, the subject taps his or her finger as rapidly as possible. Both hands are tested.

The battery could take anywhere from one to three days to administer, depending on the subject. The examiner must be well trained and highly skilled in giving the test.

Context of Development and Subsequent Use

Originally, the Halstead Battery was developed to assess "biological," or native, intelligence. Halstead observed that the behavior of organically impaired individuals showed obvious losses in aspects of functioning present in normal individuals. As a result of his observations, he developed 27 tests, later reduced to 7, to assess this phenomenon. From this original emphasis on organic impairment, the battery became increasingly useful as a diagnostic procedure. Halstead himself developed the Halstead Impairment Index as an indicator of impaired functioning. Then, first in the early 1950s, Reitan, one of Halstead's students, gave impetus to the use of this battery in an intensive program of research, focusing on the diagnostic powers of the test. Reitan also modified the test battery by adding the Halstead-Wepman Aphasia Screening Test (now the Reitan-Indiana Aphasia Screening Test), the Trailmaking Test, the Wechsler-Bellevue form I, and the MMPI.

To date, a tremendous amount of research has been done with the Halstead Battery. A complete list of the references would take many pages, so the present review includes only basic information on the battery. For further information and a detailed bibliography, the interested reader is referred to Reitan and Davidson (1974).

Sample

The sample on which the Halstead Impairment Index was established consisted of a group of 23 individuals, some brain-damaged and some diagnosed as psychoneurotic. Halstead validated his findings with another group of 25 brain-damaged and 25 neurotic patients (Halstead, 1947).

Scoring, Scale Norms, and Distribution

Cutoff scores were furnished by Halstead (1947) and later validated by Reitan (1955a) for discriminating normal from brain-damaged individuals.

Later research has determined that specific diagnostic categories within the brain-damaged group show different profiles on the tests of the Halstead Battery and on other tests added by Reitan, so that the specific site of the brain damage can be pinpointed by behavioral testing (Reitan and Fitzhugh, 1971; Reitan, 1964).

Formal Tests of Reliability

Studies establishing the reliability of this battery of five tests could not be located by this reviewer. There appear to be some problems in this area, and there may be some difficulty in documenting reliability. The problems lie in the nature of the tasks. The category test, for example, is one in which an abstract principle must be discovered. Once discovered, it is not readily lost. Other tasks are similar, so the effects of practice can be expected to be extremely strong in retesting. Split-half or odd-even reliability is also difficult to establish with tasks of this sort.

Formal Tests of Validity

Halstead (1947) performed a factor analysis on 13 neuropsychological tests, including the category test, the TPT, the speech sounds perception test, and the finger oscillation test already described. Four oblique factors were identified: a central integrative field factor, an abstracting factor, a power factor, and a directional factor. Goldstein and Shelly (1975) identified four factors—nonverbal memory, language ability, motor ability, and psychomotor problem solving—from a factor analysis of the Halstead Battery and the Wechsler Adult Intelligence Scale. These authors also performed a linear discriminant function analysis on the scores of the 60 brain-damaged and 60 non–brain-damaged individuals in this group. Only 48.3% of the cases were correctly classified by test scores. Also, the discriminant function performed well in differentiating young non–brain-damaged people but not so well in differentiating young brain-damaged or old brain-damaged and aged non–brain-damaged people.

Predictive Validity: Reitan (1955a) studied 50 pairs of subjects (brain-damaged individuals from various diagnostic categories versus non–brain-damaged psychiatric patients) and confirmed Halstead's findings. Reitan's data showed significant differences in scores for each of the basic five tests. The two groups in his study were matched for race, age, sex, and education. The mean age of the group was 32 years.

Chapman and Wolff (1959) confirmed the ability of the Halstead Battery to discriminate between brain-damaged and non–brain-damaged subjects. Their study revealed that the degree of impairment appeared to be directly related to the amount of the subject's brain tissue that had been affected.

Vega and Parsons (1967) compared 50 brain-damaged subjects and 50 control subjects. They noted lower performance among the control group (non–brain-damaged) than had been previously noted by other researchers. Since their group was from a different geographical region (the Southwest) than those previously tested and since the group was from a more rural setting, the authors ascribed the discrepancy to regional differences and developed their own regional norms. A closer examination of the differences between these groups has shown that the Vega and Parsons group was older by an average of about 10 years (mean age 42 years). Though Reed and Reitan (1963a) found that changes brought about by aging were not likely to be seen until age 45, it may be that the Vega and Parsons group showed reduced scores because they were older.

In a cross-national study, Klove and Lochen (Reitan and Davidson, 1974) compared brain-damaged and control subjects from Norway and Wisconsin. The brain-damaged and control groups were matched on age and education variables. The mean age of the brain-damaged groups was approximately 10 years older than that of the control groups. The test battery again discriminated significantly between the impaired and unimpaired groups, an indication that cultural background seems to have little influence on the usefulness of the tests.

Wheeler, Burke, and Reitan (1963) applied a discriminant function technique to 24 behavioral indicators, including the Halstead Battery. Tested were 140 subjects in four groups: subjects with no cerebral damage, with left cerebral damage, with right cerebral damage, or with diffuse cerebral damage. The groups were comparable in regard to sex, handedness, age, and education. Classification of subjects based on these tests was correct 98% of the time for the control group versus the brain-damaged group and over 90% of the time for comparisons between other groups.

Convergent Validity: Matthews and Booker (1972) gathered data on certain aspects of pneumoencephalographic findings and a wide range of behavioral indicators, including the Halstead Battery. Their study indicated a relationship between the size of the cerebral ventricular system and behavioral indicators when a group with large and a group with small ventricles were compared. On only three of the Halstead tests did the group with large cerebral ventricles show better scores than those with small ventricles.

Usability on Older Populations

This is a lengthy battery that may need several testing sessions with some groups of aged people. Also, there are at the present time no norms for aged populations. Since there are definite aging effects in scores within normal groups, caution must be exercised in using this test with elderly individuals.

Sensitivity to Age Differences

It should be noted that very few subjects over age 65 years old were included in the following studies. In an early study using the Halstead Battery with older subjects, Reitan (1955b) tested a group composed of 133 non–brain-damaged and 194 brain-damaged individuals ranging in age from 15 to 64 years. The brain-damaged group was composed of 101 men and 32 women. Using the Halstead Impairment Index, Reitan found that the mean scores for the brain-damaged individuals were well above the criterion level, with scores for the aged within this group showing even greater impairment. The correlation between the Impairment Index and age was .23. The correlation between age and the Impairment Index in the normal group was higher ($r = .54$). The impaired scores in the normal group began to appear in the 45- to 50-year age-group. This weak relationship between age and the Impairment Index in the brain-damaged group suggests that, when brain damage is clearly present, age is relatively insignificant. On the other hand, normal aging seems to bring with it impaired functioning.

Reed and Reitan (1963a) evaluated the performance on the Halstead Battery of 40 healthy subjects and 40 brain-damaged subjects matched on the variables of age (mean age 28 years), education (mean education 11.8 years), sex, and race. The two groups were matched with a group of 46 mature adults (mean age 44.7 years, mean education 16.6 years) and older adults (mean age 55.35 years, mean education 13.93 years). They found a significant correlation ($p < .01$) between the rank order of the tests (poorest to best performances) of the young brain-damaged group and the normal older group. Covariance analysis controlling the effect of education did not result in a change in the direction of the mean differences or the rank orders of the t ratios.

In a study of 29 aging (mean age 52.96 years) and 40 young (mean age 28.05 years) persons, the Halstead Battery was used with other tests to determine changes in psychological test performance associated with the normal aging process. Some individuals in each of these groups were hospitalized, but none of the individuals were considered to show any evidence of disordered brain functions. The results of this study indicated that the young subjects were clearly superior to the old subjects on the categories test and the tactual performance test (total score, location, and memory), i.e., on those tests dependent on adaptive ability. On the speech sounds perception and finger oscillation test, the old subjects were slightly superior to the young subjects, although these differences were not statistically significant (Reed and Reitan, 1963b).

Vega and Parsons (1967) found significant correlations ranging between $-.63$ and $-.33$ for the various Halstead measures and age within a control (non–brain-damaged) group of individuals aged 15 to 74 years (mean age 40.8 years, standard deviation 13.1). They also found significant correlations of between .58 and .33 for these measures and education.

General Comments and Recommendations

The Halstead Battery is a valid test battery for diagnosing brain damage in young adult populations. For older populations, however, norms need to be developed so that a large percentage of the aged are not labeled brain-damaged. Beyond this reservation, the Halstead

Battery has much more to offer for providing information about changes in brain functioning during the later years of life. This battery is recommended for clinical and research purposes.

References

Chapman, L. F., and H. G. Wolff. "The Cerebral Hemispheres and the Highest Integrative Functions of Man." *Archives of Neurology*, 1959, 1: 357–424.

Goldstein, G. and C. H. Shelly. "Similarities and Differences between Psychological Deficit in Aging and Brain Damage." *Journal of Gerontology*, 1975, 30: 448–55.

Halstead, W. C. *Brain and Intelligence: A Quantitative Study of the Frontal Lobes.* University of Chicago Press, Chicago: 1947.

Matthews, C. G., and H. E. Booker. (1972) "Pneumoencephalographic Measurements and Neuropsychological Test Performance in Human Adults." *Cortex*, 1972, 8: 69–92.

Reed, H, B. C., Jr., and R. M. Reitan. "A Comparison of the Effects of the Normal Aging Process with the Effects of Organic Damage on Adaptive Abilities." *Journal of Gerontology*, 1963a, 18: 177–79.

———. "Changes in Psychological Test Performance Associated with the Normal Aging Process." *Journal of Gerontology*, 1963b, 18: 271–74.

Reitan R. M. "Investigation of the Validity of Halstead's Measure of Biological Intelligence." *A.M.A. Archives of Neurology and Psychiatry*, 1955a, 73: 28–35.

———. "The Distribution According to Age of a Psychologic Measure Dependent upon Organic Brain Functions." *Journal of Gerontology*, 1955b, 10: 338–40.

———. "Psychological Changes Associated with Aging and in Cerebral Damage." *Mayo Clinic Proceedings*, 1967, 42: 653–73.

———. "Psychological Deficits Resulting from Cerebral Lesions in Man." In *The Frontal Granular Cortex and Behavior*, J. M. Warren and K. Akert (eds.), pp. 295–312. New York: McGraw-Hill, 1964.

Reitan, R. M., and L. A. Davidson. *Clinical Neuropsychology: Current Status and Applications.* Washington, D.C.: V. H. Winston and Sons, 1974.

Reitan, R. M., and K. B. Fitzhugh. "Behavioral Deficits in Groups with Cerebral Vascular Lesions." *Journal of Consulting Clinical Psychology*, 1971, 37: 215–23.

Vega, A. T., and O. A. Parsons. "Cross-validation of the Halstead-Reitan Tests for Brain Damage." *Journal of Consulting Psychology*, 1967, 31: 619–25.

Wheeler, L., C. J. Burke, and R. M. Reitan. "An Application of Discriminate Functions to the Problem of Predicting Brain Damage Using Behavioral Variables." *Perception and Motor Skills*, 1963, 16: 417–40.

Instrument

This copyrighted instrument is available from the Neuropsychology Laboratory, Mercer Island, Wash.

HOOPER VISUAL ORGANIZATION TEST (VOT)
H. E. Hooper, 1952

Definition of Variable

The presence or absence of brain damage, as indicated by the ability to identify disorganized visual representations, is measured.

Description of Instrument

The test uses 30 pictures of common objects, each broken into at least two pieces and, in most cases, more. The pieces are printed in a jumbled fashion, and the subject must be able to rearrange them in his or her mind in order to name the object. The items are ordered according to increasing difficulty.

Method of Administration

The test is in booklet form, with instructions printed on the front. The subject must write down the name of the object in the picture in the space provided. The test generally requires about 10 to 20 minutes to complete.

Context of Development and Subsequent Use

The VOT was developed to differentiate organically impaired individuals from psychotic and normal individuals. It has been used for that purpose in research and in clinical settings since its initial development.

Sample

The original sample consisted of a group of 70 brain-damaged patients and a group of 140 schizophrenics and psychoneurotic patients (Hooper, 1952).

Scoring, Scale Norms, and Distribution

The score is the number of correct responses, with half-credits given in some instances. Scores are interpreted according to the scale provided in the test manual (Hooper, 1958). No particular skill is necessary for administering or scoring this test. A score of 25–30 indicates no impairment, 20–24.5 indicates mild impairment, 10–19.5 indicates moderate impairment, and 0–9.5 indicates severe impairment (Hooper, 1958). Mason and Ganzler (1964) have developed a regression formula for use with the VOT that takes into account age and education variables.

Formal Tests of Reliability/Homogeneity

Split-half reliability (Spearman-Brown formula) in a group of 166 college students was .82. In a group of 74 psychoneurotic patients, the split-half correlation was .78 (Hooper, 1958).

Formal Tests of Validity

Convergent Validity: In a sample of 100 people between 16 and 70 years of age, Aftanas and Royce (1969) factor analyzed a large number of tests typically used to diagnose brain damage. In this analysis, the Hooper loaded +.549 on the first factor, interpreted as perceptual organization, i.e., the ability to integrate or organize the relevant aspects of the perceptual field. Upon examination of the tests that loaded there, memory was seen to be an important component of this factor. Perceptual integration would facilitate proficiency on those tests involving a memory component. Also, the authors concluded that organization was seen to be the important factor, since tests of pure perception loaded minimally on perceptual organization.

Predictive Validity: Performance on the VOT resulted in a 23% overlap between a group of brain-damaged individuals and a group of schizophrenic and psychoneurotic patients (Hooper, 1958). All of the overlap occurred in the scoring range of 20–24 points, the range indicated as mild impairment by Hooper. With a cutoff score of 20, there were 3% false positives for a group of 30 junior high school students. For a group of college students, 6% were falsely diagnosed positive (Hooper, 1958).

In a group with 210 controls (1958) and 70 organics, Hooper found a cutoff score of 20 yielded no false positives among the nonorganics and 21% false negatives for the organics.

Usability on Older Populations

This is an easily administered, untimed perceptual test that correlates with age and has no adjustments for scores. Use of this test would result in many aged people being classified as brain-damaged.

Sensitivity to Age Differences

Hooper (1958) reported a statistically significant correlation of −.57 with age. With a cutoff score of 20, 69% of a group of "normal aged" (mean age 76.8 years; 23 females, 5 males) were diagnosed as having organic brain pathology with moderate impairment, 15% with mild impairment, and 18% with no impairment. In a study of memory and related functions, Botwinick and Storandt (1974) also found that decreasing performance on the test was related to increasing age ($p < .0001$). Those subjects with more than 12 years of formal education performed better than those with less ($p < .0001$). Ganzler (1964) found that increasing the motivation of older adults increased their scores on the VOT. However, the increase in the scores of the older group in this study did not exceed the increase in the scores of a younger group under the same highly motivating conditions.

Storandt and Wittels (1975) used the VOT to help differentiate aged individuals who had moved to a new place of residence and those who had not. As with most of the other tests used in this study, the VOT did not detect change in functioning in "movers" significantly different from "nonmovers."

General Comments and Recommendations

Though this is an untimed test and one that does not confound the factors of motor coordination and short-term memory in the perceptual performance required, the relationship of the scores on this test to age, sex, and education are serious problems in its application to research problems. Except in cases in which regression formulas, such as Mason and Ganzler's (1964), are used, further exploration of the effect of these factors, as well as socioeconomic and intellectual factors, needs to be accomplished before the test can be used widely. Norms need to be established for the various groups (age, education, etc.) to be tested. Further, qualitative performance, such as the style of verbalization and the manner of approach to the task, must be given attention.

References

Aftanas, M. S., and J. R. Royce. "A Factor Analysis of Brain Damage Tests Administered to Normal Subjects with Factor Score Comparisons across Ages." *Multivariate Behavioral Research,* 1969, 4: 459–81.

Botwinick, J., and M. Storandt. *Memory, Related Functions and Age.* Springfield, Ill.: Charles C. Thomas, 1974.

Ganzler, H. "Motivation as a Factor in Psychological Deficit of Aging." *Journal of Gerontology,* 1964, 19: 425–29.

Hooper, H. E. "Use of Hooper Visual Organization Test in Differentiation of Organic Brain Pathology from Normals, Psychoneurotics and Schizophrenic Reactions." *American Psychologist,* 1952, 7: 350.

————. *The Hooper Visual Organization Test: Manual.* Beverly Hills, Calif.: Western Psychological Services, 1958.

Mason, C. F., and H. Ganzler. "Adult Norms for the Shipley Institute of Living Scale and Hooper Visual Organization Test Based on Age and Education." *Journal of Gerontology,* 1964, 19: 419–24.

Storandt, M., and I. Wittels. "Maintenance of Function in Relocation of Community-Dwelling Older Adults." *Journal of Gerontology,* 1975, 30: 608–12.

Instrument

This copyrighted instrument is available from Western Psychological Services, Beverly Hills, Calif.

THE SHIPLEY-HARTFORD
(THE SHIPLEY INSTITUTE OF LIVING SCALE)
W. C. Shipley, 1940

Definition of Variable

The scale differentiates psychotic from nonpsychotic individuals in terms of vocabulary and abstract reasoning.

Description of Instrument

This is a two-part paper-and-pencil test. The vocabulary subtest contains 40 multiple-choice items, and the abstract reasoning test contains 20 completion items designed to measure inductive reasoning.

Method of Administration

The test is essentially self-administering. It takes about 20 minutes to complete, with 10 minutes allowed for each subtest.

Context of Development and Subsequent Use

This test was based on clinical-experimental observations indicating that ability at vocabulary tends to be affected only slightly by mental deterioration, while ability at abstract relationships declines rapidly.

Such observations led Shipley to use a difference score based on performance on subtests to assess these two functions as the index of deterioration. Though direct evidence for Shipley's assumption is not available from other sources, his test has been found to be useful in differentiating psychotics, brain-damaged individuals, and normal individuals. This test has been used in clinical work and in research.

Sample

Mental age norms were originally established on a group of 1,046 individuals who had been given a standardized group intelligence test (Otis Self-Administering Test of Mental Ability and intelligence tests already in school records). The group was composed of college, high school, and grade school students (fourth through eighth grades) (Shipley, 1940).

Norms for adults were established by Mason and Ganzler (1964) with a group of 198 male hospitalized subjects, ranging in age from 25 to 75 years, who had no known psychiatric illness or brain damage. No time limits were used with these subjects.

Scoring, Scale Norms, and Distribution

The raw score for each subtest is the number correct. The raw vocabulary scores yield a predicted abstraction-age score. The actual abstraction-age score is divided by the predicted one. This number is multiplied by 100 to eliminate decimals. This figure is the conceptual quotient. Numbers below 100, then, would indicate superior functioning in abstract ability. In the standardization group, 50% of the cases fell between conceptual quotients of 90 and 110. This range can be considered normal performance, with scores below 90 indicating impairment.

Formal Tests of Reliability

Odd-even reliability computed on the scores of a group of 322 army recruits was .87 for the vocabulary test, .89 for the abstraction test, and .92 for the entire scale (Shipley, 1940).

Formal Tests of Validity

Concurrent Validity: Total scores on this test correlated .87 with mental age (from the Otis Self-Administering Test of Mental Ability and IQs already in school records) for the group of students (Shipley, 1940).

Predictive Validity: Shipley and Burlingame (1941) indicated consistent differences for patient categories compared to normals. The lowest conceptual quotients were reported for organics, and next came the functional psychotics, while psychopathic personalities, psycho-neurotics, and alcoholics fell within normal limits.

Construct Validity: Lewinsohn (1963) measured the Shipley-Hartford performance of 45 schizophrenic patients tested before and after treatment and found that there was no change in vocabulary scores but that there was significant improvement in abstraction scores.

Usability on Older Populations

This is an easily administered test that can provide information about deterioration due to organic impairment or psychosis. When the test is used with the aged, Mason and Ganzler's formula for computing expected scores should be used, since this formula adjusts for age and education factors. In its original form, the Shipley-Hartford was a timed test, a factor that usually handicaps older subjects. However, it can be used as an untimed test.

Sensitivity to Age Differences

Mensh (1966) studied a group of older individuals (60 years and over) with IQs ranging from 68 to 150, who attended a psychiatric clinic. Declines in the subjects' scores began when they reached their mid-60s. In the groups over that age, efficiency levels for women were not beyond the 70s. For the men, some of the scores were in the 90s range, but most were below that level. There was no further breakdown in scores indicated in the study.

Mason and Ganzler (1964) have provided regression formulas for computing expected abstraction scores, which include age and education factors. This increases the amount of variance accounted for to 38%. The authors found −.292 correlation between age and abstraction scores and .183 between age and vocabulary scores in their group. Corotto (1966) found a correlation of −.14 between abstraction scores and age. Palmer (1964) found a correlation between abstraction scores and age of +.47 in a group of adolescents 12 to 28 years of age. Lewinsohn (1963) found a +.64 correlation between age and vocabulary and −.41 between age and abstraction scores in a group of 30-year-olds.

General Comments and Recommendations

This is a quick, easily administered test that could be used for screening purposes in order to gain some idea about the level of deterioration or as a supplement to other tests. The abstraction score is based on only 20 items, which might make precise discrimination difficult. Also, the test scores do not differentiate between deterioration resulting from severe mental illness and that resulting from organic disorder.

References

Bromley, D. B. "Age Differences in Conceptual Abilities." In *Processes of Aging* (vol. 1), R. H. Williams, C. Tibbitts, and W. Donahue (eds.), pp. 96–112. New York: Atheron Press, 1963.

Corotto, L. V. "Effects of Age and Sex on the Shipley Institute of Living Scale." *Journal of Consulting Psychology,* 1966, 30: 179.

Lewinsohn, P. M. "Use of the Shipley-Hartford Concept Quotient as a Measure of Intellectual Impairment." *Journal of Consulting Psychology,* 1963, 27: 444–47.

Mason, C. F., and H. Ganzler. "Adult Norms for the Shipley Institute of Living Scale and Hooper Visual Organization Test Based on Age and Education." *Journal of Gerontology,* 1964, 19: 419–24.

Mensh, I. N. "Intellectual and Other Personality Adjustments to Aging." *The Gerontologist,* 1966, 6: 104–28.

Palmer, J. O. "Standardization of Adolescent Norms for the Shipley-Hartford." *Journal of Clinical Psychology,* 1964, 20: 492–95.

Shipley, W. C. "A Self-Administering Scale for Measuring Intellectual Impairment and Deterioration." *Journal of Psychology,* 1940, 9: 371–77.

Shipley, W. C., and C. C. Burlingame. "A Convenient Self-Administering Scale for Measuring Intellectual Impairment in Psychotics." *American Journal of Psychiatry,* 1941, 97: 1313–25.

Instrument

This copyrighted instrument is available from Mrs. John C. Boyle, 1454 Filbert Avenue, Chico, Calif. 95926.

TRAILMAKING TEST (TMT)
S. G. Armitage, 1946

Definition of Variable

The test differentiates normally functioning individuals from those with brain damage.

Description of Instrument and Method of Administration

This task has two parts (A and B). The first part requires the subject to draw a line connecting in proper sequence 25 small circles numbered from 1 to 25 that are randomly arranged on an 8½-by-11-inch page. In part B there are also 25 circles. In this part, however, 13 of the circles are numbered 1 to 13 and the other 12 have letters A to L. The subject must draw a line connecting alternate numbers with alternate letters, going from 1 to A to 2 to B . . . K to 12 to L to 13, as quickly as possible.

As the subject draws lines on part A or B, errors are caught by the examiner and the subject is requested to correct errors.

Context of Development and Subsequent Use

The Trailmaking Test was developed to differentiate individuals with brain damage from those without this condition. Use of this test has usually been in clinical or research settings. The Trailmaking Test is usually included in Halstead's Neurological Test Battery.

Sample

In one of the earliest uses of this test, Armitage (1946) compared 44 patients known to have sustained brain damage, a group of 45 normals (hospital attendants), and a small group of 16 neurotics with mild affective states.

Scoring, Scale Norms, and Distribution

The score is the time taken to complete the task on each part (A and B). A table to convert seconds to scaled scores can be found in the test manual (1944). Impairment cutoffs are 39 seconds for part A and 91 seconds for part B.

Formal Tests of Validity

Predictive Validity: Using the recommended cutoff, a number of studies have indicated about a 16% overlap between groups of brain-damaged subjects and normals and between groups of brain-damaged subjects and neurotics (Armitage, 1946; Reitan, 1955; Reitan, 1958).

Reitan and Tarsches (1959) found that the TMT distinguished among three groups of brain-damaged persons: those with right hemisphere damage, left hemisphere damage, and diffuse cerebrum damage. Left-hemisphere patients did significantly better than right-hemisphere patients ($p < .05$) on part A. On part B this relationship was reversed, with those suffering diffuse damage scoring between the other two groups. No differences between group performance were significant on part B.

Reitan (1955) studied the responses of 27 brain-damaged patients and 27 patients without brain damage. Of these groups 85% were males and 15% were females. The raw scores on each part of this test were converted to 10-point-scale scores according to the Reitan manual developed for the test. With the cutoff at 12 points (the combined score for the two parts), about 17% of each group were misclassified.

Spieth (1964) found the TMT discriminated healthy men from those with impaired heart functioning in a group of 600 men, aged 23 to 59.

Usability on Older Populations

The TMT seems to be easily usable with aged subjects, although the ability to draw the lines between the circles may be impaired in some groups. Educational level influences scores, as does age. To use the test for isolating impaired functioning in aged groups would require the development of age-specific normative data.

Sensitivity to Age Differences

In a study of 540 subjects, 50 males and 40 females in each of six age decades between 20 and 80 (distribution representative of the U.S. distribution for social class and occupation), Davies (1968) used the Trailmaking Test to differentiate normal aged subjects from brain-damaged subjects. On the TMT, 92% of the men in their 70s would have been called brain-damaged if Reitan's standards had been used. Reed and Reitan (1963a, 1963b) also indicated similarity of performance between aged and brain-damaged patients on this test.

Botwinick and Storandt (1974) included the Trailmaking Test in a battery of tests designed to determine the relationship of memory to various functions over the life span. A group of 21- to 79-year-old males and females was tested. In this sample, age-groups differed significantly in their performance on both parts A and B of this test, with age accounting for 10% of the test score variance on each part. The mean for performance in part A was within the impaired range for individuals in their 60s and above. None of the means for the age-groups on part B were within the impaired range. No significant age differences were found, but educational level made a significant difference in performance ($p < .001$). Those with more than 12 years of education performed better than those with fewer years of formal education.

In a study of 122 subjects 61 to 88 years of age who had moved into a large apartment complex for the aged (Storandt, Wittels, and Botwinick, 1975), the Trailmaking Test was one of six measures that predicted well-being approximately 15 months after the move.

General Comments and Recommendations

This is an easily used test that discriminates between brain damage and normal functioning and functioning in psychopathological states. Scores seem to correlate with age, however, so that the older the individual is, the more likely it is that the person will fall into the group labeled brain-damaged. Norms must be established for the various age-groups, or the test must be used with this qualification in mind.

References

Armitage, S. G. "An Analysis of Certain Psychological Tests Used for Evaluation of Brain Injury." *Psychological Monographs*, 1946, 60, (1) (whole number 277).

Army Individual Test, Manual of Directions. War Department, the Adjutant General's Office, 1944.

Botwinick, J., and M. Storandt. *Memory, Related Functions and Age*. Springfield, Ill.: Charles C. Thomas, 1974.

Davies, A. "Measures of Mental Deterioration in Aging and Brain Damage." In *Psychological Functioning in the Normal Aging and Senile Aging*, S. M. Chown and K. Riegel (eds.). Basel: Karger, 1968.

Heron, A., and S. M. Chown. *Age and Function*. Boston: Little, Brown and Company, 1967.

Reed, H. B. C., Jr., and R. M. Reitan. "Changes in Psychological Test Performance Associated with Normal Aging Process." *Journal of Gerontology*, 1963a, 18: 271–74.

———. "A Comparison of the Effects of Organic Brain Damage on Adaptive Abilities." *Journal of Gerontology*, 1963b, 18: 177–79.

Reitan, R. M. "The Relation of the Trailmaking Test to Organic Brain Damage." *Journal of Consulting Psychology*, 1955, 19: 393–94.

———. "Validity of the Trailmaking Test as an Indicator of Organic Brain Damage." *Perceptual and Motor Skills*, 1958, 8: 271–76.

Reitan, R. M., and E. T. Tarsches. "Differential Effects of Lateralized Brain Lesions." *Journal of Nervous and Mental Diseases*, 1959, 129: 257–62.

Spieth, W. "Cardiovascular Health Status, Age and Psychological Performance." *Journal of Gerontology*, 1964, 19: 277–84.

Storandt, M., and I. Wittels. "Maintenance of Functioning in Relocation of Community-Dwelling Older Adults." *Journal of Gerontology,* 1975, 30: 608–12.

Storandt, M., I. Wittels, and J. Botwinick. "Predictors of a Dimension of Well-Being in the Relocated Healthy Aged." *Journal of Gerontology,* 1975, 30: 97–102.

Instrument

This copyrighted instrument is available from the Neuropsychology Laboratory, Mercer Island, Wash.

WECHSLER MEMORY SCALE (WMS)
D. Wechsler, 1945

Definition of Variable

This is a test of short-term verbal memory.

Description of Instrument

There are seven subtests of the Wechsler Memory Scale: (1) information, with items on personal and current information; (2) orientation, with items regarding time and place; (3) mental control, with items requiring reproduction of previously well-learned processes; (4) memory passages, requiring immediate recall of a paragraph of meaningful material; (5) digit span, requiring the subject to recite digits forward and backward; (6) visual reproduction, requiring the subject to reproduce geometric designs; and (7) associate learning, a paired associate learning task. Two alternate forms of the test (I and II) have been developed.

Method of Administration

The test should be administered individually, and the administrator should be familiar with the test. Approximately 30 minutes are needed for completing this test. An answer sheet is available.

Context of Development

This test was developed by Wechsler (1945) for use in conjunction with the Wechsler Adult Intelligence Scale in assessing preservation or deterioration of memory in the presence of organic brain damage. In normal individuals, the memory quotient (MQ) obtained by the WMS is designed to be equivalent to the IQ obtained by the Wechsler Adult Intelligence Scale. With subjects suffering from memory loss, the MQ is designed to give an indication of the degree of deterioration.

Sample

This test was originally standardized on a group of about 200 normal subjects, ages 25 to 50 years, males and females.

Scoring, Scale Norms, and Distribution

The scoring criteria are listed in the test manual (Wechsler, 1945). Age-corrected raw scores (totals) are entered in a table in the manual to obtain the memory quotient. There are age corrections in the manual for age-groups up through 64 years. These were extrapolated from the standardization group, 25 to 50 years of age. The discrepancy score (full-scale IQ minus MQ) can be used to describe the degree of memory impairment. MacCara (1953) suggested that a discrepancy of 11 or more points indicates memory impairment. Zaidel and Sperry (1974) and Milner (1975) suggested an MQ score of 12 points or more as indicative of deficit.

Formal Tests of Reliability/Homogeneity

Meer and Baker (1965) found test-retest reliability coefficients of .97 (males) and .95 (females), with an interval of 1 day, in a group of 51 male and 26 female patients, aged 60 years and older. In a group of 17 student nurses and 10 female psychoneurotics, no significant difference was found in the scores on forms I and II when the forms were administered 1 to 16 days apart. In a group of 60 college students tested 2 weeks apart on forms I and II, there were no significant differences.

Stinnett and DiGiacomo (1970) reported a Pearson correlation of .80 between the alternate forms of the WMS after an average time interval of 18.9 days, with subjects who underwent unilateral, nondominant electroconvulsive therapy between testings.

The WMS has been factor analyzed with populations of neurological and psychiatric patients (Bachrach and Mintz, 1974; Davis and Swenson, 1970; Dujovne and Levy, 1971; Kear-Colwell, 1973). At least two factors emerged rather consistently in these four studies. One was a memory factor that was a cluster of mental control and digits forward and backward subtests. The other was a freedom-from-distractability factor including logical memory, visual reproduction, and associate learning. Sometimes, a third factor included the information and orientation subtests (Prigatano, 1978). A factor analysis within a normal population yielded factors of general retentiveness, simple learning, and associated flexibility (Dujovne and Levy, 1971).

Formal Tests of Validity

Predictive Validity: Cohen (1950) did not find that this test differentiated among groups of psychoneurotic, brain-damaged organics, and schizophrenic subjects. Howard (1950) found that the WMS differentiated gross differences between normal and brain-damaged individuals. Baer, Merryman, and Gaitz (1967) found that the WMS significantly differentiated between a group of organic and schizophrenic subjects.

Usability on Older Populations

This scale has been used widely with the aged. Care must be taken in extrapolating MQ to advanced ages, since age corrections up to 64 years are extrapolated from the standardization sample aged 25 to 50 years.

Results with the Aged

Klonoff and Kennedy (1966) found that WMS scores were responsive to activity level in a group of hospitalized and nonhospitalized aged subjects. In an earlier study, Klonoff and Kennedy (1965) did not find age-correlated differences in memory scores in a group of 80- to 90-year-old veterans.

Schaie and Strother (1968) found that 25 female and 25 male community-dwelling older adults showed little decrement in memory even though they were of an advanced age (mean age of 76.5 years). The MQ of this group was 93.

Jacobs, Alvis, and Small (1972) and Jacobs, Winter, Alvis, and Small (1969) found that hyperbaric oxygenation significantly improved scores ($p < .01$) on the WMS in a group of elderly patients.

Powell (1974) found significant improvement in the WMS scores of a group of patients after a 12-week program of exercise therapy.

Storandt and Wittels (1975) used two subtests of the WMS (visual reproduction and associate learning) and other assessment procedures to determine whether residential relocation affected cognitive functioning. No significant difference was found between elderly persons who had relocated and those who had not.

General Comments and Recommendations

The investigator should be cautious when using WMS with populations of advanced age, since the standardization sample was small and it extended only to age 50. Extrapolation beyond this age is tenuous.

No separate scores are available for the factors or the types of memory involved in this test. Though the investigator can use raw subtest scores for comparisons among groups, only the overall score yields the MQ. It would seem best to differentiate between the types of memory and the clinical groups for which the specific functions fail. In addition, little is known about the effect of some of the factors (such as education, socioeconomic status, and occupation) that correlate with age on WMS scores.

References

Bachrach, H., and J. Mintz. "The Wechsler Memory Scale as a Tool for the Detection of Mild Cerebral Dysfunction." *Journal of Clinical Psychology*, 1974, 30: 58–60.

Baer, P., P. Merryman, and C. Gaitz. "Performance Deficits Related to Chronic Brain Syndrome, Schizophrenia and Age." *Journal of Gerontology*, 1967, 7: 37.

Cohen, J. "Wechsler Memory Scale Performance of Psychoneurotic, Organic and Schizophrenic Groups." *Journal of Consulting Psychology*, 1950, 414: 371–75.

Davis, L. J., and W. M. Swenson. "Factor Analysis of the Wechsler Memory Scale." *Journal of Consulting and Clinical Psychology*, 1970, 35: 430.

Dujovne, B., and B. I. Levy. "The Psychometric Structure of the Wechsler Memory Scale." *Journal of Clinical Psychology*, 1971, 27: 351–54.

Howard, A. R. "Diagnostic Value of the WMS with Selected Groups of Institutionalized Patients." *Journal of Consulting Psychology*, 1950, 14: 376–80.

Jacobs, E. A., H. J. Alvis, and S. M. Small. "Hyperoxygenation: A Central Nervous System Activator?" *Journal of Geriatric Psychiatry*, 1972, 5: 107–21.

Jacobs, E. A., P. M. Winter, H. J. Alvis, and S. M. Small. "Hyperoxygenation Effect on Cognitive Functioning in the Aged." *New England Journal of Medicine*, 1969, 281: 753–57.

Kear-Colwell, J. J. "The Structure of the Wechsler Memory Scale and Its Relationship to 'Brain Damage.' " *British Journal of Clinical Psychology*, 1973, 12: 384–92.

Klonoff, H., and M. Kennedy. "Memory and Perceptual Functioning in Octogenarians and Non-octogenarians in the Community." *Journal of Gerontology*, 1965, 20: 328–33.

———. "A Comprehensive Study of Cognitive Functioning in Old Age." *Journal of Gerontology*, 1966, 21: 239–43.

MacCara, E. "The Wechsler Memory Scale with Average and Superior Normal Adults." *Bulletin of Maritime Psychology Association*, 1953, 30–33.

Meer, B., and J. A. Baker. "Reliability of Measurements of Intellectual Functioning of Geriatric Patients." *Journal of Gerontology*, 1965, 20: 410–14.

Milner, B. "Psychological Defects Produced by Temporal Lobe Excision." *Research Publications Association for Research in Nervous and Mental Diseases*, 1968, 36: 244–57.

———. "Psychological Aspects of Focal Epilepsy and Its Neurosurgical Management." *Advances in Neurology*, 1975, 8: 299–321.

Powell, R. "Psychological Effects of Exercise Therapy upon Institutionalized Geriatric Mental Patients." *Journal of Gerontology*, 1974, 29: 157–61.

Prigatano, G. P. "Wechsler Memory Scale: A Selective Review of the Literature." *Journal of Clinical Psychology* (Special Monograph Supplement), 1978, 34: 816–32.

Schaie, K. W., and C. R. Strother. "The Limits of Optimum Psychological Functioning of Superior Normal Old Adults." In *Psychological Functioning in the Normal Aging and Senile Aging*, S. M. Chown and K. Riegel (eds.), pp. 132–50. Basel: Karger, 1968.

Shapiro, D. Y., D. A. Sadowsky, W. G. Henderson, and J. M. Van Buren. "An Assessment of Cognitive Function in Post-thalamotomy Parkinson Patients." *Confirma Neurologica*, 1973, 35: 144–66.

Stinnett, J. L., and J. N. DiGiacomo. "Daily Administered Unilateral ECT." *Biological Psychiatry*, 1970, 3: 303–6.

Storandt, M., and I. Wittels. "Maintenance of Function in Relocation of Community-Dwelling Older Adults." *Journal of Gerontology*, 1975, 30: 608–12.

Wechsler, D. "A Standardized Memory Scale for Clinical Use." *Journal of Psychology*, 1945, 19: 87–95.

Zaidel, D., and R. W. Sperry. "Memory Impairment after Commissurotomy in Man." *Brain*, 1974, 97: 263–72.

Zamora, E. N., and R. Kaelbling. "Memory and Electroconvulsive Therapy." *American Journal of Psychiatry*, 1965, 122: 546–54.

Instrument

This copyrighted instrument is available from the Psychological Corporation, New York.

CROSSING-OFF TEST
J. Botwinick and M. Storandt, 1973

Definition of Variable

The instrument measures perceptual-motor speed.

Description of Instrument

The crossing-off task is an easily administered, timed, paper-and-pencil performance test. It uses an 8½-by-11-inch piece of paper on which there are printed 12 rows of 8 short lines each.

Method of Administration

The subject is instructed to make a vertical line across each horizontal line on the paper as quickly as possible, working from right to left, one row after another. A maximum time of three minutes is allowed.

Context of Development and Subsequent Use

This task was developed as a simplified version of the speed-of-writing tasks developed by Birren and Botwinick (1951). The speed-of-writing tasks have been found to correlate with age and to differentiate psychotic from nonpsychotic elderly individuals. These tasks required the subject to write arabic numbers and simple words, a process involving both cognitive and perceptual functions. The crossing-off task was designated to reduce the demands on the subject while providing a perceptual-speed task similar to the digit symbol subtest of the WAIS.

Sample

This test was originally developed with a sample of two age-groups. The younger group consisted of 38 subjects with a mean age of 18.6 years. The older group consisted of 28 subjects with a mean age of 71 years (Botwinick and Storandt, 1973).

Scoring, Scale Norms, and Distribution

The score is the number of lines crossed out per second, multiplied by 100. No norms have been established.

Formal Tests of Validity

Principal components analysis of this task performed by Botwinick and Storandt (1973) indicated a heavy loading on a speed factor (.78, or .38 with age partialed out) and a lesser loading on a cognitive factor (.28, or .14 with age partialed out).

Convergent and Discriminant Validity: The Crossing-Off Test correlated significantly (.64) with performance on the digit symbol subtest of the WAIS (Botwinick and Storandt, 1973). However, with age partialed out, this correlation dropped to .17. Therefore, it would seem that the possible similarity in performance between the two tasks is based on their common ability to discriminate between age-groups, rather than on common performance factors.

Predictive Validity: In a discriminate function analysis of aged subjects, data on the Crossing-Off Test yielded a coefficient of –.6066, leading to maximal discrimination of those given a clinical impression rating of "played out" (Storandt, Wittels, and Botwinick, 1975).

Usability on Older Populations

This task was developed specifically for use with older populations. Though it requires motor performance, the movements need not be as well coordinated and steady as those required by writing; and in that sense the test could be seen as suitable for use with the elderly.

Sensitivity to Age Differences

In one study, Botwinick and Storandt (1973) found that the crossing-off task correlated –.70 with age.

In a study of memory and related functions among a group of 21- to 79-year-old individuals, the Crossing-Off Test showed significant effects from education, sex, and age ($p <$ .0001). The percentage of variance accounted for by age in the speed of carrying out the task was 27 (Botwinick and Storandt, 1974).

General Comments and Recommendations

This simple task has been found to differentiate individuals who are functioning well from those who are not. It is an easy task for elderly subjects to complete and deserves further work to establish its reliability; its ability to replace other, more complex tasks; and its relationship to other variables related to age.

References

Birren, J. E., and J. Botwinick. "The Relation of Writing Speed and Age and the Senile Psychoses." *Journal of Consulting Psychology,* 1951, 15: 243–49.

Botwinick, J., and M. Storandt. "Speed Functions, Vocabulary Ability, and Age." *Perceptual and Motor Skills,* 1973, 36: 1123–28.

———. *Memory, Related Functions and Age.* Springfield, Ill. Charles C. Thomas, 1974.

Storandt, M., I. Wittels, and J. Botwinick. "Predictors of a Dimension of Well-Being in the Relocated Healthy Aged." *Journal of Gerontology,* 1975, 30: 97–102.

Instrument

There is no special material for this test.

Instruments

V1.2.I.a
DRAW-A-PERSON TEST
F. L. Goodenough, 1926

This copyrighted instrument is available from Harcourt Brace Jovanovich, New York.

V1.2.I.b
FULL-RANGE PICTURE VOCABULARY TEST
R. B. Ammons and H. S. Ammons, 1948

This copyrighted instrument is available from Psychological Test Specialists, Missoula, Mont.

V1.2.I.c
KENT SERIES OF EMERGENCY SCALES
G. A. Kent, 1946

This copyrighted instrument is available from the Psychological Corporation, New York.

V1.2.I.d
PRIMARY MENTAL ABILITIES TEST
L. L. Thurstone and T. G. Thurstone, 1947

This copyrighted instrument is available from Science Research Associates, Inc., Chicago.

V1.2.I.e
PROGRESSIVE MATRICES TEST
J. C. Raven, 1960

This copyrighted instrument is available from the Psychological Corporation, New York.

V1.2.I.f
MILL HILL VOCABULARY TEST
J. C. Raven, 1943

This copyrighted instrument is available from Western Psychological Services, Beverly Hills, Calif.

V1.2.I.g
WECHSLER ADULT INTELLIGENCE SCALE
D. Wechsler, 1955

This copyrighted instrument is available from the Psychological Corporation, New York.

V1.2.II.a
BENDER VISUAL MOTOR GESTALT TEST
L. Bender, 1938

This copyrighted instrument is available from Grune and Stratton, New York.

V1.2.II.b
BENTON VISUAL RETENTION TEST
A. L. Benton, 1974

This copyrighted instrument is available from the Psychological Corporation, New York.

V1.2.II.c
GRAHAM-KENDALL MEMORY-FOR-DESIGNS TEST
F. K. Graham and B. S. Kendall, 1960

This copyrighted instrument is available from Psychological Test Specialists, Missoula, Mont.

V1.2.II.d
GUILD MEMORY TEST
J. G. Gilbert, 1968

Although this copyrighted instrument has not been published, it is available from the Unico National Mental Health Research Center, Newark, N.J.

V1.2.II.e
THE HALSTEAD BATTERY
W. C. Halstead, 1947

This copyrighted instrument is available from the Neuropsychology Laboratory, Mercer Island, Wash.

V1.2.II.f
HOOPER VISUAL ORGANIZATION TEST
H. E. Hooper, 1952

This copyrighted instrument is available from Western Psychological Services, Beverly Hills, Calif.

V1.2.II.g
THE SHIPLEY-HARTFORD
W. C. Shipley, 1940

This copyrighted instrument is available from Mrs. John C. Boyle, 1454 Filbert Avenue, Chico, Calif. 95926.

V1.2.II.h
TRAILMAKING TEST
S. G. Armitage, 1946

This copyrighted instrument is available from the Neuropsychology Laboratory, Mercer Island, Wash.

V1.2.II.i
WECHSLER MEMORY SCALE
D. Wechsler, 1945

This copyrighted instrument is available from the Psychological Corporation, New York.

V1.2.II.j
CROSSING-OFF TEST
J. Botwinick and M. Storandt, 1973

There is no special material for this instrument.

Chapter 3

Personality

Carol J. Dye

Most assessments of personality in older adults have used tests developed with, and applied to, young and mature adult populations. Apparently, it was assumed that the same dimensions were suitable for assessment over the adult span of life and that tests appropriate to young adults were legitimate tests for assessing personality in older adults. Actually, results from tests of older individuals have indicated a basic stability and continuity, in that, when changes in personality do seem to have occurred, they are likely to reflect shifts in the relative importance of the variables measured. Instead of the appearance or disappearance of specific characteristics in old age, the relative dominance of a particular trait may be different at various points in the life span.

A common change is assessed personality with advancing age is a shift in variables related in some way to "energy." For example, on the Minnesota Multiphasic Personality Inventory, the older adult group scores lowest on the mania and the psychopathic deviate scales (Postema and Schell, 1967; Brozek, 1955; Aaronson, 1958, 1960; Calden and Hokanson, 1959; Pearson, Swenson, and Rome, 1965). For the Sixteen Personality Factors Test, comparisons the test results of older and younger adults have indicated that the only factor that consistently changes with age is factor F (surgency-desurgency); i.e., older adults are more desurgent than younger adults (Botwinick, 1973). Rosen and Neugarten (1964) also found this type of result in their research with the TAT. They explored the energy dimension as it related to the individual's interpersonal involvement. Their results indicated declines in involvement and ego energy with increasing age.

On the Guilford-Zimmerman, too, factor analyses have indicated that there is greater introversion with age (Bendig, 1960).

Most of the information available on personality development in old age is cross-sectional, rather than longitudinal. This raises the possibility that cohort differences distort results across the age-groups assessed; Though it may be unnecessary to develop special tests for the elderly in assessing different personality dimensions, cohort factors may need attention. For example, the testing situation as it is perceived by the older individual may not be similar to that perceived by the younger adult. It is well known that older adults tend to take longer to respond than younger subjects (Botwinick, 1973) and that they tend to be less well educated (Riley, Johnson, and Foner, 1972). Therefore, more time must be allowed for older subjects to read and complete personality inventories. Fatigue is an important determinant of response or lack of response on the longer assessment procedures. In addition, the print on many questionnaires is quite small, and older adults may not be able to read the items and they may experience strain and fatigue when there are a large number of items on the form. In addition, the task of responding on an answer sheet can be confusing for older persons unfamiliar with tests in general.

Personality inventories for older adults are likely to be more successful when they are relatively short. Large-type editions of tests are desirable, although it is not certain whether simply increasing the size of print makes it more legible to the elderly. Current work being done by J. Vanderplas (personal communication, 1977) seems to indicate that the style and spacing of the type used also influence legibility. Alternative administrative procedures that reduce fatigue and facilitate responses in the elderly need to be explored. Procedures using a card form (Uecker, 1969) and an oral form (Wolf, Freinek, and Shaffer, 1964) are already available for the MMPI.

Projective and Objective Personality Assessments

Formal personality assessments fall into two broad categories: projective tests and objective questionnaires. In projective testing, the subject is asked to respond in his or her own way to ambiguous stimuli, with minimal instructions and usually without a restriction on time. The task may involve saying what inkblots look like, telling a story that explains a picture, reporting the first words thought after hearing a given word, or completing a sentence. The person being tested is supposed to reveal "deeper" personality constituents, less accessible to direct report, in the content and manner of his or her responses. The rationale is that, because the demand characteristics of the test have been minimized, the subject's productions are more authentic reflections of his or her own drives, conflicts, wishes, and so on.

The reliability and validity of projective tests have usually been difficult to establish. Even reliability of scoring has been found weak in the more complex tests, such as the Rorschach. Comparisons of the testing, scoring, and interpretative results of even highly and equally skilled clinicians have produced poor results.

Objective personality questionnaires are based on the assumption that people can directly and accurately express their desires, habits, preferences, and beliefs in short answers given to questions about these matters. In many cases, the only responses allowed are simple affirmation or denial that statements apply to the subject. Thus, the stimuli (statements or questions) must be made as unambiguous as possible; instructions must be detailed and restrictive; and, because many items are needed to stabilize scores, there are usually severe restrictions on the time than can be spent on each item.

The administration of personality inventories is beset with special difficulties that influence scores. Although in the one-to-one subject-examiner situation in projective testing the examiner may become aware of many behavioral cues that may be judged to influence a subject's scores, in objective testing the examiner must rely on how willing the subject is to volunteer information about himself or herself and on the subject's self-awareness. The detection of tendencies to fake responses and malinger becomes a problem. Variation due to the subject's lack of understanding presents further problems, and scores may not be reliable and can be quite different from testing to testing, depending on the physical and psychological state of the individual being tested. In addition, the interpretation of scores may not be as straightforward as the objective scores suggest. A checked item can be taken at face value (i.e., assuming that the subject *is* the way he or she responded), or it can be interpreted as something that someone with certain inferred characteristics says about himself or herself. A level of inference is required to interpret results with subjects of this latter type. As with projective techniques, with most of these inventories little information is available about the effect on scores of educational level or other variables that tend to be associated with age. However, this is a failing in applying the tests to both aged and younger populations.

Choosing between Objective and Projective Measures

Objective questionnaires are relatively easy to administer and score. Their mechanical character greatly facilitates the quantitative assessment of their reliability and validity. Projective personality assessments usually require skill and clinical experience for their administration and interpretation. Their reliance on intuitive factors makes it difficult to estimate their reliability and validity in a quantitative way. Nonetheless, these technical considerations should *not* determine a researcher's choice of objective questionnaires over projective methods, for the two approaches clearly rest on two fundamentally different and irreconcilable beliefs about how expressive behavior relates to personality. Only when a researcher is honestly convinced that personality can be adequately reflected in the kind of behavior required by objective questionnaires should he or she select this type of measure. When he or she does not share this belief, then the conveniences of objective questionnaires are mere dust in the balance. A gerontologist should have no interest whatever in the perfection of a method he or she believes to be fundamentally misguided.

Projective Tests

The projective techniques that have been used with the elderly reviewed here are: the Rorschach (Beck and Molish, 1967), the Thematic Apperception Test (TAT) (Murray, 1943), the Senior Apperception Test (SAT) (Bellak and Bellak, 1973), the Gerontological Apperception Test (GAT) (Wolk and Wolk, 1971), the Id, Ego, and Superego Test (Dombrose and Slobin, 1958), and the word-association techniques (Jung, 1910). Except for the SAT and the GAT, these tests have a long history of use with younger populations. Few special adaptions have been made to accommodate the special needs of testing the elderly. Testing sessions can be long and intensive, and fatigue factors can influence scores. In addition, the effect of other variables, such as educational level, on scores is largely unknown. It can be expected that these special factors would be important considerations in comparing the performance of aged groups to those of younger groups.

Two variations of the Thematic Apperception Test—the Gerontological Apperception Test and the Senior Apperception Test—have been specially developed for use with the aged. Tests of thematic apperception require the individual to compose stories about pictures. The assumption is that needs, conflicts, and other similar factors are revealed in the stories to the extent that the individual identifies with the main character in the picture and becomes involved in the story. The hypothesis behind the development of the GAT and the SAT is that, if more of the pictures showed older adults in situations relevant to their unique life stresses, there would be greater identification with the stimuli and hence greater productivity and richness in their stories. Therefore, the GAT and the SAT cards picture an older adult entering a nursing home, sitting alone, et cetera. One study with the GAT does not support this hypothesis (Traxler, Sweiner, and Rogers, 1974). Older adults did not show greater richness and productivity on the GAT than on the TAT. The Id, Ego, and Superego Test (Dombrose and Slobin, 1958) provides greater structure in administration and scoring than do the Rorschach and the TAT. The last projective procedure reviewed here, the word-association technique, is one projective test that is specific in its focus, emphasizing the assessment of conflict-laden areas of functioning, rather than attempting to describe the total personality.

Objective Tests

Four omnibus objective tests of personality and three specific variable tests that have been used with older people are reviewed here. Generally, there are more standardization data available on these questionnaires, compared to that available with projectives. Most of the objective tests also have some reliability data within specified groups. On the other hand, the problem of empirical validity remains, and few of the omnibus tests have been adequately validated.

The Minnesota Multiphasic Personality Inventory (Hathaway and McKinley, 1940a, 1940b; 1942a, 1942b), and the Sixteen Personality Factors Test (Cattell, Eber, and Tatsuoka, 1970) are two omnibus tests that have extensive research backgrounds. There are a great many studies on the MMPI that indicate the correlates of variations in its scores. These two tests yield a number of scores related to basic personality processes. The 16PF is factor analytically based, while the MMPI is empirically keyed. In addition to their use as whole tests, parts of these tests have been and can be used for specific research purposes. The Guilford-Zimmerman Temperament Survey (Guilford and Zimmerman, 1949) is out of date for its norms and needs additional factorial work. The Edwards Personal Preference Inventory (Edwards, 1959) presents problems in the interpretation of scores.

The four tests of specific personality variables reviewed here are the Heron Personality Inventory (Heron, 1956) which measures two variables, emotional maladjustment and sociability; the Eysenck Personality Inventory (Eysenck and Eysenck, 1963), which measures two variables of personality, extraversion-introversion and neuroticism; the Zung Self-Rating Depression Scale (Zung, 1965); and the Neuroticism Scale Questionnaire (Scheier and Cattell, 1961). All have undergone some reliability and validity testing and seem appropriate for research purposes.

Tests of Rigidity and Cautiousness

The study of the variables rigidity and cautiousness has been emphasized by gerontologists interested in personality functioning in later life, because many older persons appear to be more rigid and/or more cautious than younger adults. Rigidity in behavior is generally taken to mean the inability to respond in a way not part of a previously learned pattern. Cautiousness usually has to do with hesitancy in making decisions. These personality factors have not been especially evident in younger people, and gerontologists have devised measures used initially with the aged.

In the area of rigidity, two tests (or tasks) are reviewed here. These are the Wesley Rigidity Inventory (Wesley, 1953) and the Test of Behavioral Rigidity (Schaie, 1955). Both have some research background for various populations, normalized scores, factor loadings, et cetera. Work on the Wesley has indicated that it assesses three factors of rigidity: (1) liking for detailed work, (2) dogmatism, and (3) liking for habit. The Test of Behavioral Rigidity measures three forms of rigidity isolated by the author before the test was constructed: (1) motor-cognitive rigidity, (2) psychomotor-speed rigidity, and (3) personality-perceptual rigidity. This test uses timed tasks and questionnaires to derive scores for each of the factors.

Two tests of cautiousness are reviewed in this chapter; one (the Estimation Questionnaire) presents stimulus material of a largely impersonal sort, not highly charged with relevance to everyday choice behavior; and the other (Dilemmas of Choice Questionnaire) focuses on situations with which the respondent presumably can identify as a decision maker.

The Estimation Questionnaire (Wallach and Kogan, 1965) gives the subject a "fact" regarding some average or modal quantity occurring in daily life, such as "usually about 58 ships arrive in New York City harbor every day." The subject is then asked to estimate the maximum and minimum values of this variable. The ranges of such estimates are presumed to reflect the cautiousness or rashness of the subject. Use of this measure by Botwinick (1970) did yield evidence of greater cautiousness on the part of elderly subjects.

The Dilemmas of Choice Questionnaire (Wallach and Kogan, 1961) assesses cautiousness in an ingenious and engaging manner. The subject reads descriptions of choices to be made under conditions of uncertainty. The choices range from selecting the next play in a football game to issues of career and marriage. The subject must choose the lowest probability of a happy outcome under which he or she would choose the risky action. Use of this instrument in subsequent studies (Botwinick 1966, 1969) has made some substantial contributions to gerontology's picture of the cautiousness and rigidity that seem to accompany aging. In particular, it has provided evidence that the elderly have no greater tendency to minimize risk when they *must* take risks, but rather they tend to avoid decisions of *any* risk.

Summary

Table 3-1 lists the 18 measures of personality that are reviewed in this chapter. Most of these measures are copyrighted and so must be obtained from their publishers. The four measures that have not been copyrighted are included in this chapter.

TABLE 3-1
Instruments Reviewed in Chapter 3

Instrument	Author (date)	Code Number
I. Projective Tests		
a. Rorschach Inkblot Technique	Rorschach (1921)	Copyrighted
b. Thematic Apperception Technique	Murray (1943)	Copyrighted
c. Senior Apperception Technique	Bellak and Bellak (1973)	Copyrighted
d. Gerontological Apperception Technique	Wolk and Wolk (1971)	Copyrighted
e. Id, Ego, Superego Test	Dombrose and Slobin (1958)	Copyrighted
f. Word-Association Techniques	Jung (1910)	No standard material
II. Objective Tests, Omnibus		
a. Minnesota Multiphasic Personality Inventory	Hathaway and McKinley (1940a and 1940b)	Copyrighted
b. Sixteen Personality Factors Test	Cattell, Eber, and Tatsuoka (1957)	Copyrighted
c. Guilford-Zimmerman Temperament Survey	Guilford and Zimmerman (1949)	Copyrighted
d. Edwards Personal Preference Inventory	Edwards (1959)	Copyrighted
III. Objective Tests, Specific		
a. Heron Personality Inventory	Heron (1956)	V1.3.III.a
b. Eysenck Personality Inventory	Eysenck and Eysenck (1963)	Copyrighted
c. Zung Self-Rating Depression Scale	Zung (1965)	Copyrighted
d. Neuroticism Scale Questionnaire	Scheier and Cattell (1961)	Copyrighted

TABLE 3-1 — *Continued*

Instrument	Author (date)	Code Number
IV. Tests of Rigidity and Caution		
a. Wesley Rigidity Inventory	Wesley (1953)	V1. 3. IV. a
b. Tests of Behavioral Rigidity	Schaie (1960)	Copyrighted
c. Dilemmas of Choice Questionnaire	Wallach and Kogan (1961); Botwinick (1966)	V1. 3. IV. c
d. Estimation Questionnaire	Wallach and Kogan (1965)	V1. 3. IV. d

References

Aaronson, B. S. "Age and Sex Influences on MMPI Profile Scale Distribution on an Abnormal Population." *Journal of Consulting Psychology*, 1958, 22: 103–6.

——. "A Dimension of Personality Change with Aging." *Journal of Gerontology*, 1960, 19: 144.

Beck, S., and H. B. Molish. *Rorschach's Test*. New York: Grune and Stratton, 1967.

Bellak, L., and S. S. Bellak. *Manual for the Senior Apperception Technique*. Larchmont, N.Y.: C.P.S., 1973.

Bendig, A. W. "Age Differences in the Interscale Factor Structure of the Guilford-Zimmerman Temperament Study." *Journal of Consulting Psychology*, 1960, 24: 134–38.

Botwinick, J. "Cautiousness in Advanced Age." *Journal of Gerontology*, 1966, 21: 347–53.

——. "Disinclination to Venture versus Cautiousness in Responding: Age Differences." *Journal of Genetic Psychology*, 1969, 115: 55–62.

——. "Age Differences in Self-Ratings of Confidence." *Psychological Reports*, 1970, 27: 865–66.

——. *Aging and Behavior*. New York: Springer, 1973.

Brozek, J. "Personality Change with Age: An Item Analysis of the MMPI." *Journal of Gerontology*, 1955, 10: 194–206.

Calden, D., and J. E. Hokanson. "Influence of Age on MMPI responses." *Journal of Clinical Psychology*, 1959, 15: 194–95.

Cattell, R. B., H. W. Eber, and M. M. Tatsuoka. *The Handbook for the Sixteen Personality Factors Questionnaire* (1970 ed.). Champaign, Ill.: Institute for Personality and Ability Testing, 1970.

Dombrose, L. A., and M. S. Slobin. "The IES Test." *Perceptual and Motor Skills*, 1958, 8: 347–89 (Monograph Suppl. 3).

Edwards A. L. *Edwards Personal Preference Schedule Manual*. New York: Psychological Corporation, 1959.

Eysenck, H. J., and B. G. Eysenck, *Manual for the Eysenck Personality Inventory*. San Diego: Educational and Industrial Test Service, 1963.

Guilford, J. P., and W. S. Zimmerman. *The Guilford-Zimmerman Temperament Survey: Manual of Instruction and Interpretation*. Beverly Hills, Calif.: Sheridan, 1949.

Hathaway, S. R., and J. C. McKinley. "A Multiphasic Personality Schedule (Minnesota) I. Construction of the Schedule." *Journal of Psychology*, 1940a, 10: 240–54.

——. "A Multiphasic Personality Schedule (Minnesota) II. A Differential Study of Hypochondriasis." *Journal of Psychology*, 1940b, 10: 255–68.

——. "A Multiphasic Personality Schedule (Minnesota) III. The Measurement of Symptomatic Depression." *Journal of Psychology*, 1942a, 14: 73–84.

———. "A Multiphasic Personality Schedule (Minnesota) IV. Psychasthenia." *Journal of Applied Psychology*, 1942b, 26: 624–24.

Heron, A. "A Two-Part Personality Measure for Use as a Research Criterion." *British Journal of Psychology*, 1956, 47: 243–51.

Jung, C. G. "The Association Method." *American Journal of Psychology*, 1910, 21: 219–69.

Murray, H. A. *Thematic Apperception Test: Manual.* Cambridge, Mass.: Harvard University Press, 1943.

Pearson, J. S., and W. M. Swenson, and H. P. Rome. "Age and Sex Differences Related to MMPI Response Frequency in 25,000 Medical Patients." *American Journal of Psychiatry*, 1965, 121: 989–95.

Postema, G., and R. E. Schell. "Some MMPI Guidance of Seemingly Greater Neurotic Behavior among Older People." *Journal of Clinical Psychology*, 1967, 23: 140–43.

Riley, M. W., J. Johnson, and A. Foner. *Aging and Society* (vol. 3). New York: Russell Sage Foundation, 1972.

Rosen, J. L., and B. L. Neugarten. "Ego Functions in the Middle and Later Years: A Thematic Apperception Study." In *Personality in Middle and Late Life*, B. L. Neugarten et al., pp. 90–101. New York: Atherton Press, 1964.

Schaie, K. W. "A Test of Behavioral Rigidity." *Journal of Abnormal and Social Psychology*, 1955, 51: 604–10.

Scheier, I. H., and R. B. Cattell. *Handbook for the Neuroticism Scale Questionnaire.* Champaign, Ill.: Institute for Personality and Ability Testing, 1961.

Traxler, A., R. Sweiner, and B. Rogers. "Use of the Gerontological Apperception Test with Community-Dwelling and Institutionalized Aged." *The Gerontologist*, 1974, 14: 52.

Uecker, A. E. "Comparability of Two Methods of Administering the MMPI to Brain-Damaged Geriatric Patients." *Journal of Clinical Psychology*, 1969, 25: 1961–98.

Wallach, M. A., and N. Kogan. "Aspects of Judgment and Decision Making: Interrelationships and Changes with Age." *Behavioral Sciences*, 1961, 6: 23–36.

———. *Modes of Thinking in Young Children*, pp. 112–15. New York: Holt Rinehart, 1965.

Wesley, E. "Perseverative Behavior in a Concept-Formation Test as a Function of Manifest Anxiety and Rigidity." *Journal of Abnormal and Social Psychology*, 1953, 48: 129–34.

Wolf S., W. R. Freinek, and J. W. Shaffer. "Comparability of Complete Oral and Booklet Forms of the MMPI." *Journal of Clinical Psychology*, 1964, 20: 375–78.

Wolk, R. L., and R. B. Wolk. *Manual: The Gerontological Apperception Test.* New York: Behavioral Publications, 1971.

Zung, W. W. K. "A Self-Rating Depression Scale." *Archives of General Psychiatry*, 1965, 12: 63–70.

Abstracts

RORSCHACH INKBLOT TECHNIQUE
H. Rorschach, 1921

Description of Instrument

The Rorschach technique uses 10 cards, each bearing a chromatic or achromatic inkblot

NOTE: In the abstracts for this chapter, definitions of the variables will not be given for omnibus personality assessments unless special emphasis is given to certain dimensions of personality.

design. The first seven designs are essentially achromatic, with small areas of red appearing on cards II and III. The last three chromatic cards are printed with a variety of colors. Some of the designs are simpler than others, and some more readily suggest objects.

Method of Administration

The cards are shown to individual subjects. Although slightly different procedures can be followed in administering the test (Klopfer and Davidson, 1962; Rapaport, Gill, and Schafer, 1968), usually there are two main steps. First, the cards are given to the subject one by one in fixed succession, card I to card X, with the subject instructed to state what each inkblot looks like. This is called the free-association period. Then, the cards are presented a second time, again in fixed succession, for elaboration of the percepts. The examiner has specific questions that can be asked in order to gather the information necessary for scoring. Average time of administration is about 30 minutes.

Context of Development and Subsequent Use

This technique was developed during the early part of this century as a multilevel, wide-ranging technique for assessing personality. Since that time, it has been widely used in clinical and research work. The stimulus cards have remained unchanged since Rorschach's time.

Samples

No specific sample can be indicated for the development of this test within young and mature adult populations, though a large number of populations have been assessed. In the case of older adults, the study by Ames and associates (1973) can be used as a normative data base. The sample in that study was composed of 101, 86, and 13 individuals in their 70s, 80s and 90s, respectively. Of these 140 were men; 60 were women. About one-third were community based. All socioeconomic levels were represented, although those at the higher levels were overrepresented.

Scoring, Scale Norms, and Distribution

There are several scoring and interpretation systems. All are highly complex and require a high level of training and skill (Klopfer and Davidson, 1962; Beck and Molish, 1967; Piotrowski, 1957; Schafer, 1954; Rapaport, Gill, and Schafer, 1968). Responses are primarily scored according to the area of the inkblot focused upon in the percept (location), the factor predominant in the determinant of the percept (determinant), and the content of the response.

For young and mature adults, norms and distributions of the many scores that are obtained can be found in the discussions of the various scoring systems, which take the form of the total number of such scores expected within one protocol or the percentage of scores expected. Deviations from the expected are discussed as variations highlighting the normal personality or as indications of pathology. Norms and distributions for older adults can be found in Ames and associates (1973). Interpretation of scores is within a psychodynamic framework.

Formal Tests of Reliability

Reliability has been difficult to establish because of the character of this test and its scores. First, the examiner has a choice of several scoring systems. Then, the criteria for assigning specific scores within any of the systems allows for some variability in judgment. In a study directly addressed to the issue of reliability in scoring, Ramzy and Pickard (1949) demonstrated the variability that can arise. These investigators found 90% agreement in scoring location only after considerable discussion regarding criteria. With determinant and content scores, this agreement dropped to 75%.

Another source of difficulty arises in demonstrating the reliability of this test: to estimate the internal consistency of an instrument, it is first necessary that all responses to all items be located on a single dimension corresponding to the way in which objective questionnaire responses are classified as "pass" or "fail," or as "alpha" or "beta." Only with such a unidimensional representation of all items are the correlations that underlie internal consistency estimates defined, but the totally unconstrained nature of responses in the Rorschach makes this sort of representation difficult, if not impossible. Further discussion of the problem of establishing reliability in Rorschach testing can be found in Anastasi (1968).

Formal Tests of Validity

In assessing the validity, as in establishing the reliability, of the Rorschach results, the investigator is faced with the problem of choosing the level of scoring to test against the chosen criterion. Individual scores, ratios, relationships, and/or comparisons among scores can be used. Some workers (Anastasi, 1968; Fiske, 1959) have emphasized that interpretations, not scores, should be validated, since integrated descriptions of personality are what the test is supposed to produce. Even if agreement could be reached regarding the issue of what should be validated, a further confounding factor is that protocols may vary greatly in the total number of responses they contain. This presents a basic problem—how to equate data among protocols. Research has indicated (Fiske and Baughman, 1953) that there is not necessarily a linear relationship between the total responses and the scores obtained. The form of this relationship varies among scores. Then, too, the total number of responses varies considerably among examiners, as does the influence of their personality styles (Baughman, 1951). Generally, the results of validity studies with this test are disappointing because of the problems outlined and in part, too, because of problems in establishing criterion behaviors against which to rate the scores from the test. However, many validity studies have been done. These are too numerous to summarize here. The interested reader is referred to Suinn and Oskamp (1969), Zubin, Eron, and Schumer (1965), and Goldfried, Strickler, and Weiner (1971) for relevant studies and further discussion of psychometric issues in projective testing.

Usability on Older Populations

This technique may have little face validity with older adults who are not as "test wise" as their younger counterparts, and, therefore, it may be difficult to complete testing with some older adults (Light and Amick, 1956).

Also, when the Rorschach is being administered, it is possible that some older adults may not remember a response that was given during the free-association period when questioned about it in the inquiry. If this is suspected by the examiner, the administrative procedure can be modified so that inquiry immediately follows the free association for each card (Rapaport, Gill, and Schafer, 1968).

Sensitivity to Age Differences

There is evidence that the elderly respond differently than the general population to the Rorschach cards. Distinctions found include "intellectual impotence," "unrealism," "difficulty in interpersonal relations" (Klopfer, 1946; Light and Amick, 1956), "inability fully to use inner resources," "inconsistency in response to emotional challenge" (Klopfer, 1946), "suspicion," "anxiety," "immature introversion," "unawareness of affectional needs," and "inflexibility" (Light and Amick, 1956). It must be carefully noted that these characterizations are high-level *interpretations* of Rorschach protocols and, hence, are vulnerable to the preconceptions of the interpreters. Thus, it is not altogether clear whether the Rorschach *as an instrument* is sensitive to age differences or whether its sensitivity lies in the indispensible judgmental links of the whole chain from administration to interpretation.

At the somewhat more objective level of scoring, Ames and associates (1973) found a relatively higher frequency with aged subjects of protocols that contained either excessively high numbers of animal and form percepts or an excessively low number of positive form percepts and a paucity of responses in general. However, even in this case, there is an irreducible element of judgment about what is an excessively high or low frequency of a given response type. Such points of judgment are also points of entry for the preconceptions and values of the scorer.

Eisdorfer (1960a; 1960b; 1963) has presented evidence that hearing impairment and intelligence (as measured by the Wechsler Adult Intelligence Scale) have a stronger relationship to the deficits in Rorschach protocols than does chronological age.

General Comments and Recommendations

This is a complex test to administer, score, and interpret. It has been difficult to establish its reliability and validity, and it may have little face validity or appeal for older adults. In light of these problems, recommendations are against its use as a research instrument with elderly adults.

References

Ames, L. B., J. Learned, R. Metraux, and R. N. Walker. *Rorschach Response in Old Age.* New York: Brunner/Mazel, 1973.

Anastasi, A. *Psychological Testing* (3rd ed.). New York: Macmillan, 1968.

Baughman, E. E. "Rorschach Scores as a Function of Examiner Differences." *Journal of Projective Technique,* 1951, 15: 243–249.

Beck, S., and H. B. Molish. *Rorschach's Test.* New York: Grune and Stratton, 1967.

Eisdorfer, C. "Developmental Level and Sensory Impairment in Aged." *Journal of Projective Technique,* 1960a, 24: 129–32.

———. "Rorschach Rigidity and Sensory Decrement in a Senescent Population." *Journal of Gerontology,* 1960b, 15: 188–90.

———. "Rorschach Performance and Intellectual Functioning in the Aged." *Journal of Gerontology,* 1963, 18: 358–63.

Fiske, D. W. "Variability of Responses and the Stability of Scores and Interpretation of Projective Protocols." *Journal of Projective Technique,* 1959, 23: 263–67.

Fiske, D. W., and E. E. Baughman. "Relationship between Rorschach Scoring Categories and the Total Number of Responses." *Journal of Abnormal and Social Psychology,* 1953, 48: 25–33.

Goldfried, M. R., G. Stricker, and I. B. Weiner. *Rorschach Handbook of Clinical and Research Applications.* Englewood Cliffs, N.J.: Prentice-Hall, 1971.

Klopfer, W. G. "Personality Patterns of Old Age." *Rorschach Research Exchange,* 1946, 10: 145–66;

Klopfer B., and H. H. Davidson. *The Rorschach Technique.* New York: Harcourt Brace & World, 1962.

Kuhlen, R. G., and C. Keil. "The Rorschach Test Performance of 100 Elderly Males." *Journal of Gerontology,* 6 (supplement number 3), Program of the Second International Gerontology Congress, St. Louis, September 9–14, 1951, p. 115.

Light, B. H., and J. H. Amick. "Rorschach Responses of Normal Aged." *Journal of Projective Technique,* 1956, 20: 185–95.

Orme, J. E. "Rorschach Performances in Normal Old Age, Elderly Depressives and Senile Dementia," *Zeitschrift Diagnostische Psychologie,* 1958, 6: 132–41.

Piotrowski, Z. *Perceptanalysis.* New York: Macmillan, 1957.

Prados, M., and E. Fried. "Personality Structure of Older Age Groups." *Journal of Clinical Psychology,* 1947, 3: 113–20.

Ramzy, I., and D. M. Pickard. "A Study in the Reliability of Scoring the Rorschach Inkblot Test." *Journal of General Psychology,* 1949, 40: 3–10.

Rapaport, D., M. M. Gill, and R. Schafer. *Diagnostic Psychological Testing.* New York: International Universities Press, 1968.

Reitan, R. M. "Intellectual and Affective Changes in Essential Hypertension." *American Journal of Psychiatry,* 1954, 110: 817–25.

Rorschach, H. *Psychodiagnostics: A Diagnostic Test Based on Perception* (translated by P. Lemkau and R. Kronenburg). Berne: Huber, 1972 (1st German edition, 1921; U.S. distributor, Grune and Stratton).

Schafer, R. *Psychoanalytic Interpretation in Rorschach Testing.* New York: Grune and Stratton, 1954.

Suinn, R. M., and S. Oskamp. *The Predictive Validity of Projective Measures.* Springfield, Ill.: Charles C. Thomas, 1969.

Zubin, J., L. D. Eron, and F. Schumer. *An Experimental Approach to Projective Techniques.* New York: John Wiley and Sons, 1965.

Instrument

This copyrighted instrument is available from Grune and Stratton, New York.

THEMATIC APPERCEPTION TEST (TAT)
H. A. Murray, 1943

Description of Instrument

The TAT test consists of 31 achromatic cards on which there are pictured people of various ages in various settings. One blank card is included in the series. On some cards only one person is pictured, on others more than one. The facial expressions of the people pictured on the cards are designed to be neutral in order to allow the subject to interpret the stimuli in an idiosyncratic manner. Not all the cards are administered to every subject. Administration usually begins with card I, but after that the examiner decides which cards to use for his or her clinical or research purposes. Cards are designated for use with men, women, girls, or boys.

Method of Administration

The test is administered in an individual session, with the subject instructed to relate a story about what he or she sees. The subject is asked to include various elements in the descriptions—what might have led up to what is seen, what is happening, what are the feelings of those involved, and what is likely to be the outcome. The examiner can ask for further details while the subject views each card. The examiner must record verbatim the subject's story as it is told. Although tape recorders can be used, this makes some subjects anxious, thus affecting the amount of material given. The TAT takes various lengths of time to administer, depending on the number of cards included. A rather high level of training and skill is required to administer and score this test.

Context of Development and Subsequent Use

The test was developed as a method of determining the dominant drives, emotions, sentiments, complexes, and conflicts within the personality of the individual (Murray, 1943). Its goal is to assess the global and the specific aspects of personality, with the focus being the individual's adjustment to his or her life situation. This test has been used within this general conceptual framework by clinicians and researchers since its development.

Samples

No particular sample can be pinpointed for the original development or for special use with the aged.

Scoring, Scale Norms, and Distribution

Scoring and interpretation for clinical use are discussed by Murray (1943) and Bellak (1954). Murray (1943) recommended analysis of TAT stories by focusing on the forces emanating from the hero of the story (needs) and on those emanating from the environment (press). The clinician first determines the hero of the story; second, the motives, trends, and feelings of the hero (or heroes); third, the forces in the hero's environment; fourth, the outcomes; fifth, themes that summarize this interaction of the needs and presses; and, finally, interests and sentiments. Interpretation requires a good foundation in personality theory and an understanding of psychodynamic principles.

Bellak (1954) outlined and discussed 10 areas to be scored: the main theme, the main hero, the main needs of the hero, the conception of the environment, the perception of the figures in the pictures, the significant conflicts, the nature of anxieties, the main defenses, the severity of superego, and the integration of the ego. Interpretation of the stories within this framework depends on psychodynamic insights and judgments by the clinician. In research with the aged, as with other age-groups, specific scores have been developed by individual investigators to suit the requirements of the study. Norms in the form of time taken to respond, length of stories, themes developed, and other characteristics of performance are given by Atkinson (1958) and Henry (1956).

Formal Tests of Reliability

The many options for scoring the TAT contribute to difficulty in establishing the reliability and validity of the test. However, when one system or one score is adhered to and when pretraining on analysis and scoring is given, reliability in scoring seems reasonably high. In a review of several studies utilizing specific scores, Feld and Smith (1958) reported reliabilities ranging from .66 to .96, with a median of .89. The use of specific scores results in greater reliability than comparisons of interpretations from the scores on the test (Zubin, Eron, and Schumer, 1965).

As with most other projective techniques, the lack of constraint on responses with the TAT makes it extremely difficult to locate them on a common dimension. This virtually precludes numerical estimates of internal consistency based on interitem and item-total correlations.

Test-retest reliability requires a short interval between testings so as to avoid memory intrusions from the previous testing. On the other hand, over longer intervals legitimate personality developments can occur, and the test then appears unreliable. Thus, this form of reliability cannot be assessed in the absence of an independent distinction between true personality changes and situational disturbances of performance.

Formal Tests of Validity

The assumption behind the TAT is that responses are a reflection of the fantasies and needs of the subject. In a study by Child, Frank, and Storm (1956), measures on the TAT were not found to be related to needs and fantasies as reflected in self-reports of experiences in later childhood.

The TAT was designed to assess the basic and more enduring aspects of personality. Atkinson (1958), however, summarized data showing TAT responses to be significantly affected by conditions of hunger, deprivation of sleep, experiences of failure, and social frustration.

These issues and others regarding the determination of the TAT's validity in predicting behavior, differentiating between nosological groups, and making prognostic statements are discussed in Zubin, Eron, and Schumer (1965). That summary indicates that validation of the TAT in almost any area is beset with conceptual and procedural difficulties.

Usability on Older Populations

The TAT has been used rather widely with the aged for determining specific personality trends over the life span. Older people appear to find the task appealing. Since the cards to be used can be chosen by the researcher, the length of administration can be limited in order to avoid fatigue effects.

Sensitivity to Age Differences

This test has been used in various aged populations, some community based and some independent. Generally, the results indicate a trend toward less instrumentality or less involvement with the environment during later life, though there is much variability.

Gutmann (1964) sorted the TAT stories of a group of 40- to 70-year-old men into those reflecting "active mastery," "positive mastery," and "magical mastery" of life situations. There was some tendency for the older individuals in the group to show less active mastery of their lives. Rosen and Neugarten (1964) administered five TAT cards to 144 persons, aged 40 to 71 years. They found a significant difference between the youngest and the oldest thirds of this group with respect to what they define as indications of "ego strength." Thus, the oldest group introduced fewer nonpictured characters, less conflict, and less affect intensity into their stories than did the youngest group. They also ascribed lower activity-energy levels to their characters.

General Comments and Recommendations

The TAT has no single recognized scoring system, and few studies use the same subset of cards. Thus, comparisons among various studies are difficult to make on other than a purely qualitative or impressionistic basis. The use of this technique cannot be recommended for cases in which a psychometrically reliable and valid measure is needed.

References

Atkinson, J. W. (ed.). *Motives in Fantasy, Action and Society*. Princeton, N.J.: Van Nostrand, 1958.

Bellak, L. *The TAT and CAT in Clinical Use*. New York: Grune and Stratton, 1954.

Child, I. L., K. F. Frank, and T. Storm. "Self-Ratings and the TAT: Their Relations to Each Other and to Childhood Background." *Journal of Personality*, 1956, 25: 96-114.

Feld, S., and C. P. Smith. "An Evaluation of the Objectivity of the Method of Content Analysis." In *Motives in Fantasy, Action and Society*, J. W. Atkinson (ed.), pp. 234-41. Princeton, N.J.: Van Nostrand, 1958.

Gutmann, D. L. "An Exploration of Ego Configurations in Middle and Later Life." In *Personality in Middle and Late Life*, B. L. Neugarten et al., pp. 114-48. New York: Atherton Press, 1964.

Henry, W. E. *The Analysis of Fantasy*. New York: John Wiley and Sons, 1956.

Murray, H. A. *Thematic Apperception Test: Manual*. Cambridge, Mass.: Harvard University Press, 1943.

Rosen, J. L., and B. L. Neugarten. "Ego Functions in the Middle and Later Years: A Thematic Apperception Study." In *Personality in Middle and Late Life*, B. L. Neugarten et al., pp. 90-101. New York: Atherton Press, 1964.

Zubin, J., L. D. Eron, and F. Schumer. *An Experimental Approach to Projective Techniques*. New York: John Wiley and Sons, 1965.

Instrument

This copyrighted instrument is available from the Psychological Corporation, New York.

SENIOR APPERCEPTION TECHNIQUE (SAT)
L. Bellak and S. S. Bellak, 1973

Description of Instrument

The SAT consists of 16 cards, each with a line drawing depicting older people involved in life situations. Various themes are presented, such as loneliness, despair, rejection, sex in old age, and physical disabilities.

Method of Administration

The test is administered according to TAT instructions, and the subject is presented with one card at a time and is asked to make up a story with a beginning, a middle, and an end. The last card of the SAT (#16) is given with different instructions. The examiner says, "Here is a picture of a sleeping person having a dream. Tell me in some detail what this dream might be about—make it a lively dream." Typically, the clinician chooses a number of cards (5 to 10) with themes that he or she feels are relevant to the patient's situation. All 16 cards need not be given. After the stories have been recorded, the examiner may go back to specific cards and make additional inquiries. The duration of SAT administration is 20 to 30 minutes for 10 cards. The authors recommend a maximum of 5 minutes of storytelling per card, although subjects often use far less time.

Context of Development and Subsequent Use

This set of cards was originally developed as an alternative to the TAT, since problems faced by older individuals are not specifically included as stimulus materials in the TAT series, nor are there many older persons pictured on those cards. An attempt was made to develop a test that would touch the distinct needs, conflicts, and aspirations of older people.

Originally, 44 pictures were prepared, but only 16 of these were retained. The cards deleted were those that rarely elicited good stories and those that stimulated a very limited variety of stories.

Samples

A sample of 100 aged individuals, some working, some retired, some institutionalized, and some living at home, was used in the selection of the final 16 cards (Bellak and Bellak, 1973). There were 46 males and 54 females between the ages of 65 and 84 years.

Scoring, Scale Norms, and Distribution

Specific scoring systems for the assessment of coping and adapting have not been reported with elderly respondents, but indications of coping may be derived from scores based on effort to maintain self, kinship, and interest in people. Themes of competition, antagonism, and aggression and expressions of needs for nurturance, affiliation, and compassion can be viewed as reflections of an adaptive style. The average length of the stories for the sample group was 112 words, with the mean 138 and the mode 280. There was no indication of the differentiation between average and mean or of the distribution of scores.

The average administration time for 10 pictures ranged from 20 to 30 minutes.

Usability on Older Populations

The SAT was developed specifically for older populations. However, its usefulness for normal versus pathological groups is not as yet well documented.

Sensitivity to Age Differences

The Bellak and Bellak manual (1973) reports a thesis by Nancy Altobello in which the SAT was used to determine themes among the aged. This study indicated that the elderly showed a yearning for "connectedness" and activity and that there were aspects of hope even in the face of infirmity and death. She found no significant differences between elderly subjects and college students on five subcategories of activities and on hope and social environment. Toone (in Bellak, 1975) reported that older black women (62 to 81 years old) told more stories with positive or neutral outcomes and college-age subjects gave stories with more neutral or negative outcomes. Garland (in Bellak, 1975) found no differences between a group of college women aged 20 to 25 and women aged 65 to 81 on themes of dependency.

NOTE: Parts of this review were written by Eva Kahana, Thomas Fairchild, and Boaz Kanaha.

In another study reported in the manual (Bellak and Bellak, 1973), Lynette Ackerly used the SAT, the TAT, and the Rorschach to study a group of seven men and eight women aged 65 to 86 years. The subjects were given 21 SAT cards. The most important finding seemed to be that sexuality as an interest did not disappear with age. Sexual concerns were second highest among concerns that the TAT and highest in the SAT results. This last result emphasizes the influence of the stimuli on results, since there are many more cards with sexual themes in the SAT.

General Comments and Recommendations

The SAT is a promising although largely untried addition to the family of thematic apperception techniques. Schaie (1978) noted that the selection of the thematic cards was not based on research guidelines and that the cards reflect stereotyped views of aging and the problems of the aged.

Additional normative data are needed in order to obtain a better understanding of the stimulus pull of these pictures on different populations of subjects. Age norms within the adult span (20 to 85+) would be particularly helpful.

It would be useful to develop scales from these data to assess those variables that are currently being studied in gerontological research through questionnaires, thus allowing tests of convergent validity. Formal content analysis (i.e., computer counts of words) may also be helpful in deriving more quantifiable measures. Additional work is needed in the area of reliability (test-retest). In a limited sense, validity may be ascertained by comparison of these findings with those of other projective techniques.

References

Bellak. L. *The T.A.T., C.A.T., and S.A.T. in Clinical Use* (3rd ed.). New York: Gruen and Stratton, 1975.

Bellak, L., and S. S. Bellak. *Manual for the Senior Apperception Technique.* Larchmont, N.Y.: C.P.S., 1973.

Schaie, K. W. "The Senior Apperception Technique." In *The Eighth Mental Measurements Yearbook* (vol. 1), O. K. Buros (ed.), p. 675. Highland Park, N.J.: Gryphon Press, 1978.

Instrument

This copyrighted instrument is available from C.P.S., Larchmont, N.Y.

GERONTOLOGICAL APPERCEPTION TEST (GAT)
R. L. Wolk and R. B. Wolk, 1971

Description of Instrument

This test is made up of a series of 14 achromatic cards picturing older people in situations often faced by older individuals. Themes include those of loneliness, family relationships, rejection, sex, and need for companionship.

Method of Administration

The method of administration is the same as that for the TAT (p. 91).

Context of Development and Subsequent Use

The conceptual context of the development of the GAT is virtually the same as that of the Senior Apperception Test. The rationale is that, if the stimulus material depicts persons and situations with which the subject is particularly likely to identify, the stories produced should be richer, more varied, and more expressive of the subject's conflicts, needs, interests, and so on.

Samples

The sample within which the GAT was developed is not specified in the manual. However, Wolk (1972) indicated that this instrument was developed in an outpatient setting—the geriatric guidance clinic at the Menorah Home and Hospital for the Aged, Brooklyn, N.Y.

Scoring, Scale Norms, and Distribution

A system of scoring can be developed by the individual researcher to suit the needs of the study. No norms for the GAT have been established.

Usability on Older Populations

Like the TAT's the GAT's task of making up stories for the cards is an appealing one. The number of cards given to the subject can be varied to suit the situation and the fatigue level of the subject.

Sensitivity to Age Differences

Fitzgerald, Pasewerk, and Fleisher (1974) compared the responses of 30 older adults, 56 to 94 years old, on five cards from the GAT and five cards from the TAT matched for similarities in themes elicited. Of the five theme areas scored—loss of sexuality, loss of attractiveness, family difficulties, physical difficulties, and dependency—only in the area of physical limitations did the GAT more successfully elicit relevant themes than did the TAT.

Traxler, Sweiner, and Rogers (1974) tested community-dwelling and institutionalized aged ranging from 60 to 91 years of age with the GAT. They found that the average length of stories in the community-dwelling group was 65 words, with shorter stories in the nursing home group. For both of the groups the length of the stories was considerably shorter than the 100–200-word figure reported by Wolk and Wolk (1971) in the GAT manual. Traxler, Sweiner, and Rogers (1974) also reported that the stories tapped only superficial aspects of personality, rather than deeper levels of ego structure. These results indicate that the GAT does not present especially potent stimuli for rich responses from older adults.

General Comments and Recommendations

In the absence of more data, it is difficult to evaluate this particular variation of the thematic series. Like the other thematic tests, it is subject to problems in establishing validity and reliability. It does not appear that presenting aged individuals with more "relevant" stimuli makes a difference. Also, it is this reviewer's opinion that the test is overly weighted with depressive themes. Though loneliness and depression are important problems in old age, other processes in personality functioning need to be explored, too.

References

Fitzgerald, B. J., R. A. Pasewerk, and S. Fleisher. "Responses of an Aged Population on the Gerontological and Thematic Apperception Tests." *Journal of Personality Assessment*, 1974, 38: 234–35.

Traxler, A., R. Sweiner, and B. Rogers. "Use of the Gerontological Apperception Test with Community-Dwelling and Institutionalized Aged." *The Gerontologist*, 1974, 14:52.

Wolk, R. L., and R. B. Wolk. *Manual: The Gerontological Apperception Test.* New York: Behavioral Publications, 1971.

Instrument

This copyrighted instrument is available from Behavioral Publications, New York.

ID, EGO, SUPEREGO TEST (IES)
L. A. Dombrose and M. S. Slobin, 1958

Definition of Variable

This test assesses the relative strengths of the Freudian constructs id, ego, and superego.

Description of Instrument

This is a projective test with four subtests. The first subtest is picture title test, which consists of 12 pictures. The subject must supply a title for each. The second is the picture story completion subtest in which the subject must supply an ending for each of 13 incomplete cartoon story sequences. Two or three cartoon pictures begin the sequence. The subject must choose one of three endings to the sequence. The photo-analysis subtest consists of nine photographs of men. The subject is asked two multiple-choice questions that vary from picture to picture about the person in the photo. The fourth subtest (arrow-dot) is a perceptual-motor task consisting of a series of 23 graphic problems requiring the subject to draw the shortest line from an arrow to a dot. Between these two points are placed a variety of solid lines and black bars defined as barriers. This subtest is based on graphic symbolic representation. The arrow represents impulse forces, and the barriers represent those frustrations met in the environment.

Method of Administration

This test must be given to individual subjects and the examiner must record responses as the test proceeds. The test takes approximately 30 minutes to complete.

Context of Development and Subsequent Use

The IES test was developed as a projective test of personality within the psychoanalytic framework of personality development and psychopathology. It was designed to give measurements of the relative strength of personality constructs—impulses, ego, and superego. Each of the subtests provides an opportunity for the subject to accumulate points for each one of these constructs to that an overall picture of personality can be obtained.

Samples

Dombrose and Slobin (1958) provided scores on 183 normal adult males. They also included the scores of 161 children and 33 adolescents and those of various groups of patients, as well as some groups of aged individuals.

Scoring, Scale Norms, and Distribution

Scoring criteria are supplied for each subtest to reflect information about id, ego, and superego functioning. Only the first subtest, picture title, requires judgment in scoring. The possible responses to the other subtests are keyed to indicate whether impulse satisfactions, reality consideration, or conscience dominates. The administration, scoring, and interpretation of the test require some skill and an understanding of psychoanalytic concepts. Norms have not been established.

Formal Tests of Reliability

Test-retest reliability coefficients (in one group of 30 male patients in outpatient therapy) ranged from .39 to .83 for the 12 different scores (Dombrose and Slobin, 1958). There was an interval of 30 to 60 days between testings in this sample. Kuder-Richardson 20 split-half reliabilities for various populations for the various scores on the four subtests ranged from below .20 to .89.

Formal Tests of Validity

Construct Validity: Hypotheses regarding genetic development were partially supported in a group of 10-year-old children, adolescents, and normal adults (Charnes, 1953, in Dombrose and Slobin, 1958). Only 7 of 36 comparisons were significant beyond the $p < .05$ level of significance on t and x^2 tests.

Comparisons of the scores of three groups of males from various diagnostic groups—normals, neurotics, and schizophrenics—indicated significant ($p < .01$) differences between means when 36 comparisons were made (Dombrose and Slobin, 1958).

Three geriatric groups were compared by Ritz (1954, in Dombrose and Slobin, 1958). In a group of normals (mean age 72.3 years), an institutionalized nonpsychotic group (mean age 78.9 years), and an institutionalized psychotic group (mean age 73.9 years), it was found that age, not diagnosis, was the most important factor in differences in scores, with an increase in impulsivity, rigidity, and irrationality with increased age. Indications of significant correlations are missing in the report of the data.

Usability on Older Populations

Though it can take 30 minutes for mature adults to complete this test, it can be expected that more time will be needed for most older adults. Still, administration time is probably within fatigue limits. This test does not require the subject to make written responses and is given in individual sessions so that the examiner can maximize cooperation and motivation. On the surface, these factors seem to indicate that the IES test would be usable with older populations if it had adequate standardization.

Sensitivity to Age Differences

Dombrose and Slobin (1958) reported a study by Ritz, which included a group of 28 hospitalized aged, 28 living in a home for the aged, and 30 community-dwelling aged. No tests of significance were performed to compare scores among these groups or with younger groups.

Bortner (1963) administered the IES to 437 men 30 through 70 years of age. Five of 13 scores correlated significantly with age. Generally, there is an increase in impulsivity in old age and a decline in ego functioning. However, the author indicated that much of the variance in the test scores was not accounted for by age and came rather from other determinants of personality.

Norms are lacking. This test is not recommended for research purposes because of its inadequate standardization.

References

Bortner, R. W. "Superego Functioning and Institutional Adjustment." *Perceptual and Motor Skills*, 1962, 14: 375–579.
———. "The Relationship between Age and Measures of Id, Ego and Superego Functioning." *Journal of Gerontology*, 1963, 18: 386–89.
Dombrose, L. A., and M. S. Slobin. "The IES Test." *Perceptual and Motor Skills*, 1958, 8: 347–89 (monograph supplement number 3).
Hamilton G. V. "Changes in Personality and Psycho-sexual Phenomena with Age." In *Problems of Aging*, E. V. Cowdry (ed.), pp. 810–31. Baltimore: Williams and Wilkins, 1942.

Instrument

This copyrighted instrument is available from Psychological Test Specialists, Missoula, Mont.

WORD-ASSOCIATION TECHNIQUES
J. C. Jung, 1910

Definition of Variable

These techniques tap the conflict-laden areas in psychodynamic functioning.

Description of Instrument

There is no standard set of items used for word-association techniques. Generally, the procedure is to mix a number of words that are expected to arouse anxiety or to tap conflicts or areas of emotional disturbance among other words that have been shown to be rather neutral (Jung, 1910; Rapaport, 1946; Rosanoff, 1927). For example, in a study of older adults (Olsen and Elder, 1958), 15 target words were imbedded in a list of 60 words. The 15 words, intended to elicit specific reactions to the stresses of old age were "money," "suffer," "health," "sickness," "stomach," "heart," "old," "suicide," "death," "religion," "Bible," "afraid," "hate," "love," and "worry."

Method of Administration

The series of words selected is read aloud, one at a time, to the subject in an individual session. The subject is instructed to respond with the first word that comes to mind and to do this as rapidly as possible. Time of administration varies, depending on the length of the word list and the fluency of the subject. Proper administration of the technique requires familiarity with the various nonverbal responses to be recorded. In clinical settings the technique is usually administered by an experienced clinician, since it is considered projective in nature.

Context of Development and Subsequent Use

Originally, this technique was developed by Jung (1910). It was later elaborated upon by Rapaport (1946) and Rosanoff (1938). Word-association techniques have been used mainly in clinical settings and relatively little in research.

Samples

Rosanoff (1927) developed frequency tables for types of responses within groups of 1,000 normal subjects, 247 insane adults, 253 defective children over age 9 years, and a group of 600 white and black children between the ages of 4 and 15 years. Olsen and Elder's (1958) sample consisted of a group of 25 women, aged 60 through 80 years. Of this group 60% was aged 60 to 70 years; 40%, 70 to 80 years. This group was compared to 25 younger women between the ages of 29 and 30 years. All the subjects were wives of members of the faculty or the staff at a college.

Scoring, Scale Norms, and Distribution

Responses, time to respond, and nonverbal reactions are recorded. The number and type of "disturbed" responses are usually the variables of central concern. Criteria for determining whether a response should be scored as "disturbed" have been developed by Rapaport (1946), Rosanoff (1927), and Rotter (1957). The reader is referred to these sources for norms. Reaction time to words can also be used as a score or as a criterion for "disturbance" of response.

Formal Tests of Reliability

Tendler (1945) reported split-half reliabilities between .80 and .95 in a study of 240 adult subjects, which used the various quantifiable aspects of responses.

Usability on Older Populations

This is an easily administered task, one that can be varied to avoid fatigue.

Sensitivity to Age Differences

In a study of 25 young (20 to 30 years old) and 25 older (60 to 80 years old) women, Olsen and Elder (1958) found that the older subjects had longer reaction times for the total list and for the lists of neutral and critical words analyzed separately. There was a significant difference between the mean reaction time to neutral words and to critical words for the older group, but not for the younger group. The authors concluded that the 15 critical words were indicators of conflict areas especially important in old age.

Riegel and Birren (1965) found only transient age differences in associations to 100 Kent-Rosanoff words (Rosanoff, 1927). Their sample was composed of 30 young individuals (mean age 22.6 years) and 23 old individuals (mean age 68.3 years). The older subjects showed longer initial latencies; but, as the series continued, their latencies became similar to the young subjects'. The older subjects' early responses were unique, but later in the series they became similar to the younger subjects' responses.

There is evidence that older persons have greater affective reaction to words in general and that health status contributes to this phenomenon. Halberstam and Zaretsky (1966) had subjects rate the affective loading of 709 words. They found that all older subjects and young brain-damaged patients rated significantly more of the words as having an affective component (negative or positive), rather than a neutral one. The authors found that there were no age differences in the amount of time taken to rate the effect of words but that, with poorer health status, reaction time increased.

General Comments and Recommendations

The word-association technique does not have well-demonstrated validity and reliability, This is due in part to its projective nature and in part to the fact that there is no specific list of words used from study to study. The technique is specifically focused upon conflict or anxiety-laden areas of functioning. It does not assess total personality, nor does it provide data on the source or nature of the conflict that may be indicated.

References

Halberstam, J. L., and H. H. Zaretsky. "Rating Reliability and Affective Value of Words as a Function of Age and Brain Damage." *Journal of Gerontology*, 1966, 21: 529–36.

Jung, J. C. "The Association Method." *American Journal of Psychology*, 1910, 21: 219–69.

Olsen, I. A., and J. H. Elder. "A Word Association Test of Emotional Disturbance in Older Women." *Journal of Gerontology*, 1958, 13: 305–8.

Rapaport, D. *Diagnostic Psychological Testing* (vol. 2). Chicago: Year Book Publishing, 1946.

Riegel, K. F., and J. E. Birren. "Age Differences in Associative Behavior." *Journal of Gerontology*, 1965, 20: 125–30.

Rosanoff, A. J. *Manual of Psychiatry and Mental Hygiene.* New York: John Wiley and Sons, 1927.

Rotter, J. B. "Word Association and Sentence Completion Methods." In *An Introduction to Projective Techniques,* H. H. Anderson and G. L. Anderson (eds.), pp. 279–312. New York: Prentice-Hall, 1957.

Tendler, A. D. "Significant Features of Disturbance in Free Association." *Journal of Psychology*, 1945, 20: 65–89.

Instrument

There is no standard material for this technique.

MINNESOTA MULTIPHASIC PERSONALITY INVENTORY (MMPI)
S. R. Hathaway and J. C. McKinley, 1940a, 1940b, 1942a, 1942b

Definition of Variable

Nine psychiatric-diagnostic dimensions are assessed: hysteria (Hs), depression (D), hypochondriasis (Hy), psychopathic deviate (Pd), masculinity-femininity (Mf), paranoia (Pa), psychasthenia(pt), schizophrenia (Sc), and mania (Ma).

Description of Instrument

The MMPI is made up of 550 statements about various actions, beliefs, physical symptoms, preferences, and personal and social values. The response options are "true," "false," and "cannot say." The statements are distributed among the nine diagnostic dimensions, with a scale formed for each. Thus, the MMPI is properly categorized as a battery.

Method of Administration

The MMPI is a self-administered questionnaire with a machine-scorable answer sheet. It can also be administered as a card-sorting task.

Context of Development and Subsequent Use

The MMPI was developed through empirical keying procedures to supply diagnostic information in psychiatric populations. The responses of criterion diagnostic groups to a large pool of items were compared to the responses of "normals" and individuals hospitalized for physical complaints. Items discriminating best between these groups were included in the final test form. Subsequent use of this test included a wide range of normal populations in clinical as well as research settings. The MMPI has been used to differentiate normals from psychoneurotic and psychotic patients. It has been used to describe specific personality characteristics within each of these groups. The MMPI has been used in total and in part. More than 200 specialized scales have been developed from the MMPI item pool that are used separately from the total test. The widely used Barron Ego Strength Scale is one example of the scales derived from the MMPI.

Samples

The original data for this test were gathered on a group of midwestern American adults tested before World War II. The group included 299 men and 425 women who were accompanying patients or visiting friends and relatives at the University of Minnesota Hospitals. In the sample, 699 were in the age-group 16 to 54 and 25 were in the age-group 55 to 65 (Hathaway and McKinley, 1940a). The median age for the males in a revised sample (Hathaway and Briggs, 1957, in Dahlstrom and Welsh, 1960, p. 45) was 34.4 years and for the females it was 34.5.

Scoring, Scale Norms, and Distribution

Raw scores are converted into T scores (mean of 50, SD of 10) on a profile chart. Different conversions are made for males and females, and they are recorded on separate profile sheets. Any score of 70 or higher (falling 2 SD or more above the mean) is generally taken as the cutoff point used in the identification of pathological deviation. The clinical significance of any one scale is not important; instead, the profile of all the scores should be interpreted. Four "validity" scales are extracted from the responses along with the nine diagnostic scales. The "cannot say" scale is based on the number of items to which the response is "cannot say," and presumably it reflects evasiveness. The lie (L) scale is based on the number of extremely improbable responses: the denial of universal weaknesses and frailness or the affirmation of impossible virtues. The false (F) scale counts replies given only rarely as an index of misunderstandings, response errors, et cetera. The K scale is the subject's score on certain items associated with "false positives," i.e., "normal" persons misclassified by the MMPI as deviant. If the K score is low, there is reason to suspect that the subject is judging himself or herself with excessive severity; if it is high, he or she is probably being excessively lenient.

Formal Tests of Reliability

Test-retest reliabilities for the subscales are reported in Dahlstrom and Welsh (1960). As it might be expected, the length of the interval between testings is important for determining reliability, with shorter intervals resulting in higher reliabilities. For example, reliability coefficients ranged from .15 to .48 in a group of 337 high school students retested after a five-year interval. In another instance, reliability coefficients ranged from .52 to .93 in a group of neuropsychiatric patients retested after an interval of one or two days.

Studies providing information about interval consistency estimates (split-half) are also reported by Dahlstrom and Welsh (1960). Though there is a considerable range in the coefficients (−.05 to .96), they are generally high.

Generally, factor analyses with the MMPI have been carried out at two levels. The early studies related the scale scores. Later factor analyses were based on the intercorrelations of the individual items. Factor analyses of the scale scores generally agreed on two basic dimensions (Dahlstrom, Welsh, and Dahlstrom, 1972). Two other dimensions were determined, but there was less agreement regarding these. Welsh (1952) determined these two to be a "general anxiety" dimension and a "repression" dimension. Eichman (1961, 1962) supported Welsh's finding. Both of these studies involved hospitalized patients. Kassebaum, Couch, and Slater (1959) found the same results in a normal college population but proposed the dimensions "extroversion-introversion."

Factor analyses of the individual items have sometimes led to the development of alternate scale constructions for the items (Tryon, 1967a, 1967b, 1968; Stein, 1968; Lorr, Caffey, and Gessner, 1968). Further information regarding the factor structure of the MMPI can be found in Dahlstrom, Welsh, and Dahlstrom (1972).

Formal Tests of Validity

Many validity studies have been done with this test. Some have had to do with the effectiveness of the entire test in differentiating diagnostic and normal groups, some have had to do with other diagnostic information, and still others have focused on specific scales. These studies indicate varying levels of validity. It is possible that low validity figures may not be a reflection of the inadequacy of the MMPI but rather the result of applying the test to situations for which it is not suited and to questions too broad to answer (Dahlstrom and Welsh, 1960).

Since there are so many validity studies on the MMPI, this review on validity will focus on the D (depression) scale and on some of the studies that demonstrate its validity as examples of others that are available in the literature.

Predictive Validity: Modlin (1947) reported that 88% of the peak scores within a group of 31 males hospitalized for depression were on the depression subscale. In addition, no profile or scores among this group was considered normal. Modlin indicated that D peaks were frequent among other groups, too, especially his group of hypochondriacs.

Endicott and Jortner (1966) made independent judgments of their subjects' current depression by means of a five-point clinical rating scale that indicated the intensity of the depressive state. These ratings were made without knowledge of the subjects' scores on the D scale of the MMPI for a group of 84 hospitalized men and women and 40 outpatients. An increase in rated intensity corresponded with an increase in scores on the D scale.

Concurrent Validity: The correlation of the MMPI D scale with the Zung Self-Rating Depression Scale was .65 (Zung, 1967).

Usability on Older Populations

This test is too long even in a shortened form for use with many groups of aged individuals, since fatigue would be an important factor in performance. An alternative might be to use the special scales that have been developed from the MMPI, such as the Barron Ego Strength Scale and the Taylor Manifest Anxiety Scale, for specific research questions.

Several special forms of the MMPI have been developed that make this test more usable with older populations. An oral form of the test has been developed (Wolf, Freinek, and Shaffer, 1964) for use with older individuals who have adequate hearing. Uecker (1969) developed a card-sort procedure for use with brain-damaged geriatric patients that seems to be applicable to other individuals.

Sensitivity to Age Differences

The studies of Brozek (1955), Aaronson (1958, 1960), Calden and Hokanson (1959), Pearson, Swenson, and Rome (1965), and Postema and Schell (1967) generally agree that older adults tend to score high on the subscales of the neurotic triad and the social introversion scale and low on the remaining scales, with the Pd and the Ma being the lowest. This result was also found by Kornetsky (1963), who used the card form of the MMPI.

The study of Pearson, Swenson, and Rome (1965) involved the assessment of 25,000 medical patients at the Mayo Clinic. These data were used as the basis for establishing separate age adjustments in scores (for individuals over age 70 years). These special conversions can be found in Appendix H of Dahlstrom, Welsh, and Dahlstrom (1972).

General Comments and Recommendations

This is an extremely long test to administer whole or in part to the elderly. Studies seem to indicate that, as tests used for differential diagnosis, few separate scales are not unidimensional and that it is usual that individuals of whatever diagnostic label do not necessarily make a high score on the matching scale (Benton, 1949; Rodgers, 1972). Anastasi (1961, p. 503) indicated that "factorial analysis based on the intercorrelations of items and of scales indicate that items would be differently grouped on the basis of their empirically established interrelations."

Though interpretation of profile configurations allows for definite differentiation of a normal individual from one with pathology, such differentiation of clinical groups is less certain. A great deal of overlap occurs between diagnostic groups in scores on the test (Benton, 1949).

A shorter measure for the assessment of personality in the elderly is recommended.

References

Aaronson, B. S. "Age and Sex Influences on MMPI Profile Scale Distribution on an Abnormal Population." *Journal of Consulting Psychology*, 1958, 22: 203-6.

——. "A Dimension of Personality Change with Aging." *Journal of Gerontology*, 1960, 19: 144.

Anastasi, A. *Psychological Testing* (3rd ed.). New York: Macmillan, 1961.

Benton, A. "Review." In *The Third Mental Measurements Yearbook*, O. K. Buros (ed.), pp. 104-7. Highland Park, N.J.: Gryphon Press, 1949.

Brozek, J. "Personality Changes with Age: An Item Analysis of the MMPI." *Journal of Gerontology*, 1955, 10: 194-206.

Calden, D., and J. E. Hokanson. "Influence of Age on MMPI Responses." *Journal of Clinical Psychology*, 1959, 15: 194-95.

Dahlstrom, W. G., and G. S. Welsh. *An MMPI Handbook: A Guide to Use in Clinical Practice and Research*. Minneapolis: University of Minnesota Press, 1960.

Dahlstrom, W. G., G. S. Welsh, and L. E. Dahlstrom. *An MMPI Handbook: Clinical Interpretation* (vol. 1, rev. ed.). Minneapolis: University of Minnesota Press, 1972.

Eichman, W. J. "Replicated Factors on the MMPI with Female NP Patients." *Journal of Consulting Psychology*, 1961, 25: 55-60.

——. "Factored Scales for the MMPI: A Clinical and Statistical Manual." *Journal of Clinical Psychology*, 1962, 18: 363-95.

Endicott, N. A., and S. Jortner. "Objective Measures of Depression." *Archives of General Psychiatry*, 1966, 15: 249-55.

Hathaway, S. R., and P. F. Briggs. "Some Normative Data on New MMPI Scales." *Journal of Clinical Psychology*, 1957, 13: 364-68.

Hathaway, S. R., and J. C. McKinley. "A Multiphasic Personality Schedule (Minnesota) I. Construction of the Schedule." *Journal of Psychology*, 1940a, 10: 249-54.

——. "A Multiphasic Personality Schedule (Minnesota) II. A Differential Study of Hypochondriasis." *Journal of Psychology*, 1940b, 10: 255-68.

——. "A Multiphasic Personality Schedule (Minnesota) III. The Measurement of Symptomatic Depression." *Journal of Psychology*, 1942a, 14: 73-84.

——. "A Multiphasic Personality Schedule (Minnesota) IV. Psychasthenia." *Journal of Applied Psychology*, 1942b, 26: 614-24.

Kassebaum, G. G., A. S. Couch, and P. E. Slater. "The Factorial Dimensions of the MMPI." *Journal of Consulting Psychology*, 1959, 23: 226-36.

Kornetsky, C. "MMPI: Results Obtained from a Population of Aged Men." In *Human Aging: a Biological and Behavioral Study*, J. E. Birren, R. M. Butler, S. W. Greenhouse,

L. Sokoloff, and M. R. Yarrow (eds.), pp. 217–52. Washington, D. C.: National Institute of Mental Health, 1963.

Lorr, M., E. M. Caffey, and T. L. Gessner. "Seven Symptom Profiles." *Journal of Nervous and Mental Disease*, 1968, 147: 134-40.

Modlin, H. C. "A Study of the MMPI in Clinical Practice with Notes on the Cornell Index." *American Journal of Psychiatry*, 1947, 103: 758-69.

Pearson, J. S., W. M. Swenson, and H. P. Rome. "Age and Sex Differences Related to MMPI Response Frequency in 25,000 Medical Patients." *American Journal of Psychiatry*, 1965, 121: 989-95.

Postema, G., and R. E. Schell. "Some MMPI Evidence of Seemingly Greater Neurotic Behavior among Older People." *Journal of Clinical Psychology*, 1967, 23: 140-43.

Rodgers, D. A. "Review." In *The Seventh Mental Measurements Yearbook*, O. K. Buros (ed.), pp. 243-50. Highland Park, N.J.: Gryphon Press, 1972.

Stein, K. B. "The TSC Scales: The Outcome of a Cluster Analysis of the 550 MMPI Items." In *Advances in Psychological Assessment* (vol. 1), P. McReynolds, (ed.), pp. 80-104. Palo Alto, Calif: Science and Behavior Books, 1968.

Tryon, R. C. "Person-Clusters on Intellectual Abilities and on MMPI Attributes." *Multivariate Behavioral Research*, 1967a, 2: 5-34.

————. "Predicting Individual Differences by Cluster Analysis: Holzinger Abilities and MMPI Attributes." *Multivariate Behavioral Research*, 1967b, 2: 325-48.

————. "Comparative Cluster Analysis of Variables and Individuals: Holzinger Abilities and the MMPI." *Multivariate Behavioral Research*, 1968, 3: 115-44.

Uecker, A. E. "Comparability of Two Methods of Administering the MMPI to Brain-Damaged Geriatric Patients." *Journal of Clinical Psychology*, 1969, 25: 196-98.

Welsh, G. S. "A Factor Study of the MMPI Using Scales with Item Overlap Eliminated." *American Psychologist*, 1952, 7: 341.

Wolf, S., W. R. Freinek, and J. W. Shaffer. "Comparability of Complete Oral and Booklet Forms of the MMPI." *Journal of Clinical Psychology*, 1964, 20: 375-78.

Zung, W. W. K. "Factors Influencing the Self-Rating Depression Scale." *Archives of General Psychiatry*, 1967, 16: 543-47.

Instrument

This copyrighted instrument is available from the Psychological Corporation, New York.

SIXTEEN PERSONALITY FACTORS TEST (16PF)
R. B. Cattell, H. W. Eber, and M. M. Tatsuoka, 1957

Definition of Variable

Sixteen bipolar traits are tested: (A) reserved versus outgoing, (B) concrete thinking (low intelligence) versus abstract thinking (high intelligence), (C) affected by feelings versus emotionally stable, (E) humble versus assertive, (F) sober versus happy-go-lucky, (G) expedient versus conscientious, (H) shy versus venturesome, (I) tough-minded (realistic) versus tender-minded (sensitive), (L) trusting versus suspicious, (M) practical versus imaginative, (N) genuine but socially clumsy versus polished, (O) self-assured versus apprehensive, (Q_1) conservative versus experimenting, (Q_2) group dependent versus self-sufficient, (Q_3) undisciplined versus controlled, and (Q_4) relaxed versus tense.

Description of Instrument

In the test there are from 106 to 187 bipolar items, depending on the form being used (A, B, C, or D). The response options are selecting one or the other polar statement as more nearly true of oneself or indicating that neither statement applies more than the other.

Though each item is intended to load significantly on 1 of the 16 factors, all the items are worded so as to avoid the direct suggestion of any particular personality trait. The items of each factor are scattered throughout the test.

Method of Administration

The test uses a self-administered questionnaire with a response sheet designed to facilitate mechanical scoring.

Context of Development and Subsequent Use

Cattell developed the 16PF in the context of factor analytic studies of personality. Factor analysis of the behavior ratings of a group of 100 adults by their close associates, using an initial pool of 171 traits, yielded the first twelve factors. Factors Q_1 through Q_4 were developed by factor analysis of self-report questionnaire items.

Samples

The standardization sample included persons aged 55 years and over in numbers proportional to their percentage in the national population. The sample was also stratified with respect to geographical area, population densities, and family income.

Scoring, Scale Norms, and Distribution

The raw score for each of the 16 factors is converted into a standard score (a *sten*) with a mean of 5.5 and a range from 1 to 10. Scores of 5 and 6 are within the "normal" range. Separate standard scoring functions are available for student and adult populations. Age corrections are made for subjects over 35 years of age.

Formal Tests of Reliability

Test-retest reliabilities with intervals of 4 to 7 days ranged from .54 to .89, depending on the factor, and they were obtained on form A or B in a group of 79 employment counselors and 67 undergraduate students. Reliability within a group of 95 New Zealand subjects (18-year-old males and females) ranged from .45 to .93, depending on the scale, for both forms A and B. Test-retest with a 2-month interval yielded correlations of .43 to .85 on form A in a group of 44 individuals (Cattell, Eber, and Tatsuoka, 1970).

Correlations between forms are low, and newer revisions differ considerably from one another. One correlation between forms A and B is in the .70s, with another ranging between that one and one in the .20s.

Formal Tests of Validity

Concurrent Validity: Factor analysis of the 16PF with the Minnesota Multiphasic Personality Inventory (MMPI), the Guilford-Zimmerman Temperament Survey (GZTS), and the Eysenck Personality Inventory (EPI) is discussed in Cattell, Eber, and Tatsuoka (1970). The comparison of the 16PF with the MMPI indicates that essentially the same dimensions of personality are measured. However, there seem to be additional items on the MMPI that characterize pathological behavior. Cattell, Eber, and Tatsuoka (1970) gave regression weights for estimating GZTS and MMPI scores from the 16PF. There is much overlap of the 16PF dimensions with those of the GZTS, though divisions into traits are different in the two tests.

Construct Validity: Construct validity, calculated from the known factor loadings of the items with the factors in the original research, ranged from .73 to .96, depending on the variable measured.

Sensitivity to Age Differences

Results from the testing of about 700 persons aged from 30 to 80 years indicate: (1) a marked and steady shift in factor F from "happy-go-lucky" toward "sober," (2) a slight shift in factor G toward "conscientious," (3) a shift in factor I toward "tender-minded," (4) a late-life shift in factor O toward "self-assured," (5) a steady shift in factor Q_1 toward "experimenting," (6) a late-life shift in factor Q_3 toward "controlled," and (7) a shift in Q_4 toward "relaxed," more noticeable after 50 years of age (Cattell, Eber, and Tatsuoka, 1970). Goodwin and Schaie (1969) also reported significant age differences. Botwinick and Storandt (1974), however, failed to find significant age effects in a multivariate analysis of the 16PF scale data. (It should be pointed out that not all 16 scales were included in each of these three studies.)

General Comments and Recommendations

The test as a whole can be too long and tedious for some aged individuals. Care should be taken in using the four forms furnished as equivalent forms, as well as in using the revisions interchangeable with earlier versions of the test.

Validity data for this test are reported in the form of regression weights for predictive purposes, with indications that scales on the 16PF may not be directly comparable with those on the MMPI or the GZTS. The 16PF seems to be testing the same overall processes as other tests, and yet there are differences in conceptualization.

The lack of actual direct validity data is a drawback in light of the amount of work done to develop the test originally. The construct validity figures and the regression weights cited by the authors are not an adequate substitute for correlations with other known tests or behavior assessed in other ways.

Although Cattell has indicated that he is measuring source traits with his test, few data have been presented to support this supposition (Bouchard, 1972). What is needed is validating evidence from other behavioral measures.

References

Botwinick, J., and M. Storandt. *Memory, Related Functions and Age*. Springfield, Ill.: Charles C. Thomas, 1974.

Bouchard, T. J. "Review." In *The Seventh Mental Measurements Yearbook*, O. K. Buros (ed.), pp. 329-32. Highland Park, N.J.: Gryphon Press, 1972.

Cattell, R. B. *Description and Measurement of Personality*. Tarrytown on Hudson, N.Y.: World Book Company, 1946.

Cattell, R. B. *Personality: A Systematic, Theoretical and Factual Study*. New York: McGraw-Hill, 1950.

Cattell, R. B. *Personality and Motivation Structure and Measurement*. Tarrytown on Hudson, N.Y.: World Book Company, 1957.

Cattell, R. B., H. W. Eber, and M. M. Tatsuoka. *The Handbook for the Sixteen Personality Factors Questionnaire: Published Forms A, B, and C*. Champaign, Ill.: Institute for Personality and Ability Testing, 1957.

——. *The Handbook for the Sixteen Personality Factors Questionnaire* (1970 ed.). Champaign, Ill.: Institute for Personality and Ability Testing, 1970.

Costa, P. T., J. L. Fazard, P. R. McCrae, and R. Bosse. "Relations of Age and Personality Dimensions to Cognitive Ability Factors." *Journal of Gerontology*, 1976, 31: 663-69.

Fozard, J. L. "Predicting Age in Adult Years." *Aging and Human Development*, 1972, 3: 175-82.

Fozard, J. L., and R. L. Nuttall. "Effects of Age and SE Status Differences on 16 PF Questionnaire Scores." *American Psychologist*, 1971, 26: 1106.

Goodwin, K. S., and K. W. Schaie. "Age Differences in Personality Structure." *American Psychologist*, 1969, 24: 1121.

Peterson, D. R. "Scope and Generality of Verbally Defined Personality Factors." *Psychological Review*, 1965, 72: 48-59.

Sealy, A. P., and R. B. Cattell. "Standard Trends in the Personality Development in Men and Women of 16-70 Years Determined by 16 PF Measurements." Paper presented at the British Psychological Conference, London, April 1965.

Slater, P. E., and H. A. Scarr. "Personality in Old Age." *Genetic Psychology Monographs*, 1964, 70: 229-69.

Instrument

This copyrighted instrument is available from the Institute of Personality and Ability Testing, Champaign, Ill.

GUILFORD-ZIMMERMAN TEMPERAMENT SURVEY (GZTS)
J. P. Guilford and W. S. Zimmerman, 1949

Definition of Variable

The survey assesses 10 traits, or aspects, of personality: general activity, restraint, ascendance, sociability, emotional stability, objectivity, friendliness, thoughtfulness, personal relations, and masculinity.

Description of Instrument

The GZTS is a 300-item inventory, with 30 test items for each trait. Three validation, or verification, scales are provided for detecting falsification and carelessness in response.

Method of Administration

The survey is a self-administering questionnaire with response categories of yes and no.

Context of Development and Subsequent Use

The Guilford-Zimmerman Temperament Survey is a revision and condensation of three other tests that are still being published: the Guilford-Martin Inventory of Factors (GAMIN), the Guilford-Martin Personnel Inventory, and the Inventory of Factors (STDCR). The scales for the STDCR were developed through separate factor analyses of test items administered to various adult groups (Guilford and Guilford, 1936, 1939a, 1939b). Thirteen scales (the Guilford-Martin Temperament Survey) were the result of these analyses, but further work reduced these to the 10 scales of the Guilford-Zimmerman. All of the versions of this survey have been used in research and clinical settings.

Sample

Norms were obtained on a college population of 523 men and 389 women.

Scoring, Scale Norms, and Distribution

Raw scores are converted to C scores, which are based on the percentage of scores attained on the standardization population. The profile of scores is interpreted through the consideration of the level of the scores and the interaction of the various scores. Profile charts for each of the 10 traits are provided for men and women. Mean scores and standard deviations are given for men and women. There are no significant differences in the scores of these two groups.

Formal Tests of Reliability

Lovell (1945) reported Spearman-Brown reliability coefficients for the separate 13 scales of the earlier Guilford-Martin questionnaire ranging from .80 to .94. Stephenson (1953) reported reliabilities (type unknown) of between .70 and .85 for the various subtests.

Formal Tests of Validity

Lovell (1945) reported intercorrelations of the 13 earlier scales that ranged from −.23 to .74. Of these intercorrelations 62 were significant ($p < .01$). The Guilford-Zimmerman manual reports intercorrelations of the 10 traits as high as .61, with many around .40.

Usability on Older Populations

There are few data available on which to base judgments of the usefulness of this test with the elderly, except for the length of the test. Probably, 300 items would be taxing for many older persons.

Sensitivity to Age Differences

Factor analysis of Guilford-Zimmerman scores of a group of 400 men aged 20 through 59 (Bendig, 1960) revealed three factors: friendliness, social activity, and extraversion-introversion. There was greater introversion among older subjects.

In a study of 123 rural community-based aged, Britton (1963) used 13 items from the personal relations scale and 10 items from the sociability scale to determine the subjects' adjustment during later life. This investigator found that in his sample adjustment was related to the GZTS-derived factors of activity and sociability.

In three studies (Bendig, 1960; Titus and Goss, 1969; Wagner, 1960) performance across the age span among men was investigated. Ascendance uniformly decreased with age and restraint and personal relations increased. Friendliness and thoughtfulness were not found to be age related in any of the three studies. The other scales yielded inconsistent results among the studies.

In a very comprehensive study, Douglas and Arenberg (1978) gathered cross-sectional, longitudinal, cross-sequential, and time-sequential data for the GZTS. Cross-sectional data for 915 males, 20 to 80 years old (most of whom had a college degree and were in good health), showed three scales (general activity, ascendance, and masculinity) to be positively correlated with age, and two scales (friendliness and restraint) to be negatively correlated with age. There were different patterns of performance for the scales over the life span. Between 5.6 and 9.9 years after the first test, retests of 336 men showed an age-related decline on general activity and a non-age-related decline on friendliness, thoughtfulness, personal relations, and masculinity. Cross-sequential and time-sequential analyses indicated that the declines in general activity and masculinity appeared to be due to maturational processes. The declines in thoughtfulness and personal relations appeared to be due to cultural influences. An increase in friendliness over the life span was due both to changes in individuals and to a generational effect (successive generations start at lower levels on this dimension). Generational effects produced cross-sectional declines in restraint and increases in ascendance with age.

General Comments and Recommendations

This test needs further factorial work if it is to be truly useful to the researcher. It lacks validity data. Little work has been done on refining this test during recent years. It would seem better to use a more recently constructed and better standardized test.

References

Bendig, A. W. "Age Differences in the Interscale Factor Structure of the Guilford-Zimmerman Temperament Study." *Journal of Consulting Psychology*, 1960, 24: 134-38.

Britton, J. H. "Dimensions of Adjustment of Older Adults." *Journal of Gerontology*, 1963, 18: 60-65.

Douglas, K., and D. Arenberg. "Age Changes, Coherent Differences, and Cultural Change in the Guilford-Zimmerman Temperament Survey." *Journal of Gerontology*, 1978, 33: 737-47.

Guilford, J. P., and R. B. Guilford. "Personality Factors S.E. and M. and Their Measurement." *Journal of Psychology*, 1936, 2: 109-27.

————. "Personality Factors N and G.D." *Journal of Abnormal and Social Psychology*, 1939a, 34: 239-48.

———. "Personality Factors D, R, T, and A." *Journal of Abnormal and Social Psychology*, 1939b, 34: 21-36.

Guilford, J. B., and W. S. Zimmerman. *The Guilford-Zimmerman Temperament Survey: Manual of Instructions and Interpretations*. Beverly Hills, Calif.: Sheridan, 1949.

Lovell, C. "A Study of the Factor Structure of the 13 Personality Variables." *Educational and Psychological Measurement*, 1945, 5: 335-50.

Stephenson, W. "Review." *The Fourth Mental Measurement Yearbook*, O. K. Buros (ed.), pp. 95-96. Highland Park, N.J.: Gryphon Press, 1953.

Thurstone, L. L. "The Dimensions of Temperament: Analysis of Guilford's 13 Personality Scores." *Psychometrika*, 1951, 16: 11-20.

Titus, H. E., and R. G. Goss. "Psychometric Comparison of Old and Young Supervisors." *Psychological Reports*, 1969, 24: 727-33.

Wagner, E. E. "Differences between Old and Young Executives on Objective Psychological Test Variables." *Journal of Gerontology*, 1960, 15: 296-99.

Instrument

This copyrighted instrument is available from Sheridan Psychological Services, Beverly Hills, Calif.

EDWARDS PERSONAL PREFERENCE INVENTORY (EPPI)
A. L. Edwards, 1959

Definition of Variable

The instrument assesses the relative strengths of 15 manifest needs selected from Murray's need system (Murray, Barrett, Homburger et al., 1938): achievement, deference, order, exhibition, autonomy, affiliation, intraception, succorance, dominance, abasement, nurturance, change, endurance, heterosexuality, and aggression.

Description of Instrument

The inventory consists of 225 items, presented in a forced choice, paired comparison format. Each statement from each need area is paired twice with a statement from each other need area. The items that are paired have equal social desirability according to previously determined scale values.

Method of Administration

The test is self-administering. The time required for administration is approximately 45 minutes.

Context of Development and Subsequent Use

The EEPI was developed within the framework of H. A. Murray's (Murray et al., 1938) "need-press" theory of personality. According to Murray, a need is a "force which organizes perception, apperception, intellection, conation, and action in such a way as to transform in a certain direction an existing, unsatisfying situation" (1938, pp. 123-24). Needs, as components of personality, are like abstract drives, and they differ substantially from the traits of personality in such instruments as the Sixteen Personality Factors Test.

Samples

A college sample was obtained, which consisted of 749 men and 760 women. The age distribution was from 15 to 59 years, with only 3 respondents over age 45. Another general adult sample was taken of participants in a consumer panel used for market surveys covering 48 states (Edwards, 1959). This sample consisted of approximately 4,000 males and 5,000 females.

Scoring, Scale Norms, and Distribution

Raw scores are converted into normative standardized scores. These ipsative raw scores from the paired forced choice format of the test are measures of the strength of each need in relation to other needs, rather than absolute measures. There is some question whether conversions of these ipsative scores comparing the individual with himself or herself into T-scores that use a normative sample as a frame of reference are legitimate (Anastasi, 1961). Nonetheless, these T-score conversions are given for college students and an adult population differentiated into male and female groups. For all of these conversions, separate tables are furnished for males and females.

A consistency measure is derived by comparing choices made on a set of 15 items that appear twice within the items of the inventory. Profile stability can be determined by correlating the partial scores as they are summed for each row and each column on the answer sheet for the 15 personality variables, for a single subject and over an entire sample.

Formal Tests of Reliability

Split-half reliabilities for each of the 15 variables were computed by correlating the row and column scores for each variable with 1,509 subjects in the college group. The correlations ranged from .60 to .84 (Edwards, 1959).

Test-retest reliabilities for a one-week interval were computed for a group of 89 college students. The correlations ranged from .74 to .88 for the various subtests (Edwards, 1959).

Formal Tests of Validity

Construct Validity: Intercorrelations of variables were computed separately for men and women in the college group. Comparison of the two groups indicated that they could be combined because of similarity in scores. Correlations between the scale scores were generally low, ranging from .46 to −.36, which indicates the relative independence of the scales.

Convergent Validity: From a group of 106 college students, the subscale scores for the EPPI were correlated with the factor scores on the Guilford-Martin Personnel Inventory (which provides scores on three variables: cooperativeness, agreeableness, and objectivity) and the Taylor Manifest Anxiety Scale. Generally, the correlations with the scales of the EPPI were low, even though 17 were significant at the $p < .05$ level (no significances at the $p < .01$ level were reported). It is difficult to determine from the names of the variables how some of these are related, even though a significant correlation has been reported. For example, objectivity significantly correlated .31 with endurance. Other correlations appear to be related, such as the correlation of aggression with agreeableness (−.51). The EPPI was constructed in such a way that the responses have high social desirability. Paired items are matched on the basis of social desirability ratings. Correlations of responses on the K scale of the MMPI with responses on the EPPI, for subjects instructed to respond in a socially desirable manner on the latter, were low. Only six correlations were significant at the .05 level.

Usability on Older Populations

This is a moderately long test, a factor that might be an important consideration in using it with many groups of aged persons.

Sensitivity to Age Differences

In a sample of 80 disabled elderly people divided into four age-groups between 40 and 79 years, with 20 persons in each group and equal numbers of males and females, the aged groups (60-79 and 70-79) had significantly higher scores on deference and affiliation than those in the 40-49-year-old group. Older groups had higher succorance scores. There were significantly lower heterosexuality scores in the two older groups.

In a study comparing age-groups in a psychiatric population aged 15-59, including males and females, Gauron (1965) found that aged patients present different needs than younger patients. Older patients present guilt feelings, show absence or loss of sex drive, and are less inclined to express aggression openly.

In a study of 25 male and 25 female retired university faculty members, declines with age were significant in heterosexuality and exhibitionism and increases were significant in deference, endurance, and order (Schaie and Strother, 1968).

General Comments and Recommendations

This test has good subscale reliability. The intercorrelations of the scales are low, indicating the independence of the variables measured. However, the test's validity has yet to be established, especially insofar as it addresses its conceptualization as a test of Murray's needs system. The other objection to it has to do with the conversion of ipsative raw scores into T scores. The researcher should be cautious in regard to these objections (Anastasi, 1961).

References

Anastasi, A. *Psychological Testing* (3rd ed.). New York: Macmillan, 1961.

Edwards, A. L. *Edwards Personal Preference Schedule Manual*. New York: Psychological Corporation, 1959.

Gauron, E. F. "Changes in EPPS Needs with Age and Psychiatric Status." *Journal of Clinical Psychology*, 1965, 21: 194-96.

Murray, H. A., W. G. Barrett, E. Homburger et al. *Explorations in Personality: A Clinical and Experimental Study of Fifty Men of College Age*. New York: Oxford University Press, 1938.

Schaie, K. W., and C. R. Strother. "The Limits of Optimum Psychological Functioning of Superior Normal Old Adults." In *Psychological Functioning in the Normal Aging and Senile Aging*, S. M. Chown and K. Riegel (eds.), pp. 132-50. New York: Academic Press, 1968.

Spangler, D. P., and C. W. Thomas. "Effects of Age, Sex, and Physical Disability upon Manifest Needs." *Journal of Counseling Psychology*, 1962, 9: 313-19.

Instrument

This copyrighted instrument is available from the Psychological Corporation, New York.

HERON PERSONALITY INVENTORY
A. Heron, 1956

Definition of Variable

The instrument assesses the subject's emotional maladjustment and sociability.

Description of Instrument

The items included in this inventory were those that correlated significantly with the overall score and did not overlap the opposite area. There are 74 items on the emotional maladjustment scale, 20 of which are scored and the rest are filler items. Eight of the filler items were taken from the MMPI lie scale, and the rest from the Maudsley Medical Questionnaire. There are 36 items on the sociability scale, 12 of which are scored. All the sociability items were drawn from Guilford's R scale (Guilford and Guilford, 1939). Items are answered true or false. With so many of the items from the Maudsley Medical Questionnaire, this personality inventory conveys the overall quality of a medical questionnaire.

Method of Administration

This self-administering questionnaire takes little skill to administer and score. It takes about 20 minutes to complete (12 minutes for the emotional maladjustment part and 8 minutes for the items on sociability).

Context of Development and Subsequent Use

The inventory was developed in Britain by A. Heron as a research instrument to provide a quick assessment for screening patients and classifying levels of emotional maladjustment and sociability. As far as it could be determined, the inventory has been used chiefly by other British researchers.

Sample

The Heron Personality Inventory was originally developed and tested within a group of 100 British males and 224 British females aged 18 to 60 years (Heron, 1956). Another group of 378 individuals was also used to make further tests of reliability and validity. The second group was made up of 19 students, 27 neurotic patients, and individuals from the community.

Scoring, Scale Norms, and Distribution

The number of items marked in the keyed direction are summed for each scale. A high score on the first scale indicates maladjustment, and a high score on the second scale indicates a lack of sociability (called unsociability). There are no established norms. However, Heron (1956) indicated that it is justifiable to regard scores of 10 and above as probably maladjusted, scores from 0 to 7 as probably well adjusted, and scores of 8 or 9 as doubtful.

Formal Tests of Reliability

Odd-even reliability coefficients corrected for full lengths within a group of 378 people were .81 for emotional maladjustment and .74 for sociability (Heron, 1956). In a sample of 124 women aged 18 to 60 years, split-half reliability (corrected to full length) was .82 for the emotional maladjustment part of the test (Heron, 1955). In a group of 214 males, split-half correlation was .83. Test-retest reliability in a group of 78 men after a 6-month interval was .75 (Heron, 1955).

In a study of young individuals (20 to 39 years of age) and old individuals (60 to 79 years of age), Kuder-Richardson 20 reliability coefficients were .67 and .72, respectively, for emotional stability and .72 and .62, respectively, for sociability (Craik, 1964).

Formal Tests of Validity

Construct Validity: In a factor analysis made by Heron (1956), it was found that the sociability items contributed 11% of the variance on the emotional maladjustment factor and that the emotional maladjustment items contributed 21% of the variance on the sociability factor. In a factor analysis by Heron and Chown (1967) involving the Rigidity Inventory and many other tests, the Heron was shown to be highly saturated on the factor of temperament for males and females.

Predictive Validity: In the original group, use of the Heron classifications (Heron, 1956) categorized 251 normals as 13% probably maladjusted, 13% doubtful, and 74% probably well adjusted.

Overlap in scores between 75 symptom-free men and 55 male neurotic inpatients was 16%, and between 50 female neurotic inpatients compared to 21 normals there was a 12% overlap in scores (Heron, 1956).

Usability on Older Populations

For some groups of elderly subjects, the length of the inventory—100 items—might cause fatigue, which could influence scores.

Sensitivity to Age Differences

Heron (1956) did not find a correlation with age in a group of 18- to 60-year-olds.

Craik (1964) used the Heron Personality Inventory with a group of 240 male subjects in age-groups ranging from 20 to 79 years (40 in each decade group). The correlation between the variables emotional maladjustment and sociability decreased from .62 in the 20-29-year-old group to +.05 in the 70-79-year-old group. The relationship between the two parts of the inventory was found to decrease significantly ($p < .01$) with age. In a group of 240 females, Craik (1964) found much greater variability in scores over the life span than within the group of males. There was a slight correlation between the two scores on the Heron at each age level but no particular trend with age.

Heron and Chown (1967) used the inventory on a group of adults aged 20 to 79 years from a wide range of occupational and educational levels. There was a slight decline in emotional instability with age in their sample, which was not significant in the case of men. There was a low, barely significant (probability level not specified) correlation between unsociability and age (.14 in men and .12 in women). Unsociability scores increased from the 20s to the 40s for both men and women. Those in their 70s had lower unsociability (i.e., more sociable) scores.

General Comments and Recommendations

This test has good reliability. Sufficient validity data are as yet unavailable. The decrease in the correlations of the parts with age seems to indicate that what is sociability at one age (young) is not sociability at another age (old). The test needs additional work on its factor structure and relationships with age. The author cautioned against the use of this inventory in anything but a research context (Heron, 1956). Users of this instrument in the United States should be alerted to a few British locutions among the items (e.g., "My physique is excellent"), which may be misinterpreted by American respondents. These items should probably be reworded.

References

Craik, F. I. M. "An Observed Age Difference in Responses to a Personality Inventory." *British Journal of Psychology*, 1964, 55: 453-62.

Guilford, J. P., and R. B. Guilford. "Personality Factors D, R, T, and A." *Journal of Abnormal and Social Psychology*, 1939, 34: 21-36.

Heron, A. "The Objective Assessment of Personality among Female Unskilled Workers." *Educational Psychological Measurement*, 1955, 15: 117-26.

———. "A Two-Part Personality Measure for Use as a Research Criterion." *British Journal of Psychology*, 1956, 47: 243-51.

Heron, A., and S. M. Chown. *Age and Function*. Boston: Little, Brown and Company, 1967.

Instrument

See Instrument V1.3.III.a.

EYSENCK PERSONALITY INVENTORY (EPI)
H. J. Eysenck and B. G. Eysenck, 1963

Definition of Variable

The measure assesses the subject's extraversion-introversion and neuroticism.

Description of Instrument

The test consists of 24 items for each of the two variables, plus 9 items on a lie scale, yielding a total of three scores. There are two forms (A and B) on a yes-no response format.

Method of Administration

This test is essentially self-administering. Time for administration is approximately 30 minutes.

Context of Development and Subsequent Use

The EPI is a revision of the Maudsley Personality Inventory (MPI). In a revision (1) two forms were created, (2) the MMPI lie-scale items were added to assess test-taking attitude, and (3) the correlation between the two scales on the test was reduced. The two scales (extra-version-introversion and neuroticism) were based on extensive factor analyses. Conceptually and empirically, extraversion is related to weak superego controls and impulsivity, rather than to sociability. The test has been used widely in research, especially in Great Britain.

Samples

Something in excess of 30,000 subjects have been involved in the repeated factor analyses yielding the dimensions of the EPI (Cline, 1972). Most important demographic and psychiatric variables are represented in its development samples.

Scoring, Scale Norms, and Distribution

Percentile norms are given in the test manual for British populations and for American college students (but for no other American group). No information is available regarding the differentiation of the various groups for norms.

Formal Tests of Reliability

Test-retest reliability is reported to be between .80 and .97. Correlations between forms A and B range between .75 and .91 (Eysenck and Eysenck, 1963).

In a study of 80 American students (40 males and 40 females), Farley (1971) found no significant shifts in scores with retesting after a month. Reliability estimates for form A were .78 (for males) and .87 (for females), for either factor.

Formal Tests of Validity

Concurrent Validity: Farley (1970) reported data covering the correlation in scores between the Maudsley Personality Inventory and the Eysenck Personality Inventory. In a population of 50 males and 50 females, extraversion scores correlated .69 and .74, respectively; neuroticism scores correlated .70 and .71, respectively. Extraversion and neuroticism did not correlate on either of the tests.

In a study of 107 depressed patients who took the MPI and the EPI, Bailey and Metcalfe (1969) found that the two tests correlated .72 on the neuroticism scale and .72 on the extraversion scale on admission. At discharge these correlations changed to .82 and .64, respectively. Retesting was done 2 to 26 weeks after the initial testing (mean 6 weeks).

Fabian and Comrey (1971) found a correlation of .732 between the Eysenck Personality Inventory and the Neuroticism Scale Questionnaire anxiety factor and a correlation between the NSQ total score and the EPI neuroticism scale of .55 (no significance levels were reported).

Vingoe (1968) found the Eysenck Personality Inventory to correlate with various subtests on the California Personality Inventory. In a group of 66 female college students, extraversion-introversion correlated −.60 with social presence, .59 with social acceptance, .53 with sociability, and .45 with dominance. Neuroticism correlated −.67 with well-being, −.64 with tolerance, and .62 with intellectual efficiency. These correlations were all significant ($p < .01$).

Discriminant Validity: Eysenck (1971) found that the extraversion-introversion factor correlated −.04 with overall scores on the Progressive Matrices Test. The neuroticism score correlated .00 with those scores.

Predictive Validity: Fabian and Comrey (1971) found that the EPI significantly discriminated ($p < .01$) between three groups of males—a group of 69 normals (aged 18 to 65 years, $\overline{X}$ = 43 years), a group of 31 neuropsychiatric outpatients (aged 18 to 65 years, $\overline{X}$ = 36.7 years), and a group of 68 male neuropsychiatric inpatients (aged 18 to 65 years, $\overline{X}$ = 45.6 years).

Harrison and McLaughlin (1969) tested 243 general psychology students with the EPI. The tested students were also asked to rate themselves for introversion-extraversion and neuroticism. Correlations between the EPI scores and self-ratings were .74 for extraversion-introversion and .56 for neuroticism.

Usability on Older Populations

This is a short, apparently easily administered test that had been used in total and in part with elderly populations. It appears to be usable with the elderly. No other information is available.

Sensitivity to Age Differences

Cameron (1967) used the extraversion-introversion scale of the EPI to compare the performance of older and younger adults. He tested over 300 subjects who were differentiated into three older groups—males and females based in residential communities (mean age 70.05, SD 8.48), hospitals (mean age 80.32, SD 9.14) and a cooperative apartments (mean age 72.24, SD 7.12)—and one group of younger individuals 18 to 40 years of age (mean 30.10 years, SD 6.06). The young group was of higher socioeconomic status. In general, he found the older females to be more introverted than the younger females, and the older males to be no different than the younger males. However, the residential females were more introverted than the younger females, while the cooperative-apartment-dwelling females were similar to the younger females. The hospitalized females were the most introverted group.

Gutman (1966) used the earlier Maudsley Personality Inventory to measure extraversion-introversion and neuroticism in a group of 1,419 Canadians of the age range 17 to 94 years. The variable extraversion-introversion showed rises and falls along the age span tested in this study and a low, statistically significant correlation with age ($r = -.069$, $p < .05$). Sex differences were significant in the age-group 40–49 years only, with men showing higher extraversion scores. There was no significant correlations of neuroticism with age, though again there were rises and falls in the level of this variable along the age span. Statistically significant sex differences occurred in the 17–25- and 30–39-year-old groups. Though females always tended toward higher neuroticism, in these age-groups the trend was significant.

General Comments and Recommendations

Though this test seems to have been appropriately developed and though it represents a necessary and adequate revision of the earlier Maudsley Personality Inventory, normative data are not available for American subjects, except for a college sample. Validity estimates have not been obtained for older populations. With appropriate normative data and validity measures, this test might be useful in research with the elderly.

References

Bailey, J. E., and M. Metcalfe, "The MPI and EPI: A Comparative Study on Depressive Patients." *British Journal of Social and Clinical Psychology*, 1969, 8: 50–54.

Cameron, P. "Introversion and Egocentricity among Aged." *Journal of Gerontology*, 1967, 22: 465–68.

Cline, V. B. "Review." In *The Seventh Mental Measurements Yearbook*, O. K. Buros (ed.), pp. 162–63. Highland Park, N.J.: Gryphon Press, 1972.

Eysenck, H. "Relation between Intelligence and Personality." *Perceptual and Motor Skills*, 1971, 32: 637–38.

Eysenck, H. J., and B. G. Eysenck. *Manual for the Eysenck Personality Inventory*. San Diego: Educational and Industrial Test Service, 1963.

Fabian, J. J., and A. L. Comrey. "Construct Validation of Factored Neuroticism Scales." *Multivariate Behavioral Research*, 1971, 6: 287–99.

Farley, F. H. "Comparability of the MPI and EPI on Normal Subjects." *British Journal of Social and Clinical Psychology*, 1970, 9: 74–76.

———. "Some EPI Reliability Estimates." *Journal of Personality Assessment*, 1971, 35: 364–66.

Gideon V. C., R. A. Gordon, R. A. Jensen, and R. R. Knapp. *Eysenck Personality Inventory, American College Norms.* San Diego: Educational and Industrial Test Service, 1966.

Gutman, G. M. "A Note of the MPI." *British Journal of Social and Clinical Psychology,* 1966, 5: 128–29.

Harrison, N. W., and R. J. McLaughlin. "Self-Rating Validation of the Eysenck Personality Inventory." *British Journal of Social and Clinical Psychology,* 1969, 8: 55–58.

Vingoe, F. J. "Validity of Eysenck Extraversion Scale: Replication and Extension." *Psychological Reports,* 1968, 22: 706–8.

Instrument

This copyrighted instrument is available from the University of London Press.

ZUNG SELF-RATING DEPRESSION SCALE (ZSDS)
W. W. K. Zung, 1965

Definition of Variable

Depression as characterized by affective, cognitive, behavioral, and psychological symptoms is assessed by this scale.

Description of Instrument

The scale consists of 20 statements regarding symptoms of depression. Of the items 10 are worded negatively, 10 positively. Response options are (true of the respondent) "a little of the time," "some of the time," "a good part of the time," and "most of the time."

Method of Administration

The test uses a self-administered questionnaire and takes 5 to 10 minutes for administration and scoring.

Context of Development and Subsequent Use

The items were derived from interviews with patients and were selected as most representative of particular symptoms. The test was developed to provide a quickly and simply administered assessment of depression.

Though the instrument was originally intended to be unidimensional, a factor analysis by Morris, Wolf, and Klerman (1975) recovered two dimensions, agitation (with nine items loading between .51 and .74) and self-satisfaction (with eight items loading between .43 and .79). In the analysis, 89 persons were tested in one or both of two sessions 15 weeks apart (60 subjects were tested on both, 29 on one or the other only). The four-point response format was reduced to three in this study.

Samples

During the initial development of this scale, it was given to all patients admitted during a five-month period to the psychiatric service of a hospital with a primary diagnosis of depressive disorder upon admission (N = 56). A control group consisted of 100 individuals who were either members of the staff or patients on the medical and surgical services in the same hospital (Zung, 1965). Additional samples have been reported in other studies listed in the references.

Scoring, Scale Norms, and Distribution

Numerical values for response categories range from 0 to 4 points. Response values are summed, divided by the maximum possible score (80), and multiplied by 100. A low score (0–49) indicates the absence of depression or minimal depression; a score of 50–59 indicates mild to moderate depression; a score of 60–69 indicates moderate to severe depression; and a score of 70 and above indicates severe depression.

Formal Tests of Reliability/Homogeneity

Morris, Wolf, and Klerman (1975) obtained Kuder-Richardson 20 homogeneity estimates of .85 for their agitation subscale and .83 for their self-satisfaction subscale.

Formal Tests of Validity

Convergent Validity: The correlation with the MMPI D scale was .65 (Zung, 1967b). Zung also reported increasing correlations between the MMPI D scale and the Self-Rating Depression Scale with increasing age, with a peak in the 40- to 65-year-old group.

Discriminant Validity: The Zung was not correlated with the patient's age, sex, marital status, financial status, educational level, or intellectual level (Zung, 1967b) in a group of outpatients aged 19 to 65 years.

Predictive Validity: In the original sample, patients who were admitted and treated for depressive disorders had scores ranging from 63 to 90 (mean 74). The scores of patients admitted for depression but diagnosed and treated later for other disorders ranged from 38 to 71 (mean 53). The scores of the control group ranged from 25 to 43 (mean 33). Differences between scores were significant ($p < .01$).

Zung (1965) reported test-retest data on a group of depressed patients who underwent therapy. The scores reported seemed to indicate a significant reduction in depression after therapy, but tests of significance were not reported.

Usability on Older Populations

This is an easily understood and easily administered scale. Its brevity is an additional advantage for use with the elderly.

Sensitivity to Age Differences

The scores on this scale have been shown to be uncorrelated with age in a patient population ranging from under 19 years of age to 65 years (Zung, 1967b). However, in a study of 169 individuals over age 65 (Zung, 1967a), the range of scores on the ZSDS overlapped those of a younger patient group and extended well into the depressed range. This would seem to indicate a need for caution in interpreting the scores of older adults in this depressed range.

General Comments and Recommendations

The Zung scale has good factor reliability and convergent, discriminant, and face validity. This could be a useful instrument for research and clinical work with the elderly if norms were developed with this population.

References

Morris, J. N., R. S. Wolf, and L. V. Klerman. "Common Themes among Morale and Depression Scales." *Journal of Gerontology*, 1975, 30: 209–15.

Storandt, M., I. Wittels, and J. Botwinick. "Prediction of a Dimension of Well-Being in the Relocated Healthy Aged." *Journal of Gerontology*, 1975, 30: 97–102.

Zung, W. W. K. "A Self-Rating Depression Scale." *Archives of General Psychiatry.* 1965, 12: 63–70.

———. "Depression in Normal Aged." *Psychosomatics*, 1967a, 8: 287–92.

———. "Factors Influencing the Self-Rating Depression Scale." *Archives of General Psychiatry*, 1967b, 16: 543–47.

———. "Mood Disturbance in the Elderly." *The Gerontologist*, 1970, 10: 2–4.

Instrument

This copyrighted instrument is available from Lakeside Laboratories, Milwaukee, Wisc.

NEUROTICISM SCALE QUESTIONNAIRE (NSQ)
I. H. Scheier and R. B. Cattell, 1961

Definition of Variable

Overprotectiveness, depressiveness, submissiveness, and anxiety are assessed.

Description of Instrument

The questionnaire is made up of 40 items selected for their ability to differentiate neurotics from normals and to discriminate degrees of neurotic trend within the normal ranges and for their factor purity, high intelligibility, and ability to disguise the test's purpose. The test consists of three first-order factors (overprotectiveness, depressiveness, and submissiveness) and one second-order factor (anxiety). Separate scores are obtained for each of these four factors.

Each item has three response alternatives scored 0, 1, or 2, from a lower to a higher level of neuroticism.

Method of Administration

This is an essentially self-administering test that takes approximately 5 to 10 minutes to complete.

Context of Development and Subsequent Use

The NSQ was derived from the Sixteen Personality Factors Test. Some of the same factors are represented in the NSQ, although the items differ. The NSQ's purpose is rapid screening or rough assessment requiring little testing skill.

Sample

The original standardization sample consisted of 393 women and 675 men. The average age of the group was 32 years. The average number of years of schooling completed was 12. Subjects were drawn from 15 different geographical regions (Scheier and Cattell, 1961).

Scoring, Scale Norms, and Distribution

The NSQ is scored by a standard scoring key system. Raw scores are converted to stens (score conversions similar to stanines, but on a 10-point scale instead of a 9-point scale). Norms for converting raw scores to stens are provided separately for men and women.

The profile of sten values indicates an average range of values (sten values 5 and 6), with deviations possible above and below this level. This can be used as a criterion against which to judge neuroticism in subjects. The range of scores is from 1 to 10. Deviations from the average range are discussed in the manual for the test (Scheier and Cattell, 1961). The user can compare subject scores to those of the reference diagnostic groups indicated in the manual. Sten values for each of the factors on the NSQ, as well as the total score, are presented. Guidelines for profile analyses are also given.

Formal Tests of Homogeneity/Reliability

Split-half consistency in a group of 200 males and 100 females (average age 31 years, average education 12 years) was .67 for the total score. Split-half reliability for the separate factor scores ranged from .47 to .70 (Scheier and Cattell, 1961).

Formal Tests of Validity

Predictive Validity: The authors of the questionnaire have reported that the NSQ significantly differentiated between 1,068 normals and 102 clinically judged neurotics at the $p < .0005$ level.

Scheier and Cattell (1961) presented the scores of groups of individuals of various diagnostic groups. The scores of various types of neurotics differed significantly from the mean of the normal population. Groups of psychotics from different diagnostic categories scored closer to the group mean than to the scores of neurotics.

Discriminant Validity: The NSQ had an insignificant correlation with education (−.14) within a sample of 160 men and women (Scheier and Cattell, 1961). However, 393 women scored significantly higher than 675 men ($p < .0005$) on the total score and on every one of the subscores except anxiety (Scheier and Cattell, 1961). This result, perhaps, can be regarded as a failure of discriminant validity, since sex has no a priori expected relationship with neuroticism.

Usability on Older Populations

This short, easily administered questionnaire could be useful in research with the aged, though at this point no special adjustments or norms are included for use with aged subjects.

Sensitivity to Age Differences

The correlation between age and total NSQ scores was .24 on a sample of 160 men and women with no fewer than 55 in any group. Average scores were computed for 586 individuals in seven age-groups. The data indicates that scores remain stable in the age span from 15 to 50 years but rise sharply only after 55 to 60 years (Cattell and Scheier, 1961).

This questionnaire has been used in one study with the aged (Storandt, Wittels, and Botwinick, 1975), which sought to measure the adjustment of aged subjects who moved into an apartment complex. In this study, the NSQ did not differentiate between individuals showing various levels of adjustment. No special adjustments or norms are included for use with aged subjects.

General Comments and Recommendations

This test, taken from the larger Sixteen Personality Factors Test, seems to fail to perform its original purpose, i.e., to differentiate neurotics from normals. Though Cattell indicated that the performance of these two groups differ significantly, a great deal of overlap is evident from the actual scores of these two groups. Actually, the anxiety factor scores discriminated between these two groups much better. The other factors on the NSQ discriminate between these two groups more unevenly than the total score. This seems to be evidence to support a unidimensional approach to neuroticism rather than the multidimensional one proposed by Cattell.

References

Cattell, R. B., H. W. Eber, and M. M. Tatsuoka. *The Handbook for the Sixteen Personality Factors Questionnaire: Forms A, B, and C.* Champaign, Ill.: Institute for Personality and Ability Testing, 1957.

Cattell, R. B., and I. H. Scheier. *The Meaning and Measurement of Neuroticism and Anxiety.* New York: Ronald Press, 1961.

Scheier, I. H., and R. B. Cattell. *Handbook for the Neuroticism Scale Questionnaire.* Champaign, Ill.: Institute for Personality and Ability Testing, 1961.

Storandt, M., I. Wittels, and J. Botwinick. "Predictors of a Dimension of Well-being in the Relocated Healthy Aged." *Journal of Gerontology*, 1975, 30: 97–102.

Instrument

This copyrighted instrument is available from the Institute of Personality and Ability Testing, Champaign, Ill.

WESLEY RIGIDITY INVENTORY
E. Wesley, 1953

Definition of Variable

The instrument assesses behavioral rigidity: persistence in patterns of action without regard to their goal adequacy.

Description of Instrument

The inventory includes 41 statements to be classified as true or false (of the respondent).

Method of Administration

The test is a self-administered questionnaire. Completion time is 10 to 15 minutes.

Context of Development and Subsequent Use

Wesley presented five psychologists with 90 items, some taken from other personality tests and some of original construction. The psychologists were instructed to rate them according to the degree of rigidity expressed. The 50 items unanimously rated high in rigidity were combined with 17 filler items from the MMPI to form the original instrument. Zelen and Levitt (1954) shortened the original to 41 items without fillers. The shortened version is the one reviewed here.

Samples

The original sample to which this test was administered was a group of undergraduates in psychology classes.

Scoring, Scale Norms, and Distribution

The score is the number of items circled that indicate rigidity. No norms have been established for this technique.

Formal Tests of Reliability

Zelen and Levitt (1954) reported test-retest reliability for a 12-item shortened version of this test as .74 for a group of 31 undergraduates. Kuder-Richardson 20 reliability for a group of 284 subjects was .68; for a group of 72 subjects it was .59 (Katz, 1952); and it was .67 for a group of 453 subjects (Moldawsky, 1951).

Formal Tests of Validity

Construct Validity: In a factor analysis of the scale, Chown (1960) administered 39 items from the 41-item version, together with 15 other paper-and-pencil tasks, to 200 community-based males, aged 20 to 82 years. The items from the Wesley—factor analyzed together with chronological age, nonverbal intelligence, and vocabulary scores—yielded three factors: (1) liking for detailed work (10 items), (2) dogmatism (11 items) related to lack of intellect, and (3) liking for habit (6 items). Age had the highest loading (.63) on the last factor. These three factors significantly correlated with each other, but the magnitude of the correlation indicated essentially unrelated factors (1 and 2, $r = .23$; 1 and 3, $r = .17$; and 2 and 3, $r = .21$).

Convergent Validity: Convergent validity between the shortened version (12 items) of the scale and the California E scale was .38 (Zelen and Levitt, 1954).

In other research, the Wesley did not correlate significantly with other measures of rigidity or with a test of behavioral rigidity (Katz, 1952). Katz found a .26 correlation of the Wesley with the California E scale (significant at the .03 level).

The shortened 39-item version used by Chown (1960) correlated .73 with the 41-item inventory in a group of 123 subjects.

Usability on Older Populations

This is an easily administered and understood test of short duration. It appears usable for work with the elderly.

Sensitivity to Age Differences

Heron and Chown (1967) found that all three factors of the Wesley were related to age (liking for detailed work correlated with age .30 for men, .35 for women; dogmatism correlated with age .28 for men, .29 for women; liking for habit correlated with age .28 for men and .25 for women). Chown (1960) found a correlation between age and the total score on 39 items of .27.

General Comments and Recommendations

This inventory shows some reliability within subject groups and in factor structure. However, the concurrent validity of the scale is low.

References

Chown, S. M. "A Factor Analysis of the Wesley Rigidity Inventory." *Journal of Abnormal and Social Psychology*, 1960, 61: 491-94.

Heron, A., and S. Chown. *Age and Function.* Boston: Little, Brown and Company, 1967.

Katz, A. "A Study of the Relationships among Several Measures of Rigidity." Ph. D. dissertation, University of Iowa, 1952.

Moldawsky, S. "An Empirical Validation of a Rigidity Scale against a Criterion of Rigidity in an Interpersonal Situation." Ph. D. dissertation, University of Iowa, 1951.

Wesley, E. "Perseverative Behavior in a Concept-Formation Task as a Function of Manifest Anxiety and Rigidity." *Journal of Abnormal and Social Psychology*, 1953, 48: 129-34.

Zelen, S. L., and E. E. Levitt. "A Note on the Wesley Rigidity Scale." *Journal of Abnormal and Social Psychology*, 1954, 49: 472-73.

Instrument

See Instrument VI.3.IV.a.

TEST OF BEHAVIORAL RIGIDITY (TBR)
K. W. Schaie, 1960

Definition of Variable

The instrument assesses the "ability of the individual to adjust to the stress imposed by constant changes in the environment" (Schaie and Parham, 1975, p. 3).

Description of Instrument

The test consists of three subtests, of which two are behavioral (performance) tasks and one is a questionnaire. In the first subtest, the respondent is required to copy a paragraph once exactly as presented and then again interchanging uppercase and lowercase letters (capitals test). For each performance 150 seconds is allowed. In the second subtest, the respondent is first required to write a word opposite in meaning to each of a series of stimulus words, then a synonym for each of another series, and finally a synonym to each word in a third series when that word is presented in uppercase letters and an antonym when it is presented in lowercase letters (opposites test). Each series is to be completed in 120 seconds. The first two subtests obviously are intended to exact increasingly quick alternation between behavioral strategies. The third subtest (questionnaire) inquires about the respondent's habitual behavior.

Method of Administration

The test must be administered and scored by an examiner familiar with the testing procedure. It can be administered in groups. Completion time is approximately 30 minutes.

Context of Development and Subsequent Use

The developers of the TBR sought to isolate motor-cognitive, personality-perceptual, and psychomotor-speed rigidity by factor analysis of the capitals test (Bernstein, 1924), tests suggested by Scheier and Ferguson (1952), items on the California Psychological Inventory (Gough, 1957; Gough, McCloskey, and Meehl, 1952), and items suggested by Lankes (1915). The measures retained were those suitable for group administration and those on which social status and educational level appeared to have little influence. The factorial structure of the test battery was cross-validated by drawing a new sample and factoring the correlation matrix for the second sample. The original test battery was then shortened by deleting the two tests that contributed the lowest factor loadings to their respective factor scores.

Samples

Five hundred subjects were selected by a stratified random sampling procedure from the membership of a group medical plan (Schaie, 1956, 1958a, 1959). Subjects in this sample were estimated to represent the upper 75% of the American socioeconomic continuum. The overall age range of 20 to 70 years was divided into 5-year interval subgroups containing 25 males and 25 females each.

Scoring, Scale Norms, and Distribution

Specific scoring instructions are given in the test manual (Schaie, 1975). Raw scores are converted to weighted scores. The total of the weighted scores for each factor is a T score to be used for comparison with the norm group. In addition, scaled scores and a rigidity quotient (RQ) can be obtained for the individual factor scores and overall score. The RQ distribution has a mean of 100 and a standard deviation of 15. Conversion tables are available for age-groups arranged in 5-year intervals from 21 to 70 years of age. The RQ can be interpreted by comparison to the norm group as indicated in the manual.

Formal Tests of Reliability

Test-retest reliabilities with the group in the original sample were obtained after 7-year and 14-year intervals. These reliabilities were .67 and .68 for motor cognitive, .84 and .78 for personality-perceptual, and .88 and .88 for psychomotor speed for the 7-year and 14-year intervals, respectively (Schaie, 1975). Additional reliabilities were given for each individual subtest on the TBR for 7- and 14-year periods (Schaie, 1975). These range from .38 to .99, with little difference between the figures for the 7-year and the 14-year intervals.

Formal Tests of Validity

Predictive Validity: In a study of success among college students in the area of physical science, Schockley (1963) found significant differences between highly rigid and less rigid students in various measures of logical thinking. Mackie, Beck, and Jaredo (1964) found that normal and brain-damaged individuals differed significantly on motor-cognitive rigidity and psychomotor-speed rigidity.

Discriminant Validity: Schaie and Patterson (1972, in Schaie 1975) found the TBR composite score to correlate .28 with the Primary Mental Abilities Test composite score in a group of 230 individuals (characteristics unspecified). Schaie (1958a) found significant correlations between TBR scores and Primary Mental Abilities Test composite scores. Correlations range between .60 and .80 over the age span tested in this study, with a dip in the correlation in the age-group 61 to 65 years. Five hundred men and women ages 20 to 70 years, grouped into 5- and 10-year intervals, were evaluated in this study.

Schaie and Parham (1975) reported correlations of Primary Mental Abilities Test composite scores and the factors of the TBR as follows: with motor-cognitive score .475, with personal-perceptual score .300, and with psychomotor score .662. The correlations of the factor scores on the PMA and the factors of the TBR range between .651 and .067.

Construct Validity: Schaie (1955) isolated the three factors of rigidity within two independent samples. Oblique factor loadings were quite similar, varying not at all, by as little as one (.01) point, or at the most by nine (.09) points.

Concurrent Validity: Ramamurti and Ananthakrishnan (1967) found a significant correlation between figure reversal scores and the psychomotor-speed factor of the TBR. Patterson (1963, reported in Schaie, 1975) found the total TBR score significantly correlated with grades. In a study of normal and brain-damaged individuals, Mackie, Beck, and Jaredo (1964) found that the normals differed significantly on two factors of rigidity — motor cognitive and psychomotor speed.

Usability on Older Populations

The TBR was designed to explore one area of special interest to gerontologists. The authors stated that it is suitable over the whole adult age range and indicated that not more than a fourth-grade education is necessary to complete it. However, scores correlate significantly with IQ and educational and occupational status (Patterson, 1963; Schaie, 1958a; Schaie and Parham, 1975). Since these variables also correlate with age, these covariates must be kept in mind when age trends are being considered.

Sensitivity to Age Differences

Cross-sectional age trends generally indicate an increase in rigidity with increased age. However, a cross-sequential study (Schaie and Strother, 1968a) indicated that only psychomotor-speed rigidity increased with age and that the other previously observed increases in rigidity across the life span were probably due to cohort differences.

General Comments and Recommendations

This is one of the few tests developed to assess a variable important to conceptualizations of personality within an aged population. It is an interesting approach to the assessment of rigidity. However, work with this test has not dealt adequately with the problem of the conceptual definition of rigidity. For example, the TBR focuses upon behavioral rigidity and does not address itself to the differentiation of behavioral rigidity from defensive rigidity, physiologically based rigidity, or rigidity based on habit formation. It would seem that these should be foremost research questions. Another problem is that scores correlate highly with IQ scores and the test may be more a measure of intellectual functioning than of rigidity. Botwinick (1973) has indicated that these two variables seem to be related in other studies, also. Additional data need to be gathered on these issues.

References

Baltes, P. B., K. W. Schaie, and A. H. Nardi. "Age and Experimental Mortality in a Seven-Year Longitudinal Study of Cognitive Behavior." *Developmental Psychology*, 1971, 5: 18-26.

Bernstein, E. "Quickness and Intelligence." *British Journal of Psychology*, 1924, 3 (monograph supplement number 7).

Botwinick, J. *Aging and Behavior.* New York: Springer, 1973.

Gough, H. G. *The California Psychological Inventory.* Palo Alto, Calif.: Consulting Psychologists Press, 1957.

Gough, H. G., H. McCloskey, and P. E. Meehl. "A Personality Scale for Social Responsibility." *Journal of Abnormal and Social Psychology*, 1952, 47: 73-80.

Lankes, W. "Perseveration." *British Journal of Psychology*, 1915, 7: 387-419.

Mackie, J. B., E. C. Beck, and L. W. Jaredo. "Interrelations among Tests of Intelligence, Perception and Rigidity in Brain Damaged and Normal Individuals." *American Psychologist*, 1964, 19: 549.

Nesselroade, J. R., K. W. Schaie, and P. B. Baltes. "Ontogenetic and Generational Components of Structural and Quantitative Change in Adult Behavior." *Journal of Gerontology*, 1972, 27: 222-28.

Patterson, N. B. "Semantic Rigidity and Its Relationship to General Behavioral Rigidity." Ph. D. dissertation, University of Nebraska, 1963.

Ramamurti, P. V., and P. Ananthakrishnan. "Behavioral Rigidity and Frequency of Figure Reversals." *Indian Journal of Experimental Psychology*, 1967, 1: 8-10.

Schaie, K. W. "Measuring Behavioral Rigidity: A Factorial Study of Some Tests of Rigid Behavior." M.A. thesis, University of Washington, 1953.

––––. "A Test of Behavioral Rigidity." *Journal of Abnormal and Social Psychology*, 1955a, 51: 604-10.

––––. *Examiner Manual for the Test of Behavioral Rigidity: Form R-2.* Washington, D.C.: American Documentation Institute, document number 4651, 1955b.

––––. "Some Developmental Concommitants of Rigid Behavior." Ph.D. dissertation, University of Washington, 1956.

_____. "Rigidity-flexibility and Intelligence: A Cross-sectional Study of the Adult Life-span from 20 to 70 Years." *Psychological Monographs*, 1958a, 72 (9) (whole number 462).

_____. "Differences in Some Personal Characteristics of 'Rigid' and 'Flexible' Individuals." *Journal of Clinical Psychology*, 1958b, 14: 11-14.

_____. "Cross-sectional Methods in the Study of Psychological Aspects of Aging." *Journal of Gerontology*, 1959, 14: 208-15.

_____. *Preliminary Manual, Test of Behavioral Rigidity*. Palo Alto, Calif.: Consulting Psychologists Press, 1960.

Schaie, K. W., G. V. Labouvie, and T. J. Barrett. "Selective Attrition Effects in a Fourteen-Year Study of Adult Intelligence." *Journal of Gerontology*, 1973, 28: 328-34.

Schaie, K. W., and I. A. Parham. *Test of Behavioral Rigidity*. Palo Alto, Calif.: Consulting Psychologists Press, 1975.

Schaie, K. W., and C. R. Strother. "A Cross-sequential Study of Age Changes in Cognitive Behavior." *Psychological Bulletin*, 1968a, 70: 671-80.

_____. "The Effect of Time and Cohort Differences on the Interpretation of Age Changes in Cognitive Behavior." *Multivariate Behavioral Research*, 1968b, 3: 259-94.

_____. "The Limits of Optimum Psychological Functioning of Superior Old Adults." In *Psychological Functioning in the Normal Aging and Senile Aging*, S. M. Chown and K. Riegel (eds.), pp. 134-50. Basel: Karger, 1968c.

Scheier, I., and G. A. Ferguson. "Further Factorial Studies of Tests of Rigidity." *Canadian Journal of Psychology*, 1952, 6: 18-30.

Schockley, J. T. "Behavioral Rigidity in Relation to Student Success in College Physical Science." *Science Education*, 1963, 46: 67-70.

Storck, P. A., W. R. Looft, and F. H. Hooper. "Interrelationships among Piagetian Tasks and Traditional Measures of Cognitive Abilities in Mature and Aged Adults." *Journal of Gerontology*, 1972, 71: 461-65.

Instrument

This copyrighted instrument is available from Consulting Psychologists Press, Palo Alto, Calif.

DILEMMAS OF CHOICE QUESTIONNAIRE
M. A. Wallach and N. Kogan, 1961; J. Botwinick, 1966

Definition of Variable

Cautiousness is the tendency to avoid assuming extreme positions or taking risks.

Description of Instrument

The questionnaire consists of 24 paragraphs, each item describing a situation in which an individual must make a decision in a situation of risk. The subject must indicate the *least* chance of a favorable outcome he or she would require before making the decision in question. The response choices are that the chances are 1 in 10, 3 in 10, 5 in 10, 7 in 10, or 9 in 10 that an expectation will be realized. The subject may also respond that *no* chance should be taken. In the later Botwinick (1969) study, the last choice was omitted.

Method of Administration

This is a self-administering questionnaire. No data are presented in the studies about the length of time required to complete the questionnaire. A rough estimate is that it could take 30 minutes or more, depending on the number of items given and the ability of the subject.

Context of Development and Subsequent Use

Originally devised as a 12-item questionnaire, this technique was used by Wallach and Kogan (1961) to assess the extent to which people make extreme judgments and to examine how this relates to personality characteristics. Later studies used the questionnaire from the same conceptual point of view, though the number of items was increased and the format changed slightly. Botwinick (1966, 1969) added 12 items that pertained more specifically to the elderly and changed the response choices slightly.

Samples

Botwinick (1966) added the 12 items applicable to older adults. In his study there were 23 older men and 24 older women, 63 younger men and 48 younger women. Finally, Botwinick (1969) studied the responses of 17 older males and 21 older females, with age ranges of between 65 and 88 years (mean in mid-70s) and 13 to 15 years of schooling.

Scoring, Scale Norms, and Distribution

There is no established scoring system. The level of risk chosen for each item can serve as the score, and the average for the total questionnaire can then be obtained.

Formal Tests of Reliability

Wallach and Kogan (1959) reported a Spearman-Brown odd-even reliability of .53 for the young males in their sample, .63 for the young females, .80 for the older males, and .80 for the older females.

Usability on Older Populations

This scale was developed for research with the aged, and all three studies in which it has been used involved aged subjects.

Sensitivity to Age Differences

The results of the two earlier studies (Wallach and Kogan, 1961; Botwinick, 1966) indicate that older individuals are more conservative in their judgments.

The second study by Botwinick (1969) varied the response choices open to the subject. The choice of taking no risk at all was omitted. The results of this study indicate that, when older persons are forced to take risks, they do so in about the same manner as the young do.

General Comments and Recommendations

This is an interesting approach to the study of caution with the elderly. It has good face validity, and it relates to meaningful life situations, rather than just being a laboratory-type task. At this time, its validity information and normative data remain incomplete.

References

Botwinick, J. "Cautiousness in Advanced Age." *Journal of Gerontology*, 1966, 21: 347-53.
———. "Disinclination to Venture versus Cautiousness in Responding: Age Differences." *Journal of Genetic Psychology*, 1969, 115: 55-62.
Brim, O. G. "Attitude Content Intensity and Probability Expectations." *American Sociology Review*, 1955, 20: 68-76.
Wallach, M. A., and N. Kogan. "Sex Differences and Judgment Processes." *Journal of Personality*, 1959, 27: 555-64.
———. "Aspects of Judgment and Decision Making: Interrelationships and Changes with Age." *Behavioral Sciences*, 1961, 6: 23-36.

Instrument

See Instrument V1.3.IV.c.

ESTIMATION QUESTIONNAIRE
M. A. Wallach and N. Kogan, 1965

Definition of Variable

Conservatism is the disinclination to take extreme positions or the tendency to make judgments closely related to the facts of a situation.

Description of Instrument

There are 12 pairs of items on the questionnaire. For each pair, a "fact" is stated, such as "Most sailboats go about 9 miles per hour." This is followed by two questions that are similar from item to item. One question requires that the subject estimate the lower limit and the other requires estimation of the upper limit of the range of speed, weight, or whatever variable is involved. In this example, the subject must estimate how slowly the slowest sailboats go and how quickly the fastest might go. Multiple choices are given after each question.

Method of Administration

This is essentially a self-administering task that takes approximately 10 minutes.

Context of Development and Subsequent Use

The technique was originally developed by Pettigrew (1958) as a measure of one aspect of cognitive ability. Pettigrew developed 20 items that were then modified and simplified by Wallach and Kogan (1965) into 12 items. They applied this shortened version to a population of children to assess their conceptual ability. Botwinick (1970) used the simplified version developed by Wallach and Kogan together with other ratings that assessed confidence or cautiousness in the elderly. In the Botwinick study, the subjects were asked to rate the confidence with which they made the choices on the Estimation Questionnaire.

Samples

The 12-item version of this test was used with school children (Wallach and Caron, 1959; Wallach and Kogan, 1965). Botwinick (1970) used this technique with a group of 18, community-based adults aged 61 to 80 years and a group of 40 18- to 21-year-olds. Education in both of Botwinick's groups ranged from 12 to 15 years.

Scoring, Scale Norms, and Distribution

Multiple-choice responses are given weights depending on the extent to which they differ from the stated fact. Alternatives that represent a more extreme choice are assigned a higher number and those choices that are closest to the stated fact a lower number. Scores range from 0 to 3. The subject's scores can be summed for all 12 items. Lower scores indicate greater cautiousness. There are no norms for the scores on this instrument.

Formal Tests of Reliability

In a sample of 151 children, odd-even reliability was .76 (Wallach and Kogan, 1965). Odd-even reliability within various samples of college students yielded Spearman-Brown coefficients from .86 to .93 (Pettigrew, 1958).

Formal Tests of Validity

Convergent Validity: Pettigrew (1958) reported a correlation of .17 with the American College Entrance Exam (quantitative) scores within a sample of college students. Pettigrew (1958) also found a rank-order correlation of .57 between performance on the 20-item questionnaire and judgments of lengths of lines and weights.

Usability on Older Populations

This is a simple, easily understood and administered task. The administrative procedure seems to present no special drawbacks for use with the aged. Although the factors influencing scores are not known, it seems very likely that the respondent's knowledge of the topics involved plays a large role. Therefore, comparisons between age-groups would almost certainly be subject to uncontrolled factors.

Sensitivity to Age Differences

In the Botwinick (1970) study, the choices of the older subjects were significantly less discrepant from the stated "facts" than were those of younger subjects ($p < .01$), a fact indicating greater conservatism among the aged in making judgments. On the other hand, the scores of the older subjects showed no significant differences in the estimated level of confidence in their answers than those of younger subjects.

General Comments and Recommendations

The reliability of this questionnaire, though adequate in a population of children, has not been established in an adult population. Validity correlations are low. Although this instrument needs additional standardization information, it is an interesting technique that may have applications beyond those already explored.

References

Botwinick, J. "Age Differences in Self-Ratings of Confidence." *Psychological Reports*, 1970, 27: 865-66.

Pettigrew, T. F. "The Measurement and Correlates of Category Width as a Cognitive Variable." *Journal of Personality*, 1958, 26: 532-44.

Wallach, M. A., and J. Caron. "Attribute Criteriality and Sex-Linked Conservatism as Determinants of Psychological Similarity." *Journal of Abnormal and Social Psychology*, 1959, 59: 43-50.

Wallach, M. A., and N. Kogan. *Modes of Thinking in Young Children*, pp. 112-15. New York: Holt, Rinehart and Winston, 1965.

Instrument

See Instrument V1.3.IV.d.

Instruments

Vl.3.I.a
RORSCHACH INKBLOT TECHNIQUE
H. Rorschach, 1921

This copyrighted instrument is available from Grune and Stratton, New York.

Vl.3.I.b
THEMATIC APPERCEPTION TECHNIQUE
H. A. Murray, 1943

This copyrighted instrument is available from the Psychological Corporation, New York.

Vl.3.I.c
SENIOR APPERCEPTION TECHNIQUE
L. Bellak and S. S. Bellak, 1973

This copyrighted instrument is available from C.P.S., Larchmont, N.Y.

Vl.3.I.d
GERONTOLOGICAL APPERCEPTION TECHNIQUE
R. L. Wolk and R. B. Wolk, 1971

This copyrighted instrument is available from Behavioral Publications, New York.

V1.3.I.e
ID, EGO, AND SUPEREGO TEST
L. A. Dombrose and M. S. Slobin, 1958

This copyrighted instrument is available from Psychological Test Specialists, Missoula, Mont.

V1.3.I.f
WORD-ASSOCIATION TECHNIQUES
J. C. Jung, 1910

There is no standard material for this technique.

V1.3.II.a
MINNESOTA MULTIPHASIC PERSONALITY INVENTORY
S. R. Hathaway and J. C. McKinley, 1940, 1942

This copyrighted instrument is available from the Psychological Corporation, New York.

V1.3.II.b
SIXTEEN PERSONALITY FACTORS TEST
R. B. Cattell, H. W. Eber, and M. M. Tatsuoka, 1957

This copyrighted instrument is available from the Institute of Personality and Ability Testing, Champaign, Ill.

V1.3.II.c
GUILFORD-ZIMMERMAN TEMPERAMENT SURVEY
J. P. Guilord and W. S. Zimmerman, 1949

This copyrighted instrument is available from Sheridan Psychological Services, Beverly Hills, Calif.

V1.3.II.d
EDWARDS PERSONAL PREFERENCE INVENTORY
A. L. Edwards, 1959

This copyrighted instrument is available from the Psychological Corporation, New York.

V1.3.III.a
HERON PERSONALITY INVENTORY
A. Heron, 1956

FIRST PART (EMOTIONAL MALADJUSTMENT)	S.R.
3. I sweat very easily even on cool days	T
5. I am troubled by sick headaches	T
6. My feelings are easily hurt	T
7. Sometimes when I am not feeling well I am cross	T
9. I consider myself rather a nervous person	T
15. I never have nightmares	F
20. I wake up fresh and rested most mornings	F
23. My eyesight is sometimes blurred	T

25. I worry over possible misfortunes — T
27. It is difficult to irritate me — F
33. My bowels are not opened every day — T
44. My physique is excellent — F
46. Once in a while I think of things too bad to talk about — T
47. I often feel self-conscious in the presence of superiors — T
50. I feel that very little works out the way it should in life — T
55. I have no particular physical or health problems — F
60. I have periods of such great restlessness that I cannot sit long in a chair — T
61. My hands often feel damp and clammy — T
69. I catch cold frequently — T
72. I often jump to conclusions — T

SECOND PART (SOCIABILITY)

79. The presence of the opposite sex makes me feel shy — T
82. What others think of my actions does not bother me much — F
83. I sometimes treat my work as if it were a matter of life and death — T
84. I like to play practical jokes on people — F
86. I find it easy to act naturally at a party — F
93. I like to have time to be alone with my thoughts — T
97. I like to have a lot of social engagements — F
101. I tend to be overconscientious — T
102. I am usually a good mixer — F
103. I think of myself as a lively sort of person — F
104. When I am bored I feel like stirring up some excitement — F
109. At a gay party I can usually let myself go and have a thoroughly good time — F

SOURCE: A. Heron. "A Two-Part Personality Measure for Use as Research Criterion." *British Journal of Psychology*, 1956, 47: 250. Published by Cambridge University Press. Reprinted by permission of publisher.

V1.3.III.b
EYSENCK PERSONALITY INVENTORY
H. J. Eysenck and B. G. Eysenck, 1963

This copyrighted instrument is available from the University of London Press.

V1.3.III.c
ZUNG SELF-RATING DEPRESSION SCALE
W. W. K. Zung, 1965

This copyrighted instrument is available from Lakeside Laboratories, Milwaukee, Wisc.

V1.3.III.d
NEUROTICISM SCALE QUESTIONNAIRE
I. H. Scheier and R. B. Cattell, 1961

This copyrighted instrument is available from the Institute of Personality and Ability Testing, Champaign, Ill.

V1.3.IV.a
WESLEY RIGIDITY INVENTORY
E. Wesley, 1953

I am often the last one to give up trying to do a thing.	True*	False
There is usually only one best way to solve most problems.	True*	False
I prefer work that requires a great deal of attention to detail.	True*	False
I often become so wrapped up in something I am doing that I find it difficult to turn my attention to other matters.	True*	False
I prefer doing one thing at a time to keeping several projects going.	True*	False
I dislike to change my plans in the midst of an undertaking.	True*	False
I never miss going to church.	True*	False
I would like a position which requires frequent changes from one kind of task to another.	True	False*
I usually maintain my own opinions even though many other people may have a different point of view.	True*	False
I find it easy to stick to a certain schedule, once I have started on it.	True*	False
I believe women ought to have as much sexual freedom as men.	True	False*
I do not enjoy having to adapt myself to new and unusual situations.	True*	False
I prefer to stop and think before I act even on trifling matters.	True	False*
I would not like the kind of work which involves a large number of different activities.	True*	False
I try to follow a program of life based on duty.	True*	False
I have kept a careful diary over a period of years.	True*	False
My interests tend to change quickly.	True	False*
I usually find that my own way of attacking a problem is best, even though it doesn't always seem to work in the beginning.	True*	False
I dislike having to learn new ways of doing things.	True*	False
I like a great deal of variety in my work.	True	False*
I am a methodical person in whatever I do.	True*	False
I am usually able to keep at a job longer than most people.	True*	False
I think it is usually wise to do things in a conventional way.	True*	False
I always finish tasks I start, even if they are not very important.	True*	False
People who go about their work methodically are almost always the most successful.	True*	False
When I have undertaken a task, I find it difficult to set it aside, even for a short time.	True*	False
I often find myself thinking of the same tune or phrases for days at a time.	True*	False
I have a work and study schedule which I follow carefully.	True*	False
I usually check more than once to be sure that I have locked a door, put out the light, or something of the sort.	True*	False
I have never done anything dangerous for the thrill of it.	True*	False
It is always a good thing to be frank.	True*	False
I have a habit of collecting various kinds of objects.	True*	False
I have taken a good many courses on the spur of the moment.	True	False*
I believe that promptness is a very important personality characteristic.	True*	False
My interests change very quickly.	True	False*
I usually dislike to set aside a task that I have undertaken until it is finished.	True*	False
I am inclined to go from one activity to another without continuing with any one for too long a time.	True	False*
I prefer to do things according to a routine which I plan myself.	True*	False
I always put on and take off my clothes in the same order.	True*	False

*Answers that show rigidity.

SOURCE: E. Wesley. "Perseverative Behavior in a Concept-Formation Task as a Function of Manifest Anxiety and Rigidity." *Journal of Abnormal and Social Psychology*, 1953, 48: 129–34. Copyright 1953 by the American Psychological Association. Reprinted by permission.

V1.3.IV.b
TEST OF BEHAVIORAL RIGIDITY
K. W. Schaie 1960

This copyrighted instrument is available from Consulting Psychologists Press, Palo Alto, Calif.

V1.3.IV.c
DILEMMAS OF CHOICE QUESTIONNAIRE
M. A. Wallach and N. Kogan, 1961; J. Botwinick, 1966

1. Mr. A., an electrical engineer, who is married and has one child, has been working for a large electronics corporation since graduating from college five years ago. He is assured of a lifetime job with a modest, though adequate, salary, and liberal pension benefits upon retirement. On the other hand, it is very unlikely that his salary will increase much before he retires. While attending a convention, Mr. A. is offered a job with a small, newly founded company which has a highly uncertain future. The new job would pay more to start and would offer the possibility of a share in the ownership if the company survived the competition of the larger firms.

Imagine that you are advising Mr. A. Listed below are several probabilities or odds of the new company's proving financially sound. PLEASE CHECK THE *LOWEST* PROBABILITY THAT YOU WOULD CONSIDER ACCEPTABLE TO MAKE IT WORTHWHILE FOR MR. A TO TAKE THE NEW JOB.

_____ The chances are 1 in 10 that the company will prove financially sound.
_____ The chances are 3 in 10 that the company will prove financially sound.
_____ The chances are 5 in 10 that the company will prove financially sound.
_____ The chances are 7 in 10 that the company will prove financially sound.
_____ The chances are 9 in 10 that the company will prove financially sound.
_____ Place a check here if you think Mr. A should *not* take the new job no matter what the probabilities.

2. Mr. B. is an elderly man who has been finding that his eyesight is getting progressively worse. He goes to the doctor for an examination and finds out that the eye condition will continue to get worse and worse, until there is hardly any vision left at all. The physician suggests that an eye operation is possible. If the operation is completely successful, perfect vision would be restored and be maintained throughout the rest of his normal life. If the operation is not successful, immediate blindness would result.

Imagine that you are advising Mr. B. Listed below are several probabilities or odds that the operation will prove successful. PLEASE CHECK THE *LOWEST* PROBABILITY THAT YOU WOULD CONSIDER ACCEPTABLE FOR THE OPERATION TO BE PERFORMED.

_____ Place a check here if you think Mr. B should *not* have the operation, no matter what the probabilities.
_____ The chances are 9 in 10 that the operation will be a success.
_____ The chances are 7 in 10 that the operation will be a success.
_____ The chances are 5 in 10 that the operation will be a success.
_____ The chances are 3 in 10 that the operation will be a success.
_____ The chances are 1 in 10 that the operation will be a success.

3. Mr. C, a married man with two children, has a steady job that pays him about $6000 per year. He can easily afford the necessities of life, but few of the luxuries. Mr. C's father, who died recently, carried a $4000 life insurance policy. Mr. C would like to invest this money in stocks. He is well aware of the secure "blue chip" stocks and bonds that would pay approximately 6% on his investment. On the other hand, Mr. C has heard that the stocks of a relatively unknown Company X might double their present value if a new product currently in production is favorably received by the buying public. However, if the product is unfavorably received, the stocks would decline in value.

Imagine that you are advising Mr. C. Listed below are several probabilities or odds that Company X stocks will double their value.

PLEASE CHECK THE *LOWEST* PROBABILITY THAT YOU WOULD CONSIDER ACCEPTABLE FOR MR. C TO INVEST IN COMPANY X STOCKS.

_____ The chances are 1 in 10 that the stocks will double their value.
_____ The chances are 3 in 10 that the stocks will double their value.
_____ The chances are 5 in 10 that the stocks will double their value.
_____ The chances are 7 in 10 that the stocks will double their value.
_____ The chances are 9 in 10 that the stocks will double their value.
_____ Place a check here if you think Mr. C should *not* invest in Company X stocks, no matter what the probabilities.

4. Mr. D is president of a light metals corporation in the United States. The corporation is quite prosperous, and has strongly considered the possibilities of business expansion by building an additional plant in a new location. The choice is between building another plant in the U.S., where there would be a moderate return on the initial investment, or building a plant in a foreign country. Lower labor costs and easy access to raw materials in that country would mean a much higher return on the initial investment. On the other hand, there is a history of political instability and revolution in the foreign country under consideration. In fact, the leader of a small minority party is committed to nationalizing, that is, taking over, all foreign investments.

Imagine that you are advising Mr. D. Listed below are several probabilities or odds of continued political stability in the foreign country under consideration.

PLEASE CHECK THE *LOWEST* PROBABILITY THAT YOU WOULD CONSIDER ACCEPTABLE FOR MR. D'S CORPORATION TO BUILD A PLANT IN THAT COUNTRY.

_____ Place a check here if you think Mr. D's corporation should *not* build a plant in the foreign country, no matter what the probabilities.
_____ The chances are 9 in 10 that the foreign country will remain politically stable.
_____ The chances are 7 in 10 that the foreign country will remain politically stable.
_____ The chances are 5 in 10 that the foreign country will remain politically stable.
_____ The chances are 3 in 10 that the foreign country will remain politically stable.
_____ The chances are 1 in 10 that the foreign country will remain politically stable.

5. Mr. E would like to retire from business, but his wife does not want him to do this. Although they have been happily married for almost 40 years, his wife is afraid that Mr. E would find that he has nothing to do, and would be in her way, making it difficult to run the home. Every time Mr. E brings up the subject of retirement, his wife shows her displeasure. Mr. E feels that he must make a decision.

Imagine that you are advising Mr. E. Listed below are several probabilities or odds that the retirement will be successful and will not make for fighting and bickering.

PLEASE CHECK THE *LOWEST* PROBABILITY THAT YOU WOULD CONSIDER ACCEPTABLE FOR RETIREMENT TO BE ATTEMPTED.

_____ The chances are 1 in 10 that the retirement will be successful.
_____ The chances are 3 in 10 that the retirement will be successful.
_____ The chances are 5 in 10 that the retirement will be successful.
_____ The chances are 7 in 10 that the retirement will be successful.
_____ The chances are 9 in 10 that the retirement will be successful.
_____ Place a check here if you think Mr. E should *not* retire, no matter what the probabilities.

6. Mr. F is an old man who has been living alone since his wife died. Mr. F's son, daughter-in-law and grandchildren live nearby, and these people are his only living relatives. Mr. F is a lonely man who doesn't have enough friends or diversions, and whose main enjoyment is in seeing his grandchildren. Recently, Mr. F's son received a very fine job offer in another state. He would like to accept the new job, but feels concerned about Mr. F, his father, since it would not be feasible for Mr. F to move with them. Mr. F is healthy and self-sufficient, but loneliness and lack of diversions may be quite a problem. Mr. F's son asks his father's advice as to whether to accept the new job.

Imagine that you are advising Mr. F. Listed below are several probabilities or odds of Mr. F being able to handle his loneliness and lack of diversions when left alone.

PLEASE CHECK THE *LOWEST* PROBABILITY THAT YOU WOULD CONSIDER ACCEPTABLE FOR MR. F'S SON TO ACCEPT THE NEW JOB.

_____ Place a check here if you think Mr. F should *not* advise his son to accept the new job, no matter what the probabilities.
_____ The chances are 9 in 10 that Mr. F will manage his loneliness in an adequate way and develop friendships with others.
_____ The chances are 7 in 10 that Mr. F will manage his loneliness in an adequate way and develop friendships with others.
_____ The chances are 5 in 10 that Mr. F will manage his loneliness in an adequate way and develop friendships with others.
_____ The chances are 3 in 10 that Mr. F will manage his loneliness in an adequate way and develop friendships with others.
_____ The chances are 1 in 10 that Mr. F will manage his loneliness in an adequate way and develop friendships with others.

7. Mr. G, a college senior, has studied the piano since childhood. He has won amateur prizes and given small recitals, suggesting that Mr. G has considerable musical talent. As graduation approaches, Mr. G has the choice of going to medical school to become a physician, a profession which would bring certain prestige and financial rewards; or entering a conservatory of music for advanced training with a well-known pianist. Mr. G realizes that even upon completion of his piano studies, which would take many more years and a lot of money, success as a concert pianist would not be assured.

Imagine that you are advising Mr. G. Listed below are several probabilities or odds that Mr. G would succeed as a concert pianist.

PLEASE CHECK THE *LOWEST* PROBABILITY THAT YOU WOULD CONSIDER ACCEPTABLE FOR MR. G TO CONTINUE WITH HIS MUSICAL TRAINING.

_____ Place a check here if you think Mr. G should *not* pursue his musical training, no matter what the probabilities.
_____ The chances are 9 in 10 that Mr. G would succeed as a concert pianist.
_____ The chances are 7 in 10 that Mr. G would succeed as a concert pianist.
_____ The chances are 5 in 10 that Mr. G would succeed as a concert pianist.
_____ The chances are 3 in 10 that Mr. G would succeed as a concert pianist.
_____ The chances are 1 in 10 that Mr. G would succeed as a concert pianist.

8. Mr. H has attained a comfortable old age, realizing a life-long goal of independence and good health. Mr. H does not have to "go-out" to anyone he doesn't care to, and can be as "individual" as he likes. However, he does have a young nephew of whom he thinks a great deal. Recently this young nephew brought to Mr. H's attention the fact that he (Mr. H) has antagonized family and friends because he has become careless in his dealings with them, not seeming to care what impression he makes. His appearance has become a bit untidy and he is less careful about personal cleanliness. Upon thinking about these things, Mr. H agreed that, without realizing it, he has been drawing away from people and situations, not caring about "making impressions," as he used to care. Mr. H became confronted with the choice of making an effort to be accommodating—something he really didn't feel like doing, or didn't really need to do—or, not being accommodating, that is, not going out to people and situations. If he made the effort, he would maintain better relations with his family and friends; if he didn't make the effort, he might lose the concern and attention of family and friends, but he would be doing what he felt like doing.

Imagine that you are advising Mr. H. Listed below are several probabilities or odds that Mr. H would maintain the attention and concern of people if he continues what he really wants to do, that is, if he continues to draw away and not "go-out" to them.

PLEASE CHECK THE *LOWEST* PROBABILITY THAT YOU WOULD CONSIDER ACCEPTABLE FOR MR. H TO CONTINUE IN HIS PRESENT MANNER OF DEALING WITH PEOPLE.

_____ The chances are 1 in 10 that people will care for him even without his "going out" to them.

_____ The chances are 3 in 10 that people will care for him even without his "going out" to them.

_____ The chances are 5 in 10 that people will care for him even without his "going out" to them.

_____ The chances are 7 in 10 that people will care for him even without his "going out" to them.

_____ The chances are 9 in 10 that people will care for him even without his "going out" to them.

_____ Mr. H should *not* go out to people no matter what, if he really does not want to.

9. Mr. I is an American captured by the enemy in World War II and placed in a prisoner-of-war camp. Conditions in the camp are quite bad, with long hours of hard physical labor and a barely sufficient diet. After spending several months in this camp, Mr. I notes the possibility of escape by concealing himself in a supply truck that shuttles in and out of the camp. Of course, there is no guarantee that the escape would prove successful. Recapture by the enemy could well mean execution.

Imagine that you are advising Mr. I. Listed below are several probabilities or odds of a successful escape from the prisoner-of-war camp.

PLEASE CHECK THE *LOWEST* PROBABILITY THT YOU WOULD CONSIDER ACCEPTABLE FOR AN ESCAPE TO BE ATTEMPTED.

_____ Place a check here if you think Mr. I should *not* try to escape no matter what the probabilities.

_____ The chances are 9 in 10 that the escape would succeed.

_____ The chances are 7 in 10 that the escape would succeed.

_____ The chances are 5 in 10 that the escape would succeed.

_____ The chances are 3 in 10 that the escape would succeed.

_____ The chances are 1 in 10 that the escape would succeed.

10. Mr. J's health is failing and he is becoming a burden to his family because he needs so much help in taking care of himself. His family has not verbalized discontent, but it is apparent to him that much time and effort is required of them, and this makes him feel bad. Mr. J's awareness of all this has made him think in terms of a home of the aged. Mr. J believes that while he would rather remain where he is, the burden is too much for his family, and perhaps a home for the aged is really the place for him.

Imagine that you are advising Mr. J. Listed below are several probabilities or odds that Mr. J would make a good adjustment in a home of the aged.

PLEASE CHECK THE *LOWEST* PROBABILITY THAT YOU WOULD CONSIDER ACCEPTABLE FOR MR. J TO REQUEST INSTITUTIONALIZATION.

_____ The chances are 1 in 10 that Mr. J would make a good adjustment in a home of the aged.

_____ The chances are 3 in 10 that Mr. J would make a good adjustment in a home of the aged.

_____ The chances are 5 in 10 that Mr. J would make a good adjustment in a home of the aged.

_____ The chances are 7 in 10 that Mr. J would make a good adjustment in a home of the aged.

_____ The chances are 9 in 10 that Mr. J would make a good adjustment in a home of the aged.

_____ Place a check here if you think Mr. J should *not* request institutionalization, no matter what the probabilities.

11. Mr. K's wife died about 6 months ago, leaving him very lonely after a marriage of more than fifty years. Recently he has been visiting a friend who is a widow. He is very attracted to her and would like to ask her to marry him, feeling that she would be a comfort and companion to him for the remainder of his life. He lives with his son and daughter-in-law, but they both have jobs and he is alone during the day. Mr. K is afraid that the son and daughter-in-law might disapprove of the marriage. He feels that he doesn't have many years left to live and would like to have some comfort and pleasure in these years, but at the same time, he doesn't want to risk destroying the good relations that now exist between his son and himself.

Imagine that you are advising Mr. K. Listed below are several odds or probabilities that Mr. K can maintain his good relationship with his son and daughter-in-law after remarrying.

PLEASE CHECK THE *LOWEST* PROBABILITY THAT YOU WOULD CONSIDER ACCEPTABLE FOR MR. K TO REMARRY.

_____ Mr. K should *not* remarry, no matter what the probabilities.

_____ The chances are 9 in 10 that good relations with his son will be maintained, even if he does remarry.

_____ The chances are 7 in 10 that good relations with his son will be maintained, even if he does remarry.

_____ The chances are 5 in 10 that good relations with his son will be maintained, even if he does remarry.

_____ The chances are 3 in 10 that good relations with his son will be maintained, even if he does remarry.

_____ The chances are 1 in 10 that good relations with his son will be maintained, even if he does remarry.

12. Mr. L, a competent chess player, is participating in a national chess tournament, In an early match he draws the top-favored player in the tournament as his opponent. Mr. L has been given a relatively low ranking in view of his performance in previous tour-

naments. During the course of his play with the top-favored man, Mr. L noted the possibility of a deceptive though risky maneuver which might bring him a quick victory. At the same time, if the attempted maneuver should fail, Mr. L would be left in an exposed position and defeat would almost certainly follow.

Imagine that you are advising Mr. L. Listed below are several probabilities or odds that Mr. L's deceptive play would succeed.

PLEASE CHECK THE *LOWEST* PROBABILITY THAT YOU WOULD CONSIDER ACCEPTABLE FOR THE RISKY PLAY IN QUESTION TO BE ATTEMPTED.

_____ The chances are 1 in 10 that the play would succeed.

_____ The chances are 3 in 10 that the play would succeed.

_____ The chances are 5 in 10 that the play would succeed.

_____ The chances are 7 in 10 that the play would succeed.

_____ The chances are 9 in 10 that the play would succeed.

_____ Place a check here if you think Mr. L should *not* attempt the risky play, no matter what the probabilities.

13. Mr. M has a meager income from his old age security benefits. He has been supplementing this meager income by savings which he managed throughout most of his working life. Both sources of money, while not enough for him to do exactly as he would choose, are enough to sustain Mr. and Mrs. M. An acquaintance of Mr. M, a younger man, told him of a business he is about to start, and offered Mr. M an opportunity to invest. Mr. M knows that if the business succeeds, he will be able to live comfortably for the rest of his life, being able to enjoy luxuries such as theatre, fine food and vacations. He also knows that if the business fails, he will lose his savings and be left with only his social security benefits.

Imagine that you are advising Mr. M. Listed below are several odds or probabilities of the business succeeding.

PLEASE CHECK THE *LOWEST* PROBABILITY THAT YOU WOULD CONSIDER ACCEPTABLE FOR MR. M TO INVEST HIS MONEY.

_____ Place a check here if you think Mr. M should *not* invest in the business, no matter what the probabilities.

_____ The chances are 9 in 10 that the business he is thinking of investing in will succeed.

_____ The chances are 7 in 10 that the business he is thinking of investing in will succeed.

_____ The chances are 5 in 10 that the business he is thinking of investing in will succeed.

_____ The chances are 3 in 10 that the business he is thinking of investing in will succeed.

_____ The chances are 1 in 10 that the business he is thinking of investing in will succeed.

14. Mr. N, a 45-year-old accountant, has recently been informed by his physician that he has developed a severe heart ailment. The disease would be sufficiently serious to force Mr. N to change many of his strongest life habits—reducing his work load, drastically changing his diet, giving up favorite leisure time pursuits. The physician suggests that a delicate medical operation could be attempted which, if successful, would completely relieve the heart condition. But its success could not be assured, and in fact, the operation might prove fatal.

Imagine that you are advising Mr. N. Listed below are several probabilities or odds that the operation will prove successful.

PLEASE CHECK THE *LOWEST* PROBABILITY THAT YOU WOULD CONSIDER ACCEPTABLE FOR THE OPERATION TO BE PERFORMED.

_____ The chances are 1 in 10 that the operation will be a success.

_____ The chances are 3 in 10 that the operation will be a success.

_____ The chances are 5 in 10 that the operation will be a success.

_____ The chances are 7 in 10 that the operation will be a success.

_____ The chances are 9 in 10 that the operation will be a success.

_____ Place a check here if you think Mr. N should *not* have the operation, no matter what the probabilities.

15. Mr. O is the captain of College X's football team. College X is playing its traditional rival, College Y, in the final game of the season. The game is in its final seconds, and Mr. O's team, College X, is behind in the score. College X has time to run one more play. Mr. O, the captain, must decide whether it would be best to settle for a tie score with a play which would be almost certain to work; or, on the other hand, should he try a more complicated and risky play which could bring victory if it succeeded, but defeat if not.

Imagine that you are advising Mr. O. Listed below are several probabilities or odds that the risky play will work.

PLEASE CHECK THE *LOWEST* PROBABILITY THAT YOU WOULD CONSIDER ACCEPTABLE FOR THE RISKY PLAY TO BE ATTEMPTED.

_____ Place a check here if you think Mr. O should *not* attempt the risky play, no matter what the probabilities.

_____ The chances are 9 in 10 that the risky play will work.

_____ The chances are 7 in 10 that the risky play will work.

_____ The chances are 5 in 10 that the risky play will work.

_____ The chances are 3 in 10 that the risky play will work.

_____ The chances are 1 in 10 that the risky play will work.

16. Mr. P has an opportunity to retire from his job with a good pension—good enough to support him and his wife. Mr. P would like to retire because he is getting on in years and has been finding the work hard. However, he is of the opinion that people often "deteriorate," becoming less and less able to do things, when they retire, and is not sure what he should do.

Imagine that you are advising Mr. P. Listed below are several probabilities or odds that Mr. P will do well in retirement and not "deteriorate."

PLEASE CHECK THE *LOWEST* PROBABILITY THAT YOU WOULD CONSIDER ACCEPTABLE TO MAKE IT WORTHWHILE FOR MR. P TO RETIRE.

_____ The chances are 1 in 10 that he will do well and not get less and less capable to do things.

_____ The chances are 3 in 10 that he will do well and not get less and less capable to do things.

_____ The chances are 5 in 10 that he will do well and not get less and less capable to do things.

_____ The chances are 7 in 10 that he will do well and not get less and less capable to do things.

_____ The chances are 9 in 10 that he will do well and not get less and less capable to do things.

_____ Place a check here if you think Mr. P should *not* retire in any case.

17. Mr. Q is currently a college senior who is very eager to pursue graduate study in chemistry leading to the Doctor of Philosophy degree. He has been accepted by both Univer-

sity X and University Y. University X has a world-wide reputation for excellence in chemistry. While a degree from University X would signify outstanding training in this field, the standards are so very rigorous that only a fraction of the degree candidates actually receive the degree. University Y, on the other hand, has much less of a reputation in chemistry, but almost everyone admitted is awarded the Doctor of Philosophy degree, though the degree has much less prestige than the corresponding degree from University X.

Imagine that you are advising Mr. Q. Listed below are several probabilities or odds that Mr. Q would be awarded a degree at University X, the one with the greater prestige.

PLEASE CHECK THE *LOWEST* PROBABILITY THAT YOU WOULD CONSIDER ACCEPTABLE TO MAKE IT WORTHWHILE FOR MR. Q TO ENROLL IN UNIVERSITY X RATHER THAN UNIVERSITY Y.

_____ Place a check here if you think Mr. Q should *not* enroll in University X, no matter what the probabilities.

_____ The chances are 9 in 10 that Mr. Q would receive a degree from University X.

_____ The chances are 7 in 10 that Mr. Q would receive a degree from University X.

_____ The chances are 5 in 10 that Mr. Q would receive a degree from University X.

_____ The chances are 3 in 10 that Mr. Q would receive a degree from University X.

_____ The chances are 1 in 10 that Mr. Q would receive a degree from University X.

18. Mr. R is contemplating marriage to Miss T, a girl whom he has known for a little more than a year. Recently, however, a number of arguments have occurred between them, suggesting some sharp differences of opinion in the way each views certain matters. Indeed, they decide to seek professional advice from a marriage counselor as to whether it would be wise for them to marry. On the basis of these meetings with a marriage counselor, they realize that a happy marriage, while possible, would not be assured.

Imagine that you are advising Mr. R and Miss T. Listed below are several probabilities or odds that their marriage would prove to be a happy and successful one.

PLEASE CHECK THE *LOWEST* PROBABILITY THAT YOU WOULD CONSIDER ACCEPTABLE FOR MR. R AND MISS T TO GET MARRIED.

_____ The chances are 1 in 10 that the marriage would be happy and successful.

_____ The chances are 3 in 10 that the marriage would be happy and successful.

_____ The chances are 5 in 10 that the marriage would be happy and successful.

_____ The chances are 7 in 10 that the marriage would be happy and successful.

_____ The chances are 9 in 10 that the marriage would be happy and successful.

_____ Place a check here if you think Mr. R and Miss T should *not* marry, no matter what the probabilities.

19. Mr. S does not approve of the way in which his daughter is bringing up her children. He is extremely fond of his grandchildren and is worried about what he sees going on. In his heart he believes that he is right and his daughter wrong, and that if he keeps quiet, the grandchildren will grow up in ways that he believes wrong. However, he knows that to be effective and make his beliefs work, it will be necessary to "lay down the law" with his daughter and son-in-law. He also knows that although he can do this because they are dependent upon him in a financial way, he is running the risk of alienating their good feelings toward him. He is afraid that in the end, he might "lose" his grandchildren because of their parents' feelings toward him.

Imagine that you are advising Mr. S. Listed below are several probabilities or odds that he can "lay down the law" or advise, and not "lose" his grandchildren.

PLEASE CHECK THE *LOWEST* PROBABILITY THAT YOU WOULD CONSIDER ACCEPTABLE FOR MR. S TO "LAY DOWN THE LAW" WITH HIS DAUGHTER AND SON-IN-LAW.

_____Place a check here if you think Mr. S. should *not* advise, no matter what the probabilities.

_____The chances are 9 in 10 that he can advise and so help his grandchildren and not "lose" them.

_____The chances are 7 in 10 that he can advise and so help his grandchildren and not "lose" them.

_____The chances are 5 in 10 that he can advise and so help his grandchildren and not "lose" them.

_____The chances are 3 in 10 that he can advise and so help his grandchildren and not "lose" them.

_____The chances are 1 in 10 that he can advise and so help his grandchildren and not "lose" them.

20. Mr. T is a widower who has lived alone for a number of years. He enjoys living alone because he can do as he pleases, go to bed and get up at the time he chooses, and have meals when he wishes. He feels nervous when other people are around and becomes irritable and short-tempered when with other people for an extended period of time. Mr. T's daughter and son-in-law live in the same community and visit or call him often. They take him to buy groceries when he needs them and also take him to the doctor. Recently Mr. T's health has become worse and he is having greater difficulty in managing for himself. He considers going to live in the home of his daughter and son-in-law. He knows that he is welcome there, but fears that he will be nervous and irritable and that the welcome may be short lived. Still, he knows that poor health is making it difficult for him to live alone.

Imagine that you are advising Mr. T. Listed below are several odds or probabilities that Mr. T will be able to maintain his good relationship with his daughter and son-in-law and will make a satisfactory adjustment.

PLEASE CHECK THE *LOWEST* PROBABILITY THAT YOU WOULD CONSIDER CEPTABLE FOR MR. T TO MOVE INTO THE HOME OF HIS DAUGHTER AND SON-IN-LAW.

_____The chances are 1 in 10 that Mr. T will make a satisfactory adjustment in the home of his daughter and son-in-law.

_____The chances are 3 in 10 that Mr. T willl make a satisfactory adjustment in the home of his daughter and son-in-law.

_____The chances are 5 in 10 that Mr. T will make a satisfactory adjustment in the home of his daughter and son-in-law.

_____The chances are 7 in 10 that Mr. T will make a satisfactory adjustment in the home of his daughter and son-in-law.

_____The chances are 9 in 10 that Mr. T will make a satisfactory adjustment in the home of his daughter and son-in-law.

_____Place a check here if you feel that Mr. T should *not* move, no matter what the probabilities.

21. Mr. U has had a series of serious sicknesses since turning 65 and now, at 72 he feels broken and worn, and feels without zest for life. Mr. U was advised that if he was fortunate in escaping sickness during the next few years, he could look forward to better spirits, and a more normal aged life. However, he was also told that his severe heart condition, and severe hardening of the arteries, could act up at any moment, leaving him feeling worse than ever, if he should survive the attack. Mr. U was advised that his chances for better health would be maximum if he changed some old habits of life, as for example, stopping intake of all alcoholic beverages (his only source of escape from his misery) and by more regular eating and sleeping schedules (something he always disliked to do). Mr. U was undecided whether to give up alcohol and live a more routinized life, so that

the future may be more comfortable, or whether to continue as he was since this brought him some current satisfaction and since he was not sure he could avoid an attack in any case.

Imagine that you are advising Mr. U. Listed below are several probabilities or odds of his health improving by giving up the life-long habits and satisfactions.

PLEASE CHECK THE *LOWEST* PROBABILITY THAT HEALTH WILL IMPROVE THAT YOU WOULD CONSIDER ACCEPTABLE FOR MR. U TO GIVE UP HIS FEW CURRENT SATISFACTIONS.

_____Place a check here if you think Mr. U should *not* give up the habits, no matter what the probabilities.

_____The chances are 9 in 10 that his health will improve by giving up his satisfactions.

_____The chances are 7 in 10 that his health will improve by giving up his satisfactions.

_____The chances are 5 in 10 that his health will improve by giving up his satisfactions.

_____The chances are 3 in 10 that his health will improve by giving up his satisfactions.

_____The chances are 1 in 10 that his health will improve by giving up his satisfactions.

22. Mr. V is a successful businessman who has participated in a number of activities of considerable value to the community. Mr. V has been approached by the leaders of his political party as a possible congressional candidate in the next election. Mr. V's party is a minority party in the district, though the party has won occasional elections in the past. Mr. V would like to hold political office, but to do so would involve a serious financial sacrifice, since the party has insufficient campaign funds. He would also have to endure the attacks of his political opponents in a hot campaign.

Imagine that you are advising Mr. V. Listed below are several probabilities or odds of Mr. V's winning the election in his district.

PLEASE CHECK THE *LOWEST* PROBABILITY THAT YOU WOULD CONSIDER ACCEPTABLE TO MAKE IT WORTHWHILE FOR MR. V TO RUN FOR POLITICAL OFFICE.

_____The chances are 1 in 10 that Mr. V would win the election.

_____The chances are 3 in 10 that Mr. V would win the election.

_____The chances are 5 in 10 that Mr. V would win the election.

_____The chances are 7 in 10 that Mr. V would win the election.

_____The chances are 9 in 10 that Mr. V would win the election.

_____Place a check here if you think Mr. V should *not* run for political office, no matter what the probabilities.

23. Mr. W, a married 30-year-old research physicist, has been given a five-year appointment by a major university laboratory. As he contemplates the next five years, he realizes that he might work on a difficult long-term problem which, if a solution could be found, would resolve basic scientific issues in the field and bring high scientific honors. If no solution were found, however, Mr. W would have little to show for his five years in the laboratory, and this would make it hard for him to get a good job afterwards. On the other hand, he could, as most of his professional associates are doing, work on a series of short-term problems where solutions would be easier to find, but where the problems are of lesser scientific importance.

Imagine that you are advising Mr. W. Listed below are several probabilities or odds that a solution would be found to the difficult long-term problem that Mr. W has in mind.

PLEASE CHECK THE *LOWEST* PROBABILITY THAT YOU WOULD CONSIDER ACCEPTABLE TO MAKE IT WORTHWHILE FOR MR. W TO WORK ON THE MORE DIFFICULT LONG-TERM PROBLEM.

_____Place a check here if you think Mr. W should *not* choose the long-term difficult problem, no matter what the probabilities.

———The chances are 9 in 10 that Mr. W would solve the long-term problem.
———The chances are 7 in 10 that Mr. W would solve the long-term problem.
———The chances are 5 in 10 that Mr. W would solve the long-term problem.
———The chances are 3 in 10 that Mr. W would solve the long-term problem.
———The chances are 1 in 10 that Mr. W would solve the long-term problem.

24. Mr. X is a seventy-eight-year-old man. He has never seen his grandchildren and would like to visit them. However, Mr. X has a heart condition and was told by his physician that he must avoid activity or excitement if he wants to prolong his life. He greatly desires to see his grandchildren before he dies, and this involves a trip across the country. He is not sure whether he ought to risk the trip to fulfill his desire to see his grandchildren.

Imagine that you are advising Mr. X. Listed below are several odds or probabilities that Mr. X will *not* shorten his life by making the visit to see his grandchildren.

PLEASE CHECK THE *LOWEST* PROBABILITY THAT YOU WOULD CONSIDER ACCEPTABLE FOR MR. X TO MAKE THE VISIT.

———Place a check here if you feel that he should *not* make the visit, no matter what the probabilities.
———The chances are 1 in 10 that he can make the visit without shortening his life.
———The chances are 3 in 10 that he can make the visit without shortening his life.
———The chances are 5 in 10 that he can make the visit without shortening his life.
———The chances are 7 in 10 that he can make the visit without shortening his life.
———The chances are 9 in 10 that he can make the visit without shortening his life.

Reprinted by permission of authors.

V1.3.IV.d
ESTIMATION QUESTIONNAIRE
M. A. Wallach and N. Kogan, 1965

"This game asks you to guess about a lot of things in our world. For instance, if you knew that most grown-up men in the world are around 5 feet and 7 inches tall, you might guess that the tallest man in the world is 7 feet tall, or 8 feet tall. And you might guess that the shortest man in the world is 4 feet tall or only 3 feet tall. In this game you get a chance to guess about things like that. Why don't you just begin reading now, and circle your guesses for each of the things printed below. Take your time, and ask me any questions you want about things that aren't clear to you."

Listed below are the twelve items comprising the children's version of the category width test.

1. Most birds fly at the speed of about 17 miles per hour.
   a. How fast does the fastest bird fly?
      1. 30 miles per hour
      2. 21 miles per hour
      3. 60 miles per hour
      4. 18 miles per hour
   b. How slow does the slowest bird fly?
      1. 15 miles per hour
      2. 5 miles per hour
      3. 10 miles per hour
      4. 2 miles per hour
2. Most whales are about 65 feet long.
   a. How long is the longest whale?
      1. 69 feet

    2. 150 feet

    3. 76 feet

    4. 90 feet

  b. How short is the shortest whale?

    1. 37 feet

    2. 8 feet

    3. 51 feet

    4. 58 feet

3. Usually about 58 ships arrive in New York City harbor every day.

  a. What do you guess is the largest number of ships ever to arrive in New York City harbor in one day?

    1. 102 ships

    2. 65 ships

    3. 74 ships

    4. 60 ships

  b. What do you guess is the smallest number of ships ever to arrive in New York City harbor in one day?

    1. 5 ships

    2. 49 ships

    3. 38 ships

    4. 18 ships

4. Most dogs are about 3½ feet long.

  a. How long is the longest dog?

    1. 4½ feet

    2. 4 feet

    3. 5½ feet

    4. 6½ feet

  b. How short is the shortest dog?

    1. 1 foot

    2. 1½ feet

    3. 2½ feet

    4. 2 feet

5. Most cars are able to go about 90 miles per hour.

  a. How fast will the fastest car go?

    1. 213 miles per hour

    2. 95 miles per hour

    3. 394 miles per hour

    4. 132 miles per hour

  b. How slow will the slowest car go?

    1. 3 miles per hour

    2. 18 miles per hour

    3. 9 miles per hour

    4. ½ mile per hour

6. Most roads are about 18 feet wide.

  a. How wide is the widest road?

    1. 51 feet

    2. 27 feet

    3. 20 feet

    4. 36 feet

  b. How narrow is the narrowest road?

    1. 16 feet

    2. 7 feet

3. 2 feet
4. 11 feet

7. Most states have about 4 million people in them.
   a. How many million people are there in the largest state?
      1. 5 million
      2. 15 million
      3. 8 million
      4. 30 million
   b. How many million people are there in the smallest state?
      1. 1 million
      2. 2 million
      3. 1/8 million
      4. 3 million

8. Most buildings are about 50 feet high.
   a. How high is the tallest building?
      1. 421 feet
      2. 1253 feet
      3. 157 feet
      4. 63 feet
   b. How short is the shortest building?
      1. 40 feet
      2. 6 feet
      3. 29 feet
      4; 17 feet

9. Most windows are about 34 inches wide.
   a. How wide is the widest window?
      1. 110 inches
      2. 36 inches
      3. 43 inches
      4. 57 inches
   b. How narrow is the narrowest window?
      1. 3 inches
      2. 21 inches
      3. 12 inches
      4. 28 inches

10. Most sailboats go about 9 miles per hour.
    a. How fast will the fastest sailboat go?
       1. 22 miles per hour
       2. 39 miles per hour
       3. 11 miles per hour
       4. 14 miles per hour
    b. How slow will the slowest sailboat go?
       1. 7 miles per hour
       2. 8½ miles per hour
       3. 6 miles per hour
       4. 4½ miles per hour

11. Every year about 300 new schoolbooks are written
    a. What is the largest number of schoolbooks written in one year?
       1. 524 books
       2. 330 books
       3. 392 books
       4. 980 books

b. What is the smallest number of schoolbooks written in one year?
   1. 94 books
   2. 25 books
   3. 9 books
   4. 180 books
12. Most people spend about 55 minutes out of a whole day eating meals.
   a. What is the longest time anyone spends eating meals in a whole day?
      1. 60 minutes
      2. 105 minutes
      3. 240 minutes
      4. 73 minutes
   b. What is the shortest time anyone spends eating meals in a whole day?
      1. 3 minutes
      2. 29 minutes
      3. 47 minutes
      4. 11 minutes

SOURCE: M. A. Wallach and N. Kogan. *Modes of Thinking in Young Children.* Copyright 1965 by Holt, Rinehart and Winston, Inc. Reprinted by permission of authors and publishers.

Chapter 4

Adaptation

Eva Kahana, Thomas Fairchild, and Boaz Kahana

Current interest in understanding the process of adaptation to crises and events of adult life has led to a recognition of the need for better description, conceptualization, and operationalization of the diverse behaviors involved in the coping process (Hamburg, Coelho, and Adams, 1974). Because of the relative newness of this area of study, a comprehensive review of the use of the construct of adaptation within psychology, sociology, and gerontology is necessary for providing a theoretical background for describing efforts in measuring coping and adaptation. It should be noted that this review of the work being done on coping and adaptation has a relatively narrow focus and excludes the more general issues in the meausrement of personality. For a review of general personality measures, the reader is directed to comprehensive reviews by Chown (1968), Schaie and Marquette (1972), Neugarten (1977), and Schaie and Schaie (1977), as well as to Chapter 3 in this volume.

There are very few measures available that have been specifically designed for assessing adaptation in aged populations. Typically, measures used with younger groups are being used and in some cases modified so as to be applicable to older populations. Excellent reviews of measurement approaches to assessing coping as a general concept have been provided by Moos (1974), Lazarus, Averill, and Opton (1974), and Haan (1977). Therefore, the present discussion is restricted to approaches of interest for use with the aged, i.e., those that have already been used with aged populations or those that have served as the basis for measures currently in use with the aged.

Because the definitional problems presented by the terms *adaptation, coping,* and *defense* have been recognized, the meaning of these terms as they are used in this chapter will be specified. The terms *coping, adaptation,* and *defense* are used to suggest the efforts of the individual at solving real-life problems in the broadest sense. These terms are used interchangeably, and this definitional problem is an issue that has not yet been resolved in the emerging literature.

Although the importance of adaptive strategies for psychosocial well-being is implicit in theories of personality (Hall and Lindzey, 1970), relatively little research has been carried out to explore the specific adaptive strategies used by older people. Until recently, conceptualizations of adaptation tended to be fragmented. Styles of coping were often equated with personality traits and were seldom differentiated from success of coping or adjustment (Moos, 1974; Kahana, 1975). Furthermore, environmental demands for coping or constraints on coping were seldom considered. The emphasis of most investigators seeking to understand adjustment has been on the individual (Lieberman, 1969; Butler, 1968; Busse and Pfeiffer, 1969; Reichard, Livson, and Peterson, 1962; Lowenthal, 1971) or on the environment (Kahana and Kahana, 1970; Pincus, 1968; Lawton, 1975; Carp, 1974; Lowenthal, Thurnher, and Chiriboga, 1975).

Consideration of individual adaptation has included the personality dimension and the individual response dimension (Lazarus, Averill, and Opton, 1974). The importance of the individual response dimension for understanding coping revolved around the difficulty in interpreting seeming contradictions in response patterns and then inferring from these *samples* of coping behavior a total pattern of coping. Personality measures have been the focus of Lieberman and Cohler's (1976) attempt to measure adaptive strategies. Assessments of relevant personality characteristics include such dimensions as locus of control, frustration tolerance, affective equilibrium, and defense mechanisms called upon in response to stressful circumstances. Focus on environmental influences on adaptation has included diverse ecological variables. This can be represented by the effects of physical environment (e.g., climate), the suprapersonal environment (age integration), and situational factors (e.g., type of problems to be dealt with). Within gerontology, examples of this orientation can be seen in studies of institutional factors as they affect adaptation (Kahana and Kahana, 1970) or readjustment to housing environments (Carp, 1974; Lawton, 1975). Only recently has there been a trend in the study of adaptation toward recognizing the interaction of individual and environmental characteristics (Hamburg, Coelho, and Adams,

1974; Mechanic, 1974; Lazarus, Averill, and Opton, 1974; Lawton, 1975; Kahana and Kahana, 1979).

Within the psychological literature, coping has been regarded as an individual defense against threats aroused in individual situations (Lazarus, Averill, and Opton, 1974). Many of the psychological measurement approaches have emerged from recent developments in personality theory (Moos, 1974), which have emphasized personal striving toward environmental mastery and competence and an adaptive ego process (Hartman, Kris, and Loewenstein, 1949; White, 1959; Erikson, 1950).

Psychologists studying adaptation have focused on processes for handling both everyday life stresses and major life crises and transitions (Alker, 1968). Haan (1963) distinguished between adaptive strategies characterized by a quality of positive problem solving (i.e., coping) and strategies that are essentially maladaptive (i.e., defenses). Alker (1968, p. 985), in his elaboration on Haan's model, suggested that coping is "flexible, differentiated, reality oriented, purposive, effective and permissive of open, ordered impulsive satisfaction" while defensive behavior permits impulse gratification through subterfuge and is rigid, distorting, and maladaptive. It is assumed that both kinds of ego functioning handle conflicts.

In considerations of these conceptualizations, one questionable assumption has been that appropriate need gratification is usually within an individual's control, and so it may be seen as far more functional to change an undesirable environment in order to obtain gratification than to deny existing problems. In the case of elderly persons, whose personal and environmental options may be severely limited, the demarcation between coping and defensive behavior may be blurred.

As a sociologist, Mechanic (1974) has focused on the fit between social structure and environmental demands as it influences coping behavior, and he has emphasized the importance of culturally provided adaptive strategies. Lazarus and associates (1974) have stressed a broad range of problem-solving efforts exercised by people in response to environmental demands. Lazarus, Averill, and Opton (1974) and Hamburg, Coelho, and Adams (1974) considered the concept of adaptive tasks to be useful in providing a more thorough view of adaptation. It should be noted, however, that much of the work cited here is limited to presentations of conceptualizations without associated empirical investigations designed to test the utility of the proposed concepts. Other sociological schemes for the study of coping fit within the conceptual framework of "total institutions." For example,

Merton (1937) and Goffman (1959) offered four essential patterns of coping with institutional environments: (1) withdrawal, (2) aggression, (3) integration, and (4) acquiescence. Although most of these discussions also lack empirical validation, they help to provide a framework for the study of adaptation.

Pearlin and Schooler's (1978) work has been the most ambitious attempt within the field of sociology to study adaptive processes empirically. They have argued that coping behavior is normally learned from groups to which people belong. One may, therefore, use fruitfully concepts such as norms, values, and social rituals for understanding individual coping behavior. Thus, one can look beyond traditional psychological profiles for an understanding of the etiology of coping behavior. For the aged, social expectations, norms, and statuses are drastically changed. Coping behavior thus may be seen as a sensitive index of the changed situation of older persons in society.

Pearlin and Schooler's (1978) conceptualization directly ties coping to problematic life circumstances or social role conflicts. They attempted to specify the array of coping mechanisms that people use to deal with these problems, and they also sought to assess the efficiency of various coping strategies. Use of a sociological model suggests links between the social characteristics of individuals and their coping behavior. The importance of sex and socioeconomic status for coping strategies is stressed.

In another empirical study of adaptation that used a structural framework similar to Merton's (1937), Sharma and Kahana (1977) examined sex differences in the adaptation patterns of aged people from ethnic groups in urban environments. Structural constraints on the use of socially endorsed means of activity and socially endorsed goals of morale were examined in operationalizing Merton's adaptive modes of conformity, ritualism, innovation, and retreatism.

Existing studies in gerontology have often focused on adaptation as an outcome (Carp, 1974; Lieberman and Cohler, 1976). Adaptation is considered to be similar to adjustment, a product rather than a reflection of the *process* of trying to adjust. Although some of these authors have defined adaptation in terms of behavioral or intrapsychic processes, their techniques of assessment have been closer to definitions of outcome, (i.e., well-being, mental health, emotional equilibrium), rather than to definitions of the process by which these ends can be achieved.

Lieberman and Cohler (1976) have outlined three approaches to the measurement of the adaptive process. Each of these relates to issues of mastery and competence and provides indications of outcome.

Lawton and Nahemow (1973) and Carp (1974) have developed theoretical approaches that categorize adaptation as a response to the environment. Lowenthal, Thurnher, and Chiriboga (1975) studied typologies of adaptation in response to major life transitions and focused on personal control as an important aspect of adaptation. Quayhagen and Chiriboga (1976), however, have considered the antecedents of different styles of adaptation among the institutionalized aged.

Gerontological research on adaptation has also depended on the perspectives of activity and disengagement theories (Stephens, 1973). Some studies have suggested that personality types provide more informative predictions of various patterns of adaptation (Neugarten, 1964; Reichard, Livson, and Peterson, 1962). The adaptive value of various styles of aging has also been examined in the cross-cultural work of Gutmann (1969) and Goldstein and Gutmann (1972).

The question still remains: how can the older person successfully cope with situations and settings that may be incongruent with his or her needs and expectations? The disadvantages of the later years (i.e., reduced income, impaired health, and role loss) reduce the options and choices available to the older person for maintaining or finding an environment in keeping with his or her preferences. Major discontinuities with earlier life patterns often occur and pose challenges to the adaptive strategies of the older person. Examples of such discontinuities include retirement, widowhood, and institutionalization. How can the older person handle the disruption of his or her life-style and the frustration inherent in the reduced options that accompany aging?

Following Lewin's (1935) theoretical formulations, Kahana and Kahana (1979) postulated five general, or typical, styles of handling incongruence or discontinuity between older persons' expectations and needs and the environment. Their ongoing longitudinal study considers coping strategies as instrumental, expressive, intrapsychic, and escapist approaches to problem solving, and the inability to cope with stress.

Although the adaptive strategies of older people can be seen as rooted in earlier types of adaptation and coping, coping strategies can also be responsive to the changing demands of the environment. Therefore, they can be considered to have both *traitlike* and *dynamic* components. Furthermore, though adaptive strategies are often outlined as typologies, it should be recognized that they overlap and that all individuals use a variety of coping methods.

Both psychologists and sociologists have recognized that the variables of adaptation and coping are valuable conceptual tools in understanding how persons deal with stresses and daily problems. In fact, Pearlin and Schooler (1978) have suggested that the study of adaptation may represent a useful point of convergence between disciplines for understanding the functioning and well-being of older persons. It is hoped that the concepts and instruments outlined in this chapter will provide researchers with the necessary information and research tools for conducting studies in adaptation. Conceptualizations of adaptive strategies or processes represent a much-needed first step in understanding the dynamics of the individual side of person-environment interactions. The challenge in pursuing this line of inquiry rests in operationalizing these constructs and using them in empirical studies of the aged.

Measurement of Adaptation

Methodological Issues

Although an exhaustive review of all the methodological issues dealing with the measurement of the individual's adaptation to life crises and events cannot be provided, the authors feel that it is essential to alert the reader to some of the problems of measurement in this area. This discussion will focus upon those problems of measurement that are particularly salient to the measures being reviewed.

Definitional problems encompass the distinction between coping and defense (Haan, 1977), coping as a specific stress (Lazarus, Averill, and Opton, 1974), equating coping with instrumental skills (Mechanic, 1974), and conceptualizing coping stimulus-dependent adaptation (White, 1974). Comparisons of studies are difficult because of the multiplicity of definitions and the diversity of measurement approaches. Instrumentation has involved a wide variety of assessment techniques, including open-ended and forced rating approaches, projective methods, and naturalistic studies. Furthermore, of the instruments reviewed (with the possible exception of the various coping inventories [Quayhagen and Quayhagen, 1978; Kahana and Kahana, 1979; Pearlin and Schooler, 1978]), few have been administered to representative samples of older adults. Coping scales have also been criticized by Lazarus, Averill, and Opton (1974) because they measure the various coping strategies that a person *thinks* he or she would use when exposed to an actual threat, instead of measuring how a person *actually* handles a threatening experience.

Another problem that plagues the empirical development of this area is the failure of researchers to assess reliability and validity for most instruments. This is especially critical in an emerging area where reliability and validity estimates, as well as the descriptive and statistical characteristics of the research groups, provide data crucial in assessing the substantive findings of research.

Although psychological methods, and projective techniques particularly, are, to date, the most well developed, it should be noted that these techniques are rather time-consuming, require considerable training to administer, and yield data beyond those necessary for measuring coping or adaptation. Furthermore, open-ended approaches such as the TAT presuppose that respondents are sufficiently verbal to provide the detailed stories that are coded for adaptation. Frequently, older persons are not articulate enough to describe in detail the diversity of their coping strategies. Projective-test protocols generally have excellent test-retest reliability; clinical patients and normal subjects offer similar, if not identical, protocols over item periods ranging up to several years. Indeed, clinicians are often dismayed when they see no change in their patients' projective-test protocols after several years of therapy. Interrater reliability, however, is a problem because it requires uniformity in ratings of these open-ended interview data. Validity is a particularly troublesome issue with projective tests, since these techniques were developed to reveal unconscious fantasies, anxieties, and defenses that are not readily portrayed in everyday behavior and that, by definition, are not recognized consciously by the individual. Nevertheless, validity can be ascertained by comparisons with other projective tests that tap similar dimensions and with those aspects of overt behavior that are not readily under the subject's conscious surveillance.

Moos (1974) suggested that the goals of research on adaptation may be descriptive and oriented toward understanding and explanation or they may be oriented toward prediction of outcomes. In distinguishing measures developed from these two approaches, he suggested, investigators oriented toward understanding coping have used more complex, intuitive, clinical, and global assessment methods, whereas those oriented toward prediction have turned to simple, objective, specific, and actuarial methods. Thus, open-ended measurement techniques may tap somewhat different aspects of coping than closed-ended approaches.

Global approaches to studying adaptation usually use ratings of lengthy interviews or batteries of measures. These complex techniques were usually constructed for some other purpose and are extremely difficult to replicate. A recent study done by Gatz and associates (1977) assesses coping patterns by using a seven-test battery. Another comprehensive study of coping with life transitions (Lowenthal, Thurnher, and Chiriboga, 1975) used extensive interview batteries rated by researchers on 15 dimensions of adaptation.

Although this review has raised some critical methodological issues, it should not be interpreted as a condemnation of the instrumentation used in assessing the coping strategies of older adults. Rather, these issues have been raised with two purposes in mind. First, as in any emerging area in the social sciences, an extensive number of new research techniques must first be developed before researchers can begin to arrive at a set of satisfactory theoretically based measures. This process will be aided by the recruitment of new talent and by the advancement of measurement skills and theories. Second, researchers in the field need to examine research methodology critically, keeping in mind that different research methods are relevant to various research goals. Therefore, gerontologists need to evaluate both specific research instruments and different assessment techniques (e.g., naturalistic studies versus interview data) used in measurement. The use of multimethod-multitrait approaches to validity (Campbell and Fiske, 1959) appears to be especially useful in the development of better instrumentation.

Choosing Measures

The authors of this chapter attempted to include the measures that hold the most promise for use in future studies of the adaptive processes of older persons. In addition, they included examples of instruments that reflect different methodological approaches to the study of adaptation, including closed- and open-ended inventories, hypothetical problems, projective measures, and observational techniques. This approach permitted the inclusion of measures that reflect many theoretical and methodological issues. It should be noted that discussions of a few measures that are centrally related to adaptive processes (e.g., life events, locus of control, frustration, and tolerance) are included because they are likely to have an important influence on the individual's styles of adaptation.

Instruments labeled by their authors as measures of adjustment were excluded from this chapter when they clearly related to outcome or tapped only one aspect of adaptation (e.g., retirement or the sick role). These measures are reviewed elsewhere in this compendium.

A great deal of relevant and significant work is in progress in this area. Consequently, some of the measures included have not appeared in published form. Several ongoing or recently completed studies have made extensive contributions to the development of instrumentation in this area (Lowenthal, Thurnher, and Chiriboga, 1975; Cutler and Chiriboga, 1976; Quayhagen and Chiriboga, 1976; Quayhagen and Quayhagen, 1978; Pearlin and Schooler, 1978; Lieberman and Cohler, 1976; Kahana and Kahana, 1979; Kahana and Felton, 1976; Kiyak, Liang and Kahana, 1976). By making note of these ongoing efforts, the authors hoped to alert readers to future developments in this field.

Ten measures of coping and adaptation are reviewed in this chapter. A light plurality of the instruments use hypothetical-problems methods; this may be due to the ease with which these techniques can be used in survey research. It is interesting to note, however, that two projective tests are included, even though the instructions and ratings required by this method make it comparatively more difficult to administer. Only one observational measure is included in this review, and it is designed for use in an interview situation. The three measures that are indirectly related to coping and adaptation also readily lend themselves to use in interview situations.

Projective Tests

Among the projective tests, the Thematic Apperception Test (TAT) (Henry, 1956) has been extensively used for the assessment of coping strategies with younger persons. A number of specially designed scoring systems have been developed to assess coping (Moos, 1974; Coelho, Silber, and Hamburg, 1962). The TAT has been used in a number of gerontological studies for concepts closely related to adaptation, such as environmental mastery (Gutmann, 1969). The Geriatric Apperception Test (GAT) (Wolk and Wolk, 1971) and the Senior Apperception Test (SAT) (Bellak, 1975) are variations of the TAT that were specifically designed for use with the aged. Only Gutmann's (1969) modification of the TAT is reviewed in this chapter. The GAT and SAT are reviewed in Chapter 3 of this volume. These may provide useful measures for coping and adaptation, although they have not been directly used for this purpose in previous research.

Sentence-completion measures provide another projective approach that is useful for assessing adaptation (Moos, 1974). Sentence stems constructed by Wiener (1956) and Goldstein (1959) successfully elicited coping polarities (e.g., sensitizers versus repressors, or copers versus avoiders). Schroder, Driver, and Streufert (1967) assessed coping style through the complexity of the respondent's sentence completion structure. Sentence-completion content as well as ratings of test behavior have been used as measures of adaptation with the aged (Kahana and Kiyak, 1976).

Coping Scales Based on Hypothetical Problems

Self-reporting coping scales are usually applied to hypothetical problems. Sidle and associates (1969) have developed one of the most widely used scales in this area, and modifications of this scale have been used with older persons (Quayhagen and Chiriboga, 1976; Pearlin and Schooler, 1978; Cutler and Chiriboga, 1976; Kahana and Kahana, 1979; Quayhagen and Quayhagen, 1978). These scales use short stories and closed-ended methods to elicit characteristic coping styles. The questions are not mutually exclusive, so the individual can endorse the use of a variety of coping styles. The scales provide information about a broad range of coping strategies, including steps taken by the individual preparatory to action. Finally, Gleser and Ihilievich's Defense Mechanism Inventory (1969) uses hypothetical problems for assessing defense mechanisms as one facet of coping.

Observational Techniques

Observational techniques for assessment of coping behavior have not been extensively used with any age-groups, and yet this is a potentially important area and one that demands further research. As Moos (1974, p. 335) put it, "Full understanding [of adaptation] can come only with detailed intensive study, either through interviews or through naturalistic observations of the actual day to day processes by which adaptation occurs." Kastenbaum and Sherwood's (1972) VIRO Scale has been successfully used to record behavioral data obtained during the course of an interview. Although it was not specifically designed to assess adaptation, several of its components tap this dimension. Ratings of projective test *behavior* have also been used as measures of adaptation by Kahana and Kiyak (1976).

Other Measures of Coping and Related Concepts

There are three indexes that are not easily classified with the methods already discussed. One is a sociological scale for assessing adaptation that is based on the combined scales for activity and morale (Sharma and Kahana, 1977). Two scales measuring constructs closely related to adaptation (i.e., recent life events [Kiyak, Liang, and Kahana, 1976] and internal-external locus of control [Rotter, 1966]) are also reviewed.

Summary

The ten instruments reviewed in this chapter (see Table 4-1) represent a range of empirical strategies and theoretical focuses that have been used in studies of aging and adaptation. This review of the instrumentation in the area highlights both the diversity of conceptualizations and the richness of empirical findings. By no means, however, is research on the coping patterns of older adults complete. Much work remains to be done before an integrated, cumulative body of knowledge is developed.

TABLE 4-1
Instruments Reviewed in Chapter 4

	Instrument	Author (date)	Code Number
I.	Projective Measures		
	a. Ego Styles (TAT)	Gutmann (1964)	Copyrighted
	b. Coping with Stress	Kahana and Kahana (1975)	V1.4.I.b
II.	Hypothetical Problems		
	a. Defense Mechanism Inventory	Gleser and Ihilievich (1969)	Copyrighted
	b. ECRC Coping Scale	Kahana and Kahana (1975)	V1.4.II.b
	c. Stress in Life Coping Scale	Pearlin and Schooler (1976, 1978)	V1.4.II.c
	d. Geriatric Coping Schedule	Quayhagen and Chiriboga (1976); Cutler and Chiriboga (1976)	V1.4.II.d
III.	Observational Technique		
	a. VIRO	Kastenbaum and Sherwood (1972)	V1.4.III.a
IV.	Other Indexes		
	a. Geriatric Scale of Recent Life Events	Kiyak, Liang, and Kahana (1976)	V1.4.IV.a
	b. Rotter's Internal-External Locus of Control Scale	Rotter (1966)	V1.4.IV.b
	c. Modes of Adaptation Patterns Scale	Sharma (1977)	V1.4.IV.c

References

Alker, H. A. "Coping Defense and Socially Desirable Responses." *Psychological Reports,* 1968, 22: 985–88.

Bellak, L. *The T.A.T., C.A.T. and S.A.T. in Clinical use* (3rd ed.). New York: Grune and Stratton, 1975.

Brown, B. "Who Shall I Turn To?: Help Seeking Behavior among Urban Adults." Paper presented to the 29th Annual Meeting of the Gerontological Society, New York, October 13–17, 1976.

Busse, E., and E. Pfeiffer. *Behavior and Adaptation in Late Life.* Boston: Little, Brown and Company, 1969.

Butler, R. "The Facade of Chronological Age." In *Middle Age and Aging,* B. Neugarten (ed.), pp. 235–42. Chicago: University of Chicago Press, 1968.

Campbell, D. T., and D. W. Fiske. "Convergent and Discriminant Validation by the Multitrait-Multimethod Matrix." *Psychological Bulletin,* 1959, 56: 81–105.

Carp, F. "Short-term and Long-term Prediction of Adjustment to a New Environment." *Journal of Gerontology,* 1974, 29 (4): 444–53.

Chown, S. M. "Personality and Aging." In *Theory and Methods of Research on Aging,* K. W. Schaie (ed.), pp. 134–57. Morgantown, W.Va.: West Virginia University Library, 1968.

Coelho, G., E. Silber, and D. Hamburg. "Use of the Student T.A.T. to Assess Coping Behavior in Hospitalized Normal and Exceptionally Competent College Freshmen." *Perceptual and Motor Skills,* 1962, 14: 355–65.

Cutler, L., and D. Chiriboga. "Coping Processes in the Institutionalized Aged." Paper presented to the 29th Annual Meeting of the Gerontological Society, New York, October 13–17, 1976.

Erikson, E. *Childhood and Society.* New York: Norton, 1950.

Fawcett, G., D. Stonner, and H. Zepelin. "Locus of Control, Perceived Constraint, and Morale among Institutionalized Aged." Paper presented to the 29th Annual Meeting of the Gerontological Society, New York, October 13–17, 1976.

Gatz, M., O. Barbarin, F. Tyler, J. Crawford, and A. Englemen. "Individualized and Community Competence: A Study of the Successfulness of Coping Mechanism of the Aged." Unpublished manuscript, 1977.

Gleser, G., and D. Ihilievich. "An Objective Instrument for Measuring Defense Mechanisms." *Journal of Consulting and Clinical Psychology,* 1969, 33 (1): 51–60.

Goffman E. "The Characteristics of Total Institutions." *Proceedings of the Walter Reed Institute of Research, Symposium on Preventive and Social Psychiatry,* pp. 43–84. Washington, D.C.: U.S. Government Printing Office, 1957.

Goldstein, M. J. "The Relationship between Coping and Avoiding Behavior and Response to Fear-Arousing Propaganda." *Journal of Abnormal and Social Psychology,* 1959, 58: 247–52.

Goldstein, T., and D. Gutmann. "A T.A.T. Study of Navajo Aging." *Psychiatry,* 1972, 35 (4): 373–84.

Gutmann, D. L. "The Country of Old Men: Cultural Studies in the Psychology of Later Life." *Occasional Paper in Gerontology,* number 5. Ann Arbor, Mich.: Wayne State University–University of Michigan Institute of Gerontology, 1969.

Haan, N. "Proposed Model of Ego Functioning: Coping and Defense Mechanisms in Relationship in IQ Change." *Psychological Monographs,* 1963, 77 (8): 1–23.

_____. *Coping and Defending: Processes of Self-Environment Organization.* New York: Academic Press, 1977.

Hall, C., and G. Lindzey. *Theories of Personality.* New York: John Wiley and Sons, 1970.

Hamburg, D. A., G. V. Coelho, and J. E. Adams. "Coping and Adaptation: Steps toward a

Synthesis of Biological and Social Perspectives. In *Coping and Adaptation*, G. V. Coelho, D. A. Hamburg, and J. E. Adams (eds.), pp. 403–40. New York: Basic Books, 1974.

Hartman, H., E. Kris, and R. Loewenstein. "Notes on the Theory of Aggression." *Psychoanalytic Study of the Child*, 1949, 4: 9–36.

Henry, W. *The Analysis of Fantasy*. New York: John Wiley and Sons, 1956.

Kahana, B., and A. Kiyak. "The Use of Projective Tests as an Aid to Assessing Coping Styles among the Aged." Paper presented to the 29th Annual Meeting of the Gerontological Society, New York, October, 13-17, 1976.

Kahana, E. "Matching Environments to Needs of the Aged: A Conceptual Scheme." In *Late Life: Recent Developments in the Sociology of Aging*, J. Gubruim (ed.), pp. 201–14. Springfield, Ill.: Charles C. Thomas, 1975.

Kahana, E., and B. Felton. "Continuity and Change in Coping Strategies in a Longitudinal Analysis." Paper presented to the 29th Annual Meeting of the Gerontological Society, New York, October 13-17, 1976.

Kahana, E., and B. Kahana. "Changes in Mental Status of Elderly Patients in Age-Integrated and Age-Segregated Hospital Milieus." *Journal of Abnormal Psychology*, 1970, 75 (2): 177–81.

———. "Strategies of Adaptation to Noncongruent Environments." Paper given at the 26th Annual Meeting of the Gerontological Society, Miami Beach, November 5-9, 1973.

———. *Strategies of Coping in Institutional Environments*. Summary progress report, NIH grant number MH24959-02, 1977.

———. *Strategies of Coping in Institutional Environments*. Summary progress report, NIH grant number MH24959-03, 1978.

———. *Strategies of Coping in Institutional Environments*. Final progress report, NIH grant number MH24959-04, 1979.

Kahana, E., J. Liang, B. Felton, T. Fairchild, and Z. Harel. "Perspectives of Aged on Victimization, 'Ageism' and Their Problems in Urban Society." *The Gerontologist*, 1977, 17 (2): 121–29.

Kastenbaum R., and S. Sherwood. "VIRO: A Scale for Assessing the Interview Behavior of Elderly People." In *Research Planning and Action for the Elderly*, D. Kent, R. Kastenbaum, and S. Sherwood (eds.), pp. 166–200. New York: Behavioral Publications, 1972.

Kates, W. R. "Coping Flexibility and Adaptation." Unpublished manuscript, Committee on Human Development, University of Chicago, 1977.

Kiyak A., J. Liang, and E. Kahana. "A Methodological Inquiry into the Schedule of Recent Life Events." Paper presented to the Meetings of the American Psychological Association, Washington, D.C., August 1976.

Lawton, M. P. "The Philadelphia Geriatric Center Morale Scale: A Revision." *Journal of Gerontology*, 1975, 30 (1): 85–89.

Lawton, M. P., and L. Nahemow. "Ecology and the Aging Process." In *Psychology of Adult Development and of Aging*, C. Eisdorfer and M. P. Lawton (eds.), pp. 619–74. Washington D. C.: American Psychological Association Publications, 1973.

Lazarus, R., J. Averill, and E. Opton. "The Psychology of Coping: Issues of Research and Assessment." In *Coping and Adaptation*, G. V. Coelho et al. (eds.), pp. 249–315. New York: Basic Books, 1974.

Lewin, K. *A Dynamic Theory of Personality*. New York: McGraw-Hill, 1935.

Lieberman, M. "Institutionalization of the Aged: Effects on Behavior." *Journal of Gerontology*, 1969, 24: 330–39.

Lieberman, M., and B. Cohler. *Constructing Personality Measures for Older People*. Final report, AoA grant number 93-P-57425/5, 1976.

Lowenthal, M. F. "Intentionality: Toward a Framework for the Study of Adaptation in Adulthood." *Aging and Human Development*, 1971, 2: 79–95.

Lowenthal, M. F., M. Thurnher, and D. Chiriboga. *Four Stages of Life*. San Francisco: Jossey-Bass, 1975.

Mechanic, D. "Social Structure and Personal Adaptation: Some Neglected Dimensions." In *Coping and Adaptation*, G. V. Coelho et al. (eds.), pp. 32–44. New York: Basic Books, 1974.

Merton, R. K. (ed.). *Social Theory and Social Structure*. New York: Free Press, 1937.

Moos, R. "Psychological Techniques in the Assessment of Adaptive Behavior." In *Coping and Adaptation*, G. V. Coelho et al. (eds.), pp. 334–99. New York: Basic Books, 1974.

_____. *Evaluation Treatment Environments: A Social Ecological Approach*. New York: John Wiley and Sons, 1979.

Neugarten, B. "A Developmental View of Personality Change over Adult Years." In *Relations of Development and Aging*, J. E. Birren (ed.), pp. 176–208. Springfield, Ill.: Charles C. Thomas, 1964.

_____. "Personality and Aging." In *Handbook of the Psychology of Aging*, J. E. Birren and K. W. Schaie (eds.), pp. 626–49. New York: Van Nostrand Reinhold, 1977.

Palmore, E. *Normal Aging*. Durham, N.C.: Duke University Press, 1970.

Pearlin, L., and C. Schooler. "The Structure of Coping." *Journal of Health and Social Behavior*, 1978, 19: 2–21.

Pincus, A. "The Definition and Measurement of the Institutional Environment in Homes for the Aged." *The Gerontologist*, 1968, 8: 207–10.

Quayhagen, M. P., and D. Chiriboga. "Geriatric Coping Schedule: Potential and Problems." Paper presented to the 29th Annual Meeting of the Gerontological Society, New York, October 13–17, 1976.

Quayhagen, M. P., and M. Quayhagen. "Discrepant Assessment of Institutionalized Older Adults." Paper Presented at the 31st Annual Meeting of the Gerontological Society, Dallas, November 16–20, 1978.

Reichard, S., F. Livson, and P. G. Peterson. *Aging and Personality: A Study of Eighty-Seven Older Men*. New York: John Wiley and Sons, 1962.

Robbins, R. R., and R. H. Tanck. "A Factor Analysis of Coping Behaviors." *Journal of Animal Psychology*, 1978, 34: 379–80.

Rotter, J. B. "Generalized Expectancies for Internal versus External Control of Reinforcement." *Psychological Monographs*, 1966, 80 (whole number 609).

Schaie, K. W., and B. W. Marquette. "Personality in Maturity and Old Age." In *Multivariate Personality Research: Contributions to the Understanding of Personality in Honor of Raymond Cattell*, R. M. Dreger (ed.), pp. 612–32. Baton Rouge, La.: Calitor's Publishing, 1972.

Schaie, K. W., and J. P. Schaie. "Clinical Assessment and Aging." In *Handbook of the Psychology of Aging*, J. E. Birren and K. W. Schaie (eds.), pp. 692–723. New York: Van Nostrand Reinhold, 1977.

Schroder, H., M. Driver, and S. Streufert. *Human Information Processing*. New York: Holt, Rinehart and Winston, 1967.

Sharma, S., and E. Kahana. "Sex Differences in Adaptation Patterns of Urban Aged." Paper presented to the Meeting of the Society for the Study of Social Problems, Chicago, August 1977.

Sidle, A., J. Moos, J. Adams, and P. Cady. "Development of a Coping Scale." *Archives of General Psychiatry*, 1969, 20: 226–32.

Stephens, B. J. "Loners, Losers, and Lovers: A Sociological Study of the Aged Tenants of a Slum Hotel." Ph.D. dissertation, Wayne State University, 1973.

Wiener, M., B. Carpenter, and J. Carpenter. "Determination of Defense Mechanisms for Conflict Areas from Verbal Material." *Journal of Consulting Psychology*, 1956, 20 (3): 215–19.

White, R. "Motivation Reconsidered: The Concept of Competence." *Psychological Review,* 1959, 66: 297–333.

_____. "Strategies of Adaptation: An Attempt at Systematic Description." In *Coping and Adaptation,* G. V. Coelho et al. (eds.), pp. 47–68. New York: Basic Books, 1974.

Wiener, M., B. Carpenter, and J. Carpenter. "Determination of Defense Mechanisms for Conflict Areas from Verbal Material." *Journal of Consulting Psychology,* 1956, 20: 215–19.

Wolk, R. L., and R. B. Wolk. *The Gerontological Apperception Test.* New York: Behavioral Publications, 1971.

Abstracts

EGO STYLES (TAT)
D. L. Gutmann, 1964

Definition of Variable

The instrument attempts to measure three styles of coping with the environment: (1) active, an assertive and active approach to coping with the environment; (2) passive, an approach characterized by withdrawal from aggressiveness and self-assertiveness, and (3) magical, an approach characterized by gross misinterpretations and distortions of stimuli that reflect misperceptions of the environment and ego regression. Although this measure was originally designed as an index of psychological disengagement, it is clearly a measure of environmental coping styles and adaptational ability (Gutmann, 1976).

Description of Instrument

Depending on the study he is undertaking, Gutmann uses a combination of different TAT cards, which include some of the original Murray test cards (numbers 1, 2, 6, 7BM, 10, and 17BM) and cards specially constructed to suit the cultural group to which the test is being administered. The number of cards varies from one study to the next.

Method of Administration

The test is administered according to TAT instructions. The subject is presented with one card at a time and is asked to make up a story with a beginning, a middle, and an end. The story is recorded verbatim and rated for mode of mastery.

Context of Development and Subsequent Use

This measure was developed as part of the Kansas City studies for assessment of psychological disengagement (Havighurst, Neugarten, and Tobin, 1968). Gutmann has applied this measure to other cultural groups and has demonstrated cross-cultural consistency regarding the hypothesis that universal sequences of processes and events intrinsic to the biopsychology of adult development exist and are in part independent of cultural, ecological, and social variables.

Samples

The sample sizes vary somewhat according to the cards administered. Table 4-2 presents general data from several studies.

TABLE 4-2
Makeup of Ego Styles Samples

Researcher	Sample Size	Percentage Male	Age Range	Location
Havighurst, Neugarten, and Tobin, 1968	137	53.3	50-70	Kansas City
Gutmann, 1966	62	100	35-60+	Maya Lowland
Gutmann, 1966	42	100	35-60+	Maya Highland
Goldstein and Gutmann, 1972	81	100	35-60+	Navajo
Gutmann, 1976	128	100	55-60+	Druze

Scoring, Scale Norms, and Distribution

Each card is scored as eliciting one of the three forms of mastery. Gutmann (1969) reviewed the Kansas City, Mayan, and Navajo data and presented detailed norms on three TAT cards: (1) rope climber card (Murray), (2) heterosexual card (Murray), and (3) desert scene card (specially constructed). Data for the rope climber and heterosexual cards are also available for the Druze sample (Gutmann, 1976, pp. 96-98).

The system of scoring active, passive, and magical modes of coping can be applied to any TAT-generated story. No combined score for an aggregate of cards has been developed.

Formal Tests of Reliability

Reliabilities among coders (on the Navajo data) based on percentage agreement for each card are as follows: rope climber scene, 88%; heterosexual scene, 88%; desert scene, 75% (Goldstein and Gutmann, 1972).

Formal Tests of Validity

In the Kansas City studies, "active mastery" subjects received higher ratings on a "personal preference measure" that indicated active mastery of the environment. Additional data derived from other measures used in Gutmann's studies are congruent with findings based on the TAT-derived ego styles and reflect similar age-related changes.

Usability on Older Populations

This measure was developed specifically for use with older populations. However, it can also be applied to younger age groups, thereby allowing for a life-span analysis.

Sensitivity to Age Differences

Active mastery declines with age and passive and magical mastery increase with age across all the cultures studied.

General Comments and Recommendations

This measure makes a number of important contributions to the field of adult development and aging. Findings shed light on the nature of coping processes and their variations cross-culturally and throughout the adult life cycle. Confirmation of these findings with self-reporting and behavioral measures have demonstrated the instrument's validity. Gutmann succeeded in harnessing TAT data for research purposes and providing a meaningful cross-cultural understanding of coping processes and aging. It would be useful to develop total ego-mastery scores based on several TAT cards for each individual tested.

References

Goldstein, T., and D. Gutmann. "A TAT Study of Navajo Aging." *Psychiatry*, 1972, 35(4): 373-84.

Gutmann, D. L. "An Exploration of Ego Configurations in Middle and Later Life." In

Personality in Middle and Later Life, B. L. Neugarten et al. (eds.), pp. 114–48. New York: Atherton Press, 1964.

――――. "Maya Aging—A Comparative TAT Study." *Psychiatry*, 1966, 29: 246-59.

――――. "The Country of Old Men: Cultural Studies in the Psychology of Later Life." *Occasional Papers in Gerontology*, number 5. Ann Arbor, Mich.: Wayne State University-University of Michigan, Institute of Gerontology, 1969.

――――. "Alternatives to Disengagement: The Old Men of the Highland Druze." In *Time, Roles and Self in Old Age*, J. Gubrium (ed.), pp. 88-108. New York: Human Sciences Press, 1976.

Havighurst, R., B. Neugarten, and S. Tobin. "Disengagement and Patterns of Aging." In *Middle Age and Aging*, B. L. Neugarten (ed.), pp. 161-72. Chicago: University of Chicago Press, 1968.

Instrument

This copyrighted instrument is available from Dr. David Gutmann, Institute of Psychiatry, 320 East Huron Street, Chicago, Ill. 60611.

COPING WITH STRESS
E. Kahana and B. Kahana, 1975

Definition of Variable

This sentence-completion test was designed to assess the coping behavior of an individual faced with an undesirable environment, i.e., too little or too much environmental stimulation, conflict, restrictions in affective expression, and lack of continuity between current environment and past environment.

Description of Instrument

The aim of this instrument is to measure intrapsychic, rather than behavioral, aspects of personality. Eighteen sentence stems are read to the respondent, along with instructions to complete each statement with whatever comes to mind. The time taken to respond to each item is considered to be an indication of the degree of conflict or difficulty in coping in the area suggested by the sentence.

Method of Administration

This measure can be administered in 5 to 10 minutes during individual oral interviews. It is not suitable for use in a paper-and-pencil format, since such a format would not permit assessment of response time and would reduce the spontaneity of response by allowing the respondent to reflect on the statements.

Context of Development and Subsequent Use

The sentence completions in this measure have been used to gauge coping adaptation in younger age-groups (Pollack, 1966) and to assess personality, mental health, and adjustment in older age-groups (Peck, 1959; Kahana, 1973; Carp, 1967). Some of the sentence stems from the earlier study (Kahana, 1973) were revised to assess coping with environmental incongruence in a later study of adaptation patterns (Kahana and Kahana, 1974).

Sample

The initial sample consisted of 128 elderly persons in three institutions for the elderly (Kahana, 1973). In a subsequent study, 264 elderly individuals who had recently relocated to homes or special residences for the aged were administered the revised version of the scale (Kahana and Kahana, 1974).

Scale Norms and Distribution

Five types of coping patterns were delineated and coded from content: (1) instrumental, (2) intrapsychic, (3) affective, (4) escapist, and (5) resigned helplessness. These dimensions were further subdivided into a number of coping styles on the basis of empirical data. The same coding scheme was found to be applicable to all sentence stems.

Formal Tests of Reliability

Interrater reliability indicated by coding particular responses to stems ranged from .70 to .90 for the 18 items.

Usability on Older Populations

The test was designed for use on elderly populations. The structure of the test is simple.

General Comments and Recommendations

The sentence-completion technique is a unique and potentially useful approach to measuring the intrapsychic aspects of coping behavior. The danger of social desirability biasing responses is potentially less than in self-reporting measures of a less projective nature, and the technique affords respondents an opportunity to interpret the statements in their own ways.

References

Carp, F. M. "The Applicability of an Empirical Scoring Standard for a Sentence Completion Test Administered to Two Age Groups." *Journal of Gerontology*, 1967, 22: 301-7.

Kahana, E. *Matching Environments to Needs of Aged*. Final progress report, NICHD, 1973.

Kahana, E., and B. Felton. "Continuity and Change in Coping Strategies in a Longitudinal Analysis." Paper presented to the 29th Annual Meeting of the Gerontological Society, New York, October 13-17, 1976.

Kahana, E., and B. Kahana. *Service Needs and Service Utilization of Urban Aged*. Final progress report, NIHM grant number MH21465, 1974.

_____. *Strategies of Coping in Institutional Environments*. Summary progress report, NIH grant number MH24959-02, 1978.

Kahana, E., and A. Kiyak. "Service Needs of Older Women in Urban Areas." Invited paper presented to the Cornell University Conference on Women in Midlife Crises. Ithaca, N.Y., 1976.

Peck, R. F. "Measuring the Mental Health of Normal Adults." *Genetic Psychological Monograph*, 1959, 60: 197-225.

Pollack, D. "Coping and Avoidance of Inebriated Alcoholics and Normals." *Journal of Abnormal Psychology*, 1966, 71 (6): 417-19.

Sidle, A., J. Moos, J. Adams, and P. Cady. "Development of a Coping Scale." *Archives of General Psychiatry*, 1969, 20: 226-32.

Instrument

See Instrument V1.4.I.b.

DEFENSE MECHANISM INVENTORY (DMI)
G. Gleser and D. Ihilievich, 1969

Definition of Variable

The Defense Mechanism Inventory was designed to identify various defenses used in dealing with conflicts. Five clusters of defenses are examined: (1) turning against object (TAO), (2) projection (PRO), (3) principalization (PRN), (4) turning against self (TAS), and (5) reversal (REV). The general assumption made in formulating the DMI was that the major function of defenses is to resolve conflicts between what is perceived by the individual and his or her internalized values (Gleser and Ihilievich, 1969, p. 52).

Description of Instrument

Ten stories, two for each conflict area (authority, independence, masculinity [on the male's form only] or femininity [on the female's form only], competition, and situational conflicts) are given to each subject. After reading each story, the subject is asked to respond to four questions about the types of behavior evoked by the situation described in the story: (1) proposed actual behavior, (2) impulsive behavior (in fantasy), (3) thoughts, and (4) feelings. Five possible responses representing the five defense mechanisms (i.e., the TAO, the PRO, etc.) are provided for each question. The subject is asked to indicate the reponses that are most and least characteristic of himself or herself.

Method of Administration

This test is self-administered and requires between 30 and 40 minutes to complete.

Context of Development and Subsequent Use

Although psychology's increased preoccupation with the theory of ego processes has resulted in the creation of systems for differentiating and assessing defensive and adaptive ego functioning, most such systems have not provided clear-cut criteria by which various defense mechanisms could be grouped. Furthermore, the few objective scales that have been developed to measure defenses do not seem to measure the extent to which certain defenses are employed. Faced with these problems, the authors developed the DMI for the measurement of five general defense mechanisms. Recently, Lieberman and Cohler (1976) have used an adaptation of the DMI to assess coping among 386 first- and second-generation Irish, Italian, and Polish men and women who were between the ages of 40 and 60. Kates (1977) used an instrument derived from the DMI on a subsample of 75 individuals drawn from the larger sample of Lieberman and Cohler (1976) to assess flexibility and adaptation in three hypothetical situations.

Sample

Analysis is based on three samples: 406 sophomore college students, 114 general adult subjects, and 234 psychiatric outpatients. All samples are of younger age-groups, with the average age of the groups never exceeding 32.6 years.

Scoring, Scale Norms, and Distribution

A subject marks a plus for the response most representative of his or her reaction and a minus for the one that is least representative. Answers marked with a minus sign are scored 0, unmarked responses are given the value of 1, and pluses are scored as 2. The score for any one defense can range from 0 to 80, but the sum of the scores for the five defenses must equal 200. Gleser and Ihilievich presented means and standard deviations for their three samples (1969, p. 54). College students tended to obtain higher scores on the TAO and the TAS, with lower scores being reported on the PRN and the REV (as compared to the adult sample).

Formal Tests of Reliability

Test-retest reliabilities (after a one-week interval) between the separate defense scores ranged from .85 for the PRO to .93 for the TAO; the average correlation was .89. Test-retest reliabilities after three months ranged from .69 for the PRN to .87 for the TAO, with an average correlation of .76 (Gleser and Ihilievich, 1969).

Formal Tests of Validity

Construct validity was assessed by providing three psychologists and seven social workers a list of 15 defenses and asking them to match each of the 240 responses on the DMI with one defense on the list. There was more than a 60% agreement on those responses keyed TAS, REV, and PRN, but less agreement on responses keyed TAO and PRO.

Correlations among the five DMI defenses and with many of the MMPI scales and Haan's Defense Scales were also given by the instrument's authors (1969, pp. 56–58). A sizable number of theoretically predicted correlations were noted.

Usability on Older Populations

The DMI has been used on a range of age samples and does appear suitable for at least some samples of older adults.

Sensitivity to Age Differences

Certain defense trends are correlated with age. Specifically, the TAO decreases with age and the PRN and the REV increase.

General Comments and Recommendations

This self-reporting inventory allows the researcher to infer which defenses a subject would use in a threat situation. Although this scale has been used with a variety of subjects, additional norms for the aged are still needed. The DMI may be an especially useful instrument for use in conjunction with more behaviorally oriented measures of coping and adaptation. Its value lies in its being nested in a widely used body of theory.

References

Gleser, G., and D. Ihilievich. "An Objective Instrument for Measuring Defense Mechanisms." *Journal of Consulting and Clinical Psychology,* 1969, 33 (1): 51–60.

Haan, N. *Coping and Defending: Process of Self-Environment Organization.* New York: Academic Press, 1977.

Kates, W. R. "Coping Flexibility and Adaptation." Unpublished manuscript, Committee on Human Development, University of Chicago, 1977.

Lieberman, M., and B. Cohler. *Constructing Personality Measures for Older People.* Final report, AoA grant number 93-P-57425/5, 1976.

Instrument

See Gleser and Ihilievich, 1969.

ELDERLY CARE RESEARCH CENTER (ECRC) COPING SCALE
E. Kahana and B. Kahana, 1975

Definition of Variable

Coping strategies have to do with an individual's predisposition to responding in a particular way to problems or stress situations or to mismatches between personal preferences and environmental characteristics. Coping is seen as a reflection of the process of dealing with stress, rather than as an index of the effectiveness of responses.

Description of Instrument

This scale was designed to measure a range of coping strategies that can be used by older people. The scale consists of 23 coping strategies: 10 items modified from the coping scale of Sidle and associates (1969) and the remaining 13 items designed to reflect more fully the range of coping behavior exhibited by older people in response to environmental incongruence. Respondents were asked to rate on a four-point scale how likely they would be to use each of the 23 strategies on the list. Each individual may endorse several coping strategies. In this way the scale provides an index of the variety and range of coping strategies used by individuals.

Method of Administration

The items on the scale are read to the respondent during the course of an oral interview. The scale requires approximately 15 minutes to complete.

Context of Development and Subsequent Use

Originally developed by Sidle and associates (1969) for use in assessing the coping strategies of college students, this measure is one of the few coping instruments that has any documentation of its methodological characteristics. The Kahana and Kahana (1975) modification was developed for use on older populations. The scale was expanded and modified to include 23 coping strategies that were applicable to the elderly, and the response range was reduced to a four-point scale. The modification has been used as part of a multimethod assessment of coping in a longitudinal study of adaptation to institutionalization by older persons. Predisposition toward different types of coping was considered to be a predictor of psychosocial well-being and survival following relocation to various homes for the aged.

Sample

A sample of 250 elderly persons was administered the questionnaire shortly before their relocation from the community to a home for the aged. The instrument was readministered to 160 individuals three months after their relocation.

Scoring, Scale Norms, and Distribution

Scoring is done through the simple summation of the items loading on each of three factors. Factor 1 (instrumental strategies) is composed of items 1, 2, 6, 8, and 18. Factor 2 (affective strategies) can be further delineated into aggressive (items 16 and 17) and passive (items 7, 12, 14) factors, and it can be scored as one or two scales. Factor 3 (diversionary or escape strategies) is composed of items 5, 10, 11, 15, and 23 (Kahana and Kahana, 1978).

Item means and standard deviations for two time periods are reported with the instrument. In general, respondents tend to endorse items describing positive, constructive, and instrumental behaviors (Kahana and Felton, 1976). The least frequently endorsed strategies are affective ones.

Formal Tests of Reliability

Test-retest reliability (after a one-week interval) was estimated in a sample of 23 residents of a home for the aged and 31 college students. Item correlations over time ranged from .28 to .88, with only five of the items having correlations below .50.

The factor analysis of these items provides some evidence of internal consistency, although the factor structure is somewhat unstable. For example, item 2 (talk about problem) *does not* load on the instrumental factor at time 1, but it does at time 2. Factor loadings that increased over time by at least .30 were noted for items 2, 6, and 17, while a decrease of .30 or more was noted for item 7 (Kahana and Kahana, 1978).

Cronbach's alpha was estimated for the three factor-analysis-based scales. Estimates of internal consistency are—instrumental: time 1, .713; time 2, .679; affective: time 1, .658; time 2, .563; and escape: time 1, .591; time 2, .546 (Kahana and Kahana, 1979).

Usability on Older Populations

The scale was designed specifically for use with older populations. The response range was reduced to a four-point scale to facilitate this use.

General Comments and Recommendations

This coping scale seems to be a useful instrument for assessing the range of coping strategies employed by older people, but it requires further use. Additional data on the reliability and validity of this instrument, together with further examination of its factor structure, are needed. Finally, it should be noted that this index has not been used in a situation-specific manner and does not permit measurement of the different coping strategies that may be used in response to different stressful situations.

References

Kahana, E., and B. Felton. "Continuity and Change in Coping Strategies in a Longitudinal

Analysis." Paper presented to the 29th Annual Meeting of the Gerontological Society, New York, October 13–17, 1976.

Kahana, E., and B. Kahana. *Strategies of Coping in Institutional Environments.* Summary progress report, NIH grant number MH24959-02, 1977.

———. *Strategies of Coping in Institutional Environments.* Summary progress report, NIH grant number MH24959-03, 1978.

———. *Strategies of Coping in Institutional Environments.* Final progress report, NIH grant number MH24959-04, 1979.

Sidle, A., J. Moos, J. Adams, and P. Cady. "Development of a Coping Scale." *Archives of General Psychiatry,* 1969, 20: 226–32.

Instrument

See Instrument V1.4.II.b.

STRESS IN LIFE COPING SCALE
L. Pearlin and C. Schooler, 1976, 1978a

Definition of Variable

Coping responses are the specific behaviors, cognitions, and perceptions in which people engage when they are actually contending with their daily problems, and they include any response to external strain that serves to prevent, control, or avoid emotional distress.

Description of Instrument

The scale consists of structured questions about the diverse coping strategies used in response to conflicts and frustrations in four social role areas: marriage, parenthood, household economics, and occupation. Factor analyses yielded 19 factors that can be placed into three categories: (1) those that change the situation out of which stressful experiences arise, (2) those that control the meaning of the stressful experience after it occurs but before stress emerges, and (3) those that control stress itself after it has emerged.

Method of Administration

The coping scale is administered as part of a larger interview schedule that examines the impact of psychological resources, strain, and coping responses upon stress.

Context of Development and Subsequent Use

This instrument was developed in the context of a large-scale investigation into the social origins of personal stress. During the course of open-ended interviews, over 100 subjects were asked to identify the daily problems they faced and to describe how they attempted to deal with these problems. Thematic examination of these interview materials suggested a number of coping patterns for which questions were developed, tested, and standardized.

Sample

A representative cluster sample of 2,300 Chicago residents aged 18 to 65 years was drawn. The sample was almost evenly divided by gender, and 38% of the sample was aged 50 and above. Further information about the sample is presented by Pearlin and Lieberman (1979, pp. 223–24).

Scoring, Scale Norms, and Distribution

Several scoring systems are available. The 19 coping response factors can each be scored by weighting the standardized item score by its factor loading and then summing (see the instrument). Scores within role areas (i.e., marriage, parenthood, household economics, and occupation) can then be computed by simply summing the factor scores for each role. No other data are available regarding the distributions of these measures.

Formal Tests of Reliability

Although no direct tests are available, the relatively strong factor loadings suggest internal consistency. (See Pearlin and Schooler, 1978a, or the appended instrument for a list of the factor loadings.)

Usability on Older Populations

Although this scale was not specifically developed for use with older populations, the original study did include middle-aged subjects. The difficulty of the items does not preclude the use of the scale with older persons, although the content of the items on work roles and parenting of young children may not be suitable for many older persons.

Sensitivity to Age Differences

Age-related differences in coping styles have been reported by Pearlin and Schooler (1978a). Younger subjects were found to be more self-denigrating, and they were also found to be more likely to express a sense of modesty. In coping with marital problems, the younger subjects were more likely to seek advice and to engage in emotional discharge, while older subjects were more likely to use selective avoidance. The authors have concluded that, in spite of there being substantial relationships between age and coping, neither the younger nor the older subjects appeared to have had any overall advantage in coping effectiveness.

General Comments and Recommendations

This scale represents one of the few sociological approaches to the measurement of coping. Clearly, additional data need to be collected, and attention needs to be given to reliability, validity, stability of factor structure, and norms.

Readers are advised to examine the erratum note of Pearlin and Schooler (1978b) regarding the magnitude of beta weights in the original article (1976). Furthermore, Marshall (1979) has questioned the isomorphism of the conceptual model of stress with the model actually tested and suggests that several interactions are pertinent. Pearlin and Schooler (1979) have confirmed the fact that some interactions are statistically significant, but they noted that no more than 2% of the remaining variance can be explained by adding interaction terms. Gore (1979) questioned the causal ordering implicit in the analyzed model and also questioned the gender differences in coping noted in the data (by suggesting that they are socioeconomic effects). Gender differences remain, however, when education, income, and occupational status are controlled (Pearlin and Schooler, 1979). Longitudinal data are being brought to bear on the issue of causal ordering.

Finally, it should be noted that this scale was developed from the assumption that coping responses must be distinguished from psychological resources for coping and that coping behavior needs to be identified in daily problems rather than in somewhat unusual experiences.

References

Gore, S. "Does Help-Seeking Increase Psychological Distress?" *Journal of Health and Social Behavior*, 1979, 20: 201–2.

Marshall, J. R. "Stress, Strain, and Coping." *Journal of Health and Social Behavior*, 1979, 20: 200–201.

Pearlin, L., and M. A. Lieberman. "Social Sources of Emotional Distress." In *Research in Community and Mental Health* (vol. 1), R. Simmons (ed.), pp. 217–48. Greenwich, Conn.: Jai Press, 1979.

Pearlin, L., and C. Schooler. *The Structure of Coping*. Bethesda, Md.: National Institute of Mental Health, 1976.

———. "The Structure of Coping." *Journal of Health and Social Behavior*, 1978a, 19: 2–21.

———. "The Structure of Coping: Erratum." *Journal of Health and Social Behavior*, 1978b, 19: 237.

————. "Some Extensions of 'The Structure of Coping.'" *Journal of Health and Social Behavior*, 1979, 20: 202-5.

Instrument

See Instrument V1.4.II.c.

GERIATRIC COPING SCHEDULE
M. P. Quayhagen and D. Chiriboga, 1976; L. Cutler and D. Chiriboga, 1976

Definition of Variable

This schedule elicits older persons' coping responses to stressful situations that represent loss or threat in five main areas: health, finances, competency, self-concept, and interpersonal relations. Actions and emotions are measured with this procedure.

Description of Instrument

Twelve descriptions of stressful situations representing loss or threat in five areas are read to the subject. The questions describe problems typical of a congregate living situation. The respondent is asked to describe how he or she would have felt in this situation and what he or she would have done. The respondent is also asked to select from a list of 24 emotions the one emotion that best describes how he or she would feel about the situation. Eleven coping strategy statements (10 of which were adapted from Sidle et al., 1969) are then read to the respondent, with the respondent asked to give Likert-type responses ranging from always to never for each item. Finally, the subject is asked a final open-ended question relating to how a person generally handles stress.

Method of Administration

The schedule is administered in an interview format.

Context of Development and Subsequent Use

The Geriatric Coping Schedule was developed to identify and measure the action patterns and emotional responses of older adults during the coping process, and it uses the hypothetical-problem and strategy-statement techniques to elicit responses. In a recent study by Cutler and Chiriboga (1976), the Geriatric Coping Schedule was used to measure the coping process of 15 institutionalized aged males.

Sample

Pilot work with the coping scale was done with 15 adults over 60 years of age. The final form was administered to 25 men and 65 women over 60 years of age (mean 77.4 years). All the subjects had been institutionalized less than 4 months (mean 2.5 months) and had varying degrees of physical impairment, but they were basically stable mentally.

Scoring, Scale Norms, and Distribution

The response weights of the structured coping items (items 13a-13k) are summed to produce a total score. The hypothetical-problems section (items 1-12) is coded for the frequency of appearance of selected themes and emotions within the stories. No data are given regarding the distribution of scores for the specific questions in this scale.

Formal Tests of Reliability

A retest using a subsample of 20 indicated greater consistency over time for action responses ($r = .65$) than for emotional responses ($r = .36$).

Formal Tests of Validity

During the development of this measure, 14 hypothetical-problem situations were submitted to a panel of five gerontologists, who agreed that 13 of the 14 were major stresses encountered by adults. During a pilot study of 15 adults over age 60, two of the situations were eliminated because they failed to elicit variation in response; this left 12 hypothetical-problems.

Usability on Older Populations

The schedule was developed for use with older populations, and, although it has been used only with institutionalized samples thus far, no problems have been reported.

Sensitivity to Age Differences

Analysis of variance with Duncan "a posteriori contrast" indicated significant age and sex differences in selected coping strategies (Quayhagen and Chiriboga, 1976, p. 8).

General Comments and Recommendations

This appears to be a good schedule for measuring coping responses. The Quayhagen, Chiriboga, and Cutler schedule deserves further study, especially with regard to its validity. Use with noninstitutionalized samples is recommended.

References

Cutler, L., and D. Chiriboga. "Coping Processes in the Instituticnalized Aged." Paper presented to the 29th Annual Meeting of the Gerontological Society, New York, October 13-17, 1976.

Quayhagen, M. P., and D. Chiriboga. "Geriatric Coping Schedule: Potential and Problems." Paper presented to the 29th Annual Meeting of the Gerontological Society, New York, October 13-17, 1976.

Sidle, A., J. Moos, J. Adams, and P. Cady. "Development of a Coping Scale." *Archives of General Psychiatry*, 1969, 20: 226-32.

Instrument

See Instrument V1.4.II.d.

VIRO (Vigor, Intactness, Relationship, Orientation)
R. Kastenbaum and S. Sherwood, 1972

Definition of Variable

The VIRO measures four dimensions of interview behavior: (1) vigor is the energy level manifested during the course of the interview; (2) intactness refers to the subject's cognitive functioning with respect to socially appropriate behavior; (3) relationship refers to the subject's level and style of interacting with the interviewer; and (4) orientation is a measure of cognitive functioning assessed by the subject's questioning of time, place, and interview content (Kastenbaum and Sherwood, 1972, p. 181). Although the focus of the scale is not directly on coping, many of the behaviors assessed are related to this concept.

Description of Instrument

The instrument includes 21 items scored on a four-point scale; 20 of these items are used in the four VIRO dimensions. VIRO is an observational procedure requiring an interviewer's ratings for all dimensions except orientation, which is assessed through direct questioning.

Method of Administration

This observational procedure can be included as part of any interview situation. Some VIRO items are rated within the first 60 seconds of the interview, but most items are rated on the basis of what transpires during the whole interview (with the exception of the orientation subscale).

Context of Development and Subsequent Use

The investigators have argued that both the substantive questions within the interview and the interview itself generate relevant data. The interview process allows researchers to capture data pertaining to interpersonal transactions. During the course of the development of the VIRO, a variety of scales and rating procedures that had been developed and applied in previous geriatric studies at the Cushing Geriatric Hospital in Massachusetts were used as background.

Sample

The VIRO was first used at Cushing Hospital and at the Hebrew Rehabilitation Center for the Aged (Boston) with numerous subgroups (Slater and Kastenbaum, 1966; Kastenbaum, 1964, 1966). The instrument was used to assess ethnic elderly hospitalized patients during a psychologically oriented interview. In addition, the VIRO scale was incorporated into several studies conducted by Kahana (1974), with a sample of 302 community-dwelling older persons.

Scoring, Scale Norms, and Distribution

The scale score for each VIRO dimension is the simple sum of interviewer-recorded items. High scores represent socially valued responses, and each item contributes to only one dimension. (See the instrument for exact scoring.) Profile analysis is possible by transforming the scores into a 30-point scale (Kastenbaum and Sherwood, 1972, p. 188). No information concerning distribution of sample responses for the scale is given.

Formal Tests of Validity

The authors report significant correlations between the four VIRO dimensions and functional health status, life patterns, and ratings of psychological status made by an interdisciplinary team of clinicians.

Significant correlations were found among the four VIRO dimensions, with the correlations between vigor and relationships ($r = .456$) and vigor and intactness ($r = .615$) stronger than that between vigor and orientation ($r = .366$).

Usability on Older Populations

Because this scale is based on an interviewer's observations and since it was developed to be used in a wide range of situations, it appears suitable for all age populations. It appears to be particularly valuable as a research tool for use with older impaired subjects.

General Comments and Recommendations

The VIRO appears to be a worthwhile instrument for the assessment of a previously neglected aspect of the interview process. The VIRO is currently being improved as it is used in more interview situations. Issues such as validity and reliability between interviewers should be explored. The VIRO fills a void in gerontological research and is unique, when compared to many other instruments, in that its dimensions can be assessed repeatedly.

References

Kahana, E. *The Role of Homes for the Aged in Meeting Community Needs*. Final progress report, NIMH 7R01 MH21465, 1974.

Kastenbaum, R. "Multiple Personality in Later Life—A Developmental Interpretation." *The Gerontologist*, 1964, 4: 68-71.

———. "Developmental-Field Theory and the Aged Person's Inner Experience." *The Gerontologist*, 1966, 6: 10-13.

Kastenbaum, R., and S. Sherwood. "VIRO: A Scale for Assessing the Interview Behavior of Elderly People." In *Research Planning and Action for the Elderly*, D. Kent, R. Kastenbaum, and S. Sherwood, (eds.), pp. 166-200. New York: Behavioral Publications, 1972.

Slater, P. E., and R. Kastenbaum. "Paradoxical Effects of Drugs: Some Personality and Ethnic Correlates." *Journal of the American Geriatrics Association*, 1966, 14: 1016-34.

Instrument

See Instrument V1.4.III.a.

THE GERIATRIC SCALE OF RECENT LIFE EVENTS
A. Kiyak, J. Liang, and E. Kahana, 1976

Definition of Variable

This scale is intended to measure the amount of stress, or readjustment, that results from various life events. Both the degree of readjustment and the length of time necessary to accommodate to a life event (regardless of the desirability of the event [Holmes and Masuda, 1974]) are seen as important in social readjustment.

Description of Instrument

Of the 55 items on this scale, 23 were taken directly from the Holmes and Rahe (1967) Social Readjustment Rating Scale (SRRS) and another 6 were split into 2 items (e.g., "change in health of a family member" was split into "decline in health" and "improvement in health") and 2 more were combined into 1. Additional items particularly relevant for the aged were developed from an earlier open-ended questionnaire (Kahana, Fairchild and Felton, 1976). Respondents indicate the degree of change required by a given event, as well as whether or not that event has occurred in their lives.

Method of Administration

This scale can be administered as a questionnaire or incorporated into an oral interview. The scale takes about 10 to 15 minutes for an elderly respondent to complete.

Context of Development and Subsequent Use

This study was aimed toward cross-validating stress weights for a revised SRRS (Holmes and Rahe, 1967) with two age-groups: students and elderly community residents. Readjustment scores were assigned to each event for the two samples and compared with those from previous studies. Similar rating scales have been used in studies by Muhlenkamp, Gress, and Flood (1975) and Amster and Krauss (1974).

Sample

A sample of 248 older people (60 years old and over), with a mean age of 70.8 years, comprised the elderly study group. A sample of 96 college students, with an average age of 20.8 years, provided judgments by young persons.

Scoring, Scale Norms, and Distribution

Respondents circle a number from 0 to 100 for each event, indicating the percentage of change the event would produce in an individual's usual way of life, and they also check off those events that they have experienced during the past few years.

Stress scores (weights) have been assigned to each event by a normative sample of elderly. (See the instrument.) The greater the readjustment demanded of the individual by that particular event, the greater the mean weights for that event. Mean scores for the 5 events ranged from 27.7 to 88.5 for the youths and 26.2 to 79.5 for the elderly. Standard deviations for the elderly ranged from 26 to 38. There was greater agreement among college students, with standard deviations ranging from 13 to 32. Mean readjustments for the total sample, broken down by age and gender, are included with the instrument. The total stress score is the simple sum of the stress weights for those items (events) experienced.

Formal Tests of Reliability

Pearson's correlations between the stress weights from this study and those of Holmes and Rahe (1967) ranged from .51 to .84.

Holmes and Rahe (1967) reported a Spearman's rank-order correlation of .93 between stress scores generated by the magnitude-estimation technique and those derived from paired comparisons.

Usability on Older Populations

There should be no major difficulties in applying this scale to older people. However, care must be exercised to ensure that older subjects can deal with the qualitative judgments required by magnitude estimation. Although the use of an anchor point was eliminated in the present study, occasional reference to the scale value of an anchor point may be necessary. Administration in an interview format, rather than a self-administered format, appears to be preferable with older subjects.

Sensitivity to Age Differences

It has been reported that the elderly tend to use a narrower range of scores to rate life events (Muhlenkamp, Gress, and Flood, 1975; Kiyak, Liang, and Kahana, 1976). Although there are some differences beween the ratings made by older people and those made by younger people, the ratings are highly correlated (i.e., Pearsons's $r = .74$; $rho = .70$).

General Comments and Recommendations

A unidimensional conceptualization of life events and stress is used here. Further refinement, preferably with a multidimensional conceptualization, is needed. Specifically, meaningful classification of events according to the life span's developmental stages as well as to other theoretical dimensions (such as positive versus negative, internal versus external, role gain versus role loss) should be examined. However, this appears to be a useful scale for measuring the amount of stress resulting from various life events. The scale awaits further study, especially with regard to reliability and validity.

References

Amster, L. E., and H. H. Krauss. "The Relationship between Life Crises and Mental Deterioration in Old Age." *International Journal of Aging and Human Development*, 1974, 5 (1): 51-55.

Holmes, T. H., and M. Masuda. "Life Change and Illness Susceptibility." In *Stressful Life Events*, B. S. Dohrenwend and B. P. Dohrenwend (eds.), pp. 45-73. New York: John Wiley and Sons, 1974.

Holmes, T. H., and R. H. Rahe. "The Social Readjustment Rating Scale." *Journal of Psychosomatic Research*, 1967, 11: 219-25.

Kahana, E., T. Fairchild, and B. Felton. "Positive and Negative Life Events." Paper presented to the American Psychological Association Meetings, Washington, D.C., August 1976.

Kiyak, A., J. Liang, and E. Kahana. "Methodological Inquiry into the Schedule of Recent Life Events." Paper presented to the American Psychological Association Meetings, Washington, D.C., August 1976.

Muhlenkamp, A., L. D. Gress, and M. A. Flood. "Perception of Life Change Events by the Elderly." *Nursing Research*, 1975, 2 (2): 109-13.

Instrument

See Instrument V1.4.IV.a.

ROTTER'S INTERNAL-EXTERNAL LOCUS OF CONTROL SCALE (I-E SCALE)
J. B. Rotter, 1966

Definition of Variable

Rotter's theory of "generalized expectancy for internal vs. external control of reinforcement" forms the basis of this measure. When a person perceives that events are contingent on his or her own behavior, his or her belief is in internal control. Conversely, when a person believes that he or she is not the master of his or her own destiny, his or her belief is in external control. Although locus of control should not be considered to be an adaptive or coping strategy per se, it is a critical determinant of an individual's coping responses.

Description of Instrument

The instrument was designed as a 23-item forced choice test, with 6 additional filler items. The items address the respondent's beliefs about the nature of the world, i.e., expectations about how reinforcement is controlled. Internal statements are paired with external statements, and respondents choose one of the pair as indicative of their beliefs.

Method of Administration

The scale can be self-administered, or it can be used in an interview format. It takes approximately 15 minutes to complete. It is recommended that the interview format be used with older persons.

Context of Development and Subsequent Use

An excellent history of the I-E Scale can be found in Rotter's monograph (1966). A revised instrument was needed because the early multidimensional measures of locus of control (James, 1957; Phares, 1965) focused on behavioral orientation, rather than on beliefs about internality or externality, and were correlated with social desirability (e.g., correlations of .31 to .55 between the Marlowe-Crowne Social Desirability Scale and the James instrument). In subsequent use with the aged, the shorter (10-item) version has been administered more frequently. Among the aged, Kuypers (1972) has found the I-E Scale to be correlated with coping (ego functioning), personality (Q-sort), and intellectual functioning (WAIS). Palmore and Luikart (1972) and Fawcett, Stonner, and Zepelin, (1976) found a correlation between the I-E Scale and life satisfaction. A modified version of Rotter's I-E Scale was recently developed for use with the aged (Cantor, 1977). The latter scale consists of nine positively and negatively worded items with an agree-disagree response format used. (A short form of the I-E Scale was reviewed by Powers in Chapter 6 in Volume 2 on work and retirement.)

Sample

Rotter's initial sample included 575 male and 605 female Ohio State University students taking introductory psychology classes. Biserial item/total correlations were computed with 200 males and 200 females (Rotter, 1966, pp. 11–12). In addition, the Rotter I-E Scale has been used on a variety of other samples (Joe, 1971; Lefcourt, 1966, 1972; Rotter, 1966). Modified versions of the scale have been used with diverse samples of older persons. (See the references.)

Scoring, Scale Norms, and Distribution

The score is the simple sum of the number of external responses. Based on the original sample, norms for males (mean 8.15; standard deviation 3.88) and females (mean 8.42; standard deviation 4.06) are reported by Rotter (1966, p. 15), who also summarized other studies. Rotter (1971) reported more recently that the trend is toward the external end of the scale (mean 12.5).

Formal Tests of Reliability

Rotter (1966, pp. 10–14) has summarized his own tests of reliability and those of others (including Jessor, 1966). Internal consistency estimates (split-half, Spearman-Brown, and Kuder-Richardson) range from .65 to .79, depending on gender and estimation procedure. Test-retest reliabilities range from .49 (males, two-month interval) to .83 (females, one-month interval). Fawcett, Stonner, and Zepelin (1976) have reported test-retest reliability of .76 in an elderly sample. Item-total correlations range from .004 to .521, depending on item and gender (Rotter, 1966, pp. 11-12).

A factor analysis done by Mirels (1970) resulted in two dimensions: control over one's own destiny (six items loaded on this, ranging in factor loadings from .40 to .60) and impact of social-political affairs (four items loaded on this, ranging in loadings from .44 to .70). This sample included 159 males and 157 females from undergraduate psychology classes.

Formal Tests of Validity

Rotter (1966, pp. 13-14), in summarizing his own and other research, indicated that correlations of the full I-E Scale with the Marlowe-Crowne Scale range from −.12 to −.41. Correlations of individual items from the I-E Scale with the Marlowe-Crowne Scale range from −.07 to −.35. (1966, p. 10). Associations with measures of intellectual performance ranged from −.22 to .03. Ware (reported in Rotter, 1966) found a positive correlation of .24 between the I-E Scale and the Taylor Manifest Anxiety Scale.

Usability on Older Populations

Forced choice techniques apparently present no problem for elderly subjects. The shortened (10-item) version seems more suitable for an elderly population (Fawcett, Stonner, and Zepelin, 1976; Kuypers, 1972) than the more extensive original format.

Sensitivity to Age Differences

The only study that has compared I-E Scale scores between the aged and college students (Wolk and Kurtz, 1975) found greater internal control among the aged than among college populations. This conclusion was based on the norms established by Rotter (1971).

General Comments and Recommendations

The scale has been used in a large number of studies, and a complete evaluation of this work is not possible here. It should be noted that despite Rotter's attempts to improve upon earlier internal-external scales, the high face validity of items on the Rotter I-E Scale increases tendencies toward social desirability, especially with test-wise samples (e.g., college students). Finally, Robinson and Shaver (1973) have noted that, even though methodological difficulties remain to be resolved, the Rotter I-E Scale is still valuable in measuring control expectancy.

References

Cantor, M. *The Elderly in the Inner City.* New York: New York City Office for the Aging, 1977.

Fawcett, G., D. Stonner, and H. Zepelin. "Locus of Control, Perceived Constraint, and Morale among Institutionalized Aged." Paper presented to the 29th Annual Meeting of the Gerontological Society, New York, October 13-17, 1976.

James, W. "Internal vs. External Control of Reinforcement as a Basic Variable in Learning Theory." Ph.D. dissertation, Ohio State University, 1957.

Jessor, B. Personal communication. In "Generalized Expectancies for Internal vs. External Control of Reinforcement," J. B. Rotter. *Psychological Monographs,* 1966, 80 (whole number 609).

Joe, V. C. "Review of the Internal-External Control Construct as a Personality Variable." *Psychological Reports,* 1971, 28: 619-40.

Kuypers, J. A. "Internal-External Locus of Control, Ego Functioning, and Characteristics in Old Age." *The Gerontologist,* 1972, 12 (part 1): 168-73.

Lefcourt, H. M. "Internal vs. External Control of Reinforcement: A Review." *Psychological Bulletin,* 1966, 65 (4): 206-20.

———. "Recent Developments in the Study of Locus of Control." In *Progress in Experimental Personality Research* (vol. 6), B. A. Mahler (ed.), pp. 1-39. New York: Academic Press, 1972.

Minton, H. L. "Power as a Personality Construct." In *Progress in Experimental Personality Research* (vol. 4), B. A. Maher (ed.), pp. 229-67. New York: Academic Press, 1967.

Mirels, H. L. "Dimensions of Internal vs. External Locus of Control." *Journal of Consulting and Clinical Psychology*, 1970, 34: 226-38.

Palmore, E., and C. Luikart. "Health and Social Factors Related to Life Satisfaction." *Journal of Health and Social Behavior*, 1972, 13: 68-80.

Phares, E. G. "Internal-External Control as a Determinant of Amount of Social Influence Exerted." *Journal of Personality and Social Psychology*, 1965, 2: 642-47.

Robinson, J. P., and R. Shaver. *Measures of Social Psychological Attitudes.* Ann Arbor, Mich.: Survey Research Center, Institute for Social Research, 1973.

Rotter, J. B. "Generalized Expectancies for Internal vs. External Control of Reinforcement." *Psychological Monographs*, 1966, 80 (whole number 609).

_____. "Who Rules You? External and Internal Control." *Psychology Today*, 1971, 5: 37-42.

Ware, A. Personal communication. In "Generalized Expectancies for Internal vs. External Control of Reinforcement," J. B. Rotter. *Psychological Monographs*, 1966, 80 (whole number 609).

Wolk, S., and J. Kurtz. "Positive Adjustment and Involvement during Aging and Expectancy for Internal Control." *Journal of Consulting and Clinical Psychology*, 1975, 43: 173-78.

Instrument

See Instrument V1.4.IV.b.

MODES OF ADAPTATION PATTERNS SCALE
S. Sharma, 1977

Definition of Variable

This instrument conceptualizes adaptation in terms of activity and morale. Measures of these two concepts provide a descriptive typology of the modes of adaptation that have been used by elderly persons in a community setting. The conceptualization and instrument have been used to provide a descriptive typology of styles of adaptation that represents a modification of Merton's (1937) styles of adaptation.

Description of Instrument

Adaptive styles are operationalized in terms of activity in a broad range of social roles along the lines suggested by Havighurst (1969) and in terms of morale as measured by Lawton's (1975) revised morale scale. (See Chapter 5 in this volume for a review of the Lawton scale.) The activity scale is made up of subscales related to seven different social roles.

Method of Administration

Data are gathered in personal interviews.

Context of Development and Subsequent Use

This scale was derived from Merton's (1937) means and goals schema, with activity seen as the socially desired means of achieving the desired goal or morale. Three of Merton's labels—conformist, ritualist, and retreatist—seemed appropriate with the concepts used here and were retained. A fourth label, passive-contented, was added.

Sample

Three hundred and two elderly community residents, randomly chosen from voter registration lists, and 100 residents of housing facilities for the aged comprised the sample upon which the instrument was developed. The sample was chosen from two distinct neighbor-hoods—one largely Polish, the other largely Jewish.

Scoring, Scale Norms, and Distribution

The Lawton (1975) morale scale was scored through simple summation and dichotomized into low (10 or less) and high (11 through 17) morale. For the activity scale, each of seven roles (work, parent, friend, relative, neighbor, organizations, solitary activities) is scored 0 (not active) through 2 (highly active). For example, participation in none to three solitary activities is scored 0; four or five activities, scored 1; and six to ten activities, scored 2. The scores for these seven roles are then summed, yielding a measure ranging from 0 to 14. This score was dichotomized into low (0–4) and high (5–14) activity levels.

The descriptive typology of adaptation modes is produced by cross-tabulating these two dichotomized dimensions. The following results were obtained: (1) conformist (high activity–high morale), 30.6%; (2) ritualistic (high activity–low morale, 25.5%; (3) passive-contented (low activity–high morale), 19.7%; and (4) retreatist (low activity–low morale, 24.2%).

Usability on Older Populations

Activity and morale scales have been used widely with numerous populations of older people, although the combined use to measure adaptation is unique.

Sensitivity to Age Differences

There were no significant relationships with age found in a sample of older community residents.

General Comments and Recommendations

This procedure was developed with elderly persons from diverse ethnic, religious, and socioeconomic backgrounds. It would be useful to replicate the original study with other elderly populations, as well as with populations of a much wider age range, so that norms, reliability, and validity could be established. It should be noted that this scale focuses on macroadaptation, or adaptation as a total life-style; it is not an index of coping with specific situations, problems, and stresses.

References

Havighurst, R. J., B. L. Neugarten, H. Thomae, and J. Munnichs. *Adjustment to Retirement—A Cross-National Study.* Netherlands: Van Gorkum, 1969.

Lawton, M. P. "The Philadelphia Geriatric Center Morale Scale: A Revision." *Journal of Gerontology,* 1975, 30 (1): 85–89.

Merton, R. K. "Social Structure and Anomie." In *Social Theory and Social Structure,* R. K. Merton (ed.), pp. 185–260. New York: Free Press, 1937.

Sharma, S. "Adaptation Patterns of Urban and Ethnic Aged." Ph.D. dissertation, Wayne State University, 1977.

Sharma, S., and E. Kahana. "Sex Differences in Adaptation Patterns of Urban Aged." Paper presented to the Meeting of the Society for the Study of Social Problems, Chicago, August 1977.

Instrument

See Instrument V1.4.IV.c.

Instruments

V1.4.I.a
EGO STYLES
D. L. Gutmann, 1964

This copyrighted instrument is available from Dr. David Gutmann, Institute of Psychiatry, 320 East Huron St., Chicago, Ill. 60611.

V1.4.I.b
COPING WITH STRESS
E. Kahana and B. Kahana, 1975
INSTRUCTIONS

I am going to read to you the beginnings of some statements. I'd like you to finish each statement with whatever comes into your mind. There are no right or wrong answers. Let me give you an example—Suppose I read to you the statement: "On a hot day I usually . . ." and asked you to finish it, what would you say? (AFTER R MAKES A RESPONSE): "Fine. Let's try the next one."

	Reaction	Time
1. When I am lonely, I:	1.	
2. When I am being bossed around, I:	2.	
3. I would like to be:	3.	
4. When I can't show my feelings, I:	4.	
5. I look forward to:	5.	
6. When I don't have enough privacy, I:	6.	
7. For me, sex:	7.	
8. I wish:	8.	
9. When there is too much noise, I:	9.	
10. When I miss my old friends, I:	10.	
11. When I don't get enough help making tough decisions, I:	11.	
12. When I find too much disorder, I:	12.	
13. When I have to stay in one place, I:	13.	
14. When I don't have enough time to think things over, I:	14.	
15. When there are too many people around, I:	15.	
16. When I am with people who are too much like me, I:	16.	
17. When people around me get too emotional, I:	17.	
18. When things are too quiet, I:	18.	

SOURCE: E. Kahana and B. Kahana, *Strategies of Coping in Institutional Environments.* Summary Progress Report, NIH, 1978. Reprinted by permission.

V1.4.II.a
DEFENSE MECHANISM INVENTORY
G. Gleser and D. Ihilievich, 1969

See Gleser and Ihilievich, 1969.

V1.4.II.b
ECRC COPING SCALE
E. Kahana and B. Kahana, 1975
COPING SCALE

Suppose a Mr. Green just celebrated his 70th birthday. The next morning he finds out that his house will be demolished to make way for a new highway. He is going to have to move. He may have different reactions to this situation. How would you deal with this problem if it happened to you?

			Time 1[a] $\bar{X}$ (s.d.)	Time 2[a] $\bar{X}$ (s.d.)
		Now I will ask you how likely you would be to use a number of other ways of dealing with the situation. (SHOW CARD) How likely would you be to:		
(Sidle #1)	1.	Find out more about the situation, get additional information?	3.23 (0.98)	3.21 (0.98)
(Sidle #2)	2.	How likely are you to talk with others about the problem?	3.08 (0.97)	3.12 (1.03)
(Sidle #3)	3.	How likely are you to try to see the humorous aspects of the situation?	2.48 (1.16)	2.40 (1.15)
(Sidle #4)	4.	How likely are you not to worry about it? Thinking everything will work out fine.	2.45 (1.11)	2.47 (1.16)
(Sidle #5)	5.	How likely are you to become involved in other activities to keep your mind off the problem?	2.71 (1.08)	2.50 (1.07)
(Sidle #6)	6.	How likely are you to take some positive action on the basis of your present understanding of the situation?	3.00 (1.05)	3.01 (1.02)
(Sidle #7)	7.	How likely are you to expect the worst?	2.29 (1.12)	2.32 (1.10)
(Sidle #8)	8.	How likely are you to make several alternate plans for handling the situation? After all, you never know which might work.	2.75 (1.01)	2.59 (1.06)
(Sidle #9)	9.	How likely are you to draw on your past experience? (Perhaps you have been in a similar situation before).	2.89 (1.05)	2.89 (1.08)
(Sidle #10)	10.	How likely are you to try to reduce tension, for example by drinking, smoking, eating, or exercising more?	1.73 (1.09)	1.90[b] (1.13)
	11.	How likely are you to think of new goals and forget about problems?	2.61 (1.08)	2.53 (1.02)
	12.	How likely are you to feel lost and confused about what to do next (as if in a daze)?	2.19 (1.06)	2.05 (1.05)

13.	How likely are you to stick to yourself? Stay away from friends and family?	2.06 (1.20)	2.04 (1.18)
14.	How likely are you to have a good cry and feel better?	2.25 (1.17)	2.26 (1.15)
15.	How likely are you to go out for a while to forget about the problem?	2.63 (1.17)	2.57 (1.06)
16.	How likely are you to become angry and irritable toward everyone around you?	1.69 (0.88)	1.76 (0.90)
17.	How likely are you to feel bitter, blame others for the problem?	1.61 (0.89)	1.66 (0.85)
18.	How likely are you to do something definite to deal with the situation?	2.99 (0.96)	2.93 (0.99)
19.	How likely are you to get together with other people who have the same problem?	2.47 (1.14)	2.68[b] (1.01)
20.	How likely are you to complain to the people in charge of the situation?	2.43 (1.11)	2.46 (1.11)
21.	How likely are you to wait and deal with the situation later?	2.35 (1.04)	2.44 (1.10)
22.	How likely are you to depend on people you can trust to deal with the problems for you?	2.97 (1.04)	2.89 (1.00)
23.	How likely are you to turn to religion or to pray?	2.98 (1.12)	3.03 (1.10)

a. Response options for all items are as follows: 1 = Not at all likely; 2 = Not very likely; 3 = Somewhat likely; and 4 = Very likely.

b. Difference between means significant at .05 level.

SOURCE: E. Kahana and B. Kahana, *Strategies of Coping in Institutional Environments*, p. 16. Summary Progress Report, NIH, 1978.

V1.4.II.c
STRESS IN LIFE COPING SCALE
L. Pearlin and C. Schooler, 1976, 1978

MARITAL COPING RESPONSES	Factor Loading[*]
Self-Reliance vs. Advice Seeking: In the past year or so, have you:	
1. Asked the advice of relatives about getting along in marriage?	.73
2. Asked for the advice of a friend or neighbor . . . ?	.72
3. Gone to a doctor, counselor, or other professional person . . . ?	.70
4. Have you read any books or magazines in recent months about getting along in marriage?	.39
Controlled Reflectiveness vs. Emotional Discharge	
1. How often do you yell or shout to let off steam?	.76
2. How often during a typical week do you find yourself thinking over marital problems?†	−.54
3. Have you read any books or magazines in recent months about getting along in marriage?†	−.44
4. How often do you keep out of your spouse's way for a while?	.38

Positive Comparisons
1. How would you compare your marriage to that of most other people like yourself? Better, the same, or less good? .76
2. With time, does your marriage get better, stay the same, or get less good? .74
3, How often do you appreciate your own marriage more after seeing what other marriages are like? .47

Negotiation: How often do you:
1. Try to find a fair compromise in marriage problems? .78
2. Sit down and talk things out . . .? .68

Self-Assertion vs. Passive Forbearance: When you have differences with your spouse, how often do you:
1. Keep out of his/her way for a while? .67
2. Give in more than halfway . . .? .67
3. Just keep hurt feelings to yourself . . .? .51

Selective Ignoring: How often do you:
1. Tell yourself that marital difficulties are not important? .77
2. Try to overlook your spouse's faults and pay attention only to good points? .63
3. Try to ignore difficulties by looking only at good things? .63
4. Keep so busy you don't have time to think? .57
5. Wait for time to remedy the difficulty? .52

PARENTAL COPING RESPONSES WITH CHILDREN AGES 16 TO 21

Selective Ignoring: How often do you:
1. Remind yourself that things could be worse? .66
2. Think that it's behavior that they will just outgrow? .63
3. Look around at other parents to see how much better off you are than they? .62
4. Tell yourself that something in your children's behavior is not really important? .56
5. Try to notice only the good things . . .? .56
6. Ignore what's going on when there is something troublesome in your children's behavior? .53
7. Decide there's nothing you can do to change things? .47

Nonpunitiveness vs. Reliance on Discipline: When your children's behavior is troublesome, how often do you:
1. Take away a privilege? .85
2. Scold them? .83
3. Threaten some kind of punishment? .83

Self-Reliance vs. Advice Seeking: In the past year or so have you:
1. Asked for the advice of friends or neighbors concerning difficulties in your children's behavior? .77
2. Asked for the advice of a relative . . .? .77
3. Asked for the advice of a doctor, teacher, or other professional person . . .? .58
4. Read any books or magazines . . .? .58

Positive Comparisons
1. As time goes by has being a parent generally become easier or more difficult? .80
2. Would you guess that in the next year or so being a parent will . . .? .70

3. How would you compare your experiences as a parent with other parents?
4. During a typical day, how often do you find that problems of being a parent are on your mind?   −.54

Exercise of Potency vs. Helpless Resignation
1. The way my children are turning out depends on their inner nature and there is little I can do about it.   .77
2. There is only so much I can do as a parent and after that I just accept my children as they are.   .72
3. How often do you decide there's really nothing you can do to change things?   .44

HOUSEHOLD ECONOMIC COPING RESPONSES

Devaluation of Money
1. When you are short of money how often do you borrow?   .65
2. During a typical week, about how much are money problems on your mind?   .57

How strongly do you agree or disagree that:
3. My money never seems to be enough for my wants?   .57
4. Financial success does not interest me?   −.52

Selective Ignoring: When you are short of money how often do you:
1. Concentrate on more important things in life?   .69
2. Notice people around who are worse off than you?   .67
3. Tell yourself that money isn't worth getting upset about?   .64
4. Accept the money pinch because there's little you can do about it?   .42

Positive Comparisons: Would you say your family income is higher, lower, or about the same as:
1. People with the same education as yours?   .74
2. Most of your friends?   .69
3. Most of your relatives?   .68
4. Most of your neighbors?   .60

Optimistic Faith
1. How do you think your standard of living will compare in a year or two to the one you have now: much better, about the same, or much worse?   .71
2. When you are short of money how often do you just sit back and wait for things to work out by themselves?   .58
3. When you are short of money how often do yout just accept the money pinch because there's little you can do about it?   .48

OCCUPATIONAL COPING RESPONSES

Substitution of Rewards: How strongly do you agree or disagree that:
1. The most important thing about my job is that it provides me the things I need in life?   .69
2. I can put up with a lot on my job as long as the pay is good?   .68
3. Time solves most problems on my job?   .58
4. I have to accept my job as it is because there's nothing I can do to change it?   .56
5. As soon as I leave work, I put it out of my mind?   .54
6. I don't really expect to get much pleasure out of work?   .39

Positive Comparisons
1. How does your work life compare with what it was about a year ago?   .80

2. When you think of the future, what would you say your work life will be like a year or so from now? .78
3. When you add up all the good and bad things about your job, how do you think it compares with the jobs of most other people you know? .58

Optimistic Action: When you have difficulties in your work situation, how often do you:
1. Take some action to get rid of them? .79
2. Talk to others to find a solution to difficulties? .73
3. Notice people who have more difficulties than you do? .50

Selective Ignoring: How often do you:
1. Just wait for difficulties to work themselves out? .77
2. Tell yourself that difficulties at work are not important to you? .72
3. Try to pay attention only to your duties in order to overlook difficulties in your work situation? .52
4. Remind yourself that for everything bad about your work situation there is also something good?

* Principal component analysis with varimax rotation.

SOURCE: L. Pearlin, personal communication, 1979.

†EDITOR'S NOTE: The loadings for these items were positive in L. Pearlin's communication with me, but they were negative in "The Structure of Coping," *Journal of Health and Social Behavior,* 1978, 19 (1): 20–21. I inserted the negative loadings based on item content.

V1.4.II.d
GERIATRIC COPING SCHEDULE
M. P. Quayhagen and D. Chiriboga, 1976;
L. Cutler and D. Chiriboga, 1976

Instructions: Now I am going to read you a series of stories dealing with situations people find themselves in. After each story, I want you to tell me how you would have felt and what you would have done. I will then show you a series of words, and ask you to select the one which most nearly describes how you feel about the situation (List of Emotions: disappointed, depressed, angry, resentful, worried, fearful, calm, frustrated, bothered, helpless, lonely, anxious, defeated, humiliated, uneasy, deadened, worthless, guilty, bored, jealous, hopeless, hateful, dissatisfied, cold.)

1.[a] Mrs. Smith was watching her favorite TV show when her roommate came in and changed the station.
2. Mr. Smith has found keeping money in the bank inconvenient. Therefore he keeps all his money in the house. One day there is a fire, and he loses his clothing, furniture, and all of his money.
3. Mr. Smith has always prided himself on his ability to handle his own affairs. His family has recently decided to take over his financial affairs because they feel he is unable to do so.
4. For many years Ann has been a close friend of Mrs. Jones. Mrs. Jones has always trusted Ann, but yesterday another friend told Mrs. Jones that Ann has been spreading rumors about her.
5. Mrs. Jones is very poor. She has lived in the same house for over 25 years. Recently the neighborhood has been going downhill. There have been several robberies in the houses nearby in the past week. Yesterday, the house next door was robbed.
6. Mrs. Jones has dangerously high blood pressure. To avoid complications, the doctor has prescribed medicine which makes her feel nauseous and dizzy.

7. Mr. Jones has always enjoyed long walks by himself. Recently, he has become lost on several occasions. His family now insists that he not go out alone.

8. Mrs. Smith had to go to the hospital for treatment of a health problem. All of her friends promised to come visit her, but it's been one week now, and no one has shown up.

9. Mrs. Jones has just come from a visit with her eye doctor. The doctor told Mrs. Jones that she has a progressive eye disease and will be totally blind in a year.

10. Mr. and Mrs. Jones were forced to move since they could no longer pay the high cost of living in the city. They have moved so far away they are unable to visit old friends or relatives.

11. Mrs. Jones, a woman in her 70s, was recently in an auto accident in which her face was disfigured. She has just learned that plastic surgery will not be completely successful.

12. Mrs. Jones has been staying at a convalescent hospital. She has a room to herself, a room she likes very much. One day the supervising nurse comes in and tells Mrs. Jones that she will have to move to a semi-private room. Mrs. Jones protests, but the nurse says that the decision has been made and walks away.

Instructions: Up to now we have been talking about specific situations, and how you might deal with them. Now I'd like to know how you think you deal with problems in general. I'm going to read you a list of ways in which people commonly deal with problems. For each one, please tell me if you think you *always* use it, *sometimes* use it, *rarely* use it, or *never* use it in handling your problems.

13. When dealing with problems in general, do you[b]

Always Sometimes Rarely Never

a. Try to find out more about the situation; seek additional information?

b. Try to see the humorous aspects of the situation?

c. Talk with others about the problem?

d. Don't worry about it. Everything will probably work out fine?

e. Become involved in other activities in order to keep your mind off the problem?

f. Take some positive concerted action on the basis of your present understanding of the situation?

g. Be prepared to expect the worst?

h. Make several alternative plans for handling the situation; after all, you never know what might work?

i. Draw upon your past experiences; perhaps you've been in a similar situation before?

j. Try to reduce the tension by drinking, eating, smoking, exercising?

k. Try to prepare for the event by going over it in your mind?

14. What other strategies or techniques do you use in dealing with stresses or distressful situations?

a. The three response categories for each of items 1 through 12 are a) "What would you have done?" b) "How would you have felt?" and c) "Selected emotion."

b. Items 13a through 13k are from Coping Scale of Sidle et al., 1969.

SOURCE: M. P. Quayhagen and D. Chiriboga. "Geriatric Coping Schedule: Potential and Problems." Paper presented to the 29th Annual Meeting of the Gerontological Society, New York, October 13–17, 1976. Reprinted by permission.

V1.4.III.a
VIRO
R. Kastenbaum and S. Sherwood, 1972
PART 1
VIRO IN PRECODED IBM CARD FORMAT

For each of the variables listed below, the interviewer is to rate the applicant in the ways specified and place the appropriate scores in the columns designated:

1. *First Impression (snapshot opinion) and Changes During Interview*

   DIRECTIONS FOR SCORING FIRST IMPRESSION AND CHANGE SCORE FOR EACH OF THE THREE VARIABLES (A, B, and C) LISTED IN SECTION I:

   Rate from 0 to 3 (four-point scale) your *first* impression and place the appropriate score in the column designated.

   Indicate in the columns designated (two columns provided for this purpose for each variable) whether or not change in this impression occurred during the interview:

   Code 00 if there was no apparent change.

   If a change occurred during the interview, code the *direction* (+ or −) in the *first column* provided and the *magnitude* (the greatest scale change occurring at any time during the interview) in the *second column* provided. Since we are starting out with a four-point scale, this change may vary from +3 (the maximum amount of positive change) to −3 (the maximum amount of negative change).

   Thus, +1, +2, +3 indicate the various degrees of possible positive change.
   −1, −2, −3 indicate the various degrees of possible negative change.

   Note: If change in both directions occurred during the interview, code only the *positive* change.

	FIRST IMPRESSION	CHANGE	SCORE
A. (3) Vigorous . . . (0) Feeble	cols. 21_____	22_____	23_____
B. (3) Receptive . . . (0) Closed	24 _____	25_____	26_____
C. (3) Comfortable . . . (0) In distress	27_____	28_____	29_____

   (Interviewer need not fill out rest of this page).

   PRESENTATION SCORE (Sum of cols. 21-29)   30_____   31_____

2. *Behavior and Attitudes Manifested During Interview*

   DIRECTIONS: Rate from 0 to 3 (four-point scale) each of the variables listed in Section 2 and place the appropriate score in the column designated.

   (For the first six variables in this section—A, B, C, D, E, and F—rate by averaging over the interview session)

		Column
col. 32 A.	(3) Quite Trustful. . . . . . .(0) Quite Suspicious	32_____
col. 33 B.	(3) High Energy Level . . . .(0) Low Energy Level	33_____
col. 34 C.	(3) Fluent Speech. . . . . . .(0) Minimal Speech	34_____
col. 35 D.	(3) Keen Attention . . . . . .(0) Poor Attention	35_____
col. 36 E.	(3) Controlled Thought . . . .(0) Tangential, Fragmented	36_____
col. 37 F.	(3) Eager Participation . . . .(0) Reluctant Participation	37_____

   (For the next three variables in this section—G, H, and I—rate according to their peak occurrence)

		Column
col. 38 G.	(3) Keen Self-Perspective. . . .(0) No Self-Perspective	38_____
col. 39 H.	(3) Engrossment in Own Ideas/Feelings. . . . . . .(0) No Self-Engrossment	39_____

col. 40 *I.* (3) Engrossed in
Relationship. . . . .(0) No Shared Engrossment   40_____

(For the last variable in this section — J — rate according to the termination phase of the interview)

col. 41 *J.* (3) Eager to Continue
Session or See Inter-
viewer Again. . . . .(0) Eager to End Session   41_____

---

cols. 42-43 INTERACTION SCORE (sum of cols. 32-41)   cols. 42_____ 43_____
(Interviewer need not fill out)

KEYING COLUMNS DIRECTIONS: At times *one* of the variables in Sections 1 and 2 appears to be most crucial in the interview. If *one* of these variables is clearly salient, the variable is to be coded on cols. 44-45 by recording the number of the column representing the variable in question. For section 1, record the column representing the FIRST IMPRESSION (col. 21 variable *A*, col. 24 for *B*, col. 27 for *C*)

Code 00 if there is no salient variable.

cols. 44-45 Keying columns (to be filled in by interviewer)   44_____ 45_____

3. *Mental Status Questions*

DIRECTIONS: For each of the items in Section 3 (A, B, C, D, E, F, G, and H), place the appropriate score in the column provided.

Column

col. 46 *A. Knows Own Age* (If other than Score 3, check direction)   46_____
SCORE: (3) Precisely; (2) Within 2 years; (1) Within 10 years; (0) Beyond 10
_____Underestimation; _____Overestimation

col. 47 *B. Knows Day of Week*   47_____
SCORE: (3) yes; (0) no

col. 48 *C. Knows Month*   48_____
SCORE: (3) yes; (0) no

col. 49 *D. Knows Year* (if other than Score 3, check direction)   49_____
SCORE: (3) Precisely; (2) Within 2 years; (1) Within 10 years; (0) Beyond 10
_____Underestimation; _____Overestimation

col. 50 *E. Knows Community*   50_____
SCORE: (3) yes; (0) no

col. 51 *F. Knows Street*   51_____
SCORE: (3) yes; (0) no

col. 52 *G. Remembers Examiner's Name*   52_____
SCORE: (3) yes; (2) partially; (0) no

col. 53 *H. Estimation of Duration of Interview* (If other than Score 3, check duration)
SCORE: (3) Within 5 min.; (2) Within 10 min.; (1) Within 20 min.; (0) More than 20 min.
_____Underestimation; _____Overestimation

(Interviewer need not fill out rest of this page)

cols. 54-55 ORIENTATION SCALE (Sum of cols. 46-53)   54_____ 55_____

col. 56 *Direction of error of A*
(1) underestimation; (2) overestimation; (0) no error   56_____

col. 57 *Direction of error of D*
(1) underestimation; (2) overestimation; (0) no error   57_____

Direction of error of H

underestimation; (2) overestimation; (0) within 5 min.   58_____

col. ~~59~~ VIGOR: Add the score in the following cols.:

    col. 21_____+ col. 33_____= _____(SUM=VIGOR RAW SCORE)   59_____

col. 60–61 RELATIONSHIP: Add the scores in the following cols.:

    col. 24_____+ col. 32_____+ col. 37_____+ col. 40_____+ col. 41_____=

                                        60_____ 61_____

  (SUM=RELATIONSHIP RAW SCORE)

cols. 62–63 INTACTNESS: Add the scores in the following cols.:

    col. 34_____+ col. 35_____+ col. 36_____+ col. 38_____+ col. 39_____=

                                        62_____ 63_____

(SUM=INTACTNESS RAW SCORE)

CHART I
Part 2
GUIDE TO RATING OF VIRO SCALES

Ratings are based on expectations of normal behavior but the highest score (3) is used to indicate normal OR supernormal reactions. Score of 0 indicates extremely negative or totally absent response.

Section I—Presentation

Ratings are made on basis of first impression. Less than one minute from time of initial contact.

A. Cols. 21-23   (3) Vigorous   (0) Feeble

                       Vitality scale—hearty handshake, impression of capacity for effective, decisive movement *vs.* flaccid tonus, impression of weak, slow, ineffective movement.

B. Cols. 24-26   (3) Receptive   (0) Closed

                       Welcoming gesture, facial expression that lights up at E's approach, implicit movements toward interviewer, impression of extending self and shortening distance between self and interviewer *vs.* no gestures or expressions that acknowledge presence of interviewer, or implicit aversive, shrinking-away movements, impression of withdrawing self and lengthening distance between self and interviewer.

C. Cols. 27-29   (3) Comfortable   (0) In Distress

                       Pained expression, moaning, writhing, awkward position or posture suggesting bodily discomfort *vs.* absence of these behaviors and general impression of being at ease, not preoccupied with body condition.

Section II—Confrontation (Interaction)

A. Col. 32   (3) Quite Trustful   (0) Quite Suspicious

                       Repeated questioning such as, "Why are you asking me these questions?" "What is this all about?" Repeated failure to answer questions adequately when there is no indication of mental incapacity or knowledge. Eyeing E as though E were on a mission of mischief *vs.* none of these behaviors.

B. Col. 33   (3) High Energy Level   (0) Low Energy Level

                       Both verbal and nonverbal behavior have a convincing intensity or power, intensity "output" is normal *vs.* mumbling, weakly-uttered speech, minimal intensity and output of behavior.

C. Col. 34   (3) Normal Fluent Speech   (0) Minimal Speech

                       Normal flow in which words are integrated into statements and statements into larger contextual units *vs.* "yes," "no," "don't know" responses, sentence fragments, lack of elaboration or stumbling bits of speech.

(Distinguish this item from energy level.)

D. Col. 35   (3) Keen Attention   (O) Poor Attention

(a) Applies to subjects at least moderately well-oriented.

Loses track of conversation, responds as though previous conversation had not taken place, seems to take no notice of changes in E's topic, intensity, personal behavior *vs.* seems to anticipate the next question, response indicates that previous conversation has registered, notices changes in E's speech or behavior.

(b) Applies to subjects who are disoriented and who may not be able to answer appropriately.

Listens attentively, watches interviewer when being questioned, tries to answer appropriately *vs.* wandering attention, seems to to be trying to answer, looks away from interviewer.

E. Col. 36   (3) Controlled Thought   (O) Tangential Thought

Maintains a frame of reference with fairly clear boundaries, context of statements is clear readily, thoughts follow in logical or reasonable sequence *vs.* conversation peppered with irrelevant statements and expressions, context of remarks not clear, takes off from mutual topic in idiosynchratic ways, "train of thought derailed."

F. Col. 37   (3) Eager Participation   (O) Reluctant Participation

Responsive to all questions and comments, spontaneous *vs.* choreful reaction to E's questions, volunteers nothing, complains about effort of responding. E must expend considerable energy of his own to extract responses from subject. (Distinguish from trustful suspicious dimension and energy level.)

G. Col. 38   (3) Keen Self-Perspective   (O) No Self-Perspective

Comments about his own role in the interview situation, expresses awareness of how he might look to others, wonders "How am I doing?" or expresses an opinion on that, divides his own experience into favorable and unfavorable, strong and weak, and other categories *vs.* no awareness that he is being interviewed, absence of all the other characteristics mentioned above labels his experiences or functioning as all good or all bad.

H. Col. 39   (3) Engrossed in Own Ideas/Feelings   (O) No Self Engrossment

Animated, "alive" when talking about his life or opinions, as shown in sparkling or intense eyes, appropriate gestures, body posture, speech patterning—may also be shown by deeply reflective, inward turning behavior, "lost in own thoughts and feelings" to such an extent that E's presence seems momentarily ignored. These are two different patterns of self-engrossment *vs.* flat, neutral, transient, "uncommitted" behavioral and expressive "commentary" when talking about his life or opinions, not "caught up" in his internal life. Talks about himself in same, rather uninvolved way he talks about most everything else.

I. Col. 40   (3) Engrossed in Relationship   (O) No Shared Engrossment

Direct eye contact, S&E meet on common ground, or in same universe of discourse, interested in E as a person, may affectionately touch E *vs.* absence of these characteristics, perhaps related to a type of self-engrossment that shuts off the relationship, gross disorientation, or impression of deciding to keep E at a distance.

J. Col. 41 (3) Eager to See Interviewer Again (O) Discontinue Session
Verbal expression of wishing interview to continue, or another contact to be made (with appropriate nonverbal commentary) *vs.* inquiring how much longer this is going to last, is this the final question, I hope I don't have to go through something like this again.

SOURCE: R. Kastenbaum and S. Sherwood. "VIRO: A Scale for Assessing the Interview Behavior of Elderly People." In *Research Planning and Action for the Elderly*, D. Kent, R. Kastenbaum and S. Sherwood (eds.), pp. 176–80. New York: Behavioral Publications, 1972. Reprinted by permission.

V1.4.IV.a
THE GERIATRIC SCALE OF RECENT LIFE EVENTS[a]
A. Kiyak, J. Liang, and E. Kahana, 1976

Directions: Please place a check mark (✓) next to each event listed below which you have personally experienced in the past 3 years.

Event	Young (n=96)	Old (n=267)	Young Men (n=11)	Young Women (n=85)	Old Men (n=58)	Old Women (n=209)	Total[b]
1. Minor Illness	27.7	26.6	16.3	28.6	26.9	25.8	27
2. Loss of Hearing/Vision	83.3	67.4	93.8	82.5	66.9	67.1	67
3. Difficulty Walking	65.6	53.5	61.2	65.9	50.4	53.8	53
4. Sexual Difficulty	61.4	37.6	80.0	59.9	56.7	34.6	37
5. Divorce	70.1	57.4	81.3	69.2	60.8	56.7	57
6. Separation	63.0	57.5	77.5	61.9	64.0	56.6	57
7. Family Member Ill	46.1	53.6	43.8	46.3	54.5	53.4	54
8. Gain New Family Member	53.4	45.5	60.0	53.0	47.0	45.2	45
9 Death of a Close Friend	66.5	47.0	72.5	66.1	41.9	48.2	47
10. Change Number of Family Get-Togethers	30.1	50.4	40.0	29.3	45.0	51.5	50
11. Personal Achievement of Family Member	30.7	45.2	36.3	30.3	42.2	45.8	45
12. Relinquish Financial Responsibility	54.3	58.6	57.5	54.0	49.3	60.5	59
13. Financial Difficulty	68.1	58.6	70.0	67.9	47.9	61.1	59
14. Change Work Hours/Conditions	48.8	38.4	36.3	49.8	45.2	36.8	38
15. Change Residence	59.3	51.3	45.0	60.4	36.4	54.3	52

Event	Young (n=96)	Old (n=267)	Young Men (n=11)	Young Women (n=85)	Old Men (n=58)	Old Women (n=209)	Total[b]
16. Sell Major Possessions	53.9	49.0	36.3	55.3	48.8	48.5	49
17. Personal Achievement	45.5	44.1	56.3	44.7	43.7	43.5	44
18. Reduce Recreation	54.4	47.3	56.3	54.2	60.6	45.3	47
19. Spouse Unfaithful	68.1	67.6	82.5	67.0	75.5	66.0	68
20. Fired from Job	71.2	57.5	85.0	70.1	52.9	58.5	57
21. Loss of Valuable Object	50.2	49.2	57.5	49.6	35.0	52.4	45
22. Child Married	51.4	43.3	51.3	51.4	47.3	52.3	43
23. Taking Large Loan	50.7	51.0	48.8	50.9	42.5	52.6	51
24. Minor Legal Violation	35.1	30.8	38.8	34.8	21.5	33.1	31
25. Trouble with Neighbors	30.6	40.9	16.3	31.8	36.1	42.0	41
26. Trouble with Social Security	53.3	54.2	58.8	52.9	42.7	57.2	54
27. Age Discrimination	60.8	53.4	81.3	59.2	30.7	37.7	53
28. Major Illness	82.3	64.9	80.7	82.6	61.8	65.5	65
29. Change in Sleep Habits	42.4	45.7	48.6	41.1	36.7	47.7	46
30. Change in Eating Habits	35.0	45.0	39.3	34.1	39.4	46.1	45
31. Menopause	41.3	45.6	46.4	40.3	54.2	44.1	46
32. Death of Spouse	88.2	79.5	92.9	87.2	66.9	81.8	79
33. Marriage	78.0	63.9	86.4	76.3	61.1	64.1	64
34. Marital Reconciliation	64.6	46.7	73.6	62.8	48.9	46.0	47
35. More Arguments with Spouse	53.9	41.6	56.4	53.4	33.7	44.0	42
36. Fewer Arguments with Spouse	34.1	35.0	39.3	33.1	27.5	37.0	35
37. Death of Family Member	76.1	66.5	72.1	76.9	75.5	63.5	66
38. Improvement in Family Member's Health	42.3	65.8	40.7	42.6	55.8	68.9	66
39. Trouble with Children	56.6	57.1	57.9	56.3	35.6	63.3	57
40. Victim of Crime	60.4	73.1	65.0	59.4	51.6	79.1	73
41. Improvement of Financial State	47.9	58.7	47.1	48.1	50.2	61.6	59

Event	Young (n=96)	Old (n=267)	Young Men (n=11)	Young Women (n=85)	Old Men (n=58)	Old Women (n=209)	Total[b]
42. Retirement	69.6	57.1	74.3	68.7	55.8	57.0	57
43. Less Church Activity	33.0	49.8	41.4	31.3	27.8	54.4	50
44. More Church Activity	36.5	40.3	37.1	36.3	38.9	40.4	40
45. More Recreation	37.3	44.0	52.9	34.1	38.9	45.7	44
46. Travel (Taking Vacation)	38.9	44.0	47.1	37.2	30.9	47.2	44
47. Stop Driving	65.8	68.5	73.6	64.1	60.5	70.1	68
48. Go to Jail	83.8	79.3	76.4	85.3	73.0	80.2	79
49. Unemployed One Month	61.7	42.9	43.6	65.4	36.6	44.9	43
50. Demotion	64.8	56.1	80.0	61.6	49.5	58.7	56
51. Promotion	54.6	63.9	62.9	52.9	52.0	67.2	64
52. Grandchild Married	30.0	26.5	37.9	28.3	19.2	29.0	26
53. Argument with Boss/Coworker	40.9	43.5	49.3	39.1	33.2	47.3	43
54. Move to Home for the Aged	83.3	74.6	82.9	83.4	72.4	75.3	75
55. Friends and Family Turn Away	88.5	68.3	90.7	88.1	59.3	71.5	68

a. Cell entries are the mean readjusted weights for each subgroup.

b. Total weight to be used in deriving the summary stress scores.

SOURCE: A. Kiyak, J. Liang, and E. Kahana. "A Methodological Inquiry into the Schedule of Recent Life Events." Paper presented to the American Psychological Association Meetings, Washington, D.C., August 1976. Reprinted by permission.

V1.4.IV.b
ROTTER'S INTERNAL-EXTERNAL LOCUS OF CONTROL SCALE
J. B. Rotter, 1966

"This test is available for use for research purposes only if the study is done by someone who is trained to give and interpret personality measures or supervised by someone who is trained to do so." (Condition stipulated by J. B. Rotter on permission to reprint this instrument.)

I more strongly believe that:

*1. a. Children get into trouble because their parents punish them too much.
   b. The trouble with most children nowadays is that their parents are too easy with them.

2. a. Many of the unhappy things in people's lives are partly due to bad luck.
   b. People's misfortunes result from the mistakes they make.

3. a. One of the major reasons why we have wars is because people don't take enough interest in politics.
   b. There will always be wars, no matter how hard people try to prevent them.

4. a. In the long run people get the respect they deserve in this world.
   b. Unfortunately, an individual's worth often passes unrecognized no matter how hard he tries.
5. a. The idea that teachers are unfair to students is nonsense.
   b. Most students don't realize the extent to which their grades are influenced by accidental happenings.
6. a. Without the right breaks one cannot be an effective leader.
   b. Capable people who fail to become leaders have not taken advantage of their opportunities.
7. a. No matter how hard you try some people just don't like you.
   b. People who can't get others to like them don't understand how to get along with others.
*8. a. Heredity plays the major role in determining one's personality.
   b. It is one's experiences in life which determine what one is like.
9. a. I have often found that what is going to happen will happen.
   b. Trusting to fate has never turned out as well for me as making a decision to take a definite course of action.
10. a. In the case of the well-prepared student there is rarely if ever such a thing as an unfair test.
    b. Many times exam questions tend to be so unrelated to course work that studying is really useless.
11. a. Becoming a success is a matter of hard work; luck has little or nothing to do with it.
    b. Getting a good job depends mainly on being in the right place at the right time.
12. a. The average citizen can have an influence in government decisions.
    b. This world is run by the few people in power, and there is not much the little guy can do about it.
13. a. When I make plans, I am almost certain that I can make them work.
    b. It is not always wise to plan too far ahead because many things turn out to be a matter of good or bad fortune anyhow.
*14. a. There are certain people who are just no good.
    b. There is some good in everybody.
15. a. In my case getting what I want has little or nothing to do with luck.
    b. Many times we might just as well decide what to do by flipping a coin.
16. a. Who gets to be the boss often depends on who was lucky enough to be in the right place first.
    b. Getting people to do the right things depends upon ability; luck has nothing to do with it.
17. a. As far as world affairs are concerned, most of us are the victims of forces we can neither understand nor control.
    b. By taking an active part in political and social affairs the people can control world events.
18. a. Most people don't realize the extent to which their lives are controlled by accidental happenings.
    b. There really is no such thing as "luck."
*19. a. One should always be willing to admit his mistakes.
    b. It is usually best to cover up one's mistakes.
20. a. It is hard to know whether or not a person really likes you.
    b. How many friends you have depends on how nice a person you are.
21. a. In the long run the bad things that happen to us are balanced by the good ones.
    b. Most misfortunes are the result of lack of ability, ignorance, laziness, or all three.

22. a. With enough effort we can wipe out political corruption.
    b. It is difficult for people to have much control over the things politicians do in office.
23. a. Sometimes I can't understand how teachers arrive at the grades they give.
    b. There is a direct connection between how hard I study and the grades I get.
*24. a. A good leader expects people to decide for themselves what they should do.
    b. A good leader makes it clear to everybody what their jobs are.
25. a. Many times I feel that I have little influence over the things that happen to me.
    b. It is impossible for me to believe that chance or luck plays an important role in my life.
26. a. People are lonely because they don't try to be friendly.
    b. There's not much use in trying too hard to please people; if they like you, they like you.
*27. a. There is too much emphasis on athletics in high school.
    b. Team sports are an excellent way to build character.
28. a. What happens to me is my own doing.
    b. Sometimes I feel that I don't have enough control over the direction my life is taking.
29. a. Most of the time I can't understand why politicians behave the way they do.
    b. In the long run the people are responsible for a bad government on a national, as well as local, level.

_____

*The six items preceded by an asterisk are "filler" items.

SOURCE: J. B. Rotter "Generalized Expectancies for Internal vs. External Control of Reinforcement." *Psychological Monographs*, 1966, 80 (whole number 609). Copyright 1966 by the American Psychological Association. Reprinted by permission.

V1.4.IV.c
MODES OF ADAPTATION PATTERNS SCALE
S. Sharma, 1977

1. ACTIVITY SUB-SCALE

1. Are you working for pay now?   yes no
2. Do you do any volunteer work or work that you are not paid for?   yes no
3. Friends, relatives, and neighbors sometimes do things to help each other out and make life a little easier or more enjoyable.
    a. In what ways have you done things for your children or helped them in the last years?
    b. What are some of the things you have done for your (other) relatives (Specify relation)?
4. Now let's talk about things friends do for each other. What are some of the ways you have helped out a friend in the last year?
5. How about neighbors—what things have you done for neighbors in the last year?
6. I am going to read you a list of things people sometimes do in their spare time. Would you tell me which you have done in the past month? (Only solitary)
    a. Did you paint pictures or do handicrafts during the past month?   yes no
    b. Did you play a musical instrument?   yes no
    c. Did you do a crossword or jigsaw or play solitaire?   yes no

d. Did you go to movies, theater, or plays?   yes no
e. Did you entertain in your home?   yes no
f. Did you go to a ball game or other sporting events?   yes no
g. Did you babysit with grandchildren or anyone else?   yes no
h. Play cards, bingo, pool, or other games?   yes no
i. Go for a walk?   yes no
j. Go for a ride?   yes no
k. Do exercises?   yes no
l. Eat out at a restaurant?   yes no
m. Read?   yes no
n. Watch TV?   yes no
o. Listen to radio?   yes no
p. Write letters?   yes no
q. Go to party?   yes no
r. (Ask females) Did you sew or knit?
   (Ask males) Did you do any woodwork or work in a home workshop? yes no

SOURCE: S. Sharma. "Adaptation Patterns of Urban and Ethnic Aged." Ph.D. dissertation, Wayne State University, 1977. Reprinted by permission of author.

Chapter 5

Morale and Life Satisfaction

William J. Sauer and Rex Warland

Research into the determinants of morale and life satisfaction in the elderly population has occupied a central role in the development of social gerontology. The pioneering study of Cavan and associates (1949) took as its central focus the measurement of adjustment, and this interest has continued unabated until the current time.

Despite this long tradition of interest, attention to the development of psychometrically valid and reliable instruments that measure morale, life satisfaction, and adjustment has been insufficient. Further, many attempts by scholars working in the field have tended to accept uncritically *instruments in development* as established, and many have neglected to examine and/or publish pertinent psychometric data regarding their use of a specific measurement technique. In part, this may be due to the neglect of theory regarding the *underlying* structure of morale and life satisfaction. This neglect, however, is also due to the fact that these concepts have remained rather vague (Rosow, 1977; Lawton, 1977). They have, on the one hand, been used interchangeably (Streib, 1956; Neugarten, Havighurst, and Tobin, 1961; Wood, Wylie, and Bradford, 1969), without concern for their nominal meanings. On the other hand, the measurement of a single concept has varied within the same study (Kutner et al., 1956). Further, with regard to adjustment, the concept has remained undefined nominally (Sherwood, 1977).

There are several factors to which this vagueness may be attributed, two of which will suffice in passing. First, social gerontology has focused historically on applied research. This emphasis has been primarily on problem solving and program development. Consequently, its main thrust has been empirically oriented. The second reason for this lack of clarity stems from the first. As a result of focusing on the applied dimension, efforts in theoretical development have remained, with few exceptions, implicit in nature. Although several authors (Taylor, 1977; Rosow, 1977; Nydegger, 1977) have given serious, though unheeded, consideration to the clarification of these concepts, clearly, the majority of researchers working in this area have addressed it only on the most superficial level.

The resultant situation has left the conceptualization of these concepts, on *both* the nominal and operational level, in an elusive state. Since the process of measurement is inherently a matter of determining the rules of correspondence between observable indicators and underlying concepts, the absence of conceptualization, on both the nominal and operational levels, has impeded the development of instruments.

Evaluation of Instruments

In this chapter, a number of measures of morale and life satisfaction are described and evaluated. Table 5-1 lists these instruments. There are several criteria that can be used to assess the state of the art of measures of life satisfaction and morale. These include the degree to which the theoretical domain of the construct has been specified and measured, the extent to which the instrument has been evaluated with respect to reliability and validity, the extent to which the dimensionality of the instrument has been investigated, and the degree to which the distribution of responses by subjects can be generalized. Each of these criteria will be discussed in turn.

Conceptual Clarity

There appear to have been few attempts to specify the conceptual and theoretical domains for either life satisfaction or morale. Perhaps the best examples are those of Neugarten, Havighurst, and Tobin (1961) and Bradburn (1969), who attempted to identify carefully what they believed to be the components of life satisfaction and then to develop items to measure each. In most cases, only a general definition of the concept is offered, and the sampling of the item domain is developed on the basis of intuition, experience, and empirical experimentation. In addition, the inability of researchers to agree about what conceptually constitutes life satisfaction and morale has resulted in the development of instruments that often have little in common

TABLE 5-1
Instruments Reviewed in Chapter 5

Instrument	Author (date)	Code Number
Single-Item Indicators of Life Satisfaction and Happiness	Streib (1956); Davis (1974); Cantril (1965); Rose (1955)	V1.5.I.a
Cornell Personal Adjustment Scale	Thompson, Streib, and Kosa (1960)	V1.5.I.b
Dean Morale Index	Cumming, Dean, and Newell (1958)	V1.5.I.c
Kutner Morale Scale	Kutner et al. (1956)	V1.5.I.d
Srole Anomie Scale	Srole (1956)	V1.5.I.e
Morale Scale	Clark and Anderson (1967); Pierce and Clark (1973)	V1.5.I.f
Attitude Inventory	Cavan et al. (1949)	V1.5.I.g
Affect-Balance Scale	Bradburn (1969)	V1.5.I.h
Life Satisfaction Index	Neugarten, Havighurst, and Tobin (1961)	V1.5.I.i
Philadelphia Geriatric Center Morale Scale	Lawton (1972)	V1.5.I.j

with each other. For example, the single-item measures (Streib, 1956; Davis, 1974; Cantril, 1965) have little in common with the multidimensional measures of Lawton (1975) and Neugarten, Havighurst, and Tobin (1961).

What is needed is a more systematic effort to define theoretically life satisfaction and morale. Lohmann (1976) has demonstrated that there is at the present time no "best" measure of life satisfaction and that considerable overlap exists among them. Lawton (1975) has suggested, with respect to his own measure of morale, that more items need to be added to the pool and that more dimensions that carefully measure the conceptual meaning of morale need to be developed and evaluated. In short, more attention needs to be devoted to construct validity. Only in this way can adequate measures of life satisfaction and morale be established.

Reliability

Many of the instruments discussed in this chapter have been evaluated with respect to reliability. These reports of reliability are uneven, and, in many cases, the assessment of reliability is scant. The coefficients that are reported are generally in the moderate range. In only a small number of cases have the designers of the instruments attempted to improve the reliability of their instruments (Lawton, 1975; Bradburn, 1969). Most instruments have not been revised or changed since their inception. Several of the earlier measures include only a single item (Streib, 1956; Rose, 1955), so their reliability can only be estimated by test-retest procedures. Although these measures have served their purpose, they should be replaced by instruments that tap a larger domain of the concept. Future progress in measurement requires that we can make more adequate assessments of reliability than can be afforded by simple test-retest procedures.

Yet, it would be unfair to place the burden for proving reliability solely upon those who have developed the instruments. The most glaring deficiency can be found with those who have used these measures. In most cases, researchers have not checked the reliability of the instruments on the subjects in their studies. Thus, there has been little opportunity to establish a record of instrument reliability over a series of different studies and different populations. In other fields of sociological research, confidence in a measure grows as the evidence for its reliability and validity accumulates. Until a similar tradition is established in the sociology of aging, the accumulated evidence of reliability is likely to remain scant and unstandardized.

Validity

The formal evidence for the validity of these instruments is more sparse than that for reliability. When attempts have been made to measure validity, they have often consisted of correlations between self-reports of life satisfaction or morale and independent rankings made by others. For example, the measures designed by Cavan and associates (1949), Lawton (1972), and Neugarten, Havighurst, and Tobin (1961) report these correlations as evidence of convergent validity. There have been a few attempts to establish predictive or discriminant validity (Cavan et al., 1949), but none have used multitrait-multimethod assessment techniques (Campbell and Fiske, 1959).

There have been several attempts at establishing construct validity (Adams, 1969; Lawton, 1972; Morris and Sherwood, 1975; Pierce and Clark, 1973; Lohmann, 1976). These studies were concerned with establishing the various components of life satisfaction and morale and with determining how these components relate to one another. The study by Lohmann (1976) is particularly noteworthy because it interrelated the major measures of life satisfaction and morale and found that all measures shared some aspects of the construct termed "life satisfaction."

All of these studies used factor analysis. The major significance of these studies is that they have advanced the measurement of life satisfaction and morale from a series of single items and unidimensional measures to more complex multidimensional instruments. This advancement has been one of the most important developments in the measurement of these concepts, for it has firmly established a base from which more adequate measures can be developed.

As was the case with reliability, few researchers have investigated the validity of their measures with their samples. These reports must be recorded and accumulated in the literature before confidence can be placed in *any* of these measures.

Dimensionality

Dimensionality is related to both the validity and the conceptual domain of the construct. It is encouraging to see a number of recent attempts to investigate dimensional structure. On the other hand, these analyses have been uneven and restricted to a limited number of techniques.

Careful investigations of dimensional structure have made a significant contribution to our understanding of the Philadelphia Geriatric Center's measure of morale. The original study by Lawton (1972) and the subsequent restudies by Morris and Sherwood (1975) and Lawton (1975) have enhanced our understanding of morale. After this series of studies, the concept was more clearly defined, and the next steps necessary to further improve the measurement of morale were specified (Lawton, 1975; Morris and Sherwood, 1975). These studies constitute a good model for future investigations of life satisfaction and morale.

However, there have been several deficiencies with the studies of dimensionality. In several cases (e.g., Adams, 1969), the data presented have been so sparse that it is difficult to evaluate the results of the analysis. Often, very little information concerning the initial solution to the factor analysis (e.g., the eigenvalues, the unrotated factor loadings, the initial and final communality estimates) has been provided. There has also been a tendency for researchers to use only orthogonal rotational methods. This approach can be questioned on both theoretical and empirical grounds. As Cartwright (1965) has argued, it makes little sense to force dimensions of a construct to be unrelated to each other. An alternative procedure would be to use both oblique and orthogonal rotational methods to determine whether the dimensions are correlated with each other. Oblique rotations may produce a more simple and meaningful factor structure than orthogonal rotations. In addition, oblique rotations have the advantage of allowing the derivation of higher order factors that may offer new insights into the nature of the concept being investigated.

Generalization of Distributions

To date, there have been few studies that offer much insight into how the elderly population is distributed on the various measures of life satisfaction and morale. Since many of the studies reviewed in this chapter were concerned with scale development, large national samples were not necessary. However, many other studies that have used these measures have been local. The distributions of responses in these studies cannot be generalized to the national population of the elderly. More broadly based samples will be necessary if national norms are to be estimated.

A recent nationwide survey conducted by the National Council on the Aging and Harris (1975) provides some preliminary information on the distribution of responses for the Neugarten, Havighurst, and Tobin (1961) and Bradburn (1969) scales. These data will be valuable for the further testing and development of these measures of life satisfaction and morale.

Finally, it is instructive to examine past research that has used these scales to determine those variables that are related to morale and life satisfaction. Larson (1978, pp. 119–25) reviewed the major studies investigating this issue over the past 30 years. A wide range of correlates have been examined for their predictive utility, including health, socioeconomic factors, social activity levels, age, marital status, race/ethnicity, employment status, and access to services. Simple bivariate relationships between all of these variables and morale have been demonstrated. It is apparent, however, that the use of multivariate controls tends to reduce the number of significant relationships that remain. Clearly, the research to date indicates that the primary predictors of morale are health, socioeconomic factors (primarily income), and some variation of activity level, e.g., informal, formal, or solitary. Although this evidence appears to be quite strong, there is still a need to refine the theoretical interpretation of these relationships. Furthermore, it appears that the meaning and measurement of the *predictor variables* should be critically examined in order to facilitate the development of a more broadly based theory of the structure and antecedents of morale.

Summary

It has been suggested here that more attention must be given to the theoretical domain of the concept, reliability, validity, dimensionality, and generalizability. Perhaps the most important implication of this brief overview is that the advancement of measurement is as much a responsibility of those who borrow measures as of those who create them. Those who developed the measures of life satisfaction, morale, and affect-balance were very careful to point out the weaknesses and limitations of their instruments, and they often suggested additional research necessary to improve their instruments. When those who use an instrument ignore such caveats and do not add to knowledge about its efficacy, they are not being scientifically responsible. For progress to be made in achieving strong measures of life satisfaction and morale, researchers must be more sensitive to measurement theory and the conventions of scientific reporting.

There is a need for more work on the measurement of morale and life satisfaction. For researchers whose work requires the measurement of these concepts, it is suggested that they use the Lawton (1972), Neugarten, Havighurst, and Tobin (1961), and Bradburn (1969) scales and that they include all the original scale items. They may then reanalyze the structure of the scale and share their findings with the larger research community, thus contributing to the advancement of measurement in the field of aging.

REFERENCES

Adams, D. L. "Analysis of a Life Satisfaction Index." *Journal of Gerontology,* 1969, 24: 470–74.

Bradburn, N. M. *The Structure of Psychological Well-Being.* Chicago: Aldine, 1969.

Campbell, D. T., and D. W. Fiske. "Convergent and Discriminant Validation by the Multi-trait-Multimethod Matrix." *Psychological Bulletin,* 1959, 56: 81–105.

Cantril, H. *The Patterns of Human Concerns.* New Brunswick, N.J.: Rutgers University Press, 1965.

Cartwright, D. A. "A Misapplication of Factor Analysis." *American Sociological Review,* 1965, 30: 249–51.

Cavan, R. S., E. W. Burgess, R. J. Havighurst, and H. Goldhammer. *Personal Adjustment in Old Age.* Chicago: Science Research Associates, 1949.

Clark, M., and B. G. Anderson. *Culture and Aging: An Anthropological Study of Older Americans.* Springfield, Ill.: Charles C. Thomas, 1967.

Cumming, E., L. R. Dean, and D. S. Newell. "What Is Morale? A Case History of a Validity Problem." *Human Organization,* 1958, 17 (2): 3–8.

Davis, J. A. *National Data Program for the Social Sciences.* Chicago: National Opinion Research Center, 1974.

Kutner, B., D. Fanshel, A. Togo, and T. Langner. *Five Hundred over Sixty.* New York: Russell Sage Foundation, 1956.

Larson, R. "Thirty Years of Research on the Subjective Well-Being of Older Americans." *Journal of Gerontology,* 1978, 33 (1): 109–25.

Lawton, M. P. "The Dimensions of Morale." In *Research Planning and Action for the Elderly,* D. Kent, R. Kastenbaum, and S. Sherwood (eds.), pp. 144–65. New York: Behavioral Publications.

———. "The Philadelphia Geriatric Center Morale Scale: A Revision." *Journal of Gerontology*, 1975, 30: 85–89.

———. "Morale: What Are We Measuring." In *Measuring Morale: A Guide to Effective Assessment*, C. N. Nydegger (ed.), pp. 6–14. Washington, D.C.: Gerontological Society, 1977.

Lohmann, N. "Comparison of Life Satisfaction, Morale, and Adjustment Scales on an Elderly Population." Ph.D. dissertation, Brandeis University, 1976.

Morris, J. N., and S. Sherwood. "A Retesting and Modification of the Philadelphia Geriatric Center Morale Scale." *Journal of Gerontology*, 1975, 30: 77–84.

National Council on the Aging. *The Myth and Reality of Aging in America*. Washington, D.C.: National Council on the Aging, 1975.

Neugarten, B. L., R. J. Havighurst, and S. S. Tobin. "The Measurement of Life Satisfaction." *Journal of Gerontology*, 1961, 16: 134–43.

Nunnally, J. C. *Psychometric Theory*. New York: McGraw-Hill, 1967.

Nydegger, C. N. (ed.). *Measuring Morale: A Guide to Effective Assessment*. Washington, D.C.: Gerontological Society, 1977.

Pierce, R. C., and M. M. Clark. "Measurement of Morale in the Elderly." *International Journal of Aging and Human Development*, 1973, 4: 83–101.

Rose, A. M. "Factors Associated with the Life Satisfaction of Middle Class, Middle Aged Persons." *Marriage and Family Living*, 1955, 17 (1): 15–19.

Rosow, I. "Morale: Concept and Measurement." In *Measuring Morale: A Guide to Effective Assessment*, C. N. Nydegger (ed.), pp. 39–45. Washington, D.C.: Gerontological Society, 1977.

Sherwood, S. "The Problems and Value of Morale Measurement." In *Measuring Morale: A Guide to Effective Assessment*. C. N. Nydegger (ed.), pp. 34–38. Washington, D.C.: Gerontological Society, 1977.

Srole, L. "Social Integration and Certain Corollaries." *American Sociological Review*, 1956, 21: 709–16.

Streib, G. "Morale of the Retired." *Social Problems*, 1956, 3: 270–76.

Taylor, C. "Why Measure Morale?" In *Measuring Morale: A Guide to Effective Assessment*, C. N. Nydegger (ed.), pp. 30–33. Washington, D.C.: Gerontological Society, 1977.

Thompson, W. E., G. F. Streib, and J. Kosa. "The Effect of Retirement on Personal Adjustment: A Panel Analysis." *Journal of Gerontology*, 1960, 15: 165–69.

Wood, V., M. L. Wylie, and B. Sheafor. "An Analysis of a Short Self-Report Measure of Life Satisfaction: Correlation with Rater Judgments." *Journal of Gerontology*, 1969, 24: 465–69.

Abstracts

SINGLE-ITEM INDICATORS
OF LIFE SATISFACTION AND HAPPINESS
G. Streib, 1956; J. A. Davis, 1974; H. Cantril, 1965; A. Rose, 1955

Definition of Variable

These indicators are generally conceptualized as an overall global measure of the individual's perception of his or her satisfaction with life.

Description of Instrument

Several forms of these indicators have been used. Rose (1955) asked, "In general, how satisfied are you with your life?" Streib (1956) used the following item: "On the whole, how satisfied are you with your way of life today?" Davis (1974), in the NORC general survey, posed the question: "Taken all together, how would you say things are these days—would you say that you are very happy, pretty happy, or not too happy?" The Cantril Ladder (Cantril, 1965) is a self-anchoring scale with a range of 0 to 10, on which 0 represents the worst possible life and 10 represents the best possible life.

Method of Administration

Single-item indicators of life satisfaction have been used in personal interviews, telephone interviews, and self-administered questionnaires.

Context of Development and Subsequent Use

Global measures of life satisfaction emerged in the earlier work in aging before more intensive efforts were made in measurement. More recently, they have been used as secondary analyses of larger national samples, on which these indicators generally have been the only measures available. Finally, they see frequent use as a validity criterion in the development of life satisfaction and morale scales.

Samples

These items are available in various national studies, (e.g., NORC General Social Survey, Income Dynamics Study, and the Election Studies). All of these are available through the Institute for Social Research at the University of Michigan.

The Cantril Ladder was included in the longitudinal Duke Adaptation Study of 502 males and females from the Piedmont region of North Carolina. By the end of the fourth wave of data collection, attrition had reduced the sample size to 357 cases (George, personal communication, 1977).

Scoring, Scale Norms, and Distribution

Single-item indicators are examined as percentage distributions. In general, these measures tend to be biased toward reporting high satisfaction; for example, Gurin, Veroff, and Feld (1960) reported that 89% of their national sample was "very" or "pretty" happy. Only 7% of the population scored from 0 through 3 (i.e., worst possible life) on the Cantril (1965) self-anchoring scale. Robinson (1973, pp. 12–17) has presented a detailed review of these measures and the response distributions obtained in their use with several national samples. George (personal communication, 1977) has informed us that the means and standard deviations for the four waves of data collection in the Duke Adaptation Study are as follows: wave I, $\bar{X} = 7.1$, $SD = 1.5$; wave II, $\bar{X} = 7.2$, $SD = 1.3$; wave III, $\bar{X} = 7.0$, $SD = 1.3$; and wave IV, $\bar{X} = 7.1$, $SD = 1.2$.

Formal Tests of Reliability

Wilson (1960) reported a test-retest correlation of .70 over a one-month interval and .67 over a two-year interval. Bradburn and Caplovitz (1965) reported a test-retest table that yields a Kendall's tau of .43 (eight-month interval). Converse and Robinson (in Robinson, 1973) reported a Kendall's tau of .59 over a four- to six-month interval. All of these studies used a single question with age-diverse samples.

George (personal communication, 1977) provided us with correlations of the Cantril Ladder with itself over waves of data collection. These correlations are: $r_{1,2} = .67$; $r_{1,3} = .69$; $r_{1,4} = .79$; $r_{2,3} = .74$; $r_{2,4} = .69$; $r_{3,4} = .78$. These correlations do not truly reflect test-retest reliability, since true score change may have occurred.

Formal Tests of Validity

In a sample of 641 Pennsylvania residents age 60 and older, Sauer and Warland (unpublished data) found a correlation of .40 with the Life Satisfaction Index (Neugarten, Havighurst, and Tobin, 1961) and a single-item indicator, and a correlation of .38 with the Philadelphia Geriatric Center Morale Scale (Lawton, 1972). Lohmann (1977, p. 74) reported correlations of .240 to .468 between the global indicator and nine different measures and/or scoring systems of life satisfaction, with an average correlation of .406. Bradburn (1969, p. 63) reported correlations of .34 and .38 between happiness and the Positive Affect Scale, and −.33 and −.38 between happiness and the Negative Affect Scale.

Usability on Older Populations

Single-item indicators have been used in previous research on elderly populations. However, these global indicators tend to elicit responses skewed toward high satisfaction.

Sensitivity to Age Differences

Gurin, Veroff, and Feld (1960) and Bradburn and Caplovitz (1965) reported that satisfaction decreases as age increases in age-diverse samples. George (personal communication, 1977) reported the following correlations of age with the scores on the Cantril Ladder: wave I, $r = .36$; wave II, $r = .39$; wave III, $r = .40$; wave IV, $r = .38$.

General Comments and Recommendations

The value of these indicators lies in their use with large, representative national samples; however, their validity remains to be determined.

References

Bradburn, N. M. *The Structure of Psychological Well-being.* Chicago: Aldine, 1969.

Bradburn, N., and D. Caplovitz. *Reports on Happiness.* Chicago: Aldine, 1965.

Cantril, H. *The Pattern of Human Concerns.* New Brunswick, N.J.: Rutgers University Press, 1965.

Davis, J. A. *National Data Program for the Social Sciences.* Chicago: National Opinion Research Center, 1974.

Gurin, G., J. Veroff, and S. Feld. *Americans View Their Mental Health.* New York: Basic Books, 1960.

Lawton, M. P. "The Dimensions of Morale." Chapter II in *Research Planning and Action for the Elderly,* D. Kent, R. Kastenbaum, and S. Sherwood (eds.), pp. 144–65. New York: Behavioral Publications, 1972.

Lohmann, N. "Correlations of Life Satisfaction, Morale and Adjustment Measures." *Journal of Gerontology,* 1977, 32 (1): 73–75.

Neugarten, B. L., R. J. Havighurst, and S. S. Tobin. "The Measurement of Life Satisfaction." *Journal of Gerontology,* 1961, 16: 134–43.

Robinson, J. "Life Satisfaction and Happiness." Chapter 2 in *Measures of Social Psychological Attitudes,* J. P. Robinson and R. P. Shaver (eds.), pp. 11–43. Ann Arbor, Mich.: Institute for Social Research, 1973.

Rose, A. M. "Factors Associated with the Life Satisfaction of Middle Class, Middle Aged Persons." *Marriage and Family Living,* 1955, 17 (1): 15–19.

Streib, G. "Morale of the Retired." *Social Problems,* 1956, 3 (4): 270–76.

Wilson, W. "An Attempt to Determine Some Correlates and Dimensions of Hedonic Tone." Ph.D. dissertation, Northwestern University, 1960.

Instrument

See Instrument V1.5.I.a.

CORNELL PERSONAL ADJUSTMENT SCALE
W. E. Thompson, G. F. Streib, and J. Kosa, 1960

Definition of Variable or Concept

Adjustment is defined here as a continuum ranging from satisfaction with life to hopelessness.

Description of Instrument

This scale is comprised of three separate indexes labeled satisfaction with life, dejection, and hopelessness. Each of these dimensions contains three items. The scale was devised through the use of Guttman scaling techniques, resulting in an empirical ordering of the three separate indexes.

Method of Administration

The items were included in an interview schedule designed to be self-administered. It would appear, however, that it could also be administered in personal or telephone interviews.

Context of Development and Subsequent Use

This research stems from a larger research effort conducted at Cornell University to examine occupational retirement.

Samples

The longitudinal sample of 4,032 persons working in industry was drawn from a 12-state area (representing all parts of the United States) and selected on the basis of three criteria: (1) geographic location, (2) industrial type, and (3) size of plant. The respondents selected were all those who were willing to take part in the study. Consequently, a random sample was not obtained. Streib and Schneider (1971, p. 13) presented a detailed tabulation of the study's participants by industry type at the first wave of data collection. By the fourth wave of data collection, attrition had reduced the sample to 2,603.

Scoring, Scale Norms, and Distribution

A total morale scale is obtained by summing the positive responses for each item. (See the instrument.) The three separate indexes can be obtained through simple summation of the items for the separate dimensions. Streib and Schneider used somewhat different scales; the reader is referred to their book (1971) for those details.

Formal Tests of Reliability/Homogeneity

A coefficient of reproducibility was calculated for each of the three indexes, together with an error ratio. The results are: (1) satisfaction with life, reproducibility .96; error ratio .55; (2) dejection, reproducibility .96; error ratio .49; and (3) hopelessness, reproducibility .95; error ratio .51 (Thompson, Streib, and Kosa, 1960, pp. 166–67).

Usability on Older Populations

This instrument appears to be appropriate for elderly subjects.

General Comments and Recommendations

Little use of this scale has resulted in little information on its reliability and none on its validity. Further work on these issues is recommended to those interested in working with this measure.

References

Streib, G. F., and C. Schneider. *Retirement in American Society.* Ithaca, N.Y.: Cornell University Press, 1971.

Streib, G. F., E. E. Thompson, and E. A. Suchman. "The Cornell Study of Occupational Retirement." *Journal of Social Issues*, 1958, 14: 3–17.

Thompson, W. E., and G. F. Streib. "Situational Determinants: Health and Economic Deprivation in Retirement." *Journal of Social Issues*, 1958, 14: 18–34.

Thompson, W. E., G. F. Streib, and J. Kosa. "The Effect of Retirement on Personal Adjustment: A Panel Analysis." *Journal of Gerontology*, 1960, 15: 165–69.

Instrument

See Instrument V1.5.I.b.

DEAN MORALE INDEX
E. Cumming, L. R. Dean, and D. S. Newell, 1958

Definition of Variable or Concept

Morale is defined as "the logical correlate of what we meant by success in aging" (Cumming, Dean, and Newell, 1958, p. 5).

Description of Instrument

The instrument consists of four items chosen for their concordance with an interviewer's ranking of the respondent's morale.

Method of Administration

The items are included in an interview schedule administered by trained interviewers.

Context of Development and Subsequent Use

The primary goal of the research in which this scale was developed and used was to construct inductively a theory of aging (i.e., a disengagement theory).

Samples

The initial work on this scale was conducted on a panel of 170 subjects participating in the Kansas City Study of Adult Life. The sample was drawn from a sampling frame of 8,700 dwelling units in Kansas City. It is important to note, however, that this universe was delimited by the exclusion of rural elderly, blacks, chronically ill, upper- and lower-class respondents, and individuals less than 50 or more than 70 years of age. Finally, while the selection of items used in the scale was drawn from the responses of the entire sample, validation of the scale was based on in-depth interviews with 20 respondents.

Scoring, Scale Norms, and Distribution

Scoring is accomplished by assigning a value of 1 for the appropriate response to each of the four items and then summing across all items for a total score, which ranges from 0 to 4. Cumming and Henry (1961, p. 263) reported a frequency distribution with a mean score of 1.599.

Formal Tests of Reliability/Homogeneity

When test scores were compared over a two-year period, it was found that 17% of the respondents had changed scores by 2 points, 44% had changed by 1 point, and 39% had remained unchanged. Scores following the fifth wave, which was six to nine months later, demonstrated that only 7% had changed by 2 points, 52% had changed by 1 point, and 41% had remained unchanged (Cumming and Henry, 1961, p. 266). Thus, though no correlations are provided, the authors concluded that the scale appeared quite stable over time. However, when we consider that the possible range is only 5 points, then a 2-point change forces us to seriously question the stability of the instrument.

Formal Tests of Validity

Correlations of the Dean Morale Index with interviewers' rankings of 10 subjects' morale, based on intensive interviews, produced significant *rho* correlations ranging from .51 to .82 (Cumming and Henry, 1961, p. 265). Lohmann (1977, p. 74) reported correlations between the Dean Morale Index and nine measures of life satisfaction that ranged from .24 to .63.

Usability on Older Populations

The instrument appears to be usable on older populations.

Sensitivity to Age Differences

A comparison of the percentage distribution of scores for the entire panel with those for the 70- to 80-year-old group indicates that the two distributions are similar. Thus, one would not suspect any unique effects of age upon morale for this scale.

General Comments and Recommendations

Neugarten, Havighurst, and Tobin (1961) have questioned the validity of this scale on the basis of its being constructed on so few items, being validated on a small number of cases, and reflecting resignation to the status quo. While the items in this scale tap certain dimensions of an individual's life space, they clearly do not cover the entire range that hypothetically constitutes morale or life satisfaction. Further use of this scale will require more rigorous testing.

References

Cumming, E., L. R. Dean, and D. S. Newell. "What Is Morale? A Case History of a Validity Problem." *Human Organization*, 1958, 17 (2): 3–8.

Cumming, E., and W. E. Henry. *Growing Old.* New York: Basic Books, 1961.

Lohmann, N. "Correlations of Life Satisfaction, Morale and Adjustment Measures." *Journal of Gerontology*, 1977, 32 (1): 73–75.

Neugarten, B. L., R. J. Havighurst, and S. S. Tobin. "The Measurement of Life Satisfaction." *Journal of Gerontology*, 1961, 16: 134–43.

Instrument

See Instrument V1.5.I.c.

KUTNER MORALE SCALE
B. Kutner, D. Fanshel, A. Togo, and T. Langner, 1956

Definition of Variable or Concept

This scale equates *adjustment* with *morale*. Morale is nominally defined as "a continuum of responses to life and living problems that reflect the presence or absence of satisfaction, optimism, and expanding life perspectives" (Kutner et al., 1956).

Description of Instrument

This scale is comprised of seven Guttman-type items chosen for their imputed ability to measure morale.

Method of Administration

The morale scale in this research was administered by trained interviewers. It seems plausible, however, that it could be self-administered or administered in a telephone interview.

Context of Development and Subsequent Use

The investigators were concerned with four specific problems relative to aged persons in a large metropolitan area (Kips Bay, New York City): (1) problems with personal adjustment,

(2) factors affecting or affected by health, (3) use of community services, and (4) attitudes toward health and social centers. The morale scale was developed to assess adjustment. Morale was then examined in terms of various conditioning factors (i.e., age, sex, income, economic status, health, marital status, employment, isolation, and activity).

Sample

The sample was drawn from the Kips Bay-Yorkville Health District in New York City. Two restrictions were placed on the sample. The first was based on the assumption that available or proposed services would be used more by people of relatively low socioeconomic status. Thus, it was decided that the sample should be stratified to include persons of 60% low, 30% middle, and 10% high socioeconomic levels. Second, the sample was drawn to reflect the known sex distribution of older men and women over 60. This resulted in a sample of 188 males and 312 females being included in the final analysis. Given these constraints, a random sample of older persons was selected. Of the 665 individuals contacted, 165 refused to be interviewed, leaving a total of 500 for the analysis.

Scoring, Scale Norms, and Distribution

Scoring is accomplished by assigning a value of 1 to all correct answers on the seven items making up the scale. The scale can range from 0 to 7, with 7 representing high morale. Of the sample 37% received high morale scores, 30% scored medium, and 33% received low morale scores (Kutner et al., 1956, p. 50).

Formal Tests of Reliability/Homogeneity

The coefficient of reproducibility was 90%, which is within the acceptable error range for this Guttman scale (Kutner et al., 1956).

Formal Tests of Validity

Cumming, Dean, and Newell (1958) have questioned the conceptual validity of the Kutner Morale Scale, pointing out its strong resemblance to the Srole Anomie Scale. In examining the results of their research, they found that both indexes scaled together as an unidimensional whole. They concluded that the scale did not measure morale, but rather the individual's world. They further referred to the two scales together as a "positive-thinking" scale. Lohmann (1977, p. 74) reported that correlations of the Kutner Morale Scale with nine other measures of psychological well-being ranged from .397 to .883.

Usability on Older Populations

Although this instrument has been used with older populations, the findings indicate a confounding of this measure with other concepts.

Sensitivity to Age Differences

Kutner and associates (1956, pp. 50-51) analyzed the impact of age upon morale for males and females 65 years old and older. For the men, the overall decline in morale was nonmonotonic, with a slight increase in the age-group 70 to 74. For the women, a linear decline in morale was noted.

General Comments and Recommendations

Given the work of Cumming, Dean, and Newell (1958), the continued use of this scale as a measure of morale is problematic.

References

Cumming, E., and W. E. Henry. *Growing Old*. New York: Basic Books, 1961.

Cumming, E., L. R. Dean, and D. S. Newell. "What is Morale? A Case History of a Validity Problem." *Human Organization*, 1958, 17 (2): 3-8.

Kutner, B., D. Fanshel, A. Togo, and T. Langner. *Five Hundred over Sixty.* New York: Russell Sage Foundation, 1956.

Lipman, A. "Role Conceptions and Morale of Couples in Retirement." *Journal of Gerontology,* 1961, 16: 267–71.

Lohmann, N. "Correlations of Life Satisfaction, Morale and Adjustment Measures." *Journal of Gerontology,* 1977, 32 (1): 73–75.

Instrument

See Instrument V1.5.I.d.

SROLE ANOMIE SCALE
L. Srole, 1956

Definition of Concept

Srole viewed this scale as an analytical device for placing individuals on a eunomia-anomia continuum representing variations in interpersonal integration. More specifically, he said, "This variable is conceived as referring to the individual's generalized, pervasive sense of 'self-to-others belongingness' as one extreme compared with 'self-to-others distance' and 'self-to-others alienation' at the other pole of the continuum" (Srole, 1956, p. 711).

Description of Instrument

The original scale consisted of five items, each measuring one dimension of anomia. Revised versions (see the instrument) include additional items. The questions are designed to solicit an opinion response, with the response categories being agree, disagree, and can't decide.

Method of Adminstration

The scale was presented in questionnaire format and administered by trained interviewers. It could also be completed as part of a self-report schedule or in a telephone interview.

Context of Development and Subsequent Use

This research was part of a larger study conducted in Springfield, Mass., which dealt with attitudes toward minorities. The hypothesis that anomia was related to negative attitudes toward minorities was tested and confirmed.

Sample

The sample was drawn from the public-transit-riding population aged 16 to 69 who used the facility four or more times each week. Because the study focused on attitudes toward minority groups, the sample was restricted to white, Christian, native-born transit riders. A two-stage sampling procedure was used: first randomized blocks were selected within walking distance of transit lines, and then the selection of respondents was based on age-sex quotas within those blocks. This procedure resulted in a sample of 401 individuals, ages 16 to 69 (mean 40.3 years, standard deviation 14.5 years), who were interviewed in their homes.

Scoring, Scale Norms, and Distribution

The original scale consists of five items presented as opinion statements, with possible answers agree, disagree, and can't decide. Only an unequivocal agree receives a score of 1. The range, therefore, is 0 to 5, with 0 indicating low anomie and 5 representing high anomie. Srole (1956) reported a mean score of 2.1, and Miller and Butler (1966) reported a mean score of 1.7. Nahemow and Kogan (1971) reported the following means and standard deviations for a 10-item version of the Anomie Scale as it was used on an elderly inner-city sample: (1) total sample, $\bar{X} = 9.8$; $SD = 4.9$; $N = 1,552$; (2) white respondents, $\bar{X} = 9.8$; $SD =$

5.1; N = 766; (3) black respondents, $\bar{X}$ = 9.5; SD = 4.8; N = 580; and (4) Spanish respondents, $\bar{X}$ = 10.7; SD = 4.6; N = 205).

Formal Tests of Reliability/Homogeneity

The unidimensionality of the original scale was demonstrated through the use of latent structure analysis. Further analysis, on a New York sample, indicated that the scale met Guttman-type requirements. Further research by Streuning and Richardson (1965) and Miller and Butler (1966) has verified the unidimensional character of the scale through the use of factor analysis. Bell (1957) reported that in his work the scale items produced a coefficient of reproducibility of .90 and a coefficient of scaleability of .65. Nahemow and Kogan (1971), who used a 10-item expanded Srole scale on an elderly inner-city sample, reported the following alpha coefficients: (1) total, .77; (2) white, .79; (3) black, .76; and (4) Spanish, .76. Sauer and Warland (unpublished data), on a state-wide sample of 641 participants in a congregate meals program in Pennsylvania, found the five items in the Srole scale produced an alpha of .25. Further, when two items, ". . . the lot of the average man is getting worse" and ". . . a person has to live . . . for today . . . ," were presented, phrased both positively and negatively, the low correlation between positive and negative versions of these items suggest that an acquiescence effect might have been present. Carr (1971, p. 290) also found a strong acquiescence effect. Finally, Lenski and Leggett (1960) suggested that the Srole scale illicits a response set in favor of agreeing with the items as they are presented in their current form.

Formal Tests of Validity

Though Srole (1956, p. 714) noted that the full validity of the scale had not yet been determined, he reported a tetrachoric correlation of .50 between a single indicator of latent suicide tendency and anomie. Bell (1957) found that anomie was significantly related to social isolation.

Relatively little analysis has emerged with regard to the validity of the Srole scale as it is applied to the elderly. However, Nahemow and Kogan's (1971) research, which indicated a moderate negative correlation (−.41) between anomie and life satisfaction, seems to question the convergent validity of this scale. Nahemow and Kogan (1971) also factor analyzed a modified 10-item version of the Srole Anomie Scale. Their results indicated a two-factor structure: sense of alienation and basic trust. These results are confirmed by Sauer's analysis of the structure of anomie among persons aged 60 and above in the 1974 NORC data (unpublished data).

Usability on Older Populations

This discussion would suggest that, though the scale has been administered to various elderly samples with relatively few problems, caution should be observed with regard to issues of reliability, validity, and dimensionality.

Sensitivity to Age (Including Social Age) Differences

Nahemow and Kogan (1971) reported that the anomie scale was not sensitive to age differences. Leonard (1977), in reporting the results of his analysis on the 1974 NORC Social Survey, also found that age was not related to anomie.

General Comments and Recommendations

Although this scale has seen considerable use in both sociological and gerontological research, the acquiescence effect found by Carr (1971) and Sauer and Warland (unpublished data) suggests that scholars using this scale in the future should do so with caution. For the elderly, specifically, more work is needed on the issue of acquiescence in order to determine the scale's validity.

References

Bell, W. "Anomia, Social Isolation and Class Structure." *Sociometrics*, 1957, 20: 105–16.

Carr, L. G. "The Srole Items on Acquiescence." *American Sociological Review*, 1971, 36: 287–93.

Lenski, G., and J. Leggett. "Caste, Class and Differences in the Research Interview." *American Journal of Sociology*, 1960, 65: 463–67.

Leonard, W. M. "Sociological and Social-Psychological Correlates of Anomia among a Random Sample of Aged." *Journal of Gerontology*, 1977, 32: 303–10.

MacIver, R. M. *The Ramparts We Guard*. New York: Macmillan, 1950.

Messer, M. "Race Differences in Selected Attitudinal Dimensions of the Elderly." *The Gerontologist*, 1968, 8: 245–49.

Miller, C., and E. Butler. "Anomie and Eunomia: A Methodological Evaluation of Srole's Anomia Scale." *American Sociological Review*, 1966, 31: 400–405.

Nahemow, L., and L. S. Kogan. *Reduced Face for the Elderly*. New York: City University of New York, 1971.

Srole, L. "Social Integration and Certain Corollaries: An Exploratory Study." *American Sociological Review*, 1956, 21 (6): 709–16.

Streuning, E., and A. Richardson. "A Factor Analytic Exploration of the Alienation, Anomia and Authoritarianism Domain." *American Sociological Review*, 1965, 30: 768–76.

Instrument

See Instrument V1.5.I.e.

MORALE SCALE
M. Clark and B. G. Anderson, 1967; R. C. Pierce and M. Clark, 1973

Definition of Variable or Concept

Morale is conceived of as the affective dimension of experience and is considered to be relatively independent of judgments regarding an individual's intrinsic worth. It indicates whether or not a person is happy with his or her way of life, as contrasted against judgments of self in positive or negative terms (Clark and Anderson, 1967, pp. 79–80).

Description of Instrument

The original instrument contained 45 forced choice items. Nine of the items were taken from Thompson, Streib, and Kosa (1960) and are supposed to measure satisfaction with life, dejection, and hopelessness. Another five items were the Srole (1956) anomie items. The remaining items were created by the authors and their colleagues for an extensive, multidisciplinary study of mental illness called the Geriatrics Research Project. The items were based upon (1) the substance of what subjects had said in reply to open-ended questions asked in earlier interviews and (2) the research team's intuition about other issues that they believed had some bearing on morale. The response categories for eight of the items were dichotomous, while the response categories for the remaining items were trichotomous.

Method of Administration

The questions were asked as part of a structured interview schedule.

Context of Development and Subsequent Use

Clark and Anderson (1967) were interested in the relationship of morale to mental and physical problems. At a more general level, they were investigating whether high morale was characteristic of those who most successfully adapted to aging.

Sample

The sample consisted of 435 elderly San Francisco residents who were survivors of a large sample of 1,135 elderly people who were studied longitudinally at the Langley Porter Neuropsychiatric Institute. There were 264 community-dwelling subjects and 171 hospitalized subjects. The community-dwelling subjects were chosen on a stratified basis from 18 census tracts in San Francisco. The hospitalized subjects were part of a group of elderly patients admitted to the psychiatric screening ward of San Francisco General Hospital during 1959. The sample included 206 men and 229 women ranging in age from 62 to 94, with 48% under 70 years old. The educational level for half of the sample was eighth grade or less.

Scoring, Scale Norms, and Distribution

Pierce and Clark (1973, pp. 87–89) presented the response distributions for the hospital and community samples. It is readily apparent that the community-dwelling subjects exhibited higher morale than the hospitalized subjects on most items.

The 45 items were submitted to a cluster analysis, from which eight orthogonal interpretable dimensions emerged. (1) Depression/satisfaction — high scores indicate moodiness, dejection, disinterest, and inertia and low scores represent good spirits, satisfaction with life, and feelings of worthiness and usefulness. (2) Social accessibility — low scores on this dimension indicate the *ratings made by the interviewers* of the subjects' reactions to the interview as normally cordial and cooperative; high scores are given to subjects who appear testy, withdrawn, or uncooperative. (3) Negative age is a collection of attitudes that tap stereotypes about what is wrong with growing old. (4) Equanimity items are measures of irritability, impatience, the tendency to become upset, and the tendency to be blue. (5) The social alienation dimension is composed of items that reflect a sour and pessimistic disposition; three of the Srole Anomie Scale items are included, and agreement with these items indicates alienation. (6) Will-to-live items indicate interest in life rather than death. (7) The physical decline dimension reflects the subjects' physical condition and deteriorating health. (8) Positive age items, for the most part, measure the degree to which the subjects see the advantages of growing older. The items assigned to each dimension, together with the oblique factor coefficients and communality estimates, are presented with the instrument.

Pierce and Clark (1973) also performed separate cluster analyses for the hospitalized and community-dwelling subjects. The depression/satisfaction, social accessibility, and social alienation clusters were nearly identical for the separate samples and the combined sample. Equanimity was found only for the community-dwelling subjects, and the will to live cluster appeared, in part, for only the hospitalized sample. Only part of the negative age cluster appeared for all three analyses. Physical decline and positive age did not appear in the separate analyses.

Pierce and Clark (1973) drew a distinction between "morale" and "attitudes." Based on a second-order cluster analysis for the combined samples, two second-order dimensions emerged. The first consisted of depression/satisfaction, equanimity, will to live, and physical decline. (These dimensions refer to the subject's assessment of his or her own life and, therefore, are considered measures of morale.) The other second-order dimension included social alienation, negative age, and positive age (which refer to the subject's assessment of other old people). Pierce and Clark called this "attitude" since it refers to what the subjects think of the condition of old people in general. Social accessibility bore a low communality on the second-order analysis and thus is considered by Pierce and Clark to fall outside the domain of morale. They further indicated that physical decline also falls outside the domain of morale since health, in their view, is not a component of a person's prevailing mood. Thus, their provisional definition of morale includes depression/satisfaction, equanimity, and will to live. Pierce and Clark (1973, p. 98) scored these dimensions as standard scores with a mean of 50 and a standard deviation of 10. They reported the following mean scores for the community-dwelling hospital-discharged, and hospital-inpatient samples, respectively: (1) depression/satisfaction, 46.0; 52.5; 53.9; $p < .001$; (2) equanimity, 53.8; 52.1; 50.7; $p < .01$; (3) will to live, 52.0; 51.1; 48.3; $p < .05$.

Clark and Anderson (1967, p. 116) included only the depression/satisfaction cluster as their measure of morale. For the total study sample, they classified 35% of the subjects as having high morale, 27% as having moderately high, 22% as having moderately low, and 16% as having very low.

Formal Tests of Reliability/Homogeneity

No formal tests of reliability are reported. However, the cluster analyses provide some evidence of internal consistency, since the responses that "go together" appear on the same dimension.

Formal Tests of Validity

Pierce and Clark (1973) presented some evidence of predictive validity. Cluster scores for the three morale dimensions were computed, and a one-way analysis of variance for each of the three morale dimensions for the community-dwelling, hospital-inpatient, and hospital-discharged subjects was performed. The psychiatric-disability groups were different on all three dimensions, with the community-dwelling subjects being most satisfied and most equable and having the greatest will to live. The differences, however, were quite small.

Usability on Older Populations

These items were developed for older people and have been used only on older people who were well and mentally impaired. The authors have reported no difficulties.

Sensitivity to Age Differences

Clark and Anderson (1967) reported that morale (using only the depression/satisfaction dimension) was inversely related to age. Among those in their 60s, 70% reported high morale, while only 54% of those in their 70s and over reported high morale. When looking at the relationships among age, mental illness, and morale, Clark and Anderson reported that mental illness is considerably more demoralizing than increasing age.

General Comments and Recommendations

This measure of morale, according to those who developed it, should be considered more suggestive than definitive. Several technical problems with the measure suggest that those who wish to use this measure should exercise caution. Since the dimensions were developed precisely on empirical grounds, additional items with more response categories need to be developed so that these dimensions can be further investigated.

References

Clark, M., and B. G. Anderson. *Culture and Aging: An Anthropological Study of Older Americans.* Springfield, Ill.: Charles C. Thomas, 1967.

Pierce, R. C., and M. M. Clark. "Measurement of Morale in the Elderly." *International Journal of Aging and Human Development,* 1973, 4: 83–101.

Srole, L. "Social Integration and Certain Corollaries." *American Sociological Review,* 1956, 21: 709–16.

Thompson, W. E., G. F. Streib, and J. Kosa. "The Effect of Retirement on Personal Adjustment: A Panel Analysis." *Journal of Gerontology,* 1960, 15: 165–69.

Instrument

See Instrument V1.5.I.f.

ATTITUDE INVENTORY (CAVAN SCALE)
R. S. Cavan, E. W. Burgess, R. J. Havighurst, and H. Goldhammer, 1949

Definition of Variable or Concept

The Attitude Inventory, also called the Cavan Scale, was developed to measure adjustment. Personal adjustment to aging was defined as "the individual's restructuring of his attitudes and behavior in such a way as to integrate the expression of his aspiration with the expectations and demands of his society" (Cavan et al., 1949, p. 10).

Description of the Instrument

The Cavan Scale consists of eight components (health, friendship, work, finances, religion, usefulness, happiness, and family), with seven questions about each component. Thus, there are 56 items, all having a trichotomous response format — agree, disagree, or uncertain.

Method of Administration

The instrument can be administered in either written or oral form. Cavan and associates (1949) reported that most of their respondents appeared to understand the attitude questions. However, they did find that persons with little education who were not accustomed to mental activity did have some difficulty with the attitude questions.

Context of Development and Subsequent Use

The Attitude Inventory was developed to measure the personal adjustment of older people. The scale was constructed to measure several components of adjustment, including a satisfaction with activities and status, a general happiness, and a feeling of usefulness. Satisfaction with activities and status included four categories of activities (family, friendship, work, and religion) and two categories of status (health and finances). Lohmann (1976) has indicated that the Cavan Scale has been used in at least eight studies, most of which were conducted during the early 1960s, including the Duke Longitudinal Study.

Samples

Cavan and associates (1949) studied 499 white males and 759 white females. The participants were selected from lists of retired public school teachers, lists of retired Methodist ministers and the widows of Methodist ministers, the alumni of two colleges, and several other miscellaneous groups. The median age of the men was 73.5 years, compared with 71.7 years for the women. The sample included persons from all regions of the United States and all major religious groups. Compared with census data, the study group was older, more highly urbanized, and better educated and had more representatives from business and the professions than the total population. However, it closely approximated the total population with respect to percentage married, percentage widowed, place of residence, and unemployment rate.

Scoring, Scale Norms, and Distribution

For each of the eight sections of the Cavan Scale, three of the items are stated positively, three items are stated negatively, and one item is neutral. Cavan and associates (1949) examined five different scoring methods, which are highly interrelated (i.e., r's ranging from .63 to .96). They suggested that only the agree answers should be used in scoring. Thus, the score for each of the eight subscales is computed by taking the sum of the agree answers to the positive items minus the sum of the agree answers to the negative items, yielding a score ranging from -3 to $+3$ for each dimension. These can then be summed across the eight dimensions to yield a total score ranging from -24 to $+24$ (Cavan et al., 1949, pp. 118-19).

Britton and Britton (1972) presented an alternative way to score the Cavan Scale. They suggested that a constant of 3 be added to the algebraic sum of the agree responses to the positive and negative items in order that the negative number be cleared. Thus, the possible score for a section is 0 to 6, and the total possible score for the Cavan Scale is 0 to 48.

Formal Tests of Reliability/Homogeneity

Cavan and associates (1949, p. 121) reported a test-retest correlation of .72, based on 110 persons. The interval between testing varied from two weeks to two months. They also reported a split-half reliability estimate (Spearman-Brown formula) of .95, based on 200 persons. Lohmann (1976) found that 52 of the 56 items correlated greater than .20 with the total score but that only 42 of the items correlated greater than .30 with the total score. As a part of the Duke University Longitudinal Study of Aging, Palmore (personal communication, 1977) has computed the test-retest correlations for each of the eight sections of the Cavan Scale as well as the total scale score over an eight-year period (1958 to 1966). The correlation coefficients are remarkably homogeneous. For the total scale, the 10 test-retest coefficients were between .59 and .80. For the eight sections, 85% of all correlations were between .40 and .80. There is some evidence that the correlations become weaker as the time span increases. Most of the correlations under .40 were for the family and work sections on the Cavan Scale.

Cavan and associates (1949, p. 134) also examined the intercorrelations of the eight dimensions and their correlation with the total score for both men and women. Subscale–total scale correlations ranged from .29 to .70 for females and .35 to .73 for males. The reader should note, however, that these estimates were based upon an earlier version of the Attitude Inventory, which included 10 dimensions.

Formal Tests of Validity

Several tests of validity were conducted by Cavan and associates. The Cavan Scale scores for 168 subjects were correlated with three independent evaluations of the subjects' adjustment by judges who were acquainted with the subjects. The three rating instruments were a checklist describing the person's activities ($r = .50$), a set of word portraits describing the subject's characteristics ($r = .49$), and a list of symptoms indicating senility ($r = .15$). The ratings of judges who had studied the subjects' self-reports and the reports of the interviewers but had not seen the Cavan Scale correlated .74 with the total scale score (Cavan et al., 1949, p. 127). Predictive validity was estimated by relating the Cavan Scale scores to the Activity Inventory for 102 subjects. The correlation coefficient was .78 (Cavan et al., 1949, p. 132). The Activity Inventory is reviewed by Graney in Chapter 2, Volume 2, of this series.

Havighurst (1951, pp. 25–27) reported that the Attitude Inventory correlated .73 with interviewers' ratings of adjustment, .78 with the Activity Inventory, and .64 with an interviewer's checklist. Subscale–total scale correlations ranged from .14 to .84 in his sample of 98 older persons in a small midwestern city. Lohmann (1977, p. 74) examined the intercorrelations of the Attitude Inventory with nine other measures of psychological well-being. Correlations ranged from .422 to .799, with an average correlation of .664.

Usability on Older Populations

Cavan and associates (1949) indicated that older people with a high school education or better and those whose work had made them familiar with analyzing problems had no difficulty with the questions. Older people with little education and who were not accustomed to mental activity and those who were senile had some difficulty with the scale.

Sensitivity to Age Differences

The scale appears to be somewhat sensitive to age differences. Cavan and associates reported several negative correlations between age and the Cavan Scale scores. These correlations, however, are relatively low (−.05 to −.27).

General Comments and Recommendations

The Cavan Scale was the first measure of adjustment developed specifically for the aged. The scale was used extensively during the 1950s and the 1960s, but it has been less popular recently, since other scales have been developed. The Cavan Scale has been criticized for placing too much emphasis on contentment with the status quo and assuming norms that indicate that a high activity level is desirable (Lohmann, 1976). Thus, the Cavan Scale does not appear to be widely used as a measure of adjustment, and its usefulness and validity have been questioned. On the other hand, Lohmann (1977) has shown that the Cavan Scale is closely related to the Philadelphia Geriatric Center Morale Scale ($r = .77$) and the Life Satisfaction Index form A ($r = .799$), two measures discussed later in this chapter. Since there are a number of items that are unique to the Cavan Scale, it would appear that this scale does measure important aspects of a common construct. It would be useful to explore this issue in more detail, along the lines suggested by Lohmann (1976; 1977), to determine more precisely what aspects of adjustment, life satisfaction, and morale that are not currently represented in other measures are measured by the Cavan Scale.

References

Britton, J. H., and J. O. Britton. *Personality Changes in Aging.* New York: Spring Publishing Company, 1972.

Cavan, R. S., E. W. Burgess, R. J. Havighurst, and H. Goldhammer. *Personal Adjustment in Old Age.* Chicago: Science Research Associates, 1949.

Havighurst, R. J. "Validity of the Chicago Attitude Inventory as a Measure of Personal Adjustment in Old Age." *Journal of Abnormal and Social Psychology*, 1951, 46: 24–29.

Lohmann, N. "Comparison of Life Satisfaction, Morale and Adjustment Scales on an Elderly Population." Ph.D. dissertation, Brandeis University, 1976.

———. "Correlations of Life Satisfaction, Morale and Adjustment Measures." *Journal of Gerontology*, 1977, 32 (1): 73–75.

Instrument

See Instrument V1.5.I.g.

AFFECT-BALANCE SCALE
N. M. Bradburn, 1969

Definition of Concept

The general concept dealt with in this research is psychological well-being. Operationally, this concept has been defined as avowed happiness and viewed as the difference between the individual's position on two independent dimensions of positive and negative affect.

Description of Instrument

The scale consists of two sets of questions, each consisting of five items, of which one set measures positive affect and the other set measures negative affect. The items are phrased in general terms, rather than specific, since the concern is with the pleasurable or the unpleasurable character of an experience, rather than the particular content of the experience.

Method of Administration

The scale can be administered either by interview or self-reporting methods. Data have also been collected by telephone, and comparisons with nontelephone interviews have indicated no differences in response patterns (Bradburn, 1969).

Context of Development and Subsequent Use

The overall objective of this research was to apply a social psychological perspective to the study of mental health in normal populations. The author attempted to focus on individuals' life situations and their responses to those situations. In so doing, he developed and refined operational measures of psychological well-being with the intent that these measures would provide time-series data on the psychological states accompanying social changes. The goal was to examine the nature of the relationship between psychological well-being and social processes.

Sample

The sample consisted of five subsamples. Two of these were from the Detroit area, with one consisting of respondents from the suburbs containing, primarily, skilled auto workers ($N = 542$) and the other from the inner city composed basically of lower-income blacks ($N = 446$). A third sample was drawn from a working-class Chicago neighborhood experiencing an influx of black and Puerto Rican families ($N = 252$). The fourth subsample was selected from a middle-class suburban Washington, D.C., county ($N = 1,277$). The fifth subsample consisted of residents from the 10 largest metropolitan areas in the country ($N = 270$). This resulted in a total time 1 sample of 2,787. Sample attrition and selective retention of sites reduced the sample to 480 at time 2, to 2,163 at time 3, and to 448 at time 4. Response rates varied from 74% to 85%, with the lowest rates occurring in the Washington suburban and Chicago areas. Bradburn (1969, pp. 20–22) presented further information regarding the socioeconomic characteristics of the sample.

The Affect-Balance Scale has been included in the Duke Adaptation Study. The all Caucasian sample of 502 persons aged 46 to 71 years at time 1 included an approximately equal number of males and females from the Piedmont region of North Carolina. Sample attrition reduced the number of cases to 357 by the end of the fourth wave of data collection (George, personal communication, 1977).

The Harris study of aging in America (NCOA/Harris, 1975) included individuals 18 years old and older with an oversample of persons more than 55 years old. A total of 4,254 interviews were conducted, of which 2,797 were of people over 65.

Scoring, Scale Norms, and Distribution

Scoring is accomplished by giving a value of 1 for each yes response to the items making up the scale. These responses are then summed separately for those items that reflect positive affect and for those items that reflect negative affect. The difference between the scores on positive and negative affect is then computed and taken to be an indicator of the individual's level of psychological well-being. Bradburn (1969, p. 67) suggested adding a constant to remove the negative summary scale scores.

Item-response distributions for time 1, time 3, a 1965 national sample, and the 1966 10-metropolitan-area subsample were presented by Bradburn (1969, p. 56). These data show ranges from 29% to 84% for those experiencing positive affect states and 17% to 56% for those experiencing negative affect states.

George (personal communication, 1977) has provided us with means and standard deviations on the Affect-Balance Scale for the Duke Adaptation Study. Table 5-2 presents these data, together with estimates of internal consistency (Cronbach's alpha).

Formal Tests of Reliability

Bradburn (1969, pp. 75–77) examined test-retest reliability in a sample of 200. Q-values of association were computed for each item, and gamma associations for each scale (i.e., positive affect, negative affect, and affect-balance). Q-values for the items over three-day intervals ranged from .86 to .96 for positive affect items and .90 to .97 for negative affect items. Gamma associations for the scale scores are (1) positive affect, .83; (2) negative affect, .81; and (3) affect-balance, .76. There is a slight tendency for respondents to increase their positive affect responses and decrease their negative affect responses, i.e., a social desirability effect (Bradburn, 1969, p. 78).

TABLE 5-2
Means, Standard Deviations, and Reliability Estimates,
Duke Adaptation Study

		Wave I	Wave II	Wave III	Wave IV
Positive	$\bar{X}$	4.65	5.51	4.34	4.27
Affect	SD	2.99	2.64	2.77	2.58
	alpha	0.59	0.61	0.58	0.66
Negative	$\bar{X}$	1.70	2.16	1.68	1.48
Affect	SD	2.41	2.59	2.63	2.40
	alpha	0.76	0.71	0.73	0.79
Affect-	$\bar{X}$	2.91	3.12	2.87	2.83
Balance	SD	2.37	3.79	2.55	2.41
	alpha	0.57	0.59	0.52	0.60

SOURCE: L. George, personal communication, 1977.

Mangen (1977) computed internal consistency estimates (Cronbach's alpha) for the positive affect (.66) and negative affect (.70) scales for the NCOA/Harris (1975) study of aging in America.

George (personal communication, 1977) has computed Cronbach's alphas for each scale at each of four time points in the Duke Adaptation Study. These are presented in Table 5-2.

George (personal communication, 1977) has further provided us with the correlations of the Affect-Balance Scale across the four waves of data collection. These are $r_{1,2} = .52$; $r_{1,3} = .49$; $r_{1,4} = .44$; $r_{2,3} = .56$; $r_{2,4} = .47$; and $r_{3,4} = .58$. Although these correlations do not truly represent test-retest reliability since real change may have occurred, they are presented here for comparative purposes.

Bradburn (1969, p. 60) computed Q-values of association among the items in the two scales. For males, the average association among items in the positive affect dimension was .51, while the average association for the negative affect dimension was .54. For females, the average association for positive affect was .50, and it was .54 for negative affect. Correlations between scale items are low, ranging from −.28 to .27 for women and −.28 to .30 for men.

Formal Tests of Validity

Positive affect correlated (gamma) .34 (time 1) and .38 (time 3) with a single-item indicator of happiness. The corresponding values for negative affect were −.33 and −.38 (Bradburn, 1969, p. 63).

Bradburn hypothesized that positive and negative affects are distinct dimensions. This hypothesis is supported by the small gamma associations between summary scales, which ranged from .04 to .15 for men across the four interview waves. For women, the comparable values were −.10 to .04 (Bradburn, 1969, p. 61). The hypothesis is further supported by the factor analysis done by Mangen (1977) using the NCOA/Harris (1975) data, which indicated that two distinct orthogonal dimensions were present. Factor-item coefficients for the positive affect dimension ranged from .50 to .57, while the loadings for the negative affect dimension ranged from .42 to .68. No cross-loadings were present, but communalities were low (i.e., ranging from .21 to .48).

Mangen (1977) further examined the correlations of the magnitude of measurement error with social characteristics through regression analysis. Increasing errors in positive affect were generally related to increasing age, lower education, deteriorating health, lower levels of social involvement, and being single. Increasing errors in the negative affect dimension were less strongly related to social characteristics. Deteriorating health was related to increased amounts of error, but increasing age was related to *decreased* measurement error.

Moriwaki (1974) reported that the Affect-Balance Scale is positively correlated with morale ($r = .61$).

Usability on Older Populations

The instrument has been successfully used with older populations. Graney (1973) suggested that the positive and negative items be alternated in order to minimize response bias. Mangen's (1977) findings indicated that the negative affect dimension might be more appropriate for older persons.

Sensitivity to Age Differences

Graney (1975) reported that increasing social activity over time is associated with improved psychological well-being. This effect is stronger for the oldest age-group.

Bradburn's (1969, pp. 154–55) data indicate little effect of age on psychological well-being in a sample of persons under age 60.

George (personal communication, 1977) reported that age is positively correlated with the Affect-Balance Scale in the Duke sample. She cited the following correlations: time 1, .52; time 2, .51; time 3, .47; and time 4, .49).

General Comments and Recommendations

Further work with Bradburn's scale is recommended. The work of Graney (1973; 1975) and NCOA (1975) suggests that this scale is a viable technique for measuring psychological well-being in older populations, although Mangen's (1977) findings suggest that nonrandom measurement error might be a problem in making age-based comparisons. Further assessment of the factorial structure, reliability, and validity of this instrument is strongly recommended.

References

Bradburn, N. M. *The Structure of Psychological Well-being.* Chicago: Aldine, 1969.

Graney, M. J. "The Affect Balance Scale and Old Age." Paper presented to the Annual Meeting of the Midwest Sociological Society, Milwaukee, April 26, 1973.

———. "Happiness and Social Participation in Aging." *Journal of Gerontology,* 1975, 30(6): 701–6.

Mangen, D. J. "Non-random Measurement Error in the Bradburn Affect-Balance Scale: Toward the Development of a Social Historical Theory of Measurement Error." Paper presented to the 30th Annual Meeting of the Gerontological Society, San Francisco, November 18–22, 1977.

Moriwaki, S. Y. "The Affect Balance Scale: A Validity Study with Aged Samples." *Journal of Gerontology,* 1974, 29 (1): 73-78.

National Council on the Aging. *The Myth and Reality of Aging in America.* Washington, D.C.: National Council on the Aging, 1975.

Instrument

See Instrument V1.5.I.h.

LIFE SATISFACTION INDEX (LSI)
B. L. Neugarten, R. J. Havighurst, and S. S. Tobin, 1961

Definition of Variable or Concept

Life satisfaction is defined as having the following five components: zest (versus apathy), resolution and fortitude, congruence between desired and achieved goals, positive self-concept, and mood tone (Neugarten, Havighurst, and Tobin, 1961, p. 137). Thus, a person who is at the positive end of the continuum (1) takes pleasure from the activity that constitutes everyday life, (2) regards his or her life as meaningful, (3) feels that he or she has succeeded in achieving his or her major goals, (4) holds a positive image of self, and (5) maintains happy and optimistic attitudes and moods.

Description of Instrument

There are two forms of the Life Satisfaction Index—form A and form B. Life Satisfaction Index A (LSI-A) contains 20 statements with which the respondent agrees or disagrees. Life Satisfaction Index B (LSI-B) consists of 12 items with two or three response categories for each item. Two shorter forms of LSI-A have been developed; one called Life Satisfaction Index Z (LSI-Z), by Wood, Wylie, and Sheafor (1969), contains 13 items; and a second, by Adams (1969), contains 18 of the original LSI-A 20 items.

Method of Administration

These are self-reporting instruments that take only a few minutes to administer. The instruments are usually administered in a paper-and-pencil format or in personal interviews.

Context of Development and Subsequent Use

The Life Satisfaction Index was developed as part of an extensive study of the psychological and social factors involved in aging, called the Kansas City Study of Adult Life. The investigators sought to develop an index that would provide a measure of the individual's own evaluation of his or her psychological well-being, independent of his or her level of activity or social participation. Wood, Wylie, and Sheafor (1969) and Adams (1969) extended the analysis of the LSI in separate studies. Wood, Wylie, and Sheafor (1969) designed a shorter version of LSI-A for a study using a mail questionnaire. They were investigating the extent to which the aged might be mobilized for community service. Adams's restudy (1969) of the LSI-A was done with a random sample of noninstitutionalized elderly people living in a small town in Missouri.

Samples

Neugarten, Havighurst, and Tobin (1961) developed the LSI-A and LSI-B on 92 respondents, who were a representative sample of the study population of 177 elderly people. They presented sample characteristics only for the 177 subjects. Data indicate that the sample was divided nearly evenly on sex. With respect to age, 39% were under 64, 19% were between 64 and 70, 28% were between the ages of 71 and 79, and 14% were 80 years of age and older. Approximately 31% were upper-lower-class, and 28% were designated as upper-middle-class.

Wood, Wylie, and Sheafor (1969) studied 100 rural elderly Kansas subjects. They reported that 70% were women, 25% had a high school education, and 66% were 70 years or older.

Adams's sample (1969) included 508 persons. Approximately 61% were women, the median education was 8.6 years, and the median age was 74.4 years. Most had been or were blue-collar workers or farmers. Most of the men were married, while 68% of the women were widowed.

The NCOA/Harris (1975) study of aging in America included 4,254 persons, including 2,797 persons aged 65 and older.

Scoring, Scale Norms, and Distribution

Scoring is accomplished on all scales by summing the correct number of answers or the item-response weights. Neugarten, Havighurst, and Tobin (1961) reported that the mean score on the LSI-A was 12.4, with a standard deviation of 4.4. The mean score for the LSI-B was 15.1, with a standard deviation of 4.7.

The mean LSI-A score for Adams's sample (1969) was 12.5, with a standard deviation of

3.6. Adams also factor analyzed the 20-item LSI-A index to determine whether the five theoretical components specified by Neugarten, Havighurst, and Tobin (1961) were present. Unfortunately, the details provided by Adams are scant, so it is difficult to report and evaluate his results. Adams reported that he found only four clearly discernible factors after rotation. Items 3, 4, 5, 6, 7, and 18 (see the instrument) constituted the first factor. He labeled these "mood tone." The second factor contained in items 1, 8, 9, 10, 15, and 16 was called "zest for life." The third factor was named "congruence," with items 12, 13, and 19 correlating highest with this factor. Items 2, 17, and 20 were related to the fourth factor, but Adams was unable to interpret the content of this factor. Items 11 and 14 did not load on any factor, and, because of this and their poor performance in an item-reliability check, Adams suggested that these items no longer be included in the LSI-A.

Wood, Wylie, and Sheafor (1969) reported that the mean score on the 20-item LSI-A for 281 respondents was 11.6, with a standard deviation of 4.4. From the 281 respondents, the investigators selected 100 subjects for further analysis. They reduced the number of items in the LSI-A from 20 to 13 through use of an item analysis. The items discarded were items 5, 8, 10, 11, 13, 14, and 15. The shorter version of the LSI-A is called the LSI-Z.

NCOA (1975) used a scoring system of 0 through 2 for each item of the LSI-A, with high scores indicating greater satisfaction. They reported a mean score of 26.4 for the total population and 24.4 for older persons in their sample (NCOA, 1975, p. 159).

Formal Tests of Reliability/Homogeneity

Wood, Wylie, and Sheafor (1969) reported that the Kuder-Richardson 20 reliability for the LSI-Z was .79. Adams (1969) evaluated the reliability of the LSI-A, using a discrimination value (D values) and a biserial correlation between the mean of the affirmative-response groups for each item and the LSI-A mean score for the entire sample. The D values indicate that all items except item 11 fell within the acceptable range from 20% to 80%. With the biserial correlation standard, all items are deemed reliable but items 11 and 14.

Formal Tests of Validity

Neugarten, Havighurst, and Tobin (1961) presented several tests of validity. First, they correlated the LSI-A and the LSI-B with expert ratings called the Life Satisfaction Ratings (LSR). This instrument consists of five rating scales for the five components of satisfaction (zest, resolution and fortitude, congruence between desired and achieved goals, positive self-concept, and mood tone). Ratings are based not on the respondent's self-reports but on inferences drawn by the judge or rater from all information available, including information on the respondents' interpersonal relationships and how others reacted to the respondent. Thus, the correlations of the LSI-A (r = .55) and the LSI-B (r = .58) with LSR constitute weak evidence of content validity.

Neugarten, Havighurst, and Tobin (1961) compared scores on the Life Satisfaction Index to ratings made by a clinical psychologist. The correlations were .39 and .41, respectively, for forms A and B.

Wood, Wylie, and Sheafor (1969) reported that the correlation between their LSI-Z and LSR was .57.

Lohmann (1977, p. 74) examined the correlations of the LSI-A, the LSI-B, the LSI-Z, and the Adams revision with each other and with six other measures of psychological well-being. The correlations of the LSI-A were as follows: LSI-B, .628; LSI-Z, .941; and Adams's revision, r = .989. The unique correlations of the LSI-B are: LSI-Z, .635; and Adams's revision, .644. Finally, the LSI-Z correlates very highly (.952), as expected, with the Adams revision. Correlations of these measures with the other indicators of life satisfaction ranged from .385 to .883.

Usability on Older Populations

The scales appear to be easy to administer to older populations.

Sensitivity to Age Differences

Neugarten, Havighurst, and Tobin (1961) reported that the indexes are more successful instruments for use with persons over 65 than with younger persons. Wood, Wylie, and Sheafor (1969) reported the same pattern in their study. They also indicated that the scale is more successful for use with men than with women.

General Comments and Recommendations

The evidence to date suggests that using all 20 items of the LSI-A may not be advisable. Adams (1969) has indicated that at least two items should be dropped; and Wood, Wylie, and Sheafor (1969) have shown that a 13-item scale may work as well as the original scale. As with the morale scales, it is evident that much more study is needed before the LSI scales can be considered reliable and valid measures of life satisfaction. The evidence with respect to reliability and validity is scant and rather weak. The attempt to establish the dimensional structure of the LSI-A is, at best, very preliminary and marred by errors of omission. Little, if any, further investigation of the LSI-B has been carried out. Thus, substantial conceptual and empirical work is needed. It is suggested that those who wish to use these instruments do so cautiously. Users are urged to further investigate the structure of this measure of life satisfaction.

References

Adams, D. L. "Analysis of a Life Satisfaction Index." *Journal of Gerontology,* 1969, 24: 470-74.

Lohmann, N. "Correlations of Life Satisfaction, Morale and Adjustment Measures." *Journal of Gerontology,* 1977, 32 (1): 73-75.

National Council on the Aging. *The Myth and Reality of Aging in America.* Washington, D.C.: National Council on the Aging, 1975.

Neugarten, B. L., R. J. Havighurst, and S. S. Tobin. "The Measurement of Life Satisfaction." *Journal of Gerontology,* 1961, 16: 134-43.

Wood, V., M. L. Wylie, and B. Sheafor. "An Analysis of a Short Self-Report Measure of Life Satisfaction: Correlation with Rater Judgments." *Journal of Gerontology,* 1969, 24: 465-69.

Instrument

See Instrument V1.5.I.i.

PHILADELPHIA GERIATRIC CENTER MORALE SCALE
(PGC MORALE SCALE)
M. P. Lawton, 1972

Definition of Variable or Concept

Morale is considered to be a multidimensional concept. High morale is defined as (1) a basic sense of satisfaction with oneself, (2) a feeling that there is a place in the environment for oneself, and (3) an acceptance of what cannot be changed (Lawton, 1972, p. 148). This scale was not, however, developed from an underlying theory of morale.

Description of Instrument

The original Lawton (1972) instrument contained 22 items, all having a dichotomous (i.e., yes-no) response format. Further analyses by Morris and Sherwood (1975) and Lawton (1975) have resulted in two revised versions of the scale. One is a 15-item scale as revised by

Morris and Sherwood (1975). The other is a 17-item scale called the Revised Philadelphia Geriatric Center Morale Scale (Lawton, 1975).

Method of Administration

The instrument can be administered in either written or oral form. This scale was designed to measure morale among the very old; thus, the items were designed to be comprehensible to very old subjects. The scale is relatively short so as not to result in fatigue or inattention. Lawton (1972) reported that his testing was done individually or in small groups of 10 to 15 subjects. When testing was done in small groups, Lawton indicated, items frequently had to be read or explained by proctors.

Context of Development and Subsequent Use

The original PGC Morale Scale was included in a study that attempted to clarify the conceptual meaning of "adjustment" in older persons. The study also sought to construct a scale that would be an appropriate measure of morale among very old persons.

Morris and Sherwood (1975) included the PGC Morale Scale in longitudinal impact-evaluation studies of applicants to the Hebrew Rehabilitation Center for the Aged (HRCA) and to a medically oriented low-income housing project for the physically impaired and elderly. Lawton (1975) further analyzed his PGC Morale Scale in a study of housing for the elderly.

Samples

Lawton's (1972) sample included 300 residents of institutions. The sample was predominantly female, with an average age of 78.2 years. Lawton's revision (1975) was carried out with a sample of 1,086 residents of public housing, as well as community residents.

Morris and Sherwood (1975) studied 269 applicants to a home for the aged and 406 applicants to a public housing project designed for the elderly and the handicapped.

Scoring, Scale Norms, and Distribution

Lawton (1972) reported that the mean morale score for those judged to be above average in morale was 16.54 (standard deviation 4.02). The mean score for those judged to be below average in morale was 12.75 (standard deviation 4.64). Lawton (1972) submitted the 22 items from his morale scale to a factor analysis. Using a principal-component analysis and a varimax rotation, he extracted six factors. The items and their respective factor loadings are summarized in Table 5-3.

The six factors, or components, include: (1) surgency—items that describe an optimistic ideology, a feeling of readiness to remain active, and freedom from anxiety and depression; (2) attitude toward own aging—items that measure self-perceived change (or lack of change) as one ages and the evaluation of the quality of these changes; (3) acceptance of status quo —items that measure general satisfaction with the way things are; (4) agitation—items that relate to anxiety and a dysphoric mood; (5) easygoing optimism—items that relate to the capacity for the enjoyment of immediate pleasures; and (6) lonely dissatisfaction—items that reflect the extent to which an individual feels lonely and dissatisfied with life.

Morris and Sherwood (1975), using two new samples, attempted to reproduce the 22-item PGC factor structure reported by Lawton. Using Harman's (1960) technique for measuring interfactor congruence of factor structures, they reported that none of the coefficients of congruence met the standard. The main reason for the lack of correspondence between the factor structures was that Morris and Sherwood were only able to replicate three of Lawton's components: (1) attitude toward own aging, (2) agitation, and (3) lonely dissatisfaction. Morris and Sherwood (1975) suggested several revisions to improve the reliability and validity of the PGC Morale Scale. First, they suggested that items 3, 5, 7, 16, and 12 (see Table 5-3) be dropped from the instrument because they appeared to be peripheral to the concept of

TABLE 5-3
Rotated Principal Components Analysis of
Philadelphia Geriatric Center Morale Scale Items

Item	Correct Response	I	II	III	IV	V	VI	h²
Component I								
10. I sometimes feel that life isn't worth living.	No	40	33	35	16	22	00	46
12. Most days I have plenty to do.	Yes	53	12	33	22	20	24	55
13. I have a lot to be sad about.	No	55	07	08	35	04	24	50
15. I am afraid of a lot of things.	No	73	03	08	28	06	12	64
Component II								
1. Things keep getting worse as I get older.	No	−02	65	14	14	15	00	49
2. I have as much pep as I did last year.	Yes	−07	70	01	11	11	09	53
6. As you get older, you are less useful.	No	05	74	00	14	01	−05	57
9. As I get older, things are (better, worse, same) than/as I thought they would be.	Better	33	49	30	−14	17	15	51
16. My health is (good, not so good).	Good	10	64	−01	13	07	13	46
Component III								
7. If you could live where you wanted, where would you live?	Here	−01	06	54	−14	18	40	51
14. People had it better in the old days.	No	04	−07	81	14	−14	−03	70
Component IV								
4. Little things bother me more this year.	No	15	36	19	54	06	10	49
8. I sometimes worry so much that I can't sleep.	No	31	20	00	55	13	13	47
17. I get mad more than I used to.	No	07	20	19	57	10	−11	43
20. I take things hard.	No	10	15	−06	71	10	18	59
23. I get upset easily.	No	02	−04	−03	71	−09	08	52
Component V								
11. I am happy now as I was when I was younger.	Yes	00	33	04	12	53	31	50

TABLE 5-3—*Continued*

Item	Correct Response	I	II	III	IV	V	VI	h²
Component V (continued)								
18. Life is hard for me most of the time.	No	33	29	12	33	39	08	46
21. A person has to live for today and not worry about tomorrow.	Yes	03	−08	−02	01	85	−05	74
Component VI								
3. How much do you feel lonely? (not much, a lot).	Not much	04	09	13	27	01	65	52
5. I see enough of my friends and relatives.	Yes	04	09	−07	−02	−02	72	54
19. How satisfied are you with your life today? (not satisfied, satisfied).	Satisfied	24	−06	28	20	17	46	42
Percentage of covariance accounted for by component		7.7	12.2	6.7	11.7	6.5	7.6	

SOURCE: Data from M. P. Lawton. "The Dimensions of Morale." In *Research Planning and Action for the Elderly,* D. Kent, R. Kastenbaum, and S. Sherwood (eds.), pp. 152–53. New York: Behavioral Publications, 1972.

morale and thus lacked face validity. The remaining 17 items were then factor analyzed using both Lawton's original data and two new samples for replication purposes. Two stable factors were extracted; one called the *tranquillity* factor and the other called the *satisfaction with life progression* component. The tranquillity factor contained all five of Lawton's original agitation items and items 13, 15, 18, and 19 (see Table 5-3). The satisfaction with life progression factor contained four original attitude toward own aging items plus items 4, 10, and 11. Items 14 and 21 did not load on either factor. The primary advantage of this revision, according to Morris and Sherwood (1975), is that the two new subscales are much longer than the original six subscales and, hence, are more reliable. In a companion paper in the same journal, Lawton (1975) reported further analysis of his PGC Morale Scale and suggested several revisions. Using several combinations of items and data bases, Lawton investigated five different factor structures. These are reproduced in Table 5-4.

The first three-factor solution (PGC2) includes 17 of the PGC items given to 872 housing subjects from the 1,086 community-resident elderly subjects. The next solution (PGC1) includes the 17 Morris-Sherwood items on the 300 York House and Lutheran Home subjects. The HRCA solution involves rehabilitation center applicants. The FR solution includes the 17 Morris-Sherwood items on 406 housing study subjects. Finally, the PGC2 (M and S) group included the 15 Morris-Sherwood items on 899 Lawton housing subjects.

Lawton found the three-factor solution to be relatively consistent over the five groups. His revised PGC Morale Scale includes three dimensions: (1) agitation—this six-item scale is essentially the same scale as the original version's; (2) attitude toward own aging—this five-item scale is essentially the same scale as in the original version; and (3) lonely dissatisfaction—this six-item scale includes items from the original lonely dissatisfaction and surgency scales.

TABLE 5-4
Three-Factor Varimax Loadings of Morale Scale Items for
Five Combinations of Subject Groups and Item Pools

Item	Correct Response	PGC 2	PGC 1 (M&S)	HRCA (M&S)	FR (M&S)	PGC 2 (M&S)
Factor 1 — Agitation						
4. Little things bother me more this year.[a]	No	58	57	55	53	54
8. I sometimes worry so much that I can't sleep.	No	36	62	65	58	54
15. I am afraid of a lot of things.	No	45	51	45	49	50
17. I get mad more than I used to.	No	67	52	43	25	44
20. I take things hard.	No	58	71	72	76	71
22. I get upset easily.	No	71	70	72	73	72
Factor 2 — Attitude toward Own Aging						
1. Things keep getting worse as I get older.	No	66	71	62	45	68
2. I have as much pep as I had last year.	Yes	68	72	52	71	66
6. As you get older you are less useful.	No	73	72	47	67	69
9. As I get older, things are better/worse than I thought they would be.	Better	54	46	37	42	61
11. I am as happy now as when I was younger.	Yes	45	30	56	39	56
Factor 3 — Lonely Dissatisfaction						
3. How much do you feel lonely?	Not much	74	—	—	—	—
5. I see enough of my friends and relatives.	Yes	44	—	—	—	—
10. I sometimes feel that life isn't worth living.[b]	No	51	47	45	18	−12
18. Life is hard for me much of the time.[b]	No	49	51	02	67	03
19. How satisfied are you with your life today?	Satisfied	52	51	06	64	03
13. I have a lot to be sad about.[b]	No	55	40	01	55	15
14. People had it better in the old days.[b]	No	—	20	16	50	—
21. A person has to live for today and not worry about tomorrow.[b]	Yes	—	58	65	27	—

SOURCE: Data from M. P. Lawton. "The Philadelphia Geriatric Center Morale Scale: A Revision." *Journal of Gerontology*, 1975, *30* (1): 87.

NOTE: High-morale responses are indicated in parentheses.

a. Item that cross-loaded and was selected as best representing factor 1 (see Lawton, 1975, p. 87).

b. Items that cross-loaded and were selected as best representing factor 3 (see Lawton, 1975, p. 87).

Formal Tests of Reliability/Homogeneity

Lawton (1972) reported that the split-half reliability estimated for all 22 items on all 300 subjects was .79. The coefficient of internal consistency (Kuder-Richardson 20)

TABLE 5-5
Test-Retest Comparisons for PGC Morale Scale

| Scale Component | Lawton (1972)[a] | | Morris-Sherwood (1975)[b] | | Lawton (1975)[c] |
	York Sample	Lutheran Sample	Hebrew Rehabilitation Sample	Housing Sample	Housing Sample
Agitation	.67	.84	—	—	.85
Attitude toward own aging	.81	89	—	—	.81
Lonely dissatisfaction	.38	.84	—	—	.85
Surgency	.22	.81	—	—	—
Acceptance of status quo	.32	.66	—	—	—
Easygoing optimism	.58	.44	—	—	—
Tranquillity	—	—	.73	.78	—
Satisfaction with life progression	—	—	.58	.65	—
TOTAL SCORE	.75	.80	—	—	—

a. Test-retest reliability coefficients (Lawton, 1972, p. 156).

b. Kuder-Richardson 20 alpha.

c. Cronbach's alpha.

was .81. Coefficients of reliability for the various subscales and samples are presented in Table 5-5.

Formal Tests of Validity

Lawton (1972) correlated the morale scale (based on all 22 items) with independent Q-sort evaluations of morale by judges who were familiar with the subjects. The criterion validity coefficient for the York House group was .43, and it was .53 for the Lutheran Home group. Lawton also reported information on cross-validation for his original 22-item PGC Morale Scale. A judge rated 40 of the York Home subjects on the Life Satisfaction Rating Scale (Neugarten, Havighurst, and Tobin, 1961). These ratings were correlated (.57) with the subjects' responses to the morale scale. The subjects selected for cross-validation included only those on whom the judges could agree in making their morale ratings.

Lawton (1972) also suggested that his morale scale has predictive validity. Using 300 subjects from his housing study, he found that high morale was correlated with a series of variables that could be predicted to relate to morale (e.g., physical health, engagement in activities, satisfaction with level of social interaction, mobility, etc.).

Lohmann (1977, p. 74) correlated the PGC Morale Scale with nine other measures of psychological well-being. These correlations ranged from .468 to .792 for the original version and .379 to .806 for the Morris-Sherwood revision. The original version and the Morris-Sherwood revision correlated very highly (.952).

Usability on Older Populations

Since the scale was designed to be administered to the very old, it is appropriate for older populations.

Sensitivity to Age Differences

There is some tentative evidence that the scale is not sensitive to age. Lawton (1972) divided the 300 subjects into those under 75 and those over 75 and found no significant differences for either the total PGC Morale Scale score or any of the factor scores. More research is necessary before any conclusion can be reached on this issue.

General Comments and Recommendations

Of the three current versions of the PGC Morale Scale, it is recommended that the Revised PGC Morale Scale be used. Morris and Sherwood (1975) and Lawton (1975) have also suggested that this version be used. One should not conclude, however, that this scale is necessarily an adequate measure of morale. While there is some evidence of reliability, validity, and factor structure stability over several samples, a number of problems remain unsolved. Since this scale was not developed from a theoretical base, it is unclear whether the domain of morale has been adequately measured. Lawton (1975) has suggested that several additional domains be explored, including self-rated health, social accessibility, general attitude toward aging, and positive affect. The factor analyses done to date are also deficient on several counts. Only varimax rotations have been used, and so no higher order factors have been investigated. The exact interrelationship among these dimensions is not at all clear. Simple structure has been difficult to obtain, so items have, at times, been assigned to a dimension on somewhat arbitrary grounds. Further work, both conceptual and empirical, is needed before an adequate measure of morale can be specified.

References

Harman, H. H. *Modern Factor Analysis.* Chicago: University of Chicago Press, 1960.

Lawton, M. P. "The Dimensions of Morale." In *Research Planning and Action for the Elderly,* D. Kent, R. Kastenbaum, and S. Sherwood (eds.), pp. 144–65. New York: Behavioral Publications, 1972.

———. "The Philadelphia Geriatric Center Morale Scale: A Revision." *Journal of Gerontology,* 1975, 30 (1): 85–89.

Lohmann, N. "Correlations of Life Satisfaction, Morale and Adjustment Measures." *Journal of Gerontology,* 1977, 32 (1): 73–75.

Morris, J. N., and S. Sherwood. "A Retesting and Modification of the Philadelphia Geriatric Center Morale Scale." *Journal of Gerontology,* 1975, 30: 77–84.

Neugarten, B. L., R. J. Havighurst, and S. S. Tobin. "The Measurement of Life Satisfaction." *Journal of Gerontology,* 1961, 16: 134–43.

Instrument

See Instrument V1.5.I.j.

Instruments

V1.5.I.a
SINGLE-ITEM INDICATORS OF
LIFE SATISFACTION AND HAPPINESS
G. Streib, 1956; A. Rose, 1955; H. Cantril, 1965

STREIB (1956)

On the whole, how satisfied are you with your way of life today—Would you say very satisfied, fairly satisfied, or not very satisfied?

ROSE (1955)

In general, how satisfied are you with your life?

_____ Very satisfied
_____ Somewhat satisfied
_____ Average
_____ Somewhat dissatisfied
_____ Very dissatisfied

CANTRIL (1965)

Self-Anchoring Scale

All of us want certain things out of life. When you think about what really matters in your own life, what are your wishes and hopes for the future? In other words, if you imagine your future in the *best* possible light, what would your life look like then, if you are to be happy? Take your time in answering; such things aren't easy to put into words.

Now taking the other side of the picture, what are your fears and worries about the future? In other words, if you imagine your future in the *worst* possible light, what would your life look like then? Again take your time in answering.

Here is a picture of a ladder. Suppose we say that the top of the ladder (pointing to Value 10) represents the best possible life for you and the bottom (pointing to Value 0) represents the worst possible life for you.

SOURCES: G. Streib. "Morale of the Retired." *Social Problems*, 1956, 3 (4): 272; A. M. Rose. "Factors Associated with the Life Satisfaction of Middle Class, Middle-Aged Persons." *Marriage and Family Living*, 1955, 17 (1): 15; H. Cantril. *The Pattern of Human Concerns*, p. 23. New Brunswick, N.J.: Rutgers University Press, 1965.

V1.5.I.b
CORNELL PERSONAL ADJUSTMENT SCALE
W. E. Thompson, G. F. Streib, and J. Kosa, 1960

Satisfaction with Life

1. All in all, how much happiness would you say you find in life today?
   (check one)
   _____ Almost none. (−)*
   _____ Some, but not very much. (−)
   _____ A good deal. (+)
2. In general, how would you say you feel most of the time, in good spirits or in low spirits: (check one)
   _____ I am usually in good spirits. (+)
   _____ I am in good spirits some of the time and in low spirits some of the time. (−)
   _____ I am usually in low spirits. (−)
3. On the whole, how satisfied would you say you are with your way of life today? (check one)
   _____ Very satisfied. (+)
   _____ Fairly satisfied. (−)
   _____ Not very satisfied. (−)
   _____ Not very satisfied at all. (−)

Dejection

4. How often do you get the feeling that you life today is not very useful? (check one)

_____ Often. (−)
_____ Sometimes. (−)
_____ Hardly ever. (+)

5. How often do you find yourself feeling "blue"? (check one)
   _____ Often. (−)
   _____ Sometimes. (−)
   _____ Hardly ever. (+)

6. How often do you get upset by the things that happen in your day-to-day living? (check one)
   _____ Often. (−)
   _____ Sometimes. (−)
   _____ Hardly ever. (+)

Hopelessness

7. These days I find myself giving up hope of trying to improve myself. (check one)
   _____ Yes. (−)
   _____ No. (+)
   _____ Undecided. (−)

8. Almost everything these days is a racket. (check one)
   _____ Yes. (−)
   _____ No. (+)
   _____ Undecided. (−)

9. How much do you plan ahead the things that you will be doing next week or the week after? (check only one)
   _____ I make *many* plans. (+)
   _____ I make a *few* plans. (−)
   _____ I make *almost no* plans. (−)

---

*Do not include these signs on the questionnaire; they are presented here only to indicate the positive or negative nature of the item for scoring purposes.

SOURCE: W. E. Thompson, G. F. Streib, and J. Kosa. "The Effect of Retirement on Personal Adjustment: A Panel Analysis." *Journal of Gerontology*, 1960, 15: 166.

V1.5.I.c.

DEAN MORALE INDEX
E. Cumming, L. R. Dean, and D. S. Newell, 1958

Item	*Correct Responses for High Morale*
1. What age would you like to be?	The age I am.
2. If you could live anywhere you pleased, in what part of _____ (city) would you most like to live?	Prefer to live where you are or plan to move if dissatisfied.
3. Of all the things you do on the weekend, which are less interesting and enjoyable to you?	Nothing.
4. Do you wish you could see more of your relatives, friends or neighbors than you do, or would you like more time to yourself?	Satisfied.

SOURCE: E. Cumming and W. E. Henry. *Growing Old*. New York: Basic Books, 1961.

V1.5.I.d
KUTNER MORALE SCALE
B. Kutner, D. Fanshel, A. Togo, and T. Langner, 1956

Item	Response Scored + 1
1. How often do you feel there's just no point in living?	Hardly ever.
2. Things just keep getting worse and worse for me as I get older.	Disagree.
3. How much do you regret the chances you missed during your life to do a better job of living?	Not at all.
4. All in all how much unhappiness would you say you find in life today?	Almost none.
5. On the whole, how satisfied would you say you are with your way of life today?	Very satisfied.
6. How much do you plan ahead the things you will be doing next week or the week after—would you say you make many plans, a few plans, or almost none?	Many plans.
7. As you get older, would you say things seem to be better or worse than you thought they would be?	Better.

SOURCE: B. Kutner, D. Fanshel, A. Togo, and T. Langner. *Five Hundred over Sixty.* New York: Russell Sage Foundation, 1956.

V1.5.I.e
SROLE ANOMIE SCALE
L. Srole, 1956

ANOMIA

(Score 1 for agreement with each item)

1. There's little use writing to public officials because they often aren't really interested in the problems of the average man.

     Agree   Disagree

2. Nowadays a person has to live pretty much for today and let tomorrow take care of itself.
3. In spite of what some people say, the lot of the average man is getting worse, not better.
4. It's hardly fair to bring children into the world with the way things look for the future.
5. These days a person doesn't really know whom he can count on.

Four new items in the enlarged anomia scale are:

6. Most people really don't care what happens to the next fellow.
7. Next to health, money is the most important thing in life.
8. You sometimes can't help wondering whether anything is worthwhile.
9. To make money there are no right and wrong ways anymore, only easy and hard ways.

The wording of the first of the five original items has been slightly changed to read: Most public officials (people in public offices) are not really interested in the problems of the average man.

SOURCE: L. Srole. "Social Integration and Certain Corollaries: An Exploratory Study." *American Sociological Review*, 1956, 21: 709-16.

V1.5.I.f
MORALE SCALE
M. Clark and B. G. Anderson, 1967; R. C. Pierce and M. Clark, 1973

Question-Response for Each Item by Dimension (Item number represents order on interview.)	Factor Loading	Communality h^2

I. Depression/Satisfaction:

14. On the whole, how satisfied would you say you are with your way of life today? (Very satisfied, Fairly satisfied, *Not very satisfied*).* — .77 / .62

12. All in all, how much happiness would you say you find in life today? (Lots, Some, *Almost none*). — .73 / .57

13. In general, how would you say you feel most of the time, in good spirits or in low spirits? (Good spirits, Both, *Low spirits*). — .70 / .52

15. How often do you get the feeling that your life is not very useful? (Often, Some, *Hardly ever*). — – .64 / .43

10. Do you often feel moody and blue? (Yes, *No*). — – .61 / .44

11. Have you felt lately that life is not worth living? (Yes, No). — – .41 / .41

3. Do you find you are less interested lately in things like your personal appearance and table manners and things like that? (Yes, *No*). — – .40 / .23

20. How much do you plan ahead the things that you will be doing the next week or week after? (Many, Few, *Almost none*). — .37 / .34

II. Social Accessibility:

5. Interviewer's rating of the subject's reaction to interview. (Normal, *Abnormal*). — .74 / .54

6. Interviewer's rating of the subject's affectivity. (Normal, *Abnormal*). — .56 / .36

7. Interviewer's rating of the subject's cooperativeness. (Cooperative, *Uncooperative*). — .48 / .27

III. Negative Age:

44. When you get old your thinking is not as good as it used to be. (Agree, Can't say, *Disagree*). — .65 / .47

36. When you get old you begin to forget things. (Agree, Can't say, *Disagree*). — .61 / .45

43. The only good thing about being old is that you are near the end of your suffering. (Agree, Can't say, *Disagree*). — .55 / .59

Question-Response for Each Item by Dimension (Item number represents order on interview.)	Factor Loading	Communality h^2
42. When you're old you take longer to make up your mind. (Agree, Can't say, *Disagree*).	.44	.22
27. When you are old there's not much use in going to a lot of trouble to look nice. (Agree, Can't say, *Disagree*).	.35	.23
IV. Equanimity:		
16. How often do you find yourself feeling blue? (Often, Some, *Hardly ever*).	.68	.57
17. How often do you get upset by the things that happen in your day-to-day life? (Often, Some, *Hardly ever*).	.66	.47
8. Do you often feel irritable and impatient? (Yes, *No*).	.51	.32
9. Have you been worried during the past year for no reason? (Yes, *No*).	.50	.29
V. Social Alienation:		
19. Almost everything these days is a racket. (Yes, Can't say, *No*).	.64	.46
25. These days a person doesn't know who he can count on. (Agree, Can't say, *Disagree*).	.56	.37
34. Everybody takes advantage of older people. (Agree, Can't say, *Disagree*)	.48	.34
24. It's hardly fair to bring children into the world with the way things look for the future. (Agree, Can't say, *Disagree*).	.48	.31
23. In spite of what some people say, the lot of the average man is getting worse, not better. (Agree, Can't say, *Disagree*).	.46	.24
35. The main problem in old age is money. (Agree, Can't say, *Disagree*).	.44	.23
38. Young people don't realize that old people have problems. (Agree, Can't say, *Disagree*).	.39	.20
VI. Will to Live:		
28. I'd rather die than grow old. (Agree, Can't say, *Disagree*).	.63	.46
30. I'd like to live another 20 years. (Agree, Can't say, *Disagree*).	- .63	.46
VIII. Physical Decline:		
2. How has your general health been this past year? (Very good, Good, Fair, Poor, *Very poor*).	.63	.44
4. Do you have as much energy as you did a year ago? (More, Same, *Less*).	.63	.43
1. How is your appetite? (Good, Fair, *Poor*).	.41	.25

Question-Response for Each Item by Dimension (Item number represents order on interview.)	Factor Loading	Communality h^2
VIII. Positive Age:		
31. Life doesn't really begin until 60. (Agree, Can't say, *Disagree*).	.49	.26
21. There's little use in writing to public officials because often they aren't interested in the problems of the average man. (Agree, Can't say, *Disagree*).	.45	.52
29. Old people can generally solve problems better because they have more experience. (Agree, Can't say, *Disagree*).	.45	.23
40. When you're older you appreciate the world more. (Agree, Can't say, *Disagree*).	.39	.25
41. When you get old, more people go out of their way to be nice to you. (Agree, Can't say, *Disagree*).	.38	.23

Variables with Insufficient Communality:

18. These days I find myself giving up hope of trying to improve myself.
    (Yes, Can't say, *No*).
22. Nowadays a person has to live pretty much for today and let tomorrow take care of itself. (Agree, Can't say, *Disagree*).
26. Young people underestimate the capabilities of older people.
    (Agree, Can't say, *Disagree*).
32. I feel sorry for old people.
    (Agree, Can't say, *Disagree*).
33. Sometimes I wish I were 25 or 30 again.
    (Agree, Can't say, *Disagree*).
37. I have more friends now than I did when I was 50.
    (Agree, Can't say, *Disagree*).
39. Lots of old people don't seem to care about keeping themselves neat and clean. (Agree, Can't say, *Disagree*).
45. I can't think of any problems that older people have.
    (Agree, Can't say, *Disagree*).

*The underlined response is indicative of a high score on the relevant dimension. Dimensions are scored with a mean of 50 and a standard deviation of 10.

SOURCE: R. C. Pierce and M. M. Clark. "Measurement of Morale in the Elderly." *International Journal of Aging and Human Development*, 1973, 4: 83-101. The instrument is reconstructed from Table 1 (pp. 84–86), Table 2 (pp. 87–89), and Table 3 (pp. 90–91).

V1.5.I.g
ATTITUDE INVENTORY
R. S. Cavan, E. W. Burgess, R. J. Havighurst, and H. Goldhammer, 1949

Item	Correct Response[1]
Health Subscale	
1. I feel just miserable most of the time.	Disagree
2. I am perfectly satisfied with my health.	Agree
3. I never felt better in my life.	Agree
4. If I can't feel better soon, I would just as soon die.	Disagree
5. When I was younger, I felt a little better than I do now.	Neutral[2]
6. My health is just beginning to be a burden to me.	Disagree
7. I still feel young and full of spirit.	Agree
Friendship Subscale	
8. I have more friends now than I ever had before.	Agree
9. I never dreamed that I could be as lonely as I am now.	Disagree
10. I would be happier if I could see my friends more often.	Neutral[2]
11. I have no one to talk to about personal things.	Disagree
12. I have so few friends that I am lonely much of the time.	Disagree
13. My many friends make my life happy and cheerful.	Agree
14. I have all the good friends anyone could wish.	Agree
Work Subscale	
15. I am happy only when I have definite work to do.	Agree
16. I can no longer do any kind of useful work.	Disagree
17. I am satisfied with the work I do now.	Agree
18. I have no work to look forward to.	Disagree
19. I get badly flustered when I have to hurry with my work.	Neutral[2]
20. I do better work now than ever before.	Agree
21. I have more free time than I know how to use.	Disagree
Financial Subscale	
22. I am just able to make ends meet.	Disagree
23. I have enough money to get along.	Agree
24. I haven't a cent in the world.	Disagree
25. All my needs are cared for.	Agree
26. I am provided with many home comforts.	Neutral[2]
27. I have everything that money can buy.	Agree
28. I have to watch how I spend every penny.	Disagree
Religion Subscale	
29. Religion is fairly important in my life.	Agree
30. I have no use for religion.	Disagree
31. Religion is a great comfort to me.	Agree
32. Religion doesn't mean much to me.	Disagree
33. I don't rely on prayer to help me.	Disagree
34. Religion is the most important thing in my life.	Agree
35. Religion is only one of many interests.	Neutral[2]
Usefulness Subscale	
36. I am some use to those around me.	Neutral[2]

	Correct
Item	*Response*

37. My life is meaningless now. — Disagree
38. The days are too short for all I want to do. — Agree
39. Sometimes I feel there's just no point in living. — Disagree
40. My life is still busy and useful. — Agree
41. This is the most useful period of my life. — Agree
42. I can't help feeling now that my life is not very useful. — Disagree

Happiness Subscale

43. This is the dreariest time in my life. — Disagree
44. I am just as happy as when I was younger. — Agree
45. My life could be happier than it is now. — Neutral[2]
46. I seem to have less and less reason to live. — Disagree
47. These are the best years of my life. — Agree
48. My life is full of worry. — Disagree
49. My life is so enjoyable that I almost wish it would go on forever. — Agree

Family Subscale[3] — *Subscale*

50. My family likes to have me around. — Neutral[2]
51. I am perfectly satisfied with the way my family treats me. — Agree
52. I wish my family would pay more attention to me. — Disagree
53. I think my family is the finest in the world. — Agree
54. My family is always trying to boss me. — Disagree
55. I get more love and affection now than I ever did before. — Agree
56. My family does not really care for me. — Disagree

1. Response options for all items are *Agree, Disagree, Uncertain(?)*.

2. Neutral items may be answered with either agreement or disagreement, and are not included in scoring the instrument (Cavan et al., 1949:119).

3. If the respondent has no living family, the Family Subscale should be omitted.

SOURCE: R. S. Cavan, E. W. Burgess, R. J. Havighurst, and H. Goldhammer. *Personal Adjustment in Old Age*, 158–59. Chicago: Science Research Associates, 1949.

V1.5.I.h

AFFECT-BALANCE SCALE
N. M. Bradburn, 1969

During the past few weeks did you ever feel . . .

Positive Feelings:

1. Pleased about having accomplished something?[1]
2. That things were your way?
3. Proud because someone complimented you on something you had done?
4. Particularly excited or interested in something?
5. On top of the world?

Negative Feelings:

1. So restless that you couldn't sit long in a chair?
2. Bored?
3. Depressed or very unhappy?
4. Very lonely or remote from other people?
5. Upset because someone criticized you?

1. Response options for all 10 items are yes or no.

SOURCE: N. M. Bradburn. *The Structure of Psychological Well-Being*, p. 56. Chicago: Aldine, 1969.

V1.5.I.i
LIFE SATISFACTION INDEX
B. L. Neugarten, R. J. Havighurst, and S. S. Tobin, 1961

FORM A

Here are some statements about life in general that people feel differently about. Would you read each statement on the list, and if you agree with it, put a check mark in the space "AGREE." If you do not agree with a statement, put a check mark in the space under "DISAGREE." If you are not sure one way or the other, put a check mark in the space "?" PLEASE BE SURE TO ANSWER EVERY QUESTION ON THE LIST.

Key: (x = high life satisfaction response).

a) Neugarten, *et al.* (1961) score 1 point for each response marked "x."
b) Adams (1969) score 1 point for each response marked "x."
c) Wood, *et al.* (1969) score 2 points for each response marked "x"; 1 point each response marked "?" or no response.

	Agree	Disagree	?	Items Used in: LSI-A Adams	LSI-2 Wood
1. As I grow older, things seem better than I thought they would be.	X			*	*
2. I have gotten more of the breaks in life than most of the people I know.	X			*	*
3. This is the dreariest time of my life.		X		*	*
4. I am just as happy as when I was younger.	X			*	*
5. My life could be happier than it is now.		X		*	
6. These are the best years of my life.	X			*	*
7. Most of the things I do are boring or monotonous.		X		*	*
8. I expect some interesting and pleasant things to happen to me in the future.	X			*	
9. The things I do are as interesting to me as they ever were.	X			*	*
10. I feel old and somewhat tired.		X		*	
11. I feel my age, but it does not bother me.	X			*	*

	Agree	Disagree	?	*Items Used in:* LSI-A Adams	LSI-2 Wood
12. As I look back on my life I am fairly well satisfied.	X	___	___	*	*
13. I would not change my past life even if I could.	X	___	___	*	___
14. Compared to other people my age, I've made a lot of foolish decisions in my life.	___	X	___	___	___
15. Compared to other people my age, I make a good appearance.	X	___	___	*	___
16. I have made plans for things I'll be doing a month or a year from now.	X	___	___	*	*
17. When I think back over my life, I didn't get most of the important things I wanted.	___	X	___	*	*
18. Compared to other people, I get down in the dumps too often.	___	X	___	*	*
19. I've gotten pretty much what I expected out of life.	X	___	___	*	*
20. In spite of what people say, the lot of the average man is getting worse, not better.	___	X	___	*	*

FORM B
(With Scoring Key)

Would you please comment freely in answer to the following questions?

1. What are the best things about being the age you are now?
   1 . . . a positive answer
   0 . . . nothing good about it
2. What do you think you will be doing five years from now? How do you expect things will be different from the way they are now, in your life?
   2 . . . better, or no change
   1 . . . contingent — "It depends."
   0 . . . worse
3. What is the most important thing in your life right now?
   2 . . . anything outside of self, or pleasant interpretation of future
   1 . . . "Hanging on"; keeping health, or job
   0 . . . getting out of present difficulty, or "nothing now," or reference to the past
4. How would you say you are right now, compared with the earlier periods in your life?
   2 . . . This is the happiest time; all have been happy; or, hard to make a choice
   1 . . . some decrease in recent years
   0 . . . earlier periods were better, this is a bad time

5. Do you ever worry about your ability to do what people expect of you—to meet demands that people make of you?

   2 . . . no

   1 . . . qualified yes or no

   0 . . . yes

6. If you could do anything you pleased, in what part of _____ would you most like to live?   (city)

   2 . . . present location

   0 . . . any other location

7. How often do you find yourself feeling lonely?

   2 . . . never; hardly ever

   1 . . . sometimes

   0 . . . fairly often; very often

8. How often do you feel there is no point in living?

   2 . . . never; hardly ever

   1 . . . sometimes

   0 . . . fairly often; very often

9. Do you wish you could see more of your close friends than you do, or would you like more time to yourself?

   2 . . . o.k. as is

   0 . . . wish could see more of friends

   0 . . . wish more time to self

10. How much unhappiness would you say you find in your life today?

   2 . . . almost none

   1 . . . some

   0 . . . a great deal

11. As you get older, would you say things seem to be better or worse than you thought they would be?

   2 . . . better

   1 . . . about as expected

   0 . . . worse

12. How satisfied would you say you are with your way of life?

   2 . . . very satisfied

   1 . . . fairly satisfied

   0 . . . not very satisfied

SOURCE: B. L. Neugarten, R. J. Havighurst, and S. S. Tobin. "The Measurement of Life Satisfaction." *Journal of Gerontology*, 1961, 16: 141–42.

V1.5.I.j
PHILADELPHIA GERIATRIC CENTER MORALE SCALE
M. P. Lawton, 1972

(Key: Score 1 point for each correct response)

	Correct Response	Lawton Revision	Items Used in: Morris and Sherwood Revision
1. Things keep getting worse as I get older.	No	*	*
2. I have as much pep as I did last year.	Yes	*	*

3. How much do you feel lonely (not much, a lot)?	Not much	*	_____
4. Little things bother me more this year.	No	*	*
5. I see enough of my friends and relatives.	Yes	*	*
6. As you get older you are less useful.	No	*	*
7. If you could live where you wanted to where would you live?	Here	_____	_____
8. I sometimes worry so much that I can't sleep.	No	*	*
9. As I get older, things are (better, worse, same) than/as I thought they would be.	Better	*	*
10. I sometimes feel that life isn't worth living.	No	*	*
11. I am happy now as I was when I was younger.	Yes	*	*
12. Most days I have plenty to do.	No	_____	_____
13. I have a lot to be sad about.	No	*	*
14. People had it better in the old days.	No	_____	_____
15. I am afraid of a lot of things.	No	*	*
16. My health is (good, not so good).	Good	_____	_____
17. I get mad more than I used to.	No	*	*
18. Life is hard for me most of the time.	No	*	*
19. How satisfied are you with your life today (not satisfied, satisfied)?	Satisfied	*	*
20. I take things hard.	No	*	*
21. A person has to live for today and not worry about tomorrow.	Yes	_____	_____
22. I get upset easily.	No	*	*

SOURCE: M. P. Lawton. "The Dimensions of Morale." In *Research Planning and Action for the Elderly*, D. Kent, R. Kastenbaum, and S. Sherwood (eds.), pp. 152-53. New York: Behavioral Publications, 1972.

Chapter 6

Self-Concept and Self-Esteem

Linda M. Breytspraak and Linda K. George

As Ruth Wylie has pointed out in her comprehensive reviews of research on the self-concept and related constructs (1968; 1974), there are many ambiguities and inconsistencies in the usage of the constructs self-concept and self-esteem. The variety of usages can be attributed both to the wide range of theoretical perspectives bearing on self-concept and self-esteem and to the variety of measurement orientations that result. Nonetheless, increasing convergences can be noted in the definition and measurement of these constructs; this is due primarily to the impact of several excellent reviews of this area of research (e.g., Wells and Marwell, 1976; Crandall, 1973; Shaver, 1969).

The purpose of this chapter is threefold. First, the salient conceptual and methodological issues in the development of self-concept and self-esteem constructs are reviewed. Second, the instruments reviewed in this chapter are briefly discussed and grouped according to the measurement approach they use. Finally, recommendations with regard to the selection of appropriate instruments for studying self-concept and self-esteem in older people are made. It is hoped that this review will contribute to the further convergence of research in this area.

Conceptual and Methodological Issues

Definitions

The distinction between self-concept and self-esteem made in this chapter rests on a view of the self that contrasts *cognitive* and *affective* processes in self-perception. Self-concept is the cognitive component of the self and consists of the individual's self-perceptions of himself or herself as an object (i.e., "what I am really like"). Self-concept emerges as a description of one's self. Epstein (1973), for example, referred to self-concept as the theory an individual holds about himself or herself as an object. In contrast, self-esteem refers to the affect associated with a judgment or an evaluation of one's self. It may emerge from individuals' comparisons of what they are like to what they aspire to be like. It might be assessed as high or low, positive, or negative. The distinction made in this chapter restricts evaluative ratings to measures of self-esteem. To know that a person considers himself or herself to be of average intelligence provides evidence of self-concept, but it does not tell us anything about that individual's self-esteem unless there is additional information about his or her level of aspired intelligence or the affect that is associated with that self-conception. This distinction between self-concept as the cognitive component and self-esteem as the evaluative or affective component of the self is compatible with the conceptual positions taken in several recent reviews (Wells and Marwell, 1976; Crandall, 1973; Shaver, 1969; Gordon, 1968), although it is not adhered to by all the authors of the instruments reviewed in this chapter.

A variety of self-related terms are commonly discussed in the relevant literature (i.e., self-acceptance, self-regard, self-image). Explicit definitions of these related constructs will not be developed here. Such constructs are conceptually related to self-concept and self-esteem and would be expected to be empirically related to them, also. When particular instruments require the consideration of related constructs, appropriate conceptual connections are provided in the reviews.

The measurement instruments reviewed in this chapter, as well as the definitions already developed, rest upon two central assumptions. First is the assumption that *self-concept and self-esteem are consciously available to the individual.* Wylie (1974) referred to this as the phenomenal view of the self. Second, and a logical extension of the first, is the assumption that *self-concept and self-esteem can be measured by using self-reporting methods.* Both of these assumptions pervade the literature in this area; however, there are alternative views. A minority of theorists believe self-concept and related constructs to be unconscious phenomena (Wylie, 1974). Such a position implies that self-concept and self-esteem must be assessed through behavioral, rather that self-reporting, measures. Some theorists who see self-concept and self-esteem as concepts consciously available may want behavioral measurement instead of, or in addition to, self-reporting measures.

Theoretical Considerations

As it has been observed by Wells and Marwell (1976), the idea of self-concept was developed fairly recently and its development has paralleled the growth of psychology and sociology in the twentieth century. Self-concept and self-esteem are constructs important to a number of theoretical perspectives, including the psychoanalytic theories of Adler, Horney, Fromm, Sullivan, and others; the ego psychologic theories of Allport and Symonds; client-centered theories, especially those represented by the work of Rogers; the field-theory approach of Ziller that stems from Gestalt psychology; the role theory of Secord and Backman (1961); and symbolic interactionist perspectives stemming from the work of Cooley and Mead but particularly manifested in the empirical work of Kuhn and his students at the University of Iowa. A detailed discussion of these theoretical perspectives is not possible here; however, several comprehensive reviews are available to the interested reader (Wells and Marwell, 1976; Wylie, 1968, 1974).

The various definitions of self-related constructs are in large part a consequence of the number of theoretical perspectives. In addition, these conceptual differences are reflected in the development and application of measures of self-concept and self-esteem. Thus, although efforts to consolidate and synthesize the measurement of self-concept and self-esteem are useful, such efforts are limited by the wide array of theoretical perspectives that include these constructs.

The issue of the role of age in self-concept and self-esteem is of particular significance in this volume. There are no firm theoretical reasons to expect age differences in self-concept and/or self-esteem, although a few measures have been constructed to maximize age differences (e.g., Mason, 1954; Bloom, 1960). Although different theoretical paradigms suggest that a variety of variables are responsible for the development and maintenance of self-concept and self-esteem, chronological age is not, at this point, one of them. Age per se does not appear to be a direct causal agent; rather, it influences self-concept and self-esteem indirectly. Thus, the position taken in this chapter is that there are no compelling theoretical reasons to expect age differences in self-esteem and self-concept, provided that other theoretically relevant and age-related variables (such as health, retirement, and loss of spouse) have been appropriately controlled.

Dimensions of Self-Concept and Self-Esteem

Self-esteem and self-concept have been conceptualized and measured both globally and in terms of relevant dimensions. Relatively few measures of self-concept are intended to be global, or all-encompassing. Even the Twenty Statements Test (Kuhn and McPartland, 1954), which permits the subject to relate self-perceptions in an open-ended manner, claims only that subjects are reporting those aspects of self-concept most meaningful for them. The majority of self-esteem measures are global in orientation, although there are some exceptions (in particular, those measures derived from semantic differential methods). Global assessments of self-esteem measure the individual's general sense of self-worth.

Dimensions of self-concept and self-esteem are useful on both theoretical and methodological grounds. Theoretically, it is not a matter of the verity of any particular classification scheme—the utility depends on the research question under consideration. Precisely because the human agent is consciously aware of his or her own existence and able to examine reflexively any and all of his or her interactions and activities, the number of conceivable self-perceptions is infinite. Methodologically, dimensions of self-concept and self-esteem are crucial to the interpretation of research results. Most measures of self-concept are actually measures of separate dimensions of self-concept. In these situations, research results should be interpreted and generalized only in terms of the dimensions they measured.

Dimensions of self-concept and self-esteem can be derived on either theoretical or empirical grounds. The most popular theoretical classification is the distinction between actual self-concept ("what I am really like"), ideal self-concept ("what I would like to be like"), and perceived self-concept ("how others see me"). In this system of definitions, self-esteem is sometimes operationalized as the discrepancy between actual and ideal self-concepts, with a larger discrepancy assumed to reflect negative affect and self-evaluation. Wylie (1974) and others have described certain conceptual and interpretive difficulties with this approach. The most common empirical approaches to the derivation of dimensions of self-concept have been the application of factor analytic techniques (e.g., Monge, 1975) and, less frequently, other correlational procedures, such as cluster analysis (e.g., Back and Guptill, 1966).

Measurement Issues

Problems related to establishing the reliability and validity of the instruments in this chapter have been found—some common to many instruments in this volume and others specifically relevant to measures of self-concept and self-esteem.

In general, this review of the instruments bears out the observations of Wylie (1974) and Wells and Marwell (1976) that too little attention has been given in self-concept and self-esteem research to issues determining reliability. In the majority of the instruments reviewed, internal consistency and split-half and test-retest reliabilities have not been reported. Some of the authors of the instruments have indicated that their measures have been determined to be reliable, but they do not present the actual reliability estimates in their published reports. Instruments for which some useful reliability information has been published include the Tennessee Self-Concept Scale, Coopersmith's Self-Esteem Inventory, Bills's Index of Adjustment and Values, Rosenberg's Self-Esteem Scale, Shostrum's Personal Orientation Inventory, Berger's Self-Acceptance Scale, and the Duke Semantic Differential Technique. Not all of these, however, include all relevant types of reliability. Furthermore, when instruments have been developed on younger populations and later used with older groups, the reliability of the instruments in the older groups is generally not computed or reported. Wylie (1974) has emphasized that reliability figures should be relevant to the groups whose results are being interpreted.

A neglected issue of reliability, even where estimates of reliability exist, is that of whether the estimation procedure involves implicit assumptions that actually fit the theoretical construct or variable being measured. This concern is particularly relevant when test-retest correlations in self-concept and self-esteem measures are being reported, for different assumptions are made in different theoretical orientations about the extent to which the concept and the measure should be situationally and temporally unbounded. For example, Coopersmith's Self-Esteem Inventory claims to tap relatively enduring aspects of self-esteem, and, thus, we would expect test-retest reliabilities to be somewhat more salient than in an orientation based on the situational responsiveness of self-esteem.

With some exceptions, validation data on self-concept and self-esteem measures are also weak. It is not an easy task to demonstrate that concepts potentially as exclusive as self-concept and self-esteem have been adequately measured by an instrument. As Wells and Marwell (1976) have observed, the most frequent form of validation in this area is simple face validity, or substitution of faith for evidence. Crandall (1973), Wylie (1974), and Wells and Marwell (1976) have all strongly appealed for a careful validation program in self-concept and self-esteem measurement that originates in a systematic process of replication of the studies and repeated use of instruments.

This review of gerontological research can only confirm their appeals. The authors do add the further caveat, however, that the establishment of validity on one sample should not lead us to presume that the measure will be equally valid for samples with different characteristics. In general, gerontological researchers who have used measures developed on younger populations have not demonstrated the appropriateness of item content or the salience of self-concept and self-esteem dimensions for older persons.

Two further issues particularly related to the validity of self-concept and self-esteem measures must be briefly mentioned. First, the confounding of self-concept and self-esteem with social desirability measures is especially likely, although—as Crandall (1973), Wylie (1974), and Wells and Marwell (1976) have all observed—it is not entirely clear what this means. Responding in a socially desirable direction should not necessarily invalidate a self-concept or self-esteem report. It can be assumed that successful socialization leads a person to hold socially desirable traits as part of a self-assessment. Therefore, caution must be exercised in evaluating correlations of self-concept/self-esteem measures with social desirability measures. Second, self-concept and self-esteem research seems to have suffered particularly from its failure to use multitrait-multimethod approaches to validation. Wylie (1974, p. 114) evaluated 2,000 articles published between 1961 and 1971, including self-concept instruments, and found only 18 with multitrait-multimethod matrices; only 1 self-concept measure was included in the 18. Very little of the evidence reported in the reviews in this chapter under *convergent validity* would qualify as multimethod.

All of the instruments selected for review in this chapter are multi-item measures that have been used at least once in studies in later life. As noted earlier, the majority have been developed on younger samples. Instruments developed specifically for studies of aging include Mason (1954), Preston and Guidekson (1966), Kutner et al. (1956), Bloom (1960), the semantic differential measures (Back and Guptill, 1966; Monge, 1973; Kogan and Wallach, 1961), and Reichard, Livson, and Petersen (1962). The instruments are grouped according to the measurement approach they took.

Likert-Type Scales

A number of commonly used measures of self-esteem and self-concept are Likert-type scales. Respondents are required to rate descriptive statements in terms of their degrees of self-applicability, usually along a four- or five-point continuum of agreement. Responses to a series of self-rating items then are usually summed to form a total score.

Potential problems in the use of Likert measures include the weighting of items in the calculation of total scores and the establishment of a neutral point along the agreement-disagreement continuum. Item analysis and careful scale construction can effectively reduce these potential problems. (See Table 6-1.)

Forced Choice Instruments

The forced choice instruments included in this chapter require respondents to rate statements as either "like me" or "unlike me," true or false. Problems associated with forced choice instruments are that subjects may be required to make inappropriate responses (i.e., the categories presented are not relevant) and the fact that dichotomous response categories cannot make fine discriminations across subjects. In spite of these limitations, forced choice response categories are used in several standardized and commonly used measures of self-esteem and self-concept. (See Table 6-1.)

Adjective Checklists

Adjective checklists are similar to both Likert scales and forced choice instruments. Like Likert scales, adjective checklists require respondents to evaluate a series of self-descriptive items as applicable or non-applicable. Like the forced choice measures reviewed in this chapter, responses to statements on adjective checklists are limited to two choices: acceptance or rejection of the item. Most scores are summed across items to derive a total scores. Potential problems with adjective checklists include the weighting of items in forming total scores and the fact that distinctions cannot be made concerning degree of agreement. (See Table 6-1.)

Semantic Differential Scales

The semantic differential is a general method of measuring the meaning of an object or an event, which was developed by Osgood and his colleagues (Osgood and Suci, 1955; Osgood, Suci, and Tannenbaum, 1957). These investigators concentrated on the measurement of meaning and the relationships between meaning and attitude. Osgood, however, did not pursue the use of semantic differential scales for the measurement of self-concept and self-esteem; that task has been performed by other investigators.

Several approaches have been used to apply semantic differential techniques to the measurement of self-concept and self-esteem. One approach is to have respondents rate themselves along a series of bipolar adjectives, to score activity and potency items as measures of self-concept, and to use the evaluative items as measures of self-esteem. (Factor analyses done by a number of investigators have shown activity, potency, and evaluative factors to be basic dimensions of meaning.) A second approach is to present the same set of adjectives twice, requiring respondents to rate both their actual and ideal selves. Scores along the actual-self continuums are viewed as measures of self-esteem. Discrepancy scores may be calculated and used as measures of self-esteem. The use of discrepancy scores raises a variety of statistical problems (Cronbach and Furby, 1970); nonetheless, this practice is common. In other cases, the distinction made in this chapter between self-concept and self-esteem is ignored, and scores across the adjectives are viewed as either self-concept or self-esteem, depending upon the investigator's theoretical perspective. (See Table 6-1.) The Rosencranz and McNevin (1969) and Kogan and Wallach (1961) versions of the semantic differential are reviewed in Chapter 12 of this volume.

Q-Sorts

Q-sorts are frequently used to measure actual self-ideal/self-discrepancies, which are used as indicators of self-esteem. Like semantic differential scales, discrepancy scores are statistically troublesome. A general problem in the use of Q-sorts is that respondents often find the procedure difficult to understand and perform. (See Table 6-1.)

Semiprojective and Open-Ended Measures

Projective measurement techniques are open-ended and nondirective in format and are intended to tap unconscious affective states. Projective measures are not included in this chapter, although some semiprojective and open-ended instruments are reviewed. Semiprojective and open-ended techniques are defined here as being open-ended and non-directive but intended to measure consciously available self-attitudes and self-evaluations. The most common problem with these instruments is the difficulty in developing an exhaustive but mutually exclusive set of scoring categories. (See Table 6-1.)

Summary and General Recommendations

This survey of the gerontological literature of self-concept and/or self-esteem (see Table 6-1) indicates that the measures that have been most frequently used are the Tennessee Self-Concept Scale, the Rosenberg Self-Esteem Scale, the Twenty Statements Test, and the several measures following the semantic differential approach. The Tennessee Self-Concept Scale and Rosenberg's scale probably represent the best of all the measures discussed because of the amount of work that has been done to establish their validity and reliability, including their use on older populations. The Index of Adjustment and Values, the Personal Orientation Inventory, and the Self-Acceptance Scale are also recommended as measures having potential for wider use in gerontological research.

This chapter tends to reinforce the conclusions of Crandall (1973) and Wylie (1974) that there is a need to concentrate on the solid development of fewer measures of self-concept and self-esteem. The temptation to develop one's own measures is clearly a great one, but, unfortunately, this approach all too often disregards the establishment of the instrument's psychometric properties.

This is not to suggest that all research on self-concept and self-esteem in gerontology, or in any field, should focus all its efforts on two or three agreed-upon measures. There are a number of considerations that would preclude this, but only a few will be mentioned. First, the researcher needs to clarify whether he or she is interested in measures of self-concept or of self-esteem. Absolutely essential is a clear conception of what one wants to measure theoretically. Second, one must ask the question whether a dimensional or a global assessment is required by the problem's definition. If the researcher opts for the dimensional approach, he or she must question the factorial invariance and construct validity of the measure across groups (especially age-groups). Third, the question whether the measure is appropriate to the characteristics of the particular sample under consideration should be asked. For example, does one wish to study a group of healthy, fully functioning adults or a nursing home sample in which one expects to find a large number of impaired individuals that might proscribe the use of a particular instrument? Fourth, are there time limits placed on the completion of the measure? Research on learning has shown older adults to be capable learners when time pressure is not a factor. This might suggest that the use of extremely long instruments would not be appropriate for some groups of older people. Finally, more careful attention to the selection, construction, and continued validation of instruments by gerontologists wishing to study self-concept and self-esteem will contribute to the overall improved status of research on these constructs.

TABLE 6-1

Instruments Reviewed in Chapter 6

Instrument	Author (date)	Code Number
I. Likert-Type Scales		
a. Tennessee Self-Concept Scale	Fitts (1965)	Copyrighted
b. Self-Esteem Scale	Rosenberg (1965)	V1.6.I.b
c. Index of Adjustment and Values	Bills, Vance, and McLean (1951)	V1.6.I.c
d. Self-Acceptance Scale	Berger (1952)	V1.6.I.d
e. Self-Concept Questionnaire	Mason (1954)	V1.6.I.e
II. Forced Choice Questionnaires		
a. Self-Esteem Inventory	Coopersmith (1967)	Copyrighted
b. Personal Orientation Inventory	Shostrum (1964)	Copyrighted
c. Self-Perception Questionnaire	Preston and Guideksen (1966)	V1.6.II.c
d. Self-Image Scale	Kutner et al. (1956)	V1.6.II.d
III. Adjective Checklists		
a. Adjective Check List	Gough and Heilbrun (1965)	Copyrighted
b. LaFarge-Suczek Adjective Checklist	Kogan and Fordyce (1962)	V1.6.III.b
c. Adjective Checklist	Bloom (1960)	V1.6.III.c
IV. Semantic Differential Scales		
a. Duke Semantic Differential Technique	Back and Guptill (1966)	V1.6.IV.a
b. Semantic Differential Scale	Monge (1973)	V1.6.IV.b
V. Q-Sorts		
a. Adjective Q-Set for Nonprofessional Sorters	Block (1961)	Copyrighted
VI. Semiprojective and Open-Ended Measures		
a. Twenty Statements Test	Kuhn and McPartland (1954); Bugenthal and Zelen (1950)	No special material
b. Peck Sentence-Completion Test	Peck (1959)	V1.6.VI.b
c. Self-Evaluation Scale	Clark and Anderson (1967)	V1.6.IV.c
d. Self Battery	Reichard, Livson, and Peterson (1962)	V1.6.VI.d

REFERENCES

Back, K. W., and C. S. Guptill. "Retirement and Self-Ratings." In *Social Asepcts of Aging,* I. H. Simpson and J. C. McKinney (eds.), pp. 120–29. Durham, N.C.: Duke University Press, 1966.

Berger, E. M. "The Relation between Expressed Acceptance of Self and Expressed Acceptance of Others." *Journal of Abnormal and Social Psychology,* 1952, 47: 778–82.

Bills, R., E. Vance, and O. McLean. "An Index of Adjustment and Values." *Journal of Consulting Psychology,* 1951, 15: 257-61.

Block, J. *The Q-Set Method in Personality Assessment and Psychiatric Research.* Springfield, Ill.: Charles C. Thomas, 1961.

Bloom, K. L. "Some Relationships between Age and Self Perception." Ph.D. dissertation, Columbia University, 1960. (Ann Arbor, Mich: University Microfilms, number 60-3046.)

Clark, M. and B. G. Anderson. *Culture and Aging: An Anthropological Study of Older Americans.* Springfield, Ill.: Charles C. Thomas, 1967.

Coopersmith, S. *The Antecedents of Self-Esteem.* San Francisco: W. H. Freeman, 1967.

Crandall, R. "The Measurement of Self-Esteem and Related Constructs." In *Measures of Social Psychological Attitudes,* pp. 45-167. Ann Arbor, Mich.: Institute for Social Research, 1973.

Cronbach, L., and L. Furby. "Can We Measure Change—or Should We?" *Psychological Bulletin,* 1970, 74: 68-80.

Epstein, S. "The Self-Concept Revisited: Or a Theory of a Theory." *American Psychologist,* 1973, 28:404-16.

Fitts, W. *Manual: Tennessee Self-Concept Scale.* Nashville, Tenn.: Counselor Recordings and Tests, 1965.

Gordon, C. "Self-Conceptions: Configurations of Context." In *The Self in Social Interaction,* C. Gordon and K. Gergen (eds.), pp. 115-36. John Wiley and Sons, 1968.

Gough, H. G., and H. G. Heilbrun, Jr. *The Adjective Check List Manual.* Palo Alto, Calif.: Consulting Psychologists Press, 1965.

Kogan, N., and M. A. Wallach. "Age Changes in Attitudes and Values." *Journal of Gerontology,* 1961, 16: 272-79.

Kogan, W. S., and W. E. Fordyce. "The Control of Social Desirability: A Comparison of Three Different Q-Sorts and a Checklist, All Composed of the Same Items." *Journal of Consulting Psychology,* 1962, 26: 26-30.

Kuhn, M. H., and T. S. McPartland. "An Empirical Investigation of Self-Attitudes." *American Sociological Review,* 1954, 19: 68-76.

Kutner, B., D. Fanshel, A. Togo, and T. Langner. *Five Hundred over Sixty.* New York: Russell Sage Foundation, 1956.

Mason, E. P. "Some Correlates of Self-Judgments of the Aged." *Journal of Gerontology,* 1954, 9: 324-37.

Monge, R. H. "Developmental Trends in Factors of Adolescent Self-Concept." *Developmental Psychology,* 1973, 8: 382-93.

———. "Structure of Self-Concept from Adolescence through Old Age." *Experimental Aging Research,* 1975, 1: 281-91.

Osgood, C. E., and G. J. Suci. "Factor Analysis of Meaning." *Journal of Experimental Psychology,* 1955, 50: 325-28.

Osgood, C. E., G. J. Suci, and P. Tannenbaum. *The Measurement of Meaning.* Urbana, Ill.: University of Illinois Press, 1957.

Peck, R. F. "Measuring the Mental Health of Normal Adults." *Genetic Psychological Monographs,* 1959, 60: 197-225.

Preston, C. E., and K. S. Guideksen. "A Measure of Self-Perception among Older People." *Journal of Gerontology,* 1966, 21: 63-71.

Reichard, S., F. Livson, and P. G. Petersen. *Aging and Personality.* New York: John Wiley and Sons, 1962.

Rosenberg, M. *Society and the Adolescent Self-Image.* Princeton, N.J.: Princeton University Press, 1965.

Rosencranz, H. A., and T. E. McNevin. "A Factor Analysis of Attitudes toward the Aged." *The Gerontologist,* 1969, 9: 55-59.

Secord, P. F., and C. W. Backman. "Personality Theory and the Problem of Stability and

Change in Individual Behavior: An Interpersonal Approach." *Psychological Review*, 1961, 68: 21–32.

Shaver, P. R. "Measurement of Self-Esteem and Related Constructs." In *Measures of Social Psychological Attitudes*, J. Robinson and P. Shaver (eds.), pp. 45–160. Ann Arbor, Mich.: Institute for Social Research, 1969.

Shostrum, E. L. "An Inventory for the Measurement of Self-Actualization." *Educational Psychological Measurement*, 1964, 24: 207–18.

Wells, L., and G. Marwell. *Self-Esteem: Its Conceptualization and Measurement*. Beverly Hills, Calif.: Sage, 1976.

Wylie, R. "The Present Status of Self-Theory." In *Handbook of Personality Theory and Research*, E. Borgatta and W. Lambert (eds.), pp. 728–87. Chicago: Rand McNally, 1968.

——. *The Self Concept* (vol. 1). Lincoln, Neb.: University of Nebraska Press, 1974.

Abstracts

TENNESSEE SELF-CONCEPT SCALE (TSCS)
W. Fitts, 1965

Definition of Concept

Fitts approached the definition of self-concept from a clinical perspective and was concerned with the relationship between self-concept and rehabilitation. Self-concept was seen as the most salient feature of each person's phenomenal world. It is the frame of reference through which the individual interacts with the world, and it is a powerful influence on behavior. The actualization of the self and the rehabilitation of handicaps were seen as simultaneous processes (Fitts et al., 1971).

Description of Instrument

This is a 100-item scale made up of self-descriptive statements. There are five response categories for each statement: completely false, mostly false, partly false and partly true, mostly true, and completely true. Ninety of the items were developed from a larger pool of items. The items fall into 15 subscales (6 items per subscale) derived from cross-classifications of the internal frame of reference of the items (self-identity, self-satisfaction, or behavior) with its external frame of reference (physical self, moral-ethical self, personal self, family self, or social self). This part of the scale is equally divided into positive and negative items. The total positive score (based on the 90 items) reflects the overall level of self-esteem. A high score indicates liking for one's self, feeling that one has value and worth, having self-confidence, and acting accordingly. Ten items from the MMPI L scale comprise the self-criticism scale. Most people admit that the mildly derogatory statements are true of them, and high scores indicate a normal and healthy capacity for self-criticism. If the self-criticism score is low, high positive scores are suspect and are probably the result of defensive distortion (Fitts, 1965). It is also possible to derive a number of other subscales (Fitts et al., 1971).

Method of Administration

This form is self-administered and requires about 20 minutes to complete.

Context of Development and Subsequent Use

Fitts's work on self-concept extends the work of Robers and Maslow on self-actualization and is one of the few attempts to generate empirical research out of this humanistic-psychol-

ogy perspective. His original interest was in the relationship between self-concept and rehabilitation. The scale has since been used in a wide variety of contexts (including with persons
with personality pathology). Fitts attempts to act as a clearinghouse for information on the
uses of the scale.

The scale has been used with older subjects in a number of studies. Grant (1967; 1969)
explored age differences in self-concept, giving special attention to the factorial structure of
the Tennessee Self-Concept Scale and age changes within each factor. Postema (1970) compared elderly male nursing home residents with self-sufficient community-dwelling residents
with respect to reminiscing, time orientation, and self-concept. Wilson and May (reported in
Thompson, 1972) compared nursing home and community residents. Trimakas and Nicolay
(1974) investigated the relationship between self-concept and old age and altruistic behavior.
Crandall (1975) looked at the correlation of religion, marital status, income, health, and age
with level of self-concept in an active, white, male, middle-class population.

Sample

The samples that have been used with the TSCS are reviewed in Table 6-2.

TABLE 6-2
TSCS Samples

Sample Characteristics	Fitts, 1965	Grant, 1967, 1969	Postema, 1970	Trimakas and Nicolay, 1974	Crandall, 1975
Sample size	626	500	60	162	Not reported
Age range	12–68	20–60	60–80+	66–88	55–86
Gender	Both	Both	Male	Female	Male

Scoring, Scale Norms, and Distribution

Complete scoring instructions are included in the TSCS manual (Fitts, 1965).

Fitts's standardization group from which norms were developed was 626 persons, ages,
12 to 68, representing all socioeconomic and educational levels and racial groups and including approximately equal numbers of each sex. Fitts contends that there is no need to
expand the norm group because the effects of sex, age, race, education, and intelligence on
scores have been shown to be negligible.

For the standardization group, the mean on the self-criticism score was 35.54 and the
standard deviation was 6.70. The total positive score mean was 345.57 and the standard
deviation was 30.70. Complete normative data on all possible subscores are reported by Fitts
(1965, p. 14).

Formal Tests of Reliability/Homogeneity

Nunnelly (1968) used a Kuder-Richardson split-half technique and reported a reliability
coefficient of .91 for total positive scores.

Fitts has reported test-retest coefficients of .75 for the self-criticism scale and .92 for the
total positive scale over a two-week period (with 60 college students). For the various subscales making up the positive score, test-retest reliability ranges between .80 and .91.

Formal Tests of Validity

Item Selection: The items were selected from a large pool of self-descriptive items derived
from other self-concept measures and from written self-descriptions of patients and non-
patients. The items selected were those on which there was perfect agreement by seven clinical psychologists as to whether they represented a positive or a negative self-concept and
where they could be classified in the 15 subscales described earlier.

Convergent Validity: Fitts reported a correlation of –.70 between the TSCS positive score (90 items) and the Taylor Manifest Anxiety Scale. Other studies have also reported significant negative correlations between the TSCS positive score and anxiety measures (Thompson, 1972). Thompson (1972) also reported numerous studies relating measures of interpersonal relationships to TSCS. Fitts and associates (1971) reported a study by Bealmer and associates in which a strong positive relationship (*r*-value not reported) was found between the TSCS positive scores and a clear, positive sense of identity represented in responses to the "who am I?" test.

Discriminant Validity: Fitts (1965) reported a correlation of –.21 of the TSCS positive scale with the F (authoritarian personality) scale. Queen (reported in Thompson, 1972) found a correlation of .08 with a revision of the F scale. Studies of the relationship between dogmatism and the TSCS positive scores have found generally negative but insignificant relationships (Thompson, 1972).

Predictive Validity: Fitts (1965) reported data showing significant differences on almost all the subscales of TSCS between his norm group (N = 626) and a group of psychiatric patients (N = 369). The scale has also been found to differentiate between delinquents and nondelinquents, soldiers who weathered the stress of being a paratrooper and those who did not, and alcoholics and nonalcoholics.

Usability on Older Populations

The scale has been used successfully on all age-groups 12 years old and older. It has been used with samples varying across the range of psychological adjustment. It is usually completed in less than 20 minutes, which makes it attractive for use with older people.

Sensitivity to Age Differences

Although Fitts (1965) originally concluded that there are significant age differences in self-concept, more recent studies have indicated that self-concept may actually *improve* with age. Grant (1969) found that feelings reported about oneself became increasingly positive with age in her sample of 20–69-year-olds. She also noted an increase in denial with age. Trimakas and Nicolay (1974) found the TSCS positive score of their sample of sixty-six 89-year-olds to be significantly higher than that of Fitts's norm group, and they also found an increase with age within their own sample. Crandall (1975) found an improvement in self-concept with age, although it was not statistically significant.

Thompson's (1972) summary and comparison of Fitts's standardization group with samples of Postema (1970) and Wilson and May (Thompson, 1972) suggest that, although elderly groups show positive scores above average, the subscores show some variation in this pattern. Physical-self scores are below average, while self-satisfaction, moral-ethical-self, and social-self scores are particularly high. Thompson also observed standard deviations for the elderly groups to be higher than for the norm group, indicating that the elderly groups represent a more diverse and heterogeneous sample than the norm group.

General Comments and Recommendations

This scale is a particularly appealing one because of the extensive use that it has had. The possibility of computing subscores is a positive point, and it is recommended that anyone interested in performance on the TSCS as it is related to age should pay particular attention to differential changes by subscore area. However, no data have been provided by Fitts concerning the factor structure of the TSCS. A factor analysis in Grant's dissertation (1967) did extract 15 factors based on the TSCS, Cattell's 16PF Questionnaire, and several personal data items. She recommended further work to establish a scoring system for the TSCS based on the establishment of a more complete factorial structure.

Evidence has accumulated on the validity and reliability of this scale, but little has been published in studies of older samples. Further evidence on test-retest reliability and convergent and discriminant validity for older people is needed.

References

Bealmer, E., G. Bussell, H. Bussell, M. Cunningham, Z. Gideon, K. Gunderson, and M. Livingston. "Ego Identity and School Achievement: A Study of their Relationship in the Latency-Age Child and His Parents." Unpublished M.S.W. thesis, University of Louisville, (Kent School of Social Work), 1965.

Crandall, R. C. "An Exploratory Study of the Self-Concept of Male Members of Selected Senior Centers in Southeastern Michigan." Ph.D. dissertation, University of Michigan, 1975. (*Dissertation Abstracts*, 36: 1824A [1975].)

Fitts, W. *Manual: Tennessee Self-Concept Scale*. Nashville, Tenn.: Counselor Recordings and Tests, 1965.

Fitts, W. H., J. L. Adams, G. Radford, W. C. Richard, B. K. Thomas, M. M. Thomas, and W. Thompson. *The Self-Concept and Self-Actualization* (Monograph number 3). Nashville, Tenn.: Counselor Recordings and Tests, 1971.

Grant, C. R. H. "Age Differences in Self-Concept from Early Adulthood through Old Age." Ph.D. dissertation, University of Nebraska, 1967. (*Dissertation Abstracts*, 28: 1160B [1967].)

————. "Age Differences in Self-Concept from Early Adulthood through Old Age." *Proceedings of the 77th Annual Convention of the American Psychological Association*, 1969, 4: 717–18.

Nunnelly, K. G. "The Use of Multiple Therapy in Group Counseling and Psychotherapy." Ph.D. dissertation, Michigan State University, 1968. (Ann Arbor, Mich.: University Microfilms number 69–11, 139.)

Postema, L. J. "Reminiscing, Time Orientation and Self Concept in Aged Men." Ph.D. dissertation, Michigan State University, 1970.

Thompson, W. *Correlates of the Self Concept* (Monograph number 6). Nashville, Tenn.: Counselor Recordings and Tests, 1972.

Trimakas, K., and R. C. Nicolay. "Self-Concept and Altruism in Old Age." *Journal of Gerontology*, 1974, 29: 434–39.

Instrument

This copyrighted instrument is available in Fitts (1965).

SELF-ESTEEM SCALE
M. Rosenberg, 1965

Definition of Concept

Self-esteem was defined by Rosenberg (1965) as self-acceptance, a basic feeling of self-worth.

Description of Instrument

The instrument consists of 10 items reported along a four-point continuum from strongly agree to strongly disagree. The measure was designed to be scored as a Guttman scale, and the four response categories are scored dichotomously as agree or disagree. The instrument was designed to be brief (for ease of administration) and unidimensional.

Method of Administration

The instrument is self-administered and very short.

Context of Development and Subsequent Use

The instrument was originally developed as a measure of self-esteem for a study of high school students. Rosenberg (1965) reported several other related measures of potential interest, including self-stability, faith in people, and sensitivity to criticism.

Robert Atchley (1969; 1976) and his colleagues (Cottrell and Atchley, 1969) have used the Rosenberg Self-Esteem Scale in a large survey of older adults. The focus of this study was adjustment to retirement by male and female respondents with various occupational backgrounds.

Kaplan and Pokorny (1969) have used the Rosenberg Self-Esteem Scale to examine the relationship between age and self-attitude. In their work, the instrument is seen as a measurement of self-derogation, which is the opposite of self-esteem.

Ward (1977) administered the Rosenberg Self-Esteem Scale as part of a study of attitudes toward the aged, age identification, and self-esteem. His study was an attempt to apply labeling theory to the process of growing old.

Samples

In Rosenberg's study (1965), 5,024 high school juniors and seniors were randomly selected from 10 New York City public schools.

The retirement survey conducted by Atchley included 1,385 male and 2,167 female retirees, most of whom were living in Ohio. Two broad occupational categories were included—former employees of the telephone system and former public school teachers.

Kaplan and Pokorny (1969) administered the instrument to 500 respondents selected from the adult population of Harris County, Texas (which includes the city of Houston). The sample was selected by a three-stage probability design. The subjects ranged in age from under 30 to over 60, with 135 respondents over age 50.

Ward (1977) administered the instrument to 323 noninstitutionalized residents of Madison, Wisc. The subjects ranged in age from 60 to 92 years, with a mean age of 74.1. Of the sample 56% was female and 43% was married.

Scoring, Scale Norms, and Distribution

Scoring procedures have varied greatly across studies. Rosenberg (1965) has suggested that the 10 items yield six scales, which form a Guttman scale. For each item, strongly agree and agree count the same, and strongly disagree and disagree count the same. The six scale items are calculated as follows. Scale item 1 is calculated from the first three items. If a respondent answers at least two out of the three in the direction of negative self-esteem, he or she receives a positive score for scale item 1. Otherwise, he or she receives a negative score for scale item 1. Scale item 2 is calculated from items 4 and 5. At least one out of the two items answered in the direction of low self-esteem is a positive score for scale item 2. Item 6 forms scale item 3, item 7 forms scale item 4, and item 8 forms scale item 5. For each, when the respondent answers the item in the direction of negative self-esteem, the scale item is scored positively. Items 9 and 10 are combined to form scale item 6. Answering one or two of the items in the direction of negative self-esteem is scored positively.

This is a complex scoring system, but the six scale items, presumably, form a Guttman scale of negative self-esteem. Atchley (1969; 1976) and Cottrell and Atchley (1969) also used this scoring system and reported an overall mean of only .84.

Kaplan and Pokorny (1969) applied their factor loadings and simply summed the subjects' weighted responses to obtain a total self-derogation score.

Ward (1977) used the four-point response categories and summed the responses to get a total self-esteem score with a potential range of 4-40, with an observed mean of 29.4 and a standard deviation of 3.07.

Formal Tests of Reliability/Homogeneity

Rosenberg (1965) reported a reproducibility coefficient of .92 and a scaleability coefficient of .72 in his sample.

Silber and Tippett (1965) obtained a test-retest correlation of .85 when a group of college students was tested at a two-week interval.

Ward (1977) reported an alpha measure of internal consistency of .74.

Formal Tests of Validity

Kaplan and Pokorny (1969) reported a factor analysis of the 10 items. Items 1, 2, and 4 failed to load on the first and only factor extracted; the remaining seven items exhibited factor-item correlations from .37 to .77.

Silber and Tippett (1965) reported that correlations of this measure with similar measures and with clinical ratings ranged from .65 to .83.

Rosenberg (1965) reported a significant correlation between self-esteem and clinical ratings of depression in a sample of 150 volunteers.

Tippett and Silber (1965) reported no correlation between this measure and stability of perceptual performance and stability of ratings of others, thus suggesting discriminant validity.

Usability on Older Populations

From the available research, it appears that the measure is usable on older samples. The ease of administration and the brevity of the instrument increase its attractiveness as a measurement tool.

Sensitivity to Age Differences

Comparisons of the percentage distributions of low, moderate, and high self-esteem in the students examined by Rosenberg with Atchley's sample suggest that older persons exhibit somewhat higher levels of self-esteem.

Kaplan and Pokorny reported a complex interaction between self-derogation and age. Overall, there was no significant relationship between age and a sense of self-derogation. However, four variables were found to condition this relationship significantly: the experience of recent life events requiring behavioral adaptation, the congruence between current and "hoped for" standard of living, the presence or absence of fears of being left alone felt during childhood, and the nature of the respondent's household composition. These results support the position taken in this chapter that theoretical expectations of age differences in self-concept and self-esteem, given proper controls, are less than compelling.

Ward reported that both age and health are significantly correlated with self-esteem (r = .13 and .37, respectively). Relatively younger subjects and those in good health report higher levels of self-esteem.

General Comments and Recommendations

From the available evidence, it seems that further use of Rosenberg's Self-Esteem Scale with samples of older subjects is warranted. The ease of administration and the brevity of this measure are attractive features. Whether the scoring is more appropriately based on Rosenberg's Guttman scaling, the use of the four-point response categories, or the results of Kaplan and Pokorny's factor analysis is an unresolved issue in need of further inquiry. In addition, the very high levels of self-esteem reported in some studies suggest the possible confounding influence of social desirability. Nonetheless, the amount of work that has been done with this scale is impressive, and the instrument appears to be a useful measure of global self-esteem.

References

Atchley, R. C. "Respondents vs. Refusers in an Interview Study of Retired Women: An Analysis of Selected Characteristics." *Journal of Gerontology*, 1969, 24: 42–47.

——. "Selected Social and Psychological Differences between Men and Women in Later Life." *Journal of Gerontology*, 1976, 31: 204–11.

Cottrell, W. F., and R. C. Atchley. *Women in Retirement: A Preliminary Report*. Oxford, Ohio: Scripps Foundation, 1969.

Kaplan, H. B., and A. D. Pokorny. "Self-Derogation and Psychosocial Adjustment." *Journal of Nervous and Mental Disease*, 1969, 149, 421–34.

Rosenberg, M. *Society and the Adolescent Self-Image.* Princeton, N.J.: Princeton University Press, 1965.

Silber, E., and J. Tippett. "Self-Esteem: Clinical Assessment and Measurement Validation." *Psychological Reports,* 1965, 16: 1017–71.

Tippett, J., and E. Silber. "Self-Image Stability: The Problem of Validation." *Psychological Reports,* 1965, 17: 323–29.

Ward, R. A. "The Impact of Subjective Age and Stigma on Older Persons." *Journal of Gerontology,* 1977, 32: 227–32.

Instrument

See Instrument V1.6.I.b.

INDEX OF ADJUSTMENT AND VALUES (IAV)
R. Bills, E. Vance, and O. McLean, 1951

Definition of Concept

Adjustment is seen by the authors of this instrument to be the result of descrepancies between one's self-concept and a concept of an ideal self (i.e., the values toward which one is striving). The self-concept is defined as the traits and values that the individual has accepted as definitions of himself or herself.

Description of Instrument

Only the adult form of the IAV is described here, although forms also exist for high school, junior high school, and elementary school children. A sample of 124 words was taken from Allport's list of 17,953 traits—items that seemed to represent clear examples of self-concept definitions were chosen. The words were followed by three blank columns. In the first column subjects were asked to use each word in the sentence "I am a (an) _____ person" and rate its appropriateness on a five-point Likert scale. This measured concept of self. In the second column subjects were asked to indicate on a five-point scale how they felt about the description of themselves in the first blank. This sum of the two columns measured acceptance of self and was akin to our notion of self-esteem. In the third column the word was filled in the sentence "I would like to be a (an) _____ person" and a five-point rating was also attached. This measured concept of ideal self. The 49 words having the highest reliability (based on comparisons of variations in words rating with variations of subjects making the ratings) were reatained. There is also an "others" form of the adult IAV that is similar to the "self" form, except that the subject is asked to complete the index as he or she thinks the average person in his or her peer group would.

Method of Administration

The scale is self-administering and takes no more than 45 minutes.

Context of Development and Subsequent Use

The IAV was developed to test some theoretical notions about the nature of the self-concept, to be a tool for research, and to assess changes in adjustment occurring during psychotherapy. It may also tell about the impact of psychotherapy on value systems. The IAV has been widely used; however, its only known use in studies of later adulthood has been in dissertations. Kitching (1972) studies perceived and idealized self-concepts and self-acceptance in middle-aged women between 35 and 55 years old. Walter (1956) studied the relationship between degree of self-acceptance and perceived problems of retirement in a group of men facing retirement. McHugh (1971) examined the congruency between self-concept and occupational role concepts in young and middle-aged women.

Samples

Bills, Vance, and McLean (1951) used 44 college students for the original item analysis and later analyzed data on 325 college students. Data in Bills's recent manual (1975) are based on 888 adults, who came primarily from two institutions of higher education. Kitching studied 200 white, middle-class women ages 35 to 55 years in Tallahassee, Fla., who were attending one of 21 women's clubs. Walter studied 54 males within one to three years of retirement from various companies. McHugh (1971) studied 50 women who were in the final stages of professional and semiprofessional training programs at an urban community college. They were assigned to the young group when they were 28 to 25 years old and to the middle-aged group when they 35 or older.

Scoring, Scale Norms, and Distribution

For scoring purposes, the ratings on negative traits (those marked with asterisks) must first be inflected for columns 1 and 3 (self-concept and ideal self)—e.g., a rating of 1 should be changed to 5 (and vice versa) and a 2 to a 4 (and vice versa). Scores are obtained by adding each of the three columns. A discrepancy score can be obtained by finding the difference between column 1 and column 3 items and summing the differences without regard to sign. Scores are similarly obtained on the "others" form of the IAV. Bills (1975) also described a categorical score obtained by comparing column 2 scores for "self" and "others." The reader is referred to his manual (Bills, 1975) for a complete description of this scoring system.

Normative data on the adult IAV have been collected since 1950. Bills (1975, p. 69) reported norms for nine scores, including self-concept ($\overline{X} = 188.8$, $r = 25.4$), self-acceptance ($\overline{X} = 183.7$, $r = 27.0$), and ideal self ($\overline{X} = 213.6$, $r = 24.1$).

Formal Tests of Reliability

Bills (1975) reported a split-half reliability for self-concept of .53, with all other "self" and "others" scores ranging between .73 and .94.

Six-week test-retest reliabilities ranged between .83 and .92 for the "self" scores. Further reliability data were summarized by Wylie (1974).

Formal Tests of Validity

Convergent Validity: Bills, Vance, and McLean, (1951) reported giving the Rorschach examination and the IAV to 20 college females and finding a high association between presence of neurotic signs and low self-acceptance and presence of psychotic signs and high self-acceptance. Ziller and associates (1969) reported correlations of .46 and .17 for males and females, respectively, with the Coopersmith Self-Esteem Inventory and .60 and .29 for males and females, respectively, with Diggory's Self-Evaluation Questionnaire. Bills (1975) reported small but statistically significant relationships between the acceptance-of-self score and the Phillips Attitudes toward Self score (.24) and the California Test of Personality (.23). The discrepancy score showed a statistically significant correlation with the Phillips Self Score (.56) and the Washburne S-A Inventory (.43). Wylie (1974) also summarized a substantial amount of data indicating convergent validity.

Discriminant Validity: Crowne, Stephens, and Kelley (1961) found correlations of −.54 (self-acceptance) and −.47 (discrepancy) for males and −.57 (self-acceptance) and −.51 (discrepancy) for females with the Edwards Social Desirability Scores. Wylie's (1974) review contends that the discriminant validity of the IAV remains undemonstrated because multi-trait-multimethod techniques have not been applied.

Usability on Older Populations

There is no evidence to suggest that this measure is not appropriate for use with older people.

Sensitivity to Age Differences

Kitching (1972) found the perceived self-concept of women during middle-age to be positively related to increasing age, but no relationship was found between age and ideal self-concept or self-acceptance.

General Comments and Recommendations

The IAV has been used widely, and there is a substantial amount of evidence suggesting its reliability and validity, although data do not exist for older populations. An appealing feature of this approach is the inclusion of the self-acceptance rating used in conjunction with the perceived self-concept. The use of discrepancy scores in this and other measures has been questioned by Wylie (1974), Wells and Marwell (1976), and others because these derived scores represent an arbitrary transformation of the individual's responses and may not adequately preserve or describe what goes on during their self-evaluation process. Similar criticisms have been made of semantic differential measures.

This instrument is recommended as one of the better ones evaluated in this chapter. It provides a mechanism for tapping both self-concept and self-esteem as they were defined in the introduction to this chapter. The IAV could profit from further applications and psychometric data on older populations.

References

Allport, G., and H. Odbert. "Trait-names: A Psycho-lexical Study," *Psychological Monographs,* 1936, 47 (whole number 1).

Bills, R. *Manual for the Index of Adjustment and Values.* Auburn, Ala.: Alabama Polytechnical Institute, 1958.

———. *A System for Assessing Affectivity.* University, Ala.: University of Alabama Press, 1975.

Bills, R., E. Vance, and O. McLean. "An Index of Adjustment and Values." *Journal of Consulting Psychology,* 1951, 15: 157–61.

Crowne, D., M. Stephens, and R. Kelly. "The Validity and Equivalence of Tests of Self-Acceptance." *Journal of Psychology,* 1961, 51: 101–12.

Kitching, J. C. "The Self-Concept of Middle-Aged Women." Ph.D. dissertation, Florida State University, 1972. (*Dissertation Abstracts,* 33 [6] [1972].)

McHugh, W. T. "A Study of the Differences in Self-Concept and Occupational Role Concepts of Young Women and Middle-Aged Women in Occupational Training Programs." Ph.D. dissertation, University of Oregon, (*Dissertation Abstracts,* 31, 3273A [1971].)

Walter, P. D. "Pre-retirement Problems as Related to the Self-Concept of the Individual." Ph.D. dissertation, University of Pittsburgh, 1956. (*Dissertation Abstracts,* [1956] 16 [6].)

Wells, L. E., and G. Marwell. *Self-Esteem: Its Conceptualization and Measurement.* Beverly Hills, Calif.: Sage, 1976.

Wylie, R. *The Self Concept* (vol. 1). Lincoln, Neb.: University of Nebraska Press, 1974.

Ziller, R., J. Hagey, M. Smith, and B. Long. "Self-Esteem: A Self-Social Construct." *Journal of Consulting and Clinical Psychology,* 1969, 33: 84–95.

Instrument

See Instrument V1.6.I.c.

SELF-ACCEPTANCE SCALE
E. M. Berger, 1952

Definition of Concept

Self-acceptance as defined by Scheerer (1949) is characterized by feelings of self-worth, a belief in one's personal abilities, and adherence to internalized principles.

Description of Instrument

Berger prepared a 47-item instrument, which was later reduced to the 36 items that best discriminate between high and low self-acceptance. Each item ranges on a five-point Likert scale of agreement from "not at all true of myself" to "true of myself."

Method of Administration

The instrument can be administered in questionnaire form, and it could be adapted for IBM scoring. Twenty minutes should be sufficient for administration.

Context of Development and Subsequent Use

Berger's purpose was to test the hypothesis that self-acceptance is positively correlated with acceptance of others. His studies tested this proposition with college students, adults, and special groups (i.e., stutterers, counselors).

Wolk (1976) and Wolk and Telleen (1976) have used the Self-Acceptance Scale with older subjects. In these studies self-acceptance, health, activity levels, developmental task accomplishment, and perceived autonomy were examined as predictors of life satisfaction and locus of control in residents of highly structured versus relatively unorganized retirement homes.

Samples

In Berger's studies, the Self-Acceptance Scale was administered to several groups of college students and adults: 183 day-session college students, 33 evening-session college students, 33 prisoners, 38 stutterers, 7 persons with speech problems, 18 members of adult classes at a YMCA, and 3 counselors.

Wolk has administered the scale to two samples of white, ambulatory older subjects: 51 residents of a structured retirement home and 78 residents of an unstructured retirement home.

Scoring, Scale Norms, and Distribution

Scoring consists of summing all 36 items in the direction of self-acceptance (this requires the reversal of some items). This yields a potential range of 36–180.

Means in Berger's samples ranged from 102.00 (counselors) to 142.63 (evening-session college students) (Shaver, 1969, p. 115). Wolk (1976) reported means of 70.94 (structured retirement home) and 64.94 (unstructured home). These apparent age differences are misleading, since the scoring systems are reversed. If Wolk had used Berger's system, the respective means would have been 146.94 and 152.94, thus indicating greater self-acceptance for older persons.

Formal Tests of Reliability/Homogeneity

Berger reported Spearman-Brown reliability estimates of .75 or greater on his various samples.

Formal Tests of Validity

Convergent Validity: Omwake (1954) reported correlations of .73 between the Berger Self-Acceptance Scale and Phillips Self-Acceptance Scale and .49 between the Berger Self-Acceptance Scale and the Bills Self-Acceptance Index.

Berger (1952) reported that the self-acceptance scores of 20 subjects have been shown to correlate highly ($r = .89$) with judge's ratings of essays.

Some of Berger's studies (e.g., 1955) have provided indirect support for discriminant validity. Wolk (1976) found the Self-Acceptance Scale to be different from life satisfaction and locus of control ($r = .14$ and $-.08$, respectively).

Usability on Older Samples

Based upon the experience of Wolk (1976) and Wolk and Telleen (1976), the measure appears to be usable on older samples.

Sensitivity to Age Differences

This issue has not been directly tested, but comparisons of the means for Berger's and Wolk's samples suggest that older subjects may score higher on self-acceptance than younger subjects do.

General Comments and Recommendations

Based on the available empirical evidence, it appears that this instrument has sufficient validity to warrant further use on older samples. The relative ease of administration is certainly one advantage of this measure. Suggestions include administration to larger, more heterogeneous samples of older subjects and subsequent item analysis.

References

Berger, E. M. "The Relation between Expressed Acceptance of Self and Expressed Acceptance of Others." *Journal of Abnormal and Social Psychology*, 1952, 47: 778-82.
_____. "Relations among Acceptance of Self, Acceptance of Others, and MMPI Scores." *Journal of Counseling Psychology*, 1955, 2: 279-84.
Omwake, K. "The Relation between Acceptance of Self and Acceptance of Others Shown by Three Personality Inventories." *Journal of Consulting Psychology*, 1954, 18: 443-46.
Shaver, P. R. "Measurement of Self-Esteem and Related Constructs." In *Measures of Social Psychological Attitudes*, J. Robinson and P. Shaver (eds.), pp. 45-160. Ann Arbor, Mich.: Institute for Social Research, 1969.
Scheerer, E. "An Analysis of the Relationship between Acceptance of and Respect for Self and Acceptance of and Respect for Others in Ten Counseling Cases." *Journal of Consulting Psychology*, 1949, 13: 169-75.
Wolk, S. "Situational Constraint as a Moderator of the Locus of Control-Adjustment Relationship." *Journal of Consulting and Clinical Psychology*, 1976, 44: 420-27.
Wolk S., and S. Telleen. "Psychological and Social Correlates of Life Satisfaction as a Function of Residential Constraint." *Journal of Gerontology*, 1976, 31: 89-98.

Instrument

See Instrument V1.6.I.d.

SELF-CONCEPT QUESTIONNAIRE
E. P. Mason, 1954a

Definition of Concept

Self-concept depends on the way in which an individual sees himself or herself, and it includes his or her self-satisfaction. Mason defined self-concept as including both cognitive and affective components of self-perception.

Description of Instrument

Mason presented an original 26-item instrument. However, subsequent analysis has indicated that only 10 of the items significantly distinguish between older and younger subjects. Response categories are Likert in format; subjects indicate agreement with the items along a four-point continuum.

Method of Administration

The instrument can be administered in questionnaire format. A maximum of 10 minutes is required for administration.

Context of Development and Subsequent Use

Mason (1954a) investigated the relationship between self-concept and environmental variables in groups of older and younger subjects.

Anderson (1967) used the Self-Concept Questionnaire in a study of the relationship between institutionalization and self-esteem and the extent to which the relationship is conditioned by the quantity and quality of social interaction.

Samples

Mason administered the Self-Concept Questionnaire to three groups: (1) 60 indigent respondents, with a mean age of 74.22 years; (2) 30 respondents of high socioeconomic status, with a mean age of 70.22 years; and (3) 30 young adults of low socioeconomic status, with a mean age of 34. 13 years.

Anderson (1967) administered the 10-item revision of the Self-Concept Questionnaire to two samples: (1) 101 individuals residing in a church-sponsored home for the aged (mean age 82.0 years), and (2) 56 subjects on the waiting list for admittance to the same home for the aged (mean age 77.9 years).

Scoring, Scale Norms, and Distribution

Scoring consists of summing the metric values across all items (once the items have all been coded in the same direction).

Mason (1954a; 1954b) reported a few descriptive statistics based on the original 26-item pool, rather than on the 10-item version of the scale that she now advocates. The interested reader is referred to Mason's original work.

Formal Tests of Validity

Convergent Validity: Mason administered the Twenty Statements Test with the Self-Concept Questionnaire, and the means of the two instruments rank-ordered differently across the three groups in that study (1954a).

Discriminant Validity: Mason (1954a) reported that the Self-Concept Questionnaire correlates with ratings of affective mood state (range of correlation coefficients across the three groups: .32 to .49) and ratings of social maturity (range of correlation coefficients: .15 to .38).

Usability on Older Samples

The instrument appears to be usable on samples of older persons, including institutionalized respondents.

Sensitivity to Age Differences

The 10-item modified questionnaire was designed to maximize age differences across the three groups in Mason's study (1954a). However, it should be noted that *within* Mason's three groups, age was positively correlated with scores on the Self-Concept Questionnaire— a pattern that is counter to her hypothesis.

General Comments and Recommendations

The original Mason article (1954a) is cited in virtually every subsequent work concerning age differences in self-concept or self-esteem, but Anderson is the only other person known to have administered the Self-Concept Questionnaire.

Unresolved theoretical issues remain. The items in the questionnaire appear to tap both self-concept and self-esteem as they have been defined in this chapter, and so the construct measured is ambiguous. The reviewers agree with Anderson that the instrument is more closely a measure of self-esteem than of self-concept. Given the theoretical ambiguity in expectations of age differences in self-esteem, the use of an instrument designed to maximize age differences would require careful consideration.

Future use of the instrument would require more careful psychometric evaluation, as well as resolution of the theoretical issues raised.

References

Anderson, N. N. "Effects of Institutionalization of Self-Esteem." *Journal of Gerontology*, 1967, 22: 313–17.

Mason, E. P. "Some Correlates of Self-Judgments of the Aged." *Journal of Gerontology,* 1954a, 9: 324–37.

———. "Some Factors in Self-Judgments." *Journal of Clinical Psychology,* 1954b, 10: 336–40.

Instrument

See Instrument V1.6.I.e.

SELF-ESTEEM INVENTORY
S. Coopersmith, 1967

Definition of Concept

Coopersmith saw self-esteem as an evaluation or a personal judgment of worthiness expressed in the attitudes the individual holds toward him or herself. Coopersmith claimed that he was tapping the relatively enduring, and not the more transitory, aspects of self-evaluations.

Description of Instrument

A 50-item scale was developed on the basis of items selected from the Rogers and Dymond (1954) scale and several original items. Eight additional items compose a lie scale. The items are short statements, and the respondents indicate whether the description is "like me" or "unlike me." Tht items included on the inventory were ones that five psychologists classified as indicating either positive or negative self-esteem. Since the instrument was originally designed to be used with preadolescent children, the original set of items reflected self-attitudes in the area of peers, parents, school, and personal interests. In other studies some of the items have been slightly reworded to make them appropriate to all ages. The 50 items have also been reduced to 25 (form B) for an item analysis of 121 children (Coopersmith, 1967). Form C is a slightly reworded version of form B that is appropriate for adults.

Method of Administration

The measure is self-administered and takes about 10 minutes to complete (Crandall, 1973).

Context of Development and Subsequent Use

Coopersmith was interested in the development of self-esteem in children. Self-esteem was viewed as emerging from several sources: treatment by significant others, history of personal successes, individual values and aspirations, and the individual's manner of responding to devaluation. In Coopersmith's study of the antecedents of self-esteem, this scale was used in conjunction with a behavioral rating form filled out by the subjects' teachers. The Self-Esteem Inventory has subsequently been used with subjects of many ages, although only one study has been located that uses it with older people. Ernst and Kantor (1976) used it to examine the effects of a cosmetic program on institutionalized women.

Samples

The instrument was initially tested on 87 fifth- and sixth-grade boys and girls. It was subsequently administered to 1,748 children with more diverse abilities, interests, and social backgrounds. Ernst and Kantor (1976) administered a 35-item version of the instrument to 95 women in a nursing home. Their age range was not specified.

Scoring, Scale Norms, and Distribution

Form A is scored by taking the total number of responses indicating high self-esteem (a maximum of 50) and multiplying the number by 2. Scores on forms B and C (which have a maximum of 25 high self-esteem responses) are multiplied by 4.

In the sample on which the scale was originally tested, total scores ranged from 40 to

100, with a mean of 82.3 and a standard deviation of 11.6. In the larger and broader sample of children, the mean for males was 70.1 and the standard deviation was 13.8 and for females the mean was 72.2, with a standard deviation of 12.8 (Coopersmith, 1967). Thus, scores of both samples were skewed in the direction of high self-esteem. No data are reported in the Ernst and Kantor study.

Crandall (1973) reported factor analyses done on two college samples of 200 and 300 subjects that indicated the multidimensionality of the scale. He labeled the four factors that emerged "self-derogation," "leadership-popularity," "family-parents," and "assertiveness-anxiety."

Formal Tests of Reliability/Homogeneity

Coopersmith (1967, p. 10) reported a test-retest reliability on 30 fifth-grade children re-tested after five weeks, of .88 and .70 over three years. In another sample of 56 children, test-retest reliability for form C is .88 over a five-month period and .93 over a one-week period (Coopersmith, undated).

Crandall (1973) found interitem correlations for the short form to be quite low in a sample of 453 college students (the average correlation was .13). However, Taylor and Reitz (1968) found a .90 split-half reliability for the long term.

Formal Tests of Validity

Convergent Validity: Crandall (1973) reported correlations of .59 and .60 between the short form and Rosenberg scale for college students. Taylor and Reitz (1968) reported a correlation of .45 between the long form and the California Psychological Inventory self-acceptance scale. Ziller and associates (1969) found correlations between an earlier 54-item version of Coopersmith's scale and the Index of Adjustment and Values of .46 for males (but only .17 for females). The correlation with Diggory's Self-Evaluation Questionnaire was .37 for males and .23 for females. The correlation with Ziller's Social Self-Esteem Scale was only .02 for males and .04 for females.

Discriminant Validity: Taylor and Reitz (1968) found correlations of .75 with the Edwards Social Desirability Scale—which has frequently been criticized for confounding psychological content with desirability measurement (Wells and Marwell, 1976). The correlation with the Marlowe-Crowne Social Desirability Scale was .44.

Predictive Validity: Coopersmith (1967) built a nomological net in which he indicated the major antecedents of self-esteem to be total acceptance of children by parents, clearly defined and enforced limits, and respect and latitude for individual action within defined limits. Children with high self-esteem were, in turn, found to be more independent, creative, personally effective, poised, and competent. Children with high self-esteem also had lower levels of anxiety and better ability to deal with anxiety (Coopersmith, 1967, pp. 249–50).

Usability on Older Populations

Even though this scale has not been used widely with older samples, the form C version is appropriate for use with adults.

General Comments and Recommendations

This instrument has had considerable use with children but apparently very little with adults, even though an adult form now exists. Validity data are somewhat ambiguous. In particular, the relatively high correlations of the instrument with social desirability scores do not provide strong evidence of discriminant validity. These high correlations are in contrast to the lower correlations discussed under convergent validity. Considerable normative and psychometric data are needed to establish the usefulness of this instrument with adults, and particularly with older adults.

References

Coopersmith, S. *The Antecendents of Self-Esteem*. San Francisco: W. H. Freeman, 1967.
———. "Instrument for Scoring and Interpreting the Self-Esteem Inventory." Lafayette, Calif.: Self Esteem Institute, undated mimeographed paper.
Crandall, R. "The Measurement of Self-Esteem and Related Constructs." In *Measures of Social Psychological Attitudes*, J. Robinson and P. Shaver (eds.) pp. 45–167. Ann Arbor, Mich.: Institute for Social Research, 1973.
Ernst, M., and R. Kantor. "Cosmetics and the Institutionalized Woman." *Concern*, 1976, 2 (5): 19–22.
Rogers, C., and R. Dymond. *Psychotherapy and Personality Change*. Chicago: University of Chicago Press, 1954.
Taylor, J., and W. Reitz. "The Three Faces of Self-Esteem." Research bulletin number 80. London, Ontario: Department of Psychology, University of Western Ontario, 1968.
Wells, L. E., and G. Marwell. *Self-Esteem: Its Conceptualization and Measurement*. Beverly Hills, Calif: Sage, 1976.
Ziller, R., J. Hagey, M. D. Smith, and B. Long. "Self-Esteem: A Self-Social Construct." *Journal of Consulting and Clinical Psychology*, 1969, 33: 84–95.

Instrument

This copyrighted instrument is available from the Self-Esteem Institute, Lafayette, Calif.

PERSONAL ORIENTATION INVENTORY (POI)
E. L. Shostrum, 1964

Definition of Concept

Self-actualization, self-acceptance, and self-regard are three subscales of the Personal Orientation Inventory. Self-actualization is defined by Maslow (1962) as the personal qualities that maximize personal growth and development. Self-regard is defined as feelings of self-worth, the belief that one has valuable personal strengths. Self-acceptance is defined as the ability to like oneself while admitting to personal weaknesses. These three subscales are conceptually and empirically related.

Description of Instrument

A total of 12 subscales are measured by the 150 paired forced choice items on the POI: (1) inner directedness, (2) time competence, (3) self-actualizing values, (4) existentiality, (5) feelings of reactivity, (6) spontaneity, (7) self-regard, (8) self-acceptance, (9) nature of man, (10) synergy, (11) acceptance of aggression, and (12) capacity for intimate contact. The first 2 subscales are primary scales; the last 10 are secondary subscales. Only 3 subscales (dimensions 3, 7, and 8) are of direct interest to discussion of self-concept and self-esteem.

Method of Administration

The instrument is given in questionnaire form. Testing time averages about 30 minutes.

Context of Development and Subsequent Use

Most of the work done by Shostrum and associates has been normative in nature (i.e., establishing standardized scores for various subgroups). However, there has also been significant research using the POI. For a review of the research in this area, the interested reader is referred to the *Handbook for the Personal Orientation Inventory* (Knapp, 1975).

There are no normative data available on the distribution of scale scores among older subjects.

Samples

The POI has been administered to a number of samples by Shostrum and his associates

(Shostrum, 1974). These samples include: 2,607 entering college freshmen, 66 male supervisors at an electronics company, 64 student nurses, 62 Peace Corps volunteers, 150 college juniors and seniors, 412 high school students, 185 hospitalized psychiatric patients, 84 delinquent males, and 20 alcoholic males.

There are no published materials that report the use of the POI with older samples.

Scoring, Scale Norms, and Distribution

Scoring is based on complex weighting of the items, which are summed to form the 12 separate subscales. A scoring key is required (it can be purchased along with copies of the instrument).

Complete normative data are included in the POI manual. Means and standard deviations on the three self-related constructs for the samples reported in the manual are listed in Table 6-3.

TABLE 6-3
POI Means and Standard Deviations

Sample	Self-Regard	Self-Acceptance	Self-Actualization
College freshmen	11.5 (2.2)	13.7 (3.1)	18.8 (2.6)
Supervisors	12.3 (1.8)	15.4 (3.3)	20.2 (2.7)
Student nurses	11.5 (2.4)	14.5 (2.6)	19.4 (2.3)
Peace Corps volunteers	13.3 (1.3)	16.4 (3.2)	20.6 (2.3)
College juniors and seniors	12.2 (2.2)	14.8 (3.2)	19.6 (2.9)
High school students	10.9 (2.2)	14.1 (3.0)	18.2 (2.7)
Psychiatric patients	10.5 (3.1)	13.1 (3.3)	17.3 (3.2)
Delinquent males	11.3 (2.1)	14.7 (3.5)	18.1 (2.8)
Alcoholic males	9.9 (2.7)	13.8 (2.5)	18.4 (2.4)

SOURCE: Data from E. L. Shostrum. *Manual for the Personal Orientation Inventory*. San Diego: EDITS Press, 1966 (revised ed., 1974). Reprinted by permission of publisher and author.

Formal Tests of Reliability/Homogeneity

Test-retest reliability coefficients have been reported on a sample of undergraduate college students taking the test twice a week apart. Coefficients for the 12 subscales range from .52 to .82. The coefficients for the self-actualization, self-regard, and self-acceptance scales are .69, .71, and .77, respectively (Shostrum, 1966).

Formal Tests of Validity

Convergent Validity: The POI manual presents results of correlation tests between scales of the POI with scales of the MMPI, the Eysenck Personality Inventory, the Study of Values, the Sixteen Personality Factors Questionnaire, and the Guilford-Zimmerman Temperament Survey. In general, the correlations are small to moderate, but in the expected directions.

Discriminant Validity: Knapp (1965) reported correlations among the subscales of the POI, based on a sample of 138 college students. The correlations between the three subscales focused on in this description are: self-actualizating value with self-regard, .56; self-actualizing value with self-acceptance, .03; and self-regard with self-acceptance, .21.

Predictive Validity: Considerable research has suggested that overall POI scores have predictive validity (see Knapp, 1975, for a review). In particular, scores on the POI have been shown to correlate highly with independent clinical ratings. Shostrum (1966) reported and summarized 12 studies that demonstrated that scores on POI subscales are sensitive to intervention.

Usability on Older Populations

It appears that the POI could be administered to samples of older subjects.

Sensitivity to Age Differences

This issue has not been directly tested.

General Comments and Recommendations

It would be useful to have the POI administered to a sample of older persons to generate reports of normative values and distributions. This instrument appears to be theoretically meaningful and to include dimensions of self not typically tapped by other instruments. The emphasis on positive mental health over and above that described by a sense of self-worth is interesting. It may be, for example, that those persons who survive and remain relatively intact mentally and physically until quite old ages are more self-actualizing than their age peers who fare less well. In addition, empirical investigations of the three subscales of self-regard, self-acceptance, and self-actualization might prove conceptually enlightening in the general area of self-concept.

On the negative side, there are points of concern. The instrument was not constructed through a standard psychometric technique. Also, the various subscales were not designed to be orthogonal, which makes their interpretation somewhat ambiguous. The POI was reviewed somewhat negatively in Buros (1972) for these reasons. On the whole, however, this would appear to be a potentially useful instrument for future research with older subjects.

References

Buros, O. K. (ed.). *The Seventh Mental Measurements Yearbook*. Highland Park, N.J.: Gryphon Press, 1972.

Knapp, R. R. "Relationship of a Measure of Self-Actualization to Neuroticism and Extraversion." *Journal of Consulting Psychology*, 1965, 29: 168–72.

————. *Handbook for the Personal Orientation Inventory*. San Diego: EDITS Press, 1975.

Maslow, A. H. *Toward a Psychology of Being*. New York: Van Nostrand Reinhold, 1962.

Shostrum, E. L. "A Test for the Measurement of Self-Actualization." *Educational and Psychological Measurement*, 1964, 24: 207–18.

————. *Manual for the Personal Orientation Inventory*. San Diego: EDITS Press, 1966 (revised ed., 1974).

Instrument

This copyrighted instrument is available in Shostrum (1974).

SELF-PERCEPTION QUESTIONNAIRE
C. E. Preston and K. S. Guideksen, 1966

Definition of Concept

Preston and Guideksen (1966) conceptualized self-perception in broad terms. In their instrument, they identified three dimensions of self-perception: relationships with family and friends; somatic functions, intellectual functions, mood tone, and future orientation; and current interests and past experiences.

Description of Instrument

The instrument consists of 110 true-false statements. Of these 53 were described by the authors as positive qualities and 57 as negative or frustrating characteristics.

Method of Administration

The instrument has been administered in questionnaire format, and it could be adapted for IBM scoring. It would also be possible to present the items in a Q-sort format. About 45 minutes should be sufficient time to complete the questionnaire.

Context of Development and Subsequent Use

Preston and Guideksen (1966) designed the Self-Perception Questionnaire to serve as a measure of self-concept in older individuals. They compared scores on the Self-Perception Questionnaire with scores on a modified version of the LaFarge-Suczek Adjective Checklist. The authors reported that 55 of the original 110 items on their questionnaire significantly discriminated between subjects who scored high and low on the modified LaFarge-Suczek Adjective Checklist. These 55 items constitute the refined version of their questionnaire.

Samples

Preston and Guideksen administered the Self-Perception Questionnaire to a sample of 242 subjects aged 65 and older in the Seattle area (mean age 75.3 years). The subjects represented a broad range of socioeconomic conditions. All the subjects were ambulatory and capable of independent living.

Scoring, Scale Norms, and Distribution

The authors do not provide normative data describing the distribution of scores on the Self-Perception Questionnaire.

Explicit information about scoring also is not provided with this instrument. Items are intended to be negative or positive. Presumably, negative and positive items are summed within each of the three suggested dimensions.

Formal Tests of Validity

Preston and Guideksen reported a significant relationship between scores on their Self-Perception Questionnaire and scores on the modified LaFarge-Suczek Adjective Checklist in a sample of older persons. However, only 55 of the original 110 items significantly discriminated between subjects who scored high and low on the adjective checklist.

Usability on Older Populations

The instrument was designed for use with older subjects.

General Comments and Recommendations

This instrument needs to be given to a larger, more heterogeneous samples of older persons. A great deal of psychometric assessment is needed. Although there is some evidence of convergent validity, more tests of validity (particularly predictive validity) and tests of reliability are needed. The questionnaire should also be factor analyzed to determine whether the three dimensions described by the authors are empirically discernible. Finally, it is suggested that future use of the instrument be restricted to the 55 items described by the authors as significant items. This would also shorten the instrument, which would be useful.

Reference

Preston, C. E., and K. S. Guideksen. "A Measure of Self-Perception among Older People." *Journal of Gerontology*, 1966, 21: 63–71.

Instrument

See Instrument V1.6.II.c.

SELF-IMAGE SCALE
B. Kutner, D. Fanshel, A. Togo, and T. Langner, 1956

Definition of Concept

Self-image was seen by the authors as emerging from social comparisons of one's life circumstances with those of one's contemporaries. This definition does not necessarily imply an evaluation of self (i.e., self-esteem), but it comes close to this chapter's definition of self-concept.

Description of Instrument

The scale consists of three questions based on the subject's comparisons of himself or herself to others of his or her age-group or to his or her friends. The comparisons are based on feelings about age, health, and standard of living.

Method of Administration

The three questions were asked orally in Kutner's study as part of an interview.

Context of Development and Subsequent Use

Kutner developed this measure to explore the self-image concept through attitude, rather than through personality research. He was interested in factors that affect comparisons of one's self to others and in whether self-image is related to basic adjustment in older persons.

Sample

The original sample consisted of 500 residents of the Kips Bay–Yorkville Health District on the East Side of Manhattan. Respondents were a 1% sample of those over age 60. Because of the large proportion of well-to-do elderly residents in the district and the implications of the study for establishing service-oriented programs for lower-income levels, the sample was weighted for lower socioeconomic groups.

Scoring, Scale Norms, and Distribution

Positive self-image scores were given when the subject advantageously compared him or herself to others. Of the populations 65% felt younger, 50% felt their health was better, and 14% reported a better living standard than others in the peer group.

Formal Test of Reliability

Kutner reported a coefficient of reproducibility of .962.

Formal Tests of Validity

No formal tests of validity were presented. However, Kutner did report data showing that self-image is related positively to morale and socioeconomic status. Unemployed and retired persons were also found to have poorer self-images.

Usability on Older Populations

The social comparisons approach seems equally appropriate to younger and older age-groups.

General Comments and Recommendations

Although Kutner made it clear that he was concerned with the self-image that arises from social comparisons, his sampling of possible comparisons that would bear on self-image appears weak and unsystematic. This measure has been included in the chapter primarily because it suggests another approach to measuring self-concept (i.e., social comparison) and because of its historical value for gerontological research.

Reference

Kutner, B., D. Fanshel, A. M. Togo, and T. S. Langner. *Five Hundred over Sixty*. New York: Russell Sage Foundation, 1956.

Instrument

See Instrument V1.6.II.d.

ADJECTIVE CHECK LIST
H. G. Gough and A. B. Heilbrun, Jr., 1965

Definition of Concept

This adjective checklist measures a variety of self-related dimensions. One of its subscales measures the self-confidence aspect of self-esteem. Hess and Bradshaw (1970) used it as a self-concept measure indexing congruency between self and ideal. Aaronson (1966) used it as a measure of age perception.

Description of Instrument

The ACL is made up of 300 adjectives of which the respondent checks those that apply to him or her. The self-confidence scale corresponds to the poise and self-assurance scales on the California Personality Inventory. Hess and Bradshaw (1970) first had subjects check the adjectives that applied to their selves and then check those descriptive of their ideal selves. There is no limit on the number of adjectives that can be checked.

Method of Administration

The ACL is self-administered, and it takes no more than 15 minutes to go through the 300 adjectives.

Context of Development and Subsequent Use

This adjective checklist was developed in the tradition of Allport and Odbert's (1936) compilation of 17,953 words referring to personal behavior and Cattell's (1943; 1946) work on personality structure. The currently used list of 300 adjectives emerged from Cattell's study, words thought be be important for describing personality from different theoretical vantage points (e.g., those of Freud, Jung, and Murray), and comments of participants in early assessment studies. It has been used with a number of samples. The study of Hess and Bradshaw (1970) is the only one known to have used the technique with older people. Aaronson's (1966) subjects were asked to describe "the typical person" at decade intervals from 5 to 85 years of age.

Samples

The basic psychometric data were based on 56 college males, 23 college females, 100 adult men, and 34 medical students. The Hess and Bradshaw (1970) sample included 53 high school students, 63 college students, 39 persons aged 35 to 50, and 20 persons aged 55 to 65. The older subjects were healthy, fully functional, and of higher than average educational and income levels. Aaronson studied two samples of 20 persons, one aged 18 to 42 and the other, 17 to 34.

Scoring, Scale Norms, and Distribution

The self-confidence scale is scored by counting the number of words in the indicative cluster and subtracting from this total the number of words checked in the contraindicative cluster. A standard score based on sex and total number of items checked is calculated (Gough and Heilbrun, 1965). Spitzer and associates (1966) calculated a self-acceptance score (the total number of favorable adjectives checked divided by the total number of adjectives checked) and a self-criticism score (the total number of unfavorable adjectives checked divided by the total number of adjectives checked). Hess and Bradshaw (1970) also used a ratio of favorable to total adjectives for both self and ideal. They went on to calculate a congruency index, which was the self ratio divided by the ideal ratio.

Formal Tests of Reliability/Homogeneity

No explicit data on homogeneity have been reported.

Gough (1960) noted that conventional tests of internal homogeneity are problematic with this measure because its subjects may employ different descriptive elements to arrive at similar outcomes. For example, on one occasion a respondent might check capable, intelligent, and thorough and on another check clear-thinking, efficient, and steady. Although the statistical correlation would be low, the psychological similarity of the two sets would be high.

Test-retest reliabilities for the entire list range up to .89, with a mean of .54 for testing intervals of 6 months. Test-retest reliabilities for the self-confidence scale range from .163 to .73 for periods from 10 weeks to 5.5 years.

Formal Tests of Validity

Convergent Validity: This ACL correlates .38 with the California Personality Inventory self-acceptance scale (Gough and Heilbrun, 1965). Other studies have shown it to correlate in the expected direction with the MMPI (Hess and Bradshaw, 1970). Spitzer and associates (1966) reported correlations of self-acceptance and self-criticism scores with the Bills Index of Adjustment and Values, the Fiedler Semantic Differential Technique, and the Twenty Statements Test in the .30s and the .50s.

Discriminant Validity: The self-confidence scale and the Edwards Social Desirability Scale have a correlation of .40.

Spitzer and associates (1966) reported that subjects themselves felt that the ACL was a more accurate measure than the IAV, the Fiedler Semantic Differential Technique, or the TST.

Usability on Older Populations

The instrument has been used successfully with an older sample (Hess and Bradshaw, 1970).

Sensitivity to Age Differences

The data presented by Hess and Bradshaw (1970) indicate that self and ideal scores increase with age. However, Hess and Bradshaw have suggested that this may be due to their older subjects' higher educational and income attainment. No clear age trends are present in the self-ideal congruency ratios.

General Comments and Recommendations

Test-retest reliabilities for this instrument have not been particularly high. Convergence with other measures also has not been high. Further evidence is needed on most types of validity and reliability, particularly with older samples. The checklist does have the advantage of being relatively simple to administer and understand. Gough (1960) argued that the technique allows the respondent to report reactions much as he or she would in ordinary discourse—an advantage over certain other types of measures.

References

Aaronson, B. S. "Personality Stereotypes of Aging." *Journal of Gerontology,* 1966, 21: 458–62.

Allport, G., and H. Odbert. "Trait Names: A Psycho-lexical Study." *Psychological Monographs,* 1936, 47: (whole number 1).

Cattell, R. B. "The Description of Personality; 2. Basic Traits Resolved into Clusters." *Journal of Abnormal and Social Psychology,* 1943, 38: 476–507.

———. *Description and Measurement of Personality.* Yonkers-on-Hudson, N.Y.: World Book Company, 1946.

Gough, H. G. "The Adjective Check List as a Personality Assessment Research Technique." *Psychological Reports,* 1960, 6: 107–22.

Gough, H. G., and H. B. Heilbrun, Jr. *The Adjective Check List Manual.* Palo Alto, Calif.: Consulting Psychologists Press, 1965.

Hess, A. L., and H. L. Bradshaw. "Positiveness of Self-Concept and Ideal Self as a Function of Age." *The Journal of Genetic Psychology,* 1970, 177: 57–67.

Spitzer, S. P., J. R. Stratton, J. D. Fitzgerald, and B. K. Mach. "The Self-Concept: Test Equivalence and Perceived Validity." *The Sociological Quarterly,* 1966, 7: 265–80.

Instrument

This copyrighted instrument is available in Gough and Heilbrun (1965).

LAFARGE-SUCZEK ADJECTIVE CHECKLIST
R. Kogan and R. F. Fordyce, 1962

Definition of Concept

Preston and Guideksen (1966) used a modified version of the LaFarge-Suczek Adjective Checklist as a measure of self-perception. The instrument focuses upon self-perceptions of one's interpersonal relationships and attitudes toward people (Kogan and Fordyce, 1962).

Description of Instrument

The instrument consists of 64 adjectives, which the subject rates as being either true or false as self-attributes.

Method of Administration

The checklist has been administered in questionnaire and Q-sort formats. It could also be given in an interview. About 20 or 30 minutes should be sufficient time for the subjects to go through the list of adjectives.

Context of Development and Subsequent Use

LaFarge and Suczek originally developed an adjective checklist as a measure of interpersonal dimensions of personality (1955). Kogan and Fordyce (1962) later refined the instrument to 64 items and used it to test different methods of measuring and controlling social desirability in self-report instruments.

Preston and Guideksen (1966) used the adjective checklist as a measure of self-perception in a sample of older persons. Their primary purpose was to correlate scores on the checklist with scores on a self-perception questionnaire they had designed.

Samples

Preston and Guideksen administered the modified version of the LaFarge-Suczek Adjective Checklist to a sample of 242 subjects aged 65 and over in the Seattle area (mean age 75.3 years). The subjects represented a broad range of socioeconomic conditions. All the subjects were ambulatory and capable of independent living.

Scoring, Scale Norms, and Distribution

The adjectives on the list are divided into those that are positive and those that are negative and then the total numbers of positive and negative items endorsed are summed. Preston and Guideksen did not provide norms or distributions.

Formal Tests of Reliability/Homogeneity

Kogan and Fordyce (1962) indicated that their modification of the original LaFarge-Suczek Adjective Checklist was performed in order to increase the instrument's reliability as well as to make it fit more closely their particular research goals. However, reliability estimates were not reported.

Formal Tests of Validity

Convergent Validity: Preston and Guideksen (1966) reported a significant relationship between scores on the modified version of the LaFarge-Suczek Adjective Checklist and scores on the Self-Perception Questionnaire in a sample of older individuals.

Discriminant Validity: Kogan and Fordyce's (1962) article indicates that self-perceptions of interpersonal qualities can be separated from statements made to reflect socially desirable responses. This work was conducted on younger subjects and has not been replicated on an older sample.

Predictive Validity: Preston and Guideksen reported that socioeconomic status correlated with scores on both the modified version of the LaFarge-Suczek Adjective Checklist and the Self-Perception Questionnaire in an expected fashion.

Usability on Older Populations

The checklist appears to be easily used with older samples.

General Comments and Recommendations

This instrument would profit from administrations to larger, more heterogeneous samples of older individuals and also from administrations to younger subjects, which would allow for examinations of possible age differences.

The interested investigator should note that the items focus on interpersonal dimensions of personality. Therefore, the instrument should be viewed as a measure of that dimension of self-perception, rather than as a global assessment.

The checklist could also profit from a careful item analysis that would examine more closely its psychometric properties.

References

Kogan, W. S., and W. E. Fordyce. "The Control of Social Desirability: A Comparison of Three Different Q-Sorts and a Checklist, All Composed on the Same Items." *Journal of Consulting Psychology*, 1962, 26: 26–30.

LaFarge, R., and R. F. Suczek. "The Interpersonal Dimensions of Personality. III. An Interpersonal Checklist." *Journal of Personality*, 1955, 24: 95–112.

Preston, C. E., and K. S. Guideksen. "A Measure of Self-Perception among Older People." *Journal of Gerontology*, 1966, 21: 63–71.

Instrument

See Instrument V1.6.III.b.

ADJECTIVE CHECKLIST
K. L. Bloom, 1960

Definition of Concept

Self-acceptance and self-rejection are aspects of the self-concept that reflect personal adjustment. They are presumed to relate to the aging process.

Description of Instrument

The instrument is an adjective checklist developed by selecting items that a group of experts agreed would differentiate younger from older persons. The adjectives included in the final checklist were ones that over 50% of a patient sample (similar to that used in the study) rated as favorable or unfavorable with no more than 10% disagreement. The final form consisted of 111 items (63 positive, 32 negative, and 16 ambiguous items that patients rated as favorable as often as unfavorable).

Method of Administration

The instrument is self-administered. No time limits were imposed. Bloom's subjects took approximately 60 minutes.

Context of Development

The instrument was developed to test the notions of Kuhlen (1948), Buehler (1935), and Slotkin (1954) that there is a curvilinear pattern to personality development, adjustment, and self-acceptance.

Sample

Bloom's sample consisted of 83 white, male surgical patients between the ages of 20 and 69 in a VA hospital. The subjects had surgical disabilities of a nonchronic nature and had been hospitalized a short period of time. The Brown ACL was given to the patients as close as possible to their time of discharge.

Scoring, Scale Norms, and Distribution

The adjectives are checked under four different sets of directions: "the way you are" (present self), "the way you would like to be" (ideal self), "the way you were at age 25" (past self), and "the way you expect to be at age 70" (future self). Self-acceptance is defined as the total number of positive adjectives attributed to the self, and self-rejection is defined as the total number of negative adjectives checked.

Age is curvilinearly related to self-acceptance ($p < .05$) but not to self-rejection. Self-acceptance peaks at ages 40 to 49 and is lowest at ages 20 to 29.

Formal Test of Reliability

Bloom (1960) reported split-half reliabilities ranging from .74 to .96 for self-acceptance and .63 to .92 for self-rejection.

Usability on Older Populations

This checklist appears to be appropriate for older subjects, since it was designed for the purpose of detecting age differences in an adult population.

Sensitivity to Age Differences

Bloom found a significant curvilinear relationship between chronological age and self-acceptance, with self-acceptance reaching a peak during the 40-to-49-year decade and then declining. The relationship of self-rejection to age was not significant, which Bloom attributed to a probable tendency of the subjects to avoid negative items in self-ratings. Ideal and future self-perceptions showed no relationship to age on either positive or negative items. Positive items in past self-perception increased in number with chronological age, but there was no relationship between negative items and age. The adjectives that were most sensitive to age differences are indicated on the instrument.

General Comments and Recommendations

Evidence for the validity of Bloom's adjective checklist does not seem strong. If the researcher prefers to use an adjective checklist type of instrument, the approach used by Bills, Vance, and McLean in the development of the Index of Adjustment and Values is recommended.

References

Bloom, K. L. "Some Relationships between Age and Self-Perception." Ph.D. dissertation, Columbia University, 1960. (Ann Arbor, Mich.: University Microfilms, number 60-3046.)

———. "Age and the Self Concept." *American Journal of Psychiatry*, 1961, 118: 534–38.

Buehler, C. "The Curve of Life as Studied in Biographies." *Journal of Applied Psychology*, 1935, 19: 405–9.

Kuhlen, R. E. "Age Trends in Adjustment during the Adult Years as Reflected in Happiness Ratings." *American Psychologist*, 1948, 3: 307.

Slotkin, J. "Life Course in Middle Age." *Journal of Social Forces*, 1954, 33: 171–77.

Instrument

See Instrument V1.6.III.c.

DUKE SEMANTIC DIFFERENTIAL TECHNIQUE
K. W. Back and C. S. Guptill, 1966

Definition of Concept

Self-concept is the individual's perception and description of himself or herself as an object. Self-esteem is the discrepancy between actual self and ideal self.

Description of Instrument

Back and Guptill prepared a seven-item set of bipolar adjectives on which the subjects were asked to rate themselves by using the referent "myself." In later studies at Duke University, the same adjectives were administered using the referents "what I really am," "what I would like to be," and "how I appear to others."

Method of Administration

The instrument can be administered in a paper-and-pencil or an interview format. The length of time required depends on the number of referents or objects the respondent is asked to rate. Each seven-item set of adjectives should require no more than five minutes.

Context of Development and Subsequent Use

This semantic differential instrument was originally included in a study of adaptation to retirement (Simpson and McKinney, 1966).

The same set of seven bipolar adjectives was used in a large-scale longitudinal investigation of adaptation and "normal aging" in middle and late life. Self-concept and self-esteem were two of many constructs examined for change over time (a descriptive task) and as outcome variables for adaptation to life events (a hypothesis-testing approach).

The Duke Longitudinal Study is multidisciplinary, and it involves large numbers of investigators. A variety of articles, including an examination of self-concept and self-esteem, have been published. It is important to note that all of these articles are based on one of the two large data sets from the Duke Longitudinal study and the Duke Adaptation Study.

Sample

Back and Guptill (1966) examined self-concept in a work and retirement study. The sample consisted of 306 retired males and 161 males within five years of scheduled retirement. The respondents were chosen as representatives of a variety of occupational backgrounds.

Breytspraak (1974), George (1975), and Back (1971) examined self-concept and/or self-esteem in the longitudinal study of adaptation to aging. This study involves a four-wave cross-sequential panel design with data collected at two-year intervals. The original sample consisted of 502 white males and females from central North Carolina. (For a more detailed description of the sample and research design, see Palmore, 1974.) The sample is representative of the middle and upper-middle classes.

Scoring, Scale Norms, and Distribution

Back and Guptill (1966), in their work and retirement study, did not provide distributions of the semantic differential measure. They did report the results of a correlational analysis used to determine the dimensions of self-concept: involvement, optimism, and autonomy. These dimensions appear similar to the activity, evaluation, and potency dimensions suggested by Osgood and Suci (1955).

Currently, all four waves of the adaptation study have been collected and three waves have been extensively analyzed. George has (1975) reported item and construct mean scores for all three waves and a factor analysis for each wave for the 380 subjects who remained in the study. The stability of item means and factor constructs is readily apparent, but only one factor emerges for each construct and wave.

Scoring can be done in a number of ways. Scores can be summed across items, or factor loadings can be used to calculate summed scale scores. Discrepancy scores between actual and ideal ratings can be used as indicators of self-esteem. (See Back, 1971, and Breytspraak, 1974.) George (1975) reported means of 37.94, 37.34, and 37.05 for the referent "how I appear to others"; means of 36.99, 39.58, and 43.16 for the referent "what I would like to be"; and means of 37.88, 38.54, and 38.82 for the referent "what I am really like" for each of the three waves, respectively. Item means and standard deviations are available for each construct and wave in George (1975) or from the Research Instrument Bank in Aging.

Formal Tests of Reliability/Homogeneity

In the longitudinal study, internal consistency reliability coefficients (Cronbach's alpha) ranged from .76 to .84 for the three constructs in each of the three waves (George, 1975).

Cross-wave correlations of individual items ranged from .67 to .93, indicating either substantial test-retest reliability, stability in self-perception over time, or both (George, 1975).

Formal Tests of Validity

Construct Validity: Evidence of construct validity has been provided by George (1975), who factor analyzed each construct (i.e., "what I am really like," "what I would like to be," and "how I appear to others") at each measurement point. For each of the nine factor analyses, a single factor emerges. For each construct, the ranking of items remains relatively stable. A table of factor loadings for each construct at each measurement point is available in George (1975) or from the Research Instrument Bank in Aging.

Convergent Validity: Validity evidence has been provided by Back (1971), who reported similar patterns emerging between this measure and the Twenty Statements Test.

In the longitudinal study, the semantic differential sums moderately correlate with internal-external locus of control (ranging from .21 to .47), life satisfaction (ranging from .33 to .49), and anomie (ranging from .16 to .37), thus indicating that self-concept shares some covariance with these constructs and yet is distinct from them (George, 1975).

Predictive Validity: Back and Guptill (1966) have reported that semantic differential scores on the involvement factor are significantly related to work status (retired versus still working). Back (1971) reported self-concept scores on the semantic differential to be significantly related to the presence or absence of the "empty nest" for women. Breytspraak (1974) indicated that patterns of actual- and ideal-self discrepancies are significantly related to educational attainment, self-perceived health, achievement value, social contacts, and occupational mobility.

Usability on Older Populations

The instrument appears to be easily usable on samples of older persons.

Sensitivity to Age Differences

According to Back's findings with both the work and retirement sample and the subjects in the longitudinal study, the instrument is able to discriminate age differences.

General Comments and Recommendations

This version of the semantic differential technique does not empirically derive the three predicted factors of activity, potency, and evaluation, but that is not surprising since only seven adjective pairs are used. However, the instrument is easily administered and is internally consistent across constructs and time.

References

Back, K. W. "Transition to Aging and Self-Image." *Aging and Human Development*, 1971, 2: 296–304.

Back, K. W., and C. S. Guptill. "Retirement and Self-Ratings." In *Social Aspects of Aging*, I. H. Simpson and J. C. McKinney (eds.), pp. 120–29. Durham, N.C.: Duke University Press, 1966.

Breytspraak, L. M. "Achievement and Self-Concept in Middle Age." In *Normal Aging II*, E. Palmore (ed.), pp. 221–31. Durham, N.C.: Duke University Press, 1974.

George, L. K. "Subjective Awareness of Self and Age in Middle and Later Life." Ph.D. dissertation, Duke University, 1975.

Osgood, C. E., and G. J. Suci. "Factor Analysis of Meaning." *Journal of Experimental Psychology*, 1955, 50: 325–38.

Palmore, E. "Appendix A. Design of the Adaptation Study." In *Normal Aging II,* E. Palmore (ed.), Durham, N. C.: Duke University Press, 1974.

Simpson, I. H., and J. C. McKinney (eds.). *Social Aspects of Aging.* Durham, N.C.: Duke University Press, 1966.

Instrument

See Instrument V1.6.IV.a.

SEMANTIC DIFFERENTIAL SCALE
R. H. Monge, 1973

Definition of Concept

The intent of the instrument is to measure "the connotative structure of the self-concept" (Monge, 1975, p. 281).

Description of Instrument

The original instrument (Monge, 1973; 1975) consisted of 21 seven-point bipolar adjectives rated in terms of the construct "my characteristic self." Nehrke (1974) has also used this instrument and in later work (Nehrke, Hulicka, and Morganti, 1975) added several items to produce a revised 29-item, seven-point, bipolar adjective instrument. The construct rated in this work was "you, as you really are."

Method of Administration

The instrument has been administered in questionnaire format, and it could be given as part of an interview. Nehrke (personal communication, 1977) reported that the measure is easy to administer, requiring an average of 5 minutes for each referent and a maximum of 10 minutes. His experiences include the testing of institutionalized subjects.

Context of Development and Subsequent Use

Monge developed this version of the semantic differential technique to examine age and sex differences in self-concept among adolescents (1973). In later work (1975) he examined age and sex differences in self-concept structure over the major portion of the life span (ages 9 through 89 years).

Nehrke (1974) used the semantic differential to examine differences in actual and perceived self-concept across three generations. Nehrke, Hulicka, and Morganti (1975) used an expanded version of Monge's instrument to examine age differences in self-concept and the relationship between self-concept, life satisfaction, and locus of control.

Samples

Monge (1973) developed this instrument on an adolescent sample and later (1975) administered it to 2,741 females and 1,799 males, aged 9 to 89. Ten age and gender groups were included, with 177 males and 230 females aged 50 to 64 and 114 males and 221 females aged 65 to 89 in the sample.

Nehrke (1974) administerd the instrument to 25 female generational triads. The average age of the daughters (all college students) was 19 years; of the mothers, 47 years; and of the grandmothers, 74 years.

Nehrke, Hulicka, and Morganti (1975) adminstered an expanded version of this semantic differential instrument to 99 male subjects aged 50 and older and residing in a VA residential setting.

Scoring, Scale Norms, and Distribution

Monge was primarily interested in the structure of self-concept across age-groups. His early study (1973) indicated that, for adolescents, the structure of the self-concept could be described by four dimensions empirically derived by principal components analysis. In the later work (1975) principal components were extracted for each of the 10 age-sex-groups. Substantial agreement in structure was found across the 10 groups; thus, the scores were combined and one grand factor analysis was performed.

Four factors emerge that explain 50.1% of the total variance: (1) achievement/leadership, $\overline{X}$ = .797, r = .133; (2) congeniality/sociability, $\overline{X}$ = .859, r = .086; (3) adjustment, $\overline{X}$ = .858, r = .082; and (4) masculinity/femininity, $\overline{X}$ = .650, r = .214 (Monge, 1975, p. 284). All factors are scored in such a way that higher scores indicate a more positive self-evaluation. Scores can be computed within dimensions or across all items and dimensions (total). Metric (raw) scores or weighting by a component loading greater than .30 can be used (see Monge, 1975, p. 285, for the loadings resulting from the components analysis).

Nehrke, Hulicka, and Morganti (1975) reported mean scores of 151.30, 152.51, and 166.75 for the age-groups 50 to 59, 60 to 69, and 70 and over, respectively.

Formal Tests of Validity

The stability of the factor structure of this instrument is indicative on construct validity (Monge, 1975).

Nehrke, Hulicka, and Morganti (1975) reported moderate correlations between total score on the expanded semantic differential and life satisfaction (r = .48) and locus of control (r = .17).

Usability on Older Populations

The available evidence indicates that this instrument is easily administered to samples of older respondents.

Sensitivity to Age Differences

Monge (1975) reported no significant age differences in the factor structure of this semantic differential instrument. Nehrke (1974) reported no significant generational mean differences in actual self-concept in a sample of female family triads. Nehrke, Hulicka, and Morganti (1975) reported significant age differences in semantic differential scores in a sample of institutionalized males, although these differences may have been confounded with length of residence or other factors.

There is, of course, no necessary relationship between the factor structure of an instrument and the mean scores obtained on that measure. Therefore it is plausible that the factor structure would not differ across age-groups while observed age-group means would significantly differ.

General Comments and Recommendations

This version of the semantic differential technique is potentially very useful. The substantial amount of factor analysis conducted by Monge (1975), using a very large sample covering virtually the entire potential age range, is refreshing indeed. At the same time, Nehrke and colleagues have used total scores on the instrument and gotten interesting results. More work is needed in the areas of reliability and validity in order to improve confidence in the instrument.

References

Monge, R. H. "Developmental Trends in Factors of Adolescent Self-Concept." *Developmental Psychology*, 1973. 8: 382–93.

——. "Structure of the Self-Concept from Adolescence through Old Age." *Experimental Aging Research*, 1975, 1 (2): 281–91.

Nehrke, M. F. "Actual and Perceived Attitudes toward Death and Self-Concept in Three-Generational Families." Paper presented to the 27th Annual Meeting of the Gerontological Society, Portland, November 5–9, 1974.

Nehrke, M. F., I. M. Hulicka, and J. B. Morganti. "The Relationship of Age to Life Satisfaction, Locus of Control, and Self-Concept in Elderly Domiciliary Residents." Paper presented to the 28th Annual Meeting of the Gerontological Society, Louisville, October 26–30, 1975.

Instrument

See Instrument V1.6.IV.b.

ADJECTIVE Q-SET FOR NONPROFESSIONAL SORTERS
J. Block, 1961

Definition of Concept

Block (1961) designed the Q-set to be a comprehensive description of personality characteristics phrased in terms of commonly known adjectives. It can be used with instructions for self-ratings or for ratings of others. Lowenthal, Thurnher, and Chiriboga (1975) have used the Q-set as a measure of self-concept. However, they saw the adjectives as covering a relatively narrow spectrum of the total self-concept—those qualities encompassed by what Neugarten has called the "executive" functions of the ego (Neugarten, 1968).

Description of Instrument

The Q-set consists of 70 adjectives that should be familiar to a person with the equivalent of a high school education. Instead of the usual Q-sort, which requires subjects to sort statements into piles that approximate a normal distribution, Block suggested using seven piles with 10 items per pile; this results in a rectangular distribution. The instructions describe the continuum along which the subject arranges the piles (i.e., "most like me" . . . "least like me"). When multiple sorts are made using different instructions (e.g., self and ideal self), several scores result (see Block, 1971).

Method of Administration

Adjective phrases are presented to subjects either on cards for sorting (this is easier) or in questionnaire form for rating. Typically subjects finish their first sort in about 30 minutes; additional sorts require about 20 minutes.

Context of Development and Subsequent Use

Block developed the Q-set to represent a comprehensive list or personality characteristics for use in surveys.

Lowenthal, Thurnher, and Chiriboga (1975) administered the Q-set to eight life-stage and gender groups as a measure of self-concept. They had subjects perform several sorts following different instructions and used subsets of items that yielded several dimensions of self-concept: ego diffusion, feminine self-concept, masculine self-concept, negative self-concept, positive self-concept, and self-criticism. Some of these dimensions were empirically derived (i.e., on the basis of factor analysis); others were simply constructed on the basis of the items' content. These dimensions are described in an appendix to the instrument.

Samples

The book in which the Q-set was introduced (Block, 1961) contains no information about the psychometric properties of the Q-set or about the samples used in the instrument's development. However, an earlier version of the instrument was used in two studies (Block and Thomas, 1955; Chang and Block, 1960). The interested reader is encouraged to pursue those references.

Lowenthal and associates administered the Q-set to eight life-stage and gender groups of 216 subjects, who were mostly Caucasian with some college training.

Scoring, Scale Norms, and Distribution

There are numerous ways to sort Q-set responses. Numbers can be assigned by respondents. Positive and negative items can be summed. When multiple sorts are made, discrepancy scores can be calculated.

Lowenthal, Thurnher, and Chiriboga (1975) used factor analysis to derive dimensions of self-concept. (See the appendix to the instrument.) Factor scores were then used. The factor loadings have not been reported.

Neither Block (1961) nor Lowenthal, Thurnher, and Chiriboga (1975) reported distributions of self-concept scores.

Formal Tests of Validity

Lowenthal, Thurnher, and Chiriboga (1975) found that the dimensions of self-concept measured with the Q-set correlated positively and significantly with judges' ratings of adjustment.

Usability on Older Populations

The Q-set appears to be usable on samples of older adults. The common and simple adjectives used increase the applicability of the instrument to subjects with relatively little education.

Sensitivity to Age Differences

Lowenthal, Thurnher, and Chiriboga (1975) described significant sex, stage, and sex-by-stage interaction differences in several of the self-concept dimensions measuresd with the Q-set. Stage, rather than age, was used in sampling and interpretation in order to buttress the useful theoretical notion that life-stage tasks account for frequently reported age differences. However, since stage is correlated with age, the stage differences probably serve as approximations of age differences.

General Comments and Recommendations

The Block Adjective Q-Set for Nonprofessional Sorters appears to be a useful instrument for further research on the self-perceptions of older subjects. There is need for more information relevant to the instrument's reliability and validity. More item analyses and empirical searches (i.e., factor analyses) for the relevant dimensions of self-concept reflected in the 70 adjectives would be useful.

References

Block, J. *The Q-Set Method of Personality Assessment and Psychiatric Research.* Springfield, Ill.: Charles C. Thomas, 1961.

Block, J., and H. Thomas. "Is Satisfaction with Self a Measure of Adjustment?" *Journal of Abnormal and Social Psychology,* 1955, 51: 254–59.

Chang, J., and J. Block. "A Study of Identification in Male Homosexuals." *Journal of Consulting Psychology,* 1960, 24: 307–10.

Lowenthal, M. F., M. Thurnher, and D. Chiriboga. *Four Stages of Life.* San Francisco: Jossey-Bass, 1975.

Neugarten, B. L. "The Awareness of Middle Age." In *Middle Age and Aging,* B. L. Neugarten (ed.), pp. 93–98. Chicago: University of Chicago Press, 1968.

Instrument

This copyrighted instrument is available in Block (1961).

TWENTY STATEMENTS TEST (WHO AM I? WHO ARE YOU?)
M. Kuhn and T. McPartland, 1954; J. Bugental and S. Zelen, 1950

Definition of Concept

The format of the instrument suggests that self-concept is defined in terms of the self-description with which the respondent identifies himself or herself. The phrase "self-identification problem" accurately describes the focus of the instrument (Spitzer, Couch, and Stratton, 1970, p. 1). Stress is on social relationships and role identities (Wells and Marwell, 1976, p. 114).

Description of Instrument

The instrument has been used in several forms. The earliest version was the "who are you?" (W-A-Y) technique (Bugental and Zelen, 1950), which asked for three responses to the question. The Twenty Statements Test (TST) poses the question "who am I?" and requires 20 responses. A variety of coding schemes have been used in connection with the responses, and the code and the response must be taken in conjunction with each other to have a self-concept measure. Spitzer, Couch, and Stratton (1970) described a number of coding strategies. Three basic approaches are: (1) the total domain approach, which seeks to assign all response to some category in the classification system; (2) the specific category approach, which focuses on particular types of responses and excludes those that do not fit the categories; and (3) the self-rating approach, which asks respondents to code their own responses by telling whether each statement indicates something good or bad about themselves.

Method of Administration

Paper-and-pencil responses to the question "who am I?" (or "who are you?") generally take no more than 15 minutes. Limits of 12 minutes were imposed by Kuhn and McPartland (1954).

Context of Development and Subsequent Use

The general approach has grown out of two different traditions of theory and research. The W-A-Y technique stemmed from the phenomenological self-psychology tradition of Rogers, Snygg, and Combs, Raimey, and others. It is sometimes seen as a projective technique and as a communicative device between counselor and respondent. Coding categories have not been nearly as well developed as with the TST (Wells and Marwell, 1976, p. 115). The W-A-Y technique has been used in conjunction with a variety of self-concept measures by Mason (1954a; 1954b) to study correlates of self-judgments among the aged. (See the separate review of Mason's work earlier in this chapter.) The TST grew out of research by symbolic interactionists at the University of Iowa, and it was the primary mechanism for doing empirical research on the self. It derives from the tenet of symbolic interaction theory that the self-definitions of greatest significance are those made by the person himself or herself. The technique has been used widely since its development, including in a number of studies of older people. Coe (1965) studied the effects of institutionalization in three types of facilities on persons 60 years old and older. Kahana and Coe (1969) compared self-conceptions and conceptions made by professionals of institutionalized persons 50 to 92 years old. Smith (1966) studied a sample of unimpaired older people to determine the extent to which a narrowing of the subjects' social worlds had occurred. Back (1971) examined the utility of the "who am I" technique for assessing the relative impact of chronological age, retirement, and departure of children.

Spitzer, Couch, and Stratton (1970) included in their research two other studies involving older samples that used variations of the TST. Lowenthal and Berkman (1967) used the question "what sort of person would you say you are?" Clark and Anderson (1967) asked: "How would you describe yourself—that is, as a person? What sort of person would you say you are?" (See the separate review of Clark and Anderson later in this chapter.)

Samples

Data on the samples tested with the Twenty Statements Test are shown in Table 6-4.

TABLE 6-4
Twenty Statements Test Samples

Sample Characteristics	Kuhn and McPartland, 1954	Coe, 1965	Kahana and Coe, 1969	Smith, 1966	Back, 1971
Sample size	288	83	36	140	502
Age range	Undergrad	60+	59–92	65+	45–70
Health	Not reported	Not reported	Not reported	Severely impaired	Healthy

Scoring, Scale Norms, and Distribution

A variety of methods for categorizing responses has been used. The categories and dimensions used in the original study and for the four studies of older samples are these.

Kuhn and McPartland

1. Consensual (matters of common knowledge)
2. Subconsensual (responses requiring interpretations)

Coe

1. Statements referring to explicitly structured social situations
2. Statements of self-distinguishing habits, moods, and preferences
3. Identifications of physical attributes
4. Statements too comprehensive to permit meaningful differentiation

Kahana and Coe (response categories were mutually exclusive within dimensions).

1. Analytic dimension
   a. Role: kinship, profession, and group membership
   b. Affective: subjective evaluations, expressions of feelings, moods, and preferences
   c. Personality characteristics
   d. Physical and health characteristics
   e. Description of others (e.g., family)
   f. Global
2. Past vs. present orientation dimension
3. Family reference dimension
4. Professional perspectives dimension (e.g., manageability as a patient-resident)
5. General evaluations or self-description dimension

Smith

1. Number of details reported
2. Representation to self versus others

Back

1. Personal background
2. Personal characteristics
3. Personal values

Methods of scoring vary considerably among the studies, and the reader is referred to the individual studies for specific procedures.

Formal Tests of Reliability/Homogeneity

Spitzer, Couch, and Stratton (1970) found interrater reliability, when reported, to vary between 72% and 97% agreement. The extent of agreement was affected by the number of content categories, the precision of the instructions given to the raters, the number of raters, the extent of their training, and the length of the form used. Kahana and Coe (1969) reported interrater reliabilities ranging between .75 and 1.00 for subdimensions.

Spitzer, Couch, and Stratton (1970) summarized test-retest reliability reports in which correlations ranged between .38 and .85 for periods of two to three months. However, the studies they summarized used a variety of coding schemes.

Formal Tests of Validity

Convergent Validity: Spitzer and associates (1966) calculated four scores from the TST. Correlations with the Gough Adjective Checklist, the Fiedler Semantic Differential Technique, and the Bills Index of Adjustment and Values were primarily in the .20s and .30s. As Kuhn observed (Spitzer, Couch, and Stratton, (1970), correlating TST scores with other instruments may not be useful, since the TST was designed from a different theoretical orientation.

Usability on Older Populations

No difficulties have been reported in administering this instrument to older people, although, presumably, some people would be so far impaired that another person would have to record their responses.

Sensitivity to Age Differences

Smith (1966) found that the subjects in his older sample (65 and over) reported a significantly lower average number of individual details about themselves and had a more introspective orientation to their identities than did the members of a younger sample (aged 20 to 64). Back (1971) found that age differences interact with work status and sex. For example, for women personal characteristics and values appear to increase in importance and personal background appears to decline with increasing age. Mulford and Salisbury (1964) found that respondents in thier 20s and over 70 mentioned age significantly more frequently than did those in their 30s, 40s, 50s, and 60s.

General Comments and Recommendations

The instructions given in this technique appear to influence response patterns (Spitzer, Couch, and Stratton, 1970, p. 12), and so particular attention should be given to the way in which the question is posed. For example, the "who am I?" form of the TST elicited fewer total responses than a form instructing respondents to "make 20 statements about yourself, each beginning with I." Responses to the latter set of instructions elicited more responses referring to activites, likes, and goals. The number of responses has also been found to be directly related to the commitment of the interviewer—with professional pollsters obtaining fewer responses than the professional sociologists and interviewers involved directly with them (Spitzer, Couch, and Stratton, 1970).

Further work is needed on this general approach to establish its utility. Spitzer and associates (1966) reported that subjects themselves felt the TST to be a less valid measure of their self-concept than the IAV, Gough's Adjective Checklist, or Fiedler's Semantic Differential Technique. Proponents of the TST and its variations argue that a subjective definition of identity is what is important and that most other measures of self-concept depend on the researcher's definition of important dimensions of the self-concept. Here, it is suggested that the usefulness of this type of measure is determined by the organization and clarity of the coding scheme. The data cannot be understood and interpreted apart from the coding scheme.

References

Back, K. W. "Transition to Aging and the Self-Image." *Aging and Human Development*, 1971, 2: 296–304.

Bugental, J., and S. Zelen. "Investigations into the 'Self-Concept.' 1. The W-A-Y Technique." *Journal of Personality*, 1950, 18: 483-98.

Clark, M., and B. G. Anderson. *Culture and Aging: An Anthropological Study of Older Americans*. Springfield, Ill.: Charles C. Thomas, 1967.

Coe, R. "Self-Conceptions and Institutionalization." In *Older People and Their Social World*, A. M. Rose and W. A. Peterson (eds.), pp. 225–43. Philadelphia: F. A. Davis, 1965.

Kahana, E., and R. M. Coe. "Self and Staff Conceptions of Institutionalized Aged." *The Gerontologist*, 1969, 9: 264-67.

Kuhn, M. H., and T. S. McPartland. "An Empirical Investigation of Self-Attitudes." *American Sociological Review*, 1954, 19: 68-76.

Lowenthal, M. F., and P. Berkman. *Aging and Mental Disorder in San Francisco*. San Francisco: Jossey-Bass, 1967.

McPhail, C., and C. W. Tucker. "The Classification and Ordering of Responses to the Question 'Who Am I?' " *The Sociological Quarterly*, 1972, 13: 329-47.

Mason, E. P. "Some Correlates of Self-Judgments of the Aged." *Journal of Gerontology*, 1954a, 9: 324-37.

_____. "Some Factors in Self-Judgments." *Journal of Clinical Psychology*, 1954b, 10: 336-40.

Mulford, H. A., and W. W. Salisbury. "Self-Conceptions in a General Population." *Sociological Quarterly*, 1964, 5: 35–46.

Smith, J. "Narrowing Social World of the Aged." In *Social Aspect of Aging*, I. H. Simpson and J. C. McKinney (eds.), pp. 226-42. Durham, N.C.: Duke University Press, 1966.

Spitzer, S., C. Couch, and J. Stratton. *The Assessment of Self*. Iowa City, Iowa: Effective Communications, 1970.

Spitzer, S., J. Stratton, J. Fitzgerald, and B. Mach. "The Self Concept: Test Equivalence and Perceived Validity." *Sociological Quarterly*, 1966, 7: 265–80.

Wells, L., and G. Marwell. *Self-Esteem: Its Conceptualization and Measurement*. Beverly Hills, Calif.: Sage, 1976.

Instrument

There is no special material for this test.

PECK SENTENCE-COMPLETION TEST
R. F. Peck, 1959

Definition of Concept

Peck defined personal adjustment as the "net effectiveness and satisfaction with which a person is adapting to his present life situation" (1959). Carp (1963; 1967a; 1967b) has made stronger statements about the measure being a direct measure of self-perception and self-evaluation.

Description of Instrument

Peck (1959) developed the original 41-item instrument to measure self-attitudes related to personal adjustment. Each item is in the form of an incomplete sentence that the subjects must complete in terms of self-referents.

Method of Administration

The items can be administered in about 20 minutes as a paper-and-pencil instrument or as part of an interview.

Context of Development and Subsequent Use

Peck wanted to measure mental health components of personal adjustment by using standardized interview data. Peck compared two methods of determining personal adjustment: the sentence-completion test described here and clinicians' ratings of interview and Thematic Apperception Test responses. In addition to this effort at construct validation, he examined sex and age differences in item response.

Carp (1963) used the Sentence-Completion Test as a measure of self-attitude in a study of adjustment to residential relocation in a public housing project for the elderly. In addition, she examined age differences in self-attitudes (1967a; 1967b).

Samples

The Sentence-Completion Test was included in the test battery administered to subjects participating in the Kansas City Study of Adult Life. The sample was a multistage probability sample of greater Kansas City, with stratification on the factors of sex, age, and socioeconomic status. Peck (1959) selected subgroups of this larger sample for his analysis. The subgroups were selected to exhibit particular distributions of sex, age, and adjustment as determined by ratings of the interview and TAT problems. The three age-groups were 40 to 45, 50 to 55, and 60 to 65.

Carp administered the Sentence-Completion Test to 115 applicants for admission to a public housing project for the elderly. The age range was 50 to 94 years, with a median age of 72 years. Typically, subjects had attained 8 years of education, and 80% of the subjects were female. The instrument was also administered to 50 college students, with a median age of 20, 55% of whom were female.

Scoring, Scale Norms, and Distribution

Peck (1959) did not provide distributions or descriptive statistics. He found that 10 items (2, 6, 7, 8, 10, 13, 19, 34, 39, 41) differentiate between high and low adjustment, 5 items (14, 15, 23, 28, 30) exhibit significant differences across age-groups, and three items (16, 22, 32) display significant sex differences. He suggested, on the basis of post hoc examination of the data, that the 41 items form eight dimensions of personal adjustment: (1) pleasant versus unpleasant anticipation, (2) active versus passive stance, (3) clear versus vague self-conception, (4) confidence versus impotence, (5) emotional stability versus emotional instability, (6) friendly versus hostile, (7) sociable versus lonely, and (8) resonable self-indulgence versus frustration.

Carp (1963; 1967a; 1967b) used a 33-item shortened form of the instrument. She has suggested that those items form seven categories of self-attitudes: (1) dependence versus independence, (2) attitudes toward authority, (3) moral standards and guilt, (4) attitudes toward and relationships with others, (5) sources of gratification and frustration, (6) management of tension, and (7) attitudes toward the self.

Scoring requires a complex coding system that encompasses all the possible responses. Peck (1959) and Carp (1963; 1967a; 1967b) developed separate and elaborate coding systems. Because the coding schemes are very long and complex, the interested reader is referred directly to those earlier works.

Formal Test of Reliability/Homogeneity

Carp (1967a) reported 90% interrater reliability in coding responses of the Sentence-Completion Test into the eight categories listed. She also reported "stable test-retest correlations" after a 15-month interval, although those correlations were not reported.

Formal Tests of Validity

Convergent Validity: Peck (1959) reported agreement in 30 of 36 cases between classifications of subjects on the Sentence-Completion Test and independent ratings of TAT responses.

Carp reported that scores on the self dimension of the Sentence-Completion Test were significantly related to self-descriptions on an adjective checklist and to qualifying phrases in TAT stories (1967b).

Predictive Validity: Carp predicted considerable change in self-attitudes following the subjects' relocation to a public housing project for the elderly. However, observed patterns of change were minimal and difficult to interpret (1967b). It is not clear whether the instrument was not sufficiently sensitive to detect change or whether the theoretical expectations of change were incorrect.

Usability on Older Populations

The instrument appears to be usable with samples of older persons.

Sensitivity to Age Differences

Peck (1959) reported that 10 of the 41 items exhibited significant age differences in a sample with an age range from 40 to 65. Carp, after using a 33-item shortened form of the Sentence-Completion Test, reported significant age differences in 13 items. The comparison was between one age-group with a median age of 20 years and a second group with a median age of 72 years (1967a).

General Comments and Recommendations

From current evidence, the most serious limitation of this instrument seems to be the ambiguity of the construct being measured. "Self-attitudes" is a vague term, and there is little evidence that the items tap any unidimensional construct of self-concept or self-esteem. Furthermore, the dimensions included in the items should be empirically derived by factor analysis or a similar technique. Finally, there is little evidence that the measure is useful in a predictive sense. The most attractive feature of the instrument is its semiprojective nature, which ensures that subjects provide their own meaning for the items. The instrument could best be used in exploratory or hypothesis-generating investigations. Much more work would be required before the instrument could be confidently recommended for rigorous hypothesis testing.

References

Carp, F. M. *A Future for the Aged.* Austin, Tex.: University of Texas Press, 1963.

———. "The Applicability of an Empirical Standard for a Sentence Completion Test Administered to Two Age Groups." *Journal of Gerontology,* 1967a, 22: 301–7.

———. "Attitudes of Old Persons toward Themselves and toward Others." *Journal of Gerontology,* 1967b, 22: 308–12.

Peck, R. F. "Measuring the Mental Health of Normal Adults." *Genetic Psychology Monographs,* 1959, 60: 197-225.

Instrument

See Instrument V1.6.VI.b.

SELF-EVALUATION SCALE
M. Clark and B. Anderson, 1967

Definition of Concept

Self-evaluation is treated as a positive or negative judgment of one's self. It tells whether the subject thinks he or she is good or bad, valuable or worthless. It is distinguished from morale, which tells whether or not the person is happy with his or her way of life. Mental health is presumed to be based on self-esteem.

Description of Instrument

Two open-ended questions were asked as part of a general social interview:

(1) "How would you describe yourself—that is, as a person? What sort of a person would you say you are?" (2) "How would you describe yourself when you were about 50—the kind of person you were then?" Only general probes were used, such as "can you think of anything else?" Intensive interviews were conducted with a subsample. Subjects were asked to recount different periods of their lives and how they and others would describe themselves at that period. They were also asked to describe their strong points and weaknesses at various stages of their lives. The measure of self-evaluation was a rating of each self-image response on a five-point scale from strongly negative to strongly positive. The explicit criteria for categorizing the responses was not reported by Clark and Anderson (1967). For purposes of analysis in Clark and Anderson's book, the five categories were compressed into three—positive, neutral, and negative.

Method of Administration

The questions were asked as part of an open-ended interview.

Context of Development

Clark and Anderson were interested in testing the hypothesis that a positive self-appraisal is essential to good adaptation to aging. They were also exploring the relationship between mental and physical problems and a weakened self-image.

Sample

The sample was composed of 435 persons who were survivors of a larger sample of 1,134 old people studied longitudinally at the Langley Porter Neuropsychiatric Institute. Of these, 264 were nonhospitalized, community-dwelling subjects and 171 were originally members of a hospitalized group (81 were still in state psychiatric hospitals and 90 had been discharged). There were 206 men and 229 women who ranged in age from 62 to 94, with nearly half over age 70. All educational levels were represented, but half had an eighth grade education or less.

Norms

About 10% of the sample rated themselves as negative, about 65% as positive, and the remainder as neutral.

Formal Test of Reliability

Clark and Anderson reported that ratings of self-image responses were highly reliable, with a *rho* correlation of 1.0 based on 35% reliability subsample.

Formal Tests of Validity

On the predictive validity of the instrument, Clark and Anderson reported that positive self-reports were given by 71% of the community-dwelling sample, 55% of the discharged sample, and 46% of the inpatients.

Usability on Older Populations

This approach was developed and used on older persons, both those who were well and those who were mentally impaired.

Sensitivity to Age Differences

Clark and Anderson found no relationship between age and self-evaluation. However, they were dealing only with an older sample of persons aged 62 to 94.

General Comments and Recommendations

Although this measure is open-ended in approach and so difficult to provide adequate reliability or validity data on, it has been included because of its use in an important study of aging. It is similar to the Twenty Statements Test in the type of self-reflection it elicits, although its approach to coding responses appears to be much more simplistic than those used in most TST studies. It would be helpful to have data on the convergent validity between this type of approach and some of the structured measures described in other sections of this chapter.

Reference

Clark, M., and B. G. Anderson. *Culture and Aging: An Anthropological Study of Older Americans.* Springfield, Ill.: Charles C. Thomas, 1967.

Instrument

See the description of the instrument above.

SELF BATTERY
S. Reichard, F. Livson, and P. G. Petersen, 1962

Definition of Concept

Reichard, Livson, and Petersen conceptualized the self in broad terms, such as attitudes toward one's life, the happiness one has attained, feelings about other people, and perceptions of one's past, present, and future.

Description of Instrument

This instrument consists of 16 open-ended questions, several with multiple parts, all focused on the broad topic of self-attitudes.

Method of Administration

The Self Battery was administered in interview form. Responses were open-ended, and they were recorded by an interviewer.

Context of Development and Subsequent Use

Reichard, Livson, and Petersen conducted an in-depth investigation of social and psychological characteristics of the aging and correlates of adjustment to aging, particularly retirement.

Samples

Reichard, Livson, and Petersen studied a sample of 87 white males, aged 55 to 84, from the San Francisco metropolitan area. All of the subjects were in good health. Of the subjects 42 had retired before the study, 45 were still employed.

Scoring, Scale Norms, and Distribution

The authors did not present normative statistics concerning the subjects' responses to that portion of the interview pertaining to the self.

Scoring the open-ended questions required the development of a complex coding system. There is no clear presentation of the scoring system used by Reichard, Livson, and Petersen; therefore, further research would require the development of new coding categories.

Formal Test of Reliability/Homogeneity

Reichard, Livson, and Petersen reported interrater reliability of .68 for the interview schedule as a whole.

Usability on Older Populations

The questions appear to be usable on samples of older subjects.

General Comments and Recommendations

This battery appears to be significant in two ways. First, Reichard, Livson, and Petersen's volume is an important pioneering study of social gerontology. In that sense, the emphasis the authors placed upon self-attitudes as a dimension of adjustment is conceptually significant. Second, use of the battery would appear feasible in exploratory, hypothesis-generating studies. In these situations, unstructured questions might prove useful. Beyond this, the battery appears less adequate. The very nature of the battery prohibits more refined psychometric application or assessment.

Reference

Richard, S., F. Livson, and P. G. Petersen. *Aging and Personality*. New York: John Wiley and Sons, 1962.

Instrument

See Instrument V1.6.VI.d.

Instruments

V1.6.I.a

TENNESSEE SELF-CONCEPT SCALE
W. Fitts, 1965

This copyrighted instrument is available in Fitts (1965).

V1.6.I.b

SELF-ESTEEM SCALE
M. Rosenberg, 1965

Response Categories: 1. Strongly agree
2. Agree
3. Disagree
4. Strongly disagree

	Kaplan and Pokorny
Items	*Factor Loadings*
1. I feel that I'm a person of worth, at least on an equal plane with others. (agree = high self-esteem)	0.08
2. I feel that I have a number of good qualities. (agree = high self-esteem)	−0.02
3. All in all, I am inclined to feel that I am a failure. (disagree = high self-esteem)	0.46
4. I am able to do things as well as most other people. (agree = high self-esteem)	0.05
5. I feel I do not have much to be proud of. (disagree = high self-esteem)	0.37
6. I take a positive attitude toward myself. (agree = high self-esteem)	0.41
7. On the whole, I am satisfied with myself. (agree = high self-esteem)	0.44
8. I wish I could have more respect for myself. (disagree = high self-esteem)	0.61
9. I certainly feel useless at times. (disagree = high self-esteem)	0.76
10. At times I think I am no good at all. (disagree = high self-esteem)	0.77

SOURCE: M. Rosenberg. *Society and the Adolescent Self-Image*, pp. 305–7. Princeton, N.J.: Princeton University Press, 1965. Reprinted by permission of Princeton University Press and author.

V1.6.I.c

INDEX OF ADJUSTMENT AND VALUES
R. Bills, E. Vance, and O. McLean, 1951

The respondent puts each of the following words into the following three sentences. Then he/she rates how descriptive the sentence is on a 1 to 5 scale.

1. I am a (an) _____person.
   The scale is as follows:

5	4	3	2	1
Most of the time	Good deal of the time	Half the time	Occasionally	Seldom

2. How do you accept yourself as described in the first rating?

Very much like being as I am in this respect	Like	Neither like nor dislike	Dislike	Very much dislike

3. I would like to be a (an) _____person.

5	4	3	2	1
Most of the time	Good deal of the time	Half the time	Occasionally	Seldom

Adjective List

acceptable	*fearful	*reckless
accurate	friendly	responsible
alert	fashionable	*sarcastic
ambitious	helpful	sincere
*annoying	intellectual	stable
busy	kind	studious
calm	logical	successful
charming	*meddlesome	*stubborn
clever	merry	tactful
competent	mature	teachable
confident	*nervous	useful
considerate	normal	worthy
*cruel	optimistic	broadminded
democratic	poised	businesslike
dependable	purposeful	competitive
economical	reasonable	*faultfinding
efficient		

Scoring for the self ratings is in the socially desirable direction. Most of the words are positive. A higher rating indicates higher esteem for all the words except those marked with an asterisk (*).

SOURCE: R. Bills, E. Vance, and O. McLean. "An Index of Adjustment and Values." *Journal of Consulting Psychology*, 1951, 15: 157–61. Copyright 1951 by the American Psychological Association. Reprinted by permission.

V1.6.I.d
SELF-ACCEPTANCE SCALE
E. M. Berger, 1952

(Berger reports 36 items that measure self-acceptance and 28 items which measure acceptance of others. Only the self-acceptance measures are reproduced below. Numbers in parentheses at the end of each item indicate the value for high self-acceptance.)

This is a study of some of your attitudes. Of course, there is no right answer for any statement. The best answer is what you feel is true of yourself. You are to respond to each question on the answer sheet according to the following scheme:

1	2	3	4	5
Not at all true of myself	Slightly true of myself	About halfway true of myself	Mostly true of myself	True of myself

Remember, the best answer is the one which applies to you.

1. I'd like it if I could find someone who would tell me how to solve my personal problems. (1)
2. I don't question my worth as a person, even if I think others do. (5)
3. When people say nice things about me, I find it difficult to believe they really mean it. I think maybe they're kidding me, or just aren't being sincere. (1)
4. If there is any criticism or anyone says anything about me, I just can't take it. (1)
5. I don't say much at social affairs because I'm afraid that people will criticize me or laugh if I say the wrong thing. (1)
6. I realize that I'm not living very effectively, but I just don't believe I've got it in me to use my energies in better ways. (1)
7. I look on most of the feelings and impulses I have toward people as being quite natural and acceptable. (5)
8. Something inside me just won't let me be satisfied with any job I've done—if it turns out well, I get a very smug feeling that this is beneath me, I shouldn't be satisfied with this, this isn't a fair test. (1)
9. I feel different from other people. I'd like to have the feeling of security that comes from knowing I'm not too different from others. (1)
10. I'm afraid for people that I like to find out what I'm really like, for fear they'd be disappointed in me. (1)
11. I am frequently bothered by feelings of inferiority. (1)
12. Because of other people, I haven't been able to achieve as much as I should have. (1)
13. I am quite shy and self-conscious in social situations. (1)
14. In order to get along and be liked, I tend to be what people expect me to be rather than anything else. (1)
15. I seem to have a real inner strength in handling things. I'm on a pretty solid foundaion and it makes me pretty sure of myself. (5)
16. I feel self-conscious when I'm with people who have a superior position to mine in business or at school. (1)
17. I think I'm neurotic or something. (1)
18. Very often, I don't try to be friendly with people because I think they won't like me. (1)
19. I feel that I'm a person of worth, on an equal plane with others. (5)
20. I can't avoid feeling guilty about the way I feel toward certain people in my life. (1)
21. I'm not afraid of meeting new people. I feel that I'm a worthwhile person and there's no reason why they should dislike me. (5)
22. I sort of only half-believe in myself. (1)
23. I'm very sensitive. People say things and I have a tendency to think they're criticizing me or insulting me in some way and later when I think of it, they may not have meant anything like that at all. (1)
24. I think I have certain abilities and other people say so too. I wonder if I'm not giving them an importance way beyond what they deserve. (1)
25. I feel confident that I can do something about the problems that may arise in the future. (5)

26. I guess I put on a show to impress people. I know I'm not the person I pretend to be. (1)
27. I do not worry or condemn myself if other people pass judgment against me. (5)
28. I don't feel very normal, but I want to feel normal. (1)
29. When I'm in a group I usually don't say much for fear of saying the wrong thing. (1)
30. I have a tendency to sidestep my problems. (1)
31. Even when people do think well of me, I feel sort of guilty because I know I must be fooling them—that if I were really to be myself, they wouldn't think well of me. (1)
32. I feel that I'm on the same level as other people and that helps to establish good relations with them. (5)
33. I feel that people are apt to react differently to me than they would normally react to other people. (1)
34. I live too much by other people's standards. (1)
35. When I have to address a group, I get self-conscious and have difficulty saying things well. (1)
36. If I didn't always have such hard luck, I'd accomplish much more than I have. (1)

SOURCE: E. M. Berger. "The Relation between Expressed Acceptance of Self and Expressed Acceptance of Others." *Journal of Abnormal and Social Psychology*, 1952, 47: 778-82. Copyright 1952 by the American Psychological Association. Reprinted by permission.

V1.6.I.e
SELF-CONCEPT QUESTIONNAIRE
E. P. Mason, 1954

The ten-item modified version of the Self-Concept Questionnaire is reproduced below. Responses are scored along a four-point continuum of agreement, which does not include a neutral response:

Strongly disagree	Disagree	Agree	Strongly agree
1	2	3	4

Items:

1. I am able to do things as well as most other people.
2. I would usually rather be by myself than with other people.
3. I enjoy living now as much as I used to.
4. I do not feel I have the energy to do the things I would like.
5. Nobody pays much attention to what I do or say.
6. My day is filled with useful activities.
7. I am unhappy much of the time.
8. I find I am the type of person who feels as close to my family now as I ever have.
9. I worry about physical pain and suffering.
10. I am hardly ever very excited or thrilled.

SOURCE: E. P. Mason. "Some Factors in Self-Judgment." *Journal of Clinical Psychology*, 1954, 10: 336–40. Copyright 1954 by the American Psychological Association. Reprinted by permission.

V1.6.II.a
SELF-ESTEEM INVENTORY
S. Coopersmith, 1967

This copyrighted instrument is available from the Self-Esteem Institute, Lafayette, Calif.

V1.6.II.b
PERSONAL ORIENTATION INVENTORY
E. L. Shostrum, 1964

This copyrighted instrument is available in Shostrum (1974).

V1.6.II.c
SELF-PERCEPTION QUESTIONNAIRE
C. E. Preston and K. S. Guideksen, 1966

The authors do not provide instructions. Items which Preston and Guideksen found to significantly discriminate between high and low scores on the modified version of the LaFarge-Suczek Adjective Checklist have been starred.

Relationships with Family and Friends

*1. My children or relatives are concerned about my well-being.
*2. I have some friends who come to see me regularly.
*3. I frequently visit my relatives and/or friends.
*4. I can accept help from others without feeling like a burden to them.
*5. I regularly send greeting cards to my friends and relatives.
*6. I have hobbies like bridge, bingo, gold, etc. that provide companionship.
*7. I attend some social gathering, party, picnic, etc. at least once a month.
*8. Other people's anniversaries (birthdays, weddings, etc.) are less important to me than to most people my age.
*9. It is difficult for me to make myself interesting to other people.
*10. I am not active in clubs or organizations which meet regularly.
*11. Sympathy and understanding of others are not very comforting to me when I am sad.
*12. It is frustrating for me to be as dependent on others for help as I am.
*13. I am rarely visited by members of my family.
*14. I feel that I have less affection and respect from others than I used to have.
*15. All my real friends are dead now.
*16. My relatives show little affection for me.
*17. Often I feel lonely or sad.
*18. I rarely attend social gatherings such as picnics, parties, etc.
19. I do something helpful for a friend or relative at least once a month.
20. I am able to make new friends when this opportunity arises.
21. I am usually satisfied with the amount of contact I have with friends.
22. I like to keep up with important happenings to other people around me.
23. Most people seem to like me most of the time.
24. I enjoy talking and listening to other people.
25. Being a widow is not harder for me to bear than it is for most people.
26. Being bored and lonely is no more a problem for me than it is for most people my age.
27. Life's greatest hardship is the loss of loved ones.
28. The greatest source of help in times of stress is the sympathy of others.
29. Most of the time I feel like a burden to other people.
30. My children and grandchildren seem to neglect or ignore me.
31. It is difficult for me to be interested in talking with other people or listening to their conversation.

32. Since the loss of my spouse, I have never found anyone or anything worth living for.
33. I often feel that other people do not like me.

Somatic, Intellectual Functions, Mood Tone, Future Orientation

*34. Each day usually brings something I can look forward to and enjoy.
*35. I feel that the future holds something worth living for.
*36. I expect to be doing some pleasure traveling in the near future.
*37. I cannot see well enough to do the fine or skilled work I enjoy.
*38. I often worry about being constipated.
*39. I am not strong enough to do the heavy work I enjoy.
*40. I can't hear as well as most people my age.
*41. I seem to be shorter of breath than most people my age.
*42. I seem to catch colds more often than most people my age.
*43. Much of the time I am in physical pain.
*44. I have less physical strength than most people my age.
*45. In the morning I am strong, but I tend to get tired as the day wears on.
*46. Although I usually feel sad and blue in the morning, things look brighter as the day wears on.
*47. Often I wake up in the middle of the night and can't go back to sleep.
*48. The days seem to drag by slowly.
*49. Often I find getting up in the morning difficult.
*50. I am not happy living where I am at the present time.
*51. At my age there is not much point in making plans for the future.
*52. Death would be welcome to me any time now.
*53. Sometimes worries about the future overwhelm me.
*54. I frequently worry about becoming an invalid.
*55. The future does not look very bright to me.
*56. Failing eyesight is no more of a problem for me than for most people my age.
57. I feel "blue" or downhearted more than most people my age.
58. My health is reasonably good.
59. I have a good appetite.
60. My height is about the same as it used to be.
61. My weight has not decreased greatly in the past year or so.
62. I can concentrate on what I read or hear about as well as most people my age.
63. I am able to remember recent happenings about as well as most people my age.
64. It is no more difficult for me to concentrate than for most people my age.
65. I have no more difficulty with my memory than most people my age.
66. I do not find myself worrying too much about the future.
67. I hope to live as long as I am in good health.
68. I feel cheerful most of the time.
69. I am unable to dress, bathe, or take care of my personal hygiene.
70. I seem to have more physical defects and disabilities than most people my age.
71. I wish I could die right now.
72. Growing old seems to be harder for me than for others my age.

Current Interests and Past Experiences

*73. My education was sufficient for my needs.
*74. I think there are more advantages than disadvantages to being retired.
*75. At least once a month I attend a play, concert or lectue.
*76. My faith in God and prayer has been the source of comfort to me in times of trial.
*77. I go to church at least once a month.

*78. I am not interested in hobbies which seem to interest most people.
*79. I am not able to do much reading.
*80. I do not go to church regularly.
*81. I have been dissatisfied with one or more of my spouses.
*82. Nothing interesting or important has happened to me in the past five years.
*83. Often I feel like a "shut-in."
*84. I am not able to find comfort in religious faith.
*85. I feel that I would be better off working than retired as I am now.
*86. Some event has occurred in the past five years that saddened me very deeply.
  87. All things considered, I feel that my life has been successful.
  88. I feel that being active "doing something" is the greatest help to me when I am troubled.
  89. I feel my current income covers most of my needs.
  90. I wish I had had more children.
  91. Some event has occurred in the past five years that made me very happy.
  92. I keep up with current events through newspapers or magazines.
  93. I enjoy my own company at times.
  94. I feel fairly content with my daily pattern of activities.
  95. I find satisfaction in activities which I pursue myself.
  96. My children's development has been satisfactory to me.
  97. I enjoy most of the jobs (job) I did as my major occupation.
  98. I do (or help my spouse with) most household chores.
  99. Public transportation serves my needs.
 100. My usual reading includes one book a month.
 101. I have some favorite radio or television programs I follow regularly.
 102. I take an active interest in my former occupation (or if formerly a housewife—I still enjoy reading about new recipes or homemaking skills).
 103. I began to prepare for this time in my life years ago.
 104. If I could relive my life I would not have married (or if single, I would have married).
 105. I wish I had had fewer children.
 106. I cannot move about my home or place of residence without help from others.
 107. Even on nice days I am unable to get out of doors.
 108. I am unable to prepare my own or my spouse's meals.
 109. I do not do light gardening work.
 110. I am unable to keep up with household chores.

SOURCE: C. E. Preston and K. S. Guideksen. "A Measure of Self-Perception among Older People." *Journal of Gerontology*, 1966, 21: 71. Reprinted by permission of authors and publisher.

V 1.6.II.d
SELF-IMAGE SCALE
B. Kutner, D. Fanshel, A. Togo, and T. Langner, 1956

  1. Would you say you feel older or younger than most people your age?
  2. Do you think your health is better or worse than that of people your age?
  3. Would you say your standard of living is better, or worse than the standard of living of most of your friends and acquaintances?

SOURCE: B. Kutner, D. Fanshel, A. M. Togo, and T. L. Langner. *Five Hundred over Sixty*, p. 303. New York: Russell Sage Foundation, 1956. Reprinted by permission of the publisher.

V1.6.III.a
ADJECTIVE CHECK LIST
H. G. Gough and A. B. Heilbrun, Jr., 1965

This copyrighted instrument is available in Gough and Heilbrun (1965).

V1.6.III.b
LAFARGE-SUCZEK ADJECTIVE CHECKLIST
R. Kogan and R. F. Fordyce, 1962

1. T F often admired
2. T F expects everyone to admire him
3. T F likes to compete with others
4. T F can be indifferent to others
5. T F proud and satisfied
6. T F hard-boiled when necessary
7. T F very anxious to be approved of
8. T F admires and imitates others
9. T F eager to get along with others
10. T F too easily influenced
11. T F spoils people with kindness
12. T F enjoys taking care of others
13. T F too lenient with others
14. T F wants everyone's love
15. T F lets others make decisions
16. T F very respectful of authority
17. T F can complain if necessary
18. T F likes to be taken care of
19. T F can be frank and honest
20. T F can be strict if necessary
21. T F shrewd and calculating
22. T F often helped by others
23. T F overprotective of others
24. T F kind and reassuring
25. T F forgives anything
26. T F lacks self-confidence
27. T F able to criticize self
28. T F gives freely of self
29. T F will confide in anyone
30. T F touchy and easily hurt
31. T F resents being bossed
32. T F able to doubt others
33. T F acts important
34. T F dominating
35. T F good leader
36. T F manages others
37. T F forceful
38. T F boastful
39. T F independent
40. T F self-confident

41. T F sarcastic
42. T F often unfriendly
43. T F outspoken
44. T F self-seeking
45. T F irritable
46. T F skeptical
47. T F frequently disappointed
48. T F resentful
49. T F hard to impress
50. T F apologetic
51. T F clinging vine
52. T F respected by others
53. T F cold and unfeeling
54. T F appreciative
55. T F warm
56. T F oversympathetic
57. T F likes everybody
58. T F modest
59. T F can be obedient
60. T F fond of everyone
61. T F friendly all the time
62. T F obeys too willingly
63. T F shy
64. T F spineless

SOURCE: C. E. Preston and K. S. Guideksen. "A Measure of Self-Perception among Older People." *Journal of Gerontology*, 1966, 21: 71. Reprinted by permission of authors and publisher.

V1.6.III.c
ADJECTIVE CHECKLIST
K. L. Bloom, 1960

This list of words can be used to describe people. You are asked to check the list under different sets of directions.

PUT A CHECK _____ in front of each word that would apply to you according to the directions given below.

PUT A ZERO _____ in front of each word that would not apply to you.

DO NOT OMIT ANY ITEMS

CHECK THE WORDS THAT DESCRIBE _____

ZERO THE WORDS THAT DO NOT DESCRIBE _____

_____ unnecessary*	_____ sickly	_____ inadequate
_____ cultured	_____ romantic	_____ muscular
_____ defective	_____ eager	_____ respectable
_____ gloomy	_____ modern	_____ lively
_____ feeble	_____ stubborn*	_____ mischievous*
_____ radical*	_____ unimportant	_____ old-fashioned
_____ tired	_____ particular	_____ afraid
_____ sure	_____ tough	_____ patient

—— fast	—— proud	—— unsuccessful
—— confident	—— dependent	—— healthy
—— active	—— natural	—— empty
—— weary	—— careless	—— flexible
—— daring	—— helpless	—— energetic
—— bent	—— stable	—— rash
—— independent	—— busy	—— strong
—— pitiful	—— thoughtful	—— forlorn
—— hopeless	—— fashionable	—— ambitious
—— initiative	—— quiet**	—— productive
—— enthusiastic	—— slow	—— fearful
—— efficient	—— modest	—— game
—— reliable	—— attractive	—— mellow**
—— athletic*	—— suffering	—— lucky
—— industrious	—— calm**	—— weak
—— spontaneous	—— careful	—— dignified**
—— alert	—— useless	—— experienced
—— peaceable	—— cautious**	—— conventional**
—— unchanged	—— progressive	—— aggressive
—— deliberate	—— lonely	—— reasonable
—— thinking	—— kind	—— courageous
—— working	—— bold	—— reckless*
—— shy	—— idle	—— bitter
—— serious	—— religious	—— important
—— hopeful	—— broken	—— manly
—— adventurous	—— wise**	—— gentle
—— understanding	—— rigid	—— quick
—— mature**	—— hasty	—— haggard
—— beaten	—— sensible	—— worthless

*Younger subjects (20–39) chose significantly more often than older (50–69).

**Older subjects chose significantly more often than younger.

SOURCE: K. L. Bloom. "Some Relationships between Age and Self Perception." Ph.D. dissertation, Columbia University, 1960. (Ann Arbor, Mich.: University Microfilms number 60-3046.) Reprinted by permission.

V1.6.IV.a

DUKE SEMANTIC DIFFERENTIAL TECHNIQUE
K. W. Back and C. S. Guptill, 1966

I will show you a set of cards with opposite words like "Inactive-Busy" and a scale from 1 to 7. For this scale 1 means very inactive and 7 means very busy. I want you to point to the number along the scale that shows where you think you appear to others (would like to be, really am). For example, if you think you appear somewhat busy to others, point to 4, and so on.

The subject responds to the same set of seven bipolar adjectives for each of three referents:
How I Appear to Others
What I Would Like to Be
What I Really Am

The seven bipolar adjectives are:

inactive-busy
not free to do things—free to do things
useless-useful
look to the past—look to the future
ineffective-effective
dissatisfied with life—satisfied with life
disregarded-repected

The order of several of the adjective pairs was reversed in order to prevent the more socially desirable response from always being presented on a single end of the continuum.

SOURCE: K. W. Back and C. S. Guptill. "Retirement and Self-Ratings." In *Social Aspects of Aging*, I. H. Simpson and J. C. McKinney (eds.), pp. 120–29. Durham, N.C.: Duke University Press, 1966. Copyright 1966 by Duke University Press. Reprinted by permission of authors and publisher.

V1.6.IV.b
SEMANTIC DIFFERENTIAL SCALE
R. H. Monge, 1973

Adjectives are presented to subjects for rating along seven-point continuums:

1. Confident-Unsure
2. Good-Bad
3. Strong-Weak
4. Leader-Follower
5. Steady-Shaky
6. Success-Failure
7. Nice-Awful
8. Rugged-Delicate
9. Sharp-Dull
10. Healthy-Sick
11. Happy-Sad
12. Valuable-Worthless
13. Kind-Cruel
14. Hard-Soft
15. Superior-Inferior
16. Relaxed-Nervous
17. Stable-Unstable
18. Friendly-Unfriendly
19. Satisfied-Dissatisfied
20. Smart-Dumb
21. Refreshed-Tired

Adjectives added to above list by Nehrke, Hulicka, and Morganti (1975):

Secure-Insecure
Loved-Hated
Interested-Bored
Appreciated-Unappreciated
Creative-Uncreative
Recognized-Unrecognized

Serene-Troubled
Productive-Unproductive
Independent-Dependent
Hopeful-Hopeless
Popular-Unpopular

Nehrke, Hulicka, and Morganti deleted the following adjectives, which were included by Monge:

Healthy-Sick
Rugged-Delicate
Hard-Soft

SOURCE: R. H. Monge. "Structure of the Self-Concept from Adolescence through Old Age." Experimental Aging Research, 1975, 1 (2): 281–91. Reprinted by permission of author and publisher.

V1.6.V.a
ADJECTIVE Q-SET FOR NONPROFESSIONAL SORTERS
J. Block, 1961

This copyrighted instrument is available in Block (1961).

V1.6.VI.a
TWENTY STATEMENTS TEST
M. Kuhn and T. McPartland, 1954; J. Bugental and S. Zelen, 1950

There is no special material for this test.

V1.6.VI.b
PECK SENTENCE-COMPLETION TEST
R. F. PECK, 1959

Sentence Stems:

1. It makes me happy to	22. Guns sometimes
2. Other people usually	23. To be old is
3. When it comes to seeing things	24. If people only knew
4. I miss	25. My work has been
5. Being younger would	26. Loving someone
6. When they avoided me	27. Weakness comes from
7. As for my legs	28. When I see hills, I
8. The past seems	29. When I let go
9. My father was a man who	30. Getting older
10. It is tiring to	31. The most important thing about me is
11. If they tell me it's dangerous	32. I wish my family
12. People think of me as	33. A woman my age should
13. What gets me into trouble is	34. I suffer most from
14. Children would be better off if	35. As for my heart
15. Being middle aged means	36. It is fun to
16. My best friend	37. A man my age should
17. People who run things should be	38. There are times when I
18. Walking barefoot in the sand	39. Being with other people
19. I get down in the dumps when	40. If I only had
20. Someday I	41. The thing I like about myself is
21. My mother usually	

SOURCE: R. F. Peck. "Measuring the Mental Health of Normal Adults." *Genetic Psychology Monographs*, 1959, 60: 223. Reprinted by permission of author and publisher.

Carp's Version of the Peck Sentence-Completion Test:

Although Carp used Peck's instrument, the modifications were significant. Therefore the entire instrument used by Carp is reproduced below.

1. The average person is	5. _____ makes me feel sad
2. _____ makes me feel happy	6. My friends are
3. People thing of me as	7. The easiest way to get money is to
4. When I let go I	8. My mother was

9. What gets me into trouble is
10. Being with other people is
11. _____ makes me feel angry
12. My best quality is my
13. Bosses are
14. Someday I will
15. My father was
16. My body is
17. What I want to do most is
18. _____ makes me feel tense
19. Most men are
20. I'd like to be a child again so I could
21. _____ makes me feel guilty

22. Most people don't know I am
23. It's exciting to
24. My worst quality is my
25. When I have some free time, I
26. As a child I was
27. When I'm put under pressure, I
28. _____ makes me feel relaxed
29. My mind is
30. I hope I never
31. Until now I have been
32. I am
33. _____ makes me feel proud

SOURCE: F. M. Carp. "The Applicability of an Empirical Standard for a Sentence Completion Test Administered to Two Age Groups." *Journal of Gerontology*, 1967, 22: 301-7. Reprinted by permission of author and publisher.

V1.6.VI.c
SELF-EVALUATION SCALE
M. Clark and G. Anderson, 1967

See the description of the instrument in the abstract.

V1.6.VI.d
SELF BATTERY
S. Reichard, F. Livson, and P. G. Petersen, 1962

1. What kind of a person do you think you are? What are your strong points and what are your weaknesses?
2. How do you think you have changed?
3. What kind of a child were you?
4. What have the main satisfactions in your life been?
5. Everybody has had some disappointments. What have the main disappointments in your life been?
6. Do you find yourself thinking more about the past or the future?
7. What kind of a life do you think you have had on the whole?
8. If everything were to be the same, would you like to live your life over again?
9. If you were going to live your life over again, what would you change?
10. What was the happiest period in your life? What about . . . made it the happiest period? Why is it less happy now?
11. What was the unhappiest period in your life? Why? Why is it more happy now?
12. What would you say are the advantages of getting older?
13. What are the disadvantages of getting older?
14. If you could stay at the same age all your life, which age would you choose? Why?
15. How do you think you have made out in life? How do you think you made out compared to what you hoped when you started out? (Better, as well as, worse?) Why?
16. Do you think that people on the whole are able to make what they want out of their lives?

SOURCE: S. Reichard, F. Livson, and P. G. Petersen. *Aging and Personality*. New York: John Wiley and Sons, 1962. Reprinted by permission of authors and publisher.

Chapter 7

Death and Dying

Victor W. Marshall

To be human is to be mortal, and many philosophers, especially the existentialists, have suggested that many aspects of our lives are shaped by this fact. It has been argued (e.g., Marshall, 1975a, 1975b; Munnichs, 1966; Neugarten, 1970; Vischer, 1967) that increasing age is associated with the increasing salience of human mortality for other aspects of the lives of individuals. Indeed, this idea is the justification for the chapter on death in a book concerned with measurement and aging. But age does not act in any automatic way to increase the salience of death (Marshall, 1975b). Instead, a number of age-related phenomena, such as ill health and the deaths of others, serve to make the individual more aware that his or her death is drawing near. Aging and mortality are not synonymous, a fact clearly borne out by the conceptual structure of the research instruments in this domain.

A broad range of theories about death and death-related phenomena are reviewed in this chapter (see Table 7-1). The evaluation of specific instruments requires consideration of the theoretical context of the research behind them. Some general comments about research priorities can, however, be advanced.

There has been an inordinate emphasis on measuring the fear of death, with the result that investigators wishing to measure other death-related attitudes will find fewer useful measures than they would in the narrower area of fear of death. Almost none of the measures of attitudes concerning death and dying have been developed with, or even applied to, aged populations. This provides another source for both dissatisfaction and excitement about research opportunities. Many areas related to death and dying, undoubtedly, are best approached through single indicators, only a few of which can be reproduced in this chapter. However, I have attempted to refer to useful sources of appropriate single indicators. The reader may want to consult other sources that review selected single indicators and fewer other measures. There is no comprehensive review of the *entire* body of research instruments used in the field.

Only a brief overview of the theoretical model underlying the organization of the instruments can be provided here. The first four instruments focus on experiencing the deaths of others. Six measures more directly concerned with awareness of impending death are then reviewed.

With varying degrees of awareness will be associated diverse reactions to this recognition that humans are mortal. Many investigators consider anxiety and fear reactions to be paramount. Fifteen measures of anxiety and fear represent the third set of measures reviewed. Other kinds of attitudes toward death are possible, and five of these measures are also reviewed. It should be emphasized that some of the unidimensional measures of other attitudes come close to the anxiety and fear dimensions and that anxiety, fear, and acceptance dimensions are tapped by some of the multidimensional measures of attitudes toward death.

Only two measures of behavior and planning regarding death are reviewed. Death research is comparable to most social science research in North America in that attitudinal measures receive an undue amount of attention in contrast to behavioral measures or even measures of behavioral intent. It must be assumed that a primary reason for attempting to measure attitudes toward death is that such attitudes are presumed to have behavioral implications. Because of the lack of developed measures of behavior, single indicators in this area receive considerable attention in these introductory comments.

One concept omitted from the topics reviewed in this chapter is suicide potential. Therefore, a few comments may be in order. While the suicide rate is somewhat age related in some societies, such as the United States and Great Britain, it is not so related in all societies. For example, age and suicide rate are not related in Canadian society. Few attempts to predict suicide have been directed at understanding the relationship between age and suicide intent. Many believe that the best prediction of suicide comes from combining rating scales (such as those in this volume) with clinical and demographic data (a review of which is clearly beyond the scope of this volume). A thorough review of the literature on the subject produced a total of four direct measures that do not rely on clinical judgments or demographic data. These are the studies by Beck and associates (1974), Colson (1973), Cohen, Motto, and Seiden (1963), and Devries (1966). This literature, as well as the clinical literature, seems to equate suicide potential with such psychological states as depression, hopelessness, and despair. These phenomena are beyond the scope of this chapter but are pertinent to other chapters in this volume. In summary, while the criteria for inclusion or exclusion of a given topic were ultimately somewhat arbitrary, in the author's judgment suicide potential is not clearly related to age or aging in any theoretically meaningful way.

Measures of the Experience of Death

With increasing age, individuals are likely to experience more frequently the deaths of kin and friends; they are also more likely to read obituaries and attend funerals (Kalish and Reynolds, 1976). Objective data on these experiences are easily retrievable through simple questions, and there is probably little need to develop composite measures. In any case, while the Mathieu and Peterson (1970) index is of questionable validity in terms of unidimensionality and the Munnichs (1966) index is not clearly more valuable as an index than as a set of three single indicators, the Kalish and Reynolds battery contains questions on as many dimensions of death experience as one might wish to know about, and it also provides normative data by age-groups for a large representative sample. It is, therefore, the most highly recommended of these measures. (Some of the items in this battery also appear in other sources, notably in Fulton [1965] and Gorer [1965].) The Marshall Comparative Age at Death indicator attempts to tap a related but distinct domain, the relationship of a single property of the parents (age at death) to a property of the respondent (age). This measure is valid and theoretically relevant in terms of the presumed psychological meaning of aging.

Measures of Awareness of Impending Death

At least two general theoretical approaches and one more specific approach to the social psychology of aging incorporate as a concept an estimate the individual makes of the time remaining before his or her death. These approaches are disengagement theory, the developmental approach that derives from Eriksonian theory, and the life-review theory of reminiscence as postulated by Robert Butler (see Marshall, 1975b). This estimate has to be kept analytically and empirically distinct from actual distance from death, which is also employed in some formulations (e.g., Lieberman and Coplan, 1970). Most tests of the three approaches commit a rather basic error by using age as a proxy for perceived distance from death. Tests of such theory, and any attempts to develop a gerontology concerned with existential questions, must measure awareness of impending death adequately.

Several investigators have asked people how long they anticipate living as a direct single-indicator measure (see, for example, Bengtson, Cuellar, and Ragan, 1977; Kastenbaum, 1971; Reynolds and Kalish, 1974; Tolar and Murphy, 1967) or as part of a battery (Chappell, 1975; Chellam, 1964; Marshall, 1975b). Chellam's Awareness of Death Scale includes three such single indicators, but these are confounded with measures that probably reflect antecedents or consequences of such an estimate.

The remaining measures included in this section deal with a closely related but conceptually distinct issue: whether or not the individual is concerned about death. It is conceivable that someone may see death as near and yet remain unconcerned about that fact (Chappell, 1975) or that someone may be quite preoccupied with the imminency of death and yet not fear it (Klug and Boss, 1976). Moreover, Cameron, Stewart, and Biber (1973) have found that death thoughts are very frequent at all ages and in many situations of everyday life. This last study casts serious doubt on the utility of paper-and-pencil measures that focus on preoccupations with death or frequency of death thoughts.

In general, it can be argued that preoccupation with death should always be used as a control variable in research on fear of death or death anxiety. If many people think little of death, perhaps because they see their own deaths as remote in time or perhaps for other reasons (or for no reason at all), then the preoccupation with measuring death fear and anxiety may well be misplaced. Such individuals may fear death when they think about it but may think about it so seldom that it has no effect on other aspects of their lives. This said, it is both theoretically interesting that so much research with college students has succeeded in identifying death fear or anxiety and methodologically irritating that so little research on death fear or anxiety has dealt with populations that might be presumed, on the basis of nearness to personal death, to be more concerned or preoccupied with it.

Measures of Death Anxiety, Fear, and Acceptance

A remarkable number of investigators presume a universal fear of death as an aspect of the human condition. If they do not find it, they presume denial of death. Much of the earlier work employing clinical judgments and projective techniques was highly susceptible to such theoretical tunnel vision (for reviews of this literature and some significant positions, see Donaldson, 1972; Dumont and Foss, 1972; Lester, 1967; Marshall, 1980; Munnichs, 1966; Vernon, 1970; Weisman, 1972; and Williams, 1966). In an early paper, Becker and Bruner (1931, pp. 828-29) suggested that in considering the individual's attitude toward death, "there are three possible emotional tendencies that are important: joy or gladness, indifference, and horror or fear." The instruments reviewed usually concentrate on measures of fear and anxiety.

Exceptions to this trend are: (1) Mathieu and Peterson's (1970) measure of attitudes toward dying and death, which, unfortunately, lacks reliability and validity; (2) Ray and Najman's (1974) measure of death acceptance; and (3) Swenson's (1961) checklist of death attitudes, which is included in this chapter because of its historical importance.

Investigators who accept the assumption that death is universally feared, but who want conceptual clarity, will find a number of measures useful (Klug and Boss, 1976; Diggory and Rothman, 1961; Collett and Lester, 1969; and especially Nelson and Nelson, 1975) or at least promising (Nehrke, 1973).

It is useful to note that a number of measures reviewed here are interrelated in that investigators include items from, react against, or cross-validate with other instruments. This research effort is relatively young but it is very active, and most investigators claim to be continuing their work in this area.

Perhaps the main dilemma facing researchers is to use (or develop) a multidimensional measure of death anxiety or fear—a measure including a broader spectrum of possible attitudes (such as indifference or acceptance)—or to focus on measuring a single construct. If a given theoretical model incorporates only one of many possible dimensions of attitudes toward death (such as fear of one's own death), then the use of a very specific unidimensional measure is justified. The danger in this approach, however, is that important aspects of death attitudes might be missed because of the restricted focus.

Neither theoretical nor empirical evidence has indicated what level of fear is "normal" or "pathological" or how much might be needed to act as a "motivator," and so forth. The lack of such norms inhibits the direct comparison of research efforts.

Other issues in this area include the widespread use of college-student populations in measurement development and the alternative theoretical strategies of beginning with a deduced dimensional structure (e.g., Diggory and Rothman, 1961; Swenson, 1961; Collett and Lester, 1969) or to use inductive strategies such as factor analysis (e.g., Nelson and Nelson, 1975). In considerations of the relative merit of theoretical typological dimensions versus factor analytic strategies, perhaps the best check on a typology is a factor analysis, provided that the factor analysis is not pursued through so many iterations as to remove any scale scores too far from reality. Gerontologists should recognize the importance of assessing an instrument's sensitivity to age differences, not only because of the relevance of impending death to older respondents, but also because a given attitude toward death or dying might be influenced by age-related phenomena such as ill health.

Finally, the work of Durlak (1972) in cross-validating a number of death fear/anxiety measures should stand as a model for others. More such studies are needed, especially those using older subjects as well as subjects from various social and ethnic backgrounds. This may be the place to point to a general problem in validating the instruments in this section and, more generally, in this chapter: the area of attitudes toward death is so undeveloped that the theoretical base renders attempts at establishing convergent validity hazardous. Not only are there few measures against which to attempt cross-validation, but there is little agreement as to empirical correlates of death attitudes; this prevents the extensive use of attempts at discriminant or nomological net validation. For example, if gerontologists knew that religiosity or advanced age was associated with increased fear of death, this knowledge would be valuable in attempts at validation. Unfortunately, gerontologists simply do not know whether either of these variables is associated with fear of death (and it is not terribly certain that they are associated with each other either!). Gerontologists will not know these things until they have valid, as well as reliable, measures of death fear. So the validation cycle goes around and around.

Measures of Other Attitudes toward Death

While one measure reviewed in this chapter includes a component of death fear (Spilka et al., 1976), it is not central to the scale.

Included are measures of other possible attitudes toward death. At the present time, the most valuable of these is the battery used by Riley (1970). Its value is in its having been applied to a large and representative sample, since this is the single instance when a significant set of indicators has been applied to a national sample. One other set of questions on diverse attitudes toward death is also valuable because it has been used on a representative sample of some size. This is the questionnaire employed by Kalish and Reynolds (1976), a fragment of which is reproduced in this chapter. The Kalish and Reynolds instrument has been fully reproduced, together with ethnicity, age, and sex cross-tabulations, as an appendix to their monograph. This instrument, and the excellent monograph that presents the analysis, is required reading for every researcher working in the areas reviewed in this chapter. The usefulness of the Kalish and Reynolds items and the Riley battery testifies to the fact that single indicators can occupy a very important place in the research on death and dying.

Of the scales and indexes reviewed, none is unreservedly recommended for research use. Spilka and his associates (1976) and Schafer (1976) are continuing instrument development, and their projects show promise. The Ellison (1969a; 1969b) instrument needs validation work, and the Back (1971) Death Images instrument lacks theoretical grounding.

In summary, the inadequacy in the measurement of attitudes toward death other than fear and anxiety is perhaps best seen in contrast to the much larger, and somewhat more successful, effort at measuring fear and anxiety over death.

Measures of Behavior and Planning in Response to Death

If attitudes toward death are at all important, they should be correlated with behavior and with statements of projected or preferred behavior. That is, even though the orientation one takes toward death (whether an attitude of fear, anxiety, or acceptance or some other orientation or perhaps a recognition or awareness that one's own death is near or the experience of the deaths of others) is worth studying in its own right, it gains in importance when it has meaningful consequences. Some of the postulated consequences of such orientations (following the most general definition of orientation here) have little to do with death per se, and, therefore, they are not of concern in this chapter. For example, disengagement theory argues that individuals voluntarily shed role relationships in response to their awareness of impending death. Measuring this phenomenon is not the province of this chapter. Nonetheless, the state of measurement for death-related consequences of orientation toward death is so undeveloped that almost total reliance must be placed on single indicators. Consequently, only two measures in this area are reviewed in this chapter. Some additional measures, however, can be briefly discussed in this introduction.

When death is recognized as being near (and this is increasingly the case in advanced age), the individual may wish to adjust his or her normal routines to accommodate the ultimate limitation on time that death represents. Back (1965) asked respondents these questions: "If you knew you were going to die within 30 days, what would you do?" "If you knew everybody was going to die within 30 days, what would you do?" Kalish and Reynolds (1976, p. 68) asked what people would do if they knew they were going to die in 6 months.

A number of investigators (Reynolds and Kalish, 1974; Kastenbaum, 1971; Marshall, 1975a, 1975b) have juxtaposed the respondent's personal estimation of life expectancy with his or her desired life expectancy. This was asked either in terms of additional years or in terms of the age to which the individual wanted to live. There was a tendency for respondents to round off their answers (though perhaps this is also the way they think about such matters, if they do think about them) to the 5- and 10-year intervals. Despite this, the measure formed from such a juxtaposition has been useful in examining such dimensions as acceptance of, and resignation to, impending death.

Measures of preferred style of dying can be found in the Kalish and Reynolds (1976) volume. Some older people express preferences for a particular syle of dying—whether or not they want to be told, who should be present, whether life should be prolonged. This literature is reviewed in Hinton (1967) and, together with very good data from batteries, in Kalish and Reynolds (1976). The early work of Gorer (1965) is also relevant here. The only measure in this area reported in detail is the Euthanasia Index (Preston and Williams, 1971). Though reliability and validity data for the index are lacking, the two-item index is a simple one that has been used successfully with older subjects. Vernon (1970, pp. 308-9) and Kalish (1965) also reported single-indicator data on this and related issues. In general, however, little is known about the ways in which people wish to die or the role expectations people have for others and for themselves concerning the ways in which people might die appropriately.

In considerations of specific planning for death (such as making wills, making funeral arrangements, and the like), it is quite clear from some studies (Hochschild, 1973; Marshall, 1975a, 1975b; Riley 1968) that older people sometimes, at least, make plans for death. Riley's index (1968) is the most useful instrument reviewed here, and it can be used either as an index or a battery. Kalish and Reynolds (1976) also provided questionnaire items and valuable data on these issues.

Summary

Before 32 measures related to death, dying, and adjustment to death and dying are reviewed (see Table 7-1), it is important to stress the limitations of this chapter. Projective techniques and measures developed on the basis of interviewer's or rater's judgments have been excluded, since the author feels that such measures are inevitably inferior to self-reports giving phenomenological data. It should be stressed, then, that this chapter attempts to review questionnaires and fixed choice interview schedules and does not attempt to review all the literature on attitudes toward death and dying. Much of the literature in this area does not use measurement in the sense this series of reviews does. Clinical and field studies using qualitative data gathered through unstructured interviews or observations of participants have given the field some of its most insightful analyses (e.g., Gubrium 1975; Hochschild, 1973; Weisman, 1972). Some people, of course, have argued that no one can "know" death. People do, however, have attitudes toward the death and dying of others and, in anticipation, of themselves. The key issue in measuring such attitudes is validity; this is the rock upon which so many of the studies reviewed in this chapter have foundered. The best instrument-development strategy may well involve bringing together both qualitative data (from clinical and field studies) and quantitative data (from measures such as those reviewed here (e.g., Bengtson, Cuellar, and Ragan, 1977).

This chapter has required a great deal of cooperation from the authors of the measures included in it and from several people who have been working with the measures. The measures reviewed span the period between 1958 and 1977—a period marked by considerable advancement in the measurement of attitudes toward death and in measurement theory per se. The field is young and small but growing very fast, and those who have contributed to it deserve praise. Where weaknesses in an instrument have been pointed out, it has most often been in points on which the investigators themselves acknowledged shortcomings.

TABLE 7-1
Instruments Reviewed in Chapter 7

Instrument	Author (date)	Code Number
I. Measures of the Experience of Death		
a. Experience with Dying and Death	Mathieu and Peterson (1970)	V1.7.I.a
b. Degree of Death Experience	Munnichs (1966)	V1.7.I.b
c. Encountering the Death of Others	Kalish and Reynolds (1976)	V1.7.I.c
d. Comparative Age at Death	Marshall (1975b)	Single item
II. Measures of Awareness of Impending Death		
a. Consciousness of Death	Cameron, Stewart, and Biber (1973)	V1.7.II.a
b. Awareness of Death Scale	Chellam (1964)	V1.7.II.b
c. Thought of Dying Scale	Guptill (1973) and Kalish (1963)	V1.7.II.c
d. Awareness of Death	Chappell (1975)	V1.7.II.d
e. Frequency of Death Thoughts	Jeffers and Verwoerdt (1970)	V1.7.II.e
f. Frequency of Thoughts about Death and Other Problems	Riley (1970)	Single item
III. Measures of Death Anxiety, Fear, and Acceptance		
a. Fear of Death Scale	Boyar (1964)	V1.7.III.a
b. Death Anxiety Scale	Handal (1969) and Tolar and Reznikoff (1967)	V1.7.III.b
c. Fear of Death Scale	Lester (1966)	V1.7.III.c
d. Death Anxiety Scale	Templer (1969)	V1.7.III.d
e. Death Anxiety Scale (Nehrke Modification)	Nehrke (1973)	V1.7.III.e
f. Death Concern Scale	Dickstein (1972), Klug and Boss (1976)	V1.7.III.f
g. Death Scale (Questions Relative to Death)	Feldman and Hersen (1967)	V1.7.III.g
h. Fear of Death Scale	Sarnoff and Corwin (1959)	V1.7.III.h
i. Extended Fear of Death Scale	Martin and Wrightsman (1965)	V1.7.III.i
j. Attitude toward Dying and Death Index	Mathieu and Peterson (1970)	V1.7.III.j
k. Consequences of One's Own Death	Diggory and Rothman (1961)	V1.7.III.k
l. Dimensions of Death Anxiety	Nelson and Nelson (1975)	V1.7.III.l
m. Death Acceptance Scale	Ray and Najman (1974)	V1.7.III.m
n. Checklist of Death Attitudes	Swenson (1961)	V1.7.III.n
o. Fear of Death Scale	Collett and Lester (1969)	V1.7.III.o
IV. Measures of Other Attitudes toward Death		
a. Death Scales	Hooper and Spilka (1970)	V1.7.IV.a
b. Will to Live Scale	Ellison (1969)	V1.7.IV.b
c. Images of Death	Riley (1970)	V1.7.IV.c
d. Death Images	Back (1971)	V1.7.IV.d
e. Death and Violent Interest Questionnaire	Schafer (1976)	V1.7.IV.e
V. Measures of Behavior and Planning in Response to Death		
a. Euthanasia Index	Preston and Williams (1971)	V1.7.V.a
b. Preparation for Death	Riley (1968)	V1.7.V.b

(Particular thanks are owed the following people, all of whom are mentioned within the chapter: Steve Fleming, Milton Nehrke, Bernard Spilka, and Jim Thorson. These people have assisted me beyond the call of duty and beyond reference to their own work. I would like also to thank Dr. I. Sakinofsky of McMaster University for invaluable help in reviewing the suicide potential literature.)

REFERENCES

Back, K. W. "Time Perspective and Social Attitudes." Paper presented to the annual meeting of the American Psychological Association, Chicago, September 7, 1965.

———. "Metaphors as Test of Personal Philosophy of Aging." *Sociological Focus*, 1971, 5 (1): 1-8. (Reprinted in *Normal Aging II*, E. Palmore [ed.], pp. 201-7. Durham, N.C.: Duke University Press, 1974.)

Beck, A. T., A. Weissman, D. Lester, and L. Trexler. "The Measurement of Pessimism: The Hopelessness Scale." *Journal of Consulting and Clinical Psychology*, 1974, 42 (6): 861-65.

Becker, H. S., and D. Bruner. "Attitude toward Death and the Dead and Some Possible Causes of Ghost Fear." *Mental Hygiene*, 1931, 15: 828-37.

Bengtson, V. L., J. B. Cuellar, and P. K. Ragan. "Stratum Contrasts and Similarities in Attitudes toward Death." *Journal of Gerontology*, 1977, 32 (1): 76-88.

Cameron, P., L. Stewart, and H. Biber. "Consciousness of Death across the Life Span." *Journal of Gerontology*, 1973, 28 (1): 92-95.

Chappell, N. L. "Awareness of Death in the Disengagement Theory: A Conceptualization and an Empirical Investigation." *Omega*, 1975, 6 (4): 325-43.

Chellam, G. "The Disengagement Theory: Awareness of Death and Self-Engagement." D.S.W. dissertation, Western Reserve University, 1964. (University microfilms number 65-2318.)

Cohen, E., J. Motto, and R. H. Seiden. "An Instrument for Evaluating Suicide Potential: A Preliminary Study." Proceedings of 121st Annual Meeting of American Psychiatric Association, May 3-7, 1963.

Collett, L. J., and D. Lester. "The Fear of Death and the Fear of Dying." *Journal of Psychology*, 1969, 72: 179-81.

Colson, C. "An Objective-Analytic Approach to the Classification of Suicidal Motivation." *Acta Psychiatrica Scandinavica*, 1973, 49 (2): 107-13.

Devries, A. G. "A Potential Suicide Personality Inventory." *Psychological Reports*, 1966, 18: 731-38.

Diggory, J. C., and D. Z. Rothman. "Values Destroyed by Death." *Journal of Abnormal and Social Psychology*, 1961, 63: 205-10.

Donaldson, P. "Denying Death: A Note Regarding Some Ambiguities in the Current Discussion." *Omega*, 1972, 3: 285-90.

Dumont, R. and D. Foss. *The American View of Death: Acceptance or Denial*. Cambridge, Mass.: Schenkman, 1972.

Durlak, J. A. "Measurement of the Fear of Death: An Examination of Some Existing Scales." *Journal of Clinical Psychology*, 1972, 28: 545-47.

Ellison, D. L. "Will to Live: A Link between Social Structure and Health among the Elderly." *Sociological Symposium*, 1969a, 2 (Spring): 37-47.

———. "Alienation and the Will to Live." *Journal of Gerontology*, 1969b, 24 (3): 361-67.

Fulton, R. "The Sacred and the Secular: Attitudes of the American Public toward Death, Funerals, and Funeral Directors." In *Death and Identity*, R. Fultin (ed.), pp. 89-105. New York: John Wiley and Sons, 1965.

Gorer, G. *Death, Grief and Mourning*. New York: Doubleday, 1965.

Gubrium, J. F. *Living and Dying at Murray Manor*. New York: St. Martin's Press, 1975.

Hinton, J. *Dying*. Harmondsworth: Penguin Books, 1967.

Hochschild, A. *The Unexpected Community*. Englewood Cliffs, N.J.: Prentice-Hall, 1973.

Kalish, R. A. "The Aged and the Dying Process: The Inevitable Decisions." *Journal of Social Issues*, 1965, 21: 87-96.

Kalish, R. A., and D. K. Reynolds. *Death and Ethnicity: A Psychocultural Study*. Los Angeles: University of Southern California Press, 1976.

Kastenbaum, R. "The Foreshortened Life Perspective." *Geriatrics*, 1966, 24 (8): 126-33.

———. "Age: Getting There Ahead of Time." *Psychology Today*, 1971, 7 (5): 52-54, 82-84.

Klug, L., and M. Boss. "Factorial Structure of the Death Concern Scale." *Psychological Reports*, 1976, 38: 107-12.

Lester, D. "Experimental and Correlational Studies of the Fear of Death." *Psychological Bulletin*, 1967, 67: 27-36.

Lieberman, M. A., and A. S. Coplan. "Distance from Death as a Variable in the Study of Aging." *Developmental Psychology*, 1970, 2 (1): 71-84.

Marshall, V. W. "Socialization for Impending Death in a Retirement Village." *American Journal of Sociology*, 1975a, 80 (5): 1124-44.

———. "Age and Awareness of Finitude in Developmental Gerontology." *Omega*, 1975b, 6 (2): 113-29.

———. *Last Chapters: A Sociology of Aging and Dying*. Monterey, Calif.: Brooks/Cole, 1980.

Mathieu, J. T., and J. A. Peterson. "Death and Dying: Some Social Psychological Dimensions." Paper presented to the 23rd Annual Meeting of Gerontological Society, Toronto, October 22-24, 1970.

Munnichs, J. M. A. *Old Age and Finitude*. New York and Basel: Karger, 1966.

Nehrke, M. F. "Perceived Generational Differences in Attitudes toward Death." Paper presented to the 26th Annual Meeting of Gerontological Society, Miami Beach, November 5-9, 1973.

Nelson, L. D., and C. C. Nelson. "A Factor Analytic Inquiry into the Multidimensionality of Death Anxiety." *Omega*, 1975, 6 (2): 171-78.

Neugarten, B. L. "Dynamics of Transition of Middle to Old Age." *Journal of Geriatric Psychiatry*, 1970, 4 (1): 71-87.

Preston, C. E., and R. H. Williams. "Views of the Aged on the Timing of Death." *The Gerontologist*, 1971, 11 (4, part 1): 300-304.

Ray, J. J., and J. Najman. "Death Anxiety and Death Acceptance: A Preliminary Approach." *Omega*, 1974, 5 (4): 311-15.

Reynolds, D. K., and R. A. Kalish. "Anticipation of Futurity as a Function of Ethnicity and Age." *Journal of Gerontology*, 1974, 29 (2): 224-31.

Riley, J. W., Jr. Previously unpublished data presented in *Aging and Society* (vol. 1), M. W. Riley, A. Foner, et al. (eds.), pp.336-37. New York: Russell Sage Foundation, 1968.

———. "What People Think about Death." In *The Dying Patient*, O. Brim, Jr., H. E. Freeman, S. Levine, and N. A. Scotch (eds.), pp. 30-41. New York: Russell Sage Foundation, 1970.

Schafer, R. "Fascination with Death as a Function of Need for Novel Stimulation." *Omega*, 1976, 7 (1): 45-50.

Spilka, B., L. Stout, B. Minton, and D. Sizemore. "Death Perspectives, Death Anxiety, and Form of Personal Religion." Paper presented to the Convention of the Society for the Scientific Study of Religion, Philadelphia, October 29, 1976.

Swenson, W. M. "Attitudes toward Death in an Aged Population." *Journal of Gerontology*, 1961, 16 (1): 49-60.

Tolar, A., and V. Murphy. "Some Psychological Correlates of Subjective Life Expectancy." *Journal of Clinical Psychology*, 1967, 23: 21-24.

Vernon, G. *Sociology of Death: An Analysis of Death Related Behavior*. New York: Ronald Press, 1970.

Vischer, A. L. *On Growing Old* (G. Onn, trans.). Boston: Houghton Mifflin Company, 1967.

Weisman, A. *On Dying and Denying*. New York: Behavioral Publications, 1972.

Williams, M. "Changing Attitudes to Death: A Survey of Contributions in Psychological Abstracts over a Thirty Year Period." *Human Relations*, 1966, 19:405-23.

Abstracts

EXPERIENCE WITH DYING AND DEATH
J. T. Mathieu and J. A. Peterson, 1970

Definition of Variable

The variable being measured is "the affective involvement of dying and death with significant others" (Mathieu and Peterson, 1970).

Description of Instrument

This index was formed from 14 questionnaire items embedded in three questions addressing frequency and proximity of deaths among the subject's family and friends and discussion of death with significant others. No item-development procedures or index-development procedures were noted in the published study. The items have face validity.

Method of Administration

The items were part of a comprehensive questionnaire administered in a group setting, but they would be equally usable in an individual administration.

Context of Development

The investigators, concerned with the lack of institutional socialization for dying and death, attempted to measure factors affecting self-initiated socialization.

Sample

The sample consisted of 183 residents over 50 years old and living in Leisure World, Calif., for at least 5 years. This population was "heavily weighted in the direction of the married, white, Protestant, middle to upper-middle class."

Scoring, Scale Norms, and Distribution

See the instrument for items and norms. The instrument is scored by the summation of the 14 items, which yields an index ranging from 0 to 42.

Usability on Older Populations

This index appears to be appropriate for administration to older populations.

Sensitivity to Age Differences

No significant differences among the age-groups (aged over 50) have been reported.

General Comments and Recommendations

The authors claimed face validity for this index. However, in the absence of data, one might alternately conclude that the items dealing with talking about death represent a different conceptual domain than those dealing with the occurrence of death and that the former could be a response to the latter. Therefore, the index could be broken down into subindexes. Individual items seem promising.

This instrument should be tested on a broader age and socioeconomic range of subjects, and it should be subjected to standard instrument-development procedures, beginning with an interitem-correlation analysis. This requirement is particularly important, given the lack of alternate measures.

Reference

Mathieu, J. T., and J. A. Peterson. "Death and Dying: Some Social Psychological Dimensions." Paper presented to the 23rd Annual Meeting of the Gerontological Society, Toronto, October 22-24, 1970.

Instrument

See Instrument V1.7.I.a.

DEGREE OF DEATH EXPERIENCE
J. M. A. Munnichs, 1966

Definition of Variable

This instrument measures "a datum referring to the knowledge and experience of dying (in a metaphorical sense, of course) and similar experiences. Among those we count the following: death of a marriage partner, having had an operation during the last five years and having recently suffered a severe illness. In the analysis we made no difference between the various experiences" (Munnichs, 1966, p. 130).

Description of Instrument

The index is based on items obtained through a semistructured (open) interview procedure. No item-development or index-development procedures were given. The items are noted during a basically free-flowing interview procedure. The index is, therefore, a coding procedure.

Context of Development

The author wished to explore the relationship between the experience of death in others and the growing awareness of one's own impending death on other aspects of the lives of the aged.

Sample

A sample of 50 males and 50 females, aged 70 and older, who were residents of Nijmegen, Netherlands. Although small, the random sample is representative of the noninstitutionalized aged of that community in age, sex, and civil status. Half the respondents of each sex were married, half were widowed.

Scoring, Scale Norms, and Distribution

The score is the simple sum of the number of death experiences. Of the 100 subjects,

4 had three death experiences, 24 had two experiences, 50 had one experience, and 22 had no experience.

Usability on Older Populations

The index appears to be appropriate for older popoulatons, including the relatively old, old population.

General Comments and Recommendations

This is an easily used coding mechanism for application to relatively unstructured data. It could be converted easily into direct questions. The instrument should be tested on a broader age range of subjects and subjected to standard instrument-development procedures, beginning with an interitem-correlation analysis.

Reference

Munnichs, J. M. A. *Old Age and Finitude*. New York and Basel: Karger, 1966.

Instrument

See the definition of the variable above.

ENCOUNTERING THE DEATH OF OTHERS
R. A. Kalish and D. K. Reynolds, 1976

Description of Concept

The measure deals with the respondents' contact with dying and death.

Description of Instrument

This instrument was a battery of 10 questions included as part of a lengthy interview. The items tap the number of dead persons the subject has known and the manner of their death, the number of funerals the subject has attended, the number of grave visitations he or she has made, and the amount of contact with dying persons the subject has had.

Method of Administration

The original measure was administered as an interview, which was also translated into Japanese and Spanish.

Context of Development

The investigators wanted to learn "how a cross-section of a general population felt concerning death and bereavement . . . [and] . . . to understand better how and why groups differed in their views of death and bereavement" (Kalish and Reynolds, 1976, pp. 2-3).

Sample

The sample included 434 residents of Los Angeles County, who were interviewed in October and November 1970. Of these, 109 were black Americans, 110 Japanese Americans, 114 Mexican Americans, and 101 white Americans. Of the total, 215 were men and 219 women. The mean age was in the middle to late 40s, with 28% aged 60 and older. The sample was drawn from census tracts falling below the median income for Los Angeles County ($7,046).

Norms and Distribution

Responses for the battery are reported with the instrument at the end of this abstract.

Formal Test of Validity

Attendance at funerals correlates significantly ($r = .41$) with having visited a dying person (Kalish and Reynolds, 1976, p. 28).

Usability on Older Populations

The measure appears to be appropriate for administration across the adult life cycle.

Sensitivity to Age Differences

Age and ethnicity appear to have an interactive effect on responses to this battery.

General Comments and Recommendations

While the intentions of Kalish and Reynolds were primarily descriptive, the explanatory use of the battery would be enhanced if indexes or scales could be developed through standard techniques. The validity of these items is enhanced because they have been interpreted in the context of a great deal of additional data presented in the monograph.

Reference

Kalish, R. A., and D. K. Reynolds. *Death and Ethnicity: A Psychocultural Study*. Los Angeles: University of Southern California Press, 1976.

Instrument

See Instrument V1.7.I.c.

COMPARATIVE AGE AT DEATH
V. W. Marshall, 1975

Definition of Variable

The relationship of the respondent's own age to the age at death of his or her parents is the focus of this measure.

Description of Instrument

The instrument is a single-item indicator formed from coding based on information gathered through direct questions. Comparative age at death is established with the respondent coded as: younger than age at death of both parents; younger than age at death of one parent; older than age at death of both parents.

Method of Administration

The measure is administered in a coded interview.

Context of Development

The investigator was concerned with the relationship between the experience of death and anticipated life expectancy.

Sample

The sample was representative of residents of a retirement village, aged 64 to 96, with mean age of 80 years. This sample was advantaged socioeconomically and educationally.

Formal Tests of Validity

Predictive validity is established through a high correlation with awareness of finitude (anticipated life expectancy), which is itself highly correlated with age. Comparative age at death is a stronger predictor of awareness of finitude than is age, and it continues to add predictiveness within 10-year age categories above age 64. The results are supportive of social comparison theory, thus indicating construct validity.

Usability on Older Populations

The measure appears to be appropriate for use with older populations.

Sensitivity to Age Differences

Responses may be inferred to correlate highly with age. However, within age-groups, the predictability of awareness of finitude is maintained.

General Comments and Recommendations

The value of this indicator is in its providing a supplement to age as a predictor of awareness of finitude. A disadvantage is the fact that the measure has not been used elsewhere or for younger age-groups.

The author failed to provide a correlation matrix of this item with several other predictors of awareness of finitude, such as age, number of dead siblings, number of dead friends, and perceived health. In particular, the item should be brought together with those on death of siblings and friends for purposes of index construction. However, this is a highly "objective" single indicator with high predictive validity. The additional benefits of index construction may be so marginal as to be exceeded by the cost involved. Applicability to younger respondents has yet to be established.

References

Marshall, V. W. "Continued Living and Dying as Problematical Aspects of Old Age." Ph.D. dissertation, Princeton University, 1973. (University Microfilms number 73-18, 768.)
——. "Age and Awareness of Finitude in Developmental Gerontology." *Omega*, 1975, 6 (2): 113-29.

Instrument

See the description of the instrument above.

CONSCIOUSNESS OF DEATH
P. Cameron, L. Stewart, and H. Biber, 1973

Definition of Variable

The variable is the amount of cognitive attention given to death.

Description of Instrument

The index is based on three nested questions, allowing a differentiation between amounts of attention given to death. The responses are coded into three categories: (1) no thoughts of death, (2) passing thoughts of death, and (3) focal thoughts of death.

Method of Administration

The subjects were either "interviewed or asked to fill out a questionnaire equally-frequently across all daylight hours in the most frequent situations of daily life—in school, while engaging in recreation, at home, or at work" (Cameron, Stewart, and Biber, 1973, p. 92). Normal activites were interrupted and the questionnaire or interview was then administered—school, Sunday school, and church services were interrupted, and persons were approached in shopping areas, parks, and sports facilities. Most of the at-home sample completed the questionnaire without an interviewer's assistance, and no differences were found between those with and without assistance.

Context of Development

The authors noted that some clinicians hold that "too frequent contemplation of death is a symptom of pathology," but the authors also noted that no parameters have been established that allow judgments of how much is too much. "This study attempted to determine how often the sexes and people in various age groups think about death and dying" (Cameron, Stewart, and Biber, 1973, p. 92).

Sample

The total sample of 4,420 ranged in age from 8 to 99 years. Of the total, 2,170 were males and 2,250 were females. The distribution of the sample by site was: (1) 1,721 at home, (2) 1,438 at work, (3) 477 at school, and (4) 784 at other places. The overall rejection rate was 11%, with the highest rate (28%) for the at-home sample.

Norms and Distribution

Cameron, Stewart, and Biber (1973, p. 93) presented cross-tabulations by age and gender. In general, females and either the old (65+) or young (8-13) subjects were apt to report conscious thoughts of death.

Usability on Older Populations

The index appears to be appropriate for all age-groups.

Sensitivity to Age Differences

Older people are more apt to report passing or focal thoughts of death.

General Comments and Recommendations

The technique for gathering such data requires the interruption of ongoing activities. As a result, the ability to extend the interruption for a lengthy interview or questionnaire session is curtailed. However, the ease of administering this measure makes it readily usable in special situations. For example, in assessing the impact of the death of a statesman, a natural disaster, or a significant death-related event, this instrument can be readily administered by quickly trained interviewers gathering essentially situational data. These data can then be readily compared with the sound baseline data Cameron has made available. The technique could be extended to ascertain the content and the affective dimensions of the death thoughts reported. As it is, the instrument does not tell us whether or not the thoughts were pleasant, nor does it say anything else about their content.

References

Cameron, P. "The Imminency of Death." *Journal of Consulting and Clinical Psychology*, 1968, 32: 479-81.

Cameron, P., L. Stewart, and H. Biber. "Consciousness of Death across the Life Span." *Journal of Gerontology*, 1973, 28 (1): 92-95.

Instrument

See Instrument V1.7.II.a.

AWARENESS OF DEATH SCALE
G. Chellam, 1964

Definition of Variable

"The awareness of death is a recognition by the individual of the shortness of his life and the scarcity of time remaining to live. It causes a changed time perspective whereby he sees death as an imminent reality for himself" (Chellam, 1964, p. 28).

The instrument "gauges three aspects of the phenomenon, namely, (1) the respondent's conscious interest in and exposure to the occurrence of death, (b) his self-evaluation of his own nearness to death, (c) his realistic acceptance of death's nearness as evidenced by his plans for his immediate future and for his death" (Chellam, 1964, p. 44).

Description of Instrument

The eight items in the index vary in nature and include dichotomous, open-ended, and Likert-type questions. Three major criteria of awareness of death are measured by the instrument. These are: (1) impingement of death (death notices and obituaries read and commented on, funerals attended, deaths known about but not attended), (2) self-evaluation of time perspective (own life expectancy from fixed choice statements and lifeline), and (3) realistic acceptance (plans for immediate future and burial plans).

Method of Administration

The items are part of a comprehensive interview schedule and are probably not as suitable in a questionnaire format.

Context of Development

The instrument was developed as part of a doctoral dissertation intended to test explicitly the disengagement theory of aging. The focus of the research was on that aspect of the disengagement theory that hypothesizes that disengagement is initiated by an acute awareness of impending death.

Sample

The sample was randomly selected from an opportunistic list of available, community-dwelling persons 65 years old and older in the Cleveland area. The subjects in the sample were described as being in reasonably good health, with freedom of movement and free from financial worries (Chellam, 1964, p. 34). The random sample was further stratified in a matching process so as to yield 50 subjects scoring high on the awareness of death scale and 50 scoring low, with a high awareness of death designated by scores of 14 and over.

Scoring, Scale Norms, and Distribution

The scoring is additive and ranges from 5 to 29. Details of the scoring scheme are presented with the instrument.

Chellam (1964, p. 61) reported the dichotomized distribution of scale scores by age. The very old (80+) were more likely to score high on this scale.

Formal Tests of Reliability

Chi squares were reported for dichotomized item scores by dichotomized scale scores (Chellam, 1964, p. 59). The first two items were not significantly related to the dichotomized scale score; for the remaining six items, chi-square tests were significant ($p < .01$).

Formal Tests of Validity

In the larger study, the relationship between AD (awareness of death) and several variables were theoretically consistent with the postulates of disengagement theory. High AD was related to low social interaction and high self-engagement. Among those subjects with high AD, solitary activity was positively related to life satisfaction.

Usability on Older Populations

The index, or components of it, has been successfully used with populations above the age of 64, including the very old (Chellam, 1964; Chappell, 1975; Marshall, 1975).

General Comments and Recommendations

Attempts to assess the instrument's reliability and validity are well reported in Chellam (1964). However, the inclusion of items that do not relate to scale scores in the computation of index scores is not explained. Neither the reliability nor the validity of this instrument can be considered to have been established, and the instrument may be multidimensional. This is one of a very small number of available measures of awareness of finitude, and so it merits refinement. Particular attention should be paid to establishing unidimensionality.

References

Chappell, N. L. "Awareness of Death in the Disengagement Theory: A Conceptualization and an Empirical Investigation." *Omega*, 1975, 6 (4): 325-43.

Chellam, G. "The Disengagement Theory: Awareness of Death and Self-Engagement." D.S.W. dissertation, Western Reserve University, 1964. (University Microfilms number 65-2318.)

Marshall, V. W. "Continued Living and Dying as Problematical Aspects of Old Age." Ph.D. dissertation, Princeton University, 1973. (University Microfilms number 73-18, 768.)

——. "Age and Awareness of Finitude in Developmental Gerontology." *Omega*, 1975, 6 (2): 113-29.

Instrument

See Instrument V1.7.II.b.

THOUGHT OF DYING SCALE
C. S. Guptill, 1976; R. A. Kalish, 1963a, 1963b

Definition of Concept

This instrument measures the importance of thoughts of dying.

Description of Instrument

The scale is made up of 12 items, in a five-point agree-disagree format, related to concern with death and dying and taken by Guptill from a questionnaire developed by Richard A. Kalish (Kalish, 1963a; 1963b). It was initially used by Kalish to form a Likert-type scale on the fear of dying. The Guptill scales departs from the Kalish index by creating and applying factor scores using varimax rotation. The factor loadings appear with the instrument appended to this review.

Method of Administration

Guptill used the instrument in a community interview situation. Kalish (1963a; 1963b) used the items in a longer questionnaire format.

Context of Development

Kalish's study was largely exploratory, and Guptill was particularly interested in the apparent decline of death fears with increasing age that had been shown in several studies.

Sample

The original sample was a simple systematic sample of all households in Bangor, Maine, which yielded 233 interviews (with an 83% completion rate). Young people (17 to 34) and females were overrepresented as a result of the daytime interviewing schedule. However, 18% of the sample was aged 60 years and over.

Scoring, Scale Norms, and Distribution

The scale is scored by weighting the items by their factor loading and summing across all items. This yields a scale with a mean of 1.68.

Formal Test of Reliability

Guptill (1977, personal communication) has examined the 7 items that load most strongly on factor 1. For the 7 items, intercorrelations ranged between .482 and −.028, with a mean correlation of .224. There is little difference between the 7-item scale and the 12-item scale.

Formal Test of Validity

Predictive Validity: As predicted by the author, thoughts of dying were lower for those who were old and also lower for those subjectively defining themselves as old.

By far the greatest proportion of a respondent's scale score is accounted for by the first four items. Eliminating items, as Guptill has done by cutting the instrument down to the first seven, enhances its validity in terms of the concept's definition. Inspection of factor loadings for the other factors leads to a suspicion that factor 2 comes close to tapping a denial or avoidance attitude; factor 3, an attitude of indifference or perhaps acceptance; and factor 4, a fear of the process of dying.

Usability on Older Populations

The scale appears to be useful across the life span.

Sensitivity to Age Differences

As it was noted above, age is significantly related to thoughts of dying ($p < .05$), with older persons scoring lower on the scale. Felt age and self-rating of health are also significantly related to scale scores.

General Comments and Recommendations

Though it is still in the development stage, this instrument shows promise as a scale of frequency of death thoughts or intensity of death concerns. Consideration should be given to refining and shortening the scale by eliminating several items that contribute very little to scale scores. This would help ensure that a unidimensional construct is tapped by the items.

References

Guptill, C. S. "Aging and Attitude toward Dying." Paper presented to the 29th Annual Meeting of the Gerontological Society, October 13-17, 1976.

Kalish, R. A. "An Approach to the Study of Death Attitudes." *American Behavioral Scientist*, 1963a, 6: 68-70.

———. "Some Variables in Death Attitudes." *Journal of Social Psychology*, 1963b, 59: 27-45.

Instrument

See Instrument V1.7.II.c.

AWARENESS OF DEATH
N. L. Chappell, 1975

Definition of Concept

This instrument attempts to assess the meaning that an elderly person's knowledge of death has for his or her limited future, or the importance of the future for the individual.

Description of Instrument

The battery consists of four indicators of the individual's knowledge of his or her death. The indicators were borrowed from other authors. Chappell's indicators explicitly code for nonresponse. Nonspecific replies were "not interpreted here as indicative of the patients' lack of knowledge of their impending death but rather as indicative of the irrelevancy of the questions asking them to estimate the exact number of years remaining to them" (Chappell, 1975, p. 332).

Method of Administration

The items were part of a comprehensive interview schedule, but they would also be usable in questionnaire format.

Context of Development

Chappell was extending some work done by Marshall (1973) and Chellam (1964) and was particularly interested in the relevancy of nearness to impending death in aged, long-term hospital patients.

Sample

The population was composed of all the patients over age 60 in a long-term-care hospital who could be interviewed for 90 minutes (i.e., those who could speak, were not deaf, etc), who could speak English, and who were not classified as senile. The sample included 91.7% of the population that furnished completed interviews.

Norms and Distribution

Nonresponse to the questions ranged from 42.5% (question 4) to 82.5% (question 3).

Formal Tests of Validity

The issue of validity rests on whether or not nonresponses or nonspecific responses indicate the irrelevancy of impending death, as it was argued by Chappell. Chappell countered the alternate explanation that the respondents simply did not know the answer to these questions by noting that all but two of the respondents expected to remain in the hospital until their deaths. Only four respondents refused to answer a lengthy interview section dealing with death. Answers to other questions indicated that the respondents knew death was near and were on the whole ready to die. "In other words the sample as a whole is characterized by the knowledge that death is near. The non-specific answers to the specifically designed knowledge of death indicators are interpreted as indicative of the irrelevancy of the exact amount of time remaining" (Chappell, 1975, p. 333). Although Chappell did not make this point, her interpretation is consonant with a Wittgensteinian language-game analysis.

Usability on Older Populations

The instrument appears to be appropriate for administration to older patients, including the hospitalized chronically ill patient.

General Comments and Recommendations

Chappell (1975) found that the indicators did not correlate, but Marshall (1973) had found that they did. Reliability is therefore at issue, although Chappell did not intend the indicators to be interpreted as reflecting a unidimensional construct. In terms of validity, Chappell made a persuasive argument for the interpretation of nonresponse. Her nonresponse rates were higher than those of Marshall and Chellam, providing a kind of validation by known groups when one assumes that her respondents were more "socially dead" than those of Marshall and Chellam, and this is likely so. Chappell's interpretation is made strongly enough to be taken seriously in interpretations of any data using these measures.

The reader should refer to the recommendations for Chellam's Awareness of Death index. Further attempts to develop the use of these items is justified and could benefit from explicit attempts to correlate answers to these questions, including the nonresponse/response dichotomy, with measures of time perspective. Those for whom impending death is largely irrelevant should be characterized by low extensionality of time perspective, as well as by low levels of concrete planning for the future.

References

Chappell, N. L. "Awareness of Death in the Disengagement Theory: A Conceptualization and an Empirical Investigation." *Omega*, 1975, 6 (4): 325-43.

Chellam, G. "The Disengagement Theory: Awareness of Death and Self-Engagement." D.S.W. dissertation, Western Reserve University, 1964. (University Microfilms number 65-2318.)

Marshall, V. W. "Continued Living and Dying as Problematical Aspects of Old Age." Ph.D. dissertation, Princeton University, 1973. (University Microfilms number 73-18, 768.)

Instrument

See Instrument V1.7.II.d.

FREQUENCY OF DEATH THOUGHTS
F. C. Jeffers and A. Verwoerdt, 1970

Definition of Concept

The concept treated in the Jeffers and Verwoerdt (1970) study was the self-reported frequency of death thoughts.

Description of Instrument

The battery includes three fixed choice questions embedded in a lengthy social history.

Method of Administration

The questions are asked as part of a life history by an interviewer known to the subjects from earlier periods in a longitudinal research project.

Context of Development

The investigation reporting the use of this battery continued an earlier study (Jeffers, Nichols, and Eisdorfer, 1961) that analyzed factors associated with verbalized fear of death and belief in life after death.

Sample

The sample of 140 elderly community volunteers participating in the Duke University geriatrics research panel is described in Maddox (1970) and Palmore (1970).

Usability on Older Populations

The battery appears to be appropriate for older populations, although the Jeffers and Verwoerdt (1970) analysis, by selecting only extreme groups on question b, did not allow a full assessment of this issue.

General Comments and Recommendations

Anyone contemplating use of these questions might consider that they have not yet been thoroughly analyzed. Question b, in particular, might be useful in a battery with other indicators or possibly as an item combined with others (though probably not those in this battery) in index construction. Question b responses fall primarily into categories 2, 3, and 4, the unanalyzed categories in this study. Question a basically differentiates those who have an opinion from those who do not, and it might be more readily interpreted as an indicator of the felt importance of death, rather than of thoughts about it. Question c lacks face validity since it does not specify whether thoughts of death affect the enjoyment of life positively or negatively.

References

Jeffers, F. C., R. Nichols, and C. Eisdorfer. "Attitudes of Older Persons towards Death: A Preliminary Study." *Journal of Gerontology*, 1961, 16: 53-56.

Jeffers, F. C., and A. Verwoerdt. "Factors Associated with Frequency of Death Thoughts in Elderly Community Volunteers." In *Normal Aging*, E. Palmore (ed.), pp. 401-6. Durham, N.C.: Duke University Press, 1970.

Maddox, G. L. "Some Methodological Issues." In *Normal Aging*, E. Palmore (ed.), pp. 18-27. Durham, N.C.: Duke University Press, 1970.

Instrument

See Instrument V1.7.II.e.

FREQUENCY OF THOUGHTS ABOUT DEATH
AND OTHER PROBLEMS
J. W. Riley, Jr. 1970

Definition of Concept

The instrument was designed to indicate the extent to which thoughts of death intrude upon the everyday lives of people.

Description of Instrument

The instrument is a single-item indicator embedded in a more general question. The relevant part simply asks, "How often do you think about the uncertainty of your life or the death of someone close to you?"

Method of Administration

The instrument was included in interviews conducted by the National Opinion Research Center.

Context of Development

As part of a continuing program of basic social research, the Equitable Life Assurance Society of the United States has sponsored studies of various aspects of the meaning of time and death. This survey explored individual attitudes and orientations toward death, and the battery is concerned in part with the everyday significance of death.

Sample

The sample was made according to a standard multistage area probability design with quota sampling at the block level based on sex, age, race, and employment status. A total of 1,482 adults were interviewed (Riley, 1970), with 17% of the respondents over age 61.

Norms and Distribution

According to Riley's study (1970), 45% of older persons say that they often think about the uncertainty of life or the death of someone close to them, compared to 32% of the general population (Riley, 1970; Riley et al., 1968, pp. 332-37). Schneidman (1974, p. 215) presented data on a similar question from a *Psychology Today* survey of more than 30,000 readers, of which 22% frequently or very frequently thought of their own deaths.

Usability on Older Populations

The instrument appears to be acceptable across the adult life span.

Sensitivity to Age Differences

Riley (1970) noted that, while individuals of all ages generally report that they would be most likely to think of death at their own age, the same individuals generally believe that others think about death mainly in the later years. Thus, even young people who view their own death thoughts as atypical seem willing to answer this question frankly.

General Comments and Recommendations

This question is highly recommended. The principal reason is that baseline data are presented for a representative United States sample and for age and educational breakdowns of that sample. This question provides a criterion validity baseline for subsequent work.

References

Riley, J. W., Jr. "What People Think about Death." In *The Dying Patient*, O. Brim, Jr., H. E. Freeman, S. Levine, and N. A. Scotch (eds.), pp. 30-41. New York: Russell Sage Foundation, 1970.

Riley, M. W., A. Foner, et al. *Aging and Society* (vol. 1), pp. 332-37. New York: Russell Sage Foundation, 1968.

Schneidman, E. *Deaths of Man*. Baltimore, Md.: Penguin Books, 1974. (First published in 1973 by Quadrangle, New York.)

Instrument

See the description of the instrument in the abstract.

FEAR OF DEATH SCALE (FODS)
J. I. Boyar, 1964

Definition of Variable

According to Boyar, the scale measures the intensity of fear of death, when fear of death is defined as "the feeling of uneasiness, disquiet, anxiety, concern or dread of the act or fact of dying, the permanent ending of life in a person, or the state of being dead" (1964, p. 21).

Description of Instrument

Eighteen items are embedded in 82 other questions and administered with accompanying materials gathering demographic data and similar information. Each item may be answered yes, no, or don't know. During the instrument-development phase, scoring was on a six-point Likert Format from strongly agree to strongly disagree scored 0 through 5.

Method of Administration

The items were part of a large packet including filler items, personality measures, and demographic measures, all in questionnaire format. The questionnaires were administered in group settings.

Context of Development

The scale was developed as part of a doctoral dissertation in clinical psychology, with the purpose of developing and partially validating a scale to measure intensity of fear of death. The investigator was influenced to some extent by the work of Sarnoff and Corwin (1959) and by the psychoanalytic perspective. On theoretical grounds, a face validation strategy was selected over a factor analytic strategy, but the scale was subsequently subjected to validation (predictive) in an experimental study.

Sample

For the purpose of scale construction, 100 subjects, freshmen and sophomores in psychology classes, were sampled. For experimental validation, an experimental group of 56 and a control group of 40, again college students, were used.

Scoring, Scale Norms, and Distribution

The measure is scored through the simple summation of the items to yield an index ranging from 0 to 90.

Formal Tests of Reliability

The instrument used in the development phase had 22 items. Split-half reliability was .805; when corrected for length of test (Spearman-Brown formula), reliability equaled .893. Item-to-test correlations were calculated for the entire group and for males and females. Two items were discarded because they failed to achieve significant correlations for the male group. Another item was discarded because it had the lowest correlation, and a fourth because it correlated very highly with an item that was retained. Item-test correlations for the surviving 18 items ranged from .42 to .78, and all items were significant at the .01 level. Standard deviations were similar, ranging between 1.14 and 1.66, with the scoring 0 through 5; and mean scores ranged between 1.26 and 3.49. The scale's index scores, therefore, are not distorted by a predominance of extreme scores.

Test-retest reliability was estimated for experimental ($r = .847$) and control ($r = .886$) groups (see the section on tests of validity). Test-retest reliability with a 10-day interval was .79.

Split-half reliability for the 18-item scale was .83; when based on item statistics, this diminished to .21, suggesting that the FODS does not retain internal consistency when used to measure change (Boyar, 1964, p. 57).

Formal Tests of Validity

An attempt was made to assess construct validity through an experimental situation. An experimental group saw a film calculated to increase fear of death by exposing subjects to scenes of fatal automobile accidents. A control group saw a film about urban traffic problems. The mean scores of the experimental group on the FODS increased significantly. A smaller but still significant increase was experienced by the control group. Item analysis indicated that only 10 of the 18 items increased significantly.

Durlak (1972) found a low ($-.21$; $p < .05$) but significant correlation between the FODS and the Marlowe-Crowne Social Desirability Scale. Durlak also reported correlations of .56 with Lester's Fear of Death Scale, .65 with Sarnoff and Corwin's Fear of Death Scale, and .61 with the Handal-Tolar Death Anxiety Scale. Durlak also reported correlations of .40, .46, .58, and .69 with the four subscales of Collett and Lester's Fear of Death measure. (See reports on these last three instruments later in this chapter.) Templer (1970) found that the FODS correlates highly ($r = .74$) with his Death Anxiety Scale.

Usability on Older Populations

Nehrke, Bellucci, and Gabriel (1977-1978) have used the Boyar scale and the Templer DAS with populations over 60 years of age. These included 40 residents from private nursing homes, 40 living independently in the community, and 40 in public housing units, with mean ages ranging from 68 years (males in community) to 84.6 years (females in nursing home). For the three residence groups and for all groups combined but analyzed by sex, there were significant correlations between the FODS and Templer's DAS, which ranged from .42 to .48. Age correlated $-.34$ for males and $-.43$ for females. For the community sample only, age was negatively correlated with the FODS ($r = -.36$), as was education with the FODS ($r = -.38$).

General Comments and Recommendations

Boyar's own conclusion is that "the failure of the FODS to retain internal consistency when used to measure change indicates the need for introducing a factor analytic approach in any further research on this scale" (Boyar, 1964, p. 64a). The index appears, from Boyar's analysis, to be multidimensional, even though the FODS reflects a narrower range of interests and life experiences than Templer's (1970) Death Anxiety Scale. The FODS contains items "which cover primarily the act of dying, the finality of death, and corpses and their burial" (Boyar, 1964, p. 622).

One virtue of the FODS is the relative thoroughness with which it has been subjected to tests of reliability and validity. One of its limitations is the infrequency with which it has been applied to non-college-age populations. However, this limitation is shared by most other measures in this area.

In summary, the Boyar FODS was of great historical importance for the measurement of attitudes toward death. (This will be apparent from a consideration of the alternatives reviewed later in this chapter.) For older populations, at least, however, it is probably of less value than other instruments, such as that of Templer (1970).

References

Boyar, J. I. "The Construction and Partial Validation of a Scale for the Measurement of the

Fear of Death." Ph.D. dissertation, University of Rochester, 1964. (University Microfilm number 64-9228.)

Durlak, J. A. "Measurement of the Fear of Death: An Examination of Some Existing Scales." *Journal of Clinical Psychology*, 1972, 28: 545-47.

Nehrke, M. F., G. Bellucci, and S. J. Gabriel. "Death Anxiety, Locus of Control and Life Satisfaction in the Elderly: Toward a Definition of Ego-Integrity." *Omega*, 1977-1978, 8 (4): 359-68.

Sarnoff, I., and S. M. Corwin. "Castration Anxiety and the Fear of Death." *Journal of Personality*, 1959, 27: 374-85.

Templer, D. I. "The Construction and Validation of a Death Anxiety Scale." *Journal of General Psychology*, 1970, 82: 165-77.

Instrument

See Instrument V1.7.III.a.

DEATH ANXIETY SCALE (DAS)
P. J. Handal, 1969; A. Tolar and M. Reznikoff, 1967

Definition of Variable

Overt death anxiety is measured by this instrument.

Description of Instrument

The 20-item Death Anxiety Scale is based on Livingston and Zimet's (1965) 24-item questionnaire, which was designed for use with medical students. The items are in an agree-disagree format on a six-point scale, with one point signifying strong disagreement and six points signifying strong agreement. The statements are balanced for response set: high- and low-anxiety statements appear in an equal number of positive and negative statements.

Method of Administration

The questionnaire is suitable for administration as part of a larger battery.

Context of Development

Livingston and Zimet (1965) devised a 24-item scale to measure death anxiety in medical students. They were influenced by psychoanalytic theory and predicted an inverse relationship between authoritarianism and overt death anxiety. They also predicted that students interested in surgery would have a lower death anxiety than those interested in psychiatry and that students would experience more death anxiety as they progressed through medical school and had more direct contact with death. These hypotheses were borne out in a sample of medical students.

Tolar (Tolar and Reznikoff, 1967) modified the instrument by dropping the four items that were specific to medical students' experiences, thus making it suitable for use with a general college-student population. His interest, with Reznikoff (1967), was in exploring the relationships between various elements in an individual's defense system.

Handal (1969; Handal and Rychlak, 1971) subsequently used the index with graduate students, investigating some psychological correlates and thereby adding to the validity data of the instrument.

Samples

Tolar and Reznikoff (1967) used a sample consisting of 79 male college students in an introductory psychology course. The age range was between 18 and 22 years.

Handal (1969) used a sample of 66 male and 50 female graduate students at a northeastern university. The male age range was 20 to 60, mean age 29.0 years; the female age range was 22 to 49, mean age 33.4 years.

Handal and Rychlak's (1971) sample 1 consisted of 43 subjects, and their sample 2 consisted of 36 subjects. Each sample was made up of a college class in undergraduate psychology, with a mean age of 20 years.

Formal Tests of Reliability

Tolar and Reznikoff (1967) reported test-retest reliability (r = .85) for a three-month interval. Fleming (1977) reported a Cronbach's alpha of only .58, indicating low internal consistency for a 20-item measure.

Formal Tests of Validity

Convergent Validity: Durlak (1972) reported correlations of the Tolar scale with the Lester scale (r = .40), the Sarnoff and Corwin scale (r = .47), the Boyar scale (r = .61), and four subscales of the Collett and Lester instrument (r = .47, .46, .39, and .40) in a sample of 94 subjects. All correlations were significant beyond the .01 level.

Discriminant Validity: Durlak (1972) reported a low (r = −.14, not significant) correlation with the Marlowe-Crowne Social Desirability Scale.

Predictive Validity: Lonetto and associates (1976) presented data for a discriminant function analysis of combined Handal and Templer items, which provided four factors amenable to meaningful interpretation. This procedure did not report separately for Handal and Templer. The discriminant function scores thus derived allowed successful placement of 91.46% of their student subjects into five groups formed on the basis of interaction between the sex of the student and the sex the student attributed to death (e.g., a male sees death as female).

Usability on Older Populations

The applicability of this scale to older samples has not been investigated, but items 14, 16, and 20 would surely be inappropriate for older subjects.

General Comments and Recommendations

Under its various names, the DAS has been widely used, but only with younger college students. As it stands now, the instrument is of unknown utility for assessing age-related changes in attitudes toward death. Some of the items in the instrument could be used in future index construction.

Fleming's (1977) observations that efforts should be directed toward improving the internal consistency of this instrument are valid. His data, as well as Lonetto and associates' (1976), are useful for this purpose.

References

Durlak, J. A. "Measurement of the Fear of Death: An Examination of Some Existing Scales." *Journal of Clinical Psychology*, 1972, 28: 545-47.

Fleming, S. "Perceptual Defensiveness and Death Anxiety." *Psychological Reports*, 1977, 41: 391-96.

Handal, P. J. "The Relationship between Subjective Life Expectancy, Death Anxiety, and General Anxiety." *Journal of Clinical Psychology*, 1969, 25: 39-42.

Handal, P. J., and J. F. Rychlak. "Curvilinearity between Dream Content and Death Anxiety and the Relationship of Death Anxiety to Repression-Sensitization." *Journal of Abnormal Psychology*, 1971, 77 (1): 11-16.

Livingston, P. B., and C. N. Zimet. "Death Anxiety, Authoritarianism and Choice of Specialty in Medical Students." *Journal of Nervous and Mental Disease*, 1965, 140 (3): 222-30.

Lonetto, R., S. Fleming, M. Clare, and M. Corman. "The Perceived Sex of Death and Concerns about Death." *Essence: Issues in the Study of Aging, Dying and Death*, 1976, 1 (1): 45-57.

Tolar, A. Unpublished data (1966) cited in P. J. Handal. "The Relationship between Subjective Life Expectancy, Death Anxiety, and General Anxiety." *Journal of Clinical Psychology*, 1969, 25: 39-42.

Tolar, A., and M. Reznikoff. "Relationship between Insight, Repression-Sensitization, Internal-External Control, and Death Anxiety." *Journal of Abnormal Psychology*, 1967, 72 (5): 426-30.

Instrument

See Instrument V1.7.III.b.

FEAR OF DEATH SCALE (FDS)
D. Lester, 1966

Definition of Variable

Lester did not define the variable, but the procedure for developing the scale asked subjects to rate statements on the degree to which each reflected a favorable attitude toward death.

Description of Instrument

The scale is based on weights given to 21 questions in an agree-disagree format. Some questions suggest a religious interpretation of death and the afterlife, while others place death into a calculus against the putative value of life or of human values (e.g., being ready to die for a best friend). Weights for the items accompany the instrument. The instrument is scored by summing the weighted items.

Context of Development

The author's intent was to produce a measure of the fear of death by using approved scale-construction procedures and then to investigate its consistency. Initially, 98 statements about death were presented to 22 students in an experimental psychology course. They were asked to judge "the degree to which each statement reflected a favorable attitude toward death." Data were used to construct an equal-interval scale. Two parallel forms of 21 statements each were given to 18 college students in an agree-disagree format employing the statements that best covered the entire 11-point range in the initial format. The two forms correlated .65 ($p < 0.01$). The best items "statistically defined" from both scales were selected to form the 21-item scale.

Sample

For purposes of scale construction, 22 students from an experimental psychology course formed the sample. Other applications have employed larger samples of college students.

Formal Tests of Reliability

Lester (1966) administered the scale to 14 psychology students. Test-retest consistency after 6 weeks was .58 ($p < 0.05$, one-tailed Spearman's *rho*).

Formal Tests of Validity

Convergent Validity: Durlak (1972) reported correlations of .56 with the Boyar FODS, .41 with Sarnoff and Corwin FDS, and .40 with Tolar-Handal DAS. The strongest correlation is with the Collett-Lester death of self subscale ($r = .78$), with the other three subscales correlating .47, .31, and .36.

Discriminant Validity: A nonsignificant correlation of $-.10$ with the Marlowe-Crowne Social Desirability Scale has been reported (Durlak, 1972).

Construct Validity: Lester (1966; 1972) reported higher scale scores for subjects with inconsistent attitudes toward death.

Usability on Older Populations

This scale's usefulness with older samples has not been demonstrated. There are no apparent face validity problems with its application to older subjects.

General Comments and Recommendations

Scale-construction procedures do not guarantee unidimensionality, and, on the fact of it, this is not a unidimensional scale. The scale offers promise of application to persons across the life span, but further development assessing its unidimensionality is warranted. Such development is especially recommended because of the high correlations with death of the self on Collett-Lester scale.

A factor analytic approach might be taken to isolate different possible dimensions measured by the scale. The presupposition that attitudes toward death vary only according to the degree of "favorableness" should be suspended. Data should be gathered across a broader age span.

References

Durlak, J. A. "Measurement of the Fear of Death: An Examination of Some Existing Scales." *Journal of Clinical Psychology*, 1972, 28: 545-47.

Lester, D. "A Scale Measuring the Fear of Death: Its Construction and Consistency." Unpublished manuscript, ADI Auxiliary Publications Project document no. 9449. Library of Congress, Washington, D.C., 1966.

———. "Inconsistency in the Fear of Death of Individuals." *Psychological Reports*, 1967a, 20: 1084.

———. "Fear of Death of Suicidal Persons." *Psychological Reports*, 1967b, 20: 1077-78.

———. "The Need to Achieve and the Fear of Death." *Psychological Reports*, 1970, 27: 516.

———. "Studies in Death Attitudes: Part Two." *Psychological Reports*, 1972, 30: 440.

Instrument

See Instrument V1.7.III.c.

DEATH ANXIETY SCALE (DAS)
D. I. Templer, 1969

Definition of Variable

The variable measured in this scale is verbalized death anxiety (sometimes referred to by the author as fear of death).

Description of Instrument

The scale consists of 15 equally weighted questions that address death, thoughts of death, disease, and time perspective.

Method of Administration

The Templer DAS is given as a paper-and-pencil questionnaire. The items can be administered as one set or embedded in other items with no apparent effects of embedding (Templer and Ruff, 1971).

Context of Development

Templer was aware of Boyar's FODS, but he constructed the DAS through different procedures. The items he selected "reflect a wider range of experiences than the FODS items which cover primarily the act of dying, the finality of death, and corpses and their burial" (Templer, 1970, p. 165).

TABLE 7-2
DAS Means and Standard Deviations in Various Studies

Sample Size	Samples	Samples	$\overline{X}$	SD
	Pandey and Templer, unpublished data			
134	Lincoln University undergraduate blacks		6.35	3.28
124	Lincoln University undergraduate whites		6.16	3.21
	Templer (1969; 1970)			
77	Murray University undergraduates		5.13	3.10
32	Heterogeneous psychiatric patients		6.78	2.97
21	High death anxiety psychiatric patients		11.62	1.96
21	Controls for high death anxiety psychiatric patients		6.77	2.74
	Templer and Dotson (1970)			
104	Western Kentucky University undergraduate males		6.07	3.12
109	Western Kentucky University undergraduate females		6.66	3.07
	Templer, Ruff, and Franks (1971)			
123	Male apartment house residents		4.85	2.88
160	Female apartment house residents		6.11	3.31
299	Adolescent males		5.72	3.07
444	Adolescent females		6.84	3.21
569	Fathers of adolescents		5.74	3.32
702	Mothers of adolescents		6.43	3.32
78	Male heterogeneous psychiatric patients		6.50	3.55
59	Female heterogeneous psychiatric patients		7.15	3.72
13	Male psychiatric aides		5.08	2.25
112	Female psychiatric aides		6.33	3.24
	Templer (1971a)			
49	Heterogeneous psychiatric patients		7.13	3.45
	Templer (1971b)			
46	Retired males		4.15	3.29
29	Retired females		4.41	3.43
	Templer, unpublished data			
217	Bloomfield College males		6.69	2.72
167	Bloomfield College females		7.84	2.99

Samples, Scoring, Scale Norms, and Distributions

The DAS is scored by giving 1 point for each answer corresponding to the key, resulting in an index varying from 0 through 15.

The instrument's initial development was conducted on several college-student samples. Subsequent research has employed the DAS with diverse populations, including those noted in Table 7-2.

Formal Tests of Reliability

Internal Consistency: Item-total point biserial correlation coefficients for three groups were used. All groups were college students. Items were retained only when they had point biserial coefficients significant at the .10 level in two of the three analyses. The probability of a truly zero correlation appearing significant at that level in two of three analyses is .028. *Phi* coefficients were calculated to ascertain the relative independence of the items. None of the coefficients for the 15 items exceeded .65. Templer, therefore, argued that there is not excessive interitem redundancy (Templer, 1970).

Test-Retest Reliability: Scores correlated .83 ($p < 0.01$) for 31 (of 37) college students retested after three weeks (Templer, 1970).

Formal Tests of Validity

Face Validity: Face validity was enhanced by the use of seven judges during the initial selection of the items. Initially, 40 items were selected. The judges rated each item by using five categories of degree of association with death anxiety. This process resulted in the selection of 31 items that had received moderate to high scores. A subsequent reduction in the number of items occurred during the process of attaining internal consistency.

Construct Validity: The unidimensionality of the scale has been placed in doubt by the low interitem correlations reported by Thorson and Perkins (1978). (See the discussion of the Death Anxiety Scale [Nehrke Modification] later in this chapter.) Moreover, the DAS loads heavily on several factors of this modification by Nehrke, which is a scale comprised of DAS and Boyar FODS items. (See also the discussion of unidimensionality tests reported by Thorson and Perkins, in the section on the Nehrke modification.)

Evidence of construct validity has been provided by the finding of no correlation between the DAS and several measures of religious affiliation, belief, and activity in a sample of college students for whom religion was believed unimportant (Templer and Dotson, 1970), while religious subjects had lower DAS scores. This suggests that religion provides a source of support against death anxiety (Templer, 1972).

The DAS scores of both males and females correlated highly with scores of their same-sex parents, and parents' scores correlated highly (Templer, Ruff, and Franks, 1971). Parent-child correlations increased as sons moved through adolescence but they decreased for daughters, suggesting that principles of learning were operant (Lester and Templer, 1972; Templer, Ruff, and Franks, 1971).

Convergent Validity: DAS correlated .74 with the Boyar FODS in a sample of 77 undergraduates. Correlations of MMPI scales with the DAS have also been reported for this sample (Templer, 1970).

Discriminant Validity: Moderate correlations with the Welsh Anxiety Scale, the Anxiety Index, the Manifest Anxiety Scale, and an "emotional words" test suggest that death anxiety differs from general anxiety (Templer, 1970). Independent validation against Galvanic skin response reactions to death words resulted in a significant correlation of .30 (Templer, 1971a).

Validation by known groups: This was assessed with a sample of 21 "presumably high death anxiety psychiatric patients" and matched controls. The patients were people who had "spontaneously verbalized fear of, or preoccupation with, death" (Templer, 1970). The mean score for the high death anxiety group was 11.62; for the control group, 6.77 (maximum score 15). The groups were statistically different on a two-tailed t test at the .01 level.

In summary, a variety of attempts to assess the validity of the DAS have suggested (1) that the construct measured by the index is related to, but independent of, general anxiety, (2) that it correlates with recognized measures of unverbalized death anxiety and with one other well-established verbal measure (the FODS), and (3) that it can be meaningfully interpreted in terms of known groups (psychiatric patients and highly religious persons).

Usability on Older Populations

Templer (1971b) included the DAS in a battery of instruments sent to a mail survey of 250 retired persons. The mean age of the 75 respondents was 69.7 years, with an age range between 51 and 92 years. The mean DAS scale score for this sample was 4.25, which is considerably lower than those for any of the other groups for whom data have been reported. One nursing home sample had a mean score of 4.08 (Nehrke, Bellucci, and Gabriel, 1977–1978). There were significant correlations between DAS scores and scores on the D (depression) scale of the MMPI ($r = .28$), as well as the psychiatric ($r = .54$) and total ($r = .34$) assessment scores for the Cornell Medical Index. The correlation with D scores led Templer to suggest "tentatively" that "high death anxiety is commonly part of a depressive syndrome in elderly persons."

The correlations between DAS scores and the Cornell Medical Inventory scores are within the range of modest but significant correlations with general anxiety and maladjustment.

Monosoff and Sterns (1973), in a cross-sectional study of respondents ranging in age from 10 to 82 years found a positive relationship between anxiety and DAS scores ($r = .44$; $p < .001$). However, the relationship was highest in the 20 to 29-year-old age bracket, and it declined steadily with increasing older groups.

These data may suggest that the DAS has some diagnostic utility. For research purposes, care should be taken with older subjects to account for the psychiatric correlates of high DAS scores.

The low response rate on the mail survey is not necessarily attributable to the inclusion of the DAS instrument, since it was but one of a large battery of instruments included.

Sensitivity to Age Differences

In general, DAS scores have not been found to correlate with age. The one study focusing on a community-based older population was inconclusive due to its low response rate. However, the lower DAS scores are consistent with a highly accepted opinion that manifest death anxiety declines among the very old.

General Comments and Recommendations

Perhaps more is known about the properties of the DAS than about any other instrument that attempts to measure death anxiety or fear of death. While such assessment is indeed a virtue, it has exposed the instrument's serious flaws—mainly its lack of unidimensionality. The continuing work so badly needed on this instrument is being done by Nehrke and Thorson. In its present form, the scale should not be used without concomitant factor analysis as a test of its unidimensionality. Continued research on the correlates of death anxiety as measured by the DAS would be welcome, as would further research on the dimensional properties of the scale and its applicability to older populations.

References

Lester, D., and D. I. Templer. "Resemblance of Parent-Child Death-Anxiety as a Function of Age and Sex of Child." *Psychological Reports*, 1972, 31: 750.

Lucas, R. A. "A Comparative Study of Measures of General Anxiety among Three Medical Groups Including Patient and Wife." *Omega*, 1974, 5 (3): 233–43.

Monosoff, R. A., and H. L. Sterns. "Death Anxiety during the Life Span." Paper presented to the 26th Annual Meeting of the Gerontological Society, Miami Beach, November 5–9, 1973.

Nehrke, M. F., G. Belucci, and S. J. Gabriel. "Death Anxiety, Locus of Control and Life Satisfaction in the Elderly: Toward a Definition of Ego-Integrity." *Omega*, 1977–1978, 8 (4): 359–68.

Templer, D. I. "Death Anxiety Scale." Paper presented to the 77th Annual Convention of the American Psychological Association, 1969.

——. "The Construction and Validation of a Death Anxiety Scale." *Journal of General Psychology*, 1970, 82: 165–77.

——. "The Relationship between Verbalized and Nonverbalized Death Anxiety." *Journal of Genetic Psychology*, 1971a, 119: 211–14.

——. "Death Anxiety as Related to Depression and Health of Retired Persons." *Journal of Gerontology*, 1971b, 26 (4): 521–23.

——. "Death Anxiety in Religiously Very Involved Persons." *Psychological Reports*, 1972, 31: 361–62.

Templer, D. I., and E. Dotson. "Religious Correlates of Death Anxiety." *Psychological Reports*, 1970, 26: 895–97.

Templer, D. I., and C. Ruff. "Death Anxiety Scale Means, Standard Deviations, and Embedding." *Psychological Reports*, 1971, 29: 173–74.

Templer, D. I., C. Ruff, and C. M. Franks. "Death Anxiety: Age, Sex and Parental Resemblances in Diverse Populations." *Developmental Psychology*, 1971, 4: 108.

Thorson, J. A., and M. Perkins. "A Factor Analytic Study of a Scale Designed to Measure Death Anxiety." Paper presented to the 30th Annual Meeting of the Gerontological Society, San Francisco, November 18–22, 1978.

Instrument

See Instrument V1.7.III.d.

DEATH ANXIETY SCALE (NEHRKE MODIFICATION)
M. F. Nehrke, 1973

Definition of Variable

This instrument combines, in a modified format, the Templer DAS and the Boyar FODS.

Description of Instrument

Nehrke's scale consists of 34 true-false items and 1 Likert item. The items were taken from the Templer DAS (1970) and the Boyar FODS (1964) (which both are described elsewhere in this chapter). The Boyar items were modified to the same true-false format used for the Templer items. There is 1 seven-point item as well (it is not discussed here).

Method of Administration

The DAS modification is a questionnaire, which can be used as part of a battery of several instruments.

Context of Development

Relevant work on the modified DAS has been done by Nehrke and Thorson. Nehrke and Gabriel (1972) gathered data from samples of older people, using both the Templer DAS and the Boyar FODS (some of their findings are discussed in the reviews of these instruments elsewhere in this chapter). Nehrke (1973) subsequently modified the FODS response format and adopted a simple true-false choice. He assessed the new instrument with a college-student population (1973) and then again with a sample of college students and their parents and grandparents (1974). Thorson and Perkins (1977; Thorson, 1977, personal communication) gathered data using Nehrke's format from opportunistic samples across a broad age range, and Thorson (1977, personal communication) provided data for the combined Boyar and Templer items, as well as for the Likert-type item.

The work being done by Nehrke and Thorson should be seen as an extension of the earlier developmental work done by Boyar and Templer.

Samples

The Death Anxiety Scale has been tested with the samples detailed in Table 7-3.

Formal Tests of Reliability

Information on the reliability of the DAS and the FODS components in the revised scale is given elsewhere in this chapter. Thorson and Perkins (1977) presented a full correlation matrix, which showed suprisingly low correlations.

Formal Tests of Validity

The discussions of the validity of the FODS and the DAS are pertinent. Nehrke (1973) reported correlations between the FODS and the DAS ranging from .48 to .76 for varying age- and sex-groups.

Thorson (1977) reported low correlations between the index and dimensions of the Edwards Personal Preference Inventory.

The Thorson and Perkins (1977) factor analysis of these data suggests that eight factors are present; the first five explain 86.9% of the *common* variance. (See Table 7-4.)

Thorson is continuing to analyze and interpret these data. It appears that the Nehrke form of the DAS measures anxiety over the state of being dead rather than the process of dying. The six questions that load highest on Factor 1 deal with the state of death; the seventh item loading here (question 6) is ambiguous as to the state or process and loads on two other factors. Factor 2 clearly concerns fear of the process or manner of dying.

Thorson (1977, personal communication) has recognized the problem with these data. Items 6, 8, and 22 load significantly on two or more factors and could be dropped from the scale. Factors 3 and 4 seem to refer to similar things, as do factors 5 and 6. Factors 7 and 8 may not be primarily related to death or dying.

TABLE 7-3
Death Anxiety Scale Samples

Researcher	Sample Size	Average Age	Percentage Female	General Comments
Nehrke, 1973	265	19.2	65.3	Students in child psychology classes
Nehrke, 1974	25	Student, 19 Mother, 47 Grandmother, 74	100	Three-generation sample
Thorson and Perkins, 1977	659	63.3% under 35; 5.9% age 55+	73.6	Conference partici- pants and inner- city summer camp teenagers
Thorson, 1977	208	23 (median)	53.4	Undergraduate and graduate students

TABLE 7-4
Thorson-Perkins Factor Loadings of Items

Items	#1	#2	#3	#4	#5	#6	#7	#8
1. Graveyards do not bother me.				−.35				
2. The idea of never thinking again after I die frightens me.	.59							
3. The idea that I may die young does not make me anxious.								−.30
4. The feeling that I will be missing out on so much after I die disturbs me.	.44							
5. I do not mind the idea of being shut into a coffin when I die.					−.28	.69		
6. Some people are afraid to die but I am not.	−.31		.55	−.18				
7. The pain involved in dying frightens me.		.52						
8. The idea of being buried bothers me.	.37				.32	.58		
9. Not knowing what it feels like to die makes me anxious.								.40
10. I am not afraid of a long, slow dying.		−.38						
11. I have moments when I really get upset about the prospect of dying.			−.24	.40				
12. Coffins make me anxious.					.61	−.26		
13. Being totally immobile after death bothers me.	.63							
14. Never again feeling anything after I die upsets me.	.68							

TABLE 7-4—*Continued*

	#1	#2	#3	#4	#5	#6	#7	#8
15. The sight of a corpse does not make me at all anxious.					−.45			
16. I am not disturbed by the finality of death.			.42	−.15				
17. The total isolation of death is frightening to me.	.49							
18. What will happen to my body after I die does not bother me						.48		
19. Sometimes I am afraid to go to sleep at night.				.42				
20. I am very much afraid to die.			−.17	.51				
21. The thought of death seldom enters my mind.				−.41				
22. It doesn't make me nervous when people talk about death.				−.38	−.32			
23. I dread to think about having to have an operation.		.36						
24. I am not at all afraid to die.			.69					
25. I am not particularly afraid of getting cancer.		−.37						
26. The thought of death never bothers me.			.59					
27. I am often distressed by the way time flies so very rapidly.							.68	
28. I fear dying a painful death.		.70						
29. I am really scared of having a heart attack.				.42				
30. The subject of life after death troubles me greatly.				.37				
31. I often think about how short life really is.							.52	

TABLE 7-4—*Continued*

	#1	#2	#3	#4	#5	#6	#7	#8
32. I shudder when I hear people talking about a World War III.		.30						
33. The sight of a dead body is horrifying to me.					.38			
34. I feel that the future holds nothing for me to fear.			.39	-.14				
Percentage common variance	51.7	11.8	8.9	7.6	6.9	5.8	4.0	3.3

SOURCE: Thorson, 1977, personal communication.

Scoring, Scale Norms, and Distribution

The instrument is scored by a simple summation of the "anxious" responses, yielding an index ranging from 0 to 34. Females have shown significantly higher ($\bar{X}$ = 14.68; SD = 6.58) scores than males ($\bar{X}$ = 12.99; SD = 6.29).

Usability on Older Populations

Both Nehrke and Thorson have been successful in obtaining questionnaires from older institutionalized and noninstitutionalized subjects. Nehrke has claimed that modification of the Boyar format to a true-false format enhances the clarity of response.

Sensitivity to Age Differences

As age increases, anxiety decreases (Thorson and Perkins, 1977). An average score of 15.08 (SD = 6.39) has been noted for those under 22; this declines to 11.64 (SD = 5.73) for those over 55.

General Comments and Recommendations

This instrument is still being developed by Nehrke and Thorson. They are following Boyar's advice by introducing a factor analytic technique. The revised scale's main advantages over the FODS are the switch to a simpler response format that may be more suited to an older population and the inclusion of a broader range of phenomena as death-related stimuli. However, these advantages can be found in the Templer DAS components alone. For current research purposes, the Templer DAS is preferable to the Nehrke modification because of its greater known reliability and validity. Some support for the Templer DAS has come from efforts to combine it with the FODS, and continued instrument development along these lines is warranted.

Researchers should first determine whether a multidimensional or a unidimensional instrument is appropriate. If a multidimensional instrument is the goal, then the number of dimensions apparently retrievable with this set of 34 questions is undoubtedly less than eight. The continuing work being done seems directed at producing an instrument that will adequately measure perhaps four dimensions of death-and-dying anxiety. At a later stage in the instrument's development, it will be useful to discover the relationship between the revised instrument and a multidimensional instrument such as the Collett-Lester scale.

References

Boyar, J. I. "The Construction and Partial Validation of a Scale for the Measurement of the Fear of Death." Ph.D. dissertation, University of Rochester, 1964. (University Microfilm number 64-9288.)

Durlak, J. A. "Measurement of the Fear of Death: An Examination of Some Existing Scales." *Journal of Clinical Psychology*, 1969, 25: 39–42.

Nehrke, M. F. "Perceived Generational Differences in Attitudes toward Death." Paper presented to the 26th Annual Meeting of the Gerontological Society, Miami Beach, November 5–9, 1973.

———. "Actual and Perceived Attitudes toward Death and Self Concept in Three-Generational Families." Paper presented to the 27th Annual Meeting of the Gerontological Society, Portland, November 5–9, 1974.

Nehrke, M. F., G. Bellucci, and S. J. Gabriel. "Death Anxiety, Locus of Control and Life Satisfaction in the Elderly: Toward a Definition of Ego-Integrity." *Omega*, 1977–1978, 8 (4): 359–68.

Nehrke, M. F., and S. J. Gabriel. "Attitudes toward Death and Its Correlates." Paper presented to the 25th Annual Meeting of the Gerontological Society, San Juan, Puerto Rico, December 17–21, 1972.

Templer, D. I. "The Construction and Validation of a Death Anxiety Scale." *Journal of General Psychology*, 1970, 82: 165–77.

Thorson, J. A. "Variations in Death Anxiety Related to College Students' Sex, Major Field of Study, and Certain Personality Traits." *Psychological Reports*, 1977, 40: 857–58.

Thorson, J. A., and M. Perkins. "A Factor Analytic Study of a Scale Designed to Measure Death Anxiety." Paper presented to the 30th Annual Meeting of the Gerontological Society, San Francisco, November 18–22, 1977.

Instrument

See Table 7-4 above.

DEATH CONCERN SCALE (DCS)
L. S. Dickstein, 1972; L. Klug and M. Boss, 1976

Definition of Variable

"Death concern is conceptualized as conscious contemplation of the reality of death and negative evaluation of that reality" (Dickstein, 1972, p. 564).

Description of Instrument

Thirty items in a questionnaire format were developed by Dickstein (1972); Klug and Boss (1976) formed two subscales from 14 of the items through factor analysis: (1) conscious concern for death and (2) negative evaluation of death. Response options for the first 11 items are (4) often, (3) sometimes, (2) rarely, and (1), never. For items 12-30, the alternatives are (1) "I strongly disagree," (2) "I somewhat disagree," (3) "I somewhat agree," and (4) "I strongly agree." Items 13, 16, 17, 18, 20, 21, 22, 24, and 27 are scored by simple summation. The Klug and Boss dimensions are noted with the appended instrument.

Method of Administration

The Death Concern Scale is a questionnaire that can be accompanied by other test batteries.

Context of Development

The instrument was based in part on an earlier measure (Dickstein and Blatt, 1966). The aim was to develop a reliable, internally consistent, and valid measure of death concern. The article by Klug and Boss (1976) provides scale scores on two factors.

Samples

Dickstein (1972) gave a preliminary questionnaire with 48 items to undergraduate psychology students. The top and bottom 27% of the sample were compared on each item, and the 30 most discriminating items were retained. The new 30-item instrument was given to a second sample of 193 undergraduate psychology students, who were also administered the Manifest Anxiety Scale. A further subsample of high, middle, and low scorers was given a battery of personality tests.

Klug and Boss (1976) conducted a factor analysis on the 30-item test scores with two samples (294 and 185) of Wellesley College women and two samples (70 women and 122 men) of New York City College students. These data were supplied to them by Dickstein, and the groups were pooled for the factor analysis.

Scoring, Scale Norms, and Distributions

The instrument is scored through the simple summation of the item scores to yield scores theoretically ranging from 30 to 120. For the full instrument (Dickstein, 1972) the mean scores ranged between 70.53 and 75.54; standard deviations ranged between 11.02 and 12.61; and scores ranged between 33 and 111. In summary, the four administrations produced very similar data. There were no significant sex differences in mean scores.

Formal Tests of Reliability

Internal Consistency: Dickstein (1972) reported split-half reliability between .859 and .879 in four different administrations.

Klug and Boss (1976) reported Kuder-Richardson 20 reliability of .856 for the 30-item instrument, .83 for the conscious concern subscale, .80 for the negative evaluation subscale, and .84 for all 14 items in the subscales.

Item-subscale correlations for the conscious concern subscale ranged form .425 to .655; for the negative evaluation subscale they ranged from .391 to .670 (Klug and Boss, 1976).

Test-Retest Reliability: For 151 females tested at an eight-week interval test-retest reliability was .87.

Formal Tests of Validity

Dickstein (1972) reported correlations of .36 for males and .30 for females between the DCS and the Manifest Anxiety Scale. Groups derived from DCS scores are significantly different on several psychological trait measures.

Construct Validity: Klug and Boss (1976) investigated the conceptual structure of "conscious concern" and "negative evaluation." Judges separated the items along these two dimensions; four of the five judges agreed that the 9 items labeled C (on the instrument) measured the conscious concern dimension, that the 6 labeled E measured the negative evaluation dimension, and that 1 measured neither dimension. On the remaining 14 items, the judges could not reach consensus. Klug and Boss then conducted an oblique rotation, principal components analysis allowing maximal intercorrelation of components on the full 30-item correlation matrix. Two factors with eigenvalues greater than 1.0 explained 24.7% of the total variance; these factors correlated .418. The dimensional structure hypothesized by the judges emerged exactly *with the one exception* of item 18 on the negative evaluation dimension. A factor analysis of these 14 items yielded two factors explaining 40.5% of the variance and correlating .426. All items loaded on their respective factors by at least .359 (see Table 2 in Klug and Boss, 1976).

Usability on Older Populations

The instrument has been used only with college students. Items 3, 12, and 26 could be problematic if the Dickstein version were used. Items 12 and 26 do not appear in the Klug and Boss version.

General Comments and Recommendations

The Klug and Boss version is a very promising instrument, being both highly reliable and reasonably validated. Of course, the longer instrument can be analyzed in terms of the shorter subscales. With either option, ease of administration is a virtue.

Klug and Boss have recommended that further validity studies be conducted using the full scale and the 14-item grouping. This would allow investigation of the stability of the factor structure. They also have suggested relating the negative evaluation dimension to an accepted measure of death anxiety (1976).

Refinement of the instrument for use with older subjects may require the elimination of some inappropriate items. Age norms across the life cycle are also needed.

References

Dickstein, L. S. "Death Concern: Measurement and Correlates." *Psychological Reports*, 1972, 30: 563-71.

Dickstein, L., and S. Blatt. "Death Concern, Futurity, and Anticipation." *Journal of Consulting Psychology*, 1966, 30: 11-17.

Klug, L., and M. Boss. "Factorial Structure of the Death Concern Scale." *Psychological Reports*, 1976, 38: 107-12.

Instrument

See Instrument V1.7.III.f.

DEATH SCALE (QUESTIONS RELATIVE TO DEATH)
M. J. Feldman and M. Hersen, 1967

Definition of Variable

Conscious concerns about death are measured by this instrument.

Description of Instrument

This scale is a 10-item questionnaire that stresses the frequency of thoughts about one's own death and the death of associates. Item responses vary on a six-point ordinal scale of frequency.

Method of Administration

The questionnaire is suitable for group administration.

Context of Development

Some items were borrowed from Middleton's (1936) questions, while others were added on an a priori basis. The authors wished to investigate the relationship between death concerns and frequency of nightmares.

Sample

The original sample consisted of 1,317 students in introductory psychology classes, about evenly divided by sex. Four groups of each sex were formed according to their self-reported frequency of nightmares.

Scoring, Scale Norms, and Distribution

The items are summed to yield an index ranging from 0 to 50. Item responses are never (0), seldom (1), sometimes (2), mostly (3), frequently (4), and very frequently (5).

Formal Tests of Reliability

Item analyses, using chi-square tests, were computed for the 10 items for each sex separately. Items 1, 2, 4, and 6 discriminated among nightmare groups in both sexes. Items 5, 7, and 9 discriminated among nightmare groups for women only. No other reliability data were provided by Feldman and Hersen.

Usability on Older Populations

Sharma and Jain (1969) used the instrument on a sample in India that included 62 retired persons, aged 55 and over. They did not discuss any difficulties in administration in their report. They found no difference between younger students and the retired persons in summary scores, but they did find a significant difference between those 55 to 60 years old and those older than 61, with older respondents expressing more fear. (Note that Feldman and Hersen did not claim that the index measures fear.)

General Comments and Recommendations

The face validity of this instrument is doubtful. Items appear to reflect several different dimensions, including reference to death or to dying of self or others. As it is now, the instrument cannot be recommended for general research use.

This instrument very much needs to be revised according to standard instrument-development procedures, including the use of data assessing reliability, data assessing unidimensionality, and data assessing applicability to broader populations.

References

Feldman, M J., and M. Hersen. "Attitudes toward Death in Nightmare Subjects." *Journal of Abnormal Psychology,* 1967, 72 (5): 421-25.
Middleton, W. C. "Some Reactions toward Death among College Students." *Journal of Abnormal and Social Psychology,* 1936, 31: 165-73.
Sharma, K. L., and U. C. Jain. "Religiosity and Fear of Death in Young and Retired Persons." *Indian Journal of Gerontology,* 1969, 1(4): 110-14.

Instrument

See Instrument V1.7.III.g.

FEAR OF DEATH SCALE (FDS)
I. Sarnoff and S. M. Corwin, 1959

Definition of Variable

This instrument measures the conscious fear of death.

Description of Instrument

Five items, with a six-point Likert response format, are included in this instrument.

Method of Administration

The instrument has been administered with other instruments in the context of an experimental study.

Context of Development

The measure was developed as part of a psychoanalytic study assessing the relationship between castration anxiety and fear of death. The experiment sought to measure the interaction of castration anxiety and sexual stimulation in the fear of death.

Sample

The original sample included 56 male undergraduates, who were unpaid volunteers.

Scoring, Scale Norms, and Distribution

The index is scored as the simple sum of the five items, to yield a score ranging from minus 15 to 15.

Formal Tests of Reliability

Initially, 7 items were embedded in a 22-item questionnaire. The items had been devised on an a priori basis. Item analysis led to the rejection of 2 items that failed to discriminate between high and low scorers. No further data are available.

Formal Tests of Validity

As it was predicted by the authors, a strong relationship was found between fear of death and castration anxiety (*phi* coefficient .612).

Martin and Wrightsman (1965) found scores on the Sarnoff and Corwin measure to correlate significantly (around the .46 level for different populations) with a measure of concern over death based on a sentence-completion technique.

The Sarnoff-Corwin measure correlated .41 with Lester's instrument, .65 with Boyar's FODS, and .47 with the Tolar scale. The Sarnoff-Corwin measure seems to tap fear of death of self and dying of self as measured by the Collett-Lester scale (Durlak, 1972).

Usability on Older Populations

Martin and Wrightsman (1965) used the instrument with church members varying in age from 18 to 75 years (mean age 44) and found no clear relationship between age and fear of death scores.

General Comments and Recommendations

This is an index of reasonably well known validity with younger populations. Less is known about its reliability, especially given the authors' failure to report interitem and item-test correlations. Despite these limitations, the brevity of the index could be considered a virtue for researchers interested in fear of death as one dimension among many to be measured. (See also the review of Martin and Wrightsman's extended version of this instrument, which follows.) In total, the two studies upon which this assessment has been based include data from only 114 subjects. There even are no mean-score data. Age norms would also be useful.

References

Durlak, J. A. "Measurement of the Fear of Death: An Examination of Some Existing Scales." *Journal of Clinical Psychology*, 1972, 28: 545–47.

Martin, D., and L. S. Wrightsman, Jr. "The Relationship between Religious Behavior and Concern about Death." *Journal of Social Psychology*, 1965, 65: 317–23.

Sarnoff, I., and S. M. Corwin. "Castration Anxiety and the Fear of Death." *Journal of Personality*, 1959, 27: 374–85.

Instrument

See Instrument V1.7.III.h.

EXTENDED FEAR OF DEATH SCALE
D. Martin and L. Wrightsman, 1965

Definition of Variable

This scale measures the conscious fear of death.

Description of Instrument

The 5 Sarnoff and Corwin items and 10 additional items with identical format and scoring are included in this instrument.

Method of Administration

The instrument is a questionnaire suitable for individual administration or administration in a mail-back procedure.

Context of Development

The authors wished to extend the length of the Sarnoff and Corwin (1959) Fear of Death Scale for use in a study of fear of death and religious behavior.

Sample

Fifty-eight adult members of three churches were handed packets after church services and were asked to mail them back. A response rate of 54% was noted. The age range of the sample was 18 to 75 years.

Formal Test of Reliability

Kahoe and Dunn (1975) conducted an item analysis (details were not given) that identified 10 "superior" items. For these 10, the measure had a split-half, Spearman-Brown corrected reliability of only .54.

Formal Test of Validity

The correlations between the 10 new items and the original 5 Sarnoff and Corwin items was .46, indicating only a moderate degree of convergence in content. Correlation of the extended measure with a sentence-completion measure of conscious death concern was significant but lower (.34) than the correlation between the Sarnoff and Corwin measure and the sentence-completion measure (.46). Martin and Wrightsman found their measure modestly but significantly correlated negatively with age (unlike the Sarnoff-Corwin scale), suggesting a difference in content.

Usability on Older Populations

The instruments apparently would be suitable for use with older subjects.

General Comments and Recommendations

Reliability data are completely lacking in the original report and unsatisfactory in the partial replication done by Kahoe and Dunn (1975). Both samples were extremely small. As an extension of Sarnoff and Corwin's scale, the measure "borrowed" some of the concurrent validation support mustered by Durlak (1972), but it can be considered modest at best. The instrument must, at this point, be considered highly undeveloped.

References

Durlak, J. A. "Measurement of the Fear of Death: An Examination of Some Existing Scales." *Journal of Clinical Psychology*, 1972, 28: 545–47.

Kahoe, R. D., and R. F. Dunn. "The Fear of Death and Religious Attitudes and Behavior." *Journal for the Scientific Study of Religion*, 1975, 14 (4): 379–82.

Martin, D., and L. S. Wrightsman, Jr. "The Relationship between Religious Behavior and Concern about Death." *Journal of Social Psychology*, 1965, 65: 317–23.

Sarnoff, E., and S. M. Corwin. "Castration Anxiety and the Fear of Death." *Journal of Personality*, 1959, 27: 374–85.

Instrument

See the description of the instrument above; the 10 new items are not currently available.

ATTITUDE TOWARD DYING AND DEATH INDEX
J. T. Mathieu and J. A. Peterson, 1970

Definition of Variable

This scale measures the respondent's attitude toward dying and death.

Description of Instrument

The three-item instrument is formed from these questions (the number in parentheses is percentage response for the study sample):

a. What is your attitude toward death—
   1—just don't think about it (20)

2—think about it with fear (3)
3—accept it as another life experience (65)
4—look forward to it (2)
5—a wonderful experience to look forward to (10)

b. Do you feel that death is—
1—the end of all (18)
2—an extended sleep (13)
3—a process toward a different life existence (69)

c. How do you approach death—
1—very fearful (4)
2—fairly fearful (5)
3—not very fearful (28)
4—unworried (63)

SOURCE: J. T. Mathieu and J. A. Peterson. "Death and Dying: Some Social Psychological Dimensions." Paper presented at the 23rd Annual Meeting of the Gerontological Society, Toronto, October 22-24, 1970. Reprinted by permission.

No item-development or index-development procedures were noted by the authors. Items were based on their "face validity."

Method of Administration

The index items were part of a comprehensive questionnaire administered in a group setting, but it would be equally usable in an individual administration.

Context of Development

The index was developed as part of a large study on socialization for dying and death.

Sample

The sample was made up of a total of 183 residents aged 50 and over and living in Leisure World, California, for at least 5 years. This population was "heavily weighted in the direction of the married, white, Protestant, middle to upper-middle class" (Mathieu and Peterson, 1970).

Scoring

The index score is the simple sum of the items, which theoretically ranges from 3 to 12.

Usability on Older Populations

The index appears to be appropriate for use with older populations.

General Comments and Recommendations

The inclusion of questions a and b with weighting, which suggests that this is a unidimensional index, is undoubtedly unwarranted. The instrument needs revision in both its item- and instrument-development procedures. However, the difficulties with this measure suggest that its usefulness might be limited to an examination of the component items as single-item measures.

Reference

Mathieu, J. T., and J. A. Peterson. "Death and Dying: Some Social Psychological Dimensions." Paper presented to the 23rd Annual Meeting of the Gerontological Society, Toronto, October 22–24, 1970.

Instrument

See the description of the instrument above.

CONSEQUENCES OF ONE'S OWN DEATH
J. C. Diggory and D. Z. Rothman, 1961

Definition of Variable

The variable measured by this instrument was what, specifically, is feared about death.

Description of Instrument

Originally, seven items were used in a paired comparisons format. The items were part of a larger questionnaire on attitudes toward death. The respondents indicated the member of each pair that they regarded as worse, or more distasteful, than the other.

The items are ranked, with the highest rank (1) assigned to the most frequently chosen of the pairs. Simple and cumulative frequencies are calculated, and from them a median rank score for each of the seven items can be calculated for any subgroup. The instrument does not, therefore, produce a single overall score but rather relative rankings on seven dimensions.

Method of Administration

In the original study, questionnaires were handed to individuals or groups on an opportunistic basis.

Context of Development

The instrument was based on the value theories of Dewey and von Ehrenfels, with the assumption that the utility of the self may be weighted against the loss of valued activities.

Sample

The opportunistic sample of 563 persons varied widely in age, religion, class, and marital status.

Formal Tests of Validity

The construct validity of the scale is supported by correlates in line with the hypotheses of the investigators; the reason an individual fears death is related to his or her ability to pursue goals important to self-esteem. Unlike many measures, this one is clearly consonant with an articulated theoretical perspective (see Diggory and Rothman, 1961; Diggory, 1966).

Usability on Older Populations

Since 30 of the 563 respondents were 55 years old and older and there were no reported difficulties in administration, the questionnaire apparently would be usable with older populations.

Sensitivity to Age Differences

Item D is obviously a partial function of age, and its importance does increase with age, rising from fifth to first place with increasing age (up to the age 55 and over category).

General Comments and Recommendations

This instrument rests on the assumption that death is feared. Within that limitation, however, it attempts to assess various bases for death fear. Diggory and Rothman also suggested that many things might be feared more than death. The paired comparison methodology is complex, but the statements could also be used in a modified format, for example, a rank-order or a Likert-type format. This set of questions is very valuable as a battery.

References

Diggory, J. C. *Self-Evaluation* (especially chapter 8). New York: John Wiley and Sons, 1966.

Diggory, J. C., and D. Z. Rothman. "Values Destroyed by Death." *Journal of Abnormal and Social Psychology,* 1961, 63: 105-10.

Instrument

See Instrument V1.7.III.k.

DIMENSIONS OF DEATH ANXIETY
L. D. Nelson and C. C. Nelson, 1975

Definition of Variable

Four dimensions of death anxiety are measured: 1) death avoidance, which is indicated by an unwillingness to be near or to touch the dead and by a reluctance to experience situations reminiscent of death; (2) death fear, which is indicated by overt statements of fear of death; (3) death denial, which reflects a reluctance to confront the reality of death in society and its consequences for the individual; and (4) reluctance to interact with the dying.

Description of Instrument

The instrument consists of 20 questions with a Likert-type response format that yield the four dimensions.

Method of Administration

The instrument is administered in the form of a mailed questionnaire.

Context of Development

The purpose of the study was "to identify fundamental dimensions of death anxiety through a controlled factor analytic technique and to construct a test instrument useful for social psychological research in the area" (Nelson and Nelson, 1975, p.172).

Samples

The samples included (1) 135 sociology undergraduates, who responded to an initial set of 55 death-related items; and (2) 1,279 males from a statewide probability sample in Virginia (response rate 62%), who completed a questionnaire containing 24 items retained after item analysis on the initial 55.

Scoring, Scale Norms, and Distribution

Two sets of scores are available. Unweighted scale scores are formed by summing the response scores on all 20 items. Factor scores are calculated according to the complete estimation method by adding the weighted Z scores of all the variables; thus, some variables are suppressor variables and all contribute in varying degrees to the solution. The factor scores shown in Table 7-5 represent the regression weights of each standardized variable (Z score).

TABLE 7-5
DIMENSIONS OF DEATH ANXIETY
FACTOR-SCORE-COEFFICIENTS

Variable[a]	Factor			
	1	2	3	4
1	.349	.706	.095	.242
2	.164	.001	−.160	.077

TABLE 7-5—*Continued*

Variable[a]	Factor			
	1	2	3	4
3	.025	.065	.305	.037
4	.071	.012	−.063	.299
5	.001	.020	.008	.388
6	.049	.112	.209	−.055
7	−.096	.175	.009	−.102
8	.100	.004	−.044	.125
9	.139	.001	−.079	.020
10	.066	.003	−.210	.057
11	.029	.084	.221	.006
12	.094	.012	−.039	−.015
13	.000	.076	.099	−.086
14	.232	.009	.002	.088
15	−.038	.068	.034	−.003
16	.082	.016	.044	.005
17	.104	.042	.074	.056
18	.033	.070	.052	.085
19	.240	.010	.113	−.077
20	−.019	.073	.034	.007

a. Identified by item number of question.
SOURCE: L. D. Nelson and C. C. Nelson. "A Factor Analytic Inquiry into the Multidimensionality of Death Anxiety." *Omega*, 1975, 6 (2): 175. Copyright 1975 by Baywood Publishing Company, Inc. Reprinted by permission.

Formal Tests of Reliability

From sample 1 an item-to-scale correlation analysis was performed, and items that correlated with the total index at less than the .25 level were excluded. This reduced the pool of items to 24. Identical criteria were applied to the remaining 24 items with sample 2, leading to the elimination of 4 items.

Formal Tests of Validity

The clear emergence of four dimensions of death anxiety support the construct validity of this measure. The factors are, in general, highly intercorrelated and correlated with the unfactored index. The average correlation among these five measures is .529. The unfactored index reflects death avoidance most strongly ($r = .888; \beta = .614$). The reader is referred to Nelson and Nelson (1975) for further details on the relationship among these components.

Usability on Older Populations

The overall return rate for a mailed questionnaire suggests no problems when the return rate is not greatly differentiated by age.

General Comments and Recommendations

This is a very promising instrument. The factor analytic technique avoids the problem of having to assume a particular typology of death responses, since the typology is derived from the data. The typology does, however, appear to be theoretically meaningful in the light of the general death anxiety literature. The validity of this instrument would be enhanced by data showing correlations with other accepted scales and indexes. At present, its validity is solely internal and is therefore based on face criteria. Similarly, no correlates of these death anxiety measures have yet been reported, so the instrument's predictive validity has not yet been ascertained.

Reference

Nelson, L. D., and C. C. Nelson. "A Factor Analytic Inquiry into the Multidimensionality of Death Anxiety." *Omega*, 1975, 6 (2): 171-78.

Instrument

See Instrument V1.7.III.l.

DEATH ACCEPTANCE SCALE
J. J. Ray and J. Najman, 1974

Definition of Variable

This scale measures a respondent's positive acceptance of death.

Description of Instrument

The instrument is a seven-item index in a Likert format.

Method of Administration

The scale was originally a questionnaire, which was part of larger packet of measures.

Context of Development

The authors espoused a theory "that death-acceptant people will be able to acknowledge some anxiety about death. They will not deny that it does concern them but will also be able to be positive about death" (Ray and Najman, 1974, p.312). The developers of this instrument wanted to avoid a perceived bias in some other instruments that assumed that an individual must fall into either a death-anxious or a death-denying category.

Sample

Sample consisted of 206 sociology students, males and females.

Formal Tests of Reliability

The coefficient alpha was .58, with all items correlating with the scale total (after overlap correction) at a level of significance less than .005 on a two-tailed t test. The mean interitem correlation was .162. These figures are comparable to those for the Sarnoff-Corwin and Templer scales administered to the same subjects in this study.

Formal Tests of Validity

On theoretical grounds, the investigators postulated moderate correlations between death anxiety measures and their measure of death acceptance. The correlations for their sample were $-.263$ with Templer and $-.242$ with Sarnoff and Corwin. These findings were consistent with the investigators (Templer and Sarnoff-Corwin correlated .612 with each other.)

Usability on Older Populations

No data about samples of older populations were reported by the authors. The instrument, however, should be acceptable to older subjects.

General Comments and Recommendations

Ray and Najman claimed that they had shown that death acceptance is not the categorical opposite of death anxiety but that persons can be both anxious and acceptant at the same time. Their instrument should help to assess this claim further. The instrument is short and convenient to use, and it may provide embedding items that can be used with other scales. The measure is particularly valuable in view of the fear/anxiety bias that troubles most other instruments. However, the instrument's reliability is rather low. Applications to age and class-heterogeneous samples, with norms for various age-groups, are needed, also.

Reference

Ray, J. J., and J. Najman. "Death Anxiety and Death Acceptance: A Preliminary Approach." *Omega*, 1974, 5 (4): 311-15.

Instrument

See Instrument V1.7.III.m.

CHECKLIST OF DEATH ATTITUDES
W. M. Swenson, 1961

Definition of Variable

The checklist measures the respondent's present feelings about death.

Description of Instrument

The instrument is a 35-item questionnaire checklist, which is hypothesized to measure two dimensions: a positive or forward-looking attitude, an actively evasive attitude.

Method of Administration

The checklist is administered in a questionnaire format.

Context of Development

The investigator wanted to investigate the ways in which old people deal with death. First, written essays describing attitudes toward death were gathered from a sample of 34 persons aged 50 and older. From these essays the checklist's statements were derived.

Sample

Swenson (1961) gathered data from 210 persons aged 60 and over in an opportunistic sample biased toward females, Protestants, and city dwellers. Both institutionalized and noninstitutionalized aged persons were represented. Chasin (1971) reported data from a study using the instrument with an opportunistic sample of members of several major religious denominations in an Iowa community. Her 324 responses were biased toward higher income and education, and the respondent's median age was 42 years.

Scoring, Scale Norms, and Distribution

Each of the 210 subjects in Swenson's study was given a score, which was the sum of responses in cluster A and cluster B. The respondents were then divided into three groups: group A was high in cluster A and low in cluster B and included 82 persons; group B was low in cluster A and high in cluster B, with 71 persons; and group C had either a zero or an equal score in both clusters, with 57 persons. The subjects in group C were described as persons who were either very indecisive about their attitudes toward death or were "passively evasive."

Formal Tests of Validity

There are no clearly interpretable data on the instrument's validity. The selection of items for the clusters was based on a correlational examination of all the items, but it was not clearly described by Swenson.

Usability on Older Populations

The instrument is usable for older populations.

General Comments and Recommendations

This measure is of considerable historical significance, since it was one of the first to assume the multidimensionality of death attitudes. Reliability and validity data are entirely missing, and, until they are provided, the usefulness of the instrument will be limited. On the other hand, the checklist format is a refreshing change from the other commonly used measurement techniques. It merits further attention in its own right because a change of format might prove valuable for any research that requires the completion of several batteries. The change of pace provided by the checklist format may well increase completion rates and decrease response sets.

Alternative scoring mechanisms could be used, including the conversion of the instrument into a Likert format with agree-disagree responses. Factor analytic or even cluster analytic techniques could be applied.

With its present or adapted format, the instrument requires intercorrelation with other measures to establish its construct validity.

References

Chasin, B. "Neglected Variables in the Study of Death Attitudes." *Sociological Quarterly,* 1971, 12: 107-13.
Swenson, W. M. "Attitudes toward Death in an Aged Population." *Journal of Gerontology,* 1961, 16 (1): 49-60.

Instrument

See Instrument V1.7.III.n.

FEAR OF DEATH SCALE
L. J. Collett and D. Lester, 1969

Definition of Variable

This instrument measures death fears, distinguishing between fear of death and fear of the process of dying and between fears for self and fears for others.

Description of Instrument

The measure includes four indexes formed from six-point agree-disagree statements in a Likert format, with strong agreement equaling +3 and strong disagreement equaling −3. There are 10 death of self items, 10 death of others items, 6 dying of self items, and 12 dying of others items.

Method of Administration

The instrument is administered as a questionnaire.

Context of Development

The instrument appears to have been created in an attempt to go beyond the earlier work of Lester and others, which developed presumably unidimensional measures.

Sample

Twenty-five female undergraduates, retested after an unspecified interval, constituted the instrument-development sample.

Scoring, Scale Norms, and Distributions

The individual's score is the mean score per item for each subscale. The original sample's mean scores per item for each subscale were: death of self, .48; death of others, .59; dying of self, .33; dying of others, −.78.

Formal Tests of Reliability

Item-to-test scores for each subscale were computed. Items whose correlations were not significant at the .10 level on a one-tailed t test (correlation less than .26) were eliminated.

Test-retest reliability was gauged by using a three-way analysis of variance for repeated measures on the sample (the length of the interval between tests was not given). Those terms involving the replication factor were not significant.

Formal Tests of Validity

Intercorrelations among the four subscales were generally low, ranging from .03 to .58. The subjects showed higher fear of death than fear of dying, and higher fear of death of self, rather than of others, was the referent.

Durlak (1972) used the Collett-Lester (C-L) scales in a validation study of other instruments (which are also reviewed in this chapter). Durlak's data, for 94 college students, are given in Table 7-6. The other instruments listed in Table 7-6 are Lester (LE), Boyar (BO), Sarnoff and Corwin (S-C), and Tolar (Handal) (TO).

TABLE 7-6
Correlations between the Fear of Death Scales
and the Four Subscales of the Collett-Lester Scale

C-L Subscales	Death Scales			
	LE	BO	S-C	TO
Dth-Self (death of self)	.78	.69	.55	.47
Dy-Self (dying of self)	.47	.58	.52	.46
Dth-Other (death of others)	.31	.46	.37	.39
Dy-Other (dying of others)	.36	.40	.41	.40

NOTE: With 94 subjects, r's of .20 and .26 are required for significance at the .05 and .01 levels, respectively.

SOURCE: J. A. Durlak. "Measurement of the Fear of Death: An Examination of Some Existing Scales." *Journal of Clinical Psychology,* 1972, 28: 547. Reprinted by permission.

Durlak's findings are consistent with those of Collett and Lester, and his general conclusion bears repeating: "If C-L is accepted on a face validity basis, the data indicate that the death scales are relatively stronger and better measures of personal fears and anxieties about death and dying (i.e., when the self is the referent) than they are measures of generalized fears of anxieties about death (i.e., when the other is the referent)" (Durlak, 1972, p. 547).

The validity of the death of self subscale is particularly strengthened by its high correlations with the other scales in Durlak's study.

General Comments and Recommendations

The main virtue of this instrument is its presumption of a typology of different kinds of death fears. As Nelson and Nelson (1975) have pointed out, however, this is also its weakness. The typology of four kinds of death fear is logical, but it is based on considerations of face validity rather than an empirical approach. The distinction between the four subscales is warranted by the pattern of intercorrelation, but there is no guarantee that this typology is inclusive or optimal, either theoretically or empirically, as a typology of death fears. Nonetheless, this instrument is one of the few most promising. Factor analysis would provide valuable additional data on the multidimensionality tapped by the subscales. Application over a wider age range and on populations other than college undergraduates would be helpful.

References

Collett, L. J., and D. Lester. "The Fear of Death and the Fear of Dying." *Journal of Psychology*, 1969, 72: 179–81.

————. Document NAPS-01754, ASIS National Auxiliary Publications Service (CCM Information Corporation, New York).

Durlak, J. A. "Measurement of the Fear of Death: An Examination of Some Existing Scales." *Journal of Clinical Psychology*, 1972, 28: 545–47.

Lester, D. "Studies in Death Attitudes: Part Two," *Psychological Reports*, 1972, 30: 440.

Nelson, L. D., and C. C. Nelson, "A Factor Analytic Inquiry into the Multidimensionality of Death Anxiety." *Omega*, 1975, 6 (2): 171–78.

Instrument

See Instrument V1.7.III.o.

DEATH SCALES
T. Hooper and B. Spilka, 1970

Definition of Variable

Multidimensional measures of death perspective and death anxiety are made in two related instruments.

Description of Instrument

The scales are based on items in a six-point Likert-type format (strongly disagree [1] to strongly agree [6]). There are two general parts in the measure: a death anxiety instrument containing five scales of death anxiety formed from responses to 41 questions, and a death perspective instrument containing eight scales of death perspective formed from responses to 60 questions.

In the Death Anxiety Scales, the first 18 items are those developed by Boyar (1964), and they are reproduced elsewhere in this chapter. The next 15 items are Templer's (1970) DAS items, which can also be found elsewhere in this chapter. Hooper and Spilka added the 8 extra items.

Responses to all 34 questions range from disagree strongly (moderately, slightly) to agree strongly. This system modified the specific format used by Boyar and Templar.

In the Death Perspectives Scales, 60 items appear in the same format, and from them are derived eight scales measuring perspectives toward death.

For both instruments the weighting of items to scales is complex. Details should be obtained from Dr. Spilka. The items for both instruments are, however, given in the instrument.

Context of Development

Spilka and associates have been interested in the relationship between attitudes toward death and religiosity (see the references cited below). Drawing on a contention made by Murphy (1959) that death can be viewed in seven different ways, Hooper (1962) and Hooper and Spilka (1970) developed and attempted to validate a set of 9, 18-item Likert-type measures. Later Hooper added a 10th scale. These scales were used in their initial form in several studies (Spilka, Pelligrini, and Dailey, 1968; Minton and Spilka, 1976). Editing and rewriting this initial set of 180 items led to the development of the 60 brief statements that are used in the contemporary Death Perspectives Scales (Stout, Minton, and Spilka, 1976; Spilka et al., 1976). The later research is concerned with both the Death Perspectives Scales in this tradition and with the Death Anxiety Scales. This work is continuing, and it is considered by the investigators to be work in progress, particularly the work on the Death Anxiety Scales (Spilka, 1977, personal communication).

Sample

The current form of these scales is reported in Spilka and associates (1976) and in a personal communication with Spilka. The sample for this most recent work consists of 362 persons aged 17 to 83, mean age 23.1 years, 54% male. Most were undergraduates from two private church-affiliated colleges, and most participants were religiously identified.

Formal Tests of Reliability

The death anxiety and death perspective items were separately subjected to factor analyses using the principal components approach and varimax rotation followed by oblique rotations. Items were considered significant when they loaded .3 or above on the resulting factors.

Kuder-Richardson 20 reliability coefficients for both sets of measures are given with scale items on the instruments. Only one of the Death Anxiety Scales has an acceptably high coefficient (.82).

Reliability coefficients for the Death Perspectives Scales are quite high (between .71 and .92). However, on the Death Anxiety Scales Spilka (1977, personal communication) has recently commented, "At this time, validity has not been demonstrated and substantial reliability exists only for two of the five scales. Enough is still present on the others for research purposes."

Formal Tests of Validity

The intercorrelations among the Death Anxiety Scales and the Death Perspectives Scales are low to moderate, with only 3 above .5 and 59 of the total of 78 being below .3, most of them below .1 in magnitude (Spilka et al., 1976). Modest correlations are consonant with the intentions of the investigators to develop measures of related, but distinct, dimensions of attitudes.

The construct validity of the death perspective measures is supported by intercorrelations with measures of religiosity, while this is not really the case with the death anxiety measures. Thus, 19 of 32 coefficients between death perspective and variables of personal religiosity are statistically significant, and almost all of these are in the directions predicted by the authors (Spilka et al., 1976).

Usability on Older Populations

No difficulties have been reported with using the instruments in a population with members as old as 83 years. Item 40 of the Death Anxiety Scales is probably irrelevant for most older subjects; however, the Death Anxiety Scales are not as yet completely developed.

General Comments and Recommendations

The Death Anxiety Scales are basically a valuable extension of the work of Boyar and Templer. Continuing work on the development of these scales through factor analysis should produce instruments of higher reproducibility.

The Death Perspectives Scales must be counted as one of the most useful multidimensional measures of attitudes toward death and dying. The items had to load on a factor at the .3 level or better to justify inclusion, which is not a rigorous requirement. Investigators using the instrument may wish to adopt a higher cutoff point. The combination of the use of a low cutoff point and the use of oblique rotations pushes the factors some degree away from a concrete, readily definable reality.

Test-retest reliability data and application to a wider population (more older subjects, fewer religious subjects, and fewer with a college education) would enhance the usefulness of the Death Perspectives Scales. As the investigators are the aware, Death Anxiety Scales are still at a rather provisional stage in their development. Overall, however, this package of items is one of the most promising for research in the area of attitudes toward death.

References

Boyar, J. I. "The Construction and Partial Validation of a Scale for the Measurement of the Fear of Death." Ph.D. dissertation, University of Rochester, 1964. (University Microfilm number 64-9288.)

Hooper, T. "Personal Values and Meanings of Future Time and Death among College Students." Ph.D. dissertation, University of Denver, 1962.

Hooper, T., and B. Spilka. "Some Meanings and Correlates of Future Time and Death among College Students." *Omega*, 1970, 1 (1): 49–56.

Minton, B., and B. Spilka. "Perspectives on Death in Relation to Powerlessness and Form of Personal Religion." *Omega*, 1976, 7 (1): 261–67.

Murphy, G. Discussion in *The Meaning of Death*, H. Feifel (ed.), pp. 317–40. New York, McGraw-Hill, 1959.

Spilka, B., R. J. Pelligrini, and K. Dailey. "Religion, American Values and Death Perspectives." *Sociological Symposium*, 1968, 1: 57–66.

Spilka, B., L. Stout, B. Minton, and D. Sizemore. "Death Perspectives, Death Anxiety, and Form of Personal Religion." Paper presented to the Convention of the Society for the Scientific Study of Religion, Philadelphia, October 29, 1976.

Stout, L., B. Minton, and B. Spilka. "The Construction and Validation of Multidimensional Measures of Death Anxiety and Death Perspectives." Paper presented to the convention of the Rocky Mountain Psychological Association, Phoenix, May 1976.

Templer, D. I. "The Construction and Validation of a Death Anxiety Scale." *Journal of General Psychology*, 1970, 82: 165–77.

Instrument

See Instrument V1.7.IV.a.

WILL TO LIVE SCALE
D. L. Ellison, 1969a and 1969b

Definition of Variable

The scale attempts to discriminate persons who want to live from those for whom continued life is less attractive.

Description of Instrument

The scale consists of an index formed from seven items that address attractiveness of continued life.

Method of Administration

The scale is administered as a questionnaire.

Context of Development

"Building on the work in psychosomatic medicine and social science, this writer argues that factors in the social structure contribute to the morale of individuals. Morale is expressed in an individual's will to live, and this in turn is related to his health" (Ellison, 1969a, p. 38).

Sample

Ellison's sample consisted of 108 retired male steelworkers.

Scoring, Scale Norms, and Distribution

Four points are given for a low will to live answer, no points for a high will to live answer, and 2 points for an undecided answer. The range is, therefore, 0 to 28.

In this sample, 57% exhibited a high will to live (0–9), 24% a moderate will to live (10–19), and 19% a low will to live (20–28).

Formal Tests of Reliability

The reproducibility of this cumulative scale is .92.

Formal Tests of Validity

The convergent validity of the Will to Live Scale is supported by significant relationships between scores on the instrument and on three single indicators. Two of these are direct questions about the desire to live long, and the third is an interviewers's assessment of this desire.

Usability on Older Populations

The instrument was used successfully with an older population. The response rate was not noted.

Sensitivity to Age Differences

While no direct relationships to age have been reported from this older sample, intra-sample differences in social isolation and self-reported health are correlated with the will to live. Investigators using the instrument, therefore, may wish to separate these effects from those of age.

General Comments and Recommendations

Several investigators have used single indicators to assess whether or not people wished to live long (e.g., Marshall, 1975; Teahan and Kastenbaum, 1970). The Will to Live Scale, while correlating highly with single indicators of how long people have to live, was interpreted by Ellison as a reflection of morale. The face meaning of the individual indicators is not obviously reflective of low morale, however. When the unstated assumption that the desire to die is related to low morale is suspended, this instrument provides a highly reproducible measure of the willingness to die. The validity of the instrument is, therefore, somewhat open to question.

It would be very useful to know the relationship between this and other measures of attitudes toward death, especially measures that explicitly tap acceptance of death (e.g., Ray and Najman, 1974). The meaning of the will to live has not been clearly established by Ellison as being highly related to morale. In addition, test-retest reliability data should be developed.

References

Ellison, D. L. "Will to Live: A Link between Social Structure and Health among the Elderly." *Sociological Symposium*, 1969a, 2: 37-47.

————. "Alienation and the Will to Live." *Journal of Gerontology*, 1969, 24 (3): 361-67.

Marshall, V. W. "Socialization for Impending Death in a Retirement Village." *American Journal of Sociology*, 1975, 80 (5): 1124-44.

Ray, J. J., and J. Najman. "Death Anxiety and Death Accpetance: A Preliminary Approach." *Omega*, 1974, 5 (4): 311-15.

Teahan, J., and R. Kastenbaum. "Subjective Life Expectancy and Future Time Perspective as Predictors of Job Success in the Hard-Core Unemployed." *Omega*, 1970, 1 (1): 189-200.

Instrument

See Instrument V1.7.IV.b.

IMAGES OF DEATH
J. W. Riley, Jr., 1970

Definition of Variable

The instrument assesses images of death or beliefs and attitudes toward death.

Description of Instrument

Images of Death is a battery of five agree-disagree questions usable in an interview or a questionnaire format.

In a national representative sample study, 1,482 adult Americans were asked to respond to the following request: "People's beliefs and attitudes toward death are, of course, quite varied. I'll read you a few statements, and you tell me whether you agree or disagree with each one." Table 7-7 lists data on the percentages of agreement and breakdowns of age-groups responding.

TABLE 7-7
Percentages of Agreement on Images of Death

Statement	Age 30 and Under	Age 31–40	Age 41–50	Age 51–60	Age 61+
(a) Death is sometimes a blessing.	88	88	86	92	91
(b) Death is not tragic for the person who dies, only for the survivors.	78	81	83	84	85
(c) Death is like a long sleep.	46	54	53	64	62
(d) Death always comes too soon.	51	45	65	60	51
(e) To die is to suffer.	13	10	13	18	18
Total respondents = 100%	(348)	(389)	(280)	(211)	(249)

SOURCE: M. W. Riley, A. Foner, et al. *Aging and Society* (vol. 1), p. 334. New York: Russell Sage Foundation, 1968.

Method of Administration

The instrument is administered in an interview format.

Context of Development

As part of continuing research sponsored by the Equitable Life Assurance Society, a nationwide area probability sample study was conducted.

Sample

The sample included 1,482 adults. The exact number in the sample is different in two reports of the data (Riley, 1970; Riley and Foner, 1968).

Formal Tests of Validity

No tests of validity have been reported. Its large sample size makes this study a benchmark against which the results of subsequent smaller studies can be assessed. For example, Marshall (1975) used similar statements with a small sample of retirement-village dwellers and found a degree of favorable attitudes toward death comparable to, but even higher than, those reported for older persons in the Riley study. Marshall attributed the difference to the community characteristics of the retirement village, which led to development of more favorable death attitudes.

Usability on Older Populations

The questions can be easily asked of older people.

General Comments and Recommendations

Because of the large and representative sample gathered by Riley, as well as his presentation of demographic breakdowns for these data, these questions are extremely useful in their own right as a basis for comparing small samples with national norms or as a part of a validation strategy for other measures.

References

Marshall, V. W. "Socialization for Impending Death in a Retirement Village." *American Journal of Sociology,* 1975, 80 (5): 1124-44.

Riley, J. W., Jr. "What People Think about Death." in *The Dying Patient,* O. Brim, Jr., H. Freeman, S. Levine, and N. A. Scotch (eds.), pp. 30-41. New York: Russell Sage Foundation, 1970.

Riley, M. W., A. Foner, et al. *Aging and Society* (vol. 1), pp. 332-37. New York: Russell Sage Foundation, 1968.

Instrument

See the description of the instrument above.

DEATH IMAGES
K. W. Back, 1971

Definition of Variable

The variables being tested are metaphors of death.

Description of Instrument and Method of Administration

The scale is formed from a card-sorting technique. Respondents are asked to sort 25 cards into five piles, ranging from most suitable to least suitable as images for death. The instructions for this sorting are as follows:

> Here are 25 phrases which might be used by a poet or writer to symbolize death. I would like you to look through the cards and pick out five phrases that seem to be the *best or most appropriate* images of death. (Wait until five best images are picked out.) Next, pick out five phrases that seem to be the worst or least appropriate images (pictures) of death. (Wait.) Next, pick out five phrases that are fairly bad images of death. (Stack the piles of cards with worst on bottom and fill in numbers below later: 1 = best; 2 = fairly good; 3 = neutral; 4 = fairly bad; 5 = worst.)

A similar procedure is employed for the concept of time. The death and time metaphors appear in Table 7-8 (Back, 1971), which also shows the pattern of age and sex differences.

TABLE 7-8
Two-way Analyses of Variance Age X Sex
for 25 Time Images and 25 Death Images

Time Image	Age and/or Sex group Favoring Image	Death Image	Age and/or Sex group Favoring Image
A large revolving wheel	M*	An infinite ocean	<50**
A whirlwind	F*	A grinning butcher	M*
A road leading over a hill	M*	A glass of bitter wine	
Budding leaves		Silent birds	<50*
An old man with a cane	M*	A trumpet	
A bird in flight	F*	A hothouse full of lilies	
Weaving cloth rapidly	F*	A chilling frost	
A rope unwinding		A compassionate mother	
A speeding train		A gentle veiled lady	F*
A quiet, motionless ocean	<50*	A misty abyss	<50**
A burning candle		An understanding doctor	F*
A stairway leading upward		A falling curtain	F**

TABLE 7-8—*Continued*

Time Image	Age and/or Sex group Favoring Image	Death Image	Age and/or Sex group Favoring Image
A dashing waterfall		A cracked bell	
A jet in flight		A hangsman with bloody hands	M*
Wind-driven sand	M*	The end of a song	<50 and 50–59*; F*
An old woman spinning	M*	A leafless tree	
Drifting clouds		A shadowed doorway	
Marching feet		Windswept leaves	
A vast expanse of sky		A dreamless sleep	
The Rock of Gibraltar		A broken thread	50–59*
A fleeting thief		A toppled house of cards	
The all-swallowing monster		A satanic wrestler[b]	
A tedious song	50–59*	A bursting rocket	
A string of beads		A crumbling tower	M**
A galloping horseman	50–59*	A dark lake	

* Group liked the image more than the others at p. 05 $p < .05$.

** p. 01.

[b] Interaction between sex and age significant at $p < .05$. Older women and younger men liked it best; other interaction was not significant.

SOURCE: K. W. Back. "Metaphors as Test of Personal Philosophy of Aging." *Sociological Focus*, 1971, 5, (1):1-8. (Reprinted in *Normal Aging II*, E. Palmore (ed.), p. 203. Durham, N.C.: Duke University Press, 1974.) Reprinted by permission of author and publisher.

Research Context of Instrument Development and Sample

The metaphors were taken from Knapp (1960; Knapp and Garbutt, 1958). The research was "part of an ongoing panel study of a cross-section of the 45–70 population in Durham, North Carolina, . . . based on the first wave of study in which 502 interviews were collected" (Back, 1974 [1971], p. 202).

Usability on Older Populations

The instrument has been applied successfully with respondents up to age 70; no data beyond that period are available. However, I found that Knapp's time metaphors evoked some confusion with subjects aged 64 to 96 (unpublished material).

Sensitivity to Age Differences

Sex was found to be more important than age. Four death metaphors showed a monotonic relationship by age, as noted in Table 7-8. None of the death factors had a relationship to age.

General Comments and Recommendations

Clinically or poetically inclined investigators may find this to be an instrument of choice. The patterns identified by this instrument can be related to gerontological theory only through rather long chains of inference, which usually involve a psychodynamic theoretical base. The interpretation of data in terms of time perspective is theoretically meaningful and useful.

Test-retest reliability data would be very useful for assessing this instrument as would a series of cross-validations with other conventional measures of attitudes toward death.

References

Back, K. W. "Metaphors as Test of Personal Philosophy of Aging." *Sociological Focus*, 1971,

5 (1):1–8. (Reprinted in *Normal Aging II,* E. Palmore, (ed.), pp. 201–7. Durham, N.C.: Duke University Press, 1974.)

Knapp, R. H. "A Study of the Metaphor." *Journal of Projective Techniques,* 1960, 24: 389–95.

Knapp, R. H., and J. T. Garbutt. "Time Imagery and the Achievement Motive." *Journal of Personality,* 1958, 26: 426–34.

Instrument

See the description of the instrument and the method of administration above.

DEATH AND VIOLENT INTEREST QUESTIONNAIRE (DVIQ)
R. Schafer, 1976

Definition of Variable

An interest or a fascination with the passive observance of death and violence-related ideas and situations is measured by this instrument.

Description of Instrument

This instrument is made up of 18 Likert-type items embedded in a longer questionnaire form. Of the 18 questions 5 are negatively keyed and reverse scored.

Method of Administration

The questionnaire was administered to college students during classtime.

Context of Development

The measure was devised "in order to measure the degree to which bored, alienated, and sensation-seeking individuals were fascinated by and interested in death-related events"; questions were constructed "after reviewing various aggression and death-related scales" (Schafer, 1977, personal communication).

Sample

The original sample consisted of 69 students enrolled in psychology courses.

Formal Tests of Reliability

Kuder-Richardson 20 reliability equals .71.

Formal Tests of Validity

Two psychology professors initially checked the items for "face validity." A factor analysis was performed. The first factor was defined as measuring "the identification with concrete violence and death-related events from spatial noninvolvement." This factor accounts for .267 of the total communality. The remaining five factors "measure exceptionally limited aspects of the practice of observing death and violence" (Schafer, 1977, personal communication). None of these last five factors account for more than .086 of total communality.

Schafer is currently conducting "validation by known groups" research with the instrument, and he has reported: "It appears as though those persons who gather around automobile accidents and who view violent movies do indeed score higher on my scale than control groups" (Schafer, 1977, personal communication).

Usability on Older Populations

The applicability of this instrument to older samples is not known. Many of the questions presume spectatorship, which probably varies greatly between age-groups.

General Comments and Recommendations

The novelty of the conceptual domain of this index recommends its use as a check on other instruments measuring dimensions of attitudes toward death. This is one of a very few attempts to measure something other than fear or anxiety. As such, its use can play an important role in relation to theory concerning death attitudes during later life.

Schafer has recommended further refinement of the instrument, including the rejection of some items and the addition of others. This would depend on an attempt to construct a one-factor index or scale. It would be wise to select a population representative of different ages, sexes, and social classes for future instrument-development work. There is a heavy "spectatorship" dimension to the questions, particularly, as the author has noted, in those questions leading to factor 1. Spectatorship varies greatly according to the variables listed.

Reference

Schafer, R. "Fascination with Death as a Function of Need for Novel Stimulation." *Omega*, 1976, 7 (1): 45–50.

Instrument

See instrument V1.7.IV.e.

EUTHANASIA INDEX
C. E. Preston and R. H. Williams, 1971

Definition of Variable

The index measures attitude toward negative and positive euthanasia.

Description of Instrument

During the course of a semistructured interview, respondents are asked these questions:

1. If you were fatally ill, in great distress, and under heavy medical expense, would you want the doctors to do *nothing* to keep you alive?
2. If you were fatally ill, in great distress, and under heavy medical expenses, would you want the doctors to do *something* to shorten your life?

SOURCE: C. E. Preston and R. H. Williams. "Views of the Aged on the Timing of Death." *The Gerontologist*, 1971, 11 (4, part 1): items 8 and 9, p. 301. Reprinted by permission of authors and publisher.

Juxtaposition yields a differentiation of respondents into three categories, as follows (figures are the number of respondents in each category) (Preston and Williams, 1971, p. 302):

a. reject negative and positive euthanasia   47
b. accept negative but not positive euthanasia   25
c. accept negative and positive euthanasia   33

Method of Administration

The index is administered during a semistructured interview.

Context of Development

As part of a larger study of attitudes toward euthanasia, this study extended the subject pool to aged institutionalized persons.

Sample

The sample was made up of 35 older women and 65 older men, all Caucasians, who resided in either a VA retirement home or a private convalescent center. There is a discrepancy in the sample size reported in the article, with some cross-tabulations totaling as much as 105.

Usability on Older Populations

The authors noted that "subjects not only gave few indications of being troubled by the interview, but several spontaneously expressed feelings of comfort and relief in sharing their views on the issues raised" (Preston and Williams, 1971, p. 302).

General Comment

The index is a simple and useful measure.

Reference

Preston, C. E., and R. H. Williams. "Views of the Aged on the Timing of Death." *The Gerontologist*, 1971, 11 (4, part 1): 300–304.

Instrument

See the description of the instrument above.

PREPARATION FOR DEATH
J. W. Riley, Jr., 1968

Definition of Variable

Being disposed to plan, or having made plans, for death is measured by this index.

Description of Instrument

This four-item index concerns planning or acting in the following areas: (1) making plans about death, (2) discussing the uncertainty of life with persons close to the respondent, (3) making funeral or cemetery arrangements, and making a will. The exact wording of questions and response options is not available.

Method of Administration

The measure is administered during an interview.

Context of Development

The measure was developed as part of a continuing program of basic social research on the meaning of time and death.

Sample

The sample consisted of 1,500 adult United States citizens, interviewed in 1963.

Scoring, Scale Norms, and Distribution

The index is scored as the sum of those subjects either planning or having taken each action and ranges from 0 to 4. Item scores by age and scales scores by age and education are reported in Riley and Foner et al. (1968, pp. 336-37).

Formal Tests of Validity

As age and education increase, preparation for death increases.

Usability on Older Populations

The instrument appears to be acceptable across the life span.

General Comments and Recommendations

The indexing procedure includes one normative judgment and three bahavioral self-reports. A good rule of thumb in index construction is to avoid confusion of these two classes of report. Nonetheless, this is a useful battery and a meaningful index in terms of correlates.

Guttman-scaling techniques could be useful here, or at the very least an effort should be made to assess the instrument's unidimensionality by using interitem and item-test correlations.

Reference

Riley, J. W., Jr. Previously unpublished data presented in *Aging and Society* (vol. 1), M. W. Riley, A. Foner, et al., pp. 336-37. New York: Russell Sage Foundation, 1968.

Instrument

See the description of the instrument above.

Instruments

V1.7.I.a
EXPERIENCE WITH DYING AND DEATH
J. T. Mathieu and J. A. Peterson, 1970

EXPERIENCE DIMENSION
a.:

N = 183   Mean = 2.2   Within the past five years, how many of your close friends have died—

Response	Value	Frequency	Percentage
None	0	30	16.4
One	1	18	9.8
Two	2	24	13.1
Three or more	3	111	60.7

b.:

N = 183   Within the past five years, how often have you talked about death with your—

	Often (3)		Sometimes (2)		Never (1)		Not app. (0) No resp.		
	Freq.	(%)	Freq.	(%)	Freq.	(%)	Freq.	(%)	Year
Friends	5	2.7	66	36.1	91	49.7	21	11.5	1.3
Lawyer	0	0.0	62	33.9	95	51.9	26	14.2	1.1
Doctor	2	1.1	13	7.1	131	71.6	37	20.2	0.9
Clergyman	2	1.1	5	2.7	136	74.3	40	21.9	0.8
Children	1	0.5	39	21.3	98	53.6	45	24.6	1.0
Spouse	6	3.3	99	54.1	48	26.2	30	16.4	1.4

c.:

N = 183   If any of the following members of your family are deceased, please record the year they died—

	1966-Present (3)		1951-1965 (2)		00-1950 (1)		
	Freq.	(%)	Freq.	(%)	Freq.	(%)	Mean
Father	7	3.8	24	13.1	152	83.0	1.1
Mother	8	4.4	45	24.6	130	71.0	1.3
Spouse	10	5.5	29	15.8	144	78.7	1.2
Brother	23	12.6	32	17.5	128	68.9	1.3
Sister	19	10.4	12	6.6	152	83.1	1.3
Son	0	0.0	3	1.6	180	98.4	1.0
Daughter	0	0.0	0	0.0	183	100.0	1.0

SOURCE: J. T. Mathieu and J. A. Peterson. "Death and Dying: Some Social Psychological Dimensions." Paper presented to the 23rd Annual Meeting of the Gerontological Society, Toronto, October 22-24, 1970. Reprinted by permission of authors.

V 1.7.I.b.
DEGREE OF DEATH EXPERIENCE
J. M. A. Munnichs, 1966

See the definition of the variable in the abstract.

V1.7.I.c.
ENCOUNTERING THE DEATH OF OTHERS
R. Kalish and D. Reynolds, 1976

Item No.		Ethnicity				Age 20-39	40-59	60+	Sex Male	Female
		B.A.	J.A.	M.A.	A.A.	39	59	60+	Male	Female
014	How many persons that you knew personally died in the past two years?									
	None	10	17	19	26	25	17	10	17	19
	1-3	42	45	43	52	52	47	35	46	45
	1-7	23	24	29	14	15	21	33	22	23
	4-7	25	15	9	8	8	14	22	15	13
	8+	(.01)				(.001)			(n.s.)	
015	How many died by acccident? (Based on those knowing at least one person who died, N = 358)									
	None	60	77	66	71	60	70	74	64	72
	Any	40	23	34	29	40	30	26	36	28
		(.10)				(.10)			(n.s.)	
017	How many died in war? (Based on those knowing at least one person who died, N = 358)									
	None	86	93	90	89	86	91	92	87	93
	Any	2	7	10	11	14	9	8	13	7
		(n.s.)				(n.s.)			(n.s.)	
018	How many died by suicide? (Based on those knowing at least one person who died, N = 358)									
	None	89	97	95	98	95	97	98	97	96
	Any	2	3	5	2	5	3	2	3	4
		(n.s.)				(n.s.)			(n.s.)	
019	How many died by homicide? (Based on those knowing at least one person who died, N = 358)									
	None	89	100	96	100	91	99	97	96	96
	Any	11	0	4	0	9	1	3	4	4
		(.01)				(.01)			(n.s.)	
020	How many funerals have you attended in the past two years?									
	None	33	16	40	45	42	29	27	27	39
	1-3	44	52	43	45	51	49	36	51	41
	4-7	14	15	15	7	5	13	23	14	12
	8+	9	17	2	4	2	9	15	8	8
		(.001)				(.001)			(n.s.)	
022	How often have you visited someone's grave, other than during a burial service, during the past two years?									
	Never	71	35	56	59	70	50	43	56	54
	1-3	26	25	27	26	21	30	28	26	26
	4-10	2	22	8	10	3	12	17	11	10
	11+	2	17	9	5	6	8	12	7	10
		(.001)				(.001)			(n.s.)	

Item No.		Ethnicity				Age 20-39	40-59	60+	Sex Male	Female
		B.A.	J.A.	M.A.	A.A.					
023	How many persons who were dying did you visit or talk with during the past two years?									
	None	62	58	61	68	72	59	55	59	65
	1	22	24	25	14	18	24	22	20	22
	2+	16	17	15	18	11	17	24	21	14
		(n.s.)				(n.s.)			(n.s.)	

Legend: Numbers in tables are percentages. Numbers in parentheses are chi-square significance levels for the entire item table. B.A. = Black Americans, J.A. = Japanese Americans, M.A. = Mexican Americans, A.A. = Anglo Americans.

SOURCE: R. A. Kalish and D. K. Reynolds. *Death and Ethnicity: A Psychocultural Study,* pp. 202–3. Los Angeles: Andrus Gerontology Center, University of Southern California Press, 1976. Reprinted by permission of authors, and publisher.

V1.7.I.d
COMPARATIVE AGE AT DEATH
V. W. Marshall, 1975

See the description of the instrument in the abstract.

V1.7.II.a
CONSCIOUSNESS OF DEATH
P. Cameron, L. Stewart, and H. Biber, 1973

What were you thinking about over the past five minutes? . . .

(a) Did you thing about death or dying—even for a moment (perhaps it crossed your mind)?
(b) How would you characterize your mood over the past half hour? (happy, neutral, sad), and
(c) For the last five minutes, what has been the central focus of your thought?

(Fourteen possible responses, of which death is one response)

SOURCE: P. Cameron, L. Stewart, and H. Biber. "Consciousness of Death across the Life Span." *Journal of Gerontology,* 1973, 28(1): 92. Reprinted by permission of authors and publisher.

V1.7.II.b
AWARENESS OF DEATH SCALE
G. Chellam, 1964

1A When you read the newspapers, what sort of things do you find most interesting?_____

_____

1B Do you read any of these regularly in the newspapers?
   a. Editorials   yes____   no____
   b. Advertisements   yes____   no____
   c. Death Notices   yes____   no____
   d. Household Hints   yes____   no____
   e. Sports   yes____   no____
   f. Comics   yes____   no____
2A How many of these have you attended in last year? Who were they for? Fill in number of each group.

(a) Family   (b) Close friends   (c) Acquaintances or neighbors

Attended Did not   Attended Did not   Attended Did not

Birthday Parties _____
Graduations _____
Marriages _____
Funerals _____

2B How many were there you did not attend?

3. Suppose this is your life line. Mark an "X" at the point you think you are now.
Birth_____Death

4. Here's a piece of conversation I heard between two ladies who were in their late sixties . . .
   Lady A: "I hear that X has made her burial plans and everything is set, but I don't see any point in worrying about such things now."
   Lady B: "Well, I have my plans made. One never knows what's ahead of us. It could be any time. I like it all behind me so I can relax."
   a. Which one of these do you agree with? Lady A____ Lady B____
   b. Have you made you own plans? Yes____ No____

5. Which one of these would you say about your own future?
   a. I should be around for quite some time yet; more than ten years.
   b. I have a little while longer; oh, at least five to ten years.
   c. Not too much longer; less than five years.
   d. The end may be any time now.

6. Do you have any plans for the future; things you hope to do five years from now?
   Yes____ No____

Scoring Index

Items on the AD Scale	Scoring	Score
1. General newspaper reading	Death notices mentioned	1
2. Specified newspaper items	Death notices read regularly	1
	Additional spontaneous comments on items relating to death	1
3. Funerals attended	For each family member	3
	For each close friend	2
	For each acquaintance	1
4. Funerals known, but not attended	For each family member	3
	For each close friend	2
	For each acquaintance	1
5. Life Line	For X in last tenth of line's length	2
	For X in last fifth of line's length	1
6. Planning for death	Agrees with Lady B that plans should be made	1
	Has personally made plans	1
7. Life expectancy	Death any time now	3
	"Less than five years"	2
	"In five to ten years"	1
8. Future plans	Has none	1

SOURCE: G. Chellam. "The Disengagement Theory: Awareness of Death and Self-Engagement." D.S.W. dissertation, Western Reserve University 1964, pp. 52–53. (University Microfilms number 56–2318.) Reprinted by permission of author.

V1.7.II.c
THOUGHT OF DYING SCALE
C. S. Guptill, 1976; R. A. Kalish, 1963

INSTRUMENT AND VARIMAX ROTATED FACTOR LOADINGS

	Factor 1	Factor 2	Factor 3	Factor 4
A. Sometimes I can't get the thought of dying out of my mind.	.689	.257	.033	.047
B. I am bothered about nightmares of myself or others dying.	.642	.120	.083	.180
C. I think less about dying than most people.	−.497	.066	.309	−.106
D. I never really think about dying.	−.492	.137	.289	.076
E. I frequently worry about being in pain when I die.	.298	.269	.116	.329
F. I feel uncomfortable when people talk to me about death.	.227	.625	−.089	−.011
G. I can honestly say I'm not afraid of dying.	−.212	−.115	.625	−.063
H. At least once in my life I was really fearful I was going to die.	.162	−.084	−.029	.184
I. I would rather forget about dying until the time comes	−.109	.486	−.008	.152
J. It would be horrible to know for certain you only had a few months to live.	.087	.410	−.167	.537
K. I dread the possibility of dying a lingering death.	.006	.084	−.128	.487
L. I won't mind being dead because I can be at peace then.	.069	−.016	.505	−.127

SOURCE: C. S. Guptill, "Aging and Attitude toward Dying." Paper presented to the 29th Annual Meeting of the Gerontological Society, October 13-17, 1976. Reprinted by permission of author.

V1.7.II.d
AWARENESS OF DEATH
N. L. Chappell, 1975

1. About your own future, which one of the following statements do you think applies to you:
   a) I shall be around for some time yet; more than ten years.
   b) I have a little while longer; at least five to ten years.
   c) Not too much longer; less than five years.
   d) The end may be any time now.
   e) I don't know.
2. How old would you like to live to be?
3. How old do you think you will live to be?

4. If this line indicates your life from birth to death, mark an "X" at the place where you
   think you are now.

birth_____ death

SOURCE: N. L. Chappell. "Awareness of Death in the Disengagement Theory: A Conceptualization and an Empirical Investigation." *Omega*, 1975, 6 (4): 331. Copyright 1975
Baywood Publishing Company, Inc. Reprinted by permission.

V1.7.II.e
FREQUENCY OF DEATH THOUGHTS
F. C. Jeffers and A. Verwoerdt, 1970

TABLE: Frequency on Inventory Questions, Total Subject Group (N = 140)

	Percentage
a. How frequently do you believe people your age think about death (as compared with before 55 years old)?	
1. More often now	80
2. Less often now	1
3. Undecided	15
4. Same as ever	4
b. How often do you think about death?	
1. Never	5
2. Rarely (less than once a week)	25
3. Occasionally (once a week)	20
4. Frequently (daily)	42
5. Always in mind	7
6. Undecided	1
c. Do death thoughts affect enjoyment of life?	
1. Yes	40
2. No	47
3. Undecided	13

SOURCE: F. C. Jeffers and A. Verwoerdt. "Factors Associated with Frequency of Death
Thoughts in Elderly Community Volunteers." In *Normal Aging*, E. Palmore (ed.), p. 403.
Durham, N.C.: Duke University Press, 1970. Reprinted by permission.

V1.7.II.f
FREQUENCY OF THOUGHTS ABOUT DEATH AND OTHER PROBLEMS
J. W. Riley, Jr., 1970

See the description of the instrument in the abstract.

V1.7.III.a
FEAR OF DEATH SCALE
J. I. Boyar, 1964

1. Graveyards seem to upset many people, but they do not bother me.
2. The idea of never thinking again after I die frightens me.
3. The idea that I may die young does not affect me.
4. The feeling that I will be missing out on so much after I die disturbs me.
5. I do not mind the idea of being shut into a coffin when I die.
6. Some people are afraid to die but I am not.

7. The pain involved in dying frightens me.
8. The idea of being buried frightens me.
9. Not knowing what it feels like to die makes me anxious.
10. I am not afraid of a long, slow dying.
11. I have moments when I get really upset about dying.
12. Coffins make me anxious.
13. Being totally immobile after death bothers me.
14. Never again feeling anything after I die upsets me.
15. The sight of a corpse does not make me at all anxious.
16. I am not at all disturbed by the finality of death.
17. The total isolation of death is frightening to me.
18. What will happen to my body after I die does not concern me.

NOTE: Response options are "yes," "no," and "?."

SOURCE: J. I. Boyar. "The Construction and Partial Validation of a Scale for the Measurement of the Fear of Death." Ph.D. dissertation, University of Rochester, 1964. (University Microfilms number 64–9228.) Reprinted by permission of author.

V1.7.III.b
DEATH ANXIETY SCALE
P. J. Handal, 1969; A. Tolar and M. Reznikoff, 1967

1. When I see a funeral procession, I never particularly wonder who the dead person is.
2. My reaction to visiting the hospital where there are people who may have fatal diseases often includes certain disturbing and difficult to understand feelings of curiosity which are not altogether sympathetic.
3. There are few, if any, real dangers to one's health while working on the wards of a hospital.
4. We are kidding ourselves if we think cancer is not a hopeless disease.
5. Death hardly concerns me.
6. People should cut out smoking.
7. I hardly ever am troubled by such things as birthmarks or other marks on my body.
8. Dying people don't make me uneasy.
9. At times one has the feeling that no disease is curable and no one leaves the hospital in quite as good condition as they were before they fell ill.
10. After I am deceased I plan to donate my body to a medical school.
11. I wonder which of the diseases I know about will finally get me.
12. There is too much living to do for me to worry about death.
13. Sometimes you just don't want to see a dying person because he makes you feel pretty damned helpless.
14. Killing animals in a science course wouldn't bother me.
15. A doctor has to be stronger than most to stand up to the constant emotional pressure due to suffering and death.
16. The thought of dying young has hardly ever occurred to me.
17. I think about death often; these thoughts accompany my life like the bass accompaniment in music I do not want to hear.
18. Sometimes I've actually had some fantasies of the event of dying.
19. When I am ill it is certainly unusual for me to think of my dying.
20. I'd love to go into a field like medicine where maybe I could cure myself and live longer.

Response Alternatives

1. Strongly Disagree
2. Disagree

3. Slightly Disagree
4. Slightly Agree
5. Agree
6. Strongly Agree

SOURCE: P. J. Handal. "The Relationship between Subjective Life Expectancy, Death Anxiety, and General Anxiety." *Journal of Clinical Psychology,* 1969, 25: 39–42; Reprinted by permission of author and publisher.

V1.7.III.c
FEAR OF DEATH SCALE
D. Lester, 1966

Would you circle A or D for each of the following statements. If you agree with the statement circle A; if you disagree circle D. Try to circle a reply for each statement. Consider the death in each statement to mean your death at this present time.

1. What we call death is only the birth of the soul into a new and delightful life. (1.29)
2. One should not grieve over the dead, because they are eternally happy in heaven. (2.00)
3. Death comes to comfort us. (2.81)
4. Death will be one of the most interesting experiences of my life. (3.25)
5. A peaceful death is a fitting end to a successful life. (3.75)
6. I don't want to die right now but I'm glad that I will die someday. (4.12)
7. Death is better than a painful life. (4.59)
8. I would be willing to die to save my best friend. (5.00)
9. Death makes all men equal. (5.11)
10. Death is a great mystery. (5.58)
11. Death is neither good nor bad since there's no consciousness in it. (6.18)
12. You can't take it with you when you die. (6.85)
13. I would feel better about death if I knew what it was going to be like. (7.17)
14. It is a pity when a talented man dies, even if he has stopped creating. (7.42)
15. Death is an unwanted sleep. (7.92)
16. Death is to be feared, for it brings grief. (8.15)
17. I am afraid to die because there may be a future punishment. (9.42)
18. Nothing can be so bad that a sane man would commit suicide. (9.80)
19. Death is last and worst insult to man. (10.19)
20. I would avoid death at all costs. (10.42)
21. Death is the worst thing that could possibly happen to me. (10.76)

The numbers in parentheses are the scale weighting values for the statements.

SOURCE: D. Lester. "A Scale Measuring for Fear of Death: Its Construction and Consistency." Unpublished manuscript, ADI Auxiliary Publications Project document number 9449. Library of Congress, Washington, D. C., 1966. Reprinted by permission of author.

V1.7.III.d
DEATH ANXIETY SCALE
D. I. Templer, 1969

Key

T   1. I am very much afraid to die.
F   2. The thought of death seldom enters my mind.
F   3. It doesn't make me nervous when people talk about death.
T   4. I dread to think about having to have an operation.
F   5. I am not at all afraid to die.

F   6.   I am not particularly afraid of getting cancer.
F   7.   The thought of death never bothers me.
T   8.   I am often distressed by the way time flies so very rapidly.
T   9.   I fear dying a painful death.
T   10.   The subject of life after death troubles me greatly.
T   11.   I am really scared of having a heart attack.
T   12.   I often think about how short life really is.
T   13.   I shudder when I hear people talking about a World War III.
T   14.   The sight of a dead body is horrifying to me.
F   15.   I feel that the future holds nothing for me to fear.

SOURCE: D. I. Templer. "Death Anxiety Scale." Paper presented to the 77th Annual Convention of the American Psychological Association, 1969. Reprinted by permission of the author.

V1.7.III.e
DEATH ANXIETY SCALE (NEHRKE MODIFICATION)
M. F. Nehrke, 1973

See Table 7-4 in the abstract.

V1.7.III.f
DEATH CONCERN SCALE
L. S. Dickstein, 1972; L. Klug and M. Boss, 1976

1. I think about my own death. C
2. I think about the death of loved ones. C
3. I think about dying young. C
4. I think about the possibility of my being killed on a city street.
5. I have fantasies of my own death. C
6. I think about death just before I go to sleep. C
7. I think of how I would act if I knew I were to die within a given period of time. C
8. I think about how my relatives would act and feel upon my death. C
9. When I am sick I think about death. C
10. When I am outside during a lightning storm I think about the possibility of being struck by lightning.
11. When I am in an automobile I think about the high incidence of traffic fatalities.
12. I think people should first become concerned about death when they are old.
13. I am much more concerned about death than those around me. C
14. Death hardly concerns me.
15. My general outlook just doesn't allow for morbid thoughts. N
16. The prospect of my own death arouses anxiety in me. E
17. The prospect of my own depresses me. E
18. The prospect of the death of my loved ones arouses anxiety in me. E
19. The knowledge that I will surely die does not in any way affect the conduct in my life.
20. I envision my own death as a painful, nightmarish experience. E
21. I am afraid of dying. E
22. I am afraid of being dead. E
23. Many people become disturbed at the sight of a new grave but it does not bother me.
24. I am disturbed when I think about the shortness of life.
25. Thinking about death is a waste of time.
26. Death should not be regarded as a tragedy if it occurs after a productive life.
27. The inevitable death of man poses a serious challenge to the meaningfulness of human existence.

28. The death of the individual is ultimately beneficial because it facilitates change in society
29. I have a desire to live on after death.
30. The question of whether or not there is a future life worries me considerably.

Klug and Boss Dimensions:

C = conscious concern
E = negative evaluation
N = neither

SOURCE: L. Klug and M. Boss. "Factorial Structure of the Death Concern Scale." *Psychological Reports,* 1976, 38: 110. And L. S. Dickstein. "Death Concern: Measurement and Correlates." *Psychological Reports,* 30: 1972, 563–71. Reprinted with permission of authors and publisher.

V1.7.III.g
DEATH SCALE (QUESTIONS RELATIVE TO DEATH)
M. J. Feldman and M. Hersen, 1967

1. How frequently do you think of your own death?
2. Do you vividly imagine yourself as dying or being dead?
3. Are you inclined to entertain thoughts of some specific disease which might cause your death?
4. Are you inclined to entertain thoughts of being killed in an accident?
5. Do you ever wish that you were dead?
6. Do you ever have nocturnal dreams of dying or being dead?
7. How frequently do you read death poems or death stories?
8. Do you have a strong fear or horror of death; are you absolutely unafraid and resigned to your fate, or is your attitude towards death one of indifference?
9. Do you think about the death of relatives or close friends?
10. Have you secretly wished for the death of a relative or close friend?

Each item had six stems ranging from never to very frequently, and scores were arbitrarily assigned from 0 to 5 points with the highest score denoting the most concerned response.

SOURCE: M. J. Feldman and M. Hersen. "Attitudes toward Death in Nightmare Subjects." *Journal of Abnormal Psychology,* 1967, 72 (5): 422. Copyright 1967 by the American Psychological Association. Reprinted by permission.

V1.7.III.h
FEAR OF DEATH SCALE
I. Sarnoff and S. M. Corwin, 1959

1. I tend to worry about the death toll when I travel on highways.
2. I find it difficult to face up to the ultimate fact of death.
3. Many people become disturbed at the sight of a new grave, but it does not bother me. (reversed scores)
4. I find the preoccupation with death at funerals upsetting.
5. I am disturbed when I think of the shortness of life.

Scoring: six-point scale with responses ranging from +3 (strongly agree) to –3 (strongly disagree)

SOURCE: I. Sarnoff and S. M. Corwin. "Castration Anxiety and the Fear of Death." *Journal of Personality,* 1959, 27: 378. Reprinted by permission of authors and publisher.

V1.7.III.i
EXTENDED FEAR OF DEATH SCALE
D. Martin and L. Wrightsman, 1965

See the description of the instrument in the abstract. The 10 new items are not currently available.

V1.7.III.j
ATTITUDE TOWARD DYING AND DEATH INDEX
J. T. Mathieu and J. A. Peterson, 1970

See the description of the instrument in the abstract.

V1.7.III.k
CONSEQUENCES OF ONE'S OWN DEATH
J. C. Diggory and D. Z. Rothman, 1961

A. I could no longer have any experiences.
B. I am uncertain as to what might happen to me if there is a life after death.
C. I am afraid of what might happen to my body after death.
D. I could no longer care for my dependents.
E. My death would cause grief to my relatives and friends.
F. All my plans and projects would come to an end.
G. The process of dying might be painful.

SOURCE: J. C. Diggory and Doreen Z. Rothman. "Values Destroyed by Death." *Journal of Abnormal and Social Psychology*, 1961, 63: 207. Copyright 1961 by the American Psychological Association. Reprinted by permission.

V1.7.III.l
DIMENSIONS OF DEATH ANXIETY
L. D. Nelson and C. C. Nelson, 1975

1. I am very much afraid to die.
2. Seeing a dead body would not bother me.
3. I would want the best casket available so my body would be well protected.
4. I would not mind working with dying persons.
5. I would willingly talk to a dying person about his coming death if he wished to discuss it.
6. Children should be protected from death as long as possible.
7. Everyone in his right mind is afraid to die.
8. I would touch a dead body.
9. Funerals do not affect me much.
10. Viewing the body in an open casket is a good practice.
11. I think dying persons should be in a hospital even if they are not receiving any real treatment.
12. I like the thought of walking through a graveyard.
13. Everyone should fight against death as much as possible.
14. I could sleep in the room with a dead body.
15. I am afraid to be put to sleep for an operation.
16. Being alone in a completely dark room for several hours would be relaxing to me.
17. It does not make me nervous when people talk about death.
18. I would hate to visit a dying friend.

19. I could lie down in a coffin without experiencing any negative feelings.
20. I worry a lot about dying a painful death.

SOURCE: L. D. Nelson and C. C. Nelson. "A Factor Analytic Inquiry into the Multidimensionality of Death Anxiety." *Omega*, 1975, 6 (2): 177–78. Reprinted by permission of authors and publisher.

V1.7.III.m
DEATH ACCEPTANCE SCALE
J. J. Ray and J. Najman, 1974

1. Since you only do it once death should at least be interesting.
2. I know that I have nothing to fear when I die.
3. Death is not something terrible.
4. Death is a friend.
5. Death is a good thing because it leaves the way for younger men to have their chance.
6. To fear pain makes sense but death is merely relief from pain.
7. People who worry about death must have nothing better to do.

SOURCE: J. J. Ray and J. Najman. "Death Anxiety and Death Acceptance: A Preliminary Approach." *Omega*, 1974, 5 (4): 313. Reprinted by permission of authors and publisher.

V1.7.III.n
CHECKLIST OF DEATH ATTITUDES
W. M. Swenson, 1961

We all think about death at some time or other. Below are a number of words or phrases that can be used in some way to describe your atittudes or feelings as you think of death. Go through the list quickly and put a mark (X) in front of any word or phrase that describes your present feelings about death. Don't spend too much time on any one, but be sure to check all those which describe your feelings. You can help most by being as frank and as truthful as you can. Remember, your name doesn't appear anywhere on these sheets.

1. Happiness.
B2. Don't think about it.
A3. Glorious happy life.
4. Pleasant.
5. Sadness.
6. The end of everything.
7. Fear leaving loved ones.
A8. It will be wonderful.
A9. All troubles will be over.
10. Something you face every day.
11. Promise of new and better life.
12. Terror overcomes me.
13. Very difficult to accept it.
A14. Most beautiful experience of all.
B15. I don't think about death.
16. Everyone's time is set.
17. I fear death.
B18. Don't dwell on it at my age.
A19. I look forward to death.
A20. Peaceful bliss.
21. Many more "living" things to think about.
A22. Enter into true Paradise.
23. Think of Hell's torments.
B24. Don't waste time thinking about it.
B25. Feel fine and no reason to think about it.
26. It disturbs me a great deal.
A27. It gladdens my heart.
28. Have nothing to do with the subject.
29. Deliverance from all this pain and difficulty.
30. All God's wonderful promises will come true.
31. No doubt a grim experience.
B32. Still a long way off.
33. Death is as sure as taxes.
34. Dread the thought of it.
35. All that I read in the Bible will come true.

NOTE: Items marked A or B indicate placement into that cluster group. See the scoring in the abstract.

SOURCE: W. M. Swenson. "Attitudes toward Death in an Aged Population." *Journal of Gerontology*, 1961, 16 (1):50. Reprinted by permission of author and publisher.

V1.7.III.o
FEAR OF DEATH SCALE
L. J. Collett and D. Lester, 1969

Instructions

Here is a series of general statements. You are to indicate how much you agree or disagree with them. Record your opinions in the blank space in front of each item according to the following scale:

1 slight agreement	−1 slight disagreement
2 moderate agreement	−2 moderate disagreement
3 strong agreement	−3 strong disagreement

Read each item and decide *quickly* how you feel about it; then record the extent of your agreement or disagreement. Put down your first impressions.

The Items For Form C of the Collett-Lester Fear of Death Scale

(It is for the user to order the items in a suitable manner. They are presented here in terms of content. Note also that some are keyed positively and some negatively.)

Death of Self:

I would avoid death at all costs
The total isolation of death frightens me
I am disturbed by the shortness of life
The feeling that I might be missing out on so much after I die bothers me
I would not mind dying young
I view death as a release from earthly suffering
Not knowing what it feels like to be dead does not bother me
The idea of never thinking or experiencing again after I die does not make me anxious
I am not disturbed by death being the end of life as I know it

Death of Others:

I would experience a great loss if someone close to me died
I would like to be able to communicate with the spirit of a friend who has died
I would never get over the death of someone close to me
If someone close to me died I would miss him/her very much
I could not accept the finality of the death of a friend
I accept the death of others as the end of their life on earth
I would easily adjust after the death of someone close to me
I would not mind having to identify the corpse of someone I knew
I do not think of dead people as having an existence of some kind
It would upset me to have to see someone who was dead

Dying of Self:

I am disturbed by the physical degeneration involved in a slow death
The pain involved in dying frightens me
The intellectual degeneration of old age disturbs me
Dying might be an interesting experience
If I had a fatal disease, I would like to be told
I am disturbed by the thought that my abilities will be limited while I lay dying

Dying of Others:

I would avoid a friend who was dying
I would feel anxious if someone who was dying talked to me about it
I would feel uneasy if someone talked to me about the approaching death of a common
    friend
If a friend were dying I would not want to be told

I would not feel anxious in the presence of someone I knew was dying

If I had a choice as to whether or not a friend should be informed he/she is dying, I would
    tell him/her

I would want to know if a friend were dying

I would visit a friend on his/her deathbed

If I knew a friend were dying, I would not know what to say to him/her

I would not like to see the physical degeneration of a friend who is dying

I would not mind visiting a senile friend

SOURCE: Personal communication. Reprinted by permission.

V1.7.IV.a
DEATH SCALES
T. Hooper and B. Spilka, 1970
DEATH ANXIETY SCALES

Scale 1: Lack of Fear of Death (K.R. 20 = .82)

1. I am not at all afraid to die.
2. Some people are afraid to die, but I am not.
3. The idea that I may die young does not affect me.
4. I am not at all disturbed by the finality of death.
5. The thought of death never bothers me.

Scale 2: Sensitivity to Death (K.R. 20 = .64)

1. I often think about how short life really is.
2. The thought of death seldom enters my mind. (−)
3. I've actually had some fantasies of the event of dying.
4. I am often distressed by the way time flies so rapidly.
5. I tend to think about the death toll from driving accidents.
6. After attending a funeral service (for other than a close relative or friend), I'm depressed
    for a considerable time.
7. I shudder when I hear people talking about World War III.

Scale 3: Fear of the Dying Process (K.R. 20 = .66)

1. I fear dying a painful death.
2. I am really scared of having a heart attack.
3. I am not particularly afraid of getting Cancer. (−)
4. The pain involved in dying frightens me.

Scale 4: Awareness of the Content of Death (K.R. 20 = .66)

1. The sight of a corpse does not make me at all anxious.
2. The sight of a dead body is horrifying to me. (−)
3. Laws which provide the death penalty for crimes are morally wrong. (−)
4. Coffins make me anxious (−)
5. Graveyards seem to upset many people, but they do not disturb me.

Scale 5: Loss of Experience and Control in Death (K.R. 20 = .86)

1. Never again feeling anything when I die upsets me.
2. Being totally immobile after death bothers me.
3. The idea of never thinking again after I die frightens me.
4. The idea of being buried frightens me.
5. The total isolation of death is frightening to me.
6. I do not mind the idea of being shut into a coffin when I die. (−)
7. The feeling that I will be missing out on so much after I die disturbs me.

(−) = reverse scoring.

DEATH PERSPECTIVES SCALES

Scale 1: Death as Pain and Loneliness (K.R. 20 = .79)

Death as . . .

1. a last agonizing moment
2. the conclusion to a time of isolation
3. the final misery
4. the fate of falling by the wayside
5. the ultimate anguish and torment
6. a lonely experience at the time of dying

Scale 2: Death as an Afterlife of Reward (K.R. 20 = .92)

Death as . . .

1. entrance to a place of ultimate satisfaction
2. leading to a cleansing and rebirth of oneself
3. leading to one's resurrection and reward
4. union with God and eternal bliss
5. opportunity to give up this life in favor of a better one
6. the doorway to heaven and ultimate happiness

Scale 3: Indifference toward Death (K.R. 20 = .71)

Death as . . .

1. unimportant in the scheme of things
2. of little consequence
3. something to be shrugged off and forgotten
4. neither feared nor welcomed
5. making no difference one way or another

Scale 4: Death as Unknown (K.R. 20 = .87)

Death as . . .

1. the biggest uncertainty of all
2. the greatest mystery
3. the end of the known and the beginning of the unknown
4. something about which one must say "I don't know"
5. a question mark
6. the most ambiguous of life's perplexities

Scale 5: Death as Forsaking Dependents plus Guilt (K.R. 20 = .78)

Death as . . .

1. leaving one's dependents vulnerable to life's trials
2. a forsaking of loved others when one dies
3. reason to feel guilty that one may not be adequately providing for future family necessities
4. a reason for feeling guilty
5. leaving the family to fend for itself

Scale 6: Death as Courage (K.R. 20 = .72)

Death as . . .

1. a chance to show that one has stood for something during life
2. an occasion to show how one can meet this last test of life
3. a great moment of truth for oneself
4. an opportunity for great accomplishment
5. a time to refuse humiliation or defeat
6. the test of commitment to one's life-values

Scale 7: Death as Failure (K.R. 20 = .77)

Death as . . .

1. an event that prevents the realization of one's potentialities
2. the end of one's hopes
3. the final failure of one's search for the meaning of life
4. the destruction of any chance to realize oneself to the fullest
5. defeat in the struggle to succeed and achieve

Scale 8: Death as a Natural End (K.R. 20 = .71)

Death as . . .

1. an experience which comes to each of us because of the normal passage of time
2. a final act in harmony with existence
3. a natural aspect of life
4. part of the cycle of life

SOURCE: B. Spilka, L. Stout, B. Minton, and D. Sizemore. "Death Perspectives, Death Anxiety, and Form of Personal Religion." Paper presented to the convention of the Society for the Scientific Study of Religion, Philadelphia, October 29, 1976.

V1.7.IV.b
WILL TO LIVE SCALE
D. L. Ellison, 1969

1. Sometimes I look forward to Passing On	Agree
2. You Sometimes Can't Help Wondering Whether Anything is Worthwhile Anymore	Agree
3. After all Our Friends & Relatives Have Passed On We Might As Well Be Gone Too	Agree
4. Sometimes It would be Better to be Gone & Away From It All	Agree
5. At My Age Continuing To Live is Not So Important	Agree
6. There Are Times When Most of Us Wish Our Lives Were Over How Often Do You Feel This Way?	Often
7. Some People Say They Want to Live Very Much; Others Say They Would Rather Be Gone. How Do You Feel About This?	Rather be Gone

Item 2 was borrowed from the questionnaire of the Midtown Manhattan Study where it was used as an indicator of "latent suicide tendency."

SOURCE: D. L. Ellison. "Alienation and the Will to Live." *Journal of Gerontology,* 1969, 24 (3): 363. Reprinted by permission of author and publisher.

V1.7.IV.c
IMAGES OF DEATH
J. W. Riley, 1970

See the description of the instrument in this abstract.

V1.7.IV.d
DEATH IMAGES
K. W. Back, 1971

See the description of the instrument and the method of administration in the abstract.

V1.7.IV.e
DEATH AND VIOLENT INTEREST QUESTIONNAIRE*
R. Schafer, 1976

1. I like watching the aggressive contact in football games. (1)
2. I would be willing to visit the morgue out of curiosity. (1)
3. I prefer not to read newspaper articles dealing with murder. (5)
4. The best parts of hockey games are the fights. (1)
5. I like to watch the news because of the exciting past events. (1)
6. I avoid going to funerals. (5)
7. I prefer watching a good detective show to a good variety show. (1)
8. I prefer to watch movies about war as opposed to movies about other kinds of historical events. (1)
9. Even though police are at the scene of an accident, I slow down to see how badly someone may be injured. (1)
10. I would be willing to witness a state execution. (1)
11. Death is something I prefer not to think about. (5)
12. I enjoy watching cars in destruction derby. (1)
13. In movies, I prefer to see a man hit with a bullet than only to see the aggressor fire the gun and then the scene cut. (1)
14. When I see a fight, I stop to watch. (1)
15. In "Roadrunner" cartoons, I like the way the wolf gets tricked. (1)
16. I prefer to see a good comedy to a good horror show. (5)
17. I prefer to shut my eyes during the violent parts of movies. (5)
18. If someone was on a hotel ledge going to commit suicide, I would stop to watch with the rest of the crowd that had gathered. (1)

*The number in parentheses indicates the keyed direction for each question.

SOURCE: R. Schafer. "Fascination with Death as a Function of Need for Novel Stimulation." *Omega*, 1976, 1 (1): 45–50. Reprinted by permission of author and publisher.

V1.7.V.a
EUTHANASIA INDEX
C. E. Preston and R. H. Williams, 1971

See the description of the instrument in the abstract.

V1.7.V.b
PREPARATION FOR DEATH
J. W. Riley, 1968

See the description of the instrument in the abstract.

Chapter 8

Environments

Paul G. Windley

This chapter reviews several research instruments that assess the relationship between older people and their large- and small-scale physical environments. The study of environment is by nature multidisciplinary, and operational definitions of the concept of environment vary among the social sciences. It is important to look briefly at these operational definitions in order to understand why the data-gathering instruments in this chapter were chosen for review. This examination is followed by an interpretive discussion of two criteria necessary if research instruments are to be effective in investigating the relationship between the elderly and the physical environments in which they live. Next follows a brief overview of research techniques currently being developed in the environment/aging field that are not reviewed in this chapter. The chapter concludes with a synopsis of the instruments reviewed.

Operational Definitions of Environment

Definitions of environment used by sociologists focus primarily on phenomena external to the individual, such as population density, age homogeneity, social relationships, geographical distribution of social problems, and structure of social organizations. These independent variables are thought to affect such factors as social disorganization and social pathology. The primary method for analysis is the social survey coupled with observation.

Anthropologists define environment in a larger cultural sense, focusing on the life-styles of groups (e.g., farmers, city dwellers, hunters) and the symbolic values held by social groups, such as their various perspectives on time, rhythm, and tempo. The primary methods used by anthropologists are participant observation, time/activity logs, maps of kinship networks, and case studies.

Psychologists define environment according to at least two schools of thought. The experimentalists treat everything outside the individual as "the stimulus." Thus, investigating the most minute properties of abstract environmental objects and artifacts is thought to explain the most elementary forms of human behavior. Experimentalists employ such laboratory equipment as tachistoscopes and galvanometers and techniques of observation under highly controlled conditions. The correlational psychologists are preoccupied with humans as dispositional creatures—the explanatory source of human behavior being found in unique individual traits. Environment to the correlationist is any social or physical dimension that forms part of a more basic behavioral trait or group of traits. The correlationist employs psychometrically derived personality and preference scales and questionnaires.

Emerging from the correlationist viewpoint are psychosocial dimensions of environment pioneered by Moos (1974) and associates at the Social Ecology Laboratory of Stanford University. This viewpoint recognizes that social situations not only mediate behaviors originally thought to belong exclusively to individual traits, but that social settings themselves possess traits. Such environmental traits as relationship potential, personal development potential, and system-maintenance and sytem-change dimensions are the most salient environmental traits in this line of research. The research instruments used in this area are also based on the psychometric model.

Researchers in the design and planning fields define environment in more physical terms. Dimensions such as square feet per person, height of building, and size of neighborhood are important factors found to affect satisfaction and general well-being among the elderly. Most investigators augment traditional social science techniques with time-lapse photography, behavioral mapping, cognitive mapping, and simulation and gaming. Many of these new techniques are discussed later in this chapter.

Instrument Development Criteria

Upon examination of the existing instruments and the current needs in the field, it was found that at least two criteria for instrument development must be met in order to study effectively the influence of environment on behavior in the elderly. Both criteria are based on the premise that a broad ecological approach must be taken to the environment/aging field. The unique approaches of the sociologist, anthropologist, psychologist, and architect/planner must be superimposed upon one another to yield a comprehensive description and analysis of behavior in environmental settings.

The first criterion requires that research instruments leave the events and the setting under investigation as conceptually intact as possible. This is not to suggest that an investigator cannot separate the psychological attributes of the individual or the social structure of the setting; it means that he or she must use instruments capable of capturing the dynamic interplay of the person and the social and physical environment. Investigators must look for person-environment units (Ittelson et al., 1974). This notion implies that the social and physical environment is not a collection of chaotic odds and ends and that the task is to bring order out of disorder. On the contrary, the task is to describe and explain the surprising amount of interplay and order that already exist between persons and their physical settings. Thus, ideal research instruments must, at one point in time, be capable of yielding a descriptive account of the interplay between multiple variables.

The second criterion argues that research instruments must be capable of accounting for change occurring both within person-environment units and between units and the larger systems of which they are parts. The assumption here is that person-environment units are systems within larger systems and that they constantly seek a state of equilibrium. Person-environment units are self-regulating. The ability to account for this dynamic is essential to understanding those factors within and outside person-environment units that create states of incongruence, as well as the mechanisms used by individuals in coping with this incongruence. Equally important is the process incongruent systems use to return to a point of equilibrium.

These two criteria argue again for the need to develop a theory that accounts for the reciprocal interaction of individual and environmental variables over time and dispels the popular notion that good instruments can precede the theories that justify them.

Various rediscovered techniques in the field approximate the two criteria just described. Some yield data capable of sophisticated, multivariate statistical procedures, and others are experimental and intuitive. All are important in describing the complexity of person-environment units.

Multivariate Procedures

Kahana (1974) and Lawton, Nahemow, and Teaff (1975) have used traditional questionnaires and interviews and submitted these data to both stepwise multiple regression and factor analytic procedures yielding sets of individual and environmental variables accounting for substantial variance in the life satisfaction and well-being of older people. Although these instruments initially did not leave the settings under investigation intact, attempts were made to reassemble dimensions of persons and settings to yield comprehensive person-environment units.

Behavior Settings

Barker's (1968) behavior setting analysis closely approximates this chapter's two criteria. His descriptive account of ecological episodes captures units of behavior occurring in situ, noting the standing pattern of behavior, significant individuals in the setting, duration of the setting, regular occurrence of the setting, and its physical boundaries. Barker's primary focus has been the social milieu of the setting; however, less attention has been paid to the physical attributes of these settings and the psychological characteristics of individuals within those settings.

Behavior Mapping

Ittelson, Rivlin, and Proshansky (1976) recorded on architectural floor plans the behavior of elderly residents in a long-term-care facility. By noting categories of behavior, the physical locations in which they occurred, and the interrelationship of these factors, important data describing and comparing person-environment units can be obtained. Behavior maps not only show areas where a predominance of a single type of activity occurs, they also show that certain kinds of behavior are distributed over a wide geographical area. Behavior maps allow the reciprocal relations between behavior and environment to be studied. In a more applied perspective, architects' plans can be examined before construction begins, and predictions about the anticipated behavior of users can be made on the basis of other studies. Postconstruction follow-up studies then can yield a wealth of information on the validity of previous design assumptions.

Cognitive Mapping

Regnier (1975) and Newcomer (1973) asked elderly individuals to outline on an area map the boundaries of their perceived neighborhoods. A consensus neighborhood map showed distinct relationships between the size and shape of the map drawn and the awareness of neighborhood services, use of services, and mobility patterns of elderly residents. Lynch (1960) and Lee (1972) found that the comprehensiveness and accuracy of cognitive maps of large city areas drawn by random individuals were strongly related to a sense of attachment to place and to life satisfaction. Research instruments exploiting the long-recognized notion that the individual screens and reacts to incoming information via personal schemata have, however, been slow to develop. Cognitive maps are able to handle simultaneously large chunks of data on personal and environmental variables and represent a summary of the accumulated experiences of the individual over time in a specific geographical place.

Simulation

Winkel and Sasanoff (1976) used an elaborate photographic arrangement to simulate a tour through a museum. Subjects participating in the simulated tour could start, stop, and choose directions to move in in order to view simulated displays. Routes taken through the simulated museum were compared to routes taken by people through the actual museum. The obvious value of such a photographic simulation would be in studying and predicting the users' behavior in specified architectural spaces under certain social conditions.

A simulation approach that perhaps more closely approximates this chapter's two criteria is the empathic model developed by Pastalan, Mautz, and Merrill (1973). The model is a set of mechanical devices (eyeglasses and earplugs) that simulate the natural vision and hearing loss that accompany old age. When worn by the investigator in various settings (such as nursing homes, single-family dwellings, and shopping centers), these devices help the investigator approximate the environmental and social experiences of older individuals in these same settings. Thus, the investigator plays the roles of the experimenter and the subject at the same time and can study the impact of the total setting on his or her own experience and behavior. The adjustment process over time can also be assessed when the investigator performs his or her daily routine while wearing the devices.

This research technique holds great promise both for identifying person-environment units and for verifying the existence of units found through other methods.

The Walk-through

Lynch and Rivkin (1976) asked several individuals to walk around a block of a large city and "free associate" about those elements in the immediate setting that seemed significant. Lynch discovered an underlying tendency for almost all the subjects to mentally organize what seemed to be discontinuous elements in the urban environment. The spacing and location of buildings, the location of open spaces, the storefronts and the contents of their windows and signs, and the texture of the sidewalk were some of the elements most commonly noticed. Lynch was able to determine the value the subjects placed on the continuity of life experience in situ, since many of the subjects' experiences were intricately interwoven with the physical and social fabric of the city. Howell (in an unpublished manuscript with no date) applied the same technique with elderly residents of a high-rise apartment building. Elderly individuals were asked to take the researcher on a tour of the building and indicate their likes and dislikes as they went along. The subjects discussed social relationships and management policies, as well as the design of the building. This technique seems promising for eliciting person-environment units.

The arguments presented here are not entirely new ones. Brunswik (1957, p. 5), in an early discussion of these issues, wrote the following:

> Both organism and environment will have to be seen as systems, each with properties of its own, yet both hewn from basically the same block. Each has surface and depth, or overt and covert regions. . . . The interrelationship between the two systems has the essential characteristic of a "coming-to-terms." And this coming-to-terms is not merely a matter of the mutual boundary or surface areas. It concerns equally as much, or perhaps even more, the rapport between the central, covert layers of the two systems. It follows that, much as psychology must be concerned with the texture of the organism or of its nervous processes and must investigate them in depth, it also must be concerned with the texture of the environment as it extends in depth away from the common boundary.

Summary

The instruments selected for review in this chapter (see Table 8-1) do not exhaust the multitude of instruments used to study the relationship of older people to their environments. They are representative, however, cutting across the entire social science spectrum.

The criteria used in the selection process were these: (1) the instrument had to assess a physical dimension of the environment, (2) the instrument and its respective study had to be readily available in

TABLE 8-1
Instruments Reviewed in Chapter 8

Instrument	Author (date)	Code Number
I. Psychometric Scales and Indexes		
a. Territorial Behavior Report Scale	Koob and Fish (1976)	V1.8.I.a
b. Need for Services Index	Lawton (1969)	V1.8.I.b
c. Environmental Description Factors	Lawton and Cohen (1974)	Not available
d. Environmental Response Inventory	McKechnie (1970)	Copyrighted
e. Privacy Preference Scale	Pastalan and Bourestom (1975)	Vi.8.I.e
f. Environmental Characteristics Factors	Schooler (1970)	Not available
g. Environmental Disposition Scales	Windley (1972)	Not reproduced
II. Questionnaires		
a. User Survey Interview Schedule	Audain and Huttman (no date)	Not reproduced
b. Satisfaction with Living Environment Questionnaire	Brody, Kleban, and Liebowitz (1975)	V1.8.II.b
c. Wish for Privacy Questionnaire	Lawton and Bader (1970)	V1.8.II.c
d. Housing Satisfaction Questionnaire	Lawton, Kleban, and Singer (1971)	Not available
e. Environmental Variables Questionnaire	Lawton, Nahemow, and Teaff (1975)	No special material
f. Indirect Assessment of Social Interaction	Lawton and Simon (1968)	No special material
g. Effect of Retirement Housing Questionnaire	Sherman (1971)	V1.8.II.g
h. Interest in Segregated Housing Questionnaire	Winiecke (1973)	V1.8.II.h
III. Single-Item Indicators		
a. Fear in Environment	Lebowitz (1975)	Single item
b. Satisfaction with the Site	Sherman et al. (1968)	Single item
IV. Checklists		
a. Factors Influencing the Abandoning of Private Homes by the Elderly	Pastalan (1977)	Not reproduced

books and journals, (3) the degree of cooperation received from authors in obtaining copies of the instruments and descriptive data were factors, and (4) value judgments were made by this author about the quality of the research in which the various instruments were used.

Given the fact that each discipline investigates the effects of physical environment within its own unique research paradigm, an accurate accounting of environmental effects requires a multidisciplinary approach. Thus, the instruments presented in this chapter range from psychometric scales to checklists of environmental amenities.

Because of the multidisciplinary nature of the aging/environment field and its recent advent as a legitimate field for inquiry, no theoretical consensus yet exists among researchers. Thus, most of the instruments reviewed reflect attempts to describe the elements in the environment that affect behavior. Due to the natural multiplicity of settings in which behaviors take place, traditional social science techniques that depend on highly controlled experimental designs are seen increasingly as inadequate for identifying environment/behavior relationships. Psychometrically reliable and valid scales are considered relatively unimportant by many in the field. Most traditional methodologies are bound to single disciplines, narrowly focused, and structured in such a way that identifying and sorting out the multiple-variable effects are difficult tasks. It would be gratifying to report that the field of aging and the environment has progressed sufficiently so that the most salient environmental dimensions are known and that all that remains is the fine tuning of existing methodologies. However, the field is not so well developed. Until a more valid and comprehensive theory can be developed in the field, research methods will continue to be basically descriptive.

REFERENCES

Audain, M. *Beyond Shelter: A Study of National Housing Act Financed Housing for the Elderly*. Canadian Council on Social Development, no date.

Barker, R. *Ecological Psychology*. Stanford, Calif.: Stanford University Press, 1968.

Brody, E. M., M. H. Kleban, and B. Liebowitz. "Living Arrangements for Older People." *American Institute of Architects Journal*, 1973, 59: 35-40.

_____. "Intermediate Housing for the Elderly: Satisfaction of Those Who Moved In and Those Who Did Not." *The Gerontologist*, 1975, 15 (4): 350.

Brunswik, E. "Scope and Aspects of the Cognitive Problem." In *Cognition: The Colorado Symposium*, H. Gruber, R. Jessor, K. Hammond (eds.). Cambridge, Mass.: Harvard University Press, 1957.

Friedman, E. P. "Spatial Proximity and Social Interaction in a Home for the Aged." *Journal of Gerontology*, 1966, 21: 556–70.

Ittelson, W. H., H. M. Proshansky, L. G. Rivlin, and G. H. Winkel (eds.). *An Introduction to Environmental Psychology*. New York: Holt, Rinehart and Winston, 1974.

Ittelson, W. H., L. G. Rivlin, and H. M. Proshansky. "The Use of Behavioral Maps in Environmental Psychology." In *Environmental Psychology: People and Their Physical Settings*, H. M. Proshansky, W. H. Ittelson, and L. G. Rivlin (eds.), pp. 340–51. New York: Holt, Rinehart and Winston, 1976.

Kahana, E. "A Congruence Model of Person-Environment Interaction." In *Theory Development in Environment and Aging*, P. G. Windley, T. Byerts, and F. G. Ernst (eds.), pp. 181–215. Washington, D.C.: Gerontological Society, 1974.

Koob, L., and G. Fish. *Measuring Territorial Behavior of Elderly People in Public Housing*. Department of Housing and Applied Design, University of Maryland, 1976.

Lawton, M. P. "Supportive Services in the Context of the Housing Environment." *The Gerontologist*, 1969, 9 (1): 15–19.

Lawton, M. P., and J. Bader. "Wish for Privacy by Young and Old." *Journal of Gerontology*, 1970, 25 (1): 48–54.

Lawton, M. P., and J. Cohen. "Environment and the Well-being of Elderly Inner-City Residents." *Environment and Behavior*, 1974, 6 (2): 194–211.

Lawton, M. P., M. H. Kleban, and M. Singer. *The Elderly Jew in an Urban Slum*. Philadelphia: Philadelphia Geriatric Center, 1970 (mimeographed report).

_____. "The Aged Jewish Person and the Slum Environment." *Journal of Gerontology*, 1971, 26 (2): 231–39.

Lawton, M. P., L. Nahemow, and J. Teaff. "Housing Characteristics and the Well-Being of Elderly Tenants in Federally Assisted Housing." *Journal of Gerontology*, 1975, 30 (5): 601–7.

Lawton, M. P., and B. Simon. "The Ecology of Social Relationships in Housing for the Elderly." *The Gerontologist*, 1968, 8: 108–15.

Lebowitz, B. D. "Age and Fearfulness: Personal and Situational Factors." *Journal of Gerontology*, 1975, 30 (6): 696–700.

Lee, T. "Psychology and Living Space." In *Image and Environment: Cognitive Mapping and Spatial Behavior*, R. Downs and D. Stea (eds.), p. 87. Chicago: Aldine: 1972.

Lynch, K. *The Image of the City*. Cambridge, Mass.: M.I.T. Press, 1960.

Lynch, K., and M. Rivkin. "A Walk around the Block." In *Environmental Psychology: People and Their Physical Settings*, H. M. Proshansky, W. Ittelson, and L. G. Rivlin (eds.), pp. 363–76. New York: Holt, Rinehart and Winston, 1976.

McKechnie, G. "Measuring Environmental Dispositions with the Environmental Response Inventory." *Proceedings of the 2nd Annual Environmental Design Research Association*, J. Archea and C. Eastman (eds.), pp. 320–26. Pittsburgh: Carnegie-Mellon University, 1970.

Marshall, N. "Environmental Components of Orientation Toward Privacy." *Proceedings of the 2nd Annual Environmental Design Research Association Conference*, J. Archea and C. Eastman (eds.), p. 246. Pittsburgh: Carnegie-Mellon University, 1970.

Moos, R., and P. M. Insel (eds.). *Issues in Social Ecology*. Palo Alto, Calif.: National Press, 1974.

Newcomer, R. J. "Housing, Services, and Neighborhood Activities." Paper presented to the

26th Annual Meeting of the Gerontological Society, Miami Beach, November 5-9, 1973.

Pastalan, L. A. "Privacy as an Expression of Human Territoriality." Paper presented to the Colloquium on Spatial-Behavioral Relationships as Related to Older People. Institute of Gerontology, University of Michigan, Ann Arbor, 1970.

_____. Factors Influencing the Abandoning of Private Homes by the Elderly. Ann Arbor, Mich.: Institute of Gerontology, University of Michigan, 1977.

Pastalan, L. A., and N. Bourestom. Forced Relocation: Setting, Staff, and Patients. Ann Arbor, Mich.: Institute of Gerontology, University of Michigan, 1975.

Pastalan, L. A., R. K. Mautz, and J. Merrill. "The Simulation of Age Related Sensory Losses: A New Approach to the Study of Environmental Barriers." In Environmental Design Research, W. F. E. Preiser (ed.), pp. 383-91. Stroudsburgh: Dowden, Hutchinson and Ross, 1973.

Regnier, V. "Neighborhood Settings and Neighborhood Use: Cognitive Mapping as a Method for Identifying the Macro Environment of Older People." Paper presented to the 28th Annual Meeting of the American Gerontological Society, Portland, November 5-9, 1975.

Schooler, K. S. "The Relationship between Social Interaction and Morale of the Elderly as a Function of Environmental Characteristics." The Gerontologist, 1969, 9: 25-29.

_____. "Effect of Environment on Morale." The Gerontologist, 1970, 10 (3, part 1): 194-97.

Sherman, S. "The Choice of Retirement Housing among the Well Elderly." Aging and Human Development, 1971, 2 (2): 118-38.

Sherman, S. R., W. P. Mangum, Jr., S. Dodds, R. P. Walkley, and D. M. Wilner. "Psychological Effects of Retirement Housing." The Gerontologist, 1968, 8 (3, part 1): 170-75.

Walkley, R. P., W. P. Mangum, Jr., S. R. Sherman, S. Dodds, and D. M. Wilner. Retirement Housing in California. Berkeley, Calif.: Diablo Press, 1966.

Windley, P. G. "Environmental Dispositions of Older People." Ph.D. dissertation, University of Michigan, 1972.

_____. "Measuring Environmental Dispositions of Elderly Females." In Environmental Design Research, W. F. E. Preiser (ed.), p. 214. Stroudsburgh: Dowden, Hutchinson and Ross, 1973.

Winiecke, L. "The Appeal of Age Segregated Housing to the Elderly Poor." International Journal of Aging and Human Development, 1973, 4 (4): 293-305.

Winkel, G. H., and R. Sasanoff. "An Approach to an Objective Analysis of Behaviors in Architectural Space." In Environmental Psychology: People and Their Physical Settings, H. M. Proshansky, W. H. Ittelson, and L. G. Rivlin (eds.), pp. 351-62. New York: Holt, Rinehart and Winston, 1976.

Abstracts

TERRITORIAL BEHAVIOR REPORT SCALE (TBRS)
L. Koob and G. Fish, 1976

Definition of Variable or Concept

This instrument assesses the territorial behavior of elderly people in public housing. Territoriality is the positioning of self, the distance kept between self and others, and the placement of objects in a setting so as to regulate social interaction and possess and control the setting.

Description of Instrument

This scale contains the following subscales: control, demarcation, and defense. Each subscale contains 15 items with a five-point response format (almost never, rarely, sometimes, often, almost always). A pool of items was developed to reflect territorial behavior as experienced by researchers. A refined pool of items was then selected by judges and on the basis of group discrimination scores and reliability estimates.

Method of Administration

The instrument is administered in a self-report or an interview situation. Approximately 30 minutes is required for administration; no special instructions for administration were mentioned.

Context of Development and Subsequent Use

In order to design better housing for the elderly, sponsors, planners, and architects need to know more about the territorial behavior of elderly people. This instrument was developed to measure individual differences in the use of space, structures, and words to claim territories as a means of control over social interaction in a public housing apartment building for the elderly. The implication was that territorial behavior relates to the variable of well-being.

Sample

The sample was comprised of 47 randomly selected public housing tenants age 62 and over. The sample contained both black and white subjects, as well as males and females.

Formal Test of Reliability

Kuder-Richardson 20 reliability estimates for the three subscales and the combined scale are as follows: control, .72; demarcation, .82; defense, .77; and combined scale, .88.

Formal Tests of Validity

The three intercorrelations of the subscales are as follows: control with demarcation, $r = .53$; control with defense, $r = .50$; and demarcation with defense, $r = .48$.

Reference

Koob, L., and G. Fish. *Measuring Territorial Behavior of Elderly People in Public Housing.* Department of Housing and Applied Design, University of Maryland, 1976.

Instrument

See Instrument V1.8.I.a.

NEED FOR SERVICES INDEX
M. P. Lawton, 1969

Definition of Variable or Concept

The Need for Services Index measures preference for medical, food, housekeeping, social, and recreational services in housing for the elderly.

Description of Instrument

This factor analytically derived index is comprised of 10 items with a fixed response format of would like/would not like.

Method of Administration

The instrument is administered by interview and takes approximately 20 minutes to complete. No special skills or instructions for administration were mentioned.

Context of Development and Subsequent Use

Government policymakers, housing sponsors, and gerontologists have been divided on the issue of whether to include supportive services in housing for the elderly. This instrument was developed to answer these questions: (1) For which people is the provision for services life sustaining? (2) For which people does the provision of services encourage dependency and ultimately erode competence? (3) To what extent does the existence of an on-site service determine the characteristics of the people who apply to live at the housing site? (4) To what extent does the existence of an on-site service change the environment in such a way as to affect those who do not utilize the service as well as those who do utilize it?

Sample

The sample was comprised of 1,400 elderly tenants from seven housing sites and from the community.

Scoring

Apparently, the number of desired services is added into a composite index.

Formal Tests of Validity

Factor loadings for the 10 services ranged from .29 to .56 (Lawton, 1969, p. 18).

Scale-Development Statistics

The items, with their respective factor loadings, are as follows: would eat lunch frequently if it were available on site, .56; wants social worker added to staff, .53; wishes meal service on site, .53; wants activity worker added to staff, .53; would utilize social worker, .46; prefers extensive medical service, .39; not enough activities on site, .37; wants maid service on site, .36; will like the new building (preoccupancy), .30; and site not near enough to shopping, .29.

Reference

Lawton, M. P. "Supportive Services in the Context of the Housing Environment." *The Gerontologist*, 1969, 9 (1): 15-19.

Instrument

See Instrument V1.8.I.b.

ENVIRONMENTAL DESCRIPTION FACTORS
M. P. Lawton and J. Cohen, 1974

Definition of Variable or Concept

The six environmental description factors were part of a study attempting to relate a number of quality-of-life criteria to three domains of independent variables: demography, health, and environment.

Description of Instrument

The instrument comprises six factor analytically derived scales that describe urban environmental characteristics among older people: Jewish concentration, distance from facilities, independent household, busy location, well-kept neighborhood, and residential block. The factors contain from three to five items each, and the item-response format varies for each item. Data are gathered from interviews and *distance mapping* of the neighborhood.

Context of Development and Subsequent Use

This study was an attempt to extend earlier instruments developed by Schooler (1969) to investigations of the dynamic interplay of environmental characteristics and the individual. It is hypothesized that environmental factors may be related to morale and other variables through perceptual and cognitive processes.

Sample

The sample was comprised of 115 Jewish elderly residents aged 60 and over who lived in a high-crime area. Seventy-four were females. The mean age was 72 years.

Scoring, Scale Norms, and Distribution

Standardized item scores are weighted by the factor loading (for the factor with the highest loading) and summed to give factor scores. Average scores for the six dimensions are: Jewish concentration, mean 1.5, standard deviation 2.0; distance from facilities, mean 0.1, standard deviation 2.0; independent household, mean −0.2, standard deviation 2.4; busy location, mean 0.7, standard deviation 2.2; well-kept neighborhood, mean 0.6, standard deviation 2.2; and residential block, mean −0.2, standard deviation 1.4 (Lawton and Cohen, 1974, p. 202).

Usability on Older Populations

The instrument is most appropriate for use with noninstitutionalized elderly subjects.

References

Lawton, M. P., and J. Cohen. "Environment and the Well-Being of Elderly Inner-City Residents." *Environment and Behavior*, 1974, 6 (2): 194–211.

Schooler, K. S. "The Relationship between Social Interaction and Morale of the Elderly as a Function of Environmental Characteristics." *The Gerontologist*, 1969, 9: 25–29.

Instrument

The exact form of this instrument is not available at this time.

ENVIRONMENTAL RESPONSE INVENTORY (ERI)
George McKechnie, 1970

Definition of Variable or Concept

These scales were designed to assess dispositions toward the manufactured and the natural environment. Dispositions are defined as relatively stable and traitlike attitudes toward the environment.

Description of Instrument

The instrument is comprised of five factor analytically derived subscales for men (pastoralism, urbanism, environmental adaptation, stimulus seeking, and environmental well-being) and six subscales for women (pastoralism, environmental security, environmental stimulation, abstract conservationism, modernism, and urbanism). There are a total of 184 items on all the subscales, to which respondents indicate that they strongly agree, agree, are neutral, disagree, or strongly disagree.

Method of Administration

The instrument is primarily group administered and self-reporting, and it takes 90 minutes to administer. No special requirements for administration were mentioned.

Context of Development and Subsequent Use

In an attempt to account for more variance in human behavior, psychologists are exploring attitudes toward the manufactured and the natural environment. The ERI is an attempt to tap individual traitlike dispositions toward the physical environment.

Sample

The item-pool was administered to a group of approximately 800 subjects (400 male, 400 female), which included university students, faculty members, registered nurses, and several other groups of people.

Formal Tests of Validity

The ERI scales have been found to correlate with the California Psychological Inventory, the Myers-Briggs Type Indicator, and the Study of Values.

Usability on Older Populations

The complete test is too long and some of the items are inappropriate for older people.

Sensitivity to Age Differences

Although the original sample contained some adult subjects, several of the scales would need some alteration before they would apply to the elderly as a group.

Reference

McKechnie, G. "Measuring Environmental Dispositions with the Environmental Response Inventory." *Proceedings of the 2nd Annual Environmental Design Research Association*, J. Archea and C. Eastman (eds.), pp. 320–26. Pittsburgh: Carnegie-Mellon University, 1970.

Instrument

This copyrighted instrument is available from the Consulting Psychologists Press, Palo Alto, Calif.

PRIVACY PREFERENCE SCALE
L. A. Pastalan and N. Bourestom, 1975

Definition of Variable or Concept

This instrument assesses the desire for privacy as a multidimensional concept. Environmental amenities in institutional settings are viewed as resources, and four dimensions of privacy are included: solitude (desire to be alone), intimacy (desire to be alone with one or more people), anonymity (getting lost in a crowd), and reserve (psychological withdrawal from others).

Description of Instrument

The Privacy Preference Scale is composed of four subscales of five items each, to which subjects respond with a yes or a no answer. This scale is an adaptation of Marshall's (1970) Privacy Preference Scale, which was developed through factor analytic techniques.

Method of Administration

The instrument is administered by interview in approximately 15 minutes. No special requirements or interview skills were mentioned.

Context of Development and Subsequent Use

This scale was part of a larger questionnaire administered to institutionalized elderly people to assess the effects of forced relocation on their mortality and morbidity. A loss of privacy was thought to be associated with mortality and morbidity rates.

Sample

The sample of 128 elderly people was selected from three institutional settings. Of the sample 36% were male, 90% were white, and most of the people in the sample were widowed.

References

Marshall, N. "Environmental Components of Orientation toward Privacy." *Proceedings of the 2nd Annual Environmental Design Research Association Conference*, J. Archea and C. Eastman (eds.), p. 246. Pittsburgh: Carnegie-Mellon University, 1970.

Pastalan, L. A., and N. Bourestom. *Forced Relocation: Setting, Staff, and Patients.* Ann Arbor, Mich.: Institute of Gerontology, University of Michigan, 1975.

Instrument

See Instrument V1.8.I.e.

ENVIRONMENTAL CHARACTERISTICS FACTORS
K. Schooler, 1970

Definition of Variable or Concept

Six environmental characteristics are measured: distance to facilities—bank, barbershop, and stores; condition of dwelling unit—state of repair of dwelling unit and surrounding grounds and style, size, and condition of furniture; convenience—accessibility of location to facilities, friends, and relatives; features—safety and convenience features, opportunities for socialization, and number of floors in dwelling unit; awareness of services; and size of dwelling unit.

Description of Instrument

The six analytically derived factors comprised part of a larger instrument that measured social relations and morale.

Method of Administration

The instrument is administered by interview. No time estimate can be made, and no special skills or instructions for administration were mentioned.

Sample

The sample was comprised of 4,000 elderly persons, aged 65 or over, selected in an area probability sample of all noninstitutionalized elderly people living in the United States.

Scoring, Scale Norms, and Distribution

Items are weighted in proportion to the factor loadings and summed (Schooler, 1970, p. 195).

Formal Tests of Validity

The factor structure matrices for males and females are "almost identical."

References

Schooler, K. "The Relationship between Social Interaction and Morale of the Elderly as a Function of Environmental Characteristics." *The Gerontologist*, 1969, 9: 25–29.

_____. "Effect of Environment on Morale." *The Gerontologist*, 1970, 10 (3, part 1): 194–97.

Instrument

The exact form of the instrument is not available at this time.

ENVIRONMENTAL DISPOSITION SCALES
P. G. Windley, 1972

Definition of Variable or Concept

Four environmental disposition scales (preferences for privacy, environmental complexity, environmental stability, and environmental manipulation) were combined, yielding a measure of the disengagement of elderly people from their environment. Environmental dispositions are defined as those relatively enduring attitudes toward objects and settings in the natural and manufactured environment.

Description of the Instrument

Each scale contains 20 items. The privacy, complexity, and stability scales each contain five visual items comprised of sketches of environmental objects and settings for which the subject indicates a preference. A five-point response format is available for each item (strongly agree, agree, neutral, disagree, strongly disagree). A pool of items was assembled for each scale on the basis of face validity and expert judgments. Each pool was then administered to a sample of 50. The final items were selected through the use of an item-discrimination index and item-total score correlations.

Method of Administration

The instrument is administered by interview or self-report in approximately 60 minutes. There are no special requirements for administration.

Context of Development and Subsequent Use

Much of the research concerning disengagement behavior has not investigated the contribution of the physical environment to disengagement. The four scales were developed to assess an environmental component of disengagement among the elderly. A person who is "environmentally disengaged" could be expected to score low on preference for privacy and low on preference for complexity and to score high on preference for environmental stability and low on preference for environmental manipulation.

Sample

The total sample was comprised of 160 white females. Eighty were elderly, with an average age of 82 years, and 80 were university students, with an average age of 21 years. The samples were matched on socioeconomic status, but they differed in education, age, and marital status.

Scoring, Scale Norms, and Distribution

The four scales are scored as the summation of item weights. Means and standard deviations for the elderly (E) and the student (S) samples are as follows—privacy: E: $\bar{X} = 60.3$, $SD = 6.0$; S: $\bar{X} = 58.6$, $SD = 7.8$; complexity: E: $\bar{X} = 47.7$, $SD = 6.4$; S: $\bar{X} = 66.1$, $SD = 7.4$; stability: E: $\bar{X} = 53.6$, SD 8.6; S: $\bar{X}$ 51.6, $SD = 11.6$; and manipulation: E: $\bar{X} = 60.6$, $SD = 6.6$; S: $\bar{X} = 63.4$. $SD = 6.0$.

Formal Tests of Reliability

The coefficient alpha was computed for the scales with the following results: privacy, .40; complexity, .78; stability, .75; and manipulation, .50.

Formal Tests of Validity

Correlations among the scales are relatively low, ranging from −0.15 (complexity with privacy) to 0.35 (manipulation with complexity).

References

Windley, P. G. "Environmental Dispositions of Older People." Ph.D. dissertation, University of Michigan, 1972.

_____ . "Measuring Environmental Dispositions of Elderly Females." In *Environmental Design Research*, W. F. E. Preiser (ed.), p. 214. Stroudsburgh: Dowden, Hutchinson and Ross, 1973.

Instrument

This instrument includes line drawings for each item, and so it is too long to be reproduced here.

USER SURVEY INTERVIEW SCHEDULE
M. J. Audain and E. Huttman, no date

Definition of Variable or Concept

The user's perception, use, and reaction to physical aspects of housing as a service for the elderly are measured by this instrument.

Description of Instrument

This battery of 75 questions contains both open- and closed-ended items. No information about the instrument's development procedure was offered in the report.

Method of Administration

Data are collected primarily through an interview, which requires approximately 50 minutes to complete. No special skills or requirements are needed for administration.

Context of Development and Subsequent Use

This battery of questions was part of the Canadian Council of Social Development's attempt to assess comprehensively the status of housing for the elderly in the Atlantic provinces, Quebec, Ontario, the prairies, and British Columbia. The entire survey assesses development characteristics, resident characteristics, facilities, services, staffing, social participation, and management finances.

Sample

The sample was comprised of a probability sample of 303 residents. Sixty percent of the respondents were aged 75 years and over. Sixty-eight percent lived in nonprofit developments, and 73% lived in urban areas.

Usability on Older Populations

The whole questionnaire is too intense for one sitting with the elderly.

Reference

Audain, M. Beyond Shelter: *A Study of National Housing Act Financed Housing for the Elderly.* Canadian Council on Social Development, no date.

Instrument

This instrument, with its elaborate tabular format, is too long to be reproduced here.

SATISFACTION WITH LIVING ENVIRONMENT QUESTIONNAIRE
E. M. Brody, M. H. Kleban, and B. Liebowitz, 1975

Definition of Variable or Concept

Four variables are thought to measure satisfaction with living environment: neighborhood satisfaction, apartment/house/living space satisfaction, overall living arrangement satisfaction, and degree to which a person is willing to move.

Description of Instrument

The environment Satisfaction Questionnaire is comprised of four closed-ended questions with response alternatives.

Method of Administration

The instrument is administered by interview. No special administration procedures were mentioned.

Context of Development and Subsequent Use

This four-question instrument was part of a larger questionnaire used to assess the impact of housing upon self-concept, morale, and other factors in a premove-postmove study. The type of housing under investigation was "intermediate housing" (housing between a private home and an institution).

Sample

The sample was comprised of 87 older people aged 62 and over who had applied for intermediate housing. Experimental and control groups did not differ significantly in age, number of children, income, or marital status, but they differed significantly in sex distribution.

Usability on Older Populations

No difficulties were mentioned; this instrument seems most appropriate for noninstitutionalized elderly subjects.

References

Brody, E. M., M. H. Kleban, and B. Liebowitz. "Living Arrangements for Older People." *American Institute of Architects Journal*, 1973, 59: 35–40.
————. "Intermediate Housing for the Elderly: Satisfaction of Those Who Moved In and Those Who Did Not." *The Gerontologist*, 1975, 15 (4): 350.

Instrument

See Instrument V1.8.II.b.

WISH FOR PRIVACY QUESTIONNAIRE
M. P. Lawton and J. Bader, 1970

Definition of Variable or Concept

Privacy is defined as self-determination of self-control over one's surroundings. This control is viewed as a form of striving for identity among institutionalized elderly people.

Description of Instrument

The questionnaire is a battery of four questions, with both fixed and open-ended response formats.

Method of Administration

No special requirements for the administration of the interview were mentioned.

Context of Development and Subsequent Use

It has been hypothesized that spatial privacy and territorial behavior are two forms of identity striving that tend to decrease with an increasing degree of institutionalization. This phenomenon is thought to be mediated by age, socioeconomic status, institutional status, present roommate status, health, wish for oneself versus prescription for others, and subcultural differences.

Samples

The samples were comprised of 438 institutionalized elderly, 56 applicants to a home for the elderly, and 345 community residents. Of the institutionalized sample 76% was female, and 65% of the community sample was female.

Scoring, Scale Norms, and Distribution

Lawton and Bader (1970, pp. 50–51) presented data on the percentage of respondents aged 60, 70, and 80 and older who preferred privacy. In general, the respondents wanted privacy.

Usability on Older Populations

No special problems were mentioned.

Reference

Lawton, M. P., and J. Bader. "Wish for Privacy by Young and Old." *Journal of Gerontology*, 1970, 25 (1): 48–54.

Instrument

See Instrument VI.8.II.c.

HOUSING SATISFACTION QUESTIONNAIRE
M. P. Lawton, M. H. Kleban, and M. Singer, 1971

Definition of Variable or Concept

Housing satisfaction is defined as how well the respondents like the dwelling unit and the neighborhood, whether they want to move, and whether they looked for a new place during the previous year.

Description of Instrument

The four-item questionnaire has both open- and closed-ended responses. No special procedures for question development were mentioned.

Method of Administration

The questions are administered in approximately 10 to 15 minutes by interview. No special skills for administration are necessary.

Context of Development and Subsequent Use

This study deals with how urban elderly people cope with their physical environment, which increasingly fails to support their special needs as the individuals get older. Housing satisfaction is seen as one indicator of successful coping.

Sample

The sample consisted of 115 low-income, Jewish elderly people aged 60 and over.

References

Lawton, M. P., M. H. Kleban, and M. Singer. *The Elderly Jew in an Urban Slum.* Philadelphia: Philadelphia Geriatric Center, 1970 (mimeographed report).
_____ . "The Aged Jewish Person and the Slum Environment." *Journal of Gerontology*, 1971, 26 (2): 231–39.

Instrument

The exact form of this instrument is not available at this time.

ENVIRONMENTAL VARIABLES QUESTIONNAIRE
M. P. Lawton, L. Nahemow, and J. Teaff 1975

Definition of Variable or Concept

This instrument is designed to measure four physical characteristics of planned housing environments and their neighborhoods: sponsorship (public housing versus housing built by nonprofit organizations under section 202 of the 1959 Housing Act), community size (total population), building size (the number of units for the elderly), and building height (the number of floors in the building).

Description of Instrument

This four-item battery consists of a simple checklist indicating either the presence or absence of an amenity or the amount of an environmental amenity.

Method of Administration

Data are collected by observation and institutional records.

Context of Development and Subsequent Use

This instrument was part of a larger instrument used to study the relationship between the physical factors in the housing environment and the well-being of elderly tenants. Specifically, the study tested Barker's hypothesis that group size determines the intensity of participation by group members.

Sample

The sample was comprised of 2,457 elderly subjects from a probability sample of 3,654 elderly people in the United States. These tenants resided in housing projects sponsored under the HUD low-rent public housing program and the section 202 program. The projects were at least three years old in 1971.

Usability on Older Populations

No special problems were discerned.

Reference

Lawton, M. P., L. Nahemow, and J. Teaff. "Housing Characteristics and the Well-being of Elderly Tenants in Federally Assisted Housing." *Journal of Gerontology*, 1975, 30 (5): 601–7.

Instrument

There is no special material for this instrument. Data on the four environmental characteristics (listed above in the definition of the variable or concept) are gathered from institutional records.

INDIRECT ASSESSMENT OF SOCIAL INTERACTION
M. P. Lawton and B. Simon, 1968

Definition of Variable or Concept

The concepts are (1) proximity—defined as the physical distance from the subject's apartment to a chosen friend's apartment expressed in terms of own-floor versus other-floor sociometric choice; (2) percentage of open apartment doors—thought to be an environmental expression of desire for interaction; and (3) percentage of tenants present in functional, social, outdoor, and common spaces.

Description of Instrument

This battery of three questions is administered by both interview and observation. The proximity question is a dichotomous choice of own floor versus other floor; the other two items involve simple incidence recording. The three items take approximately 30 minutes to complete in a moderate-size building. No special requirements for administration were mentioned.

Context of Development and Subsequent Use

An increased opportunity for social relationships is an important advantage often cited for living in planned congregate housing. Lawton's docility hypotheses—i.e., as the individual increases in competence, he or she is less affected by physical environment—suggests that certain physical features of the housing environment may facilitate or hinder the social interaction of the tenants. This portion of the study was an attempt to investigate the effects of proximity, incidence of open doors, and ecological distribution of social behavior on the social interaction of tenants.

Sample

The study sample was comprised of 464 elderly residents of housing sites in a small city and a large metropolitan area. Subjects in the sample ranged from low- to middle-income levels and were aged 62 and over.

Scoring, Scale Norms, and Distribution

Lawton and Simon (1968) presented descriptive data for this battery of items.

Formal Tests of Validity

The number of open doors was found to correlate with the number of friends mentioned and with same-floor sociometric choice.

Reference

Lawton, M. P., and B. Simon. "The Ecology of Social Relationships in Housing for the Elderly." *The Gerontologist*, 1968, 8: 108-15.

Instrument

There are no special materials for this instrument. (See the description of the instrument above.)

EFFECT OF RETIREMENT HOUSING QUESTIONNAIRE
S. Sherman, 1971

Definition of Variable or Concept

This questionnaire assesses three dimensions of housing preference: the reasons for moving into retirement housing, the advantages and disadvantages of living in retirement housing, and the most attractive and the least attractive features of the site.

Description of Instrument

This five-item questionnaire elicits open-ended responses from subjects. No item-development procedures were mentioned.

Method of Administration

The instrument is administered by interview in approximately 15 to 20 minutes. No special requirements for administration were mentioned.

Context of Development and Subsequent Use

This study has emerged from the age-integrated versus age-segregated housing controversy. Specifically, the questionnaire explores the motivation for choosing retirement housing, the choice of site, and how the housing situation matches up to the respondents' expectations.

Sample

The sample was comprised of 100 residents for each of six widely varied retirement facilities. Also studied were 600 matched controls living in conventional dwellings.

Scoring, Scale Norms, and Distribution

Sherman (1971) presented descriptive data on each question for each site. For example, 73% of the sample stressed maintenance as a reason for moving to any retirement community, while quality (68%) and proximity to services (62%) were reasons for choosing a particular site. The main advantage of living in a retirement community was the opportunity to meet people, and the main disadvantages were too many old, boring, and dying people (29%) and lack of privacy (26%).

References

Sherman, S. "The Choice of Retirement Housing among the Well Elderly." *Aging and Human Development*, 1971, 2 (2): 118–38.

Walkley, R. P., W. P. Mangum, Jr., S. R. Sherman, S. Dodds, and D. M. Wilner *Retirement Housing in California*. Berkeley, Calif.: Diablo Press, 1966.

Instrument

See Instrument V1.8.II.g.

INTEREST IN SEGREGATED HOUSING QUESTIONNAIRE
L. Winiecke, 1973

Definition of Variable or Concept

This instrument is intended to measure older people's interest in segregated housing.

Description of Instrument

This two-item questionnaire elicits both open-ended and fixed responses.

Method of Administration

No special skills or instructions for the administration of these interview questions were mentioned.

Context of Development and Subsequent Use

This instrument was part of a larger instrument used to explore the background, current activity, and morale of elderly persons who would consider living in age-dense housing as opposed to those who would not.

Sample

Data were gathered from 235 noninstitutionalized people who were approved for receiving assistance in the Old Age Assistance Program.

Scale Norms and Distribution

Winiecke (1973) presented data on the characteristics of those interested in special housing.

Usability on Older Populations

The questionnaire seems to be appropriate for the elderly; no special problems were mentioned.

Reference

Winiecke, L. "The Appeal of Age Segregated Housing to the Elderly Poor." *International Journal of Aging and Human Development*, 1973, 4 (4): 293–305.

Instrument

See Instrument V1.8.II.h.

FEAR IN ENVIRONMENT
B. D. Lebowitz, 1975

Definition of Variable or Concept

This single-item indicator assesses fear of personal and structural factors associated with walking around the subject's neighborhood.

Description of Instrument

The item is worded as follows: "Is there any area right around here—that is, within a mile—where you would be afraid to walk alone at night?"

Method of Administration

Data are collected through personal interviews.

Context of Development and Subsequent Use

Recent research in the quality of life has identified a sense of security as a significant component. Taking its negative—fear—this item assessed the personal and structural factors associated with fear in walking around the neighborhood.

Sample

Data for the study came from the National Opinion Research Center's 1973 general survey sample of 1,504 noninstitutionalized adults residing in the continental United States, of which 314 were over the age of 60.

Scale Norms and Distribution

Of those over age 60, 56% of those living alone and 41% of those living with others reported environmental fear. Other cross-tabulations are presented in Lebowitz (1975, pp. 697–99).

Usability on Older Population

No special problems were observed.

Reference

Lebowitz, B. D. "Age and Fearfulness: Personal and Situational Factors." *Journal of Gerontology*, 1975, 30 (6): 696–700.

Instrument

See the description of the instrument above.

SATISFACTION WITH THE SITE
S. R. Sherman, W. P. Mangum, Jr., S. Dodds, R. P. Walkley, and D. M. Wilner, 1968

Definition of Variable or Concept

Satisfaction with the site is considered to be an indicator of general housing satisfaction.

Description of Instrument

This single-item indicator is worded as follows: "Now that you have lived at the site for a period of time, how do you like it?" (Possible responses were a lot, quite a bit, only a little, not at all, no answer.)

Method of Administration

Data are collected through personal interviews.

Context of Development and Subsequent Use

This item was part of a larger instrument used to assess the effects of age-segregated retirement housing on social interaction and recreation.

Sample

The sample was comprised of 100 residents for each of six widely varied retirement facilities. Also studied were 600 matched controls living in conventional housing.

Scoring, Scale Norms, and Distribution

When the instrument was scored on a scale of 1–4, Sherman and associates (1968) reported an overall mean of 3.6.

Reference

Sherman, S. R., W. P. Mangum, Jr., S. Dodds, R. P. Walkley, and D. M. Wilner. "Psychological Effects of Retirement Housing." *The Gerontologist*, 1968, 8 (3, part 1): 170–75.

Instrument

See the description of the instrument above.

FACTORS INFLUENCING THE ABANDONING OF PRIVATE HOMES BY THE ELDERLY
L. A. Pastalan, 1977

Definition of Variable or Concept

This checklist is designed to identify and evaluate environmental factors exerting an important influence on elderly people deciding to abandon private housing and to seek shelter in age-segregated institutional settings.

Description of Instrument

The checklist has 17 main items, with several subitems for each. The 17 main items are: (1) type of single-family dwelling, and the condition of its (2) roof, (3) exterior walls, (4) exterior stairs, (5) interior stairs, (6) entrance doors to dwelling unit, (7) electrical system, (8) water system, (9) heating system, (10) bathroom, (11) sleeping area, (12) kitchen, (13) living room, (14) garage, (15) neighborhood and site, and the presence of (16) support services and (17) security features.

Method of Administration

Personal interviews and observation techniques are used to gather these data.

Context of Development and Subsequent Use

The ultimate purpose of the study was to develop specific guidelines for housing design and community programs that would help senior citizens continue to live independently in their own homes.

Sample

The sample consisted of 180 elderly individuals aged 62 and over who were selected from waiting lists for public housing. Of the sample 10% was black.

Reference

Pastalan, L. A. *Factors Influencing the Abandoning of Private Homes by the Elderly.* Ann Arbor, Mich.: Institute of Gerontology, University of Michigan, 1977.

Instrument

This instrument is not reproduced here because of its length and complicated graphic format.

Instruments

V1.8.I.a
TERRITORIAL BEHAVIOR REPORT SCALE
L. Koob and G. Fish, 1976

Control Sub-scale

I walk up the street to the store whenever I want to.

I say something to a stranger who does not look like a visitor.

When I see someone behaving improperly in the lobby, I speak to that person before I go to anyone else.

When someone comes to interview me, I sit at a table with them.

I talk to my neighbor directly across the hall.

I go back to my apartment when there is not a free washer for my laundry.

I do not go into the recreation room alone at night.

I tell someone who is standing in the middle of the hall that they are blocking the way for others.

I tell someone who interrupts me in my apartment to wait a minute.

I go to the mailboxes the same time many other residents do.

I walk in the opposite direction when I see someone I don't get along with.

I sit facing the door of my apartment.

I volunteer to sit at the front desk near the main entrance.

I call my friends on the phone instead of dropping in on them.

I tell others that people should not stand or sit near the main entrance.

Demarcation Sub-scale

I put a piece of furniture between my sleeping and sitting areas. (efficiencies only)

I use more than one washer for my laundry when I do it.

When someone asks, I give my opinion of color and furniture for the lounge.

When asked, I give my opinion of paint color and decoration for the recreation room.

When someone asks, I give my opinion of paint color and carpeting for the lobby.

When I go for a little walk, I go to the next hill up or down the street.

I sit so I can see out of the window of my apartment.

When someone asks, I give my opinion of paint color for another floor of the building.

I put many pictures on my walls and other things around my apartment.

I put my name on my door myself, each time I need to.

I keep flowers or other plants in front of my window.

I fold my clothes at the same place each time I do wash.

When someone asks, I give my opinion of paint color for the laundry.

I sit in the lounge.

I rearrange some of my furniture.

Defense Sub-scale

I ask to be consulted before any changes are made in my apartment.

I close the door of my bedroom when I have a visitor. (residents of one-bedrooms)

I keep a piece of furniture between my sleeping and sitting areas. (efficiencies)

I am disturbed when I hear anyone criticize this building.

When a friend stays too long I let them know when I want them to leave.

When I see someone drop paper on the recreation room floor, I tell them to pick it up.

I go to the manager when I think a neighbor is causing an insect problem.

I tell the manager if I see someone spill soap on the floor and not clean up.

When I hear a noise outside my apartment door, I look to see what is the cause.

When a neighbor is not home, I tell someone knocking at the door that no one is home and ask what they want.

I agree when anyone complains about the appearance of the lobby.

I move someone's laundry when it is in my way in the laundry.

I keep my chain lock fastened in the daytime.

I ask strangers what they want and who they are before I open my door.

When a neighbor makes too much noise in their apartment, I ask them what they are doing.

I tell the manager if I see people regularly walking across our property.

SOURCE: L. Koob and G. Fish. *Measuring Territorial Behavior of Elderly People in Public Housing*. Department of Housing and Applied Design, University of Maryland, 1976. Reprinted by permission.

V1.8.I.b
NEED FOR SERVICES INDEX
M. P. Lawton, 1969

Questions asked varied according to residence.

Community residents: There are some apartment houses for older people being built where . . . (service) is included in the rent. Would you like to live in a place like that, even if . . . (service) . . . might cost more?

Applicants and tenants in buildings where no service is offered: There are some apartment buildings being built where . . . (service) . . . is included in the rent. Would you like these arrangements in the new building, even though it might cost more?

Tenants where service was offered: Would you prefer that there was no . . . (service) . . . here?

The ten services in the composite factor apparently are: (1) Would eat lunch frequently if available on site; (2) wants social worker added to staff; (3) wishes meal service on site; (4) wants activity worker added to staff; (5) would utilize social worker; (6) prefers extensive medical service; (7) not enough activities on site; (8) wants maid service on site; (9) will like the new building (pre-occupancy); and (10) site not near enough to shopping. (Source: Lawton, 1969:18)

It appears that one additional service did not load on the composite factor: desire for a doctor or nurse to be nearby (Lawton, 1969:18).

SOURCE: M. P. Lawton. "Supportive Services in the Context of the Housing Environment." *The Gerontologist*, 1969, 9 (1): 15–19. Reprinted by permission of author and publisher.

V1.8.I.c
ENVIRONMENTAL DESCRIPTION FACTORS
M. P. Lawton and J. Cohen, 1974

The exact form of this instrument is not available at this time.

V1.8.I.d
ENVIRONMENTAL RESPONSE INVENTORY
G. McKechnie, 1970

This copyrighted instrument is available from the Consulting Psychologists Press, Palo Alto, Calif.

V1.8.I.e
PRIVACY PREFERENCE SCALE
L. A. Pastalan and N. Bourestom, 1975
PART III: PRIVACY

A. Privacy Preference Scale

LEAD IN : Solitude

    a. Would you like to have a private place which no one could enter without asking you?

        _____ Yes

        _____ No

    b. Do you dislike being completely alone?

        _____ Yes

        _____ N o

    c. Do you think there should be a place in the hospital where a person could get away from the staff for a while if he wants to?

        _____ Yes

        _____ No

    d. Do you sometimes want to get away from everyone for awhile even close friends?

        _____ Yes

        _____ No

    e. If you had curtains around your bed would you probably keep them closed most of the time?

        _____ Yes

        _____ No

S-2 : Intimacy

    a. Do you get annoyed if someone interrupts you when you are involved in a serious conversation with close friends?

        _____ Yes

        _____ No

    b. Is it important to be able to confide in someone and know that your confidence will be kept?

        _____ Yes

        _____ No

    c. Do you like to have someone who you can tell everything about yourself, even your deepest and most personal thoughts and feelings?

        _____ Yes

        _____ No

    d. Do you like to live where people do things together now and then?

        _____ Yes

        _____ No

   e. Would you be upset if a friend read something you had written without
      your permission?
      _____ Yes
      _____ No

<u>S-3</u>   : Anonymity

   a. I always like to be a part of a group.
      _____ Yes
      _____ No
   b. Is it important to you to live where you can do what you want to with-
      out bothering other people?
      _____ Yes
      _____ No
   c. Does too many people living in one room get on your nerves?
      _____ Yes
      _____ No
   d. Would you like a hospital where patients didn't visit much and it was
      difficult to get to know them?
      _____ Yes
      _____ No
   e. Do you like living in a place where people notice you coming and
      going?
      _____ Yes
      _____ No

<u>S-4</u>   : Reserve

   a. Do people who work around here often ask questions that are rude and
      personal?
      _____ Yes
      _____ No
   b. Do you mind people knowing about you and your actions, as long as
      they don't try to interfere?
      _____ Yes
      _____ No
   c. Are there times when people know you don't want to be intruded
      upon?
      _____ Yes
      _____ No
   d. Is it usually annoying when people come to see you without letting you
      know they are coming?
      _____ Yes
      _____ No
   e. When you really need to find a solution for a problem do you like to
      talk with others about it?
      _____ Yes
      _____ No

SOURCE: L. A. Pastalan and N. Bourestom. *Forced Relocation: Setting, Staff, and Patients.*
Ann Arbor, Mich.: Institute of Gerontology, University of Michigan, 1975. Reprinted by
permission.

V1.8.I.f
ENVIRONMENTAL CHARACTERISTICS FACTORS
K. Schooler, 1970

The exact form of the instrument is not available at this time.

V1.8.I.g
ENVIRONMENTAL DISPOSITION SCALES
P. G. Windley, 1972

This instrument includes line drawings for each item, and so it is too long to be reproduced here.

V1.8.II.a
USER SURVEY INTERVIEW SCHEDULE
M. J. Audain and E. Huttman, no date

This instrument, with its elaborate tabular format, is too long to be reproduced here.

V1.8.II.b
SATISFACTION WITH LIVING ENVIRONMENT QUESTIONNAIRE
E. M. Brody, M. H. Kleban, and B. Liebowitz, 1975

1. Would you say that your present living environment is: very bad; bad; average; good; very good?
2. How much do you like the neighborhood (3 point scale)?
3. How much do you like living in this house/apartment (3 point scale)?
4. With things as they are now, would you like to move? (yes or no)

SOURCE: E. M. Brody, M. H. Kleban, B. Liebowitz. "Intermediate Housing for the Elderly: Satisfaction of Those Who Moved In and Those Who Did Not." *The Gerontologist*, 1975, 15 (4): 350. Reprinted by permission of authors and publisher.

V1.8.II.c
WISH FOR PRIVACY QUESTIONNAIRE
M. P. Lawton and J. Bader, 1970

1. Do you have a roommate?
2. If you were single and in good health, and had your choice, (alternate questionnaire: and living in a home for the aged) would you rather have a room by yourself (single room), with one other person (double), or with more than one person?
3. If you were sick enough to have to stay in bed a couple of hours a day (alternate questionnaire: and you were living in a home for the aged) would you prefer living in a room by yourself (single room), with one other person (double room), or with more than one person?
4. Do you think it is better for the average older person who lives in a home for the aged to be in a room by himself, with one other person, or with more than one person?

SOURCE: M. P. Lawton and J. Bader. "Wish for Privacy by Young and Old." *Journal of Gerontology*, 1970, 25 (1): 48-54. Reprinted by permission of authors and publisher.

V1.8.II.d
HOUSING SATISFACTION QUESTIONNAIRE
M. P. Lawton, M. H. Kleban, and M. Singer, 1971

The exact form of the instrument is not available at this time.

V1.8.II.e
ENVIRONMENTAL VARIABLES QUESTIONNAIRE
M. P. Lawton, L. Nahemow, and J. Teaff, 1975

There is no special material for this instrument. Data on the four environmental characteristics (listed in the definition of the variable or concept in the abstract) are gathered from institutional records.

V1.8.II.f
INDIRECT ASSESSMENT OF SOCIAL INTERACTION
M. P. Lawton and B. Simon, 1968

There are no special materials for this instrument. (See the description of the instrument in the abstract.)

V1.8.II.g
EFFECT OF RETIREMENT HOUSING QUESTIONNAIRE
S. Sherman, 1971

Reasons for Moving

1. What were your reasons for moving to some retirement housing facility?
2. What were your reasons for choosing this particular site?

Advantages and Disadvantages in Housing

1. What do you think are the advantages of living in retirement housing?
2. What do you think are the disadvantages of living in retirement housing?

Attractiveness of the Site

1. Can you name the one thing you liked *best* about the site and the one thing you liked *least*?

SOURCE: S. Sherman. "The Choice of Retirement Housing among the Well Elderly." *Aging and Human Development*, 1971, 2 (2): 118-38. Reprinted by permission of author and publisher.

V1.8.II.h
INTEREST IN SEGREGATED HOUSING QUESTIONNAIRE
L. Winiecke, 1973

1. How do you feel about special housing centers or apartment buildings for old people? Do you think they are a good idea or not?
2. Would you ever like to try living in a place like that?

SOURCE: L. Winiecke. "The Appeal of Age Segregated Housing to the Elderly Poor." *International Journal of Aging and Human Development*, 1973, 4 (4): 293-305. Reprinted by permission.

V1.8.III.a
FEAR IN ENVIRONMENT
B. D. Lebowitz, 1975

See the description of the instrument in the abstract.

V1.8.III.b
SATISFACTION WITH THE SITE
S. R. Sherman, W. P. Mangum, Jr., S. Dodds, R. P. Walkley, and D. M. Wilner, 1968

See the description of the instrument in the abstract.

V1.8.IV.a
FACTORS INFLUENCING ABANDONMENT OF PRIVATE HOMES BY ELDERLY
L. A. Pastalan, 1977

The instrument is not reproduced here because of its length and complicated graphic format.

Chapter 9

Ethnic Group Identification

Ron Manuel

The impact of ethnicity on behavior in old age is an important area of study in social gerontology. This is due, in part, to the realization that neither theoretical understanding nor social intervention on behalf of the aged is likely to be successful unless variations in the sociocultural antecedents of present conditions among the aged are understood. This chapter focuses on the state of the art in measuring the social psychological impact of some of these antecedent cultural experiences among the aged. The chapter begins with a brief discussion of the concept of ethnic identification. This is followed by a study of the theoretical issues pertinent in establishing measures for the concept. Next, these issues are used as the basis for an evaluative overview of several specific measures of ethnic identification that have been used with older respondents. Some future directions for the study of ethnic identification of the aged are examined in the fourth section, and the chapter concludes with a systematic and detailed review of each of the three measures of ethnic identification that have been used with elderly samples.

The Concept of Ethnic Group Identification

Kurt Lewin (1948) observed that individuals need a sense of identification with an in-group in order to develop a sense of individual well-being. This is as true for the elderly as it is for the young. Moreover, an individual's group identity throughout life has definite consequences for his or her experience of life during later years. As such, ethnic identification has become an important variable for study in gerontology. Given this importance, the first question is what is an ethnic group? An ethnic group is generally understood to be a collection of persons who subjectively conceive of themselves as being similar and/or persons who are so regarded by others. Isajiw (1974), however, identified over 25 definitions of the concept. It is sufficient to conclude that most of these definitions stress the individual's distinct *sense of culture*, which is fostered by his or her participation or identification with a specified group.

Cultural factors are useful in understanding the numerous bases around which an ethnic group may be formed. Some of these factors are religious beliefs, language patterns, birthplace or national origin, minority status, and even racial characteristics. Frequently, an ethnic group is constituted as a result of a combination of these factors. For example, a Mexican American might perceive himself or herself (or be perceived by others) as unique by virtue of his or her physical characteristics, language patterns, aesthetic traditions, birthplace, and minority status.

Although such considerations are important, the objective of this chapter is not so much a sociological discussion of ethnicity as it is a social-psychological discussion. Another question, therefore, concerns the relationship of the individual to the experiences associated with the group with which he or she identifies. Erikson (1950, p. 213) observed that "the ego identity develops out of a gradual integration of all identifications." Ethnic group identity—as one among other identities—refers to the individual's affirmation of a specified group label and its associated cultural basis.

This conceptualization suggests that ethnic identity is more than merely applying a label. Herman (1977) suggested that questions must be raised in regard to (1) which group attributes the individual sees in himself or herself, (2) how he or she feels about these attributes, and (3) how he or she behaves in regard to the attributes associated with the group. It is probable, given these factors, that there is individual variation in the extent to which group identity is reflected in a particular individual. The more that the individual perceives the group attributes as belonging to himself or herself, the more he or she is favorably predisposed toward this perception; and, the more he or she acts in accordance with these attributes, the more he or she may be identified with the ethnic label. Accordingly, all persons from Polish backgrounds are not equally Polish, and all elderly black Americans are not equally black. Indeed, in the case of the marginal black, it is questionable whether he or she identifies at all—beyond a nominal reference to it—with his or her clearly observable ethnic status.

The conceptualization outlined here makes evident a clear demarcation between two approaches that have been used in measuring ethnic identification. In the first instance, the effort is merely one of identifying the ethnic label that an individual applies to himself or herself. The question is, is the respondent Polish, Jewish, Mexican American, . . . ? This procedure represents a nominal (categorical) approach to the measurement of ethnic group identification. In the second approach, the effort is one of ascertaining the extent to which one identifies with a particular ethnic label; this approach is represented—at its best—by an interval (metric) measure and—at a minimum—by an ordinal (rank) measure. Asserting that one "feels more (or much more) comfortable with Jewish persons relative to non-Jewish persons" or that one—as a black American—"has had less of a chance than whites to participate fully in American institutions" is indicative of the *extent* to which one *more or less* identifies with the culture of a group.

Like many other social scientists, social gerontologists have rarely applied ordinal or interval measures of ethnic identification. Rather, because of their limited time and resources, most gerontological studies have usually applied single-item indicators of ethnicity. The investigator may judge the ethnicity of the respondent personally. Reynolds and Kalish (1974) used this procedure in order to identify white, black, Mexican, and Asian American aged subsamples. Reynolds and Kalish indicated their concern about using this method; they noted that, in order to militate against marginally identified ethnic respondents, they selected their ethnic subsamples from census tracts with high ethnic-specific concentrations.

There is a second procedure for applying the single-item indicator of ethnicity. The investigator may permit the respondent to classify himself or herself in terms of a limited number of categories. Greeley (1974)—using information on race, religion, language, and nationality —created a categorical variable called "religious-ethnic group identification." The categories of this variable included: Protestant (British, German, Scandinavian, Irish, other), Catholic (Irish, German, Italian, Polish, Spanish-speaking, other), Jewish, black, other religion, and no religion.

In summary, a primary issue in discussing gerontological measures of ethnic identification is related to the utility of a measure in permitting observations of the extent of identification. That is, a central question is whether the measure represents information at the nominal level or at the ordinal level. Most gerontological studies, to date, have not been characterized by the study of variation in the *extent* of ethnic identification.

There are a few studies with older age cohorts that have examined the relative extensiveness of ethnic identification. It is toward the examination of the measures in these studies that the rest of this discussion is directed. The central objective is to outline the range of measures available for use by gerontologists in measuring ethnic group identification. In pursuing this objective, it is useful, first, to identify some of the major criteria that can be applied in evaluations of the relative utility of these measures.

Criteria of Evaluation

There are at least four important criteria for determining the usefulness of the various instruments used for ethnic identification measurement. The importance of measures that reflect variability in the amount of identification has been discussed, and it is not necessary to comment further on this criterion.

A second criterion is whether the measure reflects the multidimensionality that is inherent in the concept. Several investigators (e.g., Driedger, 1976a; Herman, 1977) have stressed the necessity of incorporating attitudinal, behavioral, and cognitive dimensions in measuring ethnic group identification. Other investigators have emphasized the importance of including religious measures or measures of various aesthetic traditions as dimensions around which ethnic identification can be observed. To develop a measure that incorporates both of these sets of dimensions is a task that has largely been neglected.

Actually, to reflect the complete multidimensionality of ethnic identification is an even more complex task than it has already been suggested that it is. Consider the following items: (1) "Regardless of their ability and effort, how much do you think the question of race helps or hinders the opportunity of black people in this community" (Hraba and Siegman, 1974, p. 72); (2) "I feel more comfortable with Polish people" (Sandberg, 1972, p. 62). Both statements are attitudinal and so are not distinguished by the usual dimensional constructs. The first statement implies a subjective identification of ego with a historical group experience. The second statement is ahistorical; it is concerned with a subjective identification of ego with a specifically identified and immediate other. It is sufficient, at this point, to stress the importance of being aware of which dimension of ethnic identification is being measured. To be less than aware of this criterion is to invite the possibility of contradictory conclusions about the ethnic identification of an individual merely because one investigator studies one dimension while another studies another dimension.

The cross-ethnic generality of a measure of ethnic identification is a third criterion. The primary question is whether a paper-and-pencil scale—developed to measure, say, Jewish identification among the aged—can be applied to elderly black Americans with only minor changes in a few key words. Consider the statement: "When an important newspaper insults the Jewish people, I feel that it is insulting me" (Zak, 1973, p. 896). With a minor change, the statement could be changed to: "When an important newspaper insults any black American, I feel that it is insulting me." If ethnic group identification measures could be applied cross-ethnically, a large contribution would be made toward the standardization of research involving the ethnic variable.

The standardization of measures of ethnic group identification could also be improved if investigators would supply statistical information on the accuracy of their measures for aged samples—this constitutes the fourth and final criterion by which ethnic identification measures can be evaluated. In this realm, it is important (1) to identify theoretically a wide range of items reflective of the psychological dimension, (2) to provide information on the normative response modes typical of various social categories of older people, and (3) to report on the measurement accuracy (validity and reliability) of the items. The importance of theoretically assembling a large array of items has been observed. Statistical summaries (e.g., means and standard deviations) of the response patterns to the measurement items among various social categories provide potential users with information on the applicability of the measure for their own samples. Finally, factor analysis of the responses to the measurement items has proven to be a useful procedure for gaining estimates of the measure's accuracy in other content areas. It can be expected to have similar advantages for investigators of ethnic group identification.

With this introduction to the criteria for good social-psychological measurement, it is possible to summarize the relative merits of the few measures of ethnic group identification that have been used with older samples.

An Overview of the Measures of Ethnic Group Identification

Three measures of ethnic group identification are briefly examined. These include the Group Cohesiveness Scale (Sandberg, 1972), the Ethnic Identity Questionnaire (Masuda, Matsumoto, and Meredith, 1970), and Jewish Identification (Shapiro, 1974).

The measure that seems most impressive is the Group Cohesiveness Scale. The scale is commendable largely because of the potential that it has. With only minor changes in a few key words, the scale could be made cross-ethnically versatile. For example, the item "The public schools should teach more about the contribution of Polish people to America" could easily be applied to any number of ethnic groups. Moreover, the scale items have been identified as to their relevance to cultural, national, and religious dimensions of ethnic identification. An interesting question remains, however, what is the dimensional structure of the 30-item Group Cohesiveness Scale in regard to (1) the attitudinal, cognitive, and behavioral dimensions, and (2) the historical and ahistorical components of each of the attitudinal, cognitive, and behavioral dimensions?

The Group Cohesiveness Scale is outstanding for its potential usefulness in a second area. Given the clear theoretical conceptualization represented by the scale items—despite the limitations already noted —the measure would be quite amenable to an empirical assessment of the extent to which the items do in fact represent the hypothesized dimensions. This should represent the next step in establishing the validity and reliability of the instrument.

The Ethnic Identity Questionnaire (EIQ) is also commendable because a large number of the items on the measure could easily be applied to groups other than Japanese Americans. This is true of the EIQ, however, to a much more limited extent than it is true of the Group Cohesiveness Scale. For example, a much greater number of the measurement items—albeit still a minority of the total number of items—would call for more than a few key word changes. The items that would have to be significantly revised include numbers 1, 2, 8, 9, 12, 14, 16, 18, 19, 20, 24, 26, 30, 32, 34, 41, 46, 47, and 49. Therefore, it would be necessary for potential users of these scale items to examine the applicability of each with respect to the unique cultural background factors of the ethnic groups to be studied.

Although the issue of the multidimensionality of the items was broached by the authors of the measure, they did not provide enough information to help the reader identify the items reflective of various dimensions. For example, Masuda, Hasegawa, and Matsumoto (1973) observed that some items reflect preferences for Japanese things, personality characteristics, child-rearing customs, and so forth. The potential user of the measure, however, is left with the task of theoretically identifying the dimensionality of the specific items on the measure. As was true with the Group Cohesivenes Scale, other considerations in regard to the dimensionality of the EIQ have not been addressed. Similarly, there is little information about the reliability of the measure, and moreover, there is no information about the empirical assessment of the theoretical conceptualization underlying the items.

The last measure that is reviewed is the Jewish Identification Index. With more effort than would be necessary in using the Group Cohesiveness Scale or the Ethnic Identity Questionnaire, the Jewish Identification Index could also be made useful as a cross-ethnically versatile measure. This is due largely to the religion-specific nature of the content of the items on the instrument.

The measure is a unidimensional one by theoretical and empirical design. That is, using a one-factor solution for assessing the set of theoretically hypothesized indicators, Shapiro (1974) provided the first statistically standardized measure that has been used with older respondents. This fact makes the measure a particularly attractive one, and confidence can be placed in the validity of the measure. Shapiro (1974) did not use the factor weights in applying the scale in his study; with the information given, however, the instrument would be quite amenable to further scale analysis and estimation of factor scores through regression weighting techniques.

On the other hand, given this one-factor solution, the potential user of this measure is left with the task of deciding whether the items would reflect the exact information desired. The items are almost totally attitudinal. An investigator wanting a more behaviorally oriented measure would not find this measure very helpful.

On a more practical level, the 14-item Jewish Identification Index —when compared to the 30-item Group Cohesiveness Scale and the 50-item Ethnic Identity Questionnaire—is short enough to be used easily in conjunction with additional measures among aged subjects.

In conclusion, each of these measures represents a tested set of procedures for observing ethnic group identification among elderly respondents. Although the measures have their limitations, each is an important and innovative procedure for observing the extent of ethnic group identification.

Directions for Future Research

Before proceeding to an in-depth examination of the three measures, it may be useful—given the few measures of ethnic identification that have been used by gerontologists—to refer briefly to a few of the investigations of ethnic identification described in social science literature. It is in this literature that some new directions may be found by social gerontologists who would like to consider additional procedures for measuring ethnic identification.

The study of Jewish identification has received the most concentrated attention. This is indicated by a brief look at the literature. Even during the early 1950s, Lazerwitz (1953) had identified both behavioral and attitudinal categories in Jewish identification, and Geismar (1954) had already expressed concern over establishing the validity of a 127-item questionnaire on Jewish identification. The work in this area, however, has been limited to student and/or young samples.

Experimentation in the methodology of measuring Jewish identification has also been quite evident. Hofman (1970) has used the semantic differential in his studies of Jewish identification. Rollins (1973), noting previous research that had shown that persons highly identified with an issue tend to use significantly fewer categories for sorting attitudinal items related to their issue, operationalized ethnic identification by applying the Own Categories Card Sort. In this procedure, respondents are assumed to be more ethnically identified when they use fewer categories than others of their group in categorizing attitudinal items related to their group. Recently, Zak (1976) has been concerned with the generality of Jewish identity measures. He has shown that statements can be formulated so that, with key word changes, the items can be shown to be relevant to American, Arab, or Jewish identity.

Another realm of research in the study of ethnic identification is represented by the work by Leo Driedger. Driedger (1976a) constructed a scale of ethnic self-identity. This is a promising measure because its items are constructed in such a manner that they are immediately applicable no matter what the ethnic content of a group is. For example, statements such as "I am a person who feels strong bonds with my own ethnic group" or "I am a person who is annoyed to give his ethnic identity" could be used to elicit the extent of identification from a large array of ethnically versatile samples.

Driedger's work is also important for gerontologists because he is the only investigator (to this writer's knowledge) who, in establishing the validity of his measure, has explicitly incorporated regression weights for the individual measurement items. This weighting permits the investigator to determine the individual importance of each item for the overall measure.

There is a third and final area in the social science literature on measuring ethnic identification of which gerontologists should be aware. It is important to recognize that, with limited time and resources for obtaining data from elderly samples, it may not always be feasible to consider using 30- or 50-item (or even 10- or 15-item) measures of one variable. This is especially true when ethnicity is one among a number of variables to be observed in a research instrument. It is, therefore, important that investigators be aware of short batteries of items that, although they are not as good as some other measures, still permit observations of the *extent* of variation in ethnic group identification. For example, in a study of Polish immigrants, Mostwin (1972, p. 313) included the following three items as measures of ethnic identity:

(1) Do you consider yourself primarily Polish or primarily American?
   1. Polish
   2. American
(2) How do you think Americans consider you?
   1. American
   2. Polish
(3) How do you think Poles in Poland consider you?
   1. American
   2. Polish

On the basis of their pattern of responding to these items, respondents were classified according to the consistency of the expression of their ethnic identity.

In a recent investigation, Gutmann and associates (1975, pp. 309-10), using an elderly sample, applied a battery of items for measuring ethnic identification. Their measurement indicators included:

(1) Do you consider yourself part of a nationality group, a racial group or ethnic group. (If yes) Which one?

No	Italian
White	Mexican
Black	Czech
Other Race	Hungarian
English	Jewish
Polish	German
Irish	Other Nationalization or Ethnic Group

(2) Do you feel

Very close	Moderately close
Somewhat close	Not at all close
to your group?	

(3) About how many of your friends belong to the same group?

No friends	None	1 to 5	5 to 10
All or most			

Data from this measure of ethnic identification have not, to date, been presented in any of Gutmann's analyses. It is for this reason that this measure was not included among the set of measures used with elderly samples reviewed in this chapter.

In conclusion, the reader is reminded that the measures discussed in this section have, for the most part, not been used with aged samples. The procedures represented by these measures have, however, extended the knowledge base in regard to issues that need to be considered in accurate measurements of identification among the aged.

Summary

Relatively few studies have attempted to move beyond the nominal level of measurement in assessing ethnic group identification among elderly people. The three that are reviewed in detail in the abstracts that follow provide promising leads in assessing this phenomenon. They are listed in Table 9-1.

TABLE 9-1
Instruments Reviewed in Chapter 9

Instrument	Author (date)	Code Number
Group Cohesiveness Scale	Sandberg (1972)	V1.9.I.a
Ethnic Identity Questionnaire	Masuda, Matsumoto, and Meredith (1970)	V1.9.I.b
Jewish Identification Index	Shapiro (1974)	V1.9.I.c

REFERENCES

Driedger, L. "Ethnic Self-Identity: A Comparison of Ingroup Evaluations." *Sociometry*, 1976a, 39 (2): 131-41.
————. "In Search of Cultural Identity Factors," *Canadian Review of Sociology and Anthropology*, 1976b, 12 (2): 150-62.
Erikson, E. H. *Childhood and Society*. New York: W. W. Norton, 1950.
Geismar, L. "A Scale for the Measurement of Ethnic Identification." *Jewish Social Studies*, 1954, 16 (1): 33-60.
Greeley, A. M. *Ethnicity in the United States: A Preliminary Reconnaissance*. New York: John Wiley and Sons, 1974.
Gutmann, D., J. D. Sinnott, Z. H. Carrigan, N. A. Holahan, M. J. Flynn, and J. Mullaney. *The Impact of Needs, Knowledge, Ability and Living Arrangements on Decision Making of the Elderly*. Final report, Administration on Aging, grant number 90-A-522, 1977.

Herman, S. N. *Jewish Identity: A Social Psychological Perspective.* Beverly Hills, Calif.: Sage, 1977.

Hofman, J. E. "The Meaning of Being a Jew in Israel: An Analysis of Ethnic Identity." *Journal of Personality and Social Psychology,* 1970, 15 (3): 196-202.

Hraba, J., and J. Siegman. "Black Consciousness." *Youth and Society,* 1974, 6 (1): 63-89.

Isajiw, W. W. "Definitions of Ethnicity." *Ethnicity,* 1974, 1 (2): 111-24.

Lazerwitz, B. "Some Factors in Jewish Identification." *Jewish Social Studies,* 1953, 1:3-24.

Lewin, K. *Resolving Social Conflicts.* New York: Harper, 1948.

Masuda, M., R. S. Hasegawa, and G. Matsumoto. "The Ethnic Identity Questionnaire: A Comparison of Three Japanese Age Groups in Tachikawa, Japan, Honolulu, and Seattle." *Journal of Cross-Cultural Psychology,* 1973, 4 (2): 229-45.

Masuda, M., G. Matsumoto, and G. M. Meredith. "Ethnic Identity in Three Generations of Japanese Americans." *Journal of Social Psychology,* 1970, 81 (August): 199-207.

Matsumoto, G., G. M. Meredith, and M. Masuda. "Ethnic Identification: Honolulu and Seattle Japanese Americans." *Journal of Cross-Cultural Psychology,* 1970, 1 (1): 63-76.

Mostwin, D. "In Search of Ethnic Identity." *Social Casework,* 1972, 53 (5): 307-10.

Reynolds, D. K., and R. A. Kalish. "Anticipation of Futurity as a Function of Ethnicity and Age." *Journal of Gerontoloty,* 1974, 29 (2): 224-31.

Rollins, J. H. "Reference Identification of Youth of Differing Ethnicty." *Journal of Personality and Social Psychology,* 1973, 26 (2): 222-31.

Sandberg, N. C. *Ethnic Identity and Assimilation: The Polish American Community: Case Study of Metropolitan Los Angeles.* New York: Praeger Publishers, 1972.

Shapiro, H. M. "Jewish Identification and Intellectuality: A Two Generation Analysis." *Sociological Analysis,* 1974, 33 (4): 230-38.

Zak, I. "Dimensions of Jewish-American Identity." *Psychological Reports,* 1973, 33 (3): 891-900.

_____. "Structure of Ethnic Identity of Arab-Israeli Students." *Psychological Reports,* 1976, 38 (1): 239-46.

Abstracts

GROUP COHESIVENESS SCALE
N. C. Sandberg, 1972

Definition of Variable or Concept

The scale was designed to measure the salience of identification with ethnic background experiences. Three areas of experience are reflected among the scale items: religion, nationality, and culture.

Description of Instrument

The measure includes 30 Likert-scaled items. Eight of the items are stated negatively. That is, if the statement is endorsed by the respondent, the indication is one of the absence of a feeling of identification. The remaining items are stated positively. Each item has six ordinally related response categories: strongly agree, agree, mildly agree, mildly disagree, and strongly disagree.

The items were chosen so that three separate dimensions of ethnicity were represented: religion, culture, and nationality. The religious construct was observed in terms of two subdimensions: an associational dimension and a communal dimension. The items representing each of the three major dimensions of ethnicity were intermixed to make the scale appear as one entity.

The scale was developed by a group of 20 persons with expertise in ethnic research. Items were included in the scale when they were judged by these experts to be accurate measures of ethnic identification.

Method of Administration

The scale can be self-administered or administered in a private interview. It was administered as part of a private interview by Sandberg (1972). He noted that, with a skillful interviewer, the administration of the scale takes at least 30 minutes.

Context of Development

The investigator was interested in developing a measure that would identify ethnic differences among Polish Americans and still be applicable to other ethnic groups. He noted that such a measure would provide an avenue for meaningful comparisons both between diverse ethnic categories and within ethnic boundaries. Sandberg was primarily interested in the latter topic, especially the question, are there generational and/or social-class differences within the Polish-American group? One of the research questions, for example, was concerned with whether ethnic identity diminishes with successively later generations among Polish Americans.

Sample

A stratified-purposive sampling procedure was followed. The main effort was to include a balanced cross-section of respondents according to age, sex, generational membership, income, religion, socioeconomic status, and marital status. Sandberg's report was based on 111 complete and usable interviews.

Scoring, Scale Norms, and Distribution

The individual item scores were averaged in order to determine the overall attitudinal score for each respondent. The theoretical range of the overall mean scores fell between 1 and 6. Sandberg provided data on the mean response level for his respondents on each individual item by generation. Of course, the theoretical range for the separate items was also 1 to 6. The range of these scores among the foreign-born, pre-World War II generation was between 1.60 (on scale item 7) and 4.87 (on scale item 14). The overall mean and standard deviation of these averaged scores were 2.99 and .98, respectively. The range of these scores among the fourth-generation, American-born subsample was between 2.75 (on scale item 7) and 5.25 (on scale item 27). The mean and standard deviation, respectively, were 3.89 and .70. The means and standard deviations for the respective dimensions of ethnic identity by generation are shown in Table 9-2. Only two of the five generational groups are included in the analysis. The foreign-born, pre-World War II generation was the earliest generation studied; the American-born fourth generation was the latest generation studied.

Formal Tests of Validity

The face validity of the scale was established by a panel of 20 persons who had expertise in ethnic research. These judges initially sorted a large pool of statements into ordinally related categories, each reflecting a successively higher judge's ranking of the statement in terms of the item's perceived validity. The 10 most valid items from each subindex were included in the final measure.

TABLE 9-2

Means and Standard Deviations of the Dimensional Structure
of Ethnic Identity by Generation

	Foreign-Born, Pre-World War II Generation				American-Born Fourth Generation			
	C	RA	RC	N	C	RA	RC	N
X	2.77	2.37	3.56	3.23	3.78	4.65	3.70	4.13
SD	1.30	0.30	0.70	0.81	0.49	0.22	0.85	0.55

SOURCE: The statistics are based on an analysis of data provided by N. C. Sandberg. *Ethnic Identity and Assimilation: The Polish American Community: Case Study of Metropolitan Los Angeles*, p. 65. New York: Praeger Publishers, 1972.

KEY: C = cultural dimension; RA = religious association dimension; RC = religious communal dimension; N = nationality dimension.

Usability on Older Populations

Assuming that the perspective of the ethnic researchers—who judged the validity of the items—was representative of the older sample participant's perspective, it seems that Sandberg has demonstrated the usability of the scale. This reviewer agrees—the items appear to be relevant for older populations. One problem, however, is evident—the length of the measure. The use of 30 items for one measure, especially in a large-scale survey with the aged, may not be reasonable.

Sensitivity to Age Differences

Sandberg gave no information about age differences or correlations in his report. The investigators did show variations in ethnic identification by generation. To the extent that age and generational differences are confounded in the data, it is possible to infer that the measure is sensitive to age differences.

General Comments and Recommendations

The scale represents one of the few attempts to put together a methodology that advances beyond a one-item measure of ethnic identification and that is useful for determining dimensions of ethnic identification. With slight modifications in select key words, the items would probably be applicable cross-ethnically.

Beyond its face validity, the scale shares with other measures of ethnic identification an absence of clear evidence on its measurement accuracy (validity and reliability).

Reference

Sandberg, N. C. *Ethnic Identity and Assimilation: The Polish American Community: Case Study of Metropolitan Los Angeles.* New York: Praeger Publishers, 1972.

Instrument

See Instrument V1.9.I.a.

ETHNIC IDENTITY QUESTIONNAIRE (EIQ)
M. Masuda, G. Matsumoto, and G. M. Meredith, 1970

Definition of Variable or Concept

This questionnaire was designed to measure the extent of the sense of belonging or identifying with an ethnic group. The items are particularly concerned with the sense of identification among Japanese Americans. The investigators stated that "the magnitude of one's ethnicity is a function of the extent of the individual's incorporation into his total ego identity the sense of 'Japaneseness' " (Masuda, Matsumoto, and Meredith, 1970, pp.63-64.

Description of Instrument

The index includes 50 Likert-scaled statements to which a respondent responds: strongly agree, agree, undecided, disagree, or strongly disagree. The score representing the highest identification on each item is 5; the lowest score is 1. Generally, item scores greater than 3.4 indicate positive ethnic identification, scores less than 2.60 indicate negative identification, and scores in between are considered neutral.

The total score on the questionnaire is taken as the sum of the 50 individual item scores. Twenty of the items are stated negatively, so that, when they are endorsed, low ethnic identification can be assumed; the remaining items are positive, indicating, when endorsed, identification with the Japanese-American experience.

From an initial set of 125 statements, 50 were selected by the investigators for inclusion in the final questionnaire. The items were selected so that they would be representative of a diverse array of Japanese cultural objects. some of the items refer to preferences for Japanese things (e.g., food items); other items reflect personality characteristics (e.g., spontaneity), childrearing practices, kinship patterns, community social relationships, discrimination, Japanese cultural heritage, sex roles, and interracial attitudes. No information was provided about how the specific items are associated with the hypothesized theoretical dimensions of ethnic identification.

Method of Administration

The index can be self-administered or administered by individual interviewers. The authors selected the former method in their studies.

Context of Development

The instrument was developed primarily in order to examine the influence of acculturation on the ethnic identification of Japanese Americans and to identify the important variables shaping this relationship. To examine these phenomena the investigators have applied their instrument to three generations: Issei (the earliest or elderly generation), Nisei (the middle generation), and Sansei (the latest or youngest generation).

Samples

The initial sample was drawn largely from a 1967 Japanese telephone directory for Seattle. Additional respondents were selected from a roster of church membership. Of the 514 questionnaires distributed, 125 were returned from the elderly generation; this was a return rate of 29.3%. The return rate for the middle and young-age cohorts was 33.9%. The respective mean ages and age ranges for the three generations are summarized in Table 9-3.

Additional demographic information about the initial sample was also included in subsequent publications by the investigators. For example, 55.3% of the sample was female and over 50% of the sample was Christian. The generations from earliest to latest had means of 11.7, 14.0, and 14.1 years of education, respectively (Masuda, Hasegawa, and Matsumoto, 1973).

Since the Honolulu and Tachikawa samples were, for the most part, only slightly different in terms of these characteristics, it is necessary to describe them individually. These latter samples are discussed in subsequent publications by the investigators using the same measure of ethnic identification. The Honolulu sample was studied by Masuda, Matsumoto, and Meredith (1970) and the Tachikawa sample was studied by Masuda, Hasegawa, and Matsumoto (1973).

TABLE 9-3
Age Characteristics and Generations

Generation	Number	Age Range	Mean Age
Issei	125	45-87	69.3
Nisei	114	23-66	41.6
Sansei	94	15-38	23.1

SOURCE: M. Masuda, M. Matsumoto, and G. M. Meredith. "Ethnic Identity in Three Generations of Japanese Americans." *Journal of Social Psychology,* 1970, 81: 201. Copyright 1970 by the American Psychological Association. Reprinted by permission.

Scoring, Scale Norms, and Distribution

The individual item scores are summed to derive the overall ethnic identification score. The theorectical limits of the overall scores are between 50 (indicating low identification) and 250 (indicating high identification).

In the three-generation-by-three-city comparison made by Masuda, Hasegawa, and Matsumoto (1973), there was little in the way of a city effect, but there was a clear generational effect. The Issei (first generation) averaged 152.25 in EIQ score; the Nisei (second generation) averaged 142.22; and the Sansei (third generation) averaged 133.67. The investigators noted that there were few sex differences in the scores.

Formal Tests of Validity

The face validity of the items was established by the investigators. An item was considered valid to the extent that the investigators agreed among themselves that the item was, in fact, reflective of the Japanese experience.

Usability on Older Populations

The items appear to be equally useful for older and younger populations. A shortened version of this index would be well worth the investment for use among the aged in future applications.

Sensitivity to Age Differences

There were no age relationships shown in regard to the measure. The investigators did show significant generational differences, however. To the extent that there are age differences in the analyses reported by the investigators, it is possible to infer that the measure is sensitive to age differences.

General Comments and Recommendations

Two changes in future applications of this measure among the aged are warranted. First, the dimensional structure of the items needs to be identified. Second, the numbers of items composing the measure needs to be lessened considerably. Both of these changes could be easily realized by investigators who use the measure in the future. A factor analysis of the items could be used to validate statistically several hypothetically derived dimensions. As a consequence, the factor weights of the items could be used to select a limited number of items on any one dimension.

References

Masuda, M., R. S. Hasegawa, and G. Matsumoto, "The Ethnic Identity Questionnaire: A Comparison of Three Japanese Age Groups in Tachikawa, Japan, Honolulu, and Seattle." *Journal of Cross-Cultural Psychology*, 1973, 4 (2): 229-45.

Masuda, M., G. Matsumoto, and G. M. Meredith. "Ethnic Identity in Three Generations of Japanese Americans." *Journal of Social Psychology*, 1970, 81: 199-207.

Instrument

See Instrument V1.9.I.b.

JEWISH IDENTIFICATION INDEX
H. M. Shapiro, 1974

Definition of Variable or Concept

This measure was designed to measure the effects of involvement in Jewish life. The investigator noted that the primary concern in using the measure is to determine the respondent's sense of being Jewish.

Description of Instrument

The measure includes 14 Likert-scaled statements. The respondent can respond to each item in terms of whether he or she strongly agrees (scored 1), agrees (2), disagrees (3), or strongly disagrees (4). The range of the overall (summed) scores is between 14 and 56.

The 14 items were identified through the application of factor analysis. The items represent statements that had factor loadings of .40 or greater on the one-factor solution.

Method of Administration

The index can be self-administered or administered through individual interviews. Shapiro used a survey questionnaire.

Context of Development

The high degree of Jewish intellectuality is theoretically a function of an intricate relationship between piety and study within Judaism. Generational experiences (differential social and cultural marginality) are hypothesized as factors qualifying this relationship. The research question is do Jewish identification and intellectuality vary significantly by generation?

Sample

Participants were 22- to 29-year-old Jewish residents of metropolitan St. Paul (as of December 31, 1968) and all of the fathers of the young men, who were also St. Paul residents. The list for the first group was composed of the inclusive group of males belonging to synagogues and other organizations in St. Paul. Of the sample, 183 (65% return rate) sons and 119 (63% return rate) of their fathers returned usable questionnaires.

Scoring, Scale Norms, and Distribution

Scores for the individual items ranged between 1 and 4. The overall score was derived by summing the item scores. Theoretically, this score could vary between 14 and 56. The distribution of scores for Shapiro's data is shown in Table 9-4.

The mean Jewish identification scores for the fathers and sons, respectively, were 44.2 (standard deviation 5.6) and 41.3 (standard deviation 6.5).

TABLE 9-4
Percentage Distribution of Jewish Identification Scores by Generation

| Generation | Percent in Quartiles of Possible Range | | | |
	14–24	25–35	35–46	47–56
Fathers	0	3	65	32
Sons	1	15	63	20

SOURCE: H. M. Shapiro. "Jewish Identification and Intellectuality: A Two Generation Analysis." *Sociological Analysis* 1974, 33 (4): 234. Reprinted by permission of publisher.

Formal Tests of Validity

The construct validity of the measure is indicated by the factor loadings. The loadings are shown in relation to each item on the instrument.

Usability on Older Populations

Without more information on the age range of the fathers, it would be premature to conclude that the index would be consistently useful among older Jewish samples.

Sensitivity to Age Differences

No information was given in regard to age differences or correlations.

General Comments and Recommendations

The index, as applied to older samples, represents a unique attempt, which uses factor analysis, to standardize a measure of ethnic group identification. As such, the index is one of the first of the ethnic identification measures to address methodologically the issues of validity and reliability in an objective manner. This instrument would be quite amenable to further scale analysis and estimation of factor scores via regression weighting techniques.

The cross-ethnic applicability of the index is difficult to assess theoretically. Several of the items are directly relevant to the Jewish experience. As such, revisions of the index may necessitate more than minor changes of certain key words in the index items.

Reference

Shapiro, H. M. "Jewish Identification and Intellectuality: A Two Generation Analysis. *Sociological Analysis,* 1974, 33 (4): 230-38.

Instrument

See Instrument V1.9.I.c.

Instruments

V1.9.I.a
GROUP COHESIVENESS SCALE
N. C. Sandberg, 1972

Please respond to all of the questions below by putting a number, from 1 to 6, in the box next to each item. The numbers range from 1 (strongly agree) to 6 (strongly disagree) as indicated in the following scale.

1	2	3	4	5	6
Strongly Agree	Agree	Mildly Agree	Mildly Disagree	Disagree	Strongly Disagree

+*	1.	The public schools should teach more about the contributions of Polish people to America.	C**
+	2.	I feel more comfortable in a Polish church.	RA
−	3.	We don't need stronger organizations to express the views of Polish-Americans.	N
+	4.	A Polish neighborhood is a friendlier place to live.	N
+	5.	Organizations which carry on the Polish culture are important.	C
−	6.	Polish religious education is not important for our children.	RC
+	7.	Polish music makes me want to dance.	C
+	8.	Our people should get their families to the Polish church on Sundays.	RC
+	9.	A feeling for the Polish people is "in the blood."	N
−	10.	Southern California does not need a Polish newspaper.	C
+	11.	You should belong to the Polish church even if it is far from your home.	RA
+	12.	It is not all right to change your name.	N
+	13.	I feel more comfortable with Polish people.	N
−	14.	We don't need centers where our young people can learn about Polish culture.	C
+	15.	The Polish religious tradition helps to strengthen my family life.	RA
−	16.	We don't need to know the history of the Polish people.	C
+	17.	I would rather attend a Polish Mass at Christmas.	RA
+	18.	Polish jokes bother me.	N
+	19.	It is important for me to contribute my time, talent, and finances to the Polish church.	RC
−	20.	If you're in trouble, you cannot count on Polish people to help you.	N
+	21.	We should be willing to give money to preserve the Polish tradition.	C
+	22.	It is better to marry someone of your own nationality.	N
−	23.	I should not encourage others to belong to the Polish church.	RC
+	24.	Our children should learn Polish dances and music.	C
+	25.	I prefer a church where services are in the Polish language.	RA
+	26.	It is too bad that the Polish tradition is not being carried on by many of our young people.	C
+	27.	I would vote for a Polish political candidate rather than any other nationality regardless of political party.	N
+	28.	Our children should learn to speak Polish.	C
−	29.	I don't have an obligation to help new people in the Polish parish get settled.	RC

\+   30. You can be for your own people first and still be a good American.   N

---

*Positive = a statement, which if agreed with, indicates Polish identification. Negative = a statement, which if agreed with, indicates an absence of Polish identification.

**C = cultural; N = National; RA = Religious associational; RC = Religious communal.

SOURCE: N. C. Sandberg, *Ethnic Identity and Assimilation: The Polish American Community: Case Study of Metropolitan Los Angeles*, pp. 62-63. New York: Praeger Publishers, 1972. Reprinted by permission of author and publisher.

V1.9.I.b

ETHNIC IDENTITY QUESTIONNAIRE
M. Masuda, G. Matsumoto, and G. M. Meredith, 1970

Instructions: Listed below are a number of statements about which people often have different opinions. You will discover that you agree with some, that you disagree with others. Please read each statement carefully, then circle the letter that indicates the extent to which *you* agree or disagree with it. Answer every statement, even if you have to guess at some. There is no right or wrong answer. This information will be treated as confidential.

+*   1. A good child is an obedient child.
−   2. It is all right for personal desires to come before duty to one's family.
+   3. Japanese Americans should not disagree among themselves if there are Caucasions around.
+   4. I especially like Japanese foods.
+   5. A good Japanese background helps prevent youth from getting into all kinds of trouble that other American youth have today.
−   6. It's unlucky to be born Japanese.
+   7. It would be more comfortable to live in a neighborhood which has at least a few Japanese Americans than in one which has none.
−   8. When I feel affectionate I show it.
+   9. It is a duty of the eldest son to take care of his parents in their old age.
+   10. Japanese Americans who enter into new places without any expectation of discrimination from Caucasions are naive.
+   11. I think it is all right for Japanese Americans to become Americanized, but they should retain part of their own culture.
−   12. A wife's career is just as important as the husband's career.
+   13. In regard to opportunities that other Americans enjoy, Japanese Americans are deprived of many of them because of their ancestry.
−   14. It is all right for children to question the decisions of their parents once in awhile.
+   15. In the Japanese community, human relations are generally more warm and comfortable than outside in American society.
−   16. I would not feel any more tendency to agree with the policies of the Japanese government than any other American would.
−   17. The best thing for the Japanese Americans to do is to associate more with Caucasians and identify themselves completely as Americans.
+   18. I am apt to hide my feelings in some things, to the point that people may hurt me without their knowing it.
+   19. It is a shame for a Japanese American not to be able to understand Japanese.
+   20. Japanese people have an unusual refinement and depth of feeling for nature.
+   21. I would be disturbed if Caucasians did not accept me as an equal.
+   22. It is unrealistic for a Japanese American to hope that he can become a leader of an organization composed mainly of Caucasians because they will not let him.

− 23. I don't have a strong feeling of attachment to Japan.

+ 24. I am not too spontaneous and casual with people.

− 25. It is not necessary for Japanese American parents to make it a duty to promote the preservation of Japanese cultural heritage in their children.

+ 26. An older brother's decision is to be respected more than that of a younger one.

+ 27. Socially, I feel less at ease with Caucasians than with Japanese Americans.

− 28. The Japanese are no better or no worse than any other race.

− 29. I always think of myself as an American first and as a Japanese second.

+ 30. Although children may not appreciate Japanese schools at the time, they will later when they grow up.

− 31. Life in the United States is quite ideal for Japanese Americans.

+ 32. When in need of aid, it is best to rely mainly on relatives.

+ 33. It is better that Japanese Americans date only Japanese Americans.

− 34. Parents who are very companionable with their children can still maintain respect and obedience.

+ 35. Once a Japanese always a Japanese.

− 36. Good relations between Japanese and Caucasians can be maintained without the aid of traditional Japanese organizations.

− 37. It is nice if a Japanese American learns more about Japanese culture, but it is really not necessary.

− 38. It would be better if there were no all-Japanese communities in the United States.

+ 39. Japan has a great heritage and has made contributions important to world civilization.

+ 40. Those Japanese Americans who are unfavorable toward Japanese culture have the wrong attitutde.

+ 41. I believe that, "He who does not repay a debt of gratitude cannot claim to be noble."

+ 42. To avoid being embarassed by discrimination, the best procedure is to avoid places where a person is not totally welcomed.

− 43. I usually participate in mixed group discussions.

− 44. Many of the Japanese customs, traditions, and attitudes are no longer adequate for the problems of the modern world.

+ 45. I enjoy Japanese movies.

− 46. It is a natural part of growing up to occasionally "wise-off" at teachers, policemen, and other grownups in authority.

+ 47. A person who raises too many questons interferes with the progress of a group.

+ 48. I prefer attending an all-Japanese church.

+ 49. One can never let himself down without letting the family down at the same time.

+ 50. Interracial marriages between Japanese Americans and Caucasians should be discouraged.

1	2	3	4	5
Strongly Agree	Agree	Undecided	Disagree	Strongly Disagree

*Positive = a statement, which if agreed with, indicates identification. Negative = a statement, which if agreed with, indicates an absence of identification.

SOURCE: Personal communication from Masuda.

V1.9.I.c.
JEWISH IDENTIFICATION INDEX
H. M. Shapiro, 1974

Strongly Agree	Agree	Disagree	Strongly Disagree
—* 1. It is all right for Jews to exchange gifts on Christmas.			.53**
+ 2. My thinking has been affected by Jewish ideas, beliefs, etc.			.52
+ 3. I feel a personal stake in the outcome of the Arab-Israel conflict.			.55
+ 4. I feel an attachment to the local Jewish community.			.65
+ 5. I'm opposed to Friday night dances in public schools.			.47
— 6. There's nothing wrong with Jews celebrating Christmas.			.51
+ 7. I feel an attachment to American Jewry.			.67
+ 8. Of all foreign countries, I feel the strongest ties to Israel.			.66
+ 9. If I were to learn another language, I would most like to learn Hebrew assuming I did not know it).			.67
+ 10. I feel a strong attachment to Jewish life.			.80
+ 11. It is important to marry within the Jewish faith.			.64
+ 12. The Jewish people should be an example for other people.			.43
+ 13. American Jewish ideas, values, etc. have much to contribute to the American way of life.			.41
+ 14. My general outlook has been affected by my sharing in the Jewish culture.			.62

*Positive statements, if endorsed, indicate identification with the Jewish experience; negative statements, if endorsed, indicate the absence of identification with the Jewish experience.

**Varimax factor loadings for the respective items.

SOURCE: H. M. Shapiro, "Jewish Identification and Intellectuality: A Two Generation Analysis." *Sociological Analysis*, 1974, 33 (4): 232-33. Reprinted by permission.

Chapter 10

Subjective Age Identification

Neal E. Cutler

As Kastenbaum and Durkee noted (1964, p. 251), "If there is no single, dominant way in which old age is defined at present, then there is something to be learned from the particular way in which an individual interprets the term." The concept of subjective age identification has at various times taken on various meanings. The first task in introducing the measures included in this chapter, therefore, should be to define the term. For the purposes of this review, subjective age identification is defined, somewhat narrowly, as an individual's cognitive assessment that he or she is "old." The concept of old itself is left undefined since every individual supplies that definition. The two critical elements of this definition of subjective age identification are that it is intentionally narrow and that the concept represents a *cognitive* rather than an *evaluative* attitudinal component.

These two attributes of the definition are intended to differentiate subjective age identification from two related concepts that are reviewed in other chapters of this volume—Chapters 6 and 12. In the author's opinion, both of these other concepts represent evaluative judgments made by the individual concerning others or his or her self. By contrast, subjective age identification, as it is defined here, represents only the cognitive assessment of the self as old. Whether or not the cognitive assessment of the self as old leads to an evaluative judgment of the self as good or bad is, of course, an empirical question, and it is precisely because it is an empirical *question* that the concepts must remain differentiated.

Conceptual Issues

This emphasis on the narrowness of the concept's definition and the need to keep similar (and possibly correlated) concepts analytically and operationally distinct is a consequence of the lack of clarity sometimes found in the literature. In a review of prior research in the area, for example, Peters (1971) noted that a denial of old age among chronologically older respondents was found to be associated with high morale, positive self-image, favorable reaction to life changes, and other such variables. Even though such studies indicate an empirical association between the cognitive dimension of age identification and certain affective orientations, it became easy to employ simple age identification as a more or less direct measurement of its hypothesized consequences. Phillips (1957), for example, saw old age identification itself as evidence of maladjustment, since, in his opinion, to identify oneself as old would be to accept a publicly devalued state and only a poorly adjusted person would go so far as to admit being old.

Alternatively, three studies can be briefly discussed that speak directly to the importance of keeping the concept of subjective age identification analytically distinct from such cognate concepts as self-esteem and general perceptions of aging. Kastenbaum and Durkee (1964) reviewed a number of studies of the relationship between mental health and subjective age. In some contexts those who identify themselves as old have more psychological problems, and in other contexts the subjectively old are better adjusted and have higher morale than those who deny that they are old. Clearly, the point must be that subjective age identification is not the same concept as its correlates.

Ward (1977) focused on the hypothesis that people who accept society's generally negative image of aging will deny their own aging; he also tested the impact that age-related deprivation (e.g., widowhood, retirement, health decline) had on the other variables. He found that for some individuals perceptions of aging in general were *not* predictive of subjective age. Such research is only possible when the concepts are kept separate.

Brubaker and Powers (1976) reviewed a number of studies in which stereotypes of societal aging, personal self-esteem, and subjective age were found to be interrelated. Their analysis focused on the specification and evaluation of alternative models by which the interconnections of these constructs could be displayed. Substantively, they suggested that there is no single set of causal connections among the variables. In the context of this introductory essay, however, the main point is that, unless the variables are kept analytically and operationally distinct, the various kinds of relationships and causal connections cannot be known.

In summary, this review of measures of subjective age identification is based on a narrow definition of the concept. It is precisely because gerontological researchers recognize the importance of the alternative possible causal connections among subjective age, societal images of aging, and measures of the older person's self-concept that the concepts must be carefully differentiated.

Assessment of Validity and Reliability

Most of the chapters in this compendium attempt to assess the validity and reliability of the reported measures. For the measures of subjective age identification reported in this chapter, however, such an assessment does not yield large amounts of information. Consequently, the format of the instrument review in this chapter is slightly different from that of the other chapter.

1. Since the items measure an individual's subjective feelings representing cognitive judgments about himself or herself, there is no external criterion by which validity can be assessed. *Chronological* age does not represent such a criterion, since individuals of advanced chronological age may, for a variety of reasons, be disinclined to identify themselves as old. Nonetheless, it would be strange to find that chronological age and subjective age identification are negatively correlated; consequently, correlations with (and percentages describing) chronological age are included in the description of each measure when they are available. However, since even positive correlations in this regard are unclear as to what is revealed, the information is included for general comparative interest, under the heading "norms and distribution."

2. Six of the first seven measures of subjective age identification reviewed here are single-item indicators; consequently, no internal reliability analysis can be reported. With the exception of a single methodological study (noted in comment number 4), no test-retest reliability information is available. No special assessment is made of the usability of the items for older respondents since the minor changes in item wording would do little to alter the usability of the instruments.

3. In some cases, it is tempting to speak of evidence of predictive validity or convergent validity when measures of subjective age identification are found to correlate with other variables as hypoth-

esized or predicted. The discovery of predicted relationships, however, should not be accepted as proof of true measurement validity since indicators of similar concepts may yield positive inter-correlations even when none of the indicators really measures what the analyst claims it measures, and since, alternatively, truly valid items may fail to yield the hypothesized correlations due to failures or ambiguities of theory rather than measurement problems. Despite these cautionary remarks, the results of so-called "predictive validity" tests are included under the heading "reliability/validity tests."

4. One study did focus on both reliability and validity by administering a standard single-item measure to the same sample before and after a particular task. The task itself was related to the validity test, and the test-retest results provided the information on reliability. This study is fully summarized in the first part of the instrument review. It is, however, based on a somewhat limited sample. Therefore, it must be concluded that in general the users of the measures of subjective age identification reviewed here must do so without the benefit of systematic information on reliability and validity.

Instrument Review

The instrument review presented in this chapter (see Table 10-1) contains two sets of indicators of subjective age identification. The first seven reviews describe what can be called the basic measurement of subjective age, that is, questions that have the following typical format—"Do you feel that you are: young, middle-aged, old, elderly, or what?" Though the reviews of these similar items could have been combined in a single review, they are reported separately for the following reasons. (1) There are minor variations both in the text of the lead-in question and in the exact wording of the response options. (2) Although most studies have divided the responses into two categories, there are variations in how the actual dichotomization is fashioned. (3) The samples and research contexts vary. Some studies are based on convenience samples that are generalizable to no known population, while other samples are representative of small or local populations. (4) Finally, since the theoretical interests and empirical issues of the studies vary, combining the items into a single report would hide important distinctions. The one methodological study referred to earlier (Jeffers, Eisdorfer, and Busse, 1962) is concerned with this basic measure and is the seventh review of this first set.

The second set of measures of subjective age identification includes a more diverse collection of instruments. Included is a single-item measure of comparative age identification, which is based on the concept of future time perspective; a measure based on semantic differential methodology; and a survey research multiple-item indicator. Some of these items can be used rather easily in new studies, and others would require a relatively large methodological investment. Even though these measures may be more interesting than more straightforward single-item indicators, few data on their validity and reliability are available. Unfortunately, none of the studies report direct comparisons between the items or index and the "basic" items. In short, the potential user of these items will have to make all the decisions and choices concerning which items to use in the absence of rigorously defined evidence of validity and reliability.

TABLE 10-1
Instruments Reviewed in Chapter 10

Instrument	Author (date)	Code Number
I. Basic Age-Identification Items		
a. The Early Cornell Studies	Blau (1956); Kutner et al. (1956)	Single item
b. The Duke "Age Awareness" Item	Busse, Jeffers, and Obrist (1957)	Single item
c. Perceived Age	Bloom (1961)	Single item
d. Feelings about Age	Zola (1962)	V1.10.I.d
e. Feeling Old and Social Involvement	Bell (1967)	Single item
f. Cornell Retirement Study	Streib and Schneider (1971)	Single item
g. Comparative Age Identification	Jeffers, Eisdorfer, and Busse (1962)	Single item
II. Diverse Age-Identification Instruments		
a. A Time Perspective Measure of Subjective Age	Back and Gergen (1963)	Single item
b. Semantic Age Identification	Guptill (1969)	V1.10.II.b
c. Survey Research Center "Feel Close" Items	Cutler (1974)	V1.10.II.c

Future Research

In various places throughout this chapter, item-specific suggestions are made concerning how a particular item might be used or improved in future research. There are, however, several general suggestions that should be noted.

1. The availability of both single-item (i.e., "basic" item) measures and more complex measures suggests the possibility of including more than one measure of subjective age identification in a given study. The information on convergent validity that such an analysis might provide would be a substantial improvement over what is now available.

2. Responses to the basic single-item indicator have, typically, been dichotomized, even though different studies may use different dichotomization. Therefore, it would be useful if analysis of data from a single sample would include and report any variations in substantive findings that are associated with the alternative ways in which the response options can be dichotomized. The absence of differences in substantive results when alternative dichotomizations are tried should also be reported.

3. Unfortunately, most of the studies reported here are based on small, local, and/or unique samples. Consequently, the distribution of old versus non-old subjective age identification in the national population is not generally known. The use of measures of subjective age identification in national studies would provide statistically normative data and would, consequently, give researchers greater confidence in their use of the measures in more specialized research contexts.

4. Finally, the discussion presented by Kastenbaum and Durkee may be cited again. In reviewing the somewhat discrepant findings relating subjective age identification to indicators of mental health, they suggested that at least some of the discrepancies were between older studies and more recent studies. Since societal attitudes toward old age and aging have been rapidly changing during recent years, so might have the dynamics of the personal cognition here described as subjective age identification. To paraphrase their conclusion (1964, p. 258): as a general research strategy in this area there is much to recommend the continued sampling of both national populations and similar populations at regular intervals, so that gerontologists can differentiate between constant elements in the structure of subjective age identification and those temporal elements that reflect changing societal norms and perceptions.

Prior research, it can be said, has exhibited both intriguing directions for research and some false starts. There is a need for national studies, trend studies, and replication studies. Both single-item indicators and multiple-item indicators must be explored more fully, and their reliability and validity must be more fully outlined. The increasing salience of aging in society is clearly a challenge for researchers in social gerontology. One such challenge concerns the degree to which older persons really do consider themselves as old and the conditions that account for variation in such feelings. In short, the systematic analysis of subjective age identification must now proceed apace.

REFERENCES

Brubaker, T. H., and E. A. Powers. "The Stereotype of 'Old': A Review and Alternative Approach." *Journal of Gerontology*, 1976, 31: 441-47.

Kastenbaum, R., and N. Durkee. "Elderly People View Old Age." In *New Thoughts on Old Age*, R. Kastenbaum (ed.), pp. 250–62. New York: Springer, 1964.

Peters, G. R. "Self Conceptions of the Aged, Age Identification, and Aging." *The Gerontologist*, 1971, 11: 69-73.

Phillips, B. S. "A Role Theory Approach to Adjustment in Old Age." *American Sociological Review*, 1957, 22: 212-17.

Ward, R. A. "The Impact of Subjective Age and Stigma on Older Persons." *Journal of Gerontology*, 1977, 32: 227-32.

Abstracts

THE EARLY CORNELL STUDIES (ELMIRA AND KIPS BAY)

Z. M. Blau, 1956; B. Kutner, D. Fanshel, A. M. Togo, and T.S. Langner, 1956

Definition of Concept

The investigators were primarily interested in the self-image, or the self-concept, in terms of age held by chronologically older respondents.

Description of Instrument

This is a single-item interview indicator that uses the following question: "How do you think of yourself as far as age goes—middle-aged, elderly, old, or what?" In virtually all of the analyses reported, "elderly" and "old" were combined and compared to "middle-aged" (combined with those respondents who volunteered "young" as a response).

Research Context

A number of studies have been published from the Elmira and Kips Bay research; thus, the context of the interest in age identification was varied. In general, the primary concern was with the morale and adjustment of the older person. Underlying at least some of this research was the general hypothesis that to identify oneself as old is to be maladjusted; that is, to identify oneself as old in a society that values youth is to have a negative self-image.

Samples

The Kips Bay study was based on a 500-respondent sample of the Kips Bay-Yorkville health district of New York City. The interviews took place in late 1952 and early 1953. The data represent a probability sample based upon monthly rents; the sampling procedures were weighted or stratified so that the low-middle-high rental areas yielded a ratio of 6:3:1. The Elmira study was based upon random sampling methods and yielded 468 respondents, who were interviewed in mid-1951. Both samples limited subjects to noninstitutionalized persons aged 60 and over.

Norms and Distribution

A majority (60%) of the Elmira sample identified themselves as middle-aged (Blau, 1956, p.198), and a plurality (49%) of the Kips Bay sample so identified themselves (Kutner et al., 1956, p.98). Thirty-eight percent of the Elmira sample and 42% of the Kips Bay sample identified themselves as old. Increasing age, retirement, and widowhood increased the probability of identification as old (Phillips, 1957, p. 216; Jyrkilä, 1960, p. 46).

Reliability/Validity Tests

Across the several studies cited, a number of interesting correlates of age identification can be noted; the following are examples.

1. Respondents who identified themselves as younger or denied that they were old tended to have higher morale (Kutner et al., 1956, p. 98).

2. Higher socioeconomic status, better health, and employment correlated with a more youthful orientation (Kutner et al., 1956, p. 100).

3. A higher proportion of maladjusted respondents were found among those who identified themselves as old as contrasted to middle-aged, even when controls for chronological age, marital status, and employment status were considered (Phillips, 1957, p. 216).

4. Identifying oneself as old was significantly related to believing that others think of one as old and believing that one is treated differently because of age (Jyrkilä, 1960, p.44).

5. Blau made one of the most interesting points by suggesting that age identification is a critical *intervening variable:* significant associations between chronological age and perceived change in the self or belief that others think one is old disappeared when age identification was used as control (Blau, 1956, p. 199).

General Comments and Recommendations

No formal tests of reliability or validity were reported in any of the cited reports. However, the fact that a general research project fielded similar interview studies in two cities and uncovered similar results may be reassuring as to the reliability of this single-item indicator. In both cities, fewer married, employed, and under-70-year-old respondents identified themselves as old. On the other hand, since no multivariate analyses were reported, it may be that the similarity of the age and employment distributions reflect the fact that more over-70-year-old respondents were retired. Another validity issue (which may be a problem for these studies but not necessarily for the indicator itself) concerns one of the authors' apparent confounding of method with hypothesis. It will be recalled that one of the major hypotheses predicted a positive relationship between old-age identification and maladjustment. Twelve percent of the Elmira respondents and 2% of the Kips Bay respondents refused to choose one of the offered closed-ended responses: "These individuals, who were not willing to commit themselves to a definite identification as old or elderly, were combined with the middle-aged category and other individuals who had not made a transition from a younger identification" (Phillips, 1957, p. 214). It would seem more appropriate to have simply deleted such individuals from the analysis.

References

Blau, Z. S. "Changes in Status and Age Identification." *American Sociological Review*, 1956, 21: 198–203.

Jyrkilä, F. "Society and Adjustment to Old Age: A Sociological Study on the Attitude of Society and the Adjustment of the Aged." *Transactions of the Westermarck Society*, volume 5. Copenhagen: Munksgaard, 1960.

Kutner, B., D. Fanshel, A. M. Togo, and T. S. Langner. *Five Hundred over Sixty*. New York: Russell Sage Foundation, 1956.

Phillips, B. S. "A Role Theory Approach to Adjustment in Old Age." *American Sociological Review*, 1957, 22: 212–17.

———. "Role Change, Subjective Age, and Adjustment: A Correlational Analysis." *Journal of Gerontology*, 1961, 16: 347–52.

Instrument

See the description of the instrument above.

THE DUKE "AGE AWARENESS" ITEM
E. W. Busse, F. C. Jeffers, and W. D. Obrist, 1957

Definition of Concept

Building on prior work that suggests that the self-concept is important in understanding the processes of aging, the investigators suggested that the "age-concept" is a fundamental component of the total self-concept. They further suggested that the concept is associated with subjective feelings of age awareness—this is another way of stating that a man is as old as he feels he is.

Description of Instrument

The single-item interview indicator consists of the following question: "Do you feel that you are now—a young adult person, a middle-aged person, an elderly person, an old person, an aged person?" The responses were trichotomized in the analyses presented: young and middle-aged; elderly; old and aged. This suggests that the last three responses given in the question—elderly, old, aged—were presumed to have an underlying inherent or perceived gradient, i.e., "elderly" is younger than "old" and "aged."

Research Context

The investigators and the study were part of the larger Duke University studies of normal aging. The age awareness item was included as part of the study of the self-concepts of the older respondents.

Sample

"The subjects in the present study were 134 white and 28 Negro persons, all 60 years of age or older, who volunteered to come in for a two-day series of physical, psychological, and social evaluations on the Geriatric Research Project at the Duke University School of Medicine" (Busse, Jeffers, and Obrist, 1970 [1957], p. 381).

Norms and Distribution

Because of racial differences in life expectancy and because of the small number of subjects in the black sample, the analysis of factors associated with age awareness was largely confined to the white sample. Twenty-one variables were correlated with age awareness; only three variables showed significance: chronological age, race, and feelings of health. (Among the noncorrelates were sex; IQ; socioeconomic status; marital status; religious and other activities; and attitudes toward happiness, death, family, and financial security.) The age distribution (for whites only) is shown in Table 10-2.

TABLE 10-2
Age Distribution of Responses

	Young/Middle-aged	Elderly	Old/Aged	(N)
60–64	69%	27%	4%	(26)
65–69	55%	38%	7%	(40)
70–74	28%	46%	26%	(39)
75+	24%	41%	34%	(29)

SOURCE: E. Busse, E. C. Jeffers, and W. D. Obrist. "Factors in Age Awareness." Originally presented in the *Proceedings of the Fourth Congress of the International Association of Gerontology*, 1957, pp. 349-57. Reprinted by permission of authors and publisher.

Reliability/Validity Tests

In terms of validity, only health feelings, race, and chronological age showed significant associations with the measure of age awareness. No other tests of reliability or validity were reported.

General Comments and Recommendations

The response options provided by the Duke item included elderly, old, and aged. Since "old" and "aged" were combined in the data, the assumption appears to have been that "elderly" is a younger designation than "old" or "aged." Whether "elderly" is truly less old than the other two or whether it is simply more gentle or less negative or whatever is not known, and it was not discussed by the investigators. In the methodological study reviewed later in this chapter, the reliability of judgments concerning self-placement in these categories is in fact questioned.

Reference

Busse, E. W., F. C. Jeffers, and W. D. Obrist. "Factors in Age Awareness." *Proceedings of the Fourth Congress of the International Association of Gerontology*, pp. 349–57, 1957. (Reprinted in *Normal Aging*, E. Palmore (ed.), pp. 381–89. Durham, N.C.: Duke University Press, 1970.)

Instrument

See the description of the instrument above.

PERCEIVED AGE
K. L. Bloom, 1961

Definition of Concept

The investigator was interested in the relationship of age to self-concept, and he included perceived age with chronological age in the research.

Description of Instrument

This is a single-item indicator, which was included in a questionnaire study. *"Perceived age* was based on subjects' self ratings as reported on the personal information questionnaire.

Each subject was asked to classify himself as young, middle-aged, or old" (Bloom, 1961, p. 535). The investigator reported that, since few respondents perceived themselves as "old," the responses were dichotomized as "young" versus "middle-aged and over."

Research Context

The hypothesis under investigation was that self-acceptance decreases and self-rejection increases as individuals grow older. Separate scales to measure these two concepts, based upon adjective checklists, were developed by the investigator. Based on prior research indicating that age identification was a most important factor in the emotional adjustment of the older person, the investigator included perceived age along with chronological age in the analysis.

Sample

The sample consisted of 83 white, male surgical patients at the Bronx VA Hospital in New York; all were involved with nonchronic and nondisabling surgical problems, and had been hospitalized for a relatively short period of time. Of the 83 subjects, 15 (or 18%) were 60 to 69 years old; another 15 were 50 to 59 years old. All data gathering was done as close to the date of hospital discharge as was possible; no date for the study was given.

Norms and Distribution

No age-distribution information for the perceived age measure was presented. The biserial correlation between chronological age and the dichotomized measure of perceived age was .67.

Reliability/Validity Tests

The investigator found no significant support for the hypothesis that age—chronological or perceived—was correlated with self-acceptance or self-rejection.

General Comments and Recommendations

The main significance of the inclusion of this study in the present review is its illustration of the importance of including the entire age range, from young to elderly, in the response options. Even though the investigator failed to describe the distribution of these attributes for the small number of older subjects in his initial study, a larger pool of subjects of respondents may well yield interesting data for analysis for this instrument.

Reference

Bloom, K. L. "Age and the Self Concept." *American Journal of Psychiatry*, 1961, 118: 534-38.

Instrument

See the description of the instrument above.

FEELINGS ABOUT AGE
I. K. Zola, 1962

Definition of Concept

The investigator was interested in exploring older persons' feelings and images about aging and some of the psychological sources of such images. Emphasis was on sex differences in the respondents' perceptions of their own aging in relationship to their perceptions of their own parents' aging.

Description of Instrument

This battery of items consists of five separate interview questions, with no attempt at combination or scale construction; rather, intercorrelation of the items, separately for males and females, is used for substantive analysis. The first two items require a response in terms of chronological age. The other three items solicit a dichotomous yes/no response.

(a)   How old do you feel?
(b)   What age would you most like to be?
(c)   Do you consider yourself elderly?
(d)   Did you ever feel your father was elderly?
(e)   Did you ever feel your mother was elderly?

SOURCE: I. K. Zola. "Feelings about Age among Older People." *Journal of Gerontology*, 1962, 17: 65. Used by the permission of author and publisher.

With this battery chronological age was included as a correlate. (This review does not suggest that each of these items, or all of them together, is a validated measure of subjective age identification. It is reasonable to suggest, however, that items a, c, and possibly b are acceptable indicators of subjective age identification.)

Research Context

The investigator was interested in tracing the possible sources of an older subject's image of himself or herself as older, as well as the subject's preferences with respect to age, in terms of sex differences and perceptions of parental aging. In the present context, however, items d and e are not critical to the measurement of subjective age identification.

Sample

The sample consisted of 219 volunteers from a New England gerontological research center. Although the investigator noted that the group of 100 men and 119 women was not terribly dissimilar to the population reflected in the 1950 census (national, state, or local census was never specified), it was fairly well admitted that this was a sample of convenience: "a group of noninstitutionalized older people who seemed to be members of the urban middle-class and who were concerned in some way about aging" (Zola, 1962, p. 65).

Norms and Distribution

Descriptive data for each of the items was given separately for males and females; Table 10-3 lists the means for chronological age and items a and b and the percentage giving affirmative responses to item c.

TABLE 10-3
Chronological Age and Responses to Items a, b, and c

	Males	Females
Chronological age	69.8	67.1
(a) Age felt	53.4	52.3
(b) Age desired	45.8	45.2
(c) Felt elderly	21%	20%

SOURCE: Adapted from I. K. Zola. "Feelings about Age among Older People." *Journal of Gerontology*, 1962, 17: 66. Used by permission of author and publisher.

Although the items were not treated or analyzed in terms of a single scale, intercorrelations among all items were presented. For males, correlations ranged from .05 (feel-desired) to .43 (feel-elderly). For females, correlations ranged from −.07 (desired-elderly) to .50 (feel-elderly) (Zola, 1962; p. 66).

Reliability/Validity Tests

Of all the correlations the investigator noted that the only significant male-female difference was in the correlation between chronological age and felt age: significant for women but not for men (.07 versus .22). Zola's interpretation of this distinction (p. 67), which might serve as an indicator of the external validity of the "felt age" item, is that females have the physiological evidence of menopause to reinforce feelings of oldness, while males of the same age may still be working, which may inhibit such feelings.

General Comments and Recommendations

This study represents one of the few that includes more than a single indicator. Further work of this kind is needed, in which analysis is made of the scaleability or the dimensionality of the separate items. Since the investigator found interpretable male-female differences in correlation in at least one instance, inclusion of explicit measures of life-stage events— widowhood, retirement, "empty nest," for example—might provide further validation. Additionally, the dichotomous "Do you feel elderly?" item could be replaced, within the battery, with the standard multiple-choice item with responses that range from young through elderly.

Reference

Zola, I. K. "Feelings about Age among Older People." *Journal of Gerontology*, 1962, 17: 65-68.

Instrument

See the description of the instrument above.

FEELING OLD AND SOCIAL INVOLVEMENT
T. Bell, 1967

Definition of Concept

The investigator was concerned with whether or not the subjective feeling of being old is a negative attribute associated with, or a rationalization for, the unpleasantness of old age.

Description of Instrument

The measure is a single-item interview indicator: "Do you feel yourself to be old?— yes/sometimes/no." (The yes and sometimes responses were combined in the analysis.)

Research Context

The investigator was concerned with disengagement theory, and he hypothesized that, if disengagement is correlated with subjective feelings of old age, then such age identification is indeed a self-appraisal of the disruption of actual social relationships. The study was limited to the testing of this one hypothesis and did not consider other possible causes for subjective age identification. The investigator adapted a number of social involvement indicators from the original Kansas City disengagement studies, which were included in the interviews with the single-item indicator of age identification.

Sample

The sample included 55 older respondents representing three old age residential institutions in the Santa Barbara, Calif., area. All of the unmarried residents in the three institutions were evidently considered initially; after refusals, illnesses, auditory handicaps, and other problems were considered, interviews were arranged with 10 males and 45 females. Although the investigator suggested that the speech habits and clothing of the subjects indicated that they were of general middle-class background, the study clearly was based on a sample of convenience.

Reliability / Validity Tests

The basic hypothesis of the study was generally supported: feeling old (yes and sometimes responses) was associated with low social involvement. However, since no age-descriptive information was given, it cannot be known how chronological age was related to subjective age in this study.

General Comments and Recommendations

This study is included here to illustrate both its strengths and its weaknesses. On the positive side, the connection between disengagement and subjective age identification is a plausible one, somewhat grounded in theory, and so the study suggests that even a simple measure of subjective age can be useful when the overall analytic context is well defined. On the negative side, the fact that the study arbitrarily dichotomized the responses by including sometimes feels old with yes illustrates a pitfall to be avoided in future research. The investigator admitted that this was done because the number of no responses was large and the goal was to get as even a dichotomous split as possible. His explanation, however, is not convincing: "It was also assumed that the response 'sometimes' was closer in meaning to the 'yes' answer than to the 'no' answer, so no great distortion of actual responses occurred" (Bell, 1967, p. 19). It is to avoid problems such as these that further instrumentation and test standardization research is needed.

Reference

Bell, T. "The Relationship between Social Involvement and Feeling Old among residents in Homes for the Aged." *Journal of Gerontology*, 1967, 22: 17-22.

Instrument

See the description of the instrument above.

CORNELL RETIREMENT STUDY
G. F. Streib and C. J. Schneider, 1971

Definition of Concept

The investigators were concerned with social-psychological changes associated with retirement. On the basis of prior research, subjective age identification was chosen as one social-psychological construct that may be correlated with retirement.

Description of Instrument

The single-item questionnaire indicator is: "How do you think of yourself as far as age goes—do you think of yourself as . . . middle-aged, late middle-aged, old, or elderly." For purposes of analysis, the "middle-aged" response was considered as the "younger" half of a dichotomy and the other three responses were combined as the "older" half.

Research Context

The investigators were involved in a longitudinal study of retirement in which respondents were queried initially in 1952 and then again in 1954, 1956, 1957, and 1958. Age identification was not a major element of the overall study, although its inclusion provided rare longitudinal information concerning age identification. The investigators created a somewhat different form of the standard item by including the "late middle-aged" response option; no information was given about why this form was used or what possible effect its inclusion might have had on the response distributions.

Sample

The Streib-Schneider study was a longitudinal study (1952-1958) in which five waves of questionnaires were fielded. Since it was a study of retirement, the sample selection focused on a narrow age criterion but a broad distribution of occupations and occupational sectors. Virtually all respondents were either age 63 or age 64 at the time the initial questionnaire was distributed in 1952. The authors described a complex process by which a range of companies and federal, state, and local civil service agencies were contacted. In some instances, depending upon the size of the company or agency, a sample of the target cohort was undertaken, and in others all persons meeting the age criterion were mailed inquiries and later questionnaires. The original research population included 3,793 respondents; the fifth and final wave included 1,969 respondents—about 52% of the original sample. The final sample included 75% men and 25% women. The authors described in substantial detail the procedures involved in the administration of their mail questionnaires and the substantial effort made to trace those respondents who did not respond to subsequent mailings over the course of the longitudinal study (Streib and Schneider, 1971, pp.9-28). For example, only 150 respondents from the second wave failed to return questionnaires for the third wave. Extensive checking was done with former employers and post office officials. According to the authors, "Finally, by one means or another, we learned that for this wave 110 participants had died since the previous contact with them" (Streib and Schneider, 1971, p.17). In sum, while the sample was not representative of the target age cohort as a whole, it did include a broad range of meaningful variations. Furthermore, the authors included an elaborate analysis in their chapter on research design, which compares the dropouts with the continuing participants.

Norms and Distribution

Thirty-three percent of the males and 24% of the females identified themselves as older in the first (1952) wave. By 1958, 67% of the males and 53% of the females identified themselves as old (Streib and Schneider, 1971, p.99).

Reliability/Validity Tests

The investigators noted that the longitudinal analysis demonstrated no connection between age identification and retirement, no matter whether retirement was seen as the cause or the effect of an older self-identification. That is, those who already had an older age identification in 1952 had the same rate of retirement as those who had a younger age identification in 1952; analogously, "old" identification did not increase dramatically as a consequence of the act of retirement.

One possible source of invalidity in the study should be noted. The text in Streib and Schneider's report (1971, p. 97) lists the response options to the age identification question as middle-aged, late middle-aged, old, and elderly. The first was considered the "younger" response. The questionnaire (1971, p. 202), however, presents the response options in the following order and format:

1 —Elderly
2 —Middle-aged
3 —Late middle-aged
4 —Old

To the degree that respondents might have believed that the questionnaire's ordering actually represented an implicit young-old gradient, the responses might not reflect the implicit ordering suggested in the text. When this possible problem is added to the unknown effects of the inclusion of the "late middle-aged" response option, validity (and reliability) problems may result.

General Comments and Recommendations

The inclusion of the "late middle-aged" response option could be beneficial in age identification research, in the way that the addition of working class to the standard upper-middle-lower-class subjective social class measures allowed investigators to divide up the large middle class. However, further instrument development is needed in order to map the effects of this (as well as additional) permutations of the basic age identification item.

Reference

Streib, G. F., and C. J. Schneider. *Retirement in American Society*. Ithaca, N.Y.: Cornell University Press, 1971.

Instrument

See the description of the instrument above.

AN EXAMINATION OF THE RELIABILITY AND VALIDITY OF THE STANDARD AGE IDENTIFICATION ITEM

This abstract does not follow the standardized format, because the study being reviewed described a test that is relevant to almost all of the reports already presented in this chapter. The basic age identification items ask the respondent, in an interview or a questionnaire, whether he or she perceives himself or herself to be young, middle-aged, old, elderly, aged, or what. While some items use a dichotomy, others have more elaborate response options. Those measures that begin with more than a dichotomous response option nonetheless typically dichotomize the available responses at the time of analysis. One must consider, in validity terms, whether the original responses and the subsequent dichotomization correctly assigned a respondent to the older or younger category. Of course, since the concept under consideration is that of subjective feelings of age, there is no objective criterion by which the validity of the interview/questionnaire item can be evaluated.

Jeffers, Eisdorfer, and Busse (1962), working on the Duke University project, decided to test the age awareness item used in the Duke project. They initially noted that the Duke item was really the age identification question appearing in the Burgess, Cavan, and Havighurst (1949) University of Chicago Activities and Attitudes Inventory. To test the validity of the item, the Duke researchers asked a set of subjects to respond first to the item in its traditional form. One hour later, the subjects were asked to use a card-sort technique in which they ordered the five stages listed as the response options of the original item. Finally, the subjects were again asked the standard age identification item, but this time the response options were provided in the order given by the subject's own card sort.

The subjects were 168 volunteers to the Duke University Medical Center geriatrics project. They were 60 to 94 years old, mobile, black and white, men and women, and they represented a range of occupations.

The results showed that some subjects did not agree on the meaning of the last three labels used in the basic item: elderly, old, aged. Only 26% of the subjects had card sorts that agreed with the order given by the interview item. Another 34% agreed, except for the reversal of old and aged—which was "allowable" since these two terms were combined in the Duke research into a single analytic category. Thus, at best only 60% of the subjects followed the implicit ordering of age labels used in the Duke/Chicago age identification item.

The reliability of the subjects' judgments was also called into question. After the card-sort task, the subjects were again given the age identification item, but this time with the response options ordered to match each subject's own card-sort results. As might be expected, many of the subjects did not choose the same label as in the earlier administration of the item. Table 10-4, adapted from the validity study (Jeffers, Eisdorfer, and Busse, 1962, p.438), compares the responses of the 168 subjects to the original item and their responses to the item in which each subject's questionnaire reflected his or her own card-sort ordering of the label. That is, the numbers 1 through 5 represent the original ordering (young, middle-aged, elderly, old, aged) for the top line of the table, but they represent whatever the ordering was after the card sort in the second line.

TABLE 10-4
Distribution of Self-Age Placement

	1	2	3	4	5	Mean	(Number)
Original item	2%	45%	32%	15%	6%	2.78%	(168)
Card sort format	0%	13%	43%	23%	21%	3.54%	(168)

SOURCE: Adapted from F. Jeffers, C. Eisdorfer, and E. W. Busse. "Measurement of Age Identification: A Methodologic Note." *Journal of Gerontology*, 1962, 17: Table 4, p. 438.

The results demonstrate that responses different from the original item are obtained when the subjects are involved in a subjective (card-sort) assessment of the ordering of the age labels. Clearly, the decision about where to dichotomize (or trichotomize) the array of subjective age identification responses into younger and older is affected by the subject's own subjective definitions of the labels—and such information usually is not collected when the item is used.

The results of this psychometric "experiment" are confounded somewhat by the fact that the second administration of the item, using each subject's own ordering to the response options, took place after the subjects were involved in a "consciousness-raising" set of tasks concerning the definition of age and life stages. The authors admitted that the shift toward an older subjective age identification in the second administration of the item was probably affected by the subjects' participation in the card-sort task (and no doubt by other elements of the Duke study, which included a two-day series of comprehensive physical, psychological and social evaluations).

For the researcher who is interested in using a version of the standard age identification item (several of which have been reviewed in the preceding pages), this reliability/validity study offers several challenges. First, those options that offer several synonyms (or choices) for the older end of the life cycle should be viewed with great care until further methodological work has clarified the distinctions between such choices (e.g., the difference between late middle-aged and old in the Cornell Retirement Study). Second, the analyst must be careful when reducing the data to fewer categories than were in the original item. Third, if recoding of responses is done, comparison of the different recoding patterns should be undertaken to determine whether different substantive results are produced. Fourth, if the card-sort task really did raise the subjects' age consciousness, resulting in a shift toward older age identification for the sample as a whole, then the analyst must be particularly sensitive to the placement of the age identification item in an interview or a questionnaire. Unfortunately, this is a validity question to which none of the studies reviewed have been attentive.

References

Burgess, E. W., R. S. Cavan, and R. J. Havighurst. *Your Activities and Attitudes.* Chicago: Science Research Associates, 1949.

Jeffers, F. C., C. Eisdorfer, and E. W. Busse. "Measurement of Age Identification: A Methodologic Note." *Journal of Gerontology*, 1962, 17: 437-39.

COMPARATIVE AGE IDENTIFICATION
F. C. Jeffers, C. Eisdorfer, and E. W. Busse, 1962

Definition of Concept

The investigator was generally concerned with subjective age identification, and he included an item that asks the respondent to compare feelings about his or her own age with feelings about the age of other people who are of approximately the same chronological age.

Description of Instrument

This single-item interview indicator has the following form: "Would you say you feel older or younger than most people your age?"

Research Context

The investigator was interested in role change and adjustment in older persons; age identification was important in that acceptance of an old self-identification is acceptance of the negative cultural evaluations of old age and, hence, age identification leads to maladjustment. The comparative age identification item was included in a battery of related items, including the standard age identification item ("Do you think of yourself as middle-aged, elderly, old, or what?"). In addition, the battery included an item about the respondent's general attitude toward old age—not toward the self. The items were analyzed separately (e.g., correlations were made with measures of adjustment role change, etc.), and no attempt was made to combine them into one or more summary measures.

Sample

The sample was a subsample of the Cornell Kips Bay-Yorkville health district (New York City) study described earlier. The larger sample included a 500-respondent probability sample of the area, chosen so as to have a ratio of 6:3:1 of low, middle, and high rents. All respondents were aged 60 or over. The sample for this study represented the 217 respondents who could name a close friend and for whom an interview with that friend could be completed. Given the nature of the sampling, the 217 were younger and less likely to be widowed than the sample of 500.

Norms and Distribution

No basic descriptive data concerning the sample or age distributions were given by the investigators. However, since the analysis included the correlation of the comparative age identification measure with chronological age, some information is available. Unfortunately, the intercorrelations of the various components of the investigator's battery of five items were not presented. However, for purposes of illustration, the correlation of each with chronological age may be useful (Phillips, 1961, p. 349): comparative age identification (respondent), .09; standard age identification (respondent), .39; general attitude toward old age (respondent), .12; comparative age identification (associate), −.08; and standard age identification (associate), .34.

Reliability/Validity Tests

No intercorrelation analysis across the set of age identification items was presented. Furthermore, an examination of the correlations suggests that the comparative age identification item is not significantly correlated with chronological age, as is the standard subjective age identification item. The comparative age identification item does significantly correlate with two of the substantive items in the study: adjustment and getting around now versus at age 50, but not with perception of differential treatment because of age. The same pattern of correlation emerges when the standard age identification item is correlated with these three substantive items (Philllips, 1961, p. 349).

General Comments and Recommendations

With the exception of the correlation with chronological age, the comparative age identification item seems to correlate in a similar fashion to the standard age identification item. Since the item requests a comparison by the respondent of himself or herself with a generalized other object, the analyst has no information about the standard against which the respondent is comparing himself or herself. Therefore, in future uses of this item, it might be important to use a series of other objects, some of which are specific and some of which are either general or even known only to the respondent.

References

Jeffers, F. C., C. Eisdorfer, and E. W. Busse. "Measurement of Age Identification: A Methodologic Note." *Journal of Gerontology*, 1962, 17: 437-39.

Phillips, B. S. "Role Change, Subjective Age, and Adjustment: A Correlational Analysis." *Journal of Gerontology*, 1961, 16: 347-52.

Instrument

See the description of the instrument above.

A TIME PERSPECTIVE MEASURE OF SUBJECTIVE AGE
K. W. Back and K. J. Gergen, 1963

Definition of Concept

The investigators suggested that the subjective meaning of age to an individual can be known by means of an analysis of the individual's time perspective. Thus, regardless of their chronological age, the subjectively old are those who feel that they have relatively less time ahead of them.

Description of Instrument

This instrument is an index derived through a comparison between the subject's response to a single question and the respondent's chronological age. The question is: "When does a person reach his peak of mental ability?" The response is given in terms of a chronological age, which is then compared to respondent's age, resulting in the placement of the respondent into one of two categories: "peak ahead" or "peak behind."

Sample

The sample was a standard national, cross-sectional Gallup poll, representative of the United States (in 1958). The entire adult age range was included in the sampling.

Norms and Distribution

The distribution of "peak ahead" and "peak behind" by chronological age is shown in Table 10-5.

TABLE 10-5
Distribution by Chronological Age

	"Peak Ahead"	"Peak Behind"
Under 40	98.7%	1.3%
40-59	35.6%	64.4%
60+	5.0%	95.0%

SOURCE: K. W. Back and K. J. Gergen. "Apocalyptic and Serial Time Orientations and the Structure of Opinions." *Public Opinion Quarterly*, 1963, 27: 440. Reprinted by permission of authors and publisher.

Reliability/Validity Tests

The investigators hypothesized that respondents having a shorter, rather than a longer, time perspective (hence, the peak behind rather than ahead) would have more negative views of the future, would not be supportive of public policy programs that might take a relatively long time to produce results, and would be worried about foreign-policy crises. Using four questions that were included in a 1958 Gallup poll, it was found that the "peak behind" respondents were against foreign aid, more worried about bombs, more pessimistic about the power of the United States in the world, and more likely to predict future unemployment.

General Comments and Recommendations

The measure is an intriguing one, given its relationship to the concept of future time perspectives, about which there is a substantial social-psychological literature. The fact that there is little variance with the 60 and over age-group is unfortunate. However, applications of the measure to additional samples (including specialized gerontological samples) may well reveal greater variation.

The original item used in the construction of the index refers to the mental peak of an individual. Variations of this question could refer to physical, emotional, financial, and social peaks. Similarly, the perceived peaks for men and women reported by both male and female respondents could be computed separately.

Reference

Back, K. W., and K. J. Gergen. "Apocalyptic and Serial Time Orientations and the Structure of Opinions." *Public Opinion Quarterly*, 1963, 27: 427–42.

Instrument

See the description of the instrument above.

SEMANTIC AGE IDENTIFICATION
C. S. Guptill, 1969

Definition of Concept

The investigator suggested that the standard measure of subjective age identification is inadequate since it provides no information concerning the respondent's evaluation of old age. And, since many older persons do not identify themselves as old, it is commonly thought that this "denial" of old age is a denial of society's negative valuation of old age; similarly, prior research suggests that those older persons who do identify themselves as old are maladjusted. The investigator suggested that these assumptions can only be evaluated by a measure of age identification that directly assesses the older individual's perception of self in relation to the concepts old, middle-aged, and so forth.

Description of Instrument

This measure of semantic age identification is an index computed on the basis of analysis of several semantic differential scales, each of which is applied by the respondent in three concepts. Three stages in the computation of the index are involved.

1. Seven semantic differential scales are each applied to the concepts of myself, middle-aged man, and old man. The seven bipolar scales are:

free to do things	not free to do things
useless	useful
look to future	look to past
ineffective	effective
satisfied with life	dissatisfied with life
respected	disregarded
busy	inactive

SOURCE: C. S. Guptill. "A Measure of Age Identification." *The Gerontologist*, 1969, 9: 97. Reprinted by permission of author and publisher.

2. Using standard semantic differential methods, a distance score (D) is computed

between the concept myself and the concept old man; similarly, a D score is computed for each respondent between myself and middle-aged man.

3. Since it is useful, the investigator suggested, to have a single measure representing relative identification with old man versus middle-aged man—thus producing a single variable parallel to other questionnaire/interview measures—the two D scores are combined. "The technique involved is simply subtracting each respondent's D score between *Myself* and *Old Man* from his D score between *Myself* and *Middle-Aged Man*" (Guptill, 1969, p.98). Hence, a negative score on the computed index indicates identification with middle-aged man, while a positive index score indicates greater identification with old man.

The investigator suggested that a semantic age identification index computed in this way has the advantage of being a continuous variable in which the magnitude of the index score indicates intensity of feeling; at the same time, by dichotomizing the continuum at zero, comparisons to the more standard age identifications can be taken.

Research Context

As it has already been suggested, the investigator noted that the standard multiple-choice age identification item has been interpreted in terms of whether or not the older respondent has a negative image of himself or herself, in which old is equated with negative. The semantic differential approach allows the analyst to compare directly an older respondent's evaluation of self, with parallel evaluations of such concepts as old man and middle-aged man. Furthermore, the semantic differential approach allows the analyst to see which of the specific semantic differential scales from the list of bipolar adjectives best differentiate the respondent's perception of self and the other concepts.

Sample

The sample was purposive rather than representative. The respondents were part of a group of 425 white males in North Carolina and Virginia, who ranged in age from 55 to 87 and who were participating in a study of work and retirement. The men were healthy and ambulatory, and they lived at home.

Norms and Distribution

In this study as in others of subjective age identification, the majority of respondents did not identify themselves as old. While the investigator did not give a comprehensive set of descriptive data on the sample distribution, it was reported that 30% of the under-70-year-old and 47% of the over-70-year-old respondents fell onto the old side of the index measure.

Reliability/Validity Tests

The investigator noted that the questionnaire including the semantic differential measure did not include any other measures of age identification and so direct reliability/validity comparisons were not possible. Instead, he provided detailed comparisons of the percent age of "old" respondents on the semantic differential index with the percentage of "old" respondents in several of the studies derived from the Cornell studies in the mid-1950s. By examining such background variables as retirement status, marital status, general health rating, socioeconomic status, and activity level, it is demonstrated that the direction of relationships across all of the measures, including the semantic differential index, are similar; that is, a larger percentage of respondents identify themselves as old among those who are retired, not married, in poor health, less active, and so forth. Using this kind of convergent validity test, the investigator concluded that the standard item and the semantic differential index are measuring the same phenomenon.

General Comments and Recommendations

The investigator has done a persuasive job of indicating that semantic differential bipolar items do produce differences that, when combined into a single score, seem to measure subjective age identification. The reliability of the measures and procedures has not yet been demonstrated. It would be interesting to know whether alternative sets of semantic differential adjectives, applied to self, old man, and middle-aged man, would also yield useful summary index measures. And, of course, the use of old woman and middle-aged woman, especially for female respondents, would also contribute useful information concerning reliability and validity.

Reference

Guptill, C. S. "A Measure of Age Identification." *The Gerontologist,* 1969, 9: 96-102.

Instrument

See the description of the instrument above.

SURVEY RESEARCH CENTER "FEEL CLOSE" ITEMS
N. E. Cutler, 1974

Definition of Concept

The investigator was interested in the degree to which individuals comparatively identify, or "feel close," more with old people than with young people. The items are not used to assess directly whether or not the individual actually feels old but whether or not the individual feels closer to old persons than to young persons.

Description of Instrument

This is an index based upon three "feel close" items. The individual items are: (1) "Do you feel close to old people? (yes/no)," (2) "Do you feel close to young people? (yes/no)," and (3) "Which group do you feel closer to?" The two dichotomous "feel close" items concerned with young and old were part of a 16-item series of "feel close" items. The index of subjective age identification combines these three items as follows: A subjectively old person is a person who feels close to old but *not* to young people or a person who feels close to old and young but feels closer to old people. In this way, individuals are characterized as having subjective age identification as old, as young, or as not having a predominant age identification.

Research Context

The pair of dichotomous (yes/no) "feel close" items noted above was embedded in a sequence of 16 such items in which the respondent was asked whether he or she felt close to businessmen, liberals, southerners, poor people, Catholics, Protestants, Jews, young people, whites, blacks, conservatives, women, middle-class people, working people, farmers, and old people. The third question noted above was asked after the whole sequence of dichotomous "feel close" items was asked. The focus of the overall data collection was upon the psychological and subjective placement of the individual in his or her social world. It is important to note that the whole sequence of "feel close" items was designed by Prof. Gerald Gurin (Department of Psychology, University of Michigan), whose project was not gerontological in intent or origin. The index of subjective age identification was designed as part of a very different research project for which Gurin takes no responsibility. Indeed, the index of subjective age identification was computed before the publication of any empirical analysis of the data by Gurin himself; his generosity in making the data available for gerontological research is acknowledged in the research papers cited below.

Sample

The sequence of "feel close" items was included in a nationally representative sample of the adult American population conducted by the Survey Research Center of the University of Michigan's Institute for Social Research. The survey was the 1972 national election study designed by the ISR's Center for Political Studies, and it represented the 1972 version of a series of nationally representative probability samples that have been conducted by the ISR since 1952. For a variety of technical reasons, the 1972 national sample had an unusually large number of respondents, 2,705. The data are available through the Inter-University Consortium for Political and Social Research; hence, any scholar at a member institution of the consortium can obtain the entire data set. It should be noted that the 1976 national election survey also included the sequence of "feel close" items. However, all of the information presented here is based upon research using the 1972 survey.

Norms and Distribution

The data for the total sample (Cutler, 1975a) and the older subsample (Cutler, 1975b) are shown in Tables 10-6 and 10-7.

TABLE 10−6
Total Sample Distribution

Age	Young Identification	No Identification	Old Identification	(Number)
18-40	41%	49	11	(1,011)
41-54	20%	60	20	(500)
55-75	9%	54	37	(538)
76+	5%	36	60	(109)

NOTE: Gamma = .54.
SOURCE: N. E. Cutler. "Chronological Age, Subjective Age, and Social Welfare Orientations: The Organization of Attitudes toward Society, Economics, and Politics." Paper presented to the 10th International Congress of Gerontology, Jerusalem, August 1975.

TABLE 10−7
Distribution of 50+ Subsample

Age	Old Identification	No Identification	(Number)
50-64	31%	69	(406)
65-74	51%	49	(197)
75+	62%	38	(122)

NOTE: Gamma = .43.
SOURCE: N. E. Cutler. "Socioeconomic Predictors of Subjective Age." Paper presented to the 28th Annual Meeting of the Gerontological Society, Louisville, October 2-30, 1975.

Reliability/Validity Tests

No hypotheses were presented in the research about the expected relationship between subjective age identification and sociopolitical attitudes. Three empirical patterns can be noted, however.

1. Among the chronologically old, the subjective old are more liberal on such traditional issues as federal involvement in medical programs, less liberal on such contemporary issues as abortion, and less optimistic about personal finances (Cutler, 1974).

2. The examination of various attitude clusters suggests that for matters of orientation toward the future, and control over that future, the subjectively old have more well developed ideologies (i.e., attitudinal cohesiveness) than do the nonsubjectively old (Cutler, 1975a).

3. An analysis of the proposition that old age identification is simply a function of disadvantaged social position, using multiple regression analysis, reveals that chronological age is the only sociodemographic variable that substantially contributes to the explanation of subjective age and that such variables as income, education, widowhood, and retirement explain very little of the variance in subjective age identification (Cutler, 1975b).

General Comments and Recommendations

The most important advantages of this measure of subjective age identification are that it is based on a comparison of the respondent's feelings toward both young and old and that it appears in a national survey. The latter characteristic suggests that, if it were used in local samples, comparisons with national norms could be made. Similarly, regional differences within the national data could be compared with the local data. Furthermore, since the items have already appeared in national sample surveys in 1972 and 1976, trend analyses could be calculated. Since the Feel Close Measure does not directly determine whether the respondent believes himself or herself to be old, it remains for future research to find whether this index measures the same concept as the basic item described earlier does.

References

Cutler, N. E. "The Effects of Subjective Age Identification among Old and Young: A Nationwide Study of Political, Economic, and Social Attitudes." Paper presented to the 27th Annual Meeting of the Gerontological Society, Portland, November 5-9, 1974.

———. "Chronological Age, Subjective Age, and Social Welfare Orientations: The Organization of Attitudes toward Society, Economics, and Politics." Paper presented to the 10th International Congress of Gerontology, Jerusalem, August 1975(a).

———. "Socioeconomic Predictors of Subjective Age." Paper presented to the 28th Annual Meeting of the Gerontological Society, Louisville, October 26-30, 1975(b).

Cutler, N. E., and V. L. Bengtson. "The Attitudinal Meaning of Subjective Age Identification among Young Adults." Paper presented to the Annual Meeting of the American Sociological Association, San Francisco, August 1975(c).

Instrument

See the description of the instrument above.

Instruments

V1.10.I.a
THE EARLY CORNELL STUDIES
Z. M. Blau, 1956; B. Kutner, D. Fanshel, A. M. Togo, and T. S. Langner, 1956

See the description of the instrument in the abstract.

V1.10.I.b
THE DUKE "AGE AWARENESS" ITEM
E. W. Busse, F. C. Jeffers, and W. D. Obrist, 1957

See the description of the instrument in the abstract.

V1.10.I.c
PERCEIVED AGE
K. L. Bloom, 1961

See the description of the instrument in the abstract.

V1.10.I.d
FEELINGS ABOUT AGE
I. K. Zola, 1962

See the description of the instrument in the abstract.

V1.10.I.e
FEELING OLD AND SOCIAL INVOLVEMENT
T. Bell, 1967

See the description of the instrument in the abstract.

V1.10.I.f
CORNELL RETIREMENT STUDY
G. F. Streib and C. J. Schneider, 1971

See the description of the instrument in the abstract.

V1.10.I.g
COMPARATIVE AGE IDENTIFICATION
F. C. Jeffers, C. Eisdorfer, and E. W. Busse, 1962

See the description of the instrument in the abstract.

V1.10.II.a
A TIME PERSPECTIVE MEASURE OF SUBJECTIVE AGE
K. W. Back and K. J. Gergen, 1963

See the description of the instrument in the abstract.

V1.10.II.b
SEMANTIC AGE IDENTIFICATION
C. S. Guptill, 1969

See the description of the instrument in the abstract.

V1.10.II.c
SURVEY RESEARCH CENTER "FEEL CLOSE" ITEMS
N. E. Cutler, 1974

See the description of the instrument in the abstract.

Chapter 11

Life-Phase Analysis

Gunhild O. Hagestad

In all societies, the human life span is divided into socially meaningful units through systems of age differentiation and age grading, which result in culturally recognized "punctuations of the lifeline" (Neugarten and Peterson, 1957). These socially created life phases have their associated rights, duties, and expected personal attributes. Furthermore, they divide a population into age-groups, whose relationships are structured and regulated (Riley, Johnson, and Foner, 1972). A social age system, as part of a society's culture, is transmitted to members through socialization. The age system thus becomes internalized and is a major factor in the structuring of individual lives (Neugarten and Hagestad, 1976).

This chapter examines research that has focused on socially recognized life phases in American society. It does *not* deal with psychological stage theories of development; rather, it assesses research that has attempted to elucidate socially created "demarcation points" in the span of human life—the sociocultural context of human growth, maturation, and aging.

Chapter 11 overlaps somewhat with two other chapters in this volume, Chapter 10 and Chapter 12. However, the present discussion concentrates on measures designed to assess the adult life span and not just old age.

Age Systems in Complex Societies

Theoretical overviews of social age systems in industrial societies have stressed the complexity of such systems (Cain, 1964; Neugarten and Hagestad, 1976). Three sources of complexity have been discussed: the existence of multiple age systems, intracohort variation, and intercohort change.

It has been argued that American society has no unified system of role allocation and timetables. Different institutional spheres have different age systems, which lack synchronization (Cain, 1964; Elder, 1975). For example, a man may face a prescription of adult military duties at the same time he faces a proscription against adult rights, such as buying alcoholic beverages or taking out a loan in his own name. The lack of synchronization produces age status inconsistency, to borrow a term from general work on social stratification (Lenski, 1954).

It also has been pointed out that various subsegments of the population have age systems showing systematic differences. Most commonly it is argued that any form of age grading differentiates males and females (Linton, 1942; Parsons, 1942). In complex societies, there are also likely to be regional, social class, and ethnic differences in age systems (Elder, 1975; Neugarten and Peterson, 1957; Youmans, 1971).

Finally, age systems change as a result of general social and cultural change. Thus, "different cohorts age in different ways" (Riley, Johnson, and Foner, 1972). Therefore, a diachronic approach to life-phase research is necessary (see Galtung, 1975).

Research Themes

Research into culturally created life phases has followed three main avenues: roles, norms, and perceptions. Each topic has several subtopics.

Roles

In work most closely connected with anthropological studies of age grading (e.g., Gulliver, 1968) and elaborated by Riley, Johnson, and Foner (1972), researchers have looked at age criteria for the channeling of cohorts into social roles. This work has taken three focuses.

The Three Ps: Age criteria serve as a basis for permission, proscription, and prescription (Riley, Johnson, and Foner, 1972), with regard to channeling people into social roles (Pincus, Wood, and Kondrat, 1974; Wood, 1973).

Timetables: Following the conceptual lead of Roth (1963), researchers have looked at "social clocks" for the ordering of major life events, usually role transition. Investigators have asked questions about the normal sequencing and timing of transitions; that is they have wondered what constitutes being on time, late, or early (Neugarten and Peterson, 1957; Neugarten, Moore, and Lowe, 1965).

Social Age: Attempts have been made to create summary expressions of what Kingsley Davis (1949) called one's "life station," a person's "social maturity" with regard to role "careers" in major institutional spheres, such as family and work (Bengtson and Lovejoy, 1973; Rose, 1972).

Norms

Research areas falling under roles clearly deal with norms — informal and institutionalized. However, there are questions regarding age-related norms that cannot easily be fit into a role framework.

Age-Appropriate Behavior and Life-style: What constitutes "acting one's age?" What is considered an appropriate choice of dress and grooming for men and women of different ages? (Bultena and Wood, 1969; Neugarten, Moore, and Lowe, 1965; Plath and Ikeda, 1975; Wood, 1971).

Age-group Interactions: What are the "normal" and expected relationships and interactions among members of various age-groups?

Perceptions

One research emphasis has been on assessing what major phases of adult life members of American society perceive and what characteristics differentiate these phases. Questions in this area have three focuses:

Benchmarks: How many phases are recognized? How are they labeled? What differentiates them? Are the benchmarks defined in terms of chronological age, physical characteristics, personality traits, or social role changes (Cameron, 1969; Drevenstedt, 1976; Fry, 1976; Gould, 1972; NCOA, 1975; Neugarten and Peterson, 1957; Kedar and Shanan, 1975)?

Age-Related Characteristics: Research in this category has attempted to assess the degree of consensus on *what* constitutes life phases. Other research has treated benchmarks as *given*, either in the form of chronological age categories (Bell and Stanfield, 1973; Laurence, 1964; Rosencranz and McNevin, 1969) or concepts such as "the middle-aged" or "the middle generation" (Berman,

1974; Kogan and Wallach, 1961), and then explored anticipated attributes of people in particular life phases. Ahammer and Baltes (1972) examined what were perceived as desirable traits for various target age categories. Neugarten and Peterson (1957) asked respondents to give the chronological ages they associated with a set of descriptions.

Life-Phase Comparison: In some studies, the focus is on how different life phases, or age-groups, compare on various indicators, such as attitude and outlook (Bengtson, 1971), opportunity for happiness (Cameron, 1972), general well-being (Back and Bourgue, 1970; NCOA, 1975), and power and respect (Youmans, 1971).

Methods Used in the Research

In all three topical areas, survey research has predominated. Most of the instruments discussed here are from interview schedules or questionnaires, and the majority of them apply single items or a battery of items. Few serious attempts at scale construction can be found. Exceptions to this basic trend can be noted in cases in which investigators have adapted techniques from general psychological research, such as the semantic differential (used by Laurence, 1964, and Rosencranz and McNevin, 1969), the Gough Adjective Check List (Aaronson, 1966), and the Jackson Personality Research Form (Ahammer and Baltes, 1972).

Some investigators have used content analysis with fixed categories. Some of them have studied perceptions of various age-groups in popular literature, such as magazines (e.g., Martel, 1963) and children's books (Seltzer and Atchley, 1971). Cain (1974) has examined legislation, looking for chronological age limits on roles, duties, and privileges.

Projective techniques have been applied, mostly in the study of perceptions. Researchers at the University of Chicago developed an intergenerational TAT card (see Neugarten and Gutmann, 1958); Britton and Britton (1970) also have had respondents react to pictures, as did Fennel (1974) and Kogan (1979). Back and Bourque (1970) asked people to draw "life graphs" in an approach similar to Buhler's "curve of life."

Following the suggestion of Jeffers, Eisdorfer, and Busse (1962), card sorts have been used in studies of benchmarks by Fry (1976) and of perceptions by Hickey and Kalish (1968).

An important tool for life-phase analysis that has yielded significant research falls outside the scope of this volume. Recently, a great deal of work has been generated on cohort differences and historical shifts in life-course patterns. Thus, the best work to date on the three Ps and timetables has come from secondary data analyses based on historical records (see Uhlenberg, 1974), census material (Glick, 1977; Modell, Furstenberg, and Hershberg, 1976), and social science data banks from longitudinal studies (Elder, 1974; Glenn, 1977).

Trends and Gaps in the Research

Among the research instruments discussed in this chapter, perceptions of age-related characteristics have been investigated most often. This is the focus of roughly one-third of all the instruments reviewed. (See Table 11-1.) The best-known efforts in this area are a semantic differential developed by Rosencranz and McNevin and a checklist created by Tuckman and Lorge. Both instruments ask the respondent to describe members of a given age category. These instruments have been used in a number of subsequent studies, and there is a fair amount of data on their reliability and validity. It is, however, difficult to find generalizations *across* studies of age perceptions, even when the same instruments are used. This is partly due to the lack of consistency in targets or stimuli. Often, terms such as stage, stratum, age-group, and age category are used interchangeably. Some researchers appear to have assumed that their respondents were judging the aging process; others have limited their focus to perceptions of current cohorts.

The second most common theme in the research under review is benchmarks. Following the work of the Kansas City Study of Adult Life (Neugarten and Peterson, 1957), a number of researchers have asked what constitutes the phases of adult life and how they are delineated. Considerable consensus has been found regarding three major phases—young adulthood, middle age, and old age—as well as their chronological boundaries (Cameron, 1969; Drevenstedt, 1976; NCOA, 1975; Kedar and Shanan, 1975).

As part of a card-sort procedure, Fry (1976) did not ask about the main phases of adulthood but had subjects sort cards into categories of "personas" who appeared to be in similar phases. The subjects used, on the average, six categories. Fry's article provides a useful chart showing how various scholars have conceptualized phases of adulthood in their discussions of human development.

Several researchers have compared various age-groups. Youmans (1971) and Cameron (1970b) studied the perceived power, respect,

TABLE 11–1
Instruments Reviewed in Chapter 11

Instrument	Author (date)	Code Number
I. Roles		
a. Age-Appropriate Behavior	Wood (1973)	V1.11.I.a
b. Timetables for Men and Women	Kansas City Study of Adult Life	V1.11.I.b
c. Index of Social Age Status	Bengtson and Lovejoy (1973)	V1.11.I.c
d. Social Age	Rose (1972)	V1.11.I.d
II. Norms		
a. Normative Attitudes toward the Aged Role	Bultena and Wood (1969)	V1.11.II.a
b. Age Norm Checklist	Neugarten, Moore, and Lowe (1965)	V1.11.II.b
c. Normative Expectations for Age Roles	Wood and O'Brien (no date)	V1.11.II.c
III. Perceptions		
a. Age Parameters	Cameron (1969)	V1.11.III.a
b. Onset of Adult Phases	Drevenstedt (1976)	V1.11.III.b
c. Ages of Adulthood	Fry (1976)	V1.11.III.c
d. Phases of Adult Life	Gould (1972)	V1.11.III.d
e. Onset of Old Age	NCOA (1975)	V1.11.III.e
f. Periods of Life	Kansas City Study of Adult Life	V1.11.III.f
g. Expectations about Self and Partner in Intergenerational Interactions/Perception of Self and Partner	Berman (1974)	V1.11.III.g
h. Adjective Check List	Gough and Heilbrun (1965)	Copyrighted
i. Perceptions of Adults	Hickey and Kalish (1968)	V1.11.III.i
j. Jackson Personality Research Form	Jackson (1967)	Copyrighted
k. Age Association Items	Kansas City Study of Adult Life	V1.11.III.k
l. Life Graphs	Back and Bourque (1970)	V1.11.III.l
m. Perceived Generation Gap	Bengtson (1971)	V1.11.III.m
n. Comparison of Age-Groups	Cameron (1970)	V1.11.III.n
o. Best Years of Life	NCOA (1975)	V1.11.III.o
p. Perceptions of Age-Groups' Respect and Influence	Youmans (1971)	V1.11.III.p

and influence of the young, the middle-aged, and the old. Neither of these studies distinguished between men and women as targets.

Three studies have examined perceived and expected well-being during various life stages. Harris and associates (NCOA, 1975) asked respondents to pick the best and worst decade in an average person's life. Back and Bourque (1970), in another national survey, had their respondents graphically represent "ups and downs" in the decades of *their own* lives. Cameron (1970b) asked a smaller sample to compare the young, the middle-aged, and the old on opportunities and desire for happiness and fun, as well as on perceptions of actual happiness. Bengtson (1971) asked a general, single-item question about the perceived "gap" between members of the same three age-groups studied by Cameron.

In the areas of norms and roles, there are few research efforts to review. Two attempts to create measures of social age in terms of a person's position in several "role careers" are included (Bengtson and Lovejoy, 1973; Rose, 1972), although both have serious limitations.

The only work on informal, age-based permission, proscription, and prescription for the occupancy of social roles appears to be some exploratory research by a group of investigators at the University of Wisconsin. These researchers asked about chronological age criteria for role "exits" and "entrances" in the spheres of work, education, politics, family, and friendship (Pincus, Wood, and Kondrat, 1974; Wood, 1973).

To this author's knowledge, work started by researchers at the University of Chicago represents the only effort to measure timetables and age norms. In the Kansas City Study of Adult Life, interviews included items on the optimal timing of major life events, such as getting married, starting work, and becoming a parent (Neugarten and Peterson, 1957). Later, a series of studies explored the degree of consensus regarding appropriate behavior for men and women of different ages (Neugarten, Moore, and Lowe, 1965). These age-norm items have since been used with a Japanese sample (Plath and Ikeda, 1975) and several additional American samples (McDonald, 1976; Wood, 1971). New items have since been added by other researchers (Bultena and Wood, 1969). The findings of these studies indicate an impressive degree of consensus regarding acceptable or unacceptable behavior at different ages. However, much work remains to be done on the aspects of social control in age systems. Although research has reported subjective awareness of the individual's own position vis-à-vis social timetables, such as a sense of being on time, late, or early (e.g., Sofer, 1970), there has been no systematic attempt to assess the extent to which individuals experience social constraints and sanctions in connection with timetables, informally stated three Ps, and age norms. In other words, no work has asked about age-system deviants and how they are treated.

Researchers have analyzed timing patterns on the basis of census material and other types of secondary data. They have argued that in recent decades a compression of major life transitions has occurred, particularly in early adulthood (Glick, 1977; Modell, Furstenberg, and Hershberg, 1976; Neugarten and Moore, 1968). They also have demonstrated decreasing variance around modal patterns of life-event timing and have suggested that this may indicate less flexibility in timetables during modern times, compared with earlier historical epochs. To this author's knowledge, no social psychological work has been done on the subjectively experienced intesity of age norms and timetables.

This fact appears to be related to another neglected topic in the literature under review: the relationship between age systems and social interaction. Although there is general agreement that age structures interaction patterns and that norms exist regarding relationships among age-groups, no research has looked at these aspects of social systems. For example, in spite of the informal rule putting age before beauty, no research seems to have asked about the relative power of age in structuring social interaction compared to other status criteria, such as sex and socioeconomic status. Thus, no instruments were to be found for age-group interactions. Furthermore, in the rather voluminous literature on life-phase perceptions, only two or three studies have considered the interactional correlates of such perceptions or how they might be changed as a result of interaction. Berman (1974), in a study that appears to be unique, administered attitudinal measures before and after a group session involving young and middle-aged participants in order to assess the impact of an interaction encounter.

Unresolved Issues in the Research

Little of the American age system's complexity, discussed at the beginning of this chapter, is reflected in the existing work on life phases. A few studies have recognized the existence of multiple age systems (for instance, by distinguishing between timetables in different institutional spheres, such as family and work). However, no effort has been made to explore the interaction between timetables and the *relative salience* of institutional spheres in structuring the course of individual lives.

Intracohort variation in social age systems is generally neglected, both on the target and the perceiver side. For example, the vast majority of studies on benchmarks and perceptions of age-related characteristics do not distinguish between men and women in their targets. However, when respondents *are* asked to discuss men and women separately, it is clear that the sexes indeed have distinct age systems (Drevenstedt, 1976; NCOA, 1975; Kogan, 1979; Neugarten and Peterson, 1957). It has often been assumed that timetables in the family serve as the main "life-course organizers" for women, while the sphere of work is most salient in the structuring of men's lives. The extent to which this might be changing as a result of general changes in the sex roles in the contemporary United States needs to be addressed in future research.

Besides sex differences, most types of systematic intracohort variation have been neglected in existing work because the research tends to be based on highly limited samples. However, several researchers have demonstrated that distinct differences among the social classes are found in perceptions of age-related characteristics (Hickey and Kalish, 1968; Rosencranz and McNevin, 1969), timetables (Neugarten and Peterson, 1957; Olsen and Neugarten, 1959), and benchmarks (Fry, 1976; Kedar and Shanan, 1975). Youmans (1971) and Back and Bourque (1970) demonstrated rural-urban differences in the relative evaluation of life phases. Sociocultural change, the third source of the age system's complexity, has generally been ignored by students of life phases, with the notable exception of scholars working on secondary data sources. In their work, propositions regarding changes in timetables and the three Ps have been advanced on the basis of diachronic analyses of census material and legislation (Cain, 1974; Glick, 1977; Modell, Furstenberg, and Hershberg, 1976). However, historical changes in age perceptions and informal age norms have not been dealt with in social psychological work. Several authors have pointed out that a new breed of old people is emerging as a result of twentieth-century advances in medicine and general improvements in the quality of life (Cain, 1967; Neugarten, 1974). Bernard (1976) has also argued that Americans are witnessing a new middle age, particularly among women. One would expect that perception of, and attitudes toward, these age categories would change as a result of general cohort changes. Similarly, timetables and age norms may change partly because of general cultural change and partly as a consequence of new patterns of maturation and aging in recent cohorts of adults. Thus, research runs the risk of being *cohort-centric,* with instruments that have lost their appropriateness or have taken on different meaning because of historical change. For example, some of the age-norm items developed by the Chicago group during the 1950s and 1960s are now outdated. This is due to changes in life-style, such as a general decline of age differences in dress and grooming. Instruments can also be *stage-centric.* Little or no attention has been paid to the *age equivalence* of items in studies attempting to compare perceptions of the views of age norms by respondents in different life phases.

Validity and Reliability

Most of the research just reviewed constitutes early explorations and tends to be based on batteries of items administered to small samples. Very few attempts have been made to analyze the scaleability or internal consistency of these instruments, and little or no information is available on test-retest reliability. These shortcomings may partially reflect the exploratory nature of most of the studies and the small sample sizes, but they would also appear to be related to the lack of theoretical basis for much of the work. This brings into focus the issue of validity, particularly construct validity. There is a distressing lack of consideration of focal concepts and their significance in much of the work under discussion. In other words, it is not only unclear *what* is being measured, but *why* it is being measured.

Suggestions for Future Work

In this reviewer's opinion, the first prerequisite for improvement in research on life phases in modern society is a clarification of what questions are being asked and a statement of the theoretical assumptions underlying the research. A new look at what phenomena are being addressed would lead to new efforts to specify constructs, standardize measures, and make research comparable. Only then can social scientists face up to the real challenge in the area—dealing with dynamic phenomena that require a diachronic approach.

REFERENCES

Aaronson, B. S. "Personality Stereotypes of Aging." *Journal of Gerontology*, 1966, 21: 458-62.

Ahammer, I. M., and P. B. Baltes. "Objective versus Perceived Age Differences in Personality: How Do Adolescents, Adults, and Older People View Themselves and Each Other?" *Journal of Gerontology*, 1972, 27: 46-51.

Axelrod, S., and C. Eisdorfer. "Attitudes toward Old People: An Empirical Analysis of the Stimulus-Group Validity of the Tuckman-Lorge Questionnaire." *Journal of Gerontology*, 1961, 16: 75-80.

Back, K., and L. B. Bourque. "Life Graphs: Aging and Cohort Effect." *Journal of Gerontology*, 1970, 25: 249-55.

Bell, B. D., and G. G. Stanfield. "Chronological Age in Relation to Attitudinal Judgments: An Experimental Analysis." *Journal of Gerontology*, 1973, 28: 491-96.

Bengtson, V. L. "The Generation Gap: A Review and Typology of Social-Psychological Perspectives." *Youth and Society*, 1970, 2: 7-31.

_____. "Inter-age Differences in Perception and the Generation Gap." *The Gerontologist*, 1971, 11 (4, part 2): 85-90.

Bengtson, V. L., and M. C. Lovejoy. "Values, Personality, and Social Structure." *American Behavioral Scientist*, 1973, 16: 880-912.

Berman, H. J. "Perception of Self and Others in Relation to Age." Ph.D. dissertation, Washington University, 1974.

Bernard, J. *Women, Wives, Mothers*. Chicago: Aldine, 1976.

Britton, J. O., and J. H. Britton. "Young People's Perceptions of Age and Aging." Paper presented to the 23rd Annual Meeting of the Gerontological Society, Toronto, October 22-24, 1970.

Broverman, I. K., D. M. Broverman, F. E. Clarkson, P. A. Rosenkranz, and S. R. Vogel. "Sex Role Stereotypes and Clinical Judgments of Mental Health." *Journal of Consulting and Clinical Psychology*, 1970, 34: 1-7.

Bultena, G., and V. Wood. "Normative Attitudes toward the Aged Role among Migrant and Nonmigrant Retirees." *The Gerontologist*, 1969, 9 (3): 204-8.

Cain, L. D. "Life Course and Social Structure." In *Handbook of Modern Sociology*, R. L. Faris (ed.), pp. 272-309. Chicago: Rand McNally, 1964.

_____. "Age Status and Generational Phenomena: The New Old People in Contemporary America." *The Gerontologist*, 1967, 7: 83-92.

_____. "The Growing Importance of Legal Aid in Determining the Status of the Elderly." *The Gerontologist*, 1974, 14: 167-74.

Cameron, P. "Age Parameters of Young Adult, Middle-aged, Old and Aged." *Journal of Gerontology*, 1969, 24 (2): 201-2.

_____. "The Generation Gap: Beliefs about Sexuality and Self-Reported Sexuality." *Developmental Psychology*, 1970a, 3: 272.

_____. "The Generation Gap: Which Generation is Believed Powerful versus Generational Members' Self-Appraisals of Power." *Developmental Psychology*, 1970b, 3: 403-4.

_____. "Stereotypes about Generational Fun and Happiness versus Self-Appraised Fun and Happiness." *The Gerontologist*, 1972, 12: 120-23.

_____. "Masculinity/Femininity of the Generations: As Self-Reported and as Stereotypically Appraised." *International Journal of Aging and Human Development*, 1976, 7: 143-51.

Cryns, A. G., and A. Monk. "Attitudes toward Youth as a Function of Adult Age: A Multivariate Study in Intergenerational Dynamics." *International Journal of Aging and Human Development*, 1973, 4: 23-33.

Davis K. *Human Society*. New York: Macmillan, 1949.

Drevenstedt, J. "Perceptions of Onsets of Young Adulthood, Middle Age, and Old Age." *Journal of Gerontology*, 1976, 31: 53-57.

Eisdorfer, C. "Attitudes toward Old People: A Re-analysis of Item Validity of the Stereotype Scale." *Journal of Gerontology*, 1966, 21: 455-57.

Elder, G. H., Jr. *Children of the Great Depression*. Chicago: University of Chicago Press, 1974,

_____. "Age Differentiation and the Life Course." In *Annual Review of Sociology* (vol. 1), A. Inkeles, J. Coleman, and N. Smelser (eds.), pp. 165-90. Palo Alto, Calif.: Annual Reviews, 1975.

Fennel, V. "Hierarchical Aspects of Age Relations in Curlew Point." Ph.D. dissertation, University of South Carolina, 1974.

Fry, C. L. "Age Grading in a Complex Society: A Study of the Age Status Structure of the United States." Ph.D. dissertation, University of Arizona, 1973.

_____. "The Ages of Adulthood: A Question of Numbers." *Journal of Gerontology*, 1976 31: 170-77.

———. "The Dimensions of Age: A Multidimensional Scaling Analysis." Paper presented to the 74th Annual Meeting of the American Anthropological Society, 1977.

Galtung, J. "Diachronic Correlation, Process Analysis and Causal Analysis." In *Quantitative Sociology: International Perspectives on Mathematical and Statistical Modeling*, H. M. Blalock, A. Aganbegian, F. M. Borodkin, R. Boudon, and V. Capecchi (eds.), pp. 3-47. New York: Academic Press.

Glenn, N. *Cohort Analysis.* Beverly Hills, Calif.: Sage, 1977.

Glick, P. "Updating the Family Life Cycle." *Journal of Marriage and the Family*, 1977, 39: 5-13.

Gough, H., and A. Heilbrun, Jr. *The Adjective Check List Manual.* Palo Alto, Calif.: Consulting Psychologists Press, 1965.

Gould, R. L. "The Phases of Adult Life: A Study in Developmental Psychology." *American Journal of Psychiatry*, 1972, 129 (5): 521-31.

Gulliver, P. H. "Age Differentiation." *International Encyclopedia of the Social Sciences*, 1968, 1: 157-61.

Hickey, T., and R. Kalish. "Young People's Perception of Adults." *Journal of Gerontology*, 1968, 23: 215-19.

Jackson, D. M. *Personality Research Form Manual.* Goshen, N.Y.: Research Psychology Press, 1967.

Jeffers, F., C. Eisdorfer, and E. Busse. "Measurement of Age Identification: A Methodological Note." *Journal of Gerontology*, 1962, 17: 437-39.

Kedar, H. S., and J. Shanan. "The Phenomenological Structure of the Life Span from Adolescence to Senescence as Spontaneously Reported by Different Age-Sex Groups." Paper presented to the 10th International Congress of Gerontology, Jerusalem, 1975.

Kedar, H. S., J. Shanan, M. A. Kogan, and A. Wallach. "Age Changes in Values and Attitudes." *Journal of Gerontology*, 1961, 16: 272-80.

Kogan, N. "A Study of Age Categorization." *Journal of Gerontology*, 1979, 34 (3): 358-67.

Kogan, N., and M. A. Wallach. "Age Changes in Values and Attitudes." *Journal of Gerontology*, 1961, 16: 272-80.

Laurence, M. W. "Sex Differences in the Perception of Men and Women at Four Different Ages." *Journal of Gerontology*, 1964, 19: 343-48.

Lenski, G. E. "Status Crystallization: A Non-vertical Dimension of Social Status." *American Sociological Review*, 1954, 19: 405-13.

Linton, R. A. "Age and Sex Categories." *American Sociological Review*, 1942, 7: 589-603.

McDonald, W. "A Study of Age Norms and Age Associations." Unpublished paper, Committee on Human Development, University of Chicago, 1975.

Martel, M. U. "Age-Sex Roles in American Magazine Fiction (1890-1955)." In *Middle Age and Aging*, B. L. Neugarten (ed.), pp. 47-57. Chicago: University of Chicago Press, 1968.

Modell, J., F. Furstenberg, Jr., and T. Hershberg. "Social Change and Life Course Development in Historical Perspective." *Journal of Family History*, 1976, 1: 7-32.

National Council on the Aging. *The Myth and Reality of Aging in America*. Washington, D.C.: National Council on the Aging, 1975.

Naus, P. J. "Some Correlates of Attitudes toward Old People." *International Journal of Aging and Human Development*, 1973, 4: 229-43.

Neugarten, B. L. "Age Groups in American Society and the Rise of the Young-Old." *Annals of the American Academy*, 1974, 415: 187-98.

Neugarten, B. L., and D. L. Gutmann. "Age-Sex Roles and Personality in Middle Age: A Thematic Apperception Study." In *Middle Age and Aging*, B. L. Neugarten (ed.), pp. 58-71. Chicago: University of Chicago Press, 1968.

Neugarten, B. L., and G. O. Hagestad. "Age and the Life Course." In *Handbook of Aging and the Social Sciences*, E. Shanas and R. Binstock (eds.), J. E. Birren (ed.), pp. 35-55. New York: Van Nostrand Reinhold, 1976.

Neugarten, B. L., and J. W. Moore. "The Changing Age-Status System." In *Middle Age and*

Aging, B. L. Neugarten (ed.), pp. 5-21. Chicago: University of Chicago Press, 1968.

Neugarten, B. L., J. W. Moore, and J. C. Lowe. "Age Norms, Age Constraints and Adult Socialization." *American Journal of Sociology*, 1965, 70: 710-17.

Neugarten, B. L., and W. A. Peterson. "A Study of the American Age Grading System." *Proceedings of the Fourth Congress of the International Association of Gerontology*, 1957, 3: 497-502.

Olsen, K. M., and B. L. Neugarten. "Social Class and Age-graded Behavior in Adulthood: An Empirical Study." Paper presented to the Annual Meeting of the American Sociological Association, Chicago, 1959.

Parsons, T. "Age and Sex in the Social Structure of the United States." *American Sociological Review*, 1942, 7: 604-20.

Pincus, A., V. Wood, and R. Kondrat. "Perceptions of Age Appropriate Activities and Roles." Paper presented to the 27th Annual Meeting of the Gerontological Society, Portland, November 5-9, 1974.

Plath, D. W., and K. Ikeda. "After Coming of Age: Adult Awareness of Age Norms." In *Socialization and Communication in Primary Groups*, The Hague: Mouton, 1975.

Radcliffe-Brown, A. R. "Age Organization Terminology." *Man*, 1929, 29: 21.

Riley, M. W. "Aging and Cohort Succession: Interpretations and Misinterpretations." *Public Opinion Quarterly*, 1973, 37 (Spring): 35-49.

Riley, M. W., M. E. Johnson, and A. Foner (eds.). *Aging and Society: A Sociology of Age Stratification* (vol. 3). New York: Russell Sage Foundation, 1972.

Rose, C. C. "The Measurement of Social Age." *Aging and Human Development*, 1972, 3: 153-68.

Rosencranz, A. A., and T. E. McNevin. "A Factor Analysis of Attitudes toward the Aged." *The Gerontologist*, 1969, 9: 55-59.

Roth, J. A. *Timetables*. Indianapolis: Bobbs-Merrill, 1963.

Seltzer, M. M., and R. C. Atchley. "The Concept of Old: Changing Attitudes and Stereotypes." *The Gerontologist*, 1971, 11 (3, part 1): 226-30.

Sofer, C. *Men in Mid-Career*. New York: Cambridge University Press, 1970.

Tuckman, J., and I. Lorge. "Attitudes toward Old People." *Journal of Social Psychology*, 1953, 37: 249-60.

Uhlenberg, P. R. "Cohort Variations in Family Life Cycle Experiences of United States Females." *Journal of Marriage and the Family*, 1974, 36: 284-92.

Wood, V. "Age-Appropriate Behavior for Older Persons." *The Gerontologist*, 1971, 11 (4, part 1): 74-78.

_____. "Role Allocation as a Function of Age." Paper presented to the 26th Annual Meeting of the Gerontological Society, Miami Beach, November 5-9, 1973.

Youmans, E. G. "Generation and Perceptions of Old Age: An Urban-Rural Comparison." *The Gerontologist*, 1971, 11 (4, part 1): 284-88.

Abstracts

AGE-APPROPRIATE BEHAVIOR
V. Wood, 1973

Definition of Variable or Concept

The instrument focuses on appropriate age for entry and exit into various social roles for men and women.

Description of Instrument

The battery of 41 open-ended questions asks at what age "a person"/"a man"/"a woman" is *old enough* or *too old* to occupy given social roles in three domains: political and legal, education and work, family and friendship.

Method of Administration

The instrument can be administered as an interview or a questionnaire.

Context of Development and Subsequent Use

The battery was part of a series of studies on age norms and age-appropriate behavior carried out by a group of investigators at the University of Wisconsin. One member of the team, Nahemow, has also used the instrument in a study at the University of South Carolina.

Sample

The Wisconsin research compared the perceptions of 84 college students, ages 18 to 25, and 125 residents in public housing for the elderly. The elderly sample had an age range from 60 to 95 years, with 75% age 70 to 85. Three-fourths of the elderly sample were female, and two-thirds were widowed.

Scoring, Scale Norms, and Distribution

Scoring of these open-ended data used these two systems: mean age given for role entry and exit in each item and a "constrictiveness score" assigned as follows. Score 1 if respondent denied relevance of age for the item. Score 2 if age given fell into lowest quartile of the distribution for that item in the case of items asking when a person was old enough *or* age given fell in highest quartile for items asking when a person was too old. Score 3 if age given fell into two middle quartiles. Score 4 if age given fell into uppor quartile for items asking when a person was old enough *or* in lowest quartile for items asking when a person was too old.

Formal Tests of Validity

No formal tests were reported, but it can be noted that the respondents were significantly more ready to give age limits on role entry than on role exit.

Usability on Older Populations

No problems were reported in using the instrument with an older sample.

TABLE 11−2
Adjusted Mean Constrictiveness Scores*

	Young	Elderly
Sum Entry Items (21)	2.54	3.00
Sum Exit Items (20)	2.09	2.54
Political-Legal Entry (6)	2.62	3.19
Political-Legal Exit (6)	2.06	2.44
Work-Education Entry (8)	2.31	2.88
Work-Education Exit (7)	2.14	2.61
Family-Friend Entry (7)	2.73	3.03
Family-Friend Exit (7)	2.09	2.55

*Because there were slight differences in the number of items in each category, to facilitate comparisons the mean score for each category was divided by the number or items in that category in computing the adjusted mean.
SOURCE: A. Pincus, V. Wood, and R. Kondrat. "Perceptions of Age Appropriate Activities and Roles." Paper presented to the 27th Annual Meeting of the Gerontological Society, Portland, November 5-9, 1974.

Sensitivity to Age Differences

The two samples' mean constrictiveness scores are shown in Table 11-2.

General Comments and Recommendations

The wording of the items raises questions about their equivalence. For example, one item asks when it is acceptable for a "girl" to marry and another asks when a "son" is old enough to have his own apartment.

Refrences

Pincus, A., V. Wood, and R. Kondrat. "Perceptions of Age Appropriate Activities and Roles." Paper presented to the 27th Annual Meeting of the Gerontological Society, Portland, November 5-9, 1974.

Wood, V. "Role Allocation as a Function of Age." Paper presented to the 26th Annual Meeting of the Gerontological Society, Miami Beach, November 5-9, 1973.

Instrument

See Instrument V1.11.I.a.

TIMETABLES FOR MEN AND WOMEN
Kansas City Study of Adult Life

Definition of Variable or Concept

The instrument deals with perceptions regarding optimal timing for major life events for men and women.

Description of Instrument

Battery consists of 11 open-ended questions.

Method of Administration

The instrument is administered in a personal interview.

Context of Development and Subsequent Use

The measure was part of a larger section of the interview dealing with changes in adulthood.

Sample

The sample was a random sampling of 240 residents of the metropolitan area of Kansas City, Mo., who were stratified by age, sex, and socioeconomic status. The age range was between 40 and 70 years.

Scoring, Scale Norms, and Distribution

For each item, the researchers looked at the range of ages given and the proportion of the respondents who concurred on a given age range. For most of the items, more than 80% of the respondents agreed on an age range of five years or less.

Usability on Older Populations

There were no problems reported in using this interview with older respondents.

Sensitivity to Age Differences

Few age differences were found among the responses.

General Comments and Recommendations

More work is needed on the social-control aspects of timetables (see this chapter's introduction). Furthermore, data analysis should look at *variance* around modal ages and factors contributing to such variance.

References

Neugarten, B. L., J. W. Moore, and J. C. Lowe. "Age Norms, Age Constraints and Adult Socialization." *American Journal of Sociology,* 1965, 70: 710-17.

Neugarten, B. L., and W. A. Peterson. "A Study of the American Age Grading System." *Proceedings of the Fourth Congress of the International Association of Gerontology,* 1957, 3: 497-502.

Instrument

See Instrument V1.11.I.b.

INDEX OF SOCIAL AGE STATUS
V. L. Bengtson, and M. C. Lovejoy, 1973

Definition of Variable or Concept

Social age status in terms of "careers" in various institutional spheres is studied.

Description of Instrument

The index combines five separate indicators of age status: marital status, parental status, educational status, job status, and extent of economic dependency. Within each sphere, a respondent is assigned a score, and the five scores are summed.

Method of Administration

The index is based on basic background information normally collected during survey research.

Context of Development and Subsequent Use

The index was developed as part of a large-scale study on generations carried out by the University of Southern California.

Sample

The sample consisted of 2,044 members of three-generational families, illustrated in Table 11-3.

TABLE 11−3
Index of Social Age Status Sample, by Generation

	G_1 (Grandparent)	G_2 (Parent)	G_3 (Grandchild)
N	494	686	864
Mean Age	67.02	43.82	19.44
S.D.	6.47	5.27	2.88
Sex			
Male	51.6%	46.0%	48.6%
Female	48.4%	54.0%	51.4%

SOURCE: V. L. Bengtson and M. C. Lovejoy. "Values, Personality, and Social Structure." *American Behavioral Scientist,* 1973, 16 (2): 896. Reprinted by permission of authors and publisher.

Scoring, Scale Norms, and Distribution

The social-age markers are scored as follows:

1. Marital status: never married, currently married, divorced or widowed (scores of 0, 1, and 2 are assigned, respectively.)
2. Parental status: no children, dependent children under 12 years old, dependent children under 18 years old, children "launched" and independent (scores 0-3).

3. Educational status: presently in school, education completed (scores of 0 and 1).

4. Job status: not yet entered work force, working full-time, decreased occupational status from when children were in teens, retired (scores 0-3).

5. Economic dependency: dependent on an older generation, independent, dependent on a younger generation (scores 0-2).

The five indicators are then summed to provide an Index of Social Age Status (ISAS). Scores range from 0 ("youngest") 11 ("oldest"). In the original sample, the number of respondents in each category varied considerably, from 406 in the youngest age-status category (0) to 36 in category 10 and 6 in category 11 (the "oldest" categories).

Formal Tests of Validity

Age status emerged as a salient predictor of value orientations.

Usability on Older Populations

The information on which the index is built is easy to obtain from any adult respondent.

Sensitivity to Age Differences

The measure assumes a "normal life course" and would not work on older individuals who had never been married.

General Comments and Recommendations

In addition to the comment made above, it should be noted that the metric properties of the indicators may be problematic. Particularly in the case of dependency, the assumption of additivity is problematic. The properties of an interval scale appear to be assumed. Can one assume, for example, that being dependent on an older generation is "less dependent" than relying on support from a younger generation? In all indicators equidistance is assumed; the general literature on life changes would challenge that assumption.

Reference

Bengtson, V. L., and M. C. Lovejoy. "Values, Personality, and Social Structure." *American Behavioral Scientist,* 1973, 16: 880-912.

Instrument

See the section on scoring, scale norms, and distribution above.

SOCIAL AGE
C. C. Rose, 1972

Definition of Variable or Concept

The instrument measures social age and its subdomains.

Description of Instrument

This regression analysis bases chronological age on a number of social (role) correlates of age that represent possible subdomains of social age.

Context of Development and Subsequent Use

The instrument was based on background information collected as part of the Normative Aging Study.

Sample

The sample for the Normative Aging Study consisted of 2,000 healthy male veterans from the Boston area. The age range of the sample was 28 to 83, with 42% aged 40 to 49 and 35% under 40. Only 5% were aged 60 and over.

Scoring, Scale Norms, and Distribution

The 24 variables were entered in a stepwise multiple-regression procedure, with chronological age as a dependent variable. After 10 variables entered the equation, the R^2 was .335

and changed less than .01 for any subsequent variable entered. The 10-variable equation was adopted as a significant set of predictors of chronological age. These represented 6 occupational variables and 4 family variables. (See the instrument.) (For a discussion of the technical details of the study, the reader is referred to Rose, 1972.)

Usability on Older Populations

No problems were reported with administration to older subjects.

Sensitivity to Age Differences

The initial family and occupational variables appear more geared to middle age than old age and would not seem to capture some of the social-age changes that occur during the last two decades of life.

General Comments and Recommendations

Logically, it is puzzling to see chronological age used as a dependent variable; the investigator did not offer a conceptual model that matched the statistical model. Furthermore, this "solution" to the search for a social-age measure still relies on chronological age, which is exactly what researchers have been trying to get away from.

Reference

Rose, C. C. "The Measurement of Social Age." *Aging and Human Development*, 1972, 3: 153-68.

Instrument

See instrument V1.11.I.d.

NORMATIVE ATTITUDES TOWARD THE AGED ROLE
G. Bultena and V. Wood, 1969

Definition of Variable or Concept

The instrument measures the respondents' acceptance or rejection of 80 types of behavior for older people. Two items have "man" as target, two "woman," and four "couple." Most of the items deal with informal norms for everyday social behavior.

Description of Instrument

The battery consists of eight items with yes and no as given response categories. Undecided responses are allowed, also.

Method of Administration

The battery is administered as part of an interview.

Context of Development and Subsequent Use

The battery was part of a study on retirement and migration carried out by Bultena and Wood at the University of Wisconsin.

Sample

The sample consisted of 955 retired men in Wisconsin, Florida, and Arizona. The Wisconsin subsample included 284 retired in their home communities, who were selected from a door-to-door survey of two small communities and by an area-probability sampling in a metropolitan community. The Florida and Arizona subsample included 349 respondents randomly selected from city directories in age-integrated communities and 322 respondents from age-segregated communities, selected from a random drawing from lists of residents. In these two communities, only males who had moved there following retirement in the Midwest were interviewed.

Scoring, Scale Norms, and Distribution

The items are analyzed individually and as a cumulative score of "liberalism" or "tolerance," in which each item is assigned a score of 2 for approval (yes response), 1 for undecided, and 0 for disapproval (no response). Bultena and Wood (1969) provided percentage distributions for each item and the cumulative score.

Usability on Older Populations

The items were specifically developed for an older sample, and no problems were reported.

Sensitivity to Age Differences

No analysis of within-group age differences was reported.

General Comments and Recommendations

The items raise numerous questions regarding their underlying dimensions and, therefore, their homogeneity. Item 1 deals with the three Ps, permission to enter retirement and leave the work role. Item 4 deals similarly with entry into roles, in this case remarriage. The remaining items deal with informal norms regarding behavior, mostly folkways. However, a couple of the items may not tap age-related norms at all but deal with general norms regarding proper behavior. One is item 2, which asks about regular church attendance; the other is item 3, which deals with women smoking in public. Furthermore, it is not clear how item 2 is scored. Does a yes response (indicating the sentiment that a couple *should* attend church) reflect "age-norm liberalism"?

Reference

Bultena, G., and V. Wood. "Normative Attitudes toward the Aged Role among Migrant and Nonmigrant Retirees." *The Gerontologist*, 1969, 9 (3): 204-8.

Instrument

See Instrument V1.11.II.a.

AGE NORM CHECKLIST
B. L. Neugarten, J. W. Moore, and J. C. Lowe, 1965

Definition of Variable or Concept

The checklist deals with expectations regarding age-appropriate behavior in three spheres: occupation, family, and leisure.

Description of Instrument

The battery of 48 items has two response alternatives: approve of, feel favorable and disapprove of, feel unfavorable. The respondent is asked to check one response each of three times for each item, indicating his or her feelings regarding a given type of behavior at three different chronological ages. For each item, the respondent indicates his or her own personal opinion and the opinions of "most people." Of the 48 items, 27 ask the respondent to judge behaviors of *men*, and 15 items deal with the behaviors of *women*. In the remaining 6 items, the target is a couple. The chronological ages provided in the target descriptions also vary among the items.

Method of Administration

The battery can be administered as a questionnaire or an interview.

Context of Development and Subsequent Use

The study built on earlier work on timetables and age associations in the Kansas City Study of Adult Life. The items have undergone several revisions. The most recent (1972) version is reproduced here. The checklist has been used on American samples (Neugarten, Moore, and Lowe, 1965) and one Japanese sample (Plath and Ikeda, 1975).

Samples

This measure has been used by two research teams, each of whom studied three age cohorts. The Neugarten, Moore and Lowe (1965) sample included 100 young persons (aged 20 to 29), 200 middle-aged persons (30 to 55), and 100 old persons (65 and above). This sample was evenly divded by gender.

The Plath and Ikeda (1975) sample used the same definitions for the age cohorts as noted above. Their sample included 47 young persons (55.3% female), 87 middle-aged persons (60.9% female), and 36 old persons (47.2% female).

Scoring, Scale Norms, and Distribution

During pretesting, items were developed that evoked age discrimination. Results from the pretest as well as earlier findings from the Kansas City Study of Adult Life were the basis for choosing the three chronological ages provided in each item. One of these ages was designated as the "appropriate" one, another as the "marginal" one, and the third as the "inappropriate" one (the age when the behavior usually is disapproved of and seen as a violation of age norms). A response that only disapproved of the "inappropriate" age for a given item was scored 1, and a response that not only expressed disapproval of the "inappropriate" age but also the "marginal" age received a score of 3. A score of 0 was given when the respondent approved or disapproved of the behavior at all three ages. In those instances, it was inferred that age was seen as *irrelevant* in judging the appropriateness of behavior. Theoretically, respondents' scores could range from 0 (total age irrelevance) to 144 (maximum age constraint). Plath and Ikeda (1975) converted the raw score to a standard ratio. A person perceiving maximum age constraint would have a score of 144/144 = 100%. If the raw score were 72, the ratio would be 72/144 = 50%.

Usability on Older Populations

No problems were reported in using the instrument with older respondents.

Sensitivity to Age Differences

These two studies, as well as related work by researchers at the University of Wisconsin (see the review of Wood and O'Brien's work, pp. 483-86) have found that the recognition of age as a basis for normative expectations increases with the age of the respondent. They also found that the gap between personal opinions and those of "most people" decreases with age.

General Comments and Recommendations

More work is needed to identify the spheres of behavior in which age appears to be an important basis of social norms. In this and related work, it has been assumed that age constraints fall into a linear pattern by age of targets or stimuli. However, it is possible that age norms demonstrate a curvilinear pattern. In other words, it is necessary to ask whether there is a period, possibly in mid-late adulthood, when age constraints are at a maximum while there is more flexibility in very early and very late adulthood (which might be associated with status marginality). Furthermore, researchers need to address the question of *sanctioning* in connection with expectations for age-appropriate behavior. (See the introduction to this chapter.) A general problem with items addressing life-style is relevant for this line of research — general cultural change and the possibility of items becoming outdated must be recognized as a potential problem.

References

Neugarten, B. L., J. W. Moore, and J. C. Lowe. "Age Norms, Age Constraints and Adult Socialization." *American Journal of Sociology*, 1965, 70: 710-17.

Plath, D. W. and K. Ikeda. "After Coming of Age: Adult Awareness of Age Norms." In *Socialization and Communication in Primary Groups*, T. R. Williams (ed.). The Hague: Mouton, 1975.

Instrument

See Instrument V1.11.II.b.

NORMATIVE EXPECTATIONS FOR AGE ROLES
V. Wood and J. O'Brien, no date

Definition of Variable or Concept

Expectations regarding the appropriateness of selected types of behavior for various age-groups are examined.

Description of Instrument

This battery uses the following response categories: appropriate, not appropriate, and not sure. Young, middle-aged, and old respondents are asked to rate the appropriateness of fire items for their own age-group and for the two other groups. In addition, the young adults are asked to predict how the middle-aged and old would rate the appropriateness of the young-adult items; the two older groups are asked to predict how the young adults would rate the middle-aged and old items. For the items dealing with the behavior of young adults, there are the following targets: three male, one female, and one couple. Items regarding the middle-aged have these targets: four male, and one female. For the five items dealing with the old, there are one male, two female, and two couple targets. Thus, there is some question as to target equivalence of items for the three age categories.

Method of Administration

The battery is administered as part of an interview.

Context of Development and Subsequent Use

The battery was based on age-norm items developed by University of Chicago group.

Sample

The sample consisted of 121 young adults (18 to 25 years old; 39% male), 118 middle-aged people (45 to 64 years old; 35% male), and 119 old people (65 years old and over; 43% male).

Scoring, Scale Norms, and Distribution

When the behavior described in an item is perceived as appropriate, the respondent receives a score of 2, a response of uncertain is assigned the value of 1, and the response inappropriate is scored as 0. For each respondent, the sum of the scores on the first five items constitutes his or her OP (view of old targets) score; the sum of the second five, his or her MA (views of middle-aged targets) score; and the sum of his or her judgment scores on the last five items, his or her YA (young targets) score. The means on these three scores for each item, by respondent's age-groups, are found in table 11-4. Table 11-5 shows the distribution of total summed scores (OP, MA, and YA) by respondents' ages and educational levels.

TABLE 11−4
Mean Scores, by Age-Groups

	Young Adults	Middle-aged Adults	Older Adults	Total Adults
Behavior of Older Persons (OP):				
1. A widower of 70 who re-marries even though his adult children don't approve.	1.87	1.65	1.50	1.68
2. A retired couple who wear shorts when they go shopping downtown.	.79	.47	.23	.51

TABLE 11 — 4 *Continued*
Mean Scores, by Age Groups

		Young Adults	Middle-aged Adults	Older Adults	Total Adults
3.	A recently widowed woman of 65 who buys a red convertible automobile.	1.53	1.38	1.02	1.31
4.	A retired couple who frequently attend night clubs where there's a floor show.	1.83	1.67	1.36	1.62
5.	A 68-year-old widow inviting a widower to her home for dinner.	1.98	1.86	1.74	1.86
	TOTAL	7.99	7.03	5.82	6.96
Behavior of Middle-aged persons (MA):					
6.	A financially well off man who retires at 50 because he doesn't feel like working any more.	1.77	1.38	1.19	1.45
7.	A woman of 45 who decides to have one more child.	1.07	.97	1.06	1.03
8.	A man of 62 who refuses to retire and turn his business over to his 40-year-old son.	1.61	1.44	1.57	1.54
9.	A man of 50 who risks his savings in a new business venture.	1.18	.98	.71	.96
10.	A man of 50 who feels his age entitles him to spend money on himself instead of saving it for his children.	1.53	1.53	1.29	1.44
	TOTAL	7.19	6.32	5.86	6.44
Behavior of Young Adults (YA):					
11.	A married couple of 25 who are still willing to have their parents help support them.	.40	.25	.39	.35
12.	An 18-year-old woman who goes to a large city to look for a job without her parent's permission.	1.26	.69	.58	.85
13.	A 25-year-old father and graduate student who is active in campus demonstrations and doesn't have time for a part-time job.	.52	.19	.14	.28
14.	A man who gets his first full-time job at age 25.	1.55	1.42	1.16	1.38
15.	A man of 19 who feels mature enough to take on the responsibility of fatherhood.	1.57	.86	.76	.93
	TOTAL	4.91	3.45	3.04	3.81

SOURCE: V. Wood and J. O'Brien. "Normative Expectations for Age Roles: The Views of Three Age Groups." Unpublished manuscript, University of Wisconsin, no date.

TABLE 11 — 5
Distribution of Total Summed Scores

	Young Adult	Middle-aged Adult	Old People	Row Mean
OP Score Hi Ed.[1]	8.14	7.52	5.83	7.53

TABLE 11−5 *Continued*

	Young Adult	Middle-aged Adult	Old People	Row Mean
Lo Ed.	7.17	6.48	5.82	6.21**
Col. Mean	7.99	7.03	5.82*	
Grand Mean = 6.95				
MA Score				
Hi Ed.	7.34	6.87	6.64	7.07
Lo Ed.	6.00	5.71	5.52	5.64**
Col. Mean	7.14	6.32	5.86	
Grand Mean = 6.44				
YA Score				
Hi Ed.	5.02	3.74	3.64	4.38
Lo Ed.	4.28	2.13	2.78	3.08**
Col. Mean	4.91	3.45	3.04*	
Grand Mean = 3.81***				

*Column Effects (Age) Significant at .05
**Row Effects (Education) Significant at .05
***Grand Means significantly different at .05. In no case is the interaction effect of age and education significant.
[1]Hi Ed. = Education beyond high school. Lo Ed. = High school graduation or less education.
SOURCE: V. Wood and J. O'Brien. "Normative Expectations for Age Roles: The Views of Three Age Groups." Unpublished manuscript, University of Wisconsin, no date.

Usability on Older Populations

No problems were reported in administering the battery to older persons.

Sensitivity to Age Differences

The investigators found that the greater the age of the target, the higher the rate of approval. (See Tables 11-4 and 11-5.) They also found age of respondent to be inversely related to approval, but they did not discuss the full range of perceiver/target combinations in their report (Wood and O'Brien, no date).

In a finding similar to one reported by Neugarten, Moore, and Lowe (1965), all age-groups appeared to expect others to be less tolerant than they considered themselves to be.

General Comments and Recommendations

As the researchers themselves noted in an unpublished paper, it is unclear whether the respondent is judging the appropriateness of an act, regardless of the actor's age, or whether he or she is judging a combination of the act and actor's age. (See the discussion of Bultena and Wood, pp. 480-81.) The lack of equivalence between male, female, and couple targets represents another problem. Work on the underlying dimensions and scaleability of the items is needed, as are data on the instrument's reliability.

References

Neugarten, B. L., J. W. Moore, and J. C. Lowe, "Age Norms, Age Constraints and Adult Socialization." *American Journal of Sociology*, 1965, 70: 710-17.

Wood, V. "Age-Appropriate Behavior for Older People." *The Gerontologist*, 1971, 11 (4, part 1): 74-78.

Wood, V., and J. O'Brien. "Normative Expectations for Age Roles: The Views of the Three Age Groups." Unpublished manuscript, University of Wisconsin, no date.

Instrument

See Instrument V1.11.II.c.

AGE PARAMETERS
P. Cameron, 1969

Definition of Variable or Concept

This instrument assesses the chronological age anchoring of the terms "young adult," "middle-aged," "old," and "aged."

Description of Instrument

The battery of four open-ended questions has, for all four terms, the target, *person*.

Method of Administration

The questions are asked during an interview.

Context of Development and Subsequent Use

The researcher wanted to assess the degree of consensus on the chronological boundaries for these four phases. He later used these age boundaries in his own research.

Sample

The respondents were chosen at random from the Detroit telephone directory, from a home for the aged, from on-the-street sampling, and from a group of students. The sample included 148 persons under age 30, 248 persons aged 30 to 59, and 75 persons over 59 years old. Females comprised 67.5% of the sample.

Scoring, Scale Norms, and Distribution

Cameron gave the chronological "age parameters" in mode, median, and interquartile range (1969, p. 202).

Usability on Older Populations

No problems were reported in using the questions with the older respondents.

Sensitivity to Age Differences

Benchmarks appear to increase with age of respondent.

General Comments and Recommendations

The interview instructions give "person" as the target; that is, no distinction is made between men and women. Other studies (Drevenstedt, 1976; NCOA, 1975; Neugarten and Peterson, 1957) have demonstrated that there are different benchmarks for the two sexes.

References

Cameron, P. "Age Parameters of Young Adults, Middle-aged, Old and Aged." *Journal of Gerontology*, 1969, 24 (2): 201-2.

Drevenstedt, J. "Perceptions of Onsets of Young Adulthood, Middle Age, and Old Age." *Journal of Gerontology*, 1976, 31: 53-57.

National Council on the Aging. *The Myth and Reality of Aging in America.* Washington, D.C.: National Council on Aging, 1975.

Neugarten, B. L., and W. A. Peterson. "A Study of the American Age Grading System." *Proceedings of the Fourth Congress of the International Association of Gerontology*, 1957, 3: 497-502.

Instrument

See Instrument V1.11.III.a.

ONSET OF ADULT PHASES
J. Drevenstedt, 1976

Definition of Variable or Concept

The instrument assesses chronological age benchmarks for the following terms: "young man," "young woman," "middle-aged man," "middle-aged woman," "old man," and "old woman."

Description of Instrument

The battery consists of six open-ended questionnaire items.

Method of Administration

The instrument is a self-administered questionnaire. No time restrictions are indicated in the instructions.

Context of Development and Subsequent Use

These items are being used as part of a larger study of age perception (work currently in progress).

Sample

Two samples were used: college students, about equally divided between males (N = 145) and females (N = 134); and members of senior social centers, all aged 60 and over, 30 men and 41 women. both samples were predominantly white and middle-class.

Scoring, Scale Norms, and Distribution

Means and standard deviations are calculated for ages given as the lower limit (entry point) of the three adult phases, with men and women separated both on the target and the respondent side (Drevenstedt, 1976, p. 54).

Usability on Older Populations

No problems have been reported for using the questionnaire with older respondents.

Sensitivity to Age Differences

The perceived age benchmark for a given phase increases with the respondent's own age. Women judged the onset of middle age and old age to be later than men did. The onset of young adulthood showed consensus across age-sex categories.

General Comments and Recommendations

More work is needed in relating these types of items to perceived age characteristics. Whether some of the age differences found might reflect cohort contrasts should also be examined.

Reference

Drevenstedt, J. "Perceptions of Onsets of Young Adulthood, Middle Age, and Old Age." *Journal of Gerontology,* 1976, 31 (1): 53-57.

Instrument

See Instrument V1.11.III.b.

AGES OF ADULTHOOD
C. L. Fry, 1976

Definition of Variable or Concept

The age distinctions made in adulthood and their underlying dimensions are examined by this technique.

Description of Instrument

The instrument is a card sort with 34 cards describing hypothetical target persons in terms of career and domestic characteristics. Nineteen cards describe males; 15 describe women.

Method of Administration

Respondents are asked to sort the cards into piles based on their judgments of similarities in age brackets. Once the respondent has completed the sorting, she or he is asked to name the age-group or category in each pile by indicating its chronological ranges.

Context of Development and Subsequent Use

The personas described on the cards were developed from life situations that appeared in earlier, exploratory interviews.

Sample

The original sample was a multistage area probability sample of the Lafayette, Ind., metropolitan area, which included 242 people aged 18 and over.

Scoring, Scale Norms, and Distribution

Fry looked at the number of age categories (piles) chosen by the respondent. The range was 2 to 15, with a mean of 5.7 and a standard deviation of 2.7. The mean age assigned for each persona can be found after the items on the instrument.

Formal Tests of Validity

In an attempt to assess the underlying dimensions of age categories, Fry used KYST, a multidimensional scaling procedure developed by Kruskal, Young, and Seery at Bell Laboratories. The measure of proximity used was direct proximity (1 when two cards appeared in the same group, 0 when they did not), and an incidence matrix was constructed. The one-dimension solution (stress = .111) represented chronological age, while the two-dimension solution (stress = .052) formed a horseshoe pattern, with dimensions labeled "engagement-responsibility" and "reproductive cycle." In the three-dimension solution (stress = .036), the second-dimension configuration remained intact, with a third dimension labeled "encumberment" emerging from the analysis (Fry, 1977).

Usability on Older Populations

No problems were reported when the card sort technique was used with older subjects.

Sensitivity to Age Differences

Respondent's own life stage showed a nonlinear relationship with the number of age categories chosen by the respondent (Fry, 1976, p. 174). Fewest distinctions were made during the "launching" stage of family development.

General Comments and Recommendations

This card sort represents an interesting solution to the study of culturally shared age categories without providing the categories a priori. Furthermore, the use of new scaling techniques clearly holds promise in this line of research. However, the underlying dimensions found in the two- and three-dimensional scaling reflect the initial construction of the persona descriptions on the cards. The author stated that they were deliberately centered on career and family development. If the investigator's focus was a phenomenological one, this instrument seems too narrow since it may miss other types of benchmarks for making distinctions among life phases. Some data on reliability also need to be developed.

References

Fry, C. L. "Age Grading in a Complex Society: A Study of the Age Status Structure of the United States." Ph.D. dissertation, University of Arizona, 1973.

_____. "The Ages of Adulthood: A Question of Numbers." *Journal of Gerontology*, 1976, 31: 170-77.

_____. "The Dimensions of Age: A Multidimensional Scaling Analysis." Paper presented to the 74th Annual Meeting of the American Anthropological Association, 1977.

Various unpublished papers are available from Christine L. Fry (Department of Anthropology, Loyola University, Chicago).

Instrument

See Instrument V1.11.III.c.

PHASES OF ADULT LIFE
R. L. Gould, 1972

Definition of Variable or Concept

The measure examines perceived turning points in adulthood.

Description of Instrument

The battery of items deals with (1) sense of time; relationships with (2) parents, (3) friends, (4) children, (5) spouse; and feelings about (6) respondent's personality, (7) job, (8) sex, and (9) major concerns; and (10) the relative importance of people in the respondent's life. Originally, there were 16 items in each of the 10 areas.

Method of Administration

The battery is administered as a questionnaire. The respondent is asked to rank items in terms of their subjective importance.

Context of Development and Subsequent Use

The items were developed after a study of central age-related issues in age-homogeneous groups of outpatients (aged 16 to 60) involved in group therapy at the University of Southern California at Los Angeles. Two teams (mostly made up of clinicians and medical students) were asked to characterize the key issues in these life-phase groups.

Sample

The sample consisted of 524 white, middle-class subjects. The snowball sample was obtained from a network of acquaintances of medical students and hospital volunteers. There were approximately 20 subjects for each 1-year age span between ages 16 and 22 and 20 subjects for each 3-year age span between 33 and 60. The total sample had an about-equal representation of men and women, but women were disproportionately represented among respondents over the age of 45.

Scoring, Scale Norms, and Distribution

Curves were plotted to depict the average rank ordering for each statement in each age-group. This technique was chosen to graphically represent "unstable" periods when response scores changed. Gould (1972) presented curves for the 18 items.

Usability on Older Populations

Since the respondents in the original study were all under the age of 60, it is uncertain whether the questionnaire would be appropriate for older respondents.

Sensitivity to Age Differences

Because of the investigator's decision to use relative ranking of items and comparisons of age-groups, age differences are maximized.

General Comments and Recommendations

It has to be kept in mind that some of the differences found in this cross-sectional study may reflect *cohort* change and not developmental issues. Work on the instrument's reliability and validity, particularly its construct validity, is needed.

References

Gould, R. L. "The Phases of Adult Life: A Study in Developmental Psychology." *American Journal of Psychiatry,* 1972, 129 (5): 521-31.
_____. *Transformations.* New York: Simon and Schuster, 1978.

Instrument

See Instrument V1.11.III. d.

ONSET OF OLD AGE
National Council on the Aging, 1975

Definition of Variable or Concept

The instrument assesses chronological and life-event benchmarks for the onset of old age for men and women.

Description of Instrument

The measure consists of two fixed response items, with probes.

Method of Administration

The instrument is administered as part of an interview. The respondent is given cards with response categories.

Context of Development and Subsequent Use

The instrument was part of a larger study of prevailing views on old age and the aged.

Sample

In total, 4,254 in-person, household interviews were conducted during the late spring and early summer of 1974 by trained Harris interviewers. The probability sample (multistage, random, cluster sample) of the noninstitutionalized public aged, 18 and over had four parts: (1) 1,500 adults 18+, national cross-section sample; (2) 2,400 persons 65+, oversample; (3) 360 persons 55-64, oversample; and (4) 200 persons, black, 65+, oversample. The analyzed sample was weighted to reflect known (1970 census) distributions and the oversampling procedures.

Scoring, Scale Norms, and Distribution

Univariate distributions for the weighted sample and other distributions are provided in the main report of the study, *The Myth and Reality of Aging in America* (NCOA, 1975).

Usability on Older Populations

No difficulties were reported.

Sensitivity to Age Differences

The responses to the items differed by age, but age-related bias in understanding or responding to given items was not examined.

General Comments and Recommendations

The main advantage of these items is the availability of national baseline data for 1974 with which specific samples could be compared.

References

National Council on the Aging. *The Myth and Reality of Aging in America.* Washington, D.C. : National Council on the Aging, 1975.
_____. *Codebook for "The Myth and Reality of Aging,"* a survey conducted by Louis Harris and associates for the National Council on the Aging, prepared by the Duke University Center for the Study of Aging and Human Development, 1976.

Instrument

See Instrument V1.11.III.e.

PERIODS OF LIFE
Kansas City Study of Adult Life

Definition of Variable or Concept

The questions deal with the phases of adulthood, their chronological boundaries, and associated changes.

Description of Instrument

The instrument consists of three open-ended questions. (A very similar set of questions was used by Kedar and Shanan, 1975.)

Method of Administration

The questions are part of an interview.

Context of Development and Subsequent Use

The questions were part of an interview section dealing with changes in adulthood, including perceptions and timetables.

Samples

The stratified random sample consisted of 240 subjects from the metropolitan area of Kansas City, Mo., stratified by age, sex, and socioeconomic status (Neugarten and Peterson, 1957).

Kedar and Shanan's sample was made up of 40 female and 40 male Israeli volunteers, with 10 of each gender in each of the following age-groups: (1) 11-20, (2) 21-30, (3) 46-65, and (4) 66-80.

Scoring, Scale Norms, and Distribution

Both studies looked at the *number* of periods mentioned, as well as the degree of consensus regarding their chronological boundaries. Distributions from the Israeli sample are shown in the instrument.

Usability on Older Populations

No problems were reported with using the questions for the older age-group.

Sensitivity to Age Differences

Neugarten and Peterson (1957) reported few differences between younger and older respondents. Shanan and Kedar (1980) found three age-related trends: a reduction in the number of perceived phases, a lower chronological age benchmark for entry into each phase, and a blurring of boundaries between phases. They summarized these findings as a general "de-differentiation" of adulthood in the perceptions of older respondents.

General Comments and Recommendations

Both sets of investigators found marked sex differences. In both studies, women saw clearer differentiations between life phases than did men. Neugarten and Peterson (1957) also reported social-class contrasts. Work needs to be done on factors that produce variance in the number of periods reported, as well as in their chronological boundaries. Information on reliability is also needed.

References

Kedar, H. S., and J. Shanan. "The Phenomenological Structure of the Life Span from Adolescence to Senescence as Spontaneously Reported by Different Age-Sex Groups." Paper presented to the 10th International Congress of Gerontology, Jerusalem, 1975.

Neugarten, B. L., and W. A. Peterson. "A Study of the American Age Grading System." *Proceedings of the Fourth Congress of the International Association of Gerontology,* 1957, 3: 497-502.

Shanan, J., and H. S. Kedar. "Phenomenological Structuring of the Adult Lifespand as a Function of Age and Sex." *International Journal of Aging and Human Development,* 1980, 10 (4): 343-57.

Instrument

See Instrument V1.11.III.f.

EXPECTATIONS ABOUT SELF AND PARTNER IN INTERGENERATIONAL INTERACTIONS/PERCEPTION OF SELF AND PARTNER
H. J. Berman, 1974

Definition of Variable or Concept

The instrument assesses perceptions of (1) how the respondent will behave in interactions with a member of another age-group, (2) how the member of the other group will behave, (3) how the respondent actually has behaved, and (4) how the member of the other group has behaved.

Description of Instrument

The instrument consists of five sets of Likert-type items with response categories ranging from very untrue (1) to very true (5). Four of the sets are administered prior to dyadic interaction and seek to measure (1) a young adult woman's expectations about her own behavior toward a middle-aged woman (14 items), (2) a young adult woman's expectations about a middle-aged woman's behavior (15 items), (3) a middle-aged woman's expectations about her own behavior toward a young adult woman (8 items), and (4) a middle-aged woman's expectations about a young adult woman's behavior (13 items). A final 33 items are administered to both groups of respondents following the interaction, and they seek to measure (1) each respondent's perception of the interaction and (2) each respondent's perception of the other woman's reactions. Thus, there are two sets of responses for each of the items.

Method of Administration

The questionnaire is administered in person.

Context of Development and Subsequent Use

In preliminary research, 25 young and 25 middle-aged women were given two open-ended questions asking about expectations regarding the behavior of members of the other age-group. The descriptions that were found often in these responses were included in the final instrument.

Sample

The sample consisted of two age-groups of volunteers, with 50 women in each group. The young adult college students were aged 17 to 29, and the middle-aged college alumni were aged 50-59.

Scoring, Scale Norms, and Distribution

Each item is scored on a 5-point scale. Item means and standard deviations are reported in Tables 11-6 and 11-7.

TABLE 11—6
Younger Subjects' Expectations, Means and Standard Deviations

About Partner[a]	Mean	Standard Deviation	About Self[b]	Mean	Standard Deviation
Disapprove[c]	1.84	1.06	Open	3.94	0.84

TABLE 11−6 *Continued*

About Partner[a]	Mean	Standard Deviation	About Self[b]	Mean	Standard Deviation
Like a parent	3.10	1.07	Defensive	2.26	1.10
Helpful	3.56	0.67	Cautious	3.32	1.07
Matronly	3.02	0.96	Quiet	2.66	1.17
Understanding	3.64	0.80	Superficial	1.96	0.99
Polite	4.56	0.61	Polite	4.60	0.61
Friendly	4.30	0.81	Attentive	4.54	0.73
Patronizing	2.54	0.88	Curious	4.20	1.03
Condescending	2.26	0.96	Conservative	2.86	1.01
Dogmatic	2.40	0.90	Like myself	4.08	0.99
Curious	4.04	0.83	Friendly	4.44	0.67
Interested	3.90	0.73	Try to impress	2.38	1.18
Act experienced	3.64	0.78	Respectful	4.54	0.58
Joking	2.72	0.86	Mature	4.18	0.77
Conservative	3.52	0.76			

a. $N = 50$.

b. $N = 50$.

c. All scales: 1 = very untrue to 5 = very true.

SOURCE: H. J. Berman. "Perception of Self and Others in Relation to Age," p. 179. Ph.D. dissertation, Washington University, 1975.

TABLE 11−7

Older Subjects' Expectations, Means and Standard Deviations

About Partner[a]	Mean	Standard Deviation	About Self[b]	Mean	Standard Deviation
Friendly[c]	4.34	1.08	Understanding	4.04	0.89
Courteous	4.32	1.00	Interested	4.48	0.98
Honest	4.00	1.07	Curious	4.09	1.07
Open	3.78	0.95	Polite	4.41	0.95
Curious	3.36	1.17	Open	3.86	0.90
Cautious	3.16	1.09	Honest	4.29	0.98
Straightforward	3.82	0.80	Respectful	4.39	1.02
Enthusiastic	3.14	0.88	Friendly	4.41	1.04
Polite	4.06	0.93			
Indifferent	2.60	1.07			
Critical	2.86	1.00			
Reserved	3.08	1.10			
Cool	2.32	0.91			

a. $N = 50$.

b. $N = 44$.

c. All scales: 1 = very untrue to 5 = very true.

SOURCE: H. J. Berman. "Perception of Self and Others in Relation to Age," p. 180. Ph.D. dissertation, Washington University, 1975.

Factor analysis was performed on the expectation items for self and other. Middle-aged women expected the behavior of young women to vary along two dimensions: friendliness and coolness. Young women were found to expect the behavior of middle-aged women to vary along three dimensions: curiosity-disapproval, condescension, and parental behavior. Middle-aged women expected their own behavior to vary along one dimension: friendliness. Young women expected their own behavior to vary along three dimensions: respectfulness, cautiousness, and superficiality. Tables 11-8 through 11-11 summarize the information of these factor analyses.

TABLE 11–8

Unrotated and Rotated Factor Structure Matrices of
Older Subjects' Expectations about College-Age Women

Variables	Unrotated Factors		h^2	Varimax Rotated Factors	
	1	2		1	2
1. Friendly	.84	.25	.77	.88	.01
2. Courteous	.89	.18	.82	.90	−.08
3. Honest	.74	.33	.66	.81	.10
4. Open	.61	−.24	.42	.51	−.41
5. Curious	.08	−.39	.16	−.03	−.40
6. Cautious	.22	.46	.26	.34	.38
7. Straight-forward	.59	−.19	.39	.51	−.36
8. Enthusiastic	.36	−.44	.32	.22	−.53
9. Polite	.80	.21	.68	.82	−.03
10. Indifferent	−.29	.54	.37	−.12	.60
11. Critical	−.23	.51	.31	−.07	.55
12. Reserved	.09	.74	.56	.30	.68
13. Cool	−.34	.67	.57	−.13	.74
% TOTAL VARIATION	30	18		29	19

NOTE: Loadings greater than an absolute value of .50 are italicized.

SOURCE: H. J. Berman. "Perception of Self and Others in Relation to Age," p. 188. Ph.D. dissertation, Washington University, 1975.

TABLE 11–9

Unrotated Factor Structure Matrix of 44 Older Subjects' Expectations
about Self When Interacting with College-Age Women

Variables	Unrotated Factor 1
1. Understanding	.86
2. Interested	.93
3. Curious	.77
4. Polite	.89
5. Open	.82
6. Honest	.87
7. Respectful	.88

TABLE 11—9 *Continued*

Variables	Unrotated Factor 1
8. Friendly	*.90*
% TOTAL VARIATION	

NOTE: Loadings greater than an absolute value of .50 are italicized.

SOURCE: H. J. Berman. "Perception of Self and Others in Relation to Age," p. 189, Ph.D. dissertation, Washington University, 1975.

TABLE 11—10

Unrotated and Rotated Factor Structure Matrices of 50 Younger Subjects'
Expectations about Women in Their 50s

Variables	Unrotated Factors			Varimax Rotated Factors		
	1	2	3	1	2	3
1. Disapprove	−.69	.10	.16	−.53	.31	.37
2. Like a parent	−.26	−.11	.71	−.06	−.09	.76
3. Helpful	−.19	−.23	.67	−.05	−.23	.69
4. Matronly	−.43	.34	.65	−.08	.39	.76
5. Understanding	.41	−.31	.27	.33	−.46	.13
6. Polite	.61	.38	.29	.76	.11	.08
7. Friendly	.80	.22	.17	.84	−.07	−.09
8. Patronizing	−.32	.26	−.10	−.22	.37	.01
9. Condescending	−.48	.61	−.18	−.26	.75	−.02
10. Dogmatic	−.67	.12	−.01	−.56	.33	.20
11. Curious	.71	.39	.30	.85	.10	.06
12. Interested	.67	.22	−.08	.65	−.01	−.28
13. Experienced	−.03	.64	.14	.23	.60	.15
14. Joking	−.01	−.39	.27	−.06	−.40	.26
15. Conservative	−.10	.75	.03	.16	.75	.00
% TOTAL VARIATION	25	15	12	22	16	13

NOTE: Loadings greater than an absolute value of .50 are italicized.

SOURCE: H. J. Berman. "Perception of Self and Others in Relation to Age," p. 190. Ph.D. dissertation, Washington University, 1975.

TABLE 11—11

Unrotated and Rotated Factor Structure Matrices of 50 Younger Subjects' Expectations
about Self when Interacting with Women in Their 50s

Variables	Unrotated Factors			Varimax Rotated Factors		
	1	2	3	1	2	3
1. Open	.70	−.16	.28	.55	.53	−.09
2. Defensive	−.49	.32	−.07	−.27	−.46	.25

TABLE 11−11 *Continued*

Variables	Unrotated Factors			Varimax Rotated Factors		
	1	2	3	1	2	3
3. Cautious	−.28	.49	−.40	−.04	−.69	−.03
4. Quiet	−.40	.58	−.25	−.08	−.72	.18
5. Superficial	−.50	.19	.57	−.26	−.02	.74
6. Polite	.81	.28	−.05	.83	.06	−.22
7. Attentive	.84	.17	.09	.82	.23	−.16
8. Curious	.71	−.05	.33	.62	.47	.00
9. Conservative	−.28	.58	.25	.09	−.40	.55
10. Like myself	.70	.02	−.36	.56	.05	−.54
11. Friendly	.83	.14	.10	.80	.25	−.16
12. Try to impress	−.37	.32	.55	−.08	−.09	.73
13. Respectful	.75	.46	−.18	.85	−.17	−.23
14. Mature	.67	.29	.21	.74	.14	.05
% TOTAL VARIATION	39	11	10	32	.15	14

NOTE: Loadings greater than an absolute value of .50 are italicized.

SOURCE: H. J. Berman. "Perception of Self and Others in Relation to Age," p. 191. Ph.D. dissertation, Washington University, 1975.

Formal Tests of Reliability/Validity

There is no information available on reliability beyond the factor structure. Berman discussed response set, which was significantly more pronounced among the middle-aged respondents. He attributed their tendency to give extreme responses on the perception measure (postinteraction) to social desirability. He included a careful consideration of the possible explanations for the greater tendency toward social desirability of the older subjects.

Usability on Older Populations

This instrument's appropriateness for older samples is difficult to judge. The older respondents in this study were middle-aged and college educated. Also, the items' wording presupposes a fairly sophisticated vocabulary.

Sensitivity to Age Differences

Items are not equivalent for the two age-groups.

General Comments and Recommendations

The fact that the four preinteraction checklists are all different (in length and wording of items) makes comparison and evaluation problematic, especially since the postinteraction measures are identical. The lack of equivalence between pre- and postinteraction items makes it difficult to evaluate the investigator's report that the dyadic interaction had little effect on the subjects' perceptions.

Reference

Berman, H. J. "Perception of Self and Others in Relation to Age." Ph.D. dissertation, Washington University, 1974.

Instrument

See Instrument V1.11.III.g.

ADJECTIVE CHECK LIST (ACL)
H. Gough and A. Heilbrun, Jr., 1965

Definition of Variable or Concept

The list measures self-perception. Aaronson (1966) used it as a measure of age perception.

Description of Instrument

The ACL consists of a list of 300 adjectives from which respondents choose as many as they consider to be self-descriptive. From the original list of 300 adjectives in the Gough Adjective Rating Scale, Aaronson selected 78 that fit the following criteria: (1) they were picked by more than half of the sample (N = 20) as typical for a given decade of life and, (2) across life decades, there was a range of at least 10 between the highest and lowest frequencies with which they were chosen. Aaronson's subjects were asked to describe "the typical person" at decade intervals from 5 to 85.

Method of Administration

The list can be administered as a paper-and-pencil task in group setting or as an interview. The entire instrument can usually be administered in less than 15 minutes.

Context of Development and Subsequent Use

For psychometric data on the ACL, see Gough and Heilbrun, 1965.

Sample

Aaronson used two samples, each consisting of 20 evening students. The first sample had a mean age of 29.2 years (age range 18 to 42 years); the second had a mean of 22.0 years (age range 17 to 39 years).

Scoring, Scale Norms, and Distribution

To examine changes in adjective-choice patterns for the ages rated, the frequency with which a word was chosen for a given age was related to the frequency with which it was checked for all ages. Separate matrices were created for words occurring significantly more often and significantly less often than they would by chance. Kelly's nonparametric factor analytic method was used on these data. Three factors were found when words chosen more frequently than by chance were analyzed. Factor 1 included words used to describe the first two decades of life; Aaronson called it "outgoingness." Factor 2 peacked in the ninth decade; it was labeled "anergic constriction." Factor 3 applied to the third through seventh decades, peaking in the fifth and sixth decades; it was named "socialized control" (Aaronson, 1966, p. 459).

Three factors were also found when the second matrix, with words occurring less frequently than by chance, was examined: (1) "mature restraint," which peaked in adulthood, (2) "youthfull exuberance," which peaked in the third decade, and (3) "social inefficiency," which overlapped childhood and senescence.

Formal Tests of Reliability

The frequencies with which adjectives were chosen in the two samples correlated highly (.83 to .93).

Usability on Older Populations

Aasronson's samples consisted of young adults. The use of a checklist could present some problems with very old respondents.

General Comments and Recommendations

The reader should note that the samples with which item selection was made (reducing the pool from 300 to 78) were the same 40 subjects on which further data analysis was based. The investigator did *not* use age range in raters for *any* of his analyses, although he had considerable age variance in his sample. The more serious shortcoming, however, is on the stimulus side. Research on stereotypes (Broverman et al., 1970) has found that, if respondents are asked to describe a "typical person," they will tend to describe a *male*. The lack of consideration for the stimulus or target may reflect a basic ambiguity with regard to what underlying constructs are being measured.

Refernces

Aaronson, B.S. "Personality Stereotypes of Aging." *Journal of Gerontology*, 1966, 21: 458-62.

Broverman, I. K., D. M. Broverman, F. E. Clarkson, P. A. Rosenkranz, and S. R. Vogel. "Sex Role Stereotypes and Clinical Judgments of Mental Health." *Journal of Consulting and Clinical Psychology*, 1970, 34: 1-7.

Gough, H., and A. Heilbrun, Jr. *The Adjective Check List Manual.* Palo Alto, Calif.: Consulting Psychologists Press, 1965.

Instrument

This copyrighted instrument is available from Consulting Psychologists Press, Palo Alto, Calif.

PERCEPTIONS OF ADULTS
T. Hickey and R. A. Kalish, 1968

Definition of Variable or Concept

The instrument assesses young people's attitudes toward, and perceptions of, adults at various ages.

Description of Instrument

The instrument consists of a battery of five items. Each item appears four times randomly, with these four targets: 25; 45; 65; and 85-year-old individuals.

Method of Administration

The instrument form is filled out by respondents following verbal instructions.

Context of Development and Subsequent Use

The items were developed on the basis of paragraphs written by third graders on their feelings and thoughts about old people.

Sample

A total of 335 males and females—including 78 third-grade, 83 junior high, 102 high school, and 72 college students—made up the sample.

Scoring, Scale Norms, and Distribution

The investigators found two "clusters" (after hand tallying): three "evaluative" items and two "descriptive" items. (See the instrument.) They stated that no correlation was found between responses in the two subgroups of items. Although not tested for scaleability, the items were summed across each subgroup. Hickey and Kalish (1968, p.217) presented mean scores on the evaluative and descriptive dimensions by rater's age and ratee's age.

Usability on Older Populations

These items were based on statements made by young children. It seems that they would not work with samples of adults rating their peers.

Sensitivity to Age Differences

An inverse relationship was found between age of target and evaluation by children. On the descriptive items, the age of subject was positively related to the perceived age differences.

General Comments and Recommendations

Some theoretical underpinning is needed for the distinction between descriptive and evaluative items, as is work on the reliability of a larger set of items that would seem to fall into these two general categories.

Reference

Hickey, T., and R. A. Kalish. "Young People's Perceptions of Adults." *Journal of Gerontology*, 1968, 23 (2): 215-19.

Instrument

See Instrument V1.11.III.i.

JACKSON PERSONALITY RESEARCH FORM (PRF)
D. M. Jackson, 1967

Definition of Variable or Concept

The instrument is a measure of a number of personality variables, considered within the context of trait theory. Ahammer and Baltes (1972) used it in an investigation of perceived age differences in personality.

Description of Instrument

The scale consists of 40 true-false items. The items were selected from subscales measuring affiliation, achievement, autonomy, and nurturance. In the Ahammer and Baltes (1972) research, different instructions were given to each of four independent groups. Each group was asked to rate the desirability of traits with two of the following targets: (1) how desirable they *personally* considered a given behavior (personal desirability); (2) how members of their own age- and sex-groups would judge (cohort desirability); (3) how desirable it would be for specific target ages—15-18, 34-40, 64-74 (age desirability). Each group judged one of the two other age-groups.

Method of Administration

The form is a self-administered set of true-false items. The entire PRF takes about 40 minutes to complete.

Context of Development and Subsequent Use

PRF scales have been used on a number of samples, which are described in the manual (Jackson, 1967).

Sample

Ahammer and Baltes used a sample of white, middle-class individuals in New York City, including 20 men and 20 women from the following age categories: 15-18, 34-40, 64-74.

Scoring, Scale Norms, and Distribution

Desirability judgments, using a 9-point rating scale ranging from extremely undesirable (1) through neutral (5) to extremely desirable (9), are requested in a questionnaire consisting of 40 items. In their discussion, Ahammer and Baltes considered "personal desirability" as representing objective age differences and "age desirability" as representing perceived differences. Discrepancy between the two was considered misperception. They stated that "cohort desirability" was mainly a control instruction to explore potential method effects.

ANOVAs showed misperception on the dimensions of autonomy and nurturance even though these dimensions did not show objective age differences. The adult group (34-40) was never misperceived, while the old group was most often misperceived. Ahammer and Baltes (1972, p.48) presented average scores for each dimension by target age and instruction.

Formal Tests of Reliability

The PRF showed test-retest reliability (after one week) of .88.

Formal Tests of Validity

PRF scales have been found to correlate highly with peer ratings (from .43 to .75).

Usability on Older Populations

Using the PRF as a measure of personality is outside the scope of this chapter. However, the Ahammer and Baltes research suggests some possible uses of standard personality inventories in the study of age perceptions.

General Comments and Recommendations

It is puzzling that the investigators broke down the sample into age/sex groups but did not include sex in the instructions on "age desirability." Furthermore, it is unclear what the respondent's frame of reference would be with the instruction to rate "how desirable" the traits would be for the different target groups. Does "desirable" mean socially desirable or socially useful?

References

Ahammer, I. M., and P. B. Baltes. "Objective versus Perceived Age Differences in Personality: How Do Adolescents, Adults, and Older People View Themselves and Each Other?" *Journal of Gerontology*, 1972, 27: 46-51.

Jackson, D. M. *Personality Research Form Manual*. Goshen, N.Y.: Research Psychologists Press, 1967.

Instrument

This copyrighted instrument is available from the Research Psychologists Press, Goshen, N.Y.

AGE ASSOCIATION ITEMS
Kansas City Study of Adult Life

Definition of Variable or Concept

The instrument assesses the chronological ages associated with given descriptions, which include some benchmarks.

Description of Instrument

In the descriptions, a distinction is always made between men and women. The instrument consists of 34 fill-in-the-blank items.

Method of Administration

The items are read to the respondent during an interview.

Context of Development and Subsequent Use

The instrument was part of a larger interview section dealing with changes in adulthood.

Sample

The stratified random sample of the Kansas City metropolitan area included 240 subjects.

Scoring, Scale Norms, and Distribution

For each item, the researchers looked at the age range indicated and the proportion of respondents who concurred with the age range.

Usability on Older Populations

No problems were reported.

Sensitivity to Age Differences

There is some discussion of this topic in Neugarten and Peterson (1957).

General Comments and Recommendations

These items have not been fully analyzed. *Some* discussion of the findings can be found in the two references cited.

References

Neugarten, B. L., J. W. Moore, and J. C. Lowe. "Age Norms, Age Constraints and Adult Socialization." *American Journal of Sociology*, 1965, 70: 710-17.

Neugarten, B. L., and W. A. Peterson. "A Study of the American Age Grading System." *Proceedings of the Fourth Congress of the International Association of Gerontology*, 1957, 3: 497-502.

Instrument

See Instrument V1.11.III.k.

LIFE GRAPHS
K. Back and L. B. Bourque, 1970

Definition of Variable or Concept

This instrument assesses a respondent's perception of his or her own life—its "dips, peaks, and plateaus."

Description of Instrument

This instrument uses a projective technique. The respondent is given a blank grid on a card and is asked to make his or her life into a graph—including the past, the present, and the anticipated future.

Context of Development and Subsequent Use

The instrument was part of a regular Gallup poll interview.

Sample

The national random sample included 1,503 subjects, with ages ranging between 20 and 80. The sample was weighted to be representative of the general population.

Scoring, Scale Norms, and Distribution

In the data analysis, the main emphasis was on the *height* of the curves, which were examined at five-year intervals. Subsequently, this dependent variable was standardized. Separate analyses were done on respondents who described past experiences and on those who were anticipating the future. Back and Bourque (1970, p.251) presented average graph heights by age of respondent and year described.

Usability on Older Populations

No problems were reported.

Sensitivity to Age Differences

Respondents rated their lives higher in anticipation (looking at future stages) than in retrospect. Women valued youth more than men; men valued old age more than women.

General Comments and Recommendations

It would appear that the instrument might be useful in combination with more structured measures. This combination might also shed some light on *what is being measured*, an issue not addressed by Back and Bourque.

Reference

Back, K., and L. B. Bourque. "Life Graphs: Aging and Cohort Effect." *Journal of Gerontology*, 1970, 25: 249-55.

Instrument

See Instrument V1.11.III.1.

PERCEIVED GENERATION GAP
V. L. Bengtson, 1971

Definition of Variable or Concept

The instrument measures the perceived gap between members of different age categories.

Description of Instrument

The battery of three items asks the respondent how much of a gap she or he perceives between three generations compared in three pairs. For each item, respondents indicate the perceived gap on a six-point scale ranging from 1 (no gap whatsoever) to 6 (very great gap). Subjects respond to the groups in general ("cohort' gap") and in their own families ("lineage gap").

Method of Administration

The instrument is a self-administered, mailed questionnaire (young and middle-aged respondents) and an interview (old respondents).

Context of Development and Subsequent Use

The items were part of the University of Southern California Study of Generations and Mental Health.

Sample

Members of three-generational lineages were located among metropolitan medical health plan members. Of those who were contacted, 278 individuals responded, representing a 70% response rate. The sample was mostly male, with 105 old, 95 middle-aged, and 78 young adults.

Scoring, Scale Norms, and Distribution

Table 1 in the instrument shows means and standard deviations of the perceived gap between G_3 and G_2 (young adults and middle-aged adults), G_3 and G_1 (young adults and old adults), and G_2 and G_1 (middle-aged adults and old adults) when respondents were asked to focus on the general society.

Bengtson referred to this as perceived "cohort gap." Table 2 in the instrument shows means when the focus was the *respondent's family*, referred to as "lineage gap." Bengtson did not provide significance tests and noted that this fact was due to problems in inference created by sample design.

Tests of Validity

Unpublished data (available from the investigator) showed a high correlation between perceived gap and political and religious attitudinal differences between members of two given age categories.

Usability on Older Populations

Bengtson recommended using an interview for older subjects. No problems were reported.

Sensitivity to Age Differences

There appears to be a linear effect in the perception of social distance by age, with the young seeing a greater gap than the middle-aged and the old.

General Comments and Recommendations

As is well discussed in other works by Bengtson (e.g., 1970), it is not clear what dimension is being tapped when respondents speak of a "gap."

References

Bengtson, V. L. "The Generation Gap: A Review and Typology of Social-Psychological Perspectives." *Youth and Society*, 1970, 2: 7–31.

_____. "Inter-age Perceptions and the Generation Gap." *The Gerontologist*, 1971, 11 (4, part 2): 85–89.

Instrument

See Instrument V1.11.III.m.

COMPARISON OF AGE-GROUPS
P. Cameron, 1970a and 1970b

Definition of Concept

The instrument has the respondent rate three age-groups and self on a set of characteristics.

Description of Instrument

The battery of items is concerned with power and wealth, masculinity/femininity, fun and happiness, and sexuality. There are two tasks. (1) Respondents are asked to compare young, middle-aged, and old adults and evaluate who has the most or the least of a given characteristic. (2) The respondents are asked to compare themselves to other adults of their own sex, using the following categories: above average, average, below average.

Method of Administration

The questionnaire is administered in person.

Sample

The sample consisted of 317 residents of Detroit, evenly distributed between men and women—young, middle-aged, and old. The mean ages were as follows: 21.0, 48.2, and 70.2. The respondents were mostly working-class.

Scoring, Scale Norms, and Distribution

For the comparison of age-groups, Cameron used the ratings of "first choices" and "last choices" for the three age categories. In the ratings of personal characteristics, a subject's response was scored from 1 (below average) to 3 (above average).

Usability on Older Populations

No problems were reported.

Sensitivity to Age Differences

Some of the items may reflect *cohort*, rather than *age*, differences.

General Comments and Recommendations

In publications based on the study, Cameron compared self-appraisals with stereotypes. It should be noted, however, that, given the way in which the targets are stated, the items are not equivalent. (Self-appraisal items specify the respondent's own sex; age-group items do not.)

References

Cameron, P. "The Generation Gap: Beliefs about Sexuality and Self-Reported Sexuality." *Developmental Psychology*, 1970a, 3: 272.

———. "The Generation Gap: Which Generation Is Believed Powerful versus Generational Members' Self-Appraisals of Power." *Developmental Psychology*, 1970b, 3: 403–4.

———. "Stereotypes about Generational Fun and Happiness versus Self-Appraised Fun and Happiness." *The Gerontologist*, 1972, 12 (2, part 1): 120–23.

———. "Masculinity/Femininity of the Generations: As Self-Reported and as Stereotypically Appraised." *International Journal of Aging and Human Development*, 1976, 7: 143–51.

Instrument

See Instrument V1.11.III.n.

BEST YEARS OF LIFE
National Council on the Aging, 1975

Definition of Variable or Concept

The poll asked for evaluations of the "best" and the "worst" decades of a person's life.

Description of Instrument

The poll consisted of two precoded items asking the respondent to pick a decade ranging from the teens to 70s.

Method of Administration

The poll was an interview, with probes. The respondent was handed a card with the response categories printed on it.

Context of Development and Subsequent Use

The instrument was part of a national survey of the public's views on aging.

Sample

A total of 4,254 in-person, household interviews were conducted during the late spring and early summer of 1974 by trained Harris interviewers. (For further information, see the abstract in this chapter for Onset of Old Age, p. 490.)

Scoring, Scale Norms, and Distribution

Univariate distributions by respondents' ages are provided in the main report of the study (NCOA, 1975, p. 3).

Usability on Older Populations

This study involved the administration of the items to noninstitutionalized people from 18 to over 80 years of age, and no difficulties were reported.

Sensitivity to Age Differences

Responses to items differed by age, but age-related bias in understanding or responding to given items was not examined.

General Comments and Recommendations

The main advantage of these items, in addition to their inclusion of important topics, is the availability of national baseline data for 1974, with which specific samples could be compared.

References

National Council on the Aging. *The Myth and Reality of Aging in America*. Washington, D.C.: National Council on the Aging, 1975.

――――. *Codebook for "The Myth and Reality of Aging,"* a survey conducted by Louis Harris and associates for the National Council on the Aging; prepared by the Duke University Center for the Study of Aging and Human Development, 1976.

Instrument

See Instrument V1.11.III.o.

PERCEPTIONS OF AGE-GROUPS' RESPECT AND INFLUENCE
E. G. Youmans, 1971

Definition of Variable or Concept

The instrument assesses comparisons of age-groups on perceived influence and respect: *person* in youth (up to 21), early middle age (22–45), later middle age (45–64), and older age (65+).

Description of Instrument

The battery of four items asks for age-group comparisons. The respondent is asked at what age a person is the most and least influential and respected.

Method of Administration

The original study administered the items in an interview, but they could also be included in questionnaire.

Context of Development and Subsequent Use

The items were part of a larger study of urban-rural differences in perception of old age. (See Chapter 12.)

Sample

The sample consisted of a 1969 representative cluster sample of 805 people from a metropolitan center and a rural county in Kentucky. The urban sample included 273 younger and 165 older respondents, and the rural sample included 127 younger and 276 older respondents.

Scoring, Scale Norms, and Distribution

For each item, the respondent is asked to choose one of the four life phases. Distributions are shown in the instrument, which also gives the item wording and response options.

Usability on Older Populations

The items were used on a sample of urban and rural aged people, with no difficulties reported.

Sensitivity to Age Differences

The items showed age differences, but these were mediated by urban-rural contrasts.

General Comments and Recommendations

Further information on validity and reliability is needed. The study is one of the few allowing for intracohort variation in perceptions of life phases. It points to the importance of considering regional and urban-rural differences.

References

Youmans, E. G. "Generation and Perceptions of Old Age: An Urban-Rural Comparison." *The Gerontologist*, 1971, 11 (4, part 1): 284–88.

Instrument

See Instrument V1.11.III.p.

Instruments

V1.11.I.a
AGE-APPROPRIATE BEHAVIOR
V. Wood, 1973

We are interested in knowing at what ages people think it's best to do different kinds of things. People have different opinions about at what ages a given behavior is or isn't appropriate and we'd like to get your ideas on when you think a person is either old enough or too old to do certain things.

For each question indicate a specific age which you think is generally applicable. If you have trouble deciding on when a person is "old enough," start with an age at which you are fairly certain a person is *not old enough* (e.g., you might consider a 15 year old girl not old enough to get married) and work your way up to an age where you are fairly certain a person is old enough for the specified activity. If you have trouble deciding on when a person is "too old," start with an age at which you are fairly certain a person *would not be too old* (e.g., you might consider a 35 year old man as not too old to adopt a child) and work your way up to an age where you are fairly certain a person is too old for the specified activity.

After each question please briefly note qualifications, justifications, or any other remarks which will help us understand the reasons for your answer.

Thank you for your participation and cooperation.

PART I. Here are some questions about when a person is old enough to do certain things.

1. At what age do you think it is all right for a girl to get married?
2. At what age is a person old enough to be a city councilman?
3. At what age is a person generally old enough to drive a car?
4. Suppose you moved into a new neighborhood and were looking around for a family doctor. How old would he have to be for you to feel confident about his ability?
5. After what age do you think a girl is old enough to go out alone on dates.
6. There's been a change recently on the legal voting age, but not everyone agrees with the new age. At what age do *you* think a person is old enough to vote?
7. At what age is a child old enough to decide how to spend his allowance?
8. After what age is a female old enough to take a full-time job?
9. After what age is a couple old enough to take on the responsibility of parenthood? How old should the wife be?
10. How old should the husband be?
11. After what age is it generally a good idea for a man to stick to the kind of job he's doing even if he's dissatisfied with it?
12. If he can afford it, after what age is a son old enough to move into his own apartment?
13. After what age is a man generally old enough to take on leadership responsibilities in his labor union?

14. After what age is a person old enough to choose his friends wisely?
15. How old do you think someone should be before other people begin to take their political opinions seriously?
16. After what age should a man begin to be concerned about conserving his strength?
17. After what age should someone no longer be required to attend school?
18. At what age should a young man really buckle down and work hard to get ahead in his occupation?
19. At what age do you think a person is old enough to be a U.S. Supreme Court Judge?
20. At what age do you think a man is old enough to hold down a full-time job?
21. A lot of people are thinking of retiring early these days. Others argue that a man should work as long as he's able. What do you think? After what age is it all right for a man to retire, assuming he can afford it?

Part II. Now here are some questions about when a person is too old to do certain things.

22. Suppose a woman dropped out of college when she was half-way through. Assuming she has free time and would be able to return to school, after what age do you think she is too old to go back as a full-time student to finish her degree?
23. Assuming a man has finished school and has a full-time job, after what age is he too old to continue living with his parents?
24. After what age should a person's opinions on political issues no longer be taken seriously?
25. After what age is a woman too old to return to work full time?
26. Someone recently proposed that people should lose their voting rights when they retire. What is your opinion? At what age do you think a person is too old to vote?

Suppose a couple has raised their family, but still enjoys children and misses having them around. After what age are they too old to adopt a child?

27. At what age is the wife too old?
28. At what age is the husband too old?
29. After what age should a person be required to take a driving test every few years in order to continue driving?
30. At what age do you think a person is too old to be a U.S. Supreme Court Judge?
31. Young people usually experiment with different jobs or occupations for a while. By what age should a person be settled into a permanent job or occupation?
32. After what age is a woman too old to go out on dates?
33. After what age should a man accept the fact that his health will not be as good as it used to be when he was younger?
34. When do you think a woman is too old to marry?
35. After what age should a union member stop competing with younger members for leadership in the union?
36. Suppose a son is finished with his schooling. After what age is he too old to rely on his parents for some financial support?
37. At what age do you think a man is too old to hold down a full-time job?
38. After what age do you think a person is too old to be a city councilman?
39. After what age is it too much trouble to try to make new friends?
40. After what age should a person stop pushing himself so hard to get promoted and take it easier at work?
41. After what age would you consider your family doctor to be too old for you to have confidence in his ability?

SOURCE: V. Wood. "Role Allocation as a Function of Age." Paper presented to the 26th

Annual Meeting of the Gerontological Society, Miami Beach, November 5-9, 1973. Reprinted by permission of author.

V1.11.I.b
TIMETABLES FOR MEN AND WOMEN
Kansas City Study of Adult Life

1. What do you think is the best age for a *man to marry*? Why?
2. What do you think is the best age for a *woman to marry*? Why?
3. What do you think is the best age for most *people to leave home*? Why?
4. What is the best age for most people to finish schooling and go to work? Why?
5. What do you think is the best age for most people to begin to have children?
6. At what age do you think most *men* should be settled on a *career* (job)? Why?
7. At what age do you think most *men* hold their top jobs?
8. At what age do you think most people *need* the most income? Why?
9. At what age do you think most parents should be *ready for their children to leave home*? Why?
10. At what age do you think most people should become grandparents? Why?
11. At what age do you think most people should be ready to retire? Why?

SOURCE: B. L. Neugarten and W. A. Peterson. "A study of the American Age Grading System." *Proceedings of the Fourth Congress of the International Association of Gerontology*, 1957, 3: 497-502. Reprinted by permission.

V1.11.I.c
INDEX OF SOCIAL AGE STATUS
V. L. Bengtson and M. C. Lovejoy, 1973

See the section on scoring, scale norms, and distribution in the abstract.

V1.11.I.d
SOCIAL AGE
C. C. Rose, 1972

Ten-Variable Regression Equation Predicting Age from Social Variables

Variables ranked in order of beta × r	Relation to older age	Beta	r with age	Proportion of total variance (beta × r)	Proportion of accountable variance (beta × r)/R²	F
1. Chances for advancement	Less	.283	.288	.081	.229	92.6
2. Remaining with company	More	.231	.216	.050	.140	63.4
3. Preferred retirement age	Later	.142	.257	.037	.103	16.9
4. Relocation plans	Less	.168	.214	.036	.010	33.9
5. Wife employed	More	.163	.201	.033	.092	32.1
6. Expected retirement age	Later	.135	.227	.031	.086	15.4
7. Contacts with wife's family	Less	−.130	−.228	.030	.084	17.4
8. Self-ranking in company	Higher	.139	.172	.024	.067	21.2
9. Contacts with S's family	Less	−.099	−.209	.021	.058	10.0
10. Satisfaction with salary	More	.092	.153	.014	.040	9.8

Constant 30.002

R (multiple correlation) .5962

R^2 (accountable variance) .3555

S.E. 7.346 years
SOURCE: C. C. Rose. "The Measurement of Social Age." *Aging and Human Development*, 1972, 3: 159. Copyright, 1972, Baywood Publishing Company, Inc. Reprinted by permission of author and publisher.

V1.11.II.a
NORMATIVE ATTITUDES TOWARD THE AGED ROLE
G. Bultena and V. Wood, 1969

We are interested in what you think of some of the things that some people your age are doing these days. For example:

1. Do you think a man who is financially well off should feel free to retire at age 55 just because he doesn't feel like working anymore?
           YES   NO
   RECORD COMMENTS BUT DO NOT PROBE: _____

2. Do you think a retired couple should make an effort to attend church regularly even if they don't feel like going?
           YES   NO
   RECORD COMMENTS BUT DO NOT PROBE: _____

3. Do you think it is proper for an older woman to smoke in public?
           YES   NO
   RECORD COMMENTS BUT DO NOT PROBE: _____

4. Do you think a widower should remarry even if his adult children disapprove?
           YES   NO
   RECORD COMMENTS BUT DO NOT PROBE: _____

5. Do you think it is proper for a retired couple to wear shorts when they go shopping downtown?
           YES   NO
   RECORD COMMENTS BUT DO NOT PROBE: _____

6. Do you think it is all right for an older married couple to frequently attend night clubs where there is a floor show?
           YES   NO
   RECORD COMMENTS BUT DO NOT PROBE: _____

7. Do you think it is proper for a 67-year-old woman to be seen in a bathing suit at a public beach or pool?
           YES   NO
   RECORD COMMENTS BUT DO NOT PROBE: _____

8. Do you think it is proper for an older couple to regularly invite friends into their home for a cocktail party?
           YES   NO
   RECORD COMMENTS BUT DO NOT PROBE: _____

SOURCE: G. Bultena and V. Wood. "Normative Attitudes toward the Aged Role among Migrant and Nonmigrant Retirees." *The Gerontologist*, 1969, 9 (3): 205. Reprinted by permission of authors and publisher.

V1.11.II.b
AGE NORM CHECKLIST
B. L. Neugarten, 1972

YOUR OPINIONS ABOUT AGE

This is a list of things that people sometimes do at certain ages or at certain times of their lives. We would like YOUR OPINIONS about these things. THERE ARE NO RIGHT OR

WRONG ANSWERS! Please go through the list as *quickly* as you can, and mark the answer *you feel* is appropriate—either approve or think favorably about the behavior *or* disapprove or feel unfavorable about the behavior described. Do not dwell on any one answer.

Sample Item:	Approve of, Feel Favorable	Disapprove of, Feel Unfavorable
A woman who thinks it's all right to wear shorts shopping—		
when she's 55	_____	_____
when she's 30	_____	_____
when she's 20	_____	_____

START HERE:

1a. A woman who feels it's all right at her age to wear a bikini to the beach—

when she's 45	_____	_____
when she's 30	_____	_____
when she's 18	_____	_____

1b. A man who feels he's experienced enough of life that he's entitled to write his memoirs—

when he's 35	_____	_____
when he's 50	_____	_____
when he's 65	_____	_____

2a. A woman who refuses to celebrate her birthday—

when she's 25	_____	_____
when she's 35	_____	_____
when she's 50	_____	_____

2b. A woman who decides to have another child—

when she's 45	_____	_____
when she's 37	_____	_____
when she's 30	_____	_____

3a. A man who runs for President of the United States—

when he's 65	_____	_____
when he's 50	_____	_____
when he's 37	_____	_____

3b. A man who feels too old to undertake rearing another child—

when he's 35	_____	_____
when he's 40	_____	_____
when he's 50	_____	_____

4a. A woman should be married—

when she's 20	_____	_____
when she's 25	_____	_____
when she's 30	_____	_____

	Approve of, *Feel Favorable*	*Disapprove of,* *Feel Unfavorable*
4b. A woman who is willing to see her children go their own ways —		
when she's 35	————	————
when she's 45	————	————
when she's 55	————	————
5a. A woman who becomes executive secretary to the president of a large company —		
when she's 21	————	————
when she's 28	————	————
when she's 35	————	————
5b. A man who's willing to move his family from one town to another to get ahead in his company —		
when he's 45	————	————
when he's 35	————	————
when he's 25	————	————
6a. A married woman with children who should be able to take an outside job that interests her —		
by the time she's 25	————	————
by the time she's 35	————	————
by the time she's 45	————	————
6b. A couple who are ready to have their children support them —		
when they're 55	————	————
when they're 65	————	————
when they're 75	————	————
7a. A couple who decide to move to a retirement village —		
when they're 50	————	————
when they're 60	————	————
when they're 70	————	————
7b. A man who begins to apply to himself the saying, "You can't teach an old dog new tricks" —		
when he's 55	————	————
when he's 70	————	————
8a. A man who risks his savings in a new business venture —		
when he's 60	————	————
when he's 45	————	————
when he's 30	————	————
8b. A couple who decide their age entitles them to take 6 months off from work to travel in Europe —		
when they're 35	————	————
when they're 50	————	————
when they're 65	————	————

	Approve of, Feel Favorable	Disapprove of, Feel Unfavorable
9a. A man who still prefers living with his parents rather than getting his own apartment—		
when he's 30	_____	_____
when he's 25	_____	_____
when he's 21	_____	_____
9b. A woman who thinks she can handle the chairman's job in her PTA—		
when she's 25	_____	_____
when she's 30	_____	_____
when she's 40	_____	_____
10a. A man who is thinking of what to include in his will—		
by the time he's 30	_____	_____
by the time he's 45	_____	_____
by the time he's 60	_____	_____
10b. A woman who feels it's not right for her to try to look young—		
when she's 35	_____	_____
when she's 45	_____	_____
when she's 55	_____	_____
11a. A man who makes his first visit to New York City and spends all his time visiting with his relatives—		
when he's 25	_____	_____
when he's 40	_____	_____
when he's 65	_____	_____
11b. A man who feels ready to supervise other people—		
by the time he's 40	_____	_____
by the time he's 55	_____	_____
12a. A business man who's willing to move over and make room for a younger man—		
when he's 35	_____	_____
when he's 50	_____	_____
when he's 60	_____	_____
12b. A woman who wears her hair in a pony tail—		
when she's 45	_____	_____
when she's 30	_____	_____
when she's 19	_____	_____
13a. A woman who feels experienced enough to give advice to newly married couples—		
when she's 25	_____	_____
when she's 30	_____	_____
when she's 45	_____	_____
13b. A married man who quits work to go to college full time—		
when he's 40	_____	_____
when he's 30	_____	_____
when he's 20	_____	_____

	Approve of, Feel Favorable	Disapprove of, Feel Unfavorable
14a. A man who feels his age entitles him to spend money on himself instead of saving it for his children —		
when he's 40	————	————
when he's 50	————	————
when he's 60	————	————
14b. A man who looks for a boss who will take him under his wing and show him the ropes —		
when he's 50	————	————
when he's 35	————	————
when he's 25	————	————
15a. A man who marries a 60 year old woman —		
when he's 50	————	————
when he's 55	————	————
when he's 65	————	————
15b. A man should expect to be holding his top job —		
by the time he's 30	————	————
by the time he's 40	————	————
by the time he's 50	————	————
16a. A lawyer who decides it's time to start tapering off —		
when he's 40	————	————
when he's 50	————	————
when he's 60	————	————
16b. A man who buys himself a red sports car —		
when he's 60	————	————
when he's 45	————	————
when he's 25	————	————
17a. A woman who thinks her age entitles her to wear mink —		
when she's 25	————	————
when she's 35	————	————
when she's 45	————	————
17b. A married couple who keep going to their parents for advice —		
when they're 40	————	————
when they're 30	————	————
when they're 20	————	————
18a. A married woman with children who resumes her college education full time —		
when she's 25	————	————
when she's 35	————	————
when she's 45	————	————

	Approve of, Feel Favorable	Disapprove of, Feel Unfavorable
18b. A woman who feels too young to be a grandmother—		
when she's 55	_____	_____
when she's 50	_____	_____
when she's 45	_____	_____
19a. A man who gets his first full time job—		
when he's 29	_____	_____
when he's 25	_____	_____
when he's 21	_____	_____
19b. A couple who move across the country so they can live near their married children—		
at age 40	_____	_____
at age 55	_____	_____
at age 70	_____	_____
20a. A man who feels his age entitles him to suggest changes in company policy—		
by the time he's 25	_____	_____
by the time he's 35	_____	_____
by the time he's 45	_____	_____
20b. A doctor who starts concrete planning for his retirement—		
when he's 30	_____	_____
when he's 40	_____	_____
when he's 55	_____	_____
21a. A man who feels mature enough to take on the responsibility of fatherhood—		
when he's 18	_____	_____
when he's 22	_____	_____
when he's 25	_____	_____
22a. A woman who is not yet married and feels she might as well try wholeheartedly to make a career for herself—		
when she's 25	_____	_____
when she's 30	_____	_____
when she's 35	_____	_____
22b. A man who enlists in the Navy—		
when he's 35	_____	_____
when he's 25	_____	_____
when he's 20	_____	_____
23a. A man who becomes president of a large company—		
when he's 25	_____	_____
when he's 30	_____	_____
when he's 45	_____	_____

	Approve of, *Feel Favorable*	*Disapprove of,* *Feel Unfavorable*
23b. A married couple who are still willing to have their parents help support them —		
when they're 35	_____	_____
when they're 25	_____	_____
when they're 20	_____	_____
24a. A man who becomes a general in the Army —		
when he's 35	_____	_____
when he's 50	_____	_____
when he's 60	_____	_____
24b. A woman should have had her last children —		
when she's 30	_____	_____
when she's 37	_____	_____
when she's 45	_____	_____

SOURCE: B. L. Neugarten. "Your Opinions about Age." Unpublished questionnaire, Committee on Human Development, University of Chicago, 1972.

V1.11.II.c
NORMATIVE EXPECTATIONS FOR AGE ROLES
V. Wood and J. O'Brien, no date

See the section on scoring, scale norms, and distribution in the abstract.

V1.11.III.a
AGE PARAMETERS
P. Cameron, 1969

The interview proceeded as follows. "Hello, I'm representing the Psychology Department at Wayne State University and I wonder if you'd answer four quick questions? O.K.? Although everyone uses the terms 'young adult,' 'middle-aged,' 'old,' and 'aged,' we don't know what ages are included in most people's use of the word. (a) What ages do you think of when you hear or use the words 'young adult?' That is, what's the youngest a person can be and still be a 'young adult?'_____, the oldest he can be? (b) How about 'middle-age' _____ to _____. (c) 'Old' begins at age _____. (d) 'Aged' begins at age _____. (e) Your age is _____ (f) and your sex _____."

SOURCE: P. Cameron. "Age Parameters of Young Adult, Middle-Aged, Old, and Aged." *Journal of Gerontology*, 1969, 24 (2): 201. Reprinted by permission of author and publisher.

V1.11.III.b
ONSET OF ADULT PHASES
J. Drevenstedt, 1976

Write down a *specific age in years* to each of the following questions:

1. At about what age do you consider a male becomes a "young man" in American society? _____

2. At about what age do you consider a male becomes a "middle-aged man" in American society? _____

   A female a "middle-aged woman?" _____

3. At about what age do you consider a male becomes an "old man" in American society? _____

   A female, an "old woman?" _____

SOURCE: J. Drevenstedt. "Perceptions of Onsets of Young Adulthood, Middle Age, and Old Age." *Journal of Gerontology*, 1976, 31 (1): 54. Reprinted by permission of author and publisher.

V1.11.III.c
AGES OF ADULTHOOD
C. L. Fry, 1976

The following is the instrument used to investigate the sequencing of life events without the imposition of *a priori* age categories. Included are the instructions given to each respondent as well as the card deck. Although the cards are arranged by increments of age obtained from the respondents, in the interview situation the card deck had been shuffled prior to the respondent's sorting. Code numbers were placed on the back of the cards for the purpose of recording the data. Very few respondents were aware of their existence. Interviewers were instructed to answer any questions concerning the mechanics of sorting the cards, but *not* to direct the sorting of particular cards into particular piles. Once the cards were sorted, the interviewer asked questions 1 and 2 and recorded the data for each pile of cards.

Instructions:

"People classify other people according to a number of different things. For example, we classify people by sex. That is—male or female. We can classify people by the amount of money they have. Here we would have rich, poor, comfortable, and the like. We also classify people according to age.

"I have here several cards. Each card contains a description of a person who has accomplished several things or has had several things happen to him in the course of his life. I would like you to take these cards and on the basis of the brief description of the person on each card, sort them into piles based on your guess regarding their approximate age or similarity in age-bracket. There are no number of piles or ways to sort and organize these cards. What we are interested in is how *you* would sort and organize the people described on these cards with respect to age. You might find it easier to arrange them in rough age-brackets ranging from younger to older."

Once the respondent had completed the card sort he/she was asked:

1. What would you call or what name would you give to the age-bracket or the age-group of the people you have placed in this pile? Are thre any other words you might use to describe this general age group?

2. Roughly, what is the age or range of age in terms of years of the people described in this pile?

Social Persona Deck: The mean age assigned is indicated in parentheses. (Letter or number to the left is the symbol used to represent this social persona in the multidimensional scaling solutions.)

A. A female, high school graduate, single, working, living with parents (21.4).

B. A male, high school graduate, single, in the army (21.6).

C. A male, high school graduate, single, living with parents (21.6).

D. A male, high school graduate, single, is working, living with parents (21.8).

E. A female, high school graduate, single, working, living with roommate (21.9).

F. A male, in college, single, living with a roommate (22.2).

G. A male, in college, married, no children (23.6).

H. A male, in college, single, a veteran (24.9).

I. A female, high school graduate, married, two pre-school children (26.0).

J. A male, high school graduate, working, married, two pre-school children (26.1).

K. A male, college graduate, working, married, no children (27.5).

L. A female, college graduate, working, married, no children (27.7).

M. A male, recently promoted at work, married, living with wife and children (29.7).

N. A female, married, has two school children, and is working (30.2).

O. A male, a veteran, married, living with wife and children (30.9).

P. A female, college graduate, single, recently promoted to a job of great responsibility and productivity (31.8).

Q. A male, a college graduate, recently promoted to a job of great reponsibility, married and living with wife and children (35.0).

R. A female, working, married, two high school children (37.6).

S. A female, college graduate, married, two high school children (38.3).

T. A male, working, married, two children who are recent high school graduates (39.8).

U. A female, in college, married, two children who are recent high school graduates (40.5).

V. A female, working, married, two children both of whom are in college (42.2).

W. A male, recently promoted to a job of great responsibility, married, two children both of whom are in college (42.8).

X. A female, working, married, two children both of whom have recently married (43.9).

Y. A male, recently promoted to a job of great responsibility, married, two children both of whom have recently married (45.2).

Z. A female, high school graduate, working, married, two children both of whom are married and have children of their own (49.3).

1. A male, recently promoted to a job of great responsibility, married, has two children both of whom are married and have children of their own (49.4).

2. A female, widowed, working, and living alone (50.0).

3. A male, widowed, working, living alone (51.5).

4. A male, widowed, working, living with adult children (58.5).

5. A male, single, retired, living alone (64.4).

6. A female, widowed, retired, and living alone (64.7).

7. A male, widowed, retired, living with adult children (65.4).

8. A female, widowed, retired, living in a nursing home (68.6).

SOURCE: C. L. Fry. "The Dimensions of Age: a Multidimensional Scaling Analysis." Paper presented to the 74th Annual Meeting of the American Anthropological Association, 1977. Reprinted by permission of author and publisher.

V1.11.III.d
PHASES OF ADULT LIFE
R. L. Gould, 1972

Sample Items: Respondents rank order the items within each content area. The questions included below represent Sense of Time dimension.

1. I feel that some exciting things are going to happen to me.

2. I never plan on what tomorrow may bring.

3. It hurts me to realize that I will not get some things in life I want.
4. I live for today; forget the past.
5. I think things aren't as good as they used to be.
6. I believe I will some day have everything I want in life.
7. My life doesn't change much from year to year.
8. There is little hope for the future.
9. I try to be satisfied with what I have and not to think so much about the things I probably won't be able to get.
10. I wish I could change the past.
11. I dream about life ten years from now.
12. I spend more time now thinking about the past than about the future.
13. There's still plenty of time to do most of the things I want to do.
14. I won't be content to remain as old as I am now.
15. I find myself daydreaming about good experiences in the past.
16. I will have to settle for less than I expected, but I still think I will get most things I want.

SOURCE: R. L. Gould. "The Phases of Adult Life: A Study in Developmental Psychology." *American Journal of Psychiatry*, 1972, 129 (5): 527.

V1.11.III.e
ONSET OF OLD AGE
National Council on the Aging, 1975

2a. At what age do you think the average man becomes old?

Under 40 years . . . . _____
40 to 44 years . . . . _____
45 to 49 years . . . . _____
50 to 54 years . . . . _____
55 to 59 years . . . . _____
60 to 64 years . . . . _____   (ASK 2B)
65 to 69 years . . . . _____
70 to 74 years . . . . _____
75 to 79 years . . . . _____
80 to 84 years . . . . _____
85 to 89 years . . . . _____   (ASK 2B)
90 years or older . . . . _____
Never . . . . _____
It depends . . . . _____
When he stops working . . . . _____
When his health fails . . . . _____   (SKIP TO 2C)
Other (specify) _____ . . . . . . _____
Not sure . . . . _____

2b. (IF GIVE DEFINITE AGE IN 2a) Why do you think a man becomes old at (AGE GIVEN)? Any other reason?

2c. (ASK EVERYONE) At what age do you think the average woman becomes old?

Under 40 years . . . . _____
40 to 44 years . . . . _____
45 to 49 years . . . . _____
50 to 54 years . . . . _____
55 to 59 years . . . . _____
60 to 64 years . . . . _____   (ASK 2D)

65 to 69 years. . . . . ———
70 to 74 years. . . . . ———
75 to 79 years. . . . . ———
80 to 84 years. . . . . ———
85 to 89 years. . . . . ———
90 years or older . . . . ———
Never. . . . . ———
It depends . . . . ———
When she stops working . . . . ———
When her health fails. . . . . ———
When she can't have babies
anymore; menopause. . . . . ———   (SKIP TO 2E)
Other (specify) ——————— . . . . . . ———
Not sure . . . . ———

2d. (IF GIVE DEFINITE AGE IN 2c) Why do you think a woman becomes old at (AGE GIVEN)? Any other reasons?

SOURCE: National Council on the Aging. "An Index to Available Data from the NCOA/ Harris Survey." Washington, D.C.: National Council on the Aging, 1976, pp. 6-7. Reproduced with permission from *Codebook for "The Myth and Reality of Aging,"* a survey conducted by Louis Harris and associates for the National Council on the Aging; prepared by the Duke University Center for the Study of Aging and Human Development under a grant from the Edna M. Clark Foundation.

V1.11.III.f
PERIODS OF LIFE
Kansas City Study of Adult Life

Mean Lower Age Limits, Upper Age Limits and Range Attributed to the
Various Life Periods by Different Age Groups

Life Period	Age of Subjects				Total Mean
	11–20	21–30	46–65	66+	
Adolescence:					
Mean Lower Limit	11.0	11.0	11.0	11.0	11.0
Mean Upper Limit	20.3	19.3	22.5	19.3	20.3
Range	9.3	8.3	11.5	8.3	9.3
Young Adulthood:					
Mean Lower Limit	21.0	20.7	21.3	20.1	20.8
Mean Upper Limit	30.5	29.7	28.9	27.4	29.1
Range	9.5	9.0	7.6	7.3	8.3
Adulthood:					
Mean Lower Limit	29.2	31.3	29.1	27.5	29.3
Mean Upper Limit	47.6	48.6	48.3	50.3	48.7
Range	18.4	17.3	19.2	22.8	19.4
Middle Age:					
Mean Lower Limit	45.4	49.8	45.5	45.0	46.4
Mean Upper Limit	63.1	63.0	61.5	60.4	62.0
Range	17.7	13.2	16.0	15.4	15.6

Age Limits *Continued*

Life Period	Age of Subjects				Total Mean
	11–20	21–30	46–65	66+	
Old Age:					
Mean Lower Limit	64.0	64.0	59.8	53.5	60.3
Mean Upper Limit	75.6	77.3	73.0	65.0	72.7
Range	11.6	13.3	13.2	11.5	12.4
Senescence:					
Mean Lower Limit	67.2	64.4	66.2	63.5	65.3
Mean Upper Limit*	—	—	—	—	—
Range*	—	—	—	—	—
Mean Range (not including senescing)	13.3	12.2	13.5	13.0	13.0

SOURCE: J. Shanan and H. S. Kedar. "The Phenomenological Structuring of the Adult Life-span as a Function of Age and Sex." *International Journal of Aging and Human Development*, 1980, 10 (4): 350. Reprinted by permission of authors and publisher.

PHASES OF ADULTHOOD

Interviewers: This is important. Probe!

1. What would you call the periods of life? The age periods most people go through? For instance, people first are babies, then they are children, then teen-agers . . . AFTER A PERSON IS GROWN UP, WHAT PERIODS DOES HE GO THROUGH?
2. At what age does each begin, for most people?
3. What are the important changes from one period to the next, for most people? (If R says, "just gets older," ask, "Yes, but how?")

SOURCE: B. L. Neugarten and W. A. Peterson. "A Study of the American Age Grading System." *Proceedings of the Fourth Congress of the International Association of Gerontology*, 1957, 3. Reprinted by permission.

V1.11.III.g

EXPECTATIONS ABOUT SELF AND PARTNER IN INTERGENERATIONAL INTERACTIONS/PERCEPTIONS OF SELF AND PARTNER
H. J. Berman, 1974

EXPECTATIONS ABOUT SELF AND PARTNER

We are interested in how people of different generations perceive each other. Whether or not you usually meet and talk to college age women, you probably have some definite ideas of how they will behave toward you and how you will behave toward them.

Of course, every person we meet is different and it is impossible to say for sure how we, ourselves, or anybody else will behave. But the idea of this questionnaire is to try to generalize, to try to think of similarities in the way that most younger people act toward you and similarize in the way you act toward them.

Please read each question and mark the answer form to show how true you think each statement is:

If you feel the statement is very true, put a circle around ++

If it is slightly true, put a circle around +

If you feel the statement is neither true nor untrue, or if the statement is not clear to you, put a circle around ?

If you feel the statement is slightly untrue, put a circle around   −

If you feel the statement is very untrue, put a circle around   − −

It is best to work through the statements quickly, because your first thoughts will be most useful.

Try to answer as honestly as possible.

EXPECTATIONS ABOUT SELF

In meeting and talking with a woman in her 50s, I think

I will be open with her	− − − ? + ++
I will act defensively toward her	− − − ? + ++
I will act cautiously with her	− − − ? + ++
I will be quiet with her	− − − ? + ++
I will act superficially toward her	− − − ? + ++
I will act politely toward her	− − − ? + ++
I will be attentive toward her	− − − ? + ++
I will be curious about her	− − − ? + ++
I will act conservatively toward her	− − − ? + ++
I will act like myself with her	− − − ? + ++
I will be friendly toward her	− − − ? + ++
I will try to impress her	− − − ? + ++
I will be respectful toward her	− − − ? + ++
I will act maturely with her	− − − ? + ++

EXPECTATIONS ABOUT PARTNER

In meeting and talking with a woman in her 50s, I think

She will disapprove of me	− − − ? + ++
She will act like a parent toward me	− − − ? + ++
She will act helpful toward me	− − − ? + ++
She will act matronly toward me	− − − ? + ++
She will act understandingly toward me	− − − ? + ++
She will be polite toward me	− − − ? + ++
She will be friendly toward me	− − − ? + ++
She will act patronizingly toward me	− − − ? + ++
She will act condescendingly toward me	− − − ? + ++
She will be dogmatic with me	− − − ? + ++
She will be curious about me	− − − ? + ++
She will be interested in me	− − − ? + ++
She will act experienced toward me	− − − ? + ++
She will act jokingly with me	− − − ? + ++
She will act conservatively toward me	− − − ? + ++

EXPECTATIONS ABOUT SELF

In meeting and talking with a college age woman, I think

I will be understanding toward her	− − − ? + ++
I will be interested in her	− − − ? + ++
I will be curious about her	− − − ? + ++
I will be polite toward her	− − − ? + ++
I will be open toward her	− − − ? + ++
I will be honest with her	− − − ? + ++
I will be respectful of her	− − − ? + ++
I will be friendly toward her	− − − ? + ++

EXPECTATIONS ABOUT PARTNER

In meeting and talking with a college age woman, I think

She will be friendly with me	— — — ? + ++
She will be courteous with me	— — — ? + ++
She will be honest with me	— — — ? + ++
She will be open with me	— — — ? + ++
She will be curious about me	— — — ? + ++
She will be cautious with me	— — — ? + ++
She will act straightforwardly with me	— — — ? + ++
She will be enthusiastic with me	— — — ? + ++
She will be polite with me	— — — ? + ++
She will be indifferent toward me	— — — ? + ++
She will be critical of me	— — — ? + ++
She will be reserved with me	— — — ? + ++
She will be cool toward me	— — — ? + ++

PERCEPTIONS OF SELF AND PARTNER

The purpose of this questionnaire is to obtain your reactions to the conversation you just had with your partner.

Read each question and mark the answer form to show how true you think each statement is.

If you feel the statement is *very* true, put a circle around the	++
If it is slightly true, put a circle around the	+
If it is slightly untrue, put a circle around the	—
If it is very untrue, put a circle around the	— —

You will see that each of the items has two sections: A and B. In section A the questions are direct. In section B you will be putting in the answers that you think she would give.

There will be some questions that you may find difficult because they were true or untrue sometimes, but not at other times, or because they are unclear. When this is the case, you should still try to decide whether it is in the balance true or untrue, but if you still cannot decide, you may place a circle around the (?).

It is best to do the questions quite quickly because your first thoughts will be most useful. Try to answer as honestly as possible.

1a. How true do you think the following are?
    1. I was courteous to her   — — — ? + ++
    2. She was courteous to me   — — — ? + ++
1b. How would she answer the following:
    1. "I was courteous to her."   — — — ? + ++
    2. "She was courteous to me."   — — — ? + ++
2a. How true do you think the following are?
    1. I was attentive to her   — — — ? + ++
    2. She was attentive to me.   — — — ? + ++
2b. How would she answer the following?
    1. "I was attentive toward her."   — — — ? + ++
    2. "She was attentive toward me."   — — — ? + ++
3a. How true do you think the following are?
    1. I was cautious with her   — — — ? + ++
    2. She was cautious with me   — — — ? + ++
3b. How would she answer the following?
    1. "I was cautious with her."   — — — ? + ++
    2. "She was cautious with me."   — — — ? + ++

4a. How true do you think the following are?
    1. I acted condescendingly toward her   — — — ? + ++
    2. She acted condescendingly toward me   — — — ? + ++
4b. How would she answer the following?
    1. "I acted condescendingly toward her."   — — — ? + ++
    2. "She acted consdescendingly toward me."   — — — ? + ++
5a. How true do you think the following are?
    1. I acted conservatively toward her   — — — ? + ++
    2. She acted conservatively toward me   — — — ? + ++
5b. How would she answer the following?
    1. "I acted conservatively toward her."   — — — ? + ++
    2. "She acted conservatively toward me."   — — — ? + ++
6a. How true do you think the following are?
    1. I acted cool toward her   — — — ? + ++
    2. She acted cool toward me   — — — ? + ++
6b. How would she answer the following?
    1. "I acted cool toward her."   — — — ? + ++
    2. "She acted cool toward me."   — — — ? + ++
7a. How true do you think the following are?
    1. I acted like myself toward her   — — — ? + ++
    2. She acted like herself toward me   — — — ? + ++
7b. How would she answer the following?
    1. "I acted like myself toward her."   — — — ? + ++
    2. "She acted like herself toward me."   — — — ? + ++
8a. How true do you think the following are?
    1. I was critical of her   — — — ? + ++
    2. She was critical of me   — — — ? + ++
8b. How would she answer the following?
    1. "I was critical of her."   — — — ? + ++
    2. "She was critical of me."   — — — ? + ++
9a. How true do you think the following are?
    1. I was curious about her   — — — ? + ++
    2. She was curious about me   — — — ? + ++
9b. How would she answer the following?
    1. "I was curious about her.".   — — — ? + ++
    2. "She was curious about me."   — — — ? + ++
10a. How true do you think the following are?
    1. I acted defensively toward her   — — — ? + ++
    2. She acted defensively toward me   — — — ? + ++
10b. How would she answer the following?
    1. "I acted defensively toward her."   — — — ? + ++
    2. "She acted defensively toward me."   — — — ? + ++
11a. How true do you think the following are?
    1. I disapproved of her   — — — ? + ++
    2. She disapproved of me   — — — ? + ++
11b. How would she answer the following?
    1. "I disapproved of her."   — — — ? + ++
    2. "She disapproved of me."   — — — ? + ++
12a. How true do you think the following are?
    1. I was dogmatic with her   — — — ? + ++
    2. She was dogmatic with me   — — — ? + ++

12b. How would she answer the following?
    1. "I was dogmatic with her."   —— — ? + ++
    2. "She was dogmatic with me."   —— — ? + ++
13a. How true do you think the following are?
    1. I was enthusiastic about her   —— — ? + ++
    2. She was enthusiastic about me   —— — ? + ++
13b. How would she answer the following?
    1. "I was enthusiastic about her."   —— — ? + ++
    2. "She was enthusiastic about me."   —— — ? + ++
14a. How true do you think the following are?
    1. I acted experienced toward her   —— — ? + ++
    2. She acted experienced toward me   —— — ? + ++
14b. How would she answer the following?
    1. "I acted experienced toward her."   —— — ? + ++
    2. "She acted experienced toward me." ——— ? + ++
15a. How true do you think the following are?
    1. I acted friendly toward her   —— — ? + ++
    2. She acted friendly toward me   —— — ? + ++
15b. How would she answer the following?
    1. "I acted friendly toward her."   —— — ? + ++
    2. "She acted friendly toward me."   —— — ? + ++
16a. How true do you think the following are?
    1. I was helpful to her   —— — ? + ++
    2. She was helpful to me   —— — ? + ++
16b. How would she answer the following?
    1. "I was helpful to her."   —— — ? + ++
    2. "She was helpful to me."   —— — ? + ++
17a. How true do you think the following are?
    1. I was honest with her   —— — ? + ++
    2. She was honest with me   —— — ? + ++
17b. How would she answer the following?
    1. "I was honest with her."   —— — ? + ++
    2. "She was honest with me."   —— — ? + ++
18a. How true do you think the following are?
    1. I was indifferent toward her   —— — ? + ++
    2. She was indifferent toward me   —— — ? + ++
18b. How would she answer the following?
    1. "I was indifferent toward her."   —— — ? + ++
    2. "She was indifferent toward me."   —— — ? + ++
19a. How true do you think the following are?
    1. I was interested in her   —— — ? + ++
    2. She was interested in me   —— — ? + ++
19b. How would she answer the following?
    1. "I was interested in her."   —— — ? + ++
    2. "She was interested in me."   —— — ? + ++
20a. How true do you think the following are?
    1. I acted jokingly with her   —— — ? + ++
    2. She acted jokingly with me   —— — ? + ++
20b. How would she answer the following?
    1. "I acted jokingly with her."   —— — ? + ++
    2. "She acted jokingly with me."   —— — ? + ++

21a.	How true do you think the following are?	
	1. I acted like a parent toward her	−− − ? + ++
	2. She acted like a parent toward me	−− − ? + ++
21b.	How would she answer the following?	
	1. "I acted like a parent toward her."	−− − ? + ++
	2. "She acted like a parent toward me."	−− − ? + ++
22a.	How true do you think the following are?	
	1. I acted matronly toward her	−− − ? + ++
	2. She acted matronly toward me	−− − ? + ++
22b.	How would she answer the following?	
	1. "I acted matronly toward her."	−− − ? + ++
	2. "She acted matronly toward me."	−− − ? + ++
23a.	How true do you think the following are?	
	1. I acted maturely with her	−− − ? + ++
	2. She acted maturely with me	−− − ? + ++
23b.	How would she answer the following?	
	1. "I acted maturely with her."	−− − ? + ++
	2. "She acted maturely with me."	−− − ? + ++
24a.	How true do you think the following are?	
	1. I was open with her	−− − ? + ++
	2. She was open with me	−− − ? + ++
24b.	How would she answer the following?	
	1. "I was open with her."	−− − ? + ++
	2. "She was open with me."	−− − ? + ++
25a.	How true do you think the following are?	
	1. I acted patronizingly toward her	−− − ? + ++
	2. She acted patronizingly toward me	−− − ? + ++
25b.	How would she answer the following?	
	1. "I acted patronizingly toward her."	−− − ? + ++
	2. "She acted patronizingly toward me."	−− − ? + ++
26a.	How true do you think the following are?	
	1. I was polite to her	−− − ? + ++
	2. She was polite to me	−− − ? + ++
26b.	How would she answer the following?	
	1. "I was polite to her."	−− − ? + ++
	2. "She was polite to me."	−− − ? + ++
27a.	How true do you think the following are?	
	1. I was quiet with her	−− − ? + ++
	2. She was quiet with me	−− − ? + ++
27b.	How would she answer the following?	
	1. "I was quiet with her."	−− − ? + ++
	2. "She was quiet with me."	−− − ? + ++
28a.	How true do you think the following are?	
	1. I acted reserved with her	−− − ? + ++
	2. She acted reserved with me	−− − ? + ++
28b.	How would she answer the following?	
	1. "I acted reserved with her."	−− − ? + ++
	2. "She acted reserved with me."	−− − ? + ++
29a.	How true do you think the following are?	
	1. I was respectful to her	−− − ? + ++
	2. She was respectful to me	−− − ? + ++

29b.	How would she answer the following?						
	1. "I was respectful to her."	− −	−	?	+	++
	2. "She was respectful to me."	− −	−	?	+	++
30a.	How true do you think the following are?						
	1. I was straightforward with her	− −	−	?	+	++
	2. She was straightforward with me	− −	−	?	+	++
30b.	How would she answer the following?						
	1. "I was straightforward with her."	− −	−	?	+	++
	2. "She was straightforward with me."	− −	−	?	+	++
31a.	How true do you think the following are?						
	1. I acted superficially toward her	− −	−	?	+	++
	2. She acted superficially toward me	− −	−	?	+	++
31b.	How would she answer the following?						
	1. "I acted superficially toward her."	− −	−	?	+	++
	2. "She acted superficially toward me."	− −	−	?	+	++
32a.	How true do you think the following are?						
	1. I tried to impress her	− −	−	?	+	++
	2. She tried to impress me	− −	−	?	+	++
32b.	How would she answer the following?						
	1. "I tried to impress her."	− −	−	?	+	++
	2. "She tried to impress me."	− −	−	?	+	++
33a.	How true do you think the following are?						
	1. I was understanding with her	− −	−	?	+	++
	2. She was understanding with me	− −	−	?	+	++
33b.	How would she answer the following?						
	1. "I was understanding with her."	− −	−	?	+	++
	2. "She was understanding with me."	− −	−	?	+	++

SOURCE: H. J. Berman. "Perception of Self and Others in Relation to Age." Ph.D. dissertation, Washington University, 1974.

V1.11.III.h
ADJECTIVE CHECK LIST
H. Gough and A. Heilbrun, Jr., 1965

This copyrighted instrument is available from Consulting Psychologists Press, Palo Alto, Calif.

V1.11.III.i
PERCEPTIONS OF ADULTS
T. Hickey and R. A. Kalish, 1968

EVALUATIVE

1. _____ year-old people are mean or unkind.
2. _____ year-old people like children and young people.
3. I like to help _____ year-old people.

DESCRIPTIVE

1. _____ year-old people are lonely.
2. _____ year-old people are busy.

NOTE: 25-, 45-, 65-, and 85-year-old people. Statements were listed randomly four times—each time with a different adult-ratee. The response choices, "a lot," "some," "a little," and "not much," were selected because the younger age groups had already used them on diagnostic tests in school.

SOURCE: T. Hickey and R. A. Kalish. "Young People's Perceptions of Adults." *Journal of Gerontology*, 1968, 23 (2): 219. Reprinted by permission of author and publisher.

V1.11.III.j
JACKSON PERSONALITY RESEARCH FORM
D. M. Jackson, 1967

This copyrighted instrument is available from the Consulting Psychologists Press, Goshen, N.Y.

V1.11.III.k
AGE ASSOCIATION ITEMS
Kansas City Study of Adult Life

TO THE RESPONDENT: "I have here a little game. It is a short list of things on the periods of life. I would like you to give me the age which goes best with them. There are no right or wrong answers, so just give your best guess. When I give a word, just give me the first age which comes to your mind." "*Just give the first age that pops into your head.*"

A young man _____
When a man feels the closest to his family _____
When a man begins to slow down _____
When a man tries the hardest to succeed _____
An old woman _____
When a man gets the most pleasure from his children _____
A middle-aged man _____
When a man's age makes it hard for him to find a job _____
When a man accomplishes the most _____
A mature man _____
When a man gets the most pleasure from sex _____
A grandfather _____
When a man has the most responsibilities _____
A good looking man _____
When a man has the most confidence in himself _____
A father _____
The prime of life for a man _____
A young woman _____
When a woman feels closest to her family _____
When a woman begins to slow down _____
When a woman tries the hardest to succeed _____
An old woman _____
When a woman gets the most pleasure from her children _____
A middle aged woman _____
When a woman's age makes it hard for her to find a job _____
When a woman accomplishes the most _____
A mature woman _____
When a woman gets the most pleasure from sex _____
A grandmother _____
When a woman has the most responsibilities _____

A good looking woman _____
When a woman has the most confidence in herself _____
The prime of life for a woman _____
A mother _____

SOURCE: B. L. Neugarten and W. A. Peterson. "A Study of the American Age Grading System." *Proceedings of the Fourth Congress of the International Association of Gerontology*, 1957, 3. Reprinted by permission.

V1.11.III.l
LIFE GRAPHS
K. Back and L. B. Bourque, 1970

Each S was presented with a blank-grid (Fig. 1) and was asked the following question— "Can you visualize how your life could be put into a graph? That is, ups and downs, level periods, rises and declines, etc. Assuming that you live up until at least 80 years of age, how do you think that a graph of your life will look? Indicate this by making the graph on this card."

| 10 | 20 | 30 | 40 | 50 | 60 | 70 | 80 |

Figure 1. Graph grid given to all Ss.

SOURCE: K. Back and L. B. Bourque. "Life Graphs: Aging and Cohort Effect." *Journal of Gerontology*, 1970, 25 (3): 250. Reprinted by permission of author and publisher.

V1.11.III.m
PERCEIVED GENERATION GAP
V. L. Bengtson, 1971

Some people say there is a "generation gap" between age groups in American society today.

A. How much of a gap do you think there is between the following groups?
   —Between young and middle-aged
   —Between young and old
   —Between middle-aged and old

B. In your family, how great is the gap between the three generations, in your opinion?

| 1 | 2 | 3 | 4 | 5 | 6 |

No gap whatsoever

Very great gap

Table 1
Mean Perception of "Cohort Gap" By Generation of Respondent[a]

	Between G3 − G2		Referent Between G3 − G1		Between G2 − G1		Total by Generation of Respondent
Respondent	$\bar{x}$	s.d.	$\bar{x}$	s.d.	$\bar{x}$	s.d.	$\bar{x}$
G1	3.62	1.37	3.90	1.63	3.00	1.31	3.51
G2	3.20	1.12	4.25	1.31	2.81	1.11	3.42
G3	3.28	1.35	4.42	1.44	2.95	1.19	3.55

a. "Some people say there is a 'generation gap' between age groups in American society today. How much of a 'gap' do you think there is between the following groups?" (The groups referred to are the column headings in this table.) Subjects gave responses on a six-point scale from "no gap whatsoever" (scored 1) to "very great gap" (scored 6). G1 = oldest generation (n=105); G2 = parents (n=95); G3 = grandchildren (n=78).

Table 2
Mean Perceptions of the "Lineage Gap" by Generation of Respondent[a]

	Between G3 — G2		Referent Between G3 — G1		Between G2 — G1		Total by Generation of Respondent
Respondent	$\overline{x}$	s.d.	$\overline{x}$	s.d.	$\overline{x}$	s.d.	$\overline{x}$
G1	2.19	1.24	2.06	1.23	1.81	1.19	2.02
G2	2.35	1.04	3.62	1.53	2.72	1.28	2.89
G3	2.96	1.34	3.75	1.62	2.70	1.23	3.14
Total by generation of referent	2.46	1.24	3.07	1.65	2.38	1.30	2.64

a. "In your family, how great is the 'gap' between the three generations, in your opinion?" SOURCE: V. L. Bengtson. "Inter-age Perceptions and the Generation Gap." *The Gerontologist*, 1971, 11 (4, part 2): 88. Reprinted by permission of author and publisher.

V1.11.III.n
COMPARISON OF AGE-GROUPS
P. Cameron, 1970

Examples of Some of the Items:

"How do you believe the three age-groups (young adults, middle-aged, and old) compare in
  a. femininity of personality-style;
  b. possession of feminine sorts of interests;
  c. masculinity of personality-style;
  d. possession of masculine sorts of interests;
  e. possession of feminine sorts of skills (ability to do things usually done by women in our society—as cooking, ironing, etc.);
  f. social pressure for them to do feminine sorts of things;
  g. possession of masculine sorts of skills (ability to do things usually done by men in our society—as hold a job, know how to fix a car);
  h. social pressure for them to do masculine sorts of things?"

Respondents indicated which generation they believed had the most and least of each.

Respondents were then asked to rate themselves as "above average," "average," or "below average" to the questions, "How would you compare yourself with all other adults of your sex in:
  a. femininity of personality-style;
  b. possession of feminine sorts of interests;
  c. masculinity of personality-style;
  d. possession of masculine sorts of interests;

    e. possession of feminine sorts of skills (ability to do things usually done by women in our society—cooking, ironing, etc.);

    f. social pressure on you to do feminine sorts of things;

    g. possession of masculine sorts of skills (ability to do things usually done by men in our society—as hold a job, know how to fix a car);

    h. social pressure on you to do masculine sorts of things?"

SOURCE: P. Cameron. "Masculinity/Femininity of the Generations: As Self-Reported and as Stereotypically Appraised." *International Journal of Aging and Human Development*, 1976, 7: 144–45.

"How do you believe the three age groups (young adults, middle-aged, and old) compare in:

    1. over-all happiness? _____ are the happiest; _____ are the least happy.

    2. opportunities for happiness? _____ have the most opportunities; _____ have the fewest opportunities.

    3. opportunities for fun? _____ have the most opportunities; _____ have the fewest opportunities.

    4. desire for fun? _____ want fun most; _____ want fun least.

    5. desire for happiness? _____ want happiness most; _____ want happiness least."

The self-report part of the questionnaire was a mirror of the above, consisting of a Likert scale (above average, average, below average) introduced—"How would you compare yourself with all other adults of your sex in:

    1. over-all happiness?

    2. opportunities for happiness?

    3. opportunities for fun?

    4. desire for fun?

    5. desire for happiness?"

SOURCE: P. Cameron. "Stereotypes about Generational Fun and Happiness versus Self-Appraised Fun and Happiness." *The Gerontologist*, 1972, 12 (2, part 1): 122.

V1.11.III.o
BEST YEARS OF LIFE
National Council on the Aging, 1975

1a. If you had to choose, what would you say are the best years of a person's life—his teens, 20's, 30's, 40's, 50's, 60's, 70's, or when?

Teens. . . . . _____

20's. . . . . _____

30's. . . . . _____

40's. . . . . _____

50's. . . . . _____

60's. . . . . _____

70's. . . . . _____

other (specify)

_____ . . . . . _____

Wouldn't choose any age. . . . . . (vol.)

Not sure . . . . _____

1b. Why do you feel that way? Any other reasons?

1c. And what would you say are the worst years of a person's life—his teens, 20's, 30's 40's, 50's, 60's, 70's, or when?

Teens. . . . . _____

20's. . . . . _____

```
30's. . . . . . . . . . . . . . . . . ———
40's. . . . . . . . . . . . . . . . . ———
50's. . . . . . . . . . . . . . . . . ———
60's. . . . . . . . . . . . . . . . . ———
70's. . . . . . . . . . . . . . . . . ———
other (specify)
——————————————————— . . . . . ———
Wouldn't choose any age. . . . . . (vol.)
Not sure . . . . . . . . . . . . . .———
```
1d. Why do you feel that way? Any other reasons?

SOURCE: National Council on the Aging. "An Index to Available Data from the NCOA/ Harris Survey." Washington, D.C.: National Council on the Aging, 1976, p. 6. Reproduced with permission from *Codebook for "The Myth and Reality of Aging," a survey conducted by Louis Harris and associates for the National Council on the Aging;* prepared by the Duke University Center for the Study of Aging and Human Development under a grant from the Edna M. Clark Foundation.

V1.11.III.p
PERCEPTIONS OF AGE-GROUPS' RESPECT AND INFLUENCE
E. G. Youmans, 1971

	Urban		Rural	
Perceptions	Younger (N = 237)	Older (N = 165)	Younger (N = 127)	Older (N = 276)
	%	%	%	%
1. At what age is a person				
most respected?	A	B	C	D
Youth (to age 21)	1	2	2	3
Early middle age (22-45)	31	36	37	35
Later middle age (46-64)	48	37	20	22
Older age (65 and over)	11	13	28	19
Don't know	9	12	13	21
2. At what age does a person				
have most influence?	E	F	G	H
Youth	—	2	6	3
Early middle age	31	33	34	36
Later middle age	51	50	32	28
Older age	5	2	10	5
Don't know	13	13	18	28
3. At what age is a person				
least respected?	I	J	K	L
Youth	72	33	50	20
Early middle age	2	4	7	2
Later middle age	—	1	1	—
Older age	10	28	19	52
Don't know	16	34	22	26
4. At what age does a person				
have least influence?	M	N	O	P
Youth	61	31	61	21
Early middle age	2	4	1	2

TABLE—*Continued*

Perceptions	Urban		Rural	
	Younger (N = 237) %	Older (N = 165) %	Younger (N = 127) %	Older (N = 276) %
Later middle age	1	—	3	3
Older age	21	46	14	42
Don't know	15	19	21	32

AB χ^2 = 6.29, 3 df, p < 0.05 IJ χ^2 = 62.76, 2 df, p < 0.001
CD χ^2 = 6.30, 3 df, p < 0.05 KL χ^2 = 57.84, 2 df, p < 0.001
DF χ^2 = 5.61, 3 df, p < 0.05 MN χ^2 = 41.41, 2 df, p < 0.001
GH χ^2 = 8.89, 4 df, p < 0.05 OP χ^2 = 64.64, 2 df, p < 0.001

SOURCE: E. G. Youmans. "Generation and Perceptions of Old Age: An Urban-Rural Comparison." *The Gerontologist*, 1971, 11 (4, part 1): 286. Reprinted by permission of author and publisher.

Chapter 12

Perceptions of Old People

Donald G. McTavish

Over the years since Dinkel's work on scaling children's attitudes toward their aged parents (Dinkel, 1944), there have been a substantial literature and a relatively large number of measurement approaches focused on the phenomenon variously referred to as "perceptions," "attitudes," "beliefs," "common misconceptions," "stereotypes," and "orientations" about or toward old people or old age. Most of the literature expresses a concern about negative (and sometimes positive) ageist feelings people (including older people) have about the contemporary elderly. Usually, these emotional states are considered to be prior causes of society's treatment of older people, which in turn affects the well-being of the aged themselves. The implication is that, should one be successful in turning around the more negative attitudes, a brighter existence for America's elderly people would result. Thus, there has been ever-renewed interest in ways to detect such ageist perceptions not only to identify target groups for "treatment," but to measure the effectiveness of programs designed to change these attitudes. This literature has been summarized elsewhere (e.g., Brubaker and Powers, 1976; Bennett and Eckman, 1973; McTavish, 1971).

This chapter surveys the measures of perceptions about old people. Although an attempt was made to be exhaustive, the chapter focuses on 18 of the more explicit and quantitative measures that are likely to be considered useful in gerontological research. Specifically excluded here, but discussed in other chapters (Chapters 10 and 11 in this volume and Chapters 4, 5, and 6 in volume 2), are measures of subjective age identification, age-appropriate behavior, life phases, opinions about older workers, and global societal measures. Also excluded are assessment procedures that ask subjects to fill out standard questionnaires as they think an older person or a member of some other age-group would (e.g., Ahammer and Baltes, 1972), open-ended responses to specialized materials (such as the Thematic Apperception Test pictures) that use clinical judgments in their interpretations (e.g., Neugarten and Gutmann, 1958), and studies asking respondents to rank age categories or generations according to their desirability (e.g., Tuckman and Lorge, 1953a; NCOA/Harris, 1976).

The 18 measures of primary interest are listed in Table 12-1. Several of these measures are actually families of related instruments in which the basic instruments are used, sometimes in modified forms.

TABLE 12-1
Instruments Reviewed in Chapter 12

Instrument	Author (date)	Code Number
I. Yes-No Scales		
a. Attitudes toward Old People	Tuckman and Lorge (1953a)	V1.12.I.a
b. Facts on Aging	Palmore (1977)	V1.12.I.b
II. Likert-Type Agree-Disagree Scales		
a. Kogan Attitude toward Old People Scale	Kogan (1961a)	V1.12.II.a
b. Opinions about People	Ontario Welfare Council (1971)	V1.12.II.b
c. Attitudes toward Aging	Kilty and Feld (1976)	V1.12.II.c
d. Perceptions of Old Age	Youmans (1971)	V1.12.II.d
e. Negative Attributes of Old Age and Positive Potential in Old Age	Morgan and Bengtson (1976)	V1.12.II.e
f. Images of Older People Battery	NCOA (1975)	V1.12.II.f
g. Salter View of Elderly Scale	Salter and Salter (1976)	V1.12.II.g
h. Perceptions of Aging	Bengtson et al. (1975)	V1.12.II.h
III. Semantic Differential Scales		
a. Kogan-Wallach Semantic Differential	Kogan and Wallach (1961)	V1.12.III.a
b. Eisdorfer-Altrocchi Semantic Differential	Eisdorfer and Altrocchi (1961)	V1.12.III.b
c. Across-Age Semantic Differential	Petersen (1976)	V1.12.III.c
d. Attitudes toward the Aged	Rosencranz and McNevin (1969)	V1.12.III.d
IV. Sentence-Completion and Content Analytic Procedures		
a. Golde-Kogan Sentence-Completion Assessment	Golde and Kogan (1959)	V1.12.IV.a
b. Children's Attitudes toward the Elderly	Jantz et al. (1976)	Copyrighted
c. Adjective Checklist	Aaronson (1966)	V1.12.IV.c
d. Children's Perceptions of the Elderly	Hickey, Hickey, and Kalish (1968)	V1.12.IV.d

With very few exceptions (e.g., Morgan and Bengtson, 1976), the developers and users of the scales devoted little space to the identification of the concept or concepts they intended to measure. As Hagestad noted in Chapter 11, terms that could be used in a technical sense to identify "that which is being measured" are used in a more general sense and often as synonyms. Thus, reference is made to a relatively unspecified conceptual domain, or, to put it more positively, there seems to be little indication that greater conceptual specificity is thought to be needed. For want of a more general term, this chapter in references to this general domain uses the term "perceptions" of older people.

Taken as a whole, the measures appear to treat perceptions as a property of individual respondents (although individual responses can be aggregated for analytic or social groups to indicate a common viewpoint). Analytic or convenience selections of subjects are typical, and little emphasis has been placed on verifying social-group membership or the effect of socialization on that group's perceptions. The National Council on the Aging's study (1976) is perhaps the only one that explicitly highlights the representational nature of its data. When data are aggregated, individual responses are treated as having equal importance.

Measures tend to sample from a very broad domain of possible features of older people—mental, physical, context, problems, typical behaviors, and so on. Some measures emphasize knowledge/misinformation, others emphasize affective reaction. In most instances, the treatment of the data suggests an underlying conceptualization of perceptions as ordinal and continuous and multidimensional. Virtually all the measures in this field include a directional component (e.g., favorable-unfavorable, positive-negative, for-against, agree-disagree, aware-unaware, sympathetic-unsympathetic, approach-avoid, supportive-unsupportive, etc.).

The age-related stimulus can be chronological (e.g., 50- to 70-year-old man) or a term denoting "old" age. Generally, it is such a class of individuals that is the target, rather than more specific, known older people. A few measures, however, inquire about the subject's older kin or the subject's own aging. Usually, gender is specified, but rarely is ethnic group, birth cohort, or social context.

Table 12-1 indicates that a variety of measurement approaches have been undertaken. Most popular has been the Likert agree-disagree format, in which the stimuli are statements about older people. Second most popular has been the semantic differential technique, in which a target concept is rated on several bipolar adjective-pair scales that indicate the concept's meaning to the respondent. In most cases the concept is conveyed by a word or a short phrase, rather than by a visual image, for example. Several content analyses (manually coded) of actual words have been used in characterizing older people. Some of this material is generated by open-ended sentence stems or solicited stories and word associations. The adjective checklist has been used as a structured approach to verbal description. Finally, there are a few instances of the dichotomous (yes-no) response to statements about older people.

In all of these instances, the essential task for the subject is to characterize the location of the target concept in terms of some investigator-supplied or respondent-supplied set of rating criteria. The respondents do not make comparisons between different age-groups. Such comparisons become possible through either the selection of samples of respondents of different ages or the comparison of semantic differential responses to different concepts (e.g., old man, young man). The respondent is not asked to make the comparisons directly (exceptions are the age-appropriate behavior measures and the selection of the "best" or "worst" year of life from a list of ages—methods discussed in other chapters). In both the testing and the analysis of data on perceptions, there is relatively heavy reliance on the shared meanings of most of the words. Variations in response are analyzed either as indications of the differences between respondents or (in some instances) as an indication of the different meaning of different stimuli (e.g., old person versus insane person).

One of the more frequent pursuits in the perceptions literature is a factor analytic search for underlying dimensions among time (Q analysis appears not to have been used). Table 12-2 lists the factors that have been identified by this technique. In a few instances, there has been an attempt to identify items that maintain the same factorial structure across different groups of respondents and/or different concepts being rated (e.g., Morgan and Bengtson, 1976; Kogan and Wallach, 1961; Petersen, 1976).

TABLE 12-2
Factors Identified in the Analysis of Various Perceptions
of Old People Measures

Researcher(s)	Technique	Factors
Kapos and Smith (1972)	Likert	Realistic toughness toward aging (verging on cynicism)
		Denial of the effects of aging
		Anxiety about aging
		Social distance to the old
		Family responsibility toward aged parents and relatives

TABLE 12-2—*Continued*

Researcher(s)	Technique	Factors
		Public responsibility vs. unconcern for the aged as a group
		Unfavorable stereotype of the old as inferior vs. acceptance as equals
Hickey et al. (1975)	Likert	Social distance
		Denial
		Social acceptance and responsibility
		Future orientation
		Anxiety
		Family responsibility
Kilty and Feld (1976)	Composite of scales; Likert	
		Reactions to older workers
		Srole Anomie Scale
		Positive reactions about older people
		Negative reactions about older people
Morgan and Bengtson (1976)	Likert	Negative attributes of old age
		Positive potential of old age
Kogan and Wallach (1961)	Semantic differential	Evaluative scale
Eisdorfer and Altrocchi (1961)	Semantic differential	Evaluative factor
		Self-dangerous (activity plus potency scales)
Petersen (1976)	Semantic differential	Interpersonal ability
		Instrumental ability
		Propriety (a minor factor)
Rosencranz and McNevin (1969)	Semantic differential	Autonomous-dependent
		Personal acceptability-unacceptability
		Instrumental ineffective
Aaronson (1966)	Adjective checklist	*Factors for words used more frequently than by chance:*
		Energetic outgoingness
		Socialized control
		Anergic constriction
		Factors for words used less frequently than by chance:
		Mature restraint
		Youthful exuberance
		Asocial inefficiency

Attention to measurement issues has been lacking or piecemeal, and, in general, validity and reliability information and scale norms need to be investigated and published. In a few instances, there has been an attempt to refine scale items so that chronological age categories are discriminated (Axelrod and Eisdorfer, 1961; Eisdorfer and

Altrocchi, 1961; Rosencranz and McNevin, 1969; Golde and Kogan, 1959; Aaronson, 1966). Other investigators have attempted to find scale items that show the same structure across ages or are applicable across other group boundaries (Morgan and Bengtson, 1976; Petersen, 1976; Bengtson et al., 1975). Eisdorfer and Altrocchi (1961) and Kogan (1961a) noted that the factor structure of perception items can differ across samples of respondents and by the specific concepts evaluated.

There has been some work to suggest that scale users should be wary of artifactual response effects such as response set (Kilty and Feld, 1976; Kogan, 1961a) and social desirability (Silverman, 1966). Just under half of the measures listed in Table 12-1 paid explicit attention to *some* aspect of reliability. Rarely does this involve coefficients (whole-part, split-half, internal consistency, etc.), and almost never is a test-retest procedure used. Where there are data on reliability, the results are encouraging, although much work still needs to be done.

Perhaps the primary problem with measures in this area is in their validity. It is very difficult to judge validity, because it is conceptually unclear what these measures are to identify. About half of the measures have some type of explicit, if not formal, validity assessment. Rarely is it rigorous, and most often the investigator's judgment plays a determining role. With relative frequency the outcome is mixed or contrary to the investigator's expectations. There seems to be little cumulation toward documented validity.

In terms of usage, about half of the measures have been used with only 1 sample. One family of measure (Kogan, 1961a) has been used with 8 samples, and another family (Tuckman and Lorge, 1952a) has been used on 14 samples in the literature that was surveyed for this chapter.

The most pressing question, in this writer's opinion, in why one should use any of these measures. The answer stems from a theory (or theories) that guide investigators in circumscribing a class of relevant measures. Such conceptual direction is at the root of adequate validity assessment. Once the question is phrased this way, it becomes clear that there may be several theories and several different sets of relevant measurements that may not overlap very much at all. Not only is the perceptions area not unidimensional, it may be best approached as *several* not necessarily related multidimensional theoretical domains. Thus, prior to selecting any one of the existing measurement approaches, an investigator should focus on the theoretical reasons for measuring some aspect of perceptions at all. (See Table 12-1 for a list of the instruments included in this chapter.)

REFERENCES

Aaronson, B. S. "Personality Stereotypes of Aging." *Journal of Gerontology*, 1966, 21: 458-62.

Ahammer, I. M., and P. B. Baltes. "Objective versus Perceived Age Differences in Personality: How Do Adolescents, Adults, and Older People View Themselves and Each Other?" *Journal of Gerontology*, 1972, 27: 45-51.

Axelrod, S., and C. Eisdorfer. "Attitudes toward Old People: An Empirical Analysis of the Stimulus-Group Validity of the Tuckman-Lorge Questionnaire." *Journal of Gerontology*, 1961, 16: 75-80.

Bekker, L. D., and C. Taylor. "Attitudes toward the Aged in a Multigenerational Sample." *Journal of Gerontology*, 1966, 21: 115-18.

Bengtson, V. L., J. J. Dowd, D. H. Smith, and A. Inkeles. "Modernization, Modernity, and Perceptions of Aging: A Cross-Cultural Study." *Journal of Gerontology*, 1975, 30: 688-95.

Bennett, R., and J. Eckman. "Attitudes toward Aging: A Critical Examination of Recent Literature and Implications for Future Research." In *The Psychology of Adult Development and Aging*, C. Eisdorfer and M. P. Lawton (eds.) pp. 575-97. Washington, D. C.: 1973.

Brubaker, T. H., and E. A. Powers. "The Stereotype of 'Old': A Review and Alternative Approach." *Journal of Gerontology*, 1976, 31: 441-47.

Burdman, G. D. M. "Student and Trainee Attitudes on Aging." *The Gerontologist*, 1974, 14: 65-68.

Cryns. A. G., and A. Monk. "Attitudes toward Youth as a Function of Adult Age: A Multivariate Study in Intergenerational Dynamics." *International Journal of Aging and Human Development*, 1973, 4: 23-33.

Dinkel, R. M. "Parent-Child Conflict in Minnesota Families." *American Sociological Review*, 1943, 6: 412-19.

_____. "Attitudes of Children toward Supporting Aged Parents." *American Sociological Review*, 1944, 9: 370-79.

Eisdorfer C. "Attitudes toward Old People: A Re-analysis of the Item-Validity of the Stereotype Scale." *Journal of Gerontology*, 1966, 21: 455-57.

Eisdorfer C., and J. Altrocchi. "A Comparison of Attitudes toward Old Age and Mental Illness." *Journal of Gerontology*, 1966, 21: 455-57.

Golde, P., and N. Kogan. "A Sentence Completion Procedure for Assessing Attitudes toward Old People." *Journal of Gerontology*, 1959, 14: 355-63.

Gordon, S. K., and D. S. Hallauer. "Impact of a Friendly Visiting Program on Attitudes of College Students toward the Aged." *The Gerontologist*, 1976, 16: 371-76.

Gordon, S. K., and W. E. Vinacke. "Self and Ideal Self-Concepts and Dependence in Aged Persons Residing in Institutions." *Journal of Gerontology*, 1971, 26: 337-45.

Harman, H. H. *Modern Factor Analysis*. Chicago. University of Chicago Press, 1960.

Hickey T., S. M. Bragg, W. Rakowski, and D. F. Hultsch, "Attitudes toward Aging and the Aged: An Analytical Study." 1975 (mimeographed report).

Hickey, T., L. A. Hickey, and R. A. Kalish. "Children's Perceptions of the Elderly." *Journal of Genetic Psychology*, 1968, 112: 227-35.

Hickey, T., W. Rakowski, D. F. Hultsch, and B. J. Fatula. "Attitudes toward Aging as a Function of In-Service Training and Practitioner Age." *Journal of Gerontology*, 1976, 31: 681-86.

Ivester, C., and K. King. "Attitudes of Adolescents toward the Aged." *The Gerontologist*, 1977, 17: 85-89.

Jantz, R. K., C. Seefeldt, A. Galper, and K. Serock. *Test Manual: The CATE: Children's Attitudes toward the Elderly*, Center on Aging, Division of Human and Community Resources, University of Maryland (copyrighted by Jantz and Seefeldt), 1976.

Kapos, A., and D. Smith. "Identifying Standard Attitudes toward Senescence." Paper presented to the Ninth International Congress of Gerontology, Kiev, U.S.S.R., July 2–7, 1972.

Kilty, K. M., and A. Feld. "Attitudes toward Aging and toward the Needs of Older People." *Journal of Gerontology*, 1976, 31: 586–94.

Kogan, N. "Attitudes toward Old People: The Development of a Scale and an Examination of Correlates." *Journal of Abnormal and Social Psychology*, 1961a, 62: 44–54.

———. "Attitudes toward Old People in an Older Sample." *Journal of Abnormal and Social Psychology*, 1961b, 62: 616–22.

Kogan, N., and F. C. Shelton. "Images of 'Old People' and 'People in General' in an Older Sample." *Journal of Genetic Psychology*, 1962a, 100: 3–21.

———. "Beliefs about 'Old People': A Comparative Study of Older and Younger Samples." *Journal of Genetic Psychology* 1962b, 100: 93–111.

Kogan, N., and M. A. Wallach. "Age Changes in Values and Attitudes." *Journal of Gerontology*, 1961, 16: 272–80.

Lane, B. "Attitudes of Youth toward the Aged." *Journal of Marriage and the Family*, 1964, 26: 229–31.

McTavish, D. D. "Perceptions of Old People: A Review of Research Methodologies and Findings." *The Gerontologist*, 1971, 11: 90–101.

Morgan, L. A., and V. L. Bengtson. "Measuring Perceptions of Aging Across Social Strata." Paper presented to the 29th Annual Meeting of the Gerontological Society, New York, October 13–17, 1976.

National Council on the Aging. *The Myth and Reality of Aging in America*. Washington, D. C.: National Council on the Aging, 1975.

———. *Codebook for "The Myth and Reality in Aging in America,"* a survey conducted by Louis Harris and associates for the National Council on the Aging; prepared by the Duke University Center for the Study of Aging and Human Development, 1976.

Naus, P. J. "Some Correlates of Attitudes toward Old People." *International Journal of Aging and Human Development*, 1973, 4: 229–43.

Neugarten, B. L., and D. L. Gutmann. "Age-Sex Roles and Personality in Middle Age: A Thematic Apperception Study." *Psychological Monographs*, 1958, 72 (470).

Nunnally, J. *Popular Conceptions of Mental Health: Their Development and Change*. New York: Holt, Rinehart and Winston, 1961.

Ontario Welfare Council, Section on Aging. *Opinions About People, Form A: Guidelines and Manual* (for an instrument dealing with attitudes toward aging and the aged for use in educational and training programs in the field of aging). Toronto, Ontario: January 1971.

Osgood, C. E., G. J. Suci, and P. H. Tannenbaum. *The Measurement of Meaning*. Urbana, Ill.: University of Illinois Press, 1957.

Palmore, E. "Facts on Aging: A Short Quiz." *The Gerontologist*, 1977, 17: 315–20.

Petersen, M. "A Cross-Age Semantic Differential for Social Evaluation." Paper presented to the Annual Conference of the International Communication Association, Portland, April 14–17, 1976.

Rosencranz, H. A., and T. E. McNevin. "A Factor Analysis of Attitudes toward the Aged." *The Gerontologist*, 1969, 9: 55–59.

Salter, C. A., and C. DeL. Salter. "Attitudes toward Aging and Behaviors toward the Elderly among Young People as a Function of Death Anxiety." *The Gerontologist*, 1976, 16: 232–36.

Silverman, I. "Response-Set Bias and Predictive Validity Associated with Kogan's 'Attitudes toward Old People Scale.'" *Journal of Gerontology*, 1966, 21: 86-88.

Srole, L. "Social Integration and Certain Corollaries: An Exploratory Study." *American Sociological Reveiw*, 1956, 21: 709-16.

Thorson, J. A. "Attitudes toward the Aged as a Function of Race and Social Class," *The Gerontologist*, 1975, 15: 343-44.

Thorson, J. A., and M. L. Perkins. "Attitudes toward the Aged as a Function of Personality Characteristics." Paper presented to the 29th Annual Meeting of the Gerontological Society, New York, October 13-17, 1976.

Thorson, J. A., L. Whatley, and K. Hancock. "Attitudes toward the Aged as a Function of Age and Education," *The Gerontologist*, 1974, 14: 316-18.

Tuckman, J., and I. Lorge. "The Attitudes of the Aged toward the Older Worker: For Institutionalized Adults." *Journal of Gerontology*, 1952a, 7: 559-64.

_____. "The Influence of a Course on the Psychology of the Adult on Attitudes toward Old People and Older Workers." *Journal of Educational Psychology*, 1952b, 43: 400-407.

_____. "The Effect of Institutionalization on Attitudes Toward Old People." *Journal of Abnormal and Social Psychology*, 1952c, 47: 337-44.

_____. "Attitudes toward Old People." *Journal of Social Psychology*, 1953a, 37: 249-60.

_____. "When Aging Begins and Stereotypes about Aging." *Journal of Gerontology*, 1953b, 8: 489-92.

_____. "The Effect of Changed Directions on the Attitudes about Old People and the Older Worker." *Educational Psychological Measurement*, 1953c, 13: 607-13.

_____. "The Influence of Changed Directions on Stereotypes about Aging: Before and after Instruction." *Educational and Psychological Measurement*, 1954, 14: 128-32.

_____. "The Projection of Personal Symptom into Stereotype about Aging." *Journal of Gerontology*, 1958a, 13: 70-73.

_____. "Attitude toward Aging of Individuals with Experience with the Aged." *Journal of Genetic Psychology*, 1958b, 92: 199-204.

Tuckman, J., I. Lorge, and G. A. Spooner. "The Effect of Family Environment on Attitudes toward Older People and the Older Worker." *Journal of Social Psychology*, 1953, 38: 207-18.

Youmans, E. G. "Generation and Perceptions of Old Age: An Urban-Rural Comparison. *The Gerontologist*, 1971, 11 (4, part 1): 284-88.

Abstracts

ATTITUDES TOWARD OLD PEOPLE
J. Tuckman and I. Lorge, 1953a

Definition of Variable or Concept

The instrument assesses negative stereotypes and common misconceptions about old people and attitudes about old people.

Description of Instrument

The instrument consists of 137 statements about old people, divided into 13 categories: (1) physical (including sensory, digestion, coordination, homeostasis, illness and accidents, voice, fatigue, discomfort, and death), (2) financial, (3) conservatism, (4) family, (5) attitude toward future, (6) insecurity, (7) mental deterioration, (8) activities and interests, (9) personality traits, (10) best time of life, (11) sex, (12) cleanliness, and (13) interference. Yes-no categories indicate endorsement of each statement as characteristic of older persons.

Tuckman and Lorge (1953c) also studied the effect of a 0–100 continuum response format. Their conclusion was that aggregate responses for the two response formats were not different and that the yes-no format was preferable because of the time saved in administration and simplified instructions made possible.

The instrument was based on responses to fairly unstructured interviews with 15 adults aged 21 to 65 and a series of discussions with social workers and directors of institutions for the aged, as well as on case records of older clients in a family agency and an institution for the aged and a review of the literature. Normatively deviant sexual and criminal activities were omitted. The authors noted that some statements were supported by research and others were of unknown status.

The percentage agreement was given for items overall and within various samples groups and subgroups. An overall mean percentage agreement was given for each of the 13 segments of the instrument and for the subparts of the physical segment.

Method of Administration

This self-administered paper-and-pencil instrument is given in a group setting. No special administration skill requirements are noted in the instructions. Time requirements range from an average of 15 minutes for students to an average of 30 minutes for older people. (The longest time noted by the authors was 70 minutes.) Respondents are usually instructed to answer yes in case of general agreement and no in case of general disagreement and to answer all questions, guessing in cases of uncertainty. Questions about the items are permitted during administration (at least they were in the original applications of the instrument).

The 0–100 scale response procedure took twice as long for graduate students to use, about 30 minutes (Tuckman and Lorge, 1953c, p. 608). Directions used for the procedure were: "Below are statements about old people. Read each statement, then estimate the percentage of old people to whom this statement applies. Then write this estimated percentage in the space before the statement. For example, if you think that statement No. 1, 'Old people need glasses to read,' applies to 90% of old people, write the number 90 in the space before the statement. If you think that the statement applies to 50% of old people, write the number 50, etc. Answer all questions. If you are not sure, guess."

Context of Development and Subsequent Use

The scale was developed for investigating attitudes of students toward old age. Subsequently, it has been applied to other populations; subsets of the items have also been used. For example, it has been used to examine differences in judgments made by old people in various institutional and residential contexts, to compare relationships between those with more or less experience with the aged, and to test those with various self-reported symptoms.

Samples

Tuckman and Lorge (1952c) presented the 137-item version of the instrument in a group-administered setting to three groups of older subjects: (1) a group living in a communal setting (retired, attenders of a community center): 11 men and 10 women, ages 60 to 80 (mean 71.8 years); (2) a group living in an apartment house: 5 men and 15 women ranging in age from 65 to 84 (mean 74.3 years); and (3) a group living in an institution: 29 men and 19 women aged 61 to 88 (mean 76.3 years).

In another application, Tuckman and Lorge (1952b) administered the 137 items to 92 men and 55 women graduate students in an adult psychology class (ages 20–48 [mean 29.5] for men and 20–51 [mean 33.3] for women).

In 1953, Tuckman and Lorge (1953c) gave the 137 statements with the 0–100 percentage response category system. The subjects were 31 men and 20 women graduate students, aged

21–51, with a mean age of 30.9. These data were contrasted to existing data on 147 graduate students using the yes-no response format (ages 20–51, mean age 32.5).

In 1958 (Tuckman and Lorge, 1958a), the 137 statements and the Cornell Medical Index statements were given to two samples: (1) 192 men and 202 women graduate students (mean age 32 years), and (2) 38 men and 49 women from homes, institutions, and a day-care center (mean age 74 years).

The 137 statements were examined from four samples used elsewhere: (1) 50 undergraduate students, (2) 304 graduate students, (3) 100 middle-aged subjects, (4) 88 older subjects (Tuckman and Lorge, 1953c).

Tuckman, Lorge, and Spooner (1953) gave the 137 statements to 50 sophomores (20 men and 30 women) out of 63 students in a class at Cornell, plus their parents. The samples included (1) students aged 18–42 (mean 20.4 years), (2) fathers aged 37–80 (mean 52.4 years), and (3) mothers aged 36–71 (mean 48.3 years).

Tuckman and Lorge (1958b) gave the 40 statements showing differences by age and institutionalization from the 137 to 92 agency staff members and others exposed to the aged and attending a lecture. Their ages ranged from 25 to 79, with a mean age of 56 years. These data were compared with prior data on undergraduates (mean age 19), graduates (mean age 32), middle-aged people (mean age 50), and older people (mean age 75).

The 137-item instrument was given at the beginning of a course on the psychology of the adult (Tuckman and Lorge, 1952b). The yes-no response format was used. A subset of 30 items was selected and administered with the final examination. Items used in the "after" test included those showing significant age/set differences, plus a random selection of other items. The group included students (1) under 30 (39 men and 18 women, mean age 24.6) and (2) over 30 (41 men and 26 women, mean age 36.3).

Again, the 137-item instrument was given at the beginning of a course on the psychology of the adult (Tuckman and Lorge, 1954). The 0–100 response scale indicating percentages of older people to which the statement was thought to apply was used. The "after" test used the same response format on the subset of 30 items referred to above. The sample consisted of graduate students, 29 men and 18 women, with a mean age of 32.4 and an age range of 21 to 51.

Bekker and Taylor (1966) used Axelrod and Eisdorfer's (1961) 96 items from the original 137 items with minor revisions to adapt to grandparents as a target. The instrument was given first to 800 undergraduate students, but the study focused on a matched sample of 50 undergraduates from four-generation families and 50 from three-generation families. The samples included 54 females and 46 males. No significant age differences were reported.

Axelrod and Eisdorfer (1961) administered the 137-item instrument to 280 students (170 male, 107 female, and 3 of unknown gender) in an introductory psychology class at Duke University. The average age was 19 years, and ages ranged from 18 to 23. The group was divided into random fifths, and each fifth was asked to answer the questions with respect to a different target age-group: 35, 45, 55, 65, or 75. An analysis of the patterns of response led to the selection of 96 items for which there was a monotonic increase in percentage endorsement across the stimulus ages.

Eisdorfer (1966) used two samples: (1) 88 items from the 96 selected in the Axelrod and Eisdorfer (1961) study were administered to 182 students in an introductory psychology class (111 men and 70 women, plus 1 of unknown gender); and (2) 137 items were given to a college class of 147 students (78 male, 65 female, and 4 of unknown gender). In each administration, the class was divided into random fifths, following the original Axelrod and

Eisdorfer (1961) study. The students in each fifth were asked to respond with respect to a different age-group target (35, 45, 55, 65, or 75).

Lane (1964) used a 67-item "adaptation" of the Tuckman and Lorge 137-item instrument on 400 high school and college students. A 40-item adaptation of the instrument was given for future discussion and study use.

Kilty and Feld (1976) used a combination instrument that included 15 items from the 137-item Tuckman and Lorge instrument along with items from other sources. These items were administered to two northern Pennsylvania samples, one under age 60 and one over: (1) 290 people, 18 to 59, with a mean age of 37.9 years; 47% were male; and (2) 181 people with a mean age of 70.1 years, 46% were male. A seven-point Likert scale was used, and the results were factor analyzed.

Scoring, Scale Norms, and Distribution

Since the items refer to common misconceptions or negative stereotypes, scoring usually consists of expressing the percentage of yes-responses to each item or each aggregate of items. The mean number of yes responses is also used. One study (Tuckman and Lorge, 1954) used a 0-100 "percent of old people the item applies to" scale, but no scoring data were given. Another study (Kilty and Feld, 1976) used a Likert response format (seven-point).

The distribution and norms for the initial study by Tuckman and Lorge (1953a) are given with the instrument. Item-response percentages have been given in the various studies cited below for special study groups, but these distributions are not reported here. However, three summary distributions are provided for reference in Tables 12-3, 12-4, and 12-5.

TABLE 12-3
Mean Number of Yes Responses and Standard Deviations
on Old People Questionnaire

Group	Number	Mean	SD
Community	21	61.7	24.2
Apartment House	20	66.9	19.8
Combined Institution	48	81.8	20.5
Institution (3 months)	21	80.9	20.5
Institution (5½ years)	27	82.4	20.5
Apartment House and			
Combined Institution	68	77.4	21.4

SOURCE: J. Tuckman and I. Lorge. "The Effect of Institutionalization on Attitudes toward Old People." *Journal of Abnormal and Social Psychology*, 1952, 47: 338. Copyright 1952 by the American Psychological Association. Reprinted by permission.

TABLE 12-4
Mean Scores and Standard Deviations on Old
People Questionnaire, by Age and Sex

	20-29 years	30-51 years	Male	Female
N	69	78	92	55
Mean	58.69	58.16	57.68	59.64
SD	21.71	23.60	21.50	24.86

SOURCE: J. Tuckman and I. Lorge. "Attitudes toward Old People," *Journal of Social Psychology*, 1953, 37: 251. Copyright 1953 by the American Psychological Association. Reprinted by permission.

TABLE 12-5
Mean Number of Yes Responses and Standard Deviations for Fathers, Mothers,
and Children on Old People and Older Worker Questionnaires

Group	N	Old People		Older Worker	
		Mean	SD	Mean	SD
Fathers	50	78.5	24.4	20.1	12.6
Mothers	50	76.2	22.7	19.5	11.6
Children	50	67.1	21.3	19.5	10.3
Daughters	30	64.9	24.1	19.0	12.1
Sons	20	70.4	15.7	20.4	6.9

SOURCE: J. Tuckman, I. Lorge, and G. A. Spooner. "The Effect of Family Environment on Attitudes toward Older People and the Older Worker." *Journal of Social Psychology,* 1953, 38: 209. Copyright 1953 by the American Psychological Association. Reprinted by permission.

Formal Tests of Reliability/Homogeneity

The original set of items was grouped into 13 relatively homogeneous categories according to the scale constructor's judgment. Later uses have shown some differences by and across these groups.

No test-retest reliabilities are available, although in two studies Tuckman and Lorge (1952b; 1954) reported before-and-after correlations for a subset of 40 items of .83 for percentage responses and .96 for the yes-no responses. The effects of attending the psychology classes tended to result in some increases in agreement with the scale items.

Tuckman and Lorge (1952b) reported Spearman-Brown reliability coefficients for the combined 137-item Attitudes toward Old People Scale and the 51-item Attitudes toward Older Workers Scale. They ranged form .73 for men over 30 to .88 for women over 30. The total group's Spearman-Brown coefficient of .82 apparently was for the combined before-and-after data in this study.

Formal Tests of Validity

There have been a number of studies comparing the Tuckman and Lorge scale responses by age, sex, and various other characteristics of the subjects. These, in this author's judgment, do not cumulate toward documented validity. Of possible interest, however, is a comparison of the responses to related items on the Cornell Medical Index and the Tuckman-Lorge instrument (Tuckman and Lorge, 1958a). Tuckman and Lorge reported a low correlation between reported symptoms and acceptance of old age stereotypes.

Kilty and Feld (1976), although they did not directly test the dimensionality of the Tuckman and Lorge scale, did run factor analyses on a collection of items including 15 statements from the Tuckman and Lorge instrument. They noted that the Tuckman and Lorge items appear to break into two factors, one positive and one negative.

An indication of construct validity has been provided by studies of sensitivity to differences in the target age-group. On the assumption that negative stereotypy is directed toward aging per se, it could be expected that frequency of yes responses would increase with the age of stimulus person.

Axelrod and Eisdorfer (1961) presented the 137-item instrument to random fifths of a class, asking that the students respond in relation to different age-groups (35, 45, 55, 65, and 75). Of the 137 items, 96 showed monotonic increases in the percentage endorsement with the increasing age of the target group. This led to the investigators' judgment that these items should be used in preference to the original 137.

A later study by Eisdorfer (1966) followed the same random-fifth and stimulus-age procedures on two groups, using an 88-item subset of the 96 selected for the Axelrod study, plus the 137-item original questionnaire. With the 88-item form, only 53 items differentiated significantly between target ages. But, with the 137-item form, 85 items differentiated by age. Seventy-nine items were consistently good in the original data and in the replication. Eisdorfer concluded that, since the effectiveness of items decreased with the smaller set, investigators should use the whole set of 137 items.

There appears to be a greater tendency to agree with positive items than with negative items (Tuckman and Lorge, 1953a).

Usability on Older Populations

The scale has been used with young and old samples with little noted difficulty other than the assertion that it may take somewhat longer to administer the scale to older subjects.

Sensitivity to Age (Including Social Age) Differences

The sensitivity of the items to differences in the target age-group being rated is indicated in the discussions of the Axelrod-Eisdorfer (1961) and Eisdorfer (1966) studies.

Studies using the scale have often distinguished between age-groups of respondents. Several studies have reported no significant correlation between the age of respondent and the proportion of yes responses to items (Tuckman, Lorge, and Spooner, 1953; Tuckman and Lorge, 1953a; Bekker and Taylor, 1966). Other studies have suggested age differences (Tuckman and Lorge 1958b). Tuckman and Lorge (1953b) reported a tendency for the percentages of agreement with scale items to decrease as (1) the age given as the time when old age begins increases and (2) when the respondent's age is farther from the age given as the beginning of old age. Another study (Tuckman and Lorge, 1958a) reported a low but positive correlation between reported physical symptoms on the Cornell Medical Index and the acceptance of old age stereotypes.

Scale-Development Statistics

Information on the topic was not given in any of the studies. See the instrument and the references for item-by-item percentage agreement.

General Comments and Recommendations

Further examination of the reliability and validity of the items appears to be needed, although the research has suggested that certain aspects of reliability and validity are probably satisfactory for college-student populations. Samples have tended to be small and ad hoc. A more representative sampling of a general population is needed. Some scale items appear to be culture bound, and the dimensionality of the set of items remains to be explored. Evidence that the presumed misconceptions are indeed untrue statements has yet to be mustered. Since the context of items appears to have some effect, the entire set of 137 items probably should be used, with more attention being focused on the items the literature suggests as more stable and age distinguishing.

References

Axelrod, S., and C. Eisdorfer. "Attitudes toward Old People: An Empirical Analysis of the Stimulus-Group Validity of the Tuckman-Lorge Questionnaire." *Journal of Gerontology,* 1961, 16: 75–80.

Bekker, L. D., and C. Taylor. "Attitudes toward the Aged in a Multigenerational Sample." *Journal of Gerontology,* 1966, 21: 115–18.

Eisdorfer, C. "Attitudes toward Old People: A Re-analysis of the Item-Validity of the Stereotype Scale." *Journal of Gerontology,* 1966, 21: 455–57.

Kilty, K. M., and A. Feld. "Attitudes toward Aging and toward the Needs of Older People." *Journal of Gerontology*, 1976, 31: 586–94.

Lane, B. "Attitudes of Youth toward the Aged." *Journal of Marriage and the Family*, 1964, 26: 229–31.

Tuckman, J. and I. Lorge. "The Attitudes of the Aged toward the Older Worker: For Institutionalized and Non-institutionalized Adults." *Journal of Gerontology*, 1952a, 7: 559–64.

————. "The Influence of a Course on the Psychology of the Adult on Attitudes toward Old People and Older Workers." *Journal of Educational Psychology*, 1952b, 43: 400–407.

————. "The Effect of Institutionalization on Attitudes toward Old People." *Journal of Abnormal and Social Psychology*, 1952c, 47: 337–44.

————. "Atttitudes toward Old People." *Journal of Social Psychology*, 1953a, 37: 249–60.

————. "When Aging Begins and Stereotypes about Aging." *Journal of Gerontology*, 1953b, 8: 489–92.

————. "The Effect of Changed Directions on the Attitudes about Old People and the Older Worker." *Educational and Psychological Measurement*, 1953c, 13: 607–13.

————. "The Influence of Changed Directions on Stereotypes about Aging: Before and After Instruction." *Educational and Psychological Measurement*, 1954, 14: 128–32.

————. "The Projection of Personal Symptom into Stereotype about Aging." *Journal of Gerontology*, 1958a, 13: 70–73.

————. "Attitude toward Aging of Individuals with Experiences with the Aged." *Journal of Genetic Psychology*, 1958b, 92: 199–204.

Tuckman, J., I. Lorge, and G. A. Spooner. "The Effect of Family Environment on Attitudes toward Older People and the Older Worker." *Journal of Social Psychology*, 1953, 38: 207–18.

Instrument

See Instrument V1.12.I.a.

FACTS ON AGING
E. Palmore, 1977

Definition of Variable or Concept

The variables in this measure are factual knowledge about physical, mental, and social aspects of aging and common misconceptions. The instrument is an indirect measure of bias (pro and con) about aging, as well.

Description of Instrument

The instrument is a 25-item true-false scale. The scale-development procedure was not detailed, but the items were selected from many content areas.

Method of Administration

This is a self-administered paper-and-pencil instrument, which takes about five minutes to complete. No special skills or administration requirements are noted in the instructions.

Context of Development and Subsequent Use

This instrument was developed as a reaction to problems with other perception measures, such a length and mixture of opinion and factual items. It focuses on documented facts and is relatively brief. The uses for which it was intended include (1) acting as a stimulus for group discussion, (2) determining overall level of knowledge about aging, (3) identifying the most common misconceptions, and (4) acting as an indirect measure of positive and/or negative bias toward older people.

Samples

Palmore used the instrument on: (1) 87 Duke University undergraduate students in an introductory class, (2) 44 graduate students in human development at Duke and Pennsylvania State, and (3) 11 faculty members in human development at Duke and Pennsylvania State.

Scoring, Scale Norms, and Distribution

Palmore (1977) provided information on item-response patterns as well as overall scores for the undergraduate students, graduate students, and faculty members he tested.

Sum scores are computed (correct, 1, incorrect, 0) and expressed as a percentage correct. The odd-numbered items in Table 12-6 are incorrect; the even-numbered items are true.

A second set of scores involved positive and negative bias. The *positive* bias score is the percentage (number) of errors on items 2, 4, 6, 12, and 14. The *negative* bias score is the percentage (number) of errors on items 1, 3, 5, 7, 8, 9, 10, 11, 13, 16, 17, 18, 21, 22, 24, and 25. A *net anti-aged* or *net pro-aged* score is computed by subtracting the percentage of negative errors from the percentage of positive errors. If the difference is negative, then there is a net anti-aged bias.

TABLE 12-6
Percentages of Incorrect Responses to Palmore's Items

Statement Number	Undergraduates ($N = 87$)	Graduates ($N = 44$)	Faculty ($N = 11$)
1	7	0	0
2	40	14	27
3	16	2	0
4	21	16	9
5	12	0	0
6	2	7	0
7	74	27	0
8	40	27	18
9	37	2	0
10	9	0	0
11	47	9	0
12	47	30	9
13	5	0	0
14	7	7	0
15	9	2	0
16	74	73	55
17	42	16	0
18	42	18	0
19	86	55	36
20	56	9	9
21	74	50	45
22	2	11	36
23	63	44	18
24	58	73	0
25	21	18	18

TABLE 12-6—*Continued*

	Undergraduates (N = 87)	Graduates (N = 44)	Faculty (N = 11)
Mean % "pro" errors	26	15	9
Mean % "anti" errors	33	20	11
% Pro − % Anti	−7	−6	−2
Mean % right	65	80	90
Standard deviation % right	11.2	7.5	7.7

SOURCE: E. Palmore. "Facts on Aging: A Short Quiz." *The Gerontologist*, 1977, 17 : 315–20. Reprinted by permission.

Formal Tests of Validity

Palmore provided an item-by-item discussion of the research evidence pertaining to the truth of the items, thus lending support to the face validity of this instrument.

Scale-Development Statistics

No scale-development statistics were reported, other than the distributions already mentioned.

General Comments and Recommendations

This scale represents an important clarification of the opinion-fact mix in stereotype research, and it appears to be relatively easy to use. Future work with the scale should update the research basis for each conclusion, take into account the conditions under which individual items are true or false, and consider reliability tests as well as the range of content covered. The development of national norms would be useful.

Reference

Palmore, E. "Facts on Aging: A Short Quiz." *The Gerontologist*, 1977, 17: 315–20.

Instrument

See Instrument V1.12.I.b.

KOGAN ATTITUDE TOWARD OLD PEOPLE SCALE
N. Kogan, 1961

Definition of Variable or Concept

This scale assesses attitudes toward old people with respect to both norms and individual differences, stereotypes of old people, and misconceptions about older people.

Description of Instrument

The instrument is a Likert scale, with 34 short statements (17 positive and 17 identical but negatively stated). There are six response categories: strongly disagree (scored 1), disagree (scored 2), slightly disagree (scored 3), slightly agree (scored 5), agree (scored 6), and strongly agree (scored 7). Failure to respond was scored 4.

The scale uses some items from ethnic minority stereotype research, but it substitutes old people as the referents. A range of topics is covered, including residential patterns, discomfort in associating with old people, cross-generation relations, dependence, and older persons' cognitive style, personal appearance, and personality. During their development, the items were given to three psychology-student samples, and suggestions for item modification were made after the results were analyzed (Kogan, 1961a, pp. 44–54). Two scales are used—the positive items and the negative items (OP+ and OP− scales). No exploration of dimensionality appears to have been undertaken. Later use (Silverman, 1966) reflected negatively worded items, so that an overall OP score could be used.

Method of Administration

The scale is a self-administered paper-and-pencil questionnaire. The items are generally used as a part of a longer attitude instrument with various other Likert items (authoritarianism, antiminority, anomie, conservatism, mental illness, blindness, etc.) included. No timing instructions were given, nor were any special administration requirements noted.

Context of Development and Subsequent Use

This scale represents a refinement of earlier work by making more deliberate use of scaling techniques and by seeking correlations between old people scales and other psychological attributes. Later uses have further examined response bias, applied it to older samples, and sought relationships by sex, race, and social class.

Samples

Kogan (1961a) used three samples of psychology students: (1) 128 males at Northeastern University, (2) 186 males at Northeastern University, and (3) 87 males and 81 females at Boston University.

Kogan (1961b) also used a sample of 89 males and 115 females from the Age Center of New England, Boston. Mean ages were 71 for men (54 to 92) and 68 for women (49 to 86). Their mean educational levels were 13.7 years (men) and 12.9 (women). None were institutionalized.

Silverman (1966) studied a sample of 67 males and 22 females who were introductory psychology students at a large, urban university.

Ivester and King (1977) used 270 9th graders and 142 12th graders, surveyed in May 1975 at Madison County High School, Danielsville, Ga. The sample was 51% male and 80% white, with a mode of lower-middle-class and a mean age of 15.5; 88% had one or more living grandparents.

Gordon and Hallauer (1976) sampled 60 students at a small liberal arts college in rural New York State. Class volunteers in the areas of education and child and adult development classes were used.

Thorson, Whatley, and Hancock (1974) gave the scale to 61 students and 59 practitioners in service-delivery fields.

Thorson (1975) administered the scale to a sample of 98 Atlanta high school juniors and seniors aged 16 to 18, of which 49% were black and 47% were from lower-income families. Data from the 1974 study were pooled with these data in the report, so the total sample included 218 subjects.

Thorson and Perkins (1976) sampled 212 undergraduate and graduate students from 12 classes at the University of Georgia. The median was age 23 (18 to 53), and 46% of the subjects were male.

Scoring, Scale Norms, and Distribution

The negative and positive items are usually scored separately, using simple sum scores (1 for strongly disagree). In later usage, different Likert scales have been used (e.g., using response options of 1 to 4, instead of 1 to 7), and most later uses have involved only one of the scales. Silverman (1966) used alternating positive and negative items (17 of the 34 items) and five response categories; Ivester and King (1977) used the 17 positive items and four response categories; Gordon and Hallauer (1976) used the Silverman selection of items and a five-point response scale; Thorson, Whatley, and Hancock (1974) used all 34 items in random order and a seven-point scale, with scores computed over all items (reflected and averaged to range from 1 to 7); Thorson (1975) and Thorson and Perkins (1976) used the same overall score procedure.

Formal Tests of Reliability/Homogeneity

Relatively extensive information is available on the correlation between items and their scale score (on the positive or negative scale of which the item was a part), as well as correlations between positively and negatively worded item pairs. Odd-even reliability coefficients are also available for both positive and negative scales.

The samples upon which these coefficients were computed were two samples of males and one of males and females (Kogan, 1961a) and the male-female sample plus a sample of older men and women (Kogan, 1961b). These correlations are given below.

Consistency in means and positive-negative-item-pair correlations was examined across samples; this led to some revision of item wording for the Age Center of New England sample. Negative scale items appear to have greater reliability.

Odd-even Spearman-Brown reliability coefficients for the negative scale were .76, .73, and .83, respectively, for the Boston sample (N = 168) and the Northeastern University sample 1 (N = 128) and sample 2 (N = 186). Coefficients for the positive scale for the same groups were .77, .66, and .73, respectively. Interscale correlations for the three groups were reported as .51, .52, and .46, respectively.

Formal Tests of Validity

Two kinds of examinations of validity have been conducted: (1) correlations of scales with other variables and (2) correlation of scales and later behaviors.

Authoritarianism: Kogan (1961a) reported correlations between the original F scale and a version worded in the opposite way, for three samples (a revised scale was used for the Boston sample). The correlations were in the expected direction (more authoritarian people hold less favorable attitudes toward older people) for all three samples with the originally worded F scale (.28, .21, .21, all statistically significant at the .05 level) and the *negative* OP (older person) scale. *Positive* OP scale relationships were inconsistent with these associations (opposite direction of association, inappropriately, although only one of the samples yielded a significant association, −.29). The oppositely worded F scale had low (nonsignificant) associations with both OP scales, except for an inconsistent −.22 with the negative OP scale.

Antiminority and Disability Scales: Kogan (1961a) showed correlations for both positive and negative scales and a range of attitudes toward the mentally ill, deaf, blind, and crippled and toward minorities and blacks. All the correlations were positive and significant, except for the correlation between the positive mental illness scale and the negative older people scale and between the negative mental illness scale and positive older people scale.

Anomie: Significant associations in predicted directions were found for the Srole Anomie Scale and the positive and negative OP scales (higher anomie predicts less favorable OP attutudes). The correlations were generally higher for the negative OP scale.

Religious Conservatism: Kogan (1961b) concluded that there is no clear relationship between the OP scales and authoritarianism or religious conservatism.

Silverman (1966), using a combed version of the OP scales, found a significant correlation with the Ford Social Desirability Scale for males only (the difference between males and females was not statistically significant).

Three months after the subjects had taken the revised Kogan scale, Silverman had the subjects rank kinds of people in terms of their preference for interviewing them. One of the 10 kinds of people was retired people. The correlation between the OP scale and the ranks given to retired people was .40 and, with social desirability discounted, it was .38. Both were statistically significant at .02 or more.

Usability on Older Populations

No special difficulties in using the scale with older, noninstitutionalized people were reported.

TABLE 12-7

Means, Standard Deviations, Item-Sum Correlations (r_{IS}), and Matched Item Pair Correlations (r_{NP}) for Old People Items

	BU Sample (N = 168)				NU-I Sample (N = 123)				NU-II Sample (N = 136)			
	M^c	SD	r_{IS}	r_{NP}	M	SD	r_{IS}	r_{NP}	M	SD	r_{IS}	r_{NP}
1 N[a] It would probably be better if most old people lived in residential units with people of their own age.	3.01	1.54	.40		3.25	1.78	.47		3.34	1.75	.49	
1 P[a] It would probably be better if most old people lived in residential units that also housed younger people.	3.52	1.55	.34	.26	3.53	1.61	.36	.42	3.73	1.67	.32	.32
2 N There is something different about most old people; it's hard to figure out what makes them tick.	2.90	1.40	.57		3.06	1.47	.48		3.01	1.35	.54	
2 P Most old people are really no different from anybody else; they're as easy to understand as younger people.	3.90	1.63	.61	.27	3.72	1.71	.63	.18	3.69	1.56	.57	.33
3 N Most old people get set in their ways and are unable to change.	4.89	1.46	.41		5.18	1.45	.39		3.07	1.49	.49	
3 P Most old people are capable of new adjustments when the situation demands it.	3.96	1.62	.54	.35	3.86	1.77	.33	.17	4.15	1.71	.55	.25
4 N Most old people would prefer to quit work as soon as pensions or their children can support them.	2.08	1.11	.32		2.15	1.17	.10		2.23	1.31	.30	
4 P Most old people would prefer to continue working just as long as they possibly can rather than be dependent on anybody.	2.38	1.13	.28	.38	1.99	.73	.18	.31	2.24	1.07	.32	.35
5 N Most old people tend to let their homes become shabby and unattractive.	2.22	1.15	.47		2.28	1.12	.38		2.43	1.29	.41	
5 P Most old people can generally be counted on to maintain a clean, attractive home.	2.95	1.31	.55	.42	2.69	1.20	.49	.21	2.63	1.18	.59	.32
6 N It is foolish to claim that wisdom comes with old age.	4.05	1.98	.19		3.73	2.00	.10		—	—	—	

TABLE 12-7 — *Continued*

	BU Sample (N = 168)				NU-I Sample (N = 123)				NU-II Sample (N = 136)			
	M^c	SD	r_{IS}	r_{NP}	M	SD	r_{IS}	r_{NP}	M	SD	r_{IS}	r_{NP}
6 P People grow wiser with the coming of old age.	3.71	1.49	.26	.40	4.06	1.74	.13	.41	—	—	—	—
7 N Old people have too much power in business and politics.	2.77	1.29	.49		3.36	1.67	.41		3.40	1.72	.40	
7 P^b Old people should have more power in business and politics.	5.15	1.03	.34	.12	5.22	1.19	.36	.13	5.49	1.09	.09	.24
8 N Most old people make one feel ill at ease.	2.82	1.30	.51		3.01	1.32	.50		3.03	1.37	.56	
8 P Most old people are very relaxing to be with.	3.95	1.47	.67	.30	3.65	1.51	.67	.34	3.70	1.49	.62	.42
9 N Most old people bore others by their insistence on talking about the "good old days."	3.64	1.48	.58		3.55	1.56	.53		3.53	1.60	.61	
9 P^b One of the most interesting and entertaining qualities of most old people is their accounts of their past experiences.	2.79	1.37	.27	.16	2.54	1.30	.23	.17	2.65	1.29	.32	.26
10 N Most old people spend too much time prying into the affairs of others and giving unsought advice.	3.63	1.54	.65		3.41	1.59	.70		3.95	1.57	.67	
10 P^b Most old people tend to keep to themselves and give advice only when asked.	4.84	1.38	.47	.25	4.74	1.54	.29	.23	4.67	1.51	.41	.26
11 N If old people expect to be liked, their first step is to try to get rid of their irritating faults.	3.82	1.56	.44		3.87	1.69	.48		4.17	1.56	.43	
11 P When you think about it, old people have the same faults as anybody else.	2.60	1.31	.41	.07	2.51	1.25	.49	.14	2.67	1.36	.55	.13
12 N In order to maintain a nice residential neighborhood, it would be best if too many old people did not live in it.	2.37	1.41	.48		2.69	1.65	.25		2.58	1.63	.49	

TABLE 12-7 — Continued

	BU Sample (N = 168)				NU-I Sample (N = 123)				NU-II Sample (N = 136)			
	M^c	SD	r_{IS}	r_{NP}	M	SD	r_{IS}	r_{NP}	M	SD	r_{IS}	r_{NP}
12.P You can count on finding a nice residential neighborhood when there is a sizeable number of old people living in it.	3.62	1.42	.36	.25	3.46	1.48	.34	.31	3.90	1.51	.34	.05
13 N There are a few exceptions, but in general most old people are pretty much alike.	2.60	1.56	.42	.41	3.65	1.74	.38	.41	4.05	1.63	.33	.33
13 P It is evident that most old people are very different from one another,	3.63	1.56	.42	.41	3.65	1.74	.38	.41	4.05	1.63	.33	.33
14 N Most old people should be more concerned with their personal appearance; they're too untidy.	3.01	1.36	.44		2.99	1.44	.54		3.08	1.39	.49	
14 P Most old people seem to be quite clean and neat in their personal appearance.	3.54	1.60	.57	.48	3.27	1.48	.56	.44	3.32	1.49	.59	.61
15 N Most old people are irritable, grouchy and unpleasant.	2.34	.94	.54		2.47	1.22	.46		2.69	1.45	.55	
15 P Most old people are cheerful, agreeable and good humored.	3.62	1.40	.66	.27	3.35	1.36	.64	.25	3.47	1.51	.61	.40
16 N Most old people are constantly complaining about the behavior of the younger generation.	4.89	1.62	.50		5.18	1.67	.52		5.49	1.46	.54	
16 P One seldom hears old people complaining about the behavior of the younger generation.	5.47	1.13	.49	.41	5.59	1.19	.33	.50	5.75	1.08	.25	.34
17 N Most old people make excessive demands for love and reassurance.	3.96	1.63	.46		3.96	1.68	.50		3.92	1.54	.52	
17 P Most old people need no more love and reassurance than anyone else.	4.54	1.55	.39	.19	4.41	1.79	.27	.27	4.46	1.53	.43	.11

TABLE 12-7 – Continued

	BU Sample (N = 168)				NU-I Sample (N = 123)				NU-II Sample (N = 136)			
	M^c	SD	r_{IS}	r_{NP}	M	SD	r_{IS}	r_{NP}	M	SD	r_{IS}	r_{NP}
Total negative scale (OP−)	54.87	11.04			56.84	11.00			54.17	12.28		
	3.23^d				3.35				3.40			
Total positive scale (OP+)	64.14	10.90			62.13	9.70			60.42	10.47		
	3.77				3.65				3.77			

NOTE: The magnitude of rs required for statistical significance is as follows: for $N = 168$, .15 at the .05 level and .20 at the .01 level; for $N = 123$, .17 at the .05 level and .23 at the .01 level; for $N = 136$, .14 at the .05 level and .19 at the .01 level.

a Items are listed in pairs, N representing the negatively worded form and P the positively worded form.

b Revised form of the item used with NU-II sample. The revised items read as follows:

7 P   Old people have too little power in business and politics.

9 P   One of the more interesting qualities of most old people is their accounts of their past experiences.

10 P   Most old people respect others' privacy and give advice only when asked.

c Negative and positive means were made comparable by subtracting the positive means from 8.00. By this step, higher mean values reflect more unfavorable attitudes for both positive and negative items.

d Per item means.

SOURCE: N. Kogan. "Attitudes toward Old People: The Development of a Scale and an Examination of Correlates." *Journal of Abnormal and Social Psychology*, 1961, 62: 44–54. Copyright 1961 by the American Psychological Association. Reprinted by permission of author and publisher.

Sensitivity to Age (Including Social Age) Differences

Kogan (1961b) did note that there is some evidence that there is a greater acquiescent response set among older people. There were no age differences for the negative OP scale, although there was a statistically significant one for the positive OP scale (older people were more ready to agree with the positive scale items). Kogan (1961b) expected stronger correlations between the positive and negative scales for older subjects but did not find this outcome in his study.

Scale-Development Statistics

Kogan (1961a) provided item statistics and intercorrelations. (See Table 12-7.)

General Comments and Recommendations

This scale has had considerable use, and attention has been focused on its reliability and, to some extent, its validity. Single items from the scales have been used in subsequent research, as well. Response set appears to be an important consideration, and these scales can be used to examine it. The differences between the positive scale and the negative scale, however, pose interpretative problems, and validity could well receive added attention. This is probably among the better scales for an investigator to select, in part because of the possibility of comparing results obtained with it and earlier work.

References

Gordon, S. K., and D. S. Hallauer. "Impact of a Friendly Visiting Program on Attitudes of College Students toward the Aged." *The Gerontologist,* 1976, 16: 371–76.

Ivester, C., and K. King. "Attitudes of Adolescents toward the Aged." *The Gerontologist,* 1977, 17: 85–89.

Kogan, N. "Attitudes toward Old People: The Development of a Scale and an Examination of Correlates." *Journal of Abnormal and Social Psychology,* 1961a, 62: 44–54.

Kogan, N. "Attitudes toward Old People in an Older Sample." *Journal of Abnormal and Social Psychology,* 1961b, 62: 616–22.

Silverman, I. "Response-Set Bias and Predictive Validity Associated with Kogan's 'Attitudes Toward Old People Scale.'" *Journal of Gerontology,* 1966, 21: 86–88.

Thorson, J. A. "Attitudes toward the Aged as a Function of Race and Social Class." *The Gerontologist,* 1975, 15: 343–44.

Thorson, J. A., and M. L. Perkins. "Attitudes toward the Aged as a Function of Personality Characteristics." Paper presented to the 29th Annual Meeting of the Gerontological Society, New York, October 13–17, 1976.

Thorson, J. A., L. Whatley, and K. Hancock. "Attitudes toward the Aged as a Function of Age and Education." *The Gerontologist,* 1974, 14: 316–18.

Instrument

See the scale development statistics above.

OPINIONS ABOUT PEOPLE (OAP)
Ontario Welfare Council, Section on Aging, 1971

Definition of Variable or Concept

The OAP assesses attitudes and perceptions of age and aging and attitudes toward senescence of practitioners and the general public.

Description of Instrument

The instrument is a 29-item Likert scale with 32 items (but the first 3 items are considered warm-ups and are not analyzed). The original scale used nine response categories (scored 1 for agree). Hickey and associates (1975) used nine response categories and 23 items in their analysis. (The items they used are marked with asterisks on the instrument.)

The two forms of the instrument were originally intended to be used as a pre- and post treatment assessment forms. Form A is currently available, but form B is undergoing further refinement and is not available. On the Canadian data, the two forms were judged not to be comparable.

Factor analysis of the results of each study yielded subscales, seven for the Canadian study and six for the Pennsylvania study done by Hickey and associates (1975). The seven Canadian factors (subscales) are (1) realistic toughness toward aging (six items), (2) denial of effects of aging (three items), (3) anxiety about aging (four items), (4) social distance to the old (seven items), (5) family responsibility toward aged parents and relatives (four items), (6) public responsibility for aged (six items), and (7) unfavorable stereotype of old (four items). The six Pennsylvania subscales are: (1) social distance (six items), (2) denial (three items), (3) social acceptance and responsibility (four items), (4) future orientation (three items), (5) anxiety (three items), and (6) family responsibility (four items).

Method of Administration

The OAP is a self-administered paper-and-pencil instrument. No timing or special administration skills are noted in the instructions. The Ontario Welfare Council's *Guidelines and Manual* (1971) provides some suggestions for administering and using the OAP. Most of these are straightforward descriptions of the uses that might be made for any such instrument in a discussion or evaluation setting.

Context of Development and Subsequent Use

The instrument was developed for practitioners and members of the general public. It was part of an inquiry into the consequences of attitudes for service-delivery systems, and the inquiry's goal was to isolate areas in training programs for practitioners that might be improved.

Hickey's use stemmed from an assessment of the effectiveness of Pennsylvania's training programs and hypotheses about the separation of perceptions of aging and of the aged.

Samples

Kapos and Smith's (1972) Canadian sample included 1,700 subjects. The Pennsylvanian sample (Hickey et al., 1975) consisted of 558 health-care and service-delivery personnel from the state. The instrument was administered before and after training on an experimental group and a control group. Only pretest data (1974 and 1975) were used for analysis. The controls were trained and retested.

In a second Pennsylvanian sample (Hickey et al., 1976), 332 white females (18 to 74 years old), mostly employees or volunteers in service-provider positions for the elderly in Pennsylvania, were tested. The mean age was 42.5, and the mean level of education was 15.5 years; the mean number of years as a practitioner was 6.7.

Scoring, Scale Norms, and Distribution

Several scoring procedures have been used, all involving weights for each item derived from factor analysis of the Likert scores. In the initial Canadian study, scores were attained either by (1) multiplication of the Likert score for each item by its loading on a given factor and summation of these products over all 29 items, or by (2) multiplication of the item Likert score by its loading on the factor, but with summation only over items loading significantly on that factor, or by (3) a simplified version of the second system in which the significant loadings of items on factors are replaced by integer weights. Since seven conceptually identified factors were obtained in the Canadian study, these scoring procedures yield seven subscale scores for the instrument.

The following is a list of the significantly loading items for each factor, with each item's factor loading and integral weight shown in parentheses. *Realistic toughness:* items 6 (.256, 3), 11 (.262, 3), 12 (.183, 2), 13 (.266, 3), 14 (.232, 2), and 28 (.318, 3). *Denial:*

items 15 (.402, 1), 22 (.352, 1), and 23 (.413, 1). *Anxiety*: items 19 (.398, 4), 24 (.290, 3), 27 (246, 2), and 30 (.386, 4). *Social distance*: items 8 (.486, 5), 12 (.248, 2), 13 (.171, 2), 14 (180, 2), 17 (.384, 4), 30 (.162, 2), and 31 (.169, 2). *Family responsibility*: items 10 (.161, 4), 18 (.516, 7), 20 (.213, 4), and 32 (.473, 7). *Public responsibility*: items 6 (.229, 1), 14 (.175, 1), 17 (.163, 1), 21 (.201, 1), 25 (−.480, 8), and 29 (−.241, 5). *Unfavorable stereotype*: items 7 (.603, 4), 14 (.242, 2), 20 (.157, 2), and 29 (−.215, 1).

Hickey and associates (1975) used the nine-point rating scale and "appropriate weights" (apparently the factor weights and items listed above). The lower the score on any factor, the stronger that factor's label characteristic. Cutoff points for each scale were given for practitioners' use (Table 12-8).

TABLE 12-8
Cutoff Points for Scoring Factors

Factor	Low	Uncertain	High
Realistic toughness	144	80	16
Denial	27	15	3
Anxiety	117	65	13
Social Distance	171	95	19
Family responsibility	198	110	22
Public responsibility	153	85	17
Unfavorable stereotype	81	45	9

Formal Tests of Reliability/Homogeneity

Hickey and associates (1976) noted that there was not a significant association between pre- and posttest scale scores for the control group, although there was for the experimental group. Significant factors were found, although these were different from the Canadian and Pennsylvanian data.

Formal Tests of Validity

Hickey and associates (1975) performed a confirmatory factor analysis on the responses of 558 Pennsylvania practitioners in aging and failed to obtain the same factor structure as the Canadian study had. They carried out an oblique rotation analysis, recovering the six factors listed above. Twenty-three items had loadings of absolute value not less than .30 and communalities greater than .15. A subsequent orthogonal analysis of the six factor scores yielded three higher-order factors.

Two of these factors appear to represent attitudes toward the aged, with one reflecting positive valuation and an interest in social integration. The third factor appears to reflect negative attitudes toward one's own aging or its prospect and a pessimistic outlook on the environment of the elderly. Thus, the opinion that attitudes toward the aged and toward aging as an experience ought to be conceptually distinguished is supported.

Usability on Older Populations

Apparently, the scale has been used on practitioners aged 18 to 74. No inappropriate subject-population was mentioned by the users of the scale.

Sensitivity to Age (Including Social Age) Differences

Hickey and associates (1976) reported that three (out of seven) factors have shown significant age differences in mean scores, with older persons having had lower scores. The three factors were realistic toughness, social distance, and unfavorable stereotyping.

TABLE 12-9

Opinions about People, Form A, Factor Loadings for 29 Scale Items for Seven Factors (Canadian Data)

Item Number	(1) Realistic Toughness toward Aging	(2) Denial of Effects on Aging	(3) Anxiety about Aging	(4) Social Distance to the Old	(5) Family Responsibility to the Aged Parent	(6) Public Responsibility vs. Unconcern	(7) Unfavorable Stereotype vs. Acceptance
4	-.018	.027	-.018	-.011	.054	-.064	-.008
5	-.084	-.019	.038	.015	.047	-.059	-.422
6	.256	.063	-.007	-.017	-.212	.229	-.127
7	-.044	.024	.047	.041	-.012	-.019	.603
8	.018	.018	.066	.486	-.019	.007	.062
9	.061	-.013	.028	.078	.102	.019	.050
10	.073	.061	-.047	-.003	.161	.052	-.067
11	.262	.050	.046	.075	.013	-.109	.108
12	.183	.017	.014	.248	-.054	-.051	.027
13	.266	-.091	.020	.171	.002	-.062	.066
14	.232	-.012	.005	.180	.092	.175	.242
15	.037	.402	-.020	.001	.030	-.012	.094
16	-.003	-.009	.049	.029	-.073	.083	-.009
17	.077	.012	.052	.384	.040	.163	-.029
18	.035	.052	.047	-.086	.516	.075	-.009
19	.037	-.080	.398	-.004	-.008	.013	.138
20	.098	-.044	.082	-.074	.213	.103	.157
21	-.053	.052	.117	-.073	-.168	.201	.019
22	-.080	.352	-.043	.059	-.010	.016	-.027
23	.022	.413	.017	-.015	-.006	-.014	-.032
24	.121	-.065	.290	.073	.068	-.088	-.036
25	.038	.074	.077	-.072	.079	-.480	.012
26	.112	.088	.128	.054	.080	.346	.029
27	.008	.057	.246	-.041	.061	.288	.065
28	.318	.011	.030	-.031	.054	.025	-.094
29	.145	.110	.104	-.125	.047	-.241	-.215
30	-.046	.045	.386	.162	.025	-.020	-.104
31	.068	.028	-.005	.169	.096	.072	-.002
32	-.035	-.025	.015	.081	.473	-.104	-.037

SOURCE: Personal communication from Jean Matlow, Ministry of Community and Social Services, Ontario, Canada. Reprinted by permission.

TABLE 12-10

Factor Pattern Matrix and Item Communalities for Pennsylvania Sample

Item	Factor 1	Factor 2	Factor 3	Factor 4	Factor 5	Factor 6	Communality
8	.578	.011	.117	.084	-.082	-.069	.324
7	.483	-.009	.038	.025	.087	.112	.264
17	.395	-.168	-.035	-.092	.041	.275	.323
9	.378	.078	-.047	-.055	-.146	-.026	.209
12	.348	.146	-.125	-.048	-.404	.031	.210
15	.093	.689	-.062	-.011	-.039	-.029	.485
23	.071	.509	.087	-.091	-.003	.035	.302
22	-.095	.348	.070	.136	.106	.076	.200
10	.085	.043	.439	.040	.122	-.063	.219
29	-.088	.115	.426	.055	-.025	.137	.225
5	.016	.016	.402	-.029	-.050	-.146	.198
25	-.004	-.058	.401	-.059	-.033	.038	.159
21	.004	.061	.034	-.584	-.031	.060	.362
2	.091	.131	-.025	.561	-.005	.132	.347
27	.054	.146	-.016	-.413	-.019	.159	.269
19	.009	.022	-.070	-.159	-.638	.017	.492
30	-.025	.054	-.040	.060	-.612	.068	.365
24	.084	-.129	.137	.003	-.324	.017	.164
20	.063	-.024	-.053	-.125	-.013	.538	.366
28	-.027	.006	.000	.044	-.093	.481	.239
14	.188	.001	-.119	.037	-.009	.409	.292
13	.004	.100	.066	-.025	-.007	.392	.189
6	.273	.061	-.177	-.064	.057	.126	.189

SOURCE: T. Hickey, S. M. Bragg, W. Rakowski, and D. F. Hultsch. "Attitudes toward Aging and the Aged: An Analytical Study," 1975 (mimeographed report), p. 20. Reprinted by permission of authors.

Scale-Development Statistics

Table 12-9 presents the factor weights for the Canadian sample and Table 12-10 the factor loadings for the Pennsylvania data (Hickey et al., 1975).

General Comments and Recommendations

The OAP scale is one of the more extensively examined in terms of factor analysis. Further investigation of factorial stability is needed, as is reliability and validity information.

References

Hickey, T., S. M. Bragg, W. Rakowski, and D. F. Hultsch. "Attitudes toward Aging and the Aged: An Analytical Study." 1975 (mimeographed report).

Hickey, T., W. Rakowski, D. F. Hultsch, and B. J. Fatula. "Attitudes toward Aging as a Function of In-Service Training and Practitioner Age." *Journal of Gerontology*, 1976, 31: 681–86.

Kapos, A., and D. Smith. "Identifying Standard Attitudes toward Senescence." Paper presented to the Ninth International Congress of Gerontology, Kiev, USSR, July, 2–7, 1972.

Ontario Welfare Council, Section on Aging, *Opinions about People, Form A: Guidelines and Manual* (for an instrument dealing with attitudes toward aging and the aged, for use in educational and training programs in the field of aging). Toronto, Ontario: January 1971.

Instrument

See Instrument V1.12.II.b.

ATTITUDES TOWARD AGING
K. M. Kilty and A. Feld, 1976

Definition of Variable or Concept

The instrument assesses cognitive or belief components of social attitudes toward aging and old people.

Description of Instrument

The scale includes 45 social-psychological opinion items: 15 items selected from the Tuckman and Lorge (1952a, 1953) Attitudes toward Old People Scale, 8 items from Kogan (1961), 5 new items about old people, 10 items adapted from the Srole Anomie Scale (Srole, 1956), and 7 items from the Tuckman and Lorge (1952a) scale about older workers. The items are given in a Likert format with a seven-point agree/disagree scale.

Method of Administration

It was administered as part of an interview in the original study, but it could also be self-administered. No timing information was given by the authors.

Context of Development and Subsequent Use

The scale was developed to test the factorial structure of beliefs about old people and to specify communality across age-groups.

Samples

These investigators used a modified probability sample of people from northern Pennsylvania. No response norms were given. The sample was divided into two age-groups: (1) 290 subjects 18 to 59 years old (mean age 37.9), 47% male; and (2) 181 subjects 60 and over (mean age 70.1), 46% male.

Scoring, Scale Norms, and Distribution

A seven-point (strongly agree to strongly disagree) Likert scale is used. No norms were given by the authors. At this time, the combination of these items (or subsets of these items) into scale(s) has not been attempted.

Formal Test of Reliability/Homogeneity

A factor analytic assessment of the dimensional structure (principal components with varimax rotation) was conducted, including the 45 scale items plus age, sex, years of education, income, and response set. Four main factors were identified (they are listed below).

Formal Tests of Validity

As the data below indicate, there was some item overlap among the four identified factors. The items were examined in terms of their content, source, and loading of the background items.

Factors identified were these. (1) Reactions to older workers: The defining items for this factor were from the Tuckman and Lorge Older Workers Scale. This included the response-set indicator as well. (2) Srole Anomie Scale: The defining items are from the Srole Anomie Scale, suggesting a lower than expected linkage between alienation and attitudes toward older people. The (response-set) item is also loaded on this scale—only −.16. (3) Positive reactions about older people: This is a composite of the Tuckman and Lorge Old People Scale items and those from Kogan, as well of the new items. This includes the age and response-set indicators. (4) Negative reactions about older people: The defining items for this factor come from the Tuckman and Lorge Old People Scale. This is the opposite of factor 3. Background items included are age, income, education, and response set.

The two age-groups were separately factored, and there were essentially no differences, except minor ones, in the positive factor. The results generally corroborate the original scale construction although the authors did not consider their analysis to be a test of the dimensionality of the original scales.

The investigators noted that the positive and negative factors were essentially polar opposites even though they emerged in the analysis as orthogonal. Most of the Tuckman and Lorge items were either negative or neutral. The items from Kogan's scale included five positive and three negative (they were not matched positive and negative pairs as is the case in the response-set-balanced Kogan scale). The three negative items fell on the first factor and four of the five positive items fell on the third factor, again suggesting the distinctness of the positive and negative items.

They also factored 35 items of belief especially constructed to reflect more programmatic and practical aspects of dealing with the perceived needs and concerns of older people. Again, four factors were identified: (1) general entitlements for the older person, (2) societal rejection of older people, (3) entitlement to remaining in the community, and (4) reciprocity between the elderly and the community. These items factored differently for the two age-groups, although in both cases four factors seemed appropriate. The investigators concluded that the communality in belief structure is a function of the kind of beliefs.

A factor analysis of these items was also provided by the authors. In neither case did the background items have much effect. The response set indicator was deemed "rough," being a sum of the positive responses. However, it should be noted (see tables in the instrument) that response set had relatively high loadings on several factors, at least for the younger group.

Usability on Older Populations

No special problems were noted.

Sensitivity to Age (Including Social Age) Differences

Only the needs and concerns beliefs yielded different factor structures for the two age-groups (and, to some extent, the positive old people items as well). The conclusion is that the kind of belief being examined determines whether age is a relevant consideration.

General Comments and Recommendations

Although the investigators did not treat their two sets of four-factor scales as scales that might be used by other investigators, their factor analytic analysis helped identify items of potential utility. Further validity and reliability work is needed, as well as application to other populations.

References

Kilty, K. M., and A. Feld. "Attitudes toward Aging and toward the Needs of Older People." *Journal of Gerontology*, 1976, 31: 586–94.

Kogan, N. "Attitudes toward Old People: The Development of a Scale and an Examination of Correlates." *Journal of Abnormal and Social Psychology*, 1961, 62: 44–54.

Srole, L. "Social Integration and Certain Corollaries: An Exploratory Study." *American Sociological Review*, 1956, 21: 709–16.

Tuckman, J., and I. Lorge. "The Attitudes of the Aged toward the Older Worker: For Institutionalized and Non-institutionalized Adults." *Journal of Gerontology*, 1952a, 7: 559–64.

_____. "The Effect of Institutionalization on Attitudes toward Old People." *Journal of Abnormal and Social Psychology*, 1952b, 47: 337–44.

_____. "Attitudes toward Old People." *Journal of Social Psychology*, 1953, 37: 249–60.

Instrument

See Instrument V1.12.II.c.

PERCEPTIONS OF OLD AGE
E. G. Youmans, 1971

Definition of Variable or Concept

Perceptions about older people in seven different areas are assessed by this instrument.

Description of Instrument

The scale of 21 agree/disagree items is arranged into seven content subscale areas of 3 statements each. The response categories are agree (1), don't know (2), and disagree (3), so the range of the sum score for each scale is 3 to 9. The item-generation procedures used by the author were not described. The seven areas are: (1) old age worries, (2) old age work problems, (3) old age positive (attitudes), (4) old age segregation, (5) old age organized politically, (6) old age negative (attitudes), and (7) retirement (positive).

In addition, Youmans included four questions about perceptions of age and the life cycle. Percentages for these items are shown for rural and urban, younger and older samples. These items are not part of the instrument. Responses to these items are given in Youmans (1971).

Method of Administration

The scale is administered as a personal interview. No timing or special administration skills were noted by Youmans.

Context of Development and Subsequent Use

The items were devised for use in comparisons between older and younger generations and between rural and urban subjects.

Sample

Youmans (1971) used a 1969 representative cluster sample of 805 persons from a metropolitan center and an all-rural county in Kentucky. The sample included noninstitutionalized men and women in two age-groups, 20 to 29 and 60 and over. Table 12-11 shows the characteristics of the cluster sample, and Table 12-12 shows characteristics of the respondents in the sample.

TABLE 12-11
Characteristics of the Cluster Sample

	Age 20–29	Age 60+	Total Area Population
Urban	237	165	150,000
Rural	127	276	6,500

SOURCE: Same as for Table 12-12.

TABLE 12-12
Characteristics of Respondents in 1969 Sample (in Percentages)

Characteristics	Urban		Rural	
	Younger	Older	Younger	Older
	(237)	(165)	(127)	(276)
	%	%	%	%
Sex				
Male	41	41	39	43
Female	59	59	61	57
Race				
White	95	89	99	100
Negro	5	11	1	*
Marital status				
Married	74	61	72	68
Widowed	–	33	1	28
Divorced, separated	4	2	3	1
Never married	22	4	24	3
Education (median years)	(13.8)	(10.1)	(11.1)	(7.8)
Annual income (median)	$6015.	$3885.	$3999.	$1773.
Occupation				
Professional, managerial	14	10	14	5
Clerical, sales	15	3	9	2
Skilled, semiskilled	17	4	15	3
Laborer (nonfarm)	5	1	7	1
Farm operators, tenants	–	1	6	2
Domestics	2	2	2	2
Laborer (farm)	1	1	5	3
Other (student, ill, laid off)	19	5	6	3
Housewife	27	30	36	43
Retired	–	43	–	36

* less than 0.5.

SOURCE: E. G. Youmans. "Generation and Perceptions of Old Age: An Urban-Rural Comparison." *The Gerontologist*, 1971, 11 (4, part 1): Reprinted by permission of author and publisher.

Scoring, Scale Norms and Distribution

Scale scores consisted of sum scores for each of the seven subscales: 1 for agree, 2 for don't know, 3 for disagree. Youmans (1971) reported the means and standard deviations for each of the seven scales (Table 12-13).

TABLE 12-13
Generational Differences in Perceptions of Old Age

	Urban			Rural		
	Younger	Older		Younger	Older	
	(N=237)	(N=165)	T-Value	(N=127)	(N=276)	T-Value
1. Old age worries	5.56	4.13	8.83***	4.58	3.99	4.33***
2. Old age work problems	7.89	6.50	7.59***	6.39	5.17	5.87***
3. Old age positive	6.97	5.87	5.84***	6.73	5.97	3.80***
4. Old age segregation	6.15	5.85	1.85n.s.	5.59	5.78	−1.10n.s.
5. Old age organize politically	7.60	7.35	1.55n.s.	6.80	6.65	0.71n.s.
6. Old age negative	6.70	6.51	1.08n.s.	5.86	5.26	2.70**
7. Retirement positive	5.90	5.96	−0.32n.s.	4.78	5.15	−2.11*

* $p < 0.05$ (a difference this large would occur by chance alone only five in 100 times)

** $p < 0.01$ (a difference this large would occur by chance alone only once in 100 times)

*** $p < 0.001$ (a difference this large would occur by chance alone only once in 1000 times)

n.s. = Not significant.

Lower score reveals the stronger intensity of the value.

SOURCE: E. G. Youmans. "Generation and Perceptions of Old Age: An Urban-Rural Comparison." *The Gerontologist*, 1971, 11 (4, part 1): 285. Reprinted by permission of author and publisher.

Formal Tests of Reliability/Homogeneity

Intercorrelations of items within scales (internal consistency) were reported to range from .75 to .90, with an average correlation of .84.

Usability on Older Populations

No problems were reported in the use of an older (60 and over) sample.

Sensitivity to Age (Including Social Age) Differences

Differences were found in the intercorrelation of scales by age (older persons generally report more highly intercorrelated responses), but this was not reported as a substantive finding.

Scale-Development Statistics

Scale intercorrelations for the four samples are given in Table 12-14.

TABLE 12-14

Interdependencies in Perceptions of Old Age among Younger and Older Generations

Perceptions	1	2	3	4	5	6	7
1. Old age worries	—	.046	.179	.132	.205	.078	.041
	—	.162	.048	.039	.077	.084	.046
2. Old age work problems	.171	—	.003	.278	.166	.327	.208
	.093	—	.012	.295	.239	.343	.006
3. Old age positive	.022	.064	—	.175	.311	.044	.149
	.093	.080	—	.135	.232	-.037	.171
4. Old age segregation	.076	.152	.140	—	.411	.262	.110
	.011	.009	.169	—	.326	.257	-.087
5. Old age politically	.104	.128	.245	.242	—	.298	.242
organize	.133	-.006	.147	.221	—	.374	.118
6. Old age negative	.239	.265	-.031	.228	.279	—	.197
	.162	.266	.070	.252	.176	—	.123
7. Retirement positive	.160	.319	.290	.075	.198	.174	—
	.115	.116	.227	.091	.083	.085	—

SOURCE: E. G. Youmans. "Generation and Perceptions of Old Age: An Urban-Rural Comparison." *The Gerontologist*, 1971, 11 (4, part 1): 287. Reprinted by permission of author and publisher.

NOTE: Urban correlations below diagonal; rural above diagonal. Younger generations are lower entry correlations; older generations are upper entry correlations. Correlation coefficient of .195 or more = $p < 0.05$, of .254 or more = $p < 0.01$.

The responses of the four samples to the four age/stage definition items are given in Youmans (1971).

General Comments and Recommendations

Further examination of the reliability and validity of these items seems warranted, including an analysis of dimensionality. A strength is in the representative nature of the sample, which makes contrasts potentially useful for other investigators.

Reference

Youmans, E. G. "Generation and Perceptions of Old Age: An Urban-Rural Comparison." *The Gerontologist*, 1971, 11 (4, part 1) 284–88.

Instrument

See Instrument V1.12.II.d.

NEGATIVE ATTRIBUTES OF OLD AGE and POSITIVE POTENTIAL IN OLD AGE
L. A. Morgan and V. L. Bengtson, 1976

Definition of Variable or Concept

These two scales correspond to two issues involved in research measuring the concept of perceptions of aging. Perceptions are beliefs or evaluations regarding characteristics of the aged and the process of aging. The first issue involves characteristics of the aged that are positive or negative. The second involves the functions, competence, and prestige of the aged. Perceptions are normative, expressing expectations for behavior and prescriptions or proscriptions for the aged individual. They may be stereotypic, characterizing aggregates in primarily derogatory and inaccurate ways. Morgan and Bengtson's paper (1956) elaborates on these defining characteristics.

Description of Instrument

The instrument includes two orthogonal scales: the four-item Negative Attributes of Old Age scale and the three-item Positive Potential in Old Age scale. The response categories are agree and disagree, with volunteered "depends" answers recorded as well. Some decision-maker samples were given four categories of agree-disagree.

The scales were developed from a set of 61 perception items generally reflecting the two issues noted above and taken from other stereotype and perception scales. From these a subset of 14 was used in the initial Morgan and Bengtson study and selected on the basis of a test-retest examination (plus face validity, interviewer's comments on administration problems, and reliability/validity information). Through the process of examining construct validity across age, sex, and ethnic strata and through the use of orthogonal factor analysis, the revised scales were developed, with 7 of the original 14 items being eliminated.

Method of Administration

The scales are administered as part of an interview, in the context of a 90-minute schedule. No separate timing information was given. No special skills other than interviewing competence are needed. The agree-disagree response format was used to better accommodate the ethnic and aged respondents.

Context of Development and Subsequent Use

The perceptions items were developed for use in a larger project on the social and cultural contexts of aging. No other uses have been reported thus far, although the items themselves have a long history as parts of different scales. The scale was developed because of the investigators' concern about the applicability of perception scale items across age, sex, and ethnic strata. This appears to have been the only study to undertake this kind of developmental analysis.

Samples

The sample consisted of 1,269 individuals interviewed in a large metropolitan area (Los Angeles). The stratified area probability sample was adjusted by weighting to reflect the target population. Strata were three ethnic groups (black, Mexican American, and white), three age-groups (45–54, 55–64, and 65–74), and two categories of Duncan's Socio-Economic Index.

A validity checking sample of 316 Los Angeles County "decision-makers" was also given the perception items. Date were apparently gathered in 1975/1976.

Scoring, Scale Norms, and Distribution

Sum scores are used (3 for agree, 2 for volunteered "depends," and 1 for disagree). The Negative Perceptions of Aging scale mean was 9.1 (range 4–12), and the Positive Potential of Aging scale mean was 7.3 (range 3–9).

Formal Tests of Reliability/Homogeneity

Cronbach's alpha assessment of measurement reliability is given in Table 12-15 for the two overall scales and for the scales within age, sex, and ethnicity subgroup. In addition, the authors presented Spearman rank-order correlations for the 90 students who were tested twice about three weeks apart. The correlations were .465 for the Negative Attributes Scale and .600 for the Positive Potential Scale.

TABLE 12-15

Cronbach's Alpha Assessment of Reliability of Negative Attributes
and Positive Potential

	Negative Attributes	Positive Potential
Age		
45–54	.518	.620
55–64	.650	.458
65–74	.580	.473
Sex		
Male	.543	.514
Female	.607	.550
Ethnicity		
Black	.701	.518
Mexican American	.620	.554
White	.572	.536
TOTAL	.581	.536

SOURCE: L. A. Morgan and V. L. Bengtson. "Measuring Perceptions of Aging across Social Status." Paper presented to the 29th Annual Meeting of the Gerontological Society, New York, October 13–17, 1976, Table 6. Reprinted by permission of authors.

Formal Tests of Validity

All the items were judged to be face valid. A factor analysis of the original 14 items yielded two factors, one with 4 items and the other with 2 strong and 1 weaker item (the criterion was loadings of .38 or more). These items are listed in the Table 12-16. Items that failed to achieve the .38 criterion for inclusion were most in good health, become wiser with old age, not isolated or lonely, not useful to self/others, valuable for experiences, treated like children, and can't find job, willing to work.

Table 12-16 shows the higher factor loadings for items by age/sex/ethnicity subgroups and for the decision-maker sample. These data suggest a parallel structure of the items across various subgroups. These items also have face validity in terms of the two initial issues noted earlier. Response set bias was not examined, as the authors noted. A three-way analysis of variance (age × race × sex) on the Negative Attributes items yielded no statistically significant terms, contrary to the authors' expectations. The same analysis on the Positive Potential Scale showed some stratus variation, notably for the aged 65 to 74 and for Mexican Americans, both of which were lower than the averages of other groups.

Usability on Older Populations

The scale was used on a sample with members as old as 74 years.

Sensitivity to Age (Including Social Age) Differences

An important part of the scale's development was achieving an instrument that would maintain the same perception-item scale structure across ages (45–74). Apparently, the authors were successful, except for one item in the group 45 to 54 and two items in the group 55 to 64. (See Table 12-16.)

General Comments and Recommendations

These two scales are unusual in their connection with the issues in the field and their search for stability across various kinds of groups. Investigators will want to follow Morgan and Bengtson's lead by seeking additional items to be included in each scale and by further

TABLE 12-16

Items Loading Highly (.38+) or Moderately High (.34+) (Varimax Rotation) on Factors by Strata in Main Sample and in Decision-Maker Sample

Question Factor:	Total		45-54		55-64		65-74		Male		Female		Black		Mexican-American		White		Decision-maker	
	1	2	1	2	1	2	1	2	1	2	1	2	1	2	1	2	1	2	1	2
Set in ways/unable to change	.603		.536		.641			.670		.567	.605		.734		.558		.604			.519
Spend time prying	.597		.606		.620			.494		.570	.648		.648		.526		.607			.660
Apt to complain	.415		.474		—			.415		.386	.430		.385		.584		.395			.402
Against reforms/ hang on to past	.380		—		.546			.403		.477	.374		.595		—		.371			.460
Can do job as well/ no change		.751		.948		.725	.500		.495			.769		.523		.767		.750	.870	
In job, can perform as well		.546		.461		.578	.678		.614			.592		.542		.491		.557	.734	
Can learn as well as young		.367		.474		—	.386		.411			.371		.503		.399		.362	.389	
Treated like children			.400					.368					.379		.696					
Not used to self/ others													.370							

SOURCE: L. A. Morgan and V. L. Bengtson. "Measuring Perceptions of Aging across Social Strata." Paper presented to the 29th Annual Meeting of the Gerontological Society, New York, October 13-17, 1976, Table 5. Reprinted by permission.

examining the stability of the structure across age-groups and other groups. This process could lead to improved reliability coefficients and norms for comparative populations.

Reference

Morgan, L. A., and V. L. Bengtson. "Measuring Perceptions of Aging across Social Strata." Paper presented to the 29th Annual meeting of the Gerontological Society, New York, October 13–17, 1976.

Instrument

See Instrument V1.12.II.e.

IMAGES OF OLDER PEOPLE BATTERY
National Council on the Aging, 1975

Definition of Variable or Concept

Images of older people is a rather broad and imprecise concept that includes knowledge about older people in America, opinion of personal characteristics, attribution of preference of older people for certain activities, assessment of older persons' problems, estimates of when men and women become old, and opinions about the best and worst aspects of being older. Items covering many of these areas ask about the respondent personally and for the respondent's opinion of people over 65 years old. Much of the analysis focuses on the discrepancy between self-view, view of older people, and self-view by older people; thus, in the analysis, "images" becomes a comparative misperception concept.

Description of Instrument

The battery of some 50 different items is asked in the context of a household interview schedule, and the items include eight different types of questions. The response categories vary but are of a Likert type in most instances. The items were developed by the Harris firm, which consulted with a number of gerontological researchers. The Harris report provided no descriptions of the scale-development and pretesting procedures.

Method of Administration

The battery was administered as a part of a household interview. Timing for these questions was not reported, since the items were included in a longer schedule. There were no special administration requirements other than having a generally competent interviewer and a willing respondent.

Context of Development and Subsequent Use

The items were generated specifically for the purpose of a national assessment of the views on aging held by the public aged 18 and over and especially by the older public, aged 65 and over. Its development was typical of national surveys—it was reported to NCOA (the commissioning organization) and then to the public.

Sample

A total of 4,254 in-person, household interviews were conducted during the late spring and early summer of 1974 by trained Harris interviewers. The probability sample (multistage, random, cluster sample of the noninstitutionalized public aged 18 and over) had four parts: (1) 1,500 adults 18+, national cross-section sample, (2) 2,400 persons 65+, oversample, (3) 360 persons 55–64, oversample, and (4) 200 persons, black, 65+, oversample. The analyzed sample was weighted to reflect known (1970 census) distributions and the oversampling procedures.

Scoring, Scale Norms, and Distribution

Univariate distributions for the weighted sample are provided in the main report of the study, *The Myth and Reality of Aging in America* (NCOA, 1975).

Formal Tests of Validity

No tests of validity were reported, although the contrast of views of the public in general, those 65 and over, and opinions about those 65 and over serve as a basis for judging areas of discrepancy.

Usability on Older Populations

This study involved the administration of the items to noninstitutionalized people from 18 to over 80 years of age, and no difficulties were reported.

Sensitivity to Age (Including Social Age) Differences

Responses to items differed by age, but age-related bias in understanding or responding to given items was not reported.

General Comments and Recommendations

The main advantage of these items, in addition to their inclusion of important topics, is the availability of national benchmark data for 1974 with which specific samples could be compared. The comparison of "self" and "other" views is helpful in detecting the areas and the extent of misperception about aging. Users should note that the reported benchmark is a *cross-sectional* study.

References

National Council on the Aging. *The Myth and Reality of Aging in America.* Washington, D. C.: National Council on the Aging, 1975.

———. *Codebook for "The Myth and Reality of Aging,"* A survey conducted by Louis Harris and associates for the National Council on the Aging; prepared by the Duke University Center for the Study of Aging and Human Development, 1976.

Instrument

See Instrument V1.12.II.f.

SALTER VIEW OF ELDERLY SCALE
C. A. Salter and C. deL. Salter, 1976

Definition of Variable or Concept

The scale assesses attitudes and behaviors toward the elderly.

Description of Instrument

The scale consists of a 36-item Likert scale. The response categories are from strongly disagree (1) to unsure (4) to strongly agree (7). The items are divided into six topical areas with 6 items included per area. The six areas are (1) agreement with (1971) White House Conference on Aging resolutions, (2) willingness to help the elderly, (3) absolute monthly frequency of helping the elderly, (4) agreement with stereotypes of the elderly, (5) fears of own future aging, and (6) factual questions about the elderly.

Method of Administration

The scale is administered as a paper-and-pencil instrument without introductory "biasing" comments.

Context of Development and Subsequent Use

This scale was used on the association of scores on a death anxiety scale with attitudes toward the elderly.

Scoring, Scale Norms, and Distribution

The Table 12-17 lists item means and standard deviations. The method of scale scoring used is unclear, but it appears that sum scores were created for the six separate parts of the scale and perhaps for the entire set of 36 items.

TABLE 12-17
Means and Standard Deviations for Items on Salter View of Elderly Scale

	Mean	Standard Deviation
Agreement with White House Conference on Aging Resolutions		
National awareness campaign	5.6[a]	1.4
Pre-retirement education	5.3	1.3
Health services delivery	5.6	1.3
Home property tax relief	5.1	1.5
Guaranteed minimum income	4.9	1.4
Social services program	5.2	1.5
Willingness to Help the Elderly		
Buy groceries for them	5.8[b]	1.4
Visit them	5.6	1.5
Take them to religious services	5.3	2.0
Take them to medical services	5.6	1.7
Telephone them	5.5	1.8
Run errands for them	5.1	1.9
Absolute Monthly Frequency of Helping the Elderly		
Buy groceries for them	2.6	2.4
Visit them	2.6	2.1
Take them to religious services	2.3	2.3
Take them to medical services	2.1	2.3
Telephone them	3.1	3.1
Run errands for them	2.0	2.5
Agreements with Stereotypes of the Elderly		
They become different	3.6[c]	1.9
Their needs change	4.3	2.0
Social involvement is not important	6.5	1.2
Activities are not important	6.3	1.4
Deterioration is inevitable	2.5	1.8
They become more religious	4.0	1.5
Fears of Own Future Aging		
Inadequate income	4.4[c]	1.9
Unpleasant life style changes	3.3	1.9
Being ignored by younger family	2.7	1.6
Being forced into an institution	2.3	1.6
Losing strength and vigor	3.4	2.1
Being forced into retirement	3.6	1.9
Factual Questions about the Elderly		
% of population over 65	3.1[d]	1.6
% elderly with own home	3.6	2.4

TABLE 12-17—*Continued*

	Mean	Standard Deviation
% elderly living alone	3.1	2.2
% elderly institutionalized	2.8	1.7
% elderly in poverty	3.9	2.6
% elderly with health problems	3.4	2.4

[a] % = strongly agree

[b] % = very willing

[c] % = definitely yes

[d] % = coded to a 9-point scale where 1 = 1–11%, 2 = 12–22%, 3 = 23–33%, etc.

SOURCE: C. A. Salter and C. deL. Salter. "Attitudes toward Aging and Behaviors toward the Elderly among Young People as a Function of Death Anxiety." *The Gerontologist*, 1976, 16: 234. Reprinted by permission of authors and publisher.

General Comments and Recommendations

Further testing and broader use are needed.

Reference

Salter, C. A., and C. deL. Salter. "Attitudes toward Aging and Behaviors toward the Elderly Among Young People as a Function of Death Anxiety." *The Gerontologist*, 1976, 16: 232–36.

Instrument

See the section on scoring, scale norms, and distribution above.

PERCEPTIONS OF AGING
V. L. Bengtson, J. J. Dowd, D. H. Smith, and A. Inkeles, 1975

Definition of Variable or Concept

Positive attitudes toward the aged are assessed.

Description of Instrument

Three items were used in a secondary analysis of data derived from a 438–question, cross-cultural interview schedule. The questions are: (1) on the perceived instrumental or educational value of the aged: "Some people say that a boy learns the deepest and most profound truth from old people; others say that a boy learns most from books and in school. What is your opinion?" (2) on the respondent's attitude toward his or her own aging: "Some people look forward to old age with pleasure while others dread (fear) the coming of old age. How do you personally feel about the coming of old age?" (3) and on the norms regarding deference to the aged: "What are the obligations (duties) which young people owe to old people?" (used in Bangladesh, India, Nigeria) or "How much obligation does a young man have to obey old people?" and "Do you think that contradicting an old person is incorrect?" (used in Chile, Argentina, Israel).

Method of Administration

Indigenous social scientists in each country served as interviewers during the original study. Questionnaires were backtranslated several times to ensure linguistic equivalence. See Inkeles and Smith (1974) for information on the data-gathering procedures used.

Context of Development and Subsequent Use

The items were part of the Harvard Project in the Sociocultural Aspects of Development.

Sample

The sample consisted on 5,450 male respondents aged 18 to 32 from six "developing" nations: Argentina, Chile, India, Israel, Nigeria, and Bangladesh. The samples came from three general occupational groups: cultivators, urban nonindustrial workers, and factory workers. Table 12-18 provides sample sizes for each country and occupation.

TABLE 12-18
Distribution of Respondents within Three Occupational Groups in Six Countries

| | Occupational Groups | | | |
Country	Cultivators (C)	Urban Non-Industrials (UNI)	Factory Workers (FW)	Total
Bangladesh (Pakistan)	234	112	654	1000
India	350	250	700	1300
Nigeria	100	101	519	720
Chile	109	106	668	883
Argentina	98	55	662	815
Israel	102	92	538	732
TOTALS	993	716	3741	5450

SOURCE: V. L. Bengtson, J. J. Dowd, D. H. Smith, and A. Inkeles. "Modernization, Modernity, and Perceptions of Aging: A Cross-Cultural Study." *Journal of Gerontology*, 1975, 30: 690. Reprinted by permission of authors and publisher.

TABLE 12-19
Mean Number of Obligations which Young People Owe to Old People
(by Occupation and Country)

| | Occupational Group | | | | | |
| Country | Cultivator | | Urban Non-industrial | | Urban Factory Workers | |
	X	S.D.	X	S.D.	X	S.D.
Bangladesh	2.62	0.84	2.52	0.75	2.71	0.88
India	2.15	0.63	2.26	0.73	2.01	0.61
Nigeria	2.17	0.75	2.39	0.83	2.51	0.88

NOTE: In these less-modernized nations the number of different types of obligations mentioned by the respondents were recorded; means are based on the number of obligations mentioned. The higher the mean, the higher the preceived obligation to the old on this open-ended question.

SOURCE: V. L. Bengtson, J. J. Dowd, D. H. Smith, and A. Inkeles. "Modernization, Modernity, and Perceptions of Aging: A Cross-Cultural Study." *Journal of Gerontology*, 1975, 30: 693. Reprinted by permission of authors and publisher.

TABLE 12-20
Perceptions of Amount of Duty to Obey Old People
(by Occupation and Country)

| | Occupational Group | | | | | |
| Country | Cultivator | | Urban Non-industrial | | Urban Factory Workers | |
	X	S.D.	X	S.D.	X	S.D.
Chile	3.42	0.66	3.01	0.79	3.48	0.72
Argentina	3.65	0.67	3.45	0.78	3.52	0.70
Israel	3.21	0.75	3.19	0.86	3.17	0.68

NOTE: Fixed-alternative response scored as "4" (much) to "1" (no obligation). Thus, the higher the mean, the higher the perceived obligation to obey the old.

SOURCE: V. L. Bengtson, J. J. Dowd, D. H. Smith, and A. Inkeles. "Modernization, Modernity, and Perceptions of Aging: A Cross-Cultural Study." *Journal of Gerontology*, 1975, 30: 693. Reprinted by permission of authors and publisher.

TABLE 12-21

Perceived Instrumental Value of the Aged: Percentage by Occupation
and Country Choosing "A Boy Learns Most from the Old"

Occupational Group	Country					
	Bangladesh	India	Nigeria	Chile	Argentina	Israel
Cultivators	19.8	39.4	66.0	8.83	31.6	30.0
Urban Non-Industrial Workers	30.4	39.6	59.4	7.6	18.2	14.3
Urban Factory Workers	24.0	34.1	57.8	9.8	9.5	10.0
TOTALS N	226	474	425	87	104	90
%	24.0	36.6	59.3	9.3	12.8	13.6

NOTE: Cell entries do not add up to 100% because they reflect proportions of respondents choosing only one of three alternative responses. Thus, the table should be read: Of the Bangladesh cultivators, 19.8% (35 of the 177 who responded to this question) choose the more "traditional" response, "A boy learns most from the old."

SOURCE: V. L. Bengtson, J. J. Dowd, D. H. Smith, and A. Inkeles. "Modernization, Modernity, and Perceptions of Aging: A Cross-Cultural Study." *Journal of Gerontology*, 1975, 30: 692. Reprinted by permission of authors and publisher.

TABLE 12-22

Attitude toward One's Own Aging: Percentage by Occupation and Country
Choosing "Await or Look Forward to Old Age"

Occupational Group	Country					
	Bangladesh	India	Nigeria	Chile	Argentina	Israel
Cultivators	32.8	60.5	59.0	16.5	46.9	33.6
Urban Non-Industrial Workers	37.8	46.1	67.3	24.5	16.4	45.7
Urban Factory Workers	35.8	44.4	77.2	29.7	29.2	35.4
TOTALS N	334	632	527	242	234	239
%	35.4	49.1	73.3	27.6	28.8	36.5

NOTE: Cell entries can be read as follows: Of the total sample from Bangladesh, 34.4% (334 of 943) respondents chose the "traditional" response: they "look forward to old age."

SOURCE: V. L. Bengtson, J. J. Dowd, D. H. Smith, and A. Inkeles. "Modernization, Modernity, and Perceptions of Aging: A Cross-Cultural Study." *Journal of Gerontology*, 1975, 30: 692. Reprinted by permission of authors and publisher.

Scoring, Scale Norms, and Distribution

Each item was scored differently, as follows: (1) Percentage choosing "a boy learns most from the old" (Table 12-19). (2) Mean number of obligations that young people owe to old people (Table 12-20). (3) Mean of fixed alternative response on amount of duty to obey old people; 4 for much to 1 for no obligation (Table 12-21). (4) Percentage choosing "await or look forward to old age" (Table 12-22).

General Comments and Recommendations

Though these items are not proposed as an ideal cross-cultural measure of attitudes toward older people, they are reported here because of their possible value for making contrasts with other samples.

References

Bengtson, V. L., J. J. Dowd, D. H. Smith, and A. Inkeles. "Modernization, Modernity, and Perceptions of Aging: A Cross-Cultural Study." *Journal of Gerontology,* 1975, 30: 688–95.

Inkeles, A., and D. H. Smith. *Becoming Modern.* Cambridge, Mass.: Howard University Press, 1974.

Instrument

See the description of the instrument above.

KOGAN-WALLACH SEMANTIC DIFFERENTIAL
N. Kogan and M. A. Wallach, 1961

Definition of Variable or Concept

The evaluative, potency, and activity "meaning" factors established by Osgood, Suci, and Tannenbaum (1957) are used to assess 28 concepts. Differences in the "meaning" of these concepts between young and old subjects are examined.

Description of Instrument

Twenty-five seven-point bipolar adjective pairs were selected from the work of Osgood, Suci, and Tennenbaum (1957) to reflect three dimensions of meaning. (The pairs are listed below.) Twenty-eight concepts were selected for rating. Each subject was given a set of 28 pages, each with one concept to be rated on the 25 items. A principal axes factor analysis of the 25 items was conducted, summing over all the concepts rated and all the individuals in the sample. The investigators reported as essentially identical first factor across these groups, accounting for 61% to 67% of the total variance. This was an evaluative factor with the strongest loadings for these adjective pairs: successful/unsuccessful, attractive/unattractive, warm/cold, bad/good, frustrating/rewarding, sad/happy, and sick/healthy. No further factors with a stable structure across the subject gruops were found. Thus, scores were computed for these seven adjective pairs.

Method of Administration

Younger subjects filled out the 28-page instrument in a classroom setting. Older subjects filled it out individually. No time information was given and no special administration instructions or necessary skills were noted. Osgood, Suci, and Tannenbaum (1957, pp. 82–84) standard instructions on the semantic differential were used.

Context of Development and Subsequent Use

The instrument was developed to study differences in the meaning of concepts for young and older individual subjects.

TABLE 12-23

Age Differences in Evaluative Factor Scores for all Concepts

Concepts	Mean Deviation[a]		Sigmas		t	p	Mean Deviation[a]		Sigmas		t	p
	Young Men	Older Men	Young Men	Older Men			Young Women	Older Women	Young Women	Older Women		
Work and Leisure												
Work	.47	.27	1.57	1.63	.68	—	.70	.94	2.01	1.92	.74	—
Leisure Time	-.32	-.31	1.98	1.81	.03	—	-.42	-.23	1.90	1.88	.58	—
Retirement	-1.58	-.27	2.36	2.21	3.11	.01	-1.70	-.50	2.19	2.34	3.20	.01
Majority-Minority												
Older people	-.23	-.94	2.21	2.30	1.72	.10	-.78	-.81	2.02	1.94	.10	—
Foreigner	.18	1.04	1.89	2.25	2.25	.05	.34	.49	1.55	1.78	.54	—
Negro	-.59	.44	1.84	2.19	2.74	.01	-.51	.31	1.86	2.19	2.42	.02
American	.64	.70	1.47	1.92	.20	—	1.36	.91	1.73	2.03	1.45	—
Family-Interpersonal												
Family life	.13	-.14	1.96	1.63	.83	—	-.10	.32	1.33	1.74	1.64	—
Love	.18	.10	1.95	1.64	.86	—	.58	-.18	1.76	1.83	2.57	.02
My mother	.55	-.46	1.76	1.51	3.37	.001	.09	-.61	1.65	1.73	2.49	.02
My father	-.38	-.28	1.95	1.89	.28	—	-.56	-.21	2.34	2.15	.94	—
Sex	.35	.34	1.58	1.76	.02	—	.48	.12	1.64	2.09	1.13	—
Authority	.12	.23	2.03	1.88	.31	—	.22	-.20	1.97	2.11	1.23	—
Developmental Stages												
Baby	2.24	1.75	2.81	2.67	.97	—	2.32	2.09	2.49	2.25	.58	—
Youth	.99	1.05	2.42	1.87	.14	—	1.17	1.35	1.90	2.12	.53	—
Middle age	.61	.29	1.59	1.82	1.01	—	.22	.20	1.98	1.62	.04	—
Elderly	-.77	-.69	2.50	2.07	.20	—	-1.02	-1.14	2.11	2.14	.33	—
Old age	-.97	-.11	2.03	1.65	2.54	.02	-1.79	-.30	1.71	2.09	4.71	.001
Death	-3.02	-2.25	2.76	2.96	1.46	—	-4.28	-2.33	2.68	2.49	4.53	.001

TABLE 12-23 – Continued

Concepts	Mean Deviation[a]		Sigmas		t	p	Mean Deviation[a]		Sigmas		t	p
	Young Men	Older Men	Young Men	Older Men			Young Women	Older Women	Young Women	Older Women		
Psychological-Physical Attributes												
Generosity	.01	.28	1.77	1.78	.83	—	.16	.06	1.76	1.76	.34	—
Imagination	-.63	.07	2.03	1.60	2.11	.05	-.06	.13	2.13	1.77	.60	—
Vigor	.41	.73	1.46	1.76	1.04	—	.83	.52	1.42	1.64	1.23	—
Good looks	-.80	-.97	1.27	1.47	.68	—	-.61	-.77	2.04	1.54	.55	—
Self-Concept												
Myself	1.11	.59	1.68	1.84	1.60	—	1.30	.35	1.65	2.07	3.07	.01
Ideal person	.25	-.63	1.19	1.42	3.61	.001	.49	-.72	1.43	1.45	5.07	.001
Weltanschauung												
Future	.46	-.28	1.60	1.90	2.28	.05	.73	-.28	1.32	1.77	3.91	.001
Life	.44	-.38	1.67	1.82	2.55	.02	.49	-.02	1.91	1.73	1.68	.10
Risk	.14	.04	2.16	2.11	.25	—	.35	.52	1.64	1.53	.64	—

NOTE: Ns for the four samples were as follows: 66 young men, 55 older men, 71 young women, 76 older women.

a. Deviation from the grand mean for all concepts. Positive and negative values indicate concepts evaluated favorably and unfavorably, respectively, relative to the grand mean for each sample.

SOURCE: N. Kogan and M. A. Wallach. "Age Changes in Values and Attitudes." *Journal of Gerontology*, 1961, 16: 277. Reprinted by permission of authors and publisher.

Sample

The original sample consisted of 268 subjects, including 71 Simmons College women from introductory psychology courses, 66 Northeastern University men from introductory psychology, 76 older women from the Age Center of New England (Boston), and 55 older men from the Age Center of New England. Members of the older sample were not institutionalized. Mean ages were 71.1 for the older men and 70.5 for the older women; mean years of attained schooling were 13.5 for the older men and 13.3 for the older women.

Scoring, Scale Norms, and Distribution

Seven adjective pairs were used in the final evaluative scales. Standard scores for each of the 268 subjects were computed for each of the seven scales. For each individual, a score for each rated concept was the sum of the seven standard scores used in rating that concept. Rated items were treated as equal in weight in this summing. (See Table 12-23.)

Formal Tests of Reliability/Homogeneity

The adjective pairs included in the instrument were those that had factor loadings of .60 or greater on the first factor, where other loadings were .30 or less. No other reliability information was reported.

Usability on Older Populations

This research used older, noninstitutionalized subjects, and no specific problems were reported.

Sensitivity to Age (Including Social Age) Differences

One of the authors noted that Likert and self-report response formats used for measurements of values and attitudes have response set effects. He also found (Kogan, 1961) stronger acquiescent response tendencies for older people than for younger people on Likert items when the subjects had comparable education and intelligence. Using semantic differnetial items is thought to be one way of avoiding these problems.

Scale-Development Statistics

The strongest factor in the principal axes solution for these data was an evaluative factor. It accounted for 61%, 67%, 62%, and 63% of the total variance for younger and older men and younger and older women, respectively. There were almost identical factor loading patterns for these four groups. The Kendall's coefficient of concordance among the rank-ordered loadings for the four groups was .92. The seven adjective-pair items used in this analysis all had loadings of .60 or better on the evaluative factor and .30 or less on other factors. No other factor was reported to have had a common structure across the four groups.

General Comments and Recommendations

This was one of the first scales to consider factor structure invariance over groups as a criterion for scale construction. Further work needs to be done with factors other than the evaluative one, and, as in the general case, further work on validity and reliability is needed.

References

Kogan, N. "Attitudes toward Old People in an Older Sample." *Journal of Abnormal and Social Psychology,* 1961, 62: 616–22.

Kogan, N., and A. Wallach. "Age Changes in Values and Attitudes," *Journal of Gerontology,* 1961, 16: 272–80.

Osgood, C. E., G. J. Suci, and P. H. Tannenbaum. *The Measurement of Meaning.* Urbana, Ill.: University of Illinois Press, 1957.

Instrument

See Instrument V1.12.III.a.

EISDORFER-ALTROCCHI SEMANTIC DIFFERENTIAL
C. Eisdorfer and J. Altrocchi, 1961

Definition of Variable or Concept

Attitudes toward old age are assessed.

Description of Instrument

The instrument is made up of 20 semantic differential adjective pairs selected from the work of Osgood, Suci, and Tannenbaum (1957) and Nunnally (1961), which are rated on a seven-point scale. Eight concepts are rated: average man, average woman, old man, old woman, insane man, insane woman, neurotic man, and neurotic woman.

Of the 20 items, 13 reflect Osgood's evaluative dimension of meaning, 2 his potency dimension, and 2 his activity dimension (Osgood, Suci, and Tannenbaum, 1957). The other 3 items were selected from Nunnally's understandability dimension (Nunnally, 1961). Each concept is rated on a separate page, and the items are put in random order with half of them left-right reversed.

Method of Administration

Apparently, the items are to be administered in a class setting. It is a paper-and-pencil instrument, with no time limits or special administrative skill required.

Context of Development and Subsequent Use

The authors noted that earlier findings suggest that mental deterioration is a component of attitudes toward older people. The concepts rated reflect an interest in making these kinds of comparisons. The semantic differential instrument was selected as a constant-item basis for making comparisons. The set of items was subsequently used by Burdman (1974), but with different concepts rated: old person, average person, and sick person.

Samples

Eisdorfer and Altrocchi used 103 undergraduate summer school students and nursing students at Duke University (average age 21.2).

Burdman (1974) used a stratified proportional sample of 250 (an 86% response rate yielded, $N = 214$) rehabilitation counseling graduate students and gerontology graduate trainees enrolled during the 1972/1973 school year in university training programs throughout the United States. The sample was based on doctoral dissertation research in health education at the University of Oregon in 1973. Details of the study are not given in the article.

Scoring, Scale Norms, and Distribution

Individual scores on each meaning component (potency, activity, evaluation, understandability) were computed by summing the checked point (1-7) response for each of the items and dividing by the number of items checked. Group averages were used in contrasting the rated concepts. The means have been presented graphically (see Eisdorfer and Altrocchi, 1961, p. 341).

Formal Tests of Reliability/Homogeneity

The items were factor analyzed, following Kogan and Wallach (1961), and the authors concurred with Kogan in observing that the factorial structure of these scales may differ from items used by Osgood on different populations and concepts. The evaluative factor stands out, and the activity and potency items seem to form a "self-dangerous" factor. The factor structure after the first factor may not be universal across the concepts Eisdorfer and Altrocchi used. They concluded that attitudes toward old people are qualitatively different from those toward average, insane, and neurotic individuals.

General Comments and Recommendations

Further analyses of the factor structure, reliability, and validity of this instrument appear to be needed. The set of scales is similar to that used by Kogan (1961), but it includes the added Nunnally dimension.

References

Burdman, G. D. M. "Student and Trainee Attitudes on Aging." *The Gerontologist*, 1974, 14: 65–68.

Eisdorfer, C., and J. Altrocchi. "A Comparison of Attitudes toward Old Age and Mental Illness." *Journal of Gerontology*, 1961, 16: 340–43.

Kogan, N., and M. A. Wallach. "Age Changes in Values and Attitudes." *Journal of Gerontology*, 1961, 16: 272–80.

Nunnally, J. *Popular Conceptions of Mental Health: Their Development and Change.* New York: Holt, Rinehart and Winston, 1961.

Osgood, C. E., G. J. Suci, and P. H. Tannenbaum. *The Measurement of Meaning.* Urbana, Ill.: University of Illinois Press, 1957.

Instrument

See Instrument V1.12.III.b.

ACROSS-AGE SEMANTIC DIFFERENTIAL
M. Petersen, 1976

Definition of Variable or Concept

The instrument measures the subjects' evaluation of potential young and older adult partners with whom interpersonal communications could be established. Two underlying factors are explicitly addressed: interpersonal ability and instrumental ability.

Description of Instrument

The final version of the instrument consists of 15 semantic differential items, with a seven-point rating scale, which can be used to evaluate a stimulus person.

The scale was developed from a set of 7 items selected from Osgood, Suci, and Tannenbaum (1957) and 30 items derived from suggestions made by a specially organized group of volunteers (15 young males, 15 older males, 15 young females, and 15 older females — with young defined as ages 22 through 32 and old as 60 and over). These people were all college educated and white, and no married partners were included. In addition, the item "young/old" was added as a check on the definition of the stimulus objects to be rated. Thus, 38 items were initially used. (See Table 12-24.)

Sixty subjects (a different 60 who had the same characteristics as the original group) were asked to evaluate 8 persons (each shown in a 60-second, silent videotape). The stimulus persons were white nonactors taken from television documentaries. Two young males, two older males, two young females, and two older females were shown (again, age was defined as it was above). All combinations of young and old stimulus and young and old subject were examined by factor analysis (N = 240, since each subject contributed four ratings for each condition). The focus of attention was possible interaction of concept and item or subjects and items (items having different meanings due to different stimuli or different subjects).

Three factors were extracted for each of the four conditions: (1) interpersonal ability (17 items), (2) instrumental ability (7 items), and (3) propriety (3 items). The first two factors explained between 84% and 94% of the common variance; the third factor was minor. The Harman (1960, pp. 257–59) coefficient of congruence was used to examine the similarity of factor structures across the four conditions. The first two factors were found to be sufficiently stable for all four analyses. The third factor was stable for only one of the four.

Examining the factor loadings for those with an absolute value of .50 or larger and eliminating items with across-age differences in loading of .22 or more led to the elimination of 10 items (all propriety factor items plus 7 others). Of the remaining 17, 14 were selected for the final instrument, 7 from each of the first two factors. The checking item "young/old" was suggested as an additional item where it was appropriate.

Method of Administration

Apparently, the instrument is to be administered in a group setting. No time or special requirements were noted. The final items should be put in random order, and the positive-negative orientation of items should be randomized in use.

Context of Development and Subsequent Use

The purpose of the scale's development was to derive a set of semantic differential items that was not sensitive to subject-item or stimulus-item interaction and thus could be used across differently aged adult subjects and object persons.

Sample

The sample consisted of 60 adult volunteers: 15 22- to 32-year-old males, 15 22- to 32-year-old females, 15 males over 60, and 15 females over 60.

Scoring, Scale Norms, and Distribution

Sum scores are apparently used, with unit-item weights for items included in each factor.

Formal Tests of Reliability/Homogeneity

The items selected to represent each factor have high loadings in each of the four analyses. The average factor loading across the four analyses for items included in the interpersonal factor is .72, and for the instrumental factor it is .80. No item has a loading as high as .25 on the factor it does not represent.

Formal Tests of Validity

The author reported that the interpersonal ability factor is similar to Osgood's "evaluation" factor and to the "personal acceptability/unacceptability" factor of Rosencranz and McNevin (1969). The instrumental ability factor is also similar to Osgood's "dynamism" (potency and activity factors) and to Rosencranz and McNevin's "instrumental/ineffective" factor. Recall also the across-condition stability analysis mentioned above.

Usability on Older Populations

The scale was designed to be used on young and old objects and by young and old subjects.

Sensitivity to Age (Including Social Age) Differences

The strength of the set of items is that they appear to be stable reflections of the two underlying factors across different-aged objects and subjects.

Scale-Development Statistics

Table 12-24 lists the items in the original set of 38 by the factor on which they have a .50 or larger loading, if any.

TABLE 12-24
Items and Factors in Order of Average Factor Loading

	Source
Scales with .5 or Larger Factor Loading on a Given Factor	
Interpersonal Ability Factor	
pleasant/unpleasant	Generating sample
cooperative/uncooperative	Generating sample
considerate/inconsiderate	Generating sample
flexible/inflexible	Generating sample
generous/selfish	Generating sample
nice/awful	Osgood
open-minded/closed-minded	Generating sample
understanding/nonunderstanding	Generating sample
loving/unloving	Generating sample
has good relations with people of other ages/ has poor relations with people of other ages	Generating sample
friendly/unfriendly	Generating sample
modest, humble/arrogant, know-it-all	Generating sample
nonbigoted/bigoted	Generating sample
good/bad	Osgood
noncomplainer/complainer	Generating sample
nondomineering, nonbossy/domineering, bossy	Generating sample
has sense of humor/has no sense of humor	Generating sample
Instrumental Ability Factor	
active/passive	Osgood
strong/weak	Osgood
enthusiastic/unenthusiastic	Generating sample
fast/slow	Osgood
alert/nonalert	Generating sample
independent/dependent	Generating sample
ambitious, hardworking/lacking ambition, lazy	Generating sample
Propriety Factor	
honest/dishonest	Generating sample
responsible, reliable/irresponsible, unreliable	Generating sample
financially careful/financially careless	Generating sample
Scales Eliminated Due to Loadings of Less than .50	
does physical exercise/no physical exercise	Generating sample
has desire to learn/has no desire to learn	Generating sample
healthy/unhealthy	Generating sample
well groomed/poorly groomed	Generating sample
informed about current events/ uninformed about current events	Generating sample
intelligent/unintelligent	Generating smaple
involved in civic affairs/uninvolved in civic affairs	Generating sample
mature, understands self/ immature, does not understand self	Generating sample
beautiful/ugly	Osgood
large/small	Osgood
Checking Item	
young/old	Petersen

General Comments and Recommendations

The development of across-age semantic differential items is important for making comparisons with a variety of different target concepts and subjects where age is at issue. The work needs to be replicated on general populations, and reliability and validity issues need to be addressed further. It does not solve the problem of across-age stability for content scales not included in this analysis.

References

Harman, H. H. *Modern Factor Analysis*. Chicago: University of Chicage Press, 1960.

Osgood, C. E., G. J. Suci, and P. H. Tannenbaum. *The Measurement of Meaning*. Urbana, Ill.: University of Illinois Press, 1957.

Petersen, M. "A Cross-Age Semantic Differential for Social Evaluation." Paper Presented to the Annual Conference of the International Communication Association, Portland, April 14–17, 1976.

Rosencranz, H. A., and T. E. McNevin. "A Factor Analysis of Attitudes toward the Aged." *The Gerontologist*, 1969, 9: 55–59.

Instrument

See Instrument V1.12.III.c.

ATTITUDES TOWARD THE AGED
H. A. Rosencranz and T. E. McNevin, 1969

Definition of Variable or Concept

The scale assesses the stereotypes, or perceptual predispositions of the subjects.

Description of Instrument

The semantic differential scale includes 32 items, with seven response levels. Three factors have been found: autonomous-dependent, personal acceptability-unacceptability, and instrumental-ineffective. The scale is the result of the extensive pretesting of adjective scales. Subjects compiled lists of adjective pairs (attributes or behavioral characteristics of persons of all ages). These pairs were given to 200 17- to 21-year-olds, who were asked to rate three items: a 20- to 30-year-old male, a 40- to 55-year-old male, a 70- to 85-year-old male. The resulting items were factor analyzed, and the reduced set of 32 items makes up the final instrument.

Method of Administration

The scale is a paper-and-pencil instrument administered to groups. No special time or administration procedures were noted by the authors.

Context of Development and Subsequent Use

The aim in developing the scale was reported to have been the extension of measurement beyond a single-score stereotype scale and the analysis of the effects of social experience on stereotypes of the aging individual.

Cryns and Monk (1973) used two bipolar pairs with the highest factor loadings from each factor (i.e., six pairs) in a study of attitudes toward youth among 210 males aged 27 to 70. Concepts rated were "today's young people," "our boys in Vietnam," and "college students."

Naus (1973) used 15 of the original 32 bipolar pairs and added 5 other pairs (for a total of 20) reflecting the evaluative dimension found in Osgood's earlier work with the semantic differential. Correlates of attitudes toward old people were examined. Concepts rated were "paternal grandfather," "paternal grandmother," "maternal grandfather," "maternal grandmother," "old person I like most," "old person I like least," "young person I like most," "young person I like least," "myself," "man 70–85 years old," and "man 20–30 years old."

Samples

Rosencranz and McNevin's (1969) sample consisted of 287 undergraduate students at the University of Missouri.

Naus's (1973) sample was made up of 103 undergraduate students from introductory psychology courses (ages 18 to 22, 89% male). Of these 50 participated in a second session of the study along with 4 who had not participated in the first session.

Cryns and Monk's (1973) sample consisted of 210 males, aged 27 to 70, who were married, had one or more children, and were upper-lower- to upper-middle-class. The sample had three subgroups: young-adult males ($N = 55$), average age 32; middle-aged males ($N = 102$), average age 50; aged males ($N = 53$), average age 65.

Scoring, Scale Norms, and Distribution

Each pair of adjectives was checked on a scale of 1 through 7, and these scores were used in the factor analysis. Scores on each factor were obtained by adding the weights for adjectives deemed to fall on a given factor.

Usability on Older Populations

Rosencranz and McNevin recommended the insrument's use across ages.

Scale-Development Statistics

The three factors are: instrumental-ineffective (I-I) dimension (9 items), autonomous-dependent (A-D) dimension (9 items), and personal acceptability-unacceptability (PA-U) dimension (14 items). Factor loadings were not reported.

General Comments and Recommendations

Although the instrument appears to be among the more widely used, more work is needed on its validity and reliability and on the replicability of the factor structure across age-groups and samples for the rated concepts. As the authors noted, the separate factors permit the investigator to examine the impact of variables on aspects of connotative judgment about older (or other) people.

References

Cryns, A. G., and A. Monk. "Attitudes toward Youth as a Function of Adult Age: A Multivariate Study in Intergenerational Dynamics." *International Journal of Aging and Human Development*, 1973, 4: 23–33.

Naus, P. J. "Some Correlates of Attitudes toward Old People." *International Journal of Aging and Human Development*, 1973, 4: 229–43.

Rosencranz, H. A., and T. E. McNevin. "A Factor Analysis of Attitudes toward the Aged." *The Gerontologist*, 1969, 9: 55–59.

Instrument

See Instrument V1.12.III.d.

GOLDE-KOGAN SENTENCE-COMPLETION ASSESSMENT
P. Golde and N. Kogan, 1959

Definition of Variable or Concept

The instrument assesses attitudes toward old people (and people in general) reflecting emotions, physical attributes, interpersonal qualities, and values attributed to people.

Description of Instrument

It consists of 25 matched statement stems. Each pair includes one stem for old people and one about people in general; these are referred to as the experimental form and the control form of the statement. Eight of the experimental items are noted as not having exact equivalent parallel items for the control form (items number 7, 10, 12, 14, 16, 20, 23, and 24).

Subjects are asked to provide written responses that complete each sentence stem. Any given subject responds to either the experimental or the control form, not to both.

In the initial study, experimental and control responses to each item were mixed, and content-analysis coding categories were created for each item. These categories were intended to be mutually exclusive and (with an unanalyzed miscellaneous category) exhaustive. Later studies with older people resulted in adding a few analysis categories to selected items.

Coded responses are analyzed item by item, both by making comparisons between subject groups by percentages with a chi-square test of significance and by a verbal account of responses. Experimental and control forms are compared.

Method of Administration

Students may have been given the instrument as a group paper-and-pencil task. Old subjects completed the instrument individually. No timing or special administrative skill was noted.

Context of Development and Subsequent Use

The instrument was originally created to help handle problems noticed in the Tuckman and Lorge procedures. Noteworthy is the control form for people in general that serves as a comparative base.

Samples

Golde and Kogan's (1959) sample consisted of 50 male and 50 female undergraduate students from two dormitories at Brandeis University. The age range was from 17 to 23. Twenty-five matched statements were used (on both the experimental form and the control form). Alternate halves of the sample filled out the experimental form and the control form.

The first Kogan and Shelton (1962a) sample was made up of 89 men and 109 women who were volunteer members of the Age Center of New England (a nonprofit gerontological research organization in Boston). The subjects were in good health, noninstitutionalized, and average to superior in education and intelligence. The men's ages ranged from 54 to 92 years (mean 70.7, standard deviation 7.3 years). The women's ages ranged from 49 to 86 years (mean 69.4, standard deviation 7.9). Only 20 statements were used, and both the experimental and the control forms were used.

Kogan and Shelton's (1962b) second sample included 46 men and 55 women volunteers from the Age Center of New England. They ranged in age from 50 to 92 (mean 70 years). The IQ scores of the older subjects were similar to those of the younger subjects included in the sample—44 male and 49 female undergraduate students in psychology courses at Boston University and Tufts University. Only the 20-statement experimental form was used.

Scoring, Scale Norms, and Distribution

Four judges coded the completed sentences. All the judges were told to code the first idea in the response (most responses had only one idea) and to code it into only one of the possible response/code categories that had been devised. In the 1962 studies, some additional code categories were used.

When both the experimental and the control forms were used (Kogan and Shelton,

1962a), two judges were assigned to code the statements from each form. This was intended to reduce the possibility that a given judge would attempt to create artificial differences between coded experimental and control forms. Interjudge reliability was computed separately for each form. When there were differences, a fifth judge resolved the issue.

In the Kogan and Shelton (1962b) study, two judges coded the older subjects' responses and two coded the younger subjects' responses. The outcome was expressed as a percentage of the total responses answering any given code category for each item separately.

Item distributions are given in the original articles.

Formal Tests of Reliability/Homogeneity

Intercoder reliability was computed between two coders used for each form of the instrument. For Golde and Kogan (1959), reliability ranged from 60% to 97% (average 83%) agreement for the old person experimental form and 64% to 96% (average 83%) agreement for the control form. For Kogan and Shelton (1962a), reliabilities ranged from 73% to 97% (average 86%) on the experimental form and 50% to 94% (average 81%) on the control form. For Kogan and Shelton (1962b), reliabilities ranged from 73% to 97% (average 86%) agreement for the pair of judges coding the experimental form for older subjects and 58% to 90% (average 75%) agreement for coders of the experimental form for younger subjects.

Formal Tests of Validity

Golde and Kogan (1959) used chi-square tests of significance for experimental and control forms on each item. For the 17 more exactly paired items, 16 were significantly different in response distribution between experimental and control forms. For the 8 item pairs that were not exactly matched but were "equivalent," 7 showed significant experimental-control differences.

Usability on Older Populations

No difficulty has been noted in using this instrument with healthy, noninstitutionalized older people.

Sensitivity to Age (Including Social Age) Differences

Kogan and Shelton (1962b) noted that 7 out of 20 experimental items and 9 out of 20 control items showed chi-square differences significant at the .05 level between older and younger subjects. They provided no other information on age sensitivity.

Scale-Development Statistics

Percentage distributions contrasting the experimental and control forms are given with the instrument.

General Comments and Recommendations

Although this procedure so far has not resulted in overall scale-score summaries, it does allow less experimenter control over kind of response. Unfortunately, the coding effort appears to be important in large studies. Computerized content-analysis procedures may help solve both problems and eliminate the judges' unreliability as well. Reliability (beyond coder reliability) and validity issues need to be addressed. The scores could be, but generally have not been, used in examining the relationships between variables other than the subject's age and sex.

References

Golde, P., and N. Kogan. "A Sentence Completion Procedure for Assessing Attitudes toward Old People." *Journal of Gerontology*, 1959, 14: 355–63.

Kogan, N., and F. C. Shelton. "Images of 'Old People' and 'People in General' in an Older Sample." *Journal of Genetic Psychology*, 1962a, 100: 3–21.

―――. "Beliefs about 'Old People': A Comparative Study of Older and Younger Samples." *Journal of Genetic Psychology*, 1962b, 100: 93–111.

Instrument

See Instrument V1.12.IV.a.

CHILDREN'S ATTITUDES TOWARD THE ELDERLY (CATE)
R. K. Jantz, C. Seefeldt, A. Galper, and K. Serock, 1976

Definition of Variable or Concept

The instrument assesses the cognitive, affective, and behavioral components of attitudes toward the elderly.

Description of Instrument

CATE includes four subtests, three of which measure a child's attitudes toward the elderly; the fourth measures a child's understanding of age. (1) Word-association subtest: 5 questions are asked regarding cognitive and affective aspects of old people; open-ended responses are sought. (2) Semantic differential subtest: 10 five-point bipolar scales are used to evaluate two concepts: young people and old people; a total sum score is computed. (3) Picture series subtest: Four 8-by-10-inch drawings of men at four stages of life are shown to the subjects; a series of questions is asked about the set, and the answers are recorded on an interview form. (4) Child's concept of age: 12 questions are asked, to which a yes-no answer is sought, with a follow-up probe (why?).

Responses are tape-recorded, and the examiner codes the responses according to pre-arranged categories. Apparently, the instrument was developed through a number of pre-testing phases.

Method of Administration

The subtests are supposed to take 15 minutes to administer and are given individually to children aged 3 to 11. The copyrighted test manual gives detailed instructions and wordings for questions and provides information on response coding. It appears that the examiner should be familiar with the code categories and develop some experience in using the instrument.

Context of Development and Subsequent Use

The instrument was aimed at children 3 to 11 years old. It was developed with funding from the American Association of Retired Persons and the National Retired Teachers' Association.

Sample

Twenty children were randomly selected from each of nine grades. Preschool (3- to 4-year-olds) came from a university center; students were from two public schools in the Washington, D.C., area. Sex was relatively evenly distributed; about 30% were black; about 40% lived in rural and farm areas.

Scoring, Scale Norms, and Distribution

The copyrighted test manual lists means and standard deviations on the sample for items and scales as coded from the four subtests.

Formal Tests of Reliability/Homogeneity

The manual provides statements regarding the reliability and validity of each part. The word-association subtest was reviewed and revised through consultation with experts in gerontology and measurement. With a sample of 180 3- to 11-year-olds, responses showed a consistency of understanding. Interrater reliability (for two raters) ranged from .80 to .98 on coding for open-ended responses. The subtest should be regarded as experimental until further reliability/validity testing can be accomplished.

For the semantic differential subtest, even though the authors noted the need for reliability and validity studies, they cited earlier work on semantic differential scales with children. Correlations of individual scale items with the sum scale for young people as a rated concept and for old people were given. They ranged from .48 to .67 for young people and from .45 to .70 for the concept of old people. A Cronbach's alpha for the former was .76 and for the latter was .79.

For the testing of the picture series subtest, experts judged the professional drawings of men, and graduate students in gerontology "validated" the drawings. Interrater reliability (for two raters) coding open-ended responses ranged from .72 to .98. The need for further testing was noted by the authors.

An analysis of variance on the scores of 180 children on the concept of age subtest indicated a statistically significant, expected main effect of grade on a child's level of development on the concept of age. An interrater reliability (for two raters) of .997 was noted. Further need for testing was also noted.

Formal Tests of Validity

The authors, apparently after consulting experts in aging and measurement, stated that the responses of children were consistent in every case. The concept of age subtest showed the expected developmental shifts with grade level and a significant and expected association with the conservation scale. The need for further testing was noted.

Usability on Older Populations

The instrument was designed specifically for children 3 to 11 years old, and so it is inappropriate for use with older subjects.

Sensitivity to Age (Including Social Age) Differences

Normative differences by the grade level of the children were apparent.

Scale-Development Statistics

The manual provides some information on individual items for the 180 test subjects in the original sample.

General Comments and Recommendations

The test appears to be in a preliminary state of testing, and further work and replication are needed. It seems to be short and potentially useful for testing children. The response categories and questions are apparently related to various developmental theories.

Reference

Jantz, R. K., C. Seefeldt, A. Galper, and K. Serock. *Test Manual: The CATE: Children's Attitudes toward the Elderly*. Center on Aging, Division of Human and Community Resources, University of Maryland (copyrighted by Jantz and Seefeldt), 1976.

Instrument

This copyrighted instrument is available from the authors of the study.

ADJECTIVE CHECKLIST
B. S. Aaronson, 1966

Definition of Variable or Concept

Normative expectations of what people are like at different ages are assessed.

Description of Instrument

The instrument consists of a checklist of adjectives subjects indicated as descriptive of people aged 5, 15, 25, 35, 45, 55, 65, 75, and 85 years. The adjectives were taken from the Gough Adjective Rating Scale (GARS), which lists 300 words. Eighty-six adjectives were chosen by over half of a small test sample as typical of one of the ages, and these adjectives also had a range of at least 10 from highest to lowest rating frequency (out of a sample of 20). Eight words were eliminated in a test on a second small sample. The final test includes 78 words.

Method of Administration

The respondent completes the checklist individually. No administration specifications were mentioned. Subjects are asked to check those adjectives that, in their opinion, describe the typical person at each decade interval.

Context of Development and Subsequent Use

The checklist was developed as a test of age-category differences in using adjectives.

Sample

Two samples were used and later combined: 20 evening school students, mean age 29.2, age range 18 to 42 years; and 20 similar students aged 17 to 39, mean age 22.0.

Scoring, Scale Norms, and Distribution

The frequency with which each word was checked for each age category was examined. Correlations across word use for the age-category pairs were computed. Separate nonmetric factor analyses of words used more and less frequently than by chance were conducted.

Formal Tests of Validity

The final 78 words used were those that showed some concentration and spread of usage across the age categories.

Scale-Development Statistics

The results of factoring the "less than usual" and "greater than usual" usage matrices are given in Tables 12-25 and 12-26.

TABLE 12-25
Adjectives Loading Significantly on Factors Derived from Matrix
of Words Chosen with Greater than Chance Frequency

Factor 1	Factor 2	Factor 3
Positive Loading:	*Positive Loading:*	*Positive Loading:*
1. active	1. absentminded	1. clearthinking
2. adventurous	2. calm	2. cooperative
3. aggressive	3. conservative	3. dependable
4. attractive	4. practical	4. efficient
5. careless	5. reserved	5. helpful
6. changeable	6. slow	6. logical
7. curious	7. thoughtful	7. mature
8. daring		8. organized
9. dreamy	*Negative Loading:*	9. poised
10. energetic	8. interests wide	10. realistic
11. enthusiastic		11. reliable
12. foolish		12. responsible
13. healthy		13. steady

TABLE 12-25 — *Continued*

Factor 1	Factor 2	Factor 3
Positive Loading:		
14. humorous		
15. imaginative		
16. immature		
17. impatient		
18. loud		
19. mischievous		
20. noisy		
21. pleasureseeking		

SOURCE: B. S. Aaronson. "Personality Stereotypes of Aging." *Journal of Gerontology*, 1966, 21: 459–60. Reprinted by permission of publisher.

TABLE 12-26

Adjectives Loading Significantly on Factors Derived from Matrix
of Words Chosen with Less than Chance Frequency

Factor A	Factor B	Factor C
Positive Loading:	*Positive Loading:*	*Positive Loading:*
1. calm	1. active	1. absentminded
2. capable	2. adaptable	2. careless
3. cautious	3. alert	3. curious
4. clearthinking	4. ambitious	4. foolish
5. confident	5. attractive	5. forgetful
6. conservative	6. energetic	6. immature
7. considerate	7. enthusiastic	7. impatient
8. dependable	8. good-looking	8. mischievous
9. efficient	9. healthy	9. restless
10. forgiving	10. humorous	10. stubborn
11. formal	11. intelligent	11. temperamental
12. logical	12. pleasureseeking	
13. mature	13. progressive	
14. moderate		
15. organized		
16. patient		
17. poised		
18. practical		
19. realistic		
20. reliable		
21. reserved		
22. respectable		
23. self-confident		
24. self-controlled		
25. stable		
26. steady		
27. thorough		
28. thoughtful		
29. understanding		
30. wise		

Table 12-26—*Continued*

Factor A	Factor B	Factor C

Negative Loading:
31. noisy
32. showoff

SOURCE: B. S. Aaronson. "Personality Stereotypes of Aging." *Journal of Gerontology*, 1966, 21: 459–60. Reprinted by permission of publisher.

Factors for more-frequent-than-by-chance words include (1) energetic outgoingness, (2) anergic constriction, and (3) socialized control. Factors for less frequently used words include (1) mature restraint, (2) youthful exuberance, and (3) asocial inefficiency. Each of these factors tends to be associated with characteristic age categories, which suggests the importance of age stereotypes. See Tables 12-27 and 12-28.

TABLE 12-27
Means and Standard Deviations of Choice Frequencies of Word Sets Comprising
Factors Derived from Words Chosen with Greater than by Chance Frequency

Ages	Factor 1		Factor 2		Factor 3	
	Mean	Standard Deviation	Mean	Standard Deviation	Mean	Standard Deviation
5	23.8	7.2	4.2	4.9	3.0	2.7
15	26.2	3.6	5.1	2.6	5.9	4.5
25	17.7	9.0	9.7	6.8	18.0	2.3
35	12.6	9.5	12.9	8.6	25.4	4.0
45	9.5	6.9	16.7	8.8	26.9	3.9
55	6.3	6.2	20.5	9.6	26.9	3.6
65	5.8	5.2	19.7	7.4	18.8	4.4
75	4.1	4.2	23.2	7.1	10.6	4.4
85	4.8	5.1	24.7	7.4	6.1	3.1

SOURCE: B. S. Aaronson. "Personality Stereotypes of Aging." *Journal of Gerontology*, 1966, 21: 459–60. Reprinted by permission of publisher.

TABLE 12-28
Means and Standard Deviations of Choice Frequencies of Word Sets
Comprising Factors Derived from Words Chosen with Less than Chance Frequency

Ages	Factor A		Factor B		Factor C	
	Mean	Standard Deviation	Mean	Standard Deviation	Mean	Standard Deviation
5	3.1	3.1	18.2	9.8	19.8	8.6
15	5.6	4.2	23.9	5.7	22.4	6.3
25	18.3	6.9	27.5	4.4	8.4	5.0
35	23.3	7.2	23.8	5.1	5.4	4.6
45	25.4	5.4	18.6	5.6	4.7	2.1
55	26.2	5.2	14.2	5.1	5.7	3.8
65	20.8	6.8	9.5	4.9	10.4	7.0
75	14.8	8.3	3.4	2.4	12.4	9.9
85	12.3	9.5	2.4	2.1	15.4	10.0

SOURCE: B. S. Aaronson. "Personality Stereotypes of Aging." *Journal of Gerontology*, 1966, 21: 459–60. Reprinted by permission of publisher.

General Comments and Recommendations

Although there are important validity and reliability questions to be addressed, this approach to the analysis of perceptions of aging warrants further exploration.

Reference

Aaronson, B. S. "Personality Stereotypes of Aging." *Journal of Gerontology*, 1966, 21: 458–62.

Instrument

See Tables 12-25 and 12-26 above.

CHILDREN'S PERCEPTIONS OF THE ELDERLY
T. Hickey, L. A. Hickey, and R. A. Kalish, 1968

Definition of Variable or Concept

The instrument assesses children's perceptions of the elderly, and reactions toward the elderly.

Description of Instrument

In the original study, students were asked to write papers about an "old person." The teacher mentioned grandparents as examples of old persons but said nothing more. The papers were collected when the class seemed to be finished. There were no time limits.

Method of Administration

The instrument can be administered to a class as an open-ended writing assignment.

Context of Development and Subsequent Use

The instrument was developed to study children's perceptions of the elderly.

Sample

The sample consisted of 208 third-graders from four different schools in the Los Angeles area, including 77 from an upper-class public school, 41 from an upper-class Catholic school, 43 from a lower-class public school, and 47 from a lower-class Catholic school. Half of the children in the lower-class schools were Americans of Mexican ancestry. All the others were Caucasians of European ancestry.

Scoring, Scale Norms, and Distribution

Each paper consisted of two or three sentences describing an old person. Two of the authors coded the responses by hand into two major categories—physical characteristics: (1) ambulatory differences, (2) visual and auditory differences, (3) hair and beard differences, (4) skin deterioration, and (5) general feebleness; and social characteristics: (1) kindness, (2) meanness, (3) poverty, (4) loneliness, (5) leisure time, and (6) eccentricity and/or senility.

Formal Tests of Reliability / Homogeneity

The authors noted that the two coders were in close agreement, but no magnitude of association was reported.

General Comments and Recommendations

This approach may hold promise for further development.

Reference

Hickey, T., L. A. Hickey, and R. A. Kalish. "Children's Perceptions of the Elderly." *Journal of Genetic Psychology*, 1968, 112: 227–35.

Instrument

See the description of the instrument above.

Instruments

V1.12.I.a
ATTITUDES TOWARD OLD PEOPLE
J. Tuckman and I. Lorge, 1953

The original 137 Attitude Toward Old People items are given below, including the categories of meaning that each item is intended to reflect (Tuckman and Lorge, 1953a). This listing also indicates items used in shorter assessments.

a) Tuckman and Lorge (1952a) used a set of 30 items from the original 137 (plus 10 more from the related Attitudes Toward Old Workers scale). Twenty of these were selected because they showed before-class age or sex differences and another 20 were selected at random from various sub-categories.

b) Tuckman and Lorge (1958b) used a subset of 40 of the 137 items (plus 10 from the Older Worker scale) in an assessment of professionals who worked with the elderly.

c) Axelrod and Eisdorfer (1961) identified a subset of 96 items which showed differences between rated target groups of different ages. In later work, Eisdorfer (1966) used a set of 88 of these 96 but concluded that the larger set of 137 should be used since the subset seemed to behave differently when used alone, compared to its use within the context of the 137 items.

Original Tuckman-Lorge (1952a) Statements, by Category

T-La = Retained in Tuckman and Lorge (1953a)
T-Lb = Retained in Tuckman and Lorge (1958b)
A-E = Retained in Axelrod and Eisdorfer (1961)

Category	Statement
Conservatism	15. They are set in their ways. A-E
	28. They are old fashioned. T-Lb, A-E
	42. They are conservative. T-La
	45. They are out of step with the times. T-La, A-E
	46. They like old songs on the radio.
	66. They respect tradition. A-E
	73. They hold on to their opinions. A-E
	83. They object to women smoking in public. T-La, A-E
	86. They like to think about the good old days. A-E
	94. They prefer old friends rather than make new ones. T-La, T-Lb, A-E
	97. They would like to live their lives over again.
	106. They are critical of the younger generation. A-E
	108. They dislike any changes or interference with established ways of doing things. T-Lb, A-E
	130. They feel that young parents do not know how to bring up children properly. A-E

Category	Statement
Activities and Interests	18. They vote for the political candidate who promises largest old age pensions.
	26. They are more interested in religion. T-La, A-E
	65. They like religious programs on the radio. T-La, T-Lb, A-E
	79. They collect many useless things like string, paper and old shoes. T-La, A-E
Best Time of Life	4. They are in the happiest period of their lives. T-La
	59. They would like to be young again. T-Lb, A-E
	62. They never had it better. T-La, T-Lb
	95. They love life. T-Lb
	137. They have a chance to do all the things they wanted to.
Mental Deterioration	2. They are absent minded. T-La, A-E
	7. They repeat themselves in conversation. T-Lb, A-E
	8. They cannot learn new things. T-Lb
	21. They are better off in old age homes. T-Lb, A-E
	24. They are forgetful. A-E
	32. They just like to sit and dream. A-E
	58. They cannot manage their own affairs. T-Lb, A-E
	77. They cannot remember names. T-La, A-E
	85. They like to doze in a rocking chair. T-La, A-E
	89. They are in their second childhood. T-La, A-E
	121. They cannot concentrate, even on simple tasks. T-Lb
	127. They become less intelligent. A-E
	128. They frequently talk to themsleves. T-La, A-E
	136. They are not useful to themselves or others.
Insecurity	10. They get upset easily. A-E
	11. They prefer to live alone.
	12. They prefer to be alone. T-Lb
	20. They worry about unimportant things. A-E
	25. They are easily moved to tears. T-Lb, A-E
	30. They feel sorry for themselves. T-Lb, A-E
	38. They become insane.
	52. They like to be helped across the street. A-E
	55. They are suspicious of others.
	57. They worry about their health. A-E
	74. They are afraid of the dark. T-Lb, A-E
	75. They like to be waited on. T-Lb, A-E
	78. They are lonely. A-E
	88. They are bad patients when ill. T-Lb, A-E
	92. They are fussy about food. A-E
	102. They frequently are at loose ends. T-La, A-E
	125. They feel miserable most of the time. A-E
	133. They are helpless. A-E
	134. They are insecure. A-E
	135. They have a high suicide rate.
	49. They cannot taste differences in food.
Voice	93. Their voices break. A-E

Category		Statement
Fatigue	16.	They need less sleep than younger people. T-La
	22.	They have to go to bed early. A-E
	31.	They need a nap every day. A-E
	87.	They feel tired most of the time. T-Lb, A-E
Illness and Accidents	27.	They have many accidents in the home. A-E
	40.	They never fully recover if they break any bone. A-E
	76.	They spend much time in bed because of illness. T-Lb, A-E
	103.	They develop infection easily. T-La, A-E
	122.	They have a high automobile accident rate. A-E
	131.	They die after a major operation. T-La, A-E
Sex	71.	They should not marry. T-Lb, A-E
	104.	They should not become parents. A-E
	112.	They marry persons much younger than themselves.
	120.	They have no interest in the opposite sex. T-Lb, A-E
Interference	111.	They are in the way. A-E
	117.	They meddle in other people's affairs. T-Lb, A-E
	132.	They are a nuisance to others. T-Lb, A-E
Cleanliness	39.	They never take a bath.
	100.	They are untidy and careless about their appearance.
	126.	They are careless about their table manners. T-Lb, A-E
Personality	6.	They are kind.
	19.	They are grouchy. T-Lb, A-E
	33.	They are calm.
	34.	They are hard to get along with. T-Lb, A-E
	43.	They are very talkative. A-E
	47.	They are stubborn. A-E
	53.	They like to give advice. T-La
	54.	They make friends easily.
	60.	They are touchy. T-Lb, A-E
	61.	They have few friends. A-E
	69.	They are selfish. T-Lb, A-E
	114.	They are cranky. A-E
	118.	They are bossy. A-E
	124.	They like to gossip. T-Lb, A-E
Attitude toward Future	37.	They think the world is headed for destruction. T-La, A-E
	50.	They believe in a life after death. T-Lb
	56.	They think the future is hopeless. A-E
	91.	They are afraid of death. T-Lb
	113.	They are anxious about the future.
	82.	They like to play checkers or dominoes. T-La, A-E
	96.	They spend most of their time reading or listening to the radio. T-Lb, A-E
	101.	They take a keen interest in politics.
	119.	They prefer to read newspapers rather than books.
	129.	They do not take part in sports. A-E

Category	Statement
Financial	36. They are unproductive. T-Lb, A-E
	51. They have too much power in business and politics. T-La
	84. They hide their money. A-E
	105. They worry about financial security.
	107. They are tight in money matters. A-E
	109. They are usually supported by their children or old age pensions. T-La, A-E
Family	5. They spoil their grandchildren. A-E
	14. They are proud of their children. T-La
	17. They are not important in family affairs. T-La, A-E
	23. They expect their children to support them. T-Lb, A-E
	29. They are a burden to their children. T-La, T-Lb, A-E
	41. They usually live with their children.
	63. They are good to children.
	68. They feel that their children have failed them.
	70. They frequently quarrel with their children and relatives.
	81. They get no sympathy from their relatives.
	90. They feel that their children neglect them. A-E
	116. They expect obedience and respect from their children and grandchildren.
	123. They get love and affection from their children. T-La
Physical Coordination	67. They walk slowly. T-La, A-E
	80. They have poor coordination. T-Lb, A-E
Homeostatis	35. They feel cold even in warm weather. T-La, A-E
	99. They avoid going out in bad weather. A-E
Digestion	3. They need less food than younger people.
	9. They are poor eaters. A-E
	13. They have to be careful of their diet. A-E
	64. They have lost most of their teeth. A-E
	72. They suffer from constipation. A-E
Discomfort	110. They are very sensitive to noise. A-E
	115. They suffer much discomfort. A-E
Death	48. They die soon after retirement. T-La
	98. They die of cancer or heart disease. A-E
Sensory	1. Old people need glasses to read. T-Lb, A-E
	44. They are hard of hearing. T-Lb, A-E

SOURCE: J. Tuckman and I. Lorge. "The Attitudes of the Aged toward the Older Worker: For Institutionalized and Non-institutionalized Adults." *Journal of Gerontology*, 1952, 7: 559–64. Reprinted by permission of publisher.

V1.12.I.b
FACTS ON AGING
E. Palmore, 1977

T   F   1. The majority of old people (past age 65) are senile (i.e., deficient in memory, disoriented, or demented).

T   F   2. All five senses tend to decline in old age.

T	F	3.	Most old people have no interest in, or capacity for, sexual relations.
T	F	4.	Lung capacity tends to decline in old age.
T	F	5.	The majority of old people feel miserable most of the time.
T	F	6.	Physical strength tends to decline in old age.
T	F	7.	At least one-tenth of the aged are living in long-stay institutions (i.e., nursing homes, mental hospitals, homes for the aged, etc.).
T	F	8.	Aged drivers have fewer accidents per person than drivers under age 65.
T	F	9.	Most older workers cannot work as effectively as younger workers.
T	F	10.	About eighty percent of the aged are healthy enough to carry out their normal activities.
T	F	11.	Most old people are set in their ways and unable to change.
T	F	12.	Old people usually take longer to learn something new.
T	F	13.	It is almost impossible for most old people to learn new things.
T	F	14.	The reaction time of most old people tends to be slower than reaction time of younger people.
T	F	15.	In general, most old people are pretty much alike.
T	F	16.	The majority of old people are seldom bored.
T	F	17.	The majority of old people are socially isolated and lonely.
T	F	18.	Older workers have fewer accidents than younger workers.
T	F	19.	Over 15 percent of the U.S. population are now age 65 or over.
T	F	20.	Most medical practitioners tend to give lower priority to the aged.
T	F	21.	The majority of older people have incomes below the poverty level (as defined by the Federal Government).
T	F	22.	The majority of old people are working or would like to have some kind of work to do (including housework and volunteer work).
T	F	23.	Older people tend to become more religious as they age.
T	F	24.	The majority of old people are seldom irritated or angry.
T	F	25.	The health and socioeconomic status of older people (compared to younger people) in the year 2000 will probably be about the same as now.

SOURCE: E. Palmore. "Facts on Aging: A Short Quiz." *The Gerontologist*, 1977, 17: 315–20. Reprinted by permission of author and publisher.

V1.12.II.a
KOGAN ATTITUDE TOWARD OLD PEOPLE SCALE
N. Kogan, 1961

See the scale development statistics in the abstract.

V1.12.II.b
OPINIONS ABOUT PEOPLE
Ontario Welfare Council, Section on Aging, 1971

1. Some people stay young at heart no matter how long they live.
*2. Things are getting better for most people these days.
3. You have to be old yourself to enjoy the stories old people like to tell.
4. Residences for retired persons should always work out their programs and routines with the old people concerned.
*5. The best neighbourhoods are those where young families intermingle with retired people.
*6. You can't expect other people to take care of you when you no longer can take care of yourself.

*7. No one who is retired and over 70 should be allowed to drive a car.

*8. The older people get, the more they think only of themselves.

*9. You're further ahead if you always assume that everybody is out for Number One.

*10. Most times I feel relaxed in the company of elderly people.

11. Old age is O.K. for those who are financially independent.

*12. There is no point in talking about personal matters with people who are much older or much younger than yourself.

*13. You can't cope with things the way you used to if you live to be a ripe old age.

*14. Retired people are happiest in the company of people who are their own age.

*15. Anyone could keep young if he only tried.

16. People in high offices aren't really interested in the troubles of the average person.

*17. You're likely to get bogged down if you let elderly people help you with your projects.

18. No matter what the community can do it is up to the children to see that their aging parents have every comfort.

*19. I cannot help feeling depressed at the thought of getting old.

*20. You can't expect old people to exert themselves.

*21. On the whole, people's chances in life are getting worse and not better.

*22. When you retire you realize that the best years of life are yet to come.

*23. You'll never get old if you don't let yourself go.

*24. It is rather sad to be still alive after all your friends are gone.

*25. Old age pensioners have a right to be taken care of in a dignified way even if younger people must contribute their taxes to make this possible.

26. By and large, young people don't care about anyone but themselves.

*27. The future is so uncertain that there is little point in thinking or planning ahead.

*28. People who spend all they make cannot expect much when they are no longer earning a living.

*29. All community organizations should have some older persons on their boards.

*30. It must be quite a shock to look in the mirror and find that you are showing signs of aging.

31. One shouldn't try to involve elderly people in things; all they really want is some peace and comfort.

32. Relatives who were close to the parents in former years rightly expect the children to care about their well being if they live a very long life.

SOURCE: Ontario Welfare Council, Section on Aging. *Opinions about People, Form A: Guidelines and Manual* (for an instrument dealing with attitudes toward aging and the aged, for use in educational and training programs in the field of aging). Toronto, Ontario: January 1971. Reprinted by permission.

V1.12.II.c

ATTITUDES TOWARD AGING

K. M. Kilty and A. Feld, 1976

Table 1 — Principal Components Analysis of 45 Social-Psychological Opinion Items

Variables	Varimax Rotated Factor Matrix				
	I	II	III	IV	h^2
1. Most older people are capable of new adjustments when the situation demands it. (K)	−26	−08	34	02	19
2. Older people have a chance to do all the things they wanted to do. (TLO)	27	−14	30	−09	19

Table 1 — *Continued*

Variables	Varimax Rotated Factor Matrix				
	I	II	III	IV	h^2
3. It is sad for children to have to grow up in this world the way things look for the future. (S)	07	72	12	06	54
4. Old people frequently talk to themselves. (TLO)	24	00	06	55	37
5. Older workers are suspicious of other workers. (TLW)	15	08	−17	44	25
6. The future looks bright for today's children. (S)	07	71	12	−05	53
7. Older people are generally stuck in their homes. (N)	16	32	01	28	21
8. It is useless to write public officials because your problems to not interest them. (S)	07	54	01	19	34
9. It would probably be better if most old people lived in residential units with people their own age. (K)	40	13	−01	13	20
10. One of the most interesting qualities of elderly people is their accounts of their past experiences. (K)	−27	02	12	38	24
11. Older workers are interested only in putting in their hours. (TLW)	62	07	−11	04	40
12. The government will see to it that the people of this country have a better life. (S)	40	−37	41	04	47
13. Elderly persons generally take a keen interest in politics. (TLO)	02	−12	48	12	26
14. Older people love life. (TLO)	−10	−10	60	−04	38
15. Older people prefer to read newspapers rather than books. (TLO)	05	01	24	21	10
16. People grow wise with the coming of old age. (K)	−17	05	45	19	27
17. The government should take care of elderly persons. (N)	04	24	08	18	10
18. Older persons fail in emergencies. (TLW)	60	17	−02	16	42
19. Older people are lonely. (TLO)	04	18	−02	47	25
20. You can always find something ahead of you to make life worth living. (S)	−08	−31	28	04	18
21. Older people feel that their children neglect them. (TLO)	01	18	−05	62	42
22. Old people hold on to their opinions. (TLO)	08	−07	08	46	23
23. These days a person doesn't know whom he or she can count on. (S)	09	56	16	25	41
24. You can count on finding a nice residential neighborhood when there is a sizeable number of old people living in it. (K)	01	18	57	07	37
25. Older people worry about financial security. (TLO)	−24	13	13	48	33

Table 1 — *Continued*

		Varimax Rotated Factor Matrix				
	Variables	I	II	III	IV	h²
26.	Older persons are good with children. (TLO)	−16	−01	42	04	21
27.	In spite of what people say, the life of the average person is getting worse. (S)	07	77	−05	08	60
28.	Most old people should be more concerned with their personal appearance; they're too untidy. (K)	44	11	15	−06	23 ·
29.	Most old people are very relaxing to be with. (K)	−17	09	50	04	29
30.	Old people are usually supported by their children or old-age pensions. (TLO)	14	02	06	27	10
31.	You can trust most old people. (S)	03	−33	28	−07	20
32.	Older workers take jobs away from younger workers. (TLW)	64	04	−02	−07	42
33.	Older workers make friends easily. (TLO)	06	25	40	−09	23
34.	Older workers keep younger people from getting ahead. (TLW)	63	03	−12	04	42
35.	It is useless to plan for tomorrow; all we can do is live for the present. (S)	36	47	06	−12	37
36.	Older people look forward to the future as much as any other people. (N)	−06	−15	50	04	28
37.	Older people have too much power in business and politics. (K)	52	11	−03	14	30
38.	The lives of most people will be better in the next few years. (S)	22	−67	30	−02	59
39.	Old people should not be allowed to have driver's licenses. (N)	40	−05	−13	25	24
40.	Older workers cannot take criticism without getting angry. (TLW)	51	04	−08	28	35
41.	Most older people try not to be a financial burden to their children. (N)	−22	−05	44	22	29
42.	Elderly people walk slowly. (TLO)	24	03	19	44	29
43.	Old people expect their children to support them. (TLO)	52	−04	−19	11	32
44.	Older workers increase costs of pensions for employers. (TLW)	45	−21	−07	17	28
45.	Older persons prefer to live alone. (TLO)	09	09	22	22	11
46.	Sex.	10	00	00	−07	01
47.	Age.	−13	−12	−42	29	29
48.	Years of education.	09	32	25	−10	18
49.	Income.	12	22	28	−25	20
50.	Response Set.	−52	−16	−52	−52	83
	% total variance.	8.8	8.0	7.5	6.2	30.5

NOTE: TLO = Tuckman-Lorge Old People scale; TLW = Tuckman-Lorge Older Workers scale; K = Kogan Old People scale; S = Srole Alienation scale; and N = New item. Decimals have been omitted.

Needs and Concern Scales
Table 2 — Factor 1: General Entitlements for the Older Person

Item	Younger Group (N=290)	Loading Older Group (N=181)	Combined Groups (N=471)
1. Moderate income housing should be open to who needs it without regard to age.	.44	.51	.43
2. The needs of older people are special and should be taken care of separately from the needs of other groups of citizens.	.33	.48	.44
4. Every person over the age of 40 should have a yearly medical check-up regardless of ability to pay.	.46	.52	.47
9. Property tax should be discontinued for persons over 65.	.35	.42	.46
10. There is no need for a public transportation system in this area.	−.42	−.13	−.26
16. Special community and professional groups must advocate for the needs of the elderly.	.46	.14	.33
18. In order that the nutritional needs of older people be met, congregate feeding locations should be established and transportation provided without cost for those who need it.	.53	.34	.41
21. The needs of elderly people should be taken care of by the Department of Public Welfare.	.52	.58	.57
23. In some areas of the state, public transportation programs provide free rides for older persons during certain hours of the day; this sort of program should also be made available in this area.	.62	.59	.63
24. Anyone over 60 should be entitled to a yearly medical check-up without cost.	.33	.53	.55
25. People who work with families where there has been a recent death need special training.	.48	.15	.30
26. The government should provide for the needs of the elderly.	.50	.75	.66
29. This country needs a comprehensive health plan for everyone, regardless of age.	.53	.55	.59
30. A new, cabinet-level office should be set up and given the responsibility of coordinating and developing services for the elderly.	.53	.52	.59
31. Public utilities costs for older persons should be reduced and made proportionate to ability to pay.	.48	.59	.55
32. A program providing group meals for elderly individuals would give them a useful social outlet.	.48	.16	.30

Table 2 — *Continued*

Item	Loading Younger Group (N=290)	Older Group (N=181)	Combined Groups (N=471)
33. Even if it meant an increase in taxes, this area should be provided with a public transportation program for the elderly.	.73	.37	.56
40. Response set.	−.62	−.76	−.69

Table 3 — Factor II: Societal Rejection of Older People

Item	Loading Younger Group (N=290)	Older Group (N=181)	Combined Groups (N=471)
3. Public transportation programs should be supported by those who use them regardless of age.	.46	.16	.44
7. Older persons should be housed separately from the rest of the community.	.49	.22	.37
8. The elderly are able to organize and lobby for themselves to get what they need and do not need this to be done for them.	.50	.28	.44
10. There is no need for a public transportation system in this area.	.40	.59	.47
11. An older person who cannot take care of himself or herself should be placed in a state-run home.	.51	.47	.49
12. People over 65 have diets as well-balanced as the rest of the community.	.53	.41	.53
17. Since schools are of benefit to the whole community, all residents — regardless of age — should contribute to the costs of education.	.40	.17	.36
18. In order that the nutritional needs of older people be met, congregate feeding locations should be established and transportation provided without cost for those who need it.	.09	−.41	−.03
19. Enough money is being spent in rural areas for services for the elderly in comparison to the money that is being spent in other areas.	.12	.57	.41
23. In some areas of the state, public transportation programs provide free rides for older persons during certain hours of the day; this sort of program should also be made available in this area.	−.28	−.44	−.30
32. A program providing group meals for elderly individuals would give them a useful social outlet.	.04	−.46	−.11

Table 3 — *Continued*

Item	Younger Group (N=290)	Loading Older Group (N=181)	Combined Groups (N=471)
33. Even if it meant an increase in taxes, this area should be provided with a public transportation program for the elderly.	−.12	−.56	−.29
35. The older person gets a fair break in benefits from our society.	.52	.35	.56
40. Response set.	−.47	.01	−.38

Table 4 — Factor III: Entitlement to Remaining in the Community

Item	Younger Group (N=290)	Loading Older Group (N=181)	Combined Groups (N=471)
6. It costs more money in rural than in urban areas to provide the same amount of services.	.32	.32	.41
12. People over 65 have diets as well-balanced as the rest of the community.	−.31	−.10	−.12
14. Nursing homes become dumping grounds for people who are no longer considered useful.	.62	.63	.56
15. There is just something about an apartment that makes it less comfortable to live in than a house.	.31	.46	.19
16. Special community and professional groups must advocate for the needs of the elderly.	.18	.54	.28
20. Programs should be developed which allow older people to continue living at home rather than in a nursing home.	.66	.19	.63
25. People who work with families where there has been a recent death need special training.	−.11	.46	.13
26. The government should provide for the needs of the elderly.	.31	.01	.10
27. Property taxes should be phased out over time and replaced by a progressive income tax.	.00	.58	.05
28. Nursing homes should be used as a last resort.	.45	.51	.45
30. A new, cabinet-level office should be set up and given the responsibility of coordinating and developing services for the elderly.	.31	.05	.12
34. Many people are in nursing homes who — with a little help — could be living on their own.	.58	.04	.45
37. Age.	−.06	−.23	−.41
40. Response set.	−.46	−.40	−.41

Table 5 — Factor IV: Reciprocity Between the Elderly and the Community

Item	Younger Group (N=290)	Loading Older Group (N=181)	Combined Groups (N=471)
3. Public transportation programs should be supported by those who use them, regardless of age.	−.23	−.39	−.22
5. For elderly persons who are unable to cook their own food, meals should be provided and delivered to their homes, with the older person determining the amount he can pay.	.12	−.45	−.12
9. Property tax should be discontinued for persons over 65.	.47	.56	.42
13. Special training programs are needed for people who work with older persons.	−.30	−.39	−.32
17. Since schools are of benefit to the whole community, all residents — regardless of age — should contribute to the costs of education.	−.46	−.55	.48
18. In order that the nutritional needs of older people be met, congregate feeding locations should be established and transportation provided without cost for those who need it.	.10	−.35	−.03
24. Anyone over the age of 60 should be entitled to a yearly medical check-up without cost.	.49	.36	.30
26. The government should provide for the needs of the elderly.	.35	.11	.22
35. The older person gets a fair break in benefits from our society.	−.10	−.56	−.10
37. Age.	−.13	.24	−.33
38. Years of education.	.58	.35	.59
39. Income.	.53	.06	.54

SOURCE: K. M. Kilty and A. Feld. "Attitudes toward Aging and toward the Needs of Older People." *Journal of Gerontology*, 1976, 31: 586-94. Reprinted by permission of author and publisher.

V1.12.II.d
PERCEPTIONS OF OLD AGE
E. G. Youmans, 1971

1. Old Age Worries
   Older people worry more about finances than do younger persons.
   Older people worry more about their children and relatives than do younger persons.
   Older people worry more about world problems than do younger persons.
2. Old Age Work Problems
   Old people who work at a job generally have trouble getting along with young workers.
   Old people who work at a job should step aside and let young people get jobs.
   Old people who work at a job make more mistakes than young workers.
3. Old Age Positive
   Most old people are cheerful, agreeable, and good-humored.

Most people grow wiser with the coming of old age.
Most old people can learn things quite easily.
4. Old Age Segregation
Places should be set up especially for old people to hold meetings.
Special classes should be set up for old people where they can get more schooling.
It would be best for all concerned if old people lived in old-age homes.
5. Old Age Organize Politically
More old people should run for political office.
Old people should organize to obtain more money from the government.
Old people should form a political party to take care of their interests.
6. Old Age Negative
Most old people are bossy and grouchy.
Most old people are lonely.
Most old people are miserable most of the time.
7. Retirement Positive
Generally speaking, retirement is good for an old person.
Retirement is a time in life when a person can do all the things he wants to do.
Most people look forward to the time when they can stop working and retire.

SOURCE: E. G. Youmans. "Generation and Perceptions of Old Age: An Urban-Rural Comparison." *The Gerontologist*, 1971, 11 (4, part 1): 284-88. Reprinted by permission of author and publisher.

V1.12.II.e
NEGATIVE ATTRIBUTES OF OLD AGE AND
POSITIVE POTENTIAL IN OLD AGE
L. A. Morgan and V. L. Bengtson, 1976

Note that these are the original 14 items.
The two derived scales are:
N = Negative Attributes of Old Age
P = Positive Potential in Old Age

ATTRIBUTES CHARACTERIZING THE AGED OR ELDERLY*

N　1. Most older people are set in their ways and unable to change.
　　2. Most older people are *not* isolated.
N　3. Older persons are apt to complain.
P　4. Older people can learn new things just as well as younger people can.
　　5. People become wiser with the coming of old age.
N　6. Older people are often against needed reform in our society because they want to hang on to the past.
　　7. Most older people (in this country) are in good health.
N　8. Most older people spend too much time prying into the affairs of others.

FUNCTIONS OR COMPETENCE OF THE AGED*

P　9. In most jobs, older people can perform as well as younger people.
　　10. Elderly people are often treated more like children than like adults who can make their own decisions.
　　11. Many older people cannot find a job even though they want to work.
P　12. Most older people can do a job as well as younger persons but they are just not given a chance to show what they can do.
　　13. Older people are valuable because of their experiences.
　　14. Older people are not very useful to themselves or others.

*Response alternatives: "Agree" or "Disagree." "Depends" or "Neither Agree nor Disagree" when volunteered by respondents was coded in an intermediate category, while "don't know" or "no opinion" responses were omitted from analysis. As indicated, items were recoded in this analysis to reflect negative orientations.

SOURCE: L. A. Morgan and V. L. Bengtson. "Measuring Perceptions of Aging across Social Strata." Paper presented to the 29th Annual Meeting of the American Gerontological Society, New York, October 13–17, 1976. Reprinted by permission of authors.

V1.12.II.f
IMAGES OF OLDER PEOPLE BATTERY
National Council on the Aging, 1975

1a. If you had to choose, what would you say are the best years of a person's life—his teens, 20's, 30's, 40's, 50's, 60's 70's or when?

Teens. . . . .———
20's. . . . .———
30's. . . . .———
40's. . . . .———
50's. . . . .———
60's. . . . .———
70's. . . . .———
other (specify)

————————— . . . . . .———
Wouldn't choose any age (vol.)
Not sure . . . .———

1b. Why do you feel that way? Any other reasons?

1c. And what would you say are the worst years of a person's life—his teens, 20's, 30's 40's, 50's, 60's, 70's, or when?

Teens. . . . .———
20's. . . . .———
30's. . . . .———
40's. . . . .———
50's. . .' . . . .———
60's. . . . .———
70's. . . . .———
other (specify)

————————— . . . . . .———
Wouldn't choose any age (vol.)
Not sure . . . .———

1d. Why do you feel that way? Any other reasons?

2a. At what age do you think the average man becomes old? Just think about men, not women.

Under 40 years . . . .———
40 to 44 years. . . . .———
45 to 49 years. . . . .———
50 to 54 years. . . . .———
55 to 59 years. . . . .——— (ASK 2b)
60 to 64 years. . . . .———
65 to 69 years. . . . .———
70 to 74 years. . . . .———
75 to 79 years. . . . .———

80 to 84 years . . . . _____

85 to 89 years . . . . _____   (ASK 2b)

90 years or older . . . . _____

Never . . . . _____

It depends . . . . _____

When he stops working . . . . _____

When his health fails . . . . _____   (SKIP TO 2c)

Other (specify) _____ . . . . _____

Not sure . . . . _____

2b. (IF GIVEN DEFINITE AGE IN 2a) Why do you think a man becomes old at (AGE GIVEN)? Any other reason?

2c. (ASK EVERYONE) At what age do you think the average woman becomes old?

Under 40 years . . . . _____

40 to 44 years . . . . _____

45 to 49 years . . . . _____

50 to 54 years . . . . _____

55 to 59 years . . . . _____

60 to 64 years . . . . _____   (ASK 2d)

65 to 69 years . . . . _____

70 to 74 years . . . . _____

75 to 79 years . . . . _____

80 to 84 years . . . . _____

85 to 89 years . . . . _____

90 years or older . . . . _____

Never . . . . _____

It depends . . . . _____

When she stops working . . . . _____

When her health fails . . . . _____

When she can't have babies
anymore; menopause . . . . _____   (SKIP TO 2e)

Other (specify) _____ . . . . _____

Not sure . . . . _____

2d. (IF GIVEN DEFINITE AGE IN 2c) Why do you think a woman becomes old at (AGE GIVEN)? Any other reason?

2e. (ASK EVERYONE) In your opinion, what percentage of the total United States population is 65 years of age or over?

1 to 2% . . . . _____

3 to 4% . . . . _____

5 to 7% . . . . _____

8 to 11% . . . . _____

12 to 14% . . . . _____

15 to 19% . . . . _____

20 to 24% . . . . _____

25 to 29% . . . . _____

30 to 39% . . . . _____

40 to 49% . . . . _____

50% or more . . . . _____

Not sure . . . . _____

2f. Let me read you some statements about people over 65 today compared with ten or twenty years ago. For each statement, please tell me if you tend to agree or disagree. (READ STATEMENTS AND RECORD BELOW FOR EACH.)

	Agree	Disagree	Not Sure
1. Older people make up a smaller part of the population today than they did then.	____	____	____
2. People live longer today than they did then.	____	____	____
3. Older people today are generally better educated than older people were then.	____	____	____
4. Older people today are worse off financially than older people were then.	____	____	____
5. Older people today are healthier than older people were then.	____	____	____
6. There are more older people living alone today than there were then.	____	____	____

3a. In general, what do you feel are the best things about being over 65 years of age? Anything else?

3b. And what do you feel are the worst things about being over 65 years of age? Anything else?

4a. I'm going to read to you some phrases used to describe people. For each tell me how much like that you feel most people over 65 years of age you know or have seen are. Let's start with being (READ FIRST ITEM ON LIST)—would you say most people over 65 are very (READ ITEM), somewhat or hardly at all? (RECORD BELOW AND CONTINUE WITH LIST.)

4a. Now, I'd like to ask you about other people over 65 whom you know or have seen. For the moment, don't think about yourself; just think about most people over 65. Would you say most people over 65 years of age are very (READ LIST), somewhat (REPEAT ITEM) or hardly (REPEAT ITEM) at all; (RECORD BELOW FOR EACH ITEM ON LIST.)

4b. Now, what about you personally—would you say you are very (READ LIST), somewhat or hardly at all? (RECORD BELOW AND CONTINUE WITH LIST.)

	4a. Most people over 65			
	Very	Some-what	Hardly at All	Not Sure
1. Friendly and warm	____	____	____	____
2. Physically active.	____	____	____	____
3. Bright and alert	____	____	____	____
4. Good at getting things done	____	____	____	____
5. Open-minded and adaptable	____	____	____	____
6. Sexually active	____	____	____	____
7. Wise from experience	____	____	____	____

	4b. You personally			
	Very	Some-what	Hardly at All	Not Sure
1. Friendly and warm	____	____	____	____
2. Physically active.	____	____	____	____
3. Bright and alert	____	____	____	____
4. Good at getting things done	____	____	____	____
5. Open-minded and adaptable	____	____	____	____
6. Sexually active	____	____	____	____
7. Wise from experience	____	____	____	____

5a. Now I'm going to read you some things that other people have said they do with their time. For each, would you tell me whether you personally spend a lot of time, some but not a lot, or hardly any time at all doing that. (READ LIST AND RECORD BELOW FOR EACH ITEM.)

5b. And how much time do you think most people over 65 spend (READ LIST)—a lot of time, some but not a lot, or hardly any time at all? (RECORD BELOW FOR EACH ITEM ON LIST.)

| | *5a. You personally* | | | |
	A Lot	Some But not a Lot	Hardly Any at All	Not Sure
1. Participating in recreational activites and hobbies	____	____	____	____
2. Participating in fraternal or community organizations or clubs	____	____	____	____
3. Socializing with friends.	____	____	____	____
4. Sitting and thinking.	____	____	____	____
5. Caring for younger or older members of the family	____	____	____	____
6. Participating in political activities.	____	____	____	____
7. Sleeping	____	____	____	____
8. Watching television	____	____	____	____
9. Working part-time or full-time.	____	____	____	____
10. Doing volunteer work	____	____	____	____
11. Participating in sports, like golf, tennis or swimming	____	____	____	____
12. Just doing nothing	____	____	____	____
13. Reading	____	____	____	____
14. Going for walks	____	____	____	____
15. Gardening or raising plants.	____	____	____	____

| | *5b. Most people over 65* | | | |
	A Lot	Some But not a Lot	Hardly Any at All	Not Sure
1. Participating in recreational activities and hobbies	____	____	____	____
2. Participating in fraternal or community organizations or clubs	____	____	____	____
3. Socializing with friends.	____	____	____	____
4. Sitting and thinking.	____	____	____	____
5. Caring for younger or older members of the family	____	____	____	____
6. Participating in political activities.	____	____	____	____
7. Sleeping	____	____	____	____
8. Watching television	____	____	____	____
9. Working part-time or full-time.	____	____	____	____
10. Doing volunteer work	____	____	____	____
11. Participating in sports, like golf, tennis or swimming	____	____	____	____
12. Just doing nothing	____	____	____	____

	5b. Most people over 65			
	A Lot	Some But not a Lot	Hardly Any at All	Not Sure
13. Reading	___	___	___	___
14. Going for walks	___	___	___	___
15. Gardening or raising plants.	___	___	___	___

6a. Now I'm going to read you some problems that other people have mentioned to us. For each, would you tell me whether it is a very serious problem, a somewhat serious problem, or hardly a problem at all for you personally. (READ LIST AND RECORD BELOW FOR EACH ITEM.)

6b. And how serious a problem would you say (READ LIST) is for most people over 65 these days—a very serious problem, a somewhat serious problem, or hardly a problem at all for most people over 65? (RECORD BELOW FOR EACH ITEM ON LIST.)

	6a. You personally			
	Very Serious Problem	Somewhat Serious Problem	Hardly A Problem At All	Not Sure
1. Not having enough money to live on	___	___	___	___
2. Poor health	___	___	___	___
3. Loneliness	___	___	___	___
4. Poor housing	___	___	___	___
5. Not enough clothing	___	___	___	___
6. Not enough to do to keep busy	___	___	___	___
7. Fear of crime	___	___	___	___
8. Not enough friends	___	___	___	___
9. Not feeling needed	___	___	___	___
10. Not enough education	___	___	___	___
11. Not enough job opportunities	___	___	___	___
12. Not enough medical care	___	___	___	___

	6b. Most people over 65			
	Very Serious Problem	Somewhat Serious Problem	Hardly A Problem At All	Not Sure
1. Not having enough money to live on	___	___	___	___
2. Poor health	___	___	___	___
3. Loneliness	___	___	___	___
4. Poor housing	___	___	___	___
5. Not enough clothing	___	___	___	___
6. Not enough to do to keep busy	___	___	___	___
7. Fear of crime	___	___	___	___
8. Not enough friends	___	___	___	___
9. Not feeling needed	___	___	___	___

	6b. Most people over 65			
	Very Serious Problem	Somewhat Serious Problem	Hardly A Problem At All	Not Sure
10. Not enough education	____	____	____	____
11. Not enough job opportunities. . .	____	____	____	____
12. Not enough medical care.	____	____	____	____

7. We are interested in the way people are feeling these days. Looking at your present life situation, do you ever feel (READ LIST), or not? (RECORD BELOW FOR EACH ITEM ON LIST.)

	Ever Feel	Don't Feel	Not Feel
1. Particularly excited or interested in something	____	____	____
2. So restless you can't sit long in a chair	____	____	____
3. Proud because someone complimented you on something you had done	____	____	____
4. Very lonely or remote from other people	____	____	____
5. Pleased about having accomplished something	____	____	____
6. Bored.	____	____	____
7. On top of the world	____	____	____
8. Depressed or very unhappy	____	____	____
9. That things are going your way	____	____	____
10. Upset because someone criticized you	____	____	____

	17b. Most people over 65			
	Very Serious Problem	Somewhat Serious Problem	Hardly A Problem At All	Not Sure
1. The cost of buses and subways . . .	____	____	____	____
2. Difficulty in walking and climbing stairs	____	____	____	____
3. Danger of being robbed or attacked on the street	____	____	____	____
4. No buses or subways available for where they want to go	____	____	____	____
5. Their general health.	____	____	____	____
6. Not having a car or being able to drive	____	____	____	____
7. Other problems (SPECIFY)				
_____	____	____	____	____

18a. In your opinion, what makes someone a useful member of his or her community? Anything else?

18b. On the whole, do you feel that you personally are a very useful member of your community, a somewhat useful member or not a useful member of your community at all? (RECORD BELOW.)

18c. Do you feel most people over 65 are very useful members of their communities, somewhat useful members or not useful members of their communities at all? (RECORD BELOW.)

	18b. You personally	18c. Most people over 65
Very useful	_____	_____
Somewhat useful	_____	_____
Not useful at all	_____	_____
Not sure	_____	_____

SOURCE: Reproduced with permission from *Codebook for "The Myth and Reality of Aging,"* a survey conducted by Louis Harris and associates for the National Council on the Aging; prepared by the Duke University Center for the Study of Aging and Human Development under a grant from the Edna M. Clark Foundation.

V1.12.II.g
SALTER VIEW OF ELDERLY SCALE
C. A. Salter and C. deL. Slater, 1976

See the section on scoring, scale norms, and distribution in the abstract.

V1.12.II.h
PERCEPTIONS OF AGING
V. L. Bengtson, J. J. Dowd, D. H. Smith, and A. Inkeles, 1975

See the description of the instrument in the abstract.

V1.12.III.a
KOGAN-WALLACH SEMANTIC DIFFERENTIAL
N. Kogan and M. A. Wallach, 1961

Instructions were the standard semantic differential instructions given in Osgood (1957).

The 25 7-point, adjective-pair rating items were in the following order for each concept rated. Those with an asterisk were ultimately used as the evaluative factor scales in this analysis.

*1.	successful/unsuccessful	*14.	sick/healthy
2.	demanding/undemanding	15.	concluding/beginning
*3.	bad/good	16.	dominant/submissive
*4.	attractive/unattractive	17.	clean/dirty
5.	weak/strong	18.	hostile/friendly
6.	valuable/worthless	19.	wise/foolish
*7.	frustrating/rewarding	20.	strict/lenient
*8.	sad/happy	21.	interesting/boring
9.	calm/irritable	22.	relaxed/tense
10.	dependent/independent	23.	humble/proud
*11.	warm/cold	24.	selfish/unselfish
12.	active/passive	25.	broad/narrow
13.	slow/fast		

Concepts to be rated each appeared at the top of a separate page of items. The order of the concepts was the following:

1.	work	15.	old age
2.	family life	16.	sex
3.	future	17.	death
4.	baby	18.	authority

5.	older people	19.	myself
6.	foreigner	20.	youth
7.	love	21.	retirement
8.	middle age	22.	life
9.	Negro	23.	generosity
10.	elderly	24.	vigor
11.	my mother	25.	the ideal person
12.	American	26.	imagination
13.	leisure time	27.	good looks
14.	my father	28.	risk

These concepts reflected the following groups:

    work and leisure (1, 13, 21)
    majority and minority groups (5, 6, 9, 12)
    family and interpersonal relations (2, 7, 11, 14, 16, 18)
    developmental stages of life (4, 8, 10, 15, 17, 20)
    psychological vs. physical attributes (23, 24, 26, 27)
    self concept (19, 25)
    Weltanschauung (3, 22, 28)

SOURCE: N. Kogan and M. A. Wallach. "Age Changes in Values and Attitudes." *Journal of Gerontology*, 1961, 16: 275. Reprinted by permission of author and publisher.

V1.12.III.b
EISDORFER-ALTROCCHI SEMANTIC DIFFERENTIAL
C. Eisdorfer and J. Altrocchi, 1961

The 20 semantic differential items are grouped below by the factor they are thought to reflect. In administration, the order was randomized and the scales were left-right reversed so that half were presented with the more undesirable alternative at the left.

Evaluative factor adjective pairs:

    wise/foolish
    intelligent/ignorant
    happy/sad
    trustworthy/untrustworthy
    rich/poor
    warm/cold
    clean/dirty
    safe/dangerous
    relaxed/tense
    valuable/worthless
    healthy/sick
    effective/ineffective
    good/bad

Potency factor adjective pairs:

    strong/weak
    rugged/delicate

Activity factor adjective pairs:

    active/passive
    fast/slow

Understandability factor adjective pairs:
    predictable/unpredictable
    understandable/mysterious
    familiar/strange

SOURCE: C. Eisdorfer and J. Altrocchi. "A Comparison of Attitudes toward Old Age and Mental Illness." *Journal of Gerontology*, 1961, 16: 340-43. Reprinted by permission of authors and publishers.

V1.12.III.c
ACROSS-AGE SEMANTIC DIFFERENTIAL
M. Petersen, 1976

(stimulus person)

pleasant	unpleasant
cooperative	uncooperative
considerate	inconsiderate
flexible	inflexible
open minded	closed minded
understanding	non-understanding
loving	unloving
active	passive
strong	weak
enthusiastic	unenthusiastic
fast	slow
alert	non-alert
independent	dependent
ambitious, hardworking	lacking ambition, lazy
young	old

SOURCE: M. Petersen. "A Cross-Age Semantic Differential for Social Evaluation." Paper presented to the Annual Conference of the International Communication Association, Portland, April 14-17, 1976.

V1.12.III.d
ATTITUDES TOWARD THE AGED
H. A. Rosencranz and T. E. McNevin, 1969

Below are listed a series of polar adjectives accompanied by a scale. You are asked to place a check mark along the scale at a point which in your judgment best describes the social object indicated. Make each item a separate and independent judgment. Do not worry or puzzle over individual items. Do not try to remember how you have marked earlier items even though they may seem to have been similar. It is your first impression or immediate feeling about each item that is wanted.

SOCIAL OBJECT:_____

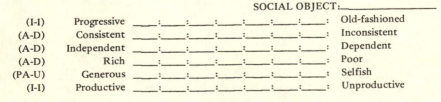

(I-I)	Progressive	___:___:___:___:___:___:___:	Old-fashioned
(A-D)	Consistent	___:___:___:___:___:___:___:	Inconsistent
(A-D)	Independent	___:___:___:___:___:___:___:	Dependent
(A-D)	Rich	___:___:___:___:___:___:___:	Poor
(PA-U)	Generous	___:___:___:___:___:___:___:	Selfish
(I-I)	Productive	___:___:___:___:___:___:___:	Unproductive

(I-I)	Busy	___:___:___:___:___:___:___:	Idle
(A-D)	Secure	___:___:___:___:___:___:___:	Insecure
(I-I)	Strong	___:___:___:___:___:___:___:	Weak
(I-I)	Healthy	___:___:___:___:___:___:___:	Unhealthy
(I-I)	Active	___:___:___:___:___:___:___:	Passive
(PA-U)	Handsome	___:___:___:___:___:___:___:	Ugly
(PA-U)	Cooperative	___:___:___:___:___:___:___:	Uncooperative
(PA-U)	Optimistic	___:___:___:___:___:___:___:	Pessimistic
(A-D)	Satisfied	___:___:___:___:___:___:___:	Dissatisfied
(I-I)	Expectant	___:___:___:___:___:___:___:	Resigned
(PA-U)	Flexible	___:___:___:___:___:___:___:	Inflexible
(PA-U)	Hopeful	___:___:___:___:___:___:___:	Dejected
(A-D)	Organized	___:___:___:___:___:___:___:	Disorganized
(PA-U)	Happy	___:___:___:___:___:___:___:	Sad
(PA-U)	Friendly	___:___:___:___:___:___:___:	Unfriendly
(PA-U)	Neat	___:___:___:___:___:___:___:	Untidy
(PA-U)	Trustful	___:___:___:___:___:___:___:	Suspicious
(A-D)	Self-Reliant	___:___:___:___:___:___:___:	Dependent
(I-I)	Liberal	___:___:___:___:___:___:___:	Conservative
(A-D)	Certain	___:___:___:___:___:___:___:	Uncertain
(PA-U)	Tolerant	___:___:___:___:___:___:___:	Intolerant
(PA-U)	Pleasant	___:___:___:___:___:___:___:	Unpleasant
(PA-U)	Ordinary	___:___:___:___:___:___:___:	Eccentric
(I-I)	Aggressive	___:___:___:___:___:___:___:	Defensive
(PA-U)	Exciting	___:___:___:___:___:___:___:	Dull
(A-D)	Decisive	___:___:___:___:___:___:___:	Indecisive

The dimension containing each scale is indicated parenthetically by the following notations:

Instrument-Ineffective Dimension = (I-I) 9 items
Autonomous-Dependent Dimension = (A-D) 9 items
Personal Acceptability-Unacceptability Dimension = (PA-U) 14 items

Each of the 32 scales was scored from 1 to 7. For example:

Progressive _1_ : _2_ : _3_ : _4_ : _5_ : _6_ : _7_ : Old-fashioned

Factor scores were obtained by adding the score values of adjectives contained in each dimension.

SOURCE: H. A. Rosencranz and T. E. McNevin. "A Factor Analysis of Attitudes toward the Aged." *The Gerontologist*, 1969, 9: 55–59. Reprinted by permission of author and publisher.

V1.12.IV.a
GOLDE-KOGAN SENTENCE-COMPLETION ASSESSMENT
P. Golde and N. Kogan, 1959

		Percent of Responses	
Item Sentence Stems	Scoring Categories	Experimental Group	Control Group
1E. Most old people's friendships are. . .	A. Enduring, deep	43.2	14.3
	B. Impermanent, shallow	13.6	28.6

GOLDE-KOGAN SENTENCE-COMPLETION ASSESSMENT — *Continued*

Item Sentence Stems	Scoring Categories	Percent of Responses Experimental Group	Percent of Responses Control Group
	C. Positive adjectives not included above	27.3	30.9
	D. Negative adjectives not included above	4.5	21.4
	E. S cites reason for friendship	11.4	4.8
		N=44	N=42
2E. In general, old people need . . .	A. Assistance (e.g. help, care)	30.2	7.9
	B. Security (e.g. personal well-being)	16.3	28.9
2C. In general, people need . . .	C. Positive responses from others (e.g. love)	53.5	63.2
		N=43	N=38
3E. When I am with an old person, I . . .	A. Negative feelings (e.g. discomfort, tension)	27.7	12.5
3C. When I am with another person, I . . .	B. Positive feelings (e.g. well-being, ease)	16.7	27.5
	C. Passive, subordinate response (e.g. respect)	38.9	2.5
	D. General outgoing response (e.g. talk)	16.7	57.5
		N=36	N=40
4E. One of the greatest fears of many old people is . . .	A. Death or dying	40.8	35.9
	B. Loneliness, isolation	30.6	12.8
4C. One of the greatest fears is . . .	C. Rejection, being disliked	6.1	20.5
	D. Anxiety response (e.g. insecurity)	4.1	28.2
	E. Loss of powers, dependence	18.4	2.6
		N=49	N=39
5E. Old people's appearance . . .	A. Important	7.4	47.6
	B. Denial or qualification of importance	7.4	19.0
5C. People's appearance . . .	C. Index of kind of person	18.5	28.6
	D. Positive descriptive adjectives	25.9	4.8
	E. Explicit age related adjectives	40.8	0.0
		N=27	N=42
6E. Old people tend to resent . . .	A. Younger people	25.0	0.0
	B. Overconcern and intrusion	10.0	34.5
6C. People tend to resent . . .	C. Rejection, lack of concern	10.0	24.1
	D. Criticism, authority	7.5	31.0
	E. Condescension, being patronized, helped	32.5	6.9
	F. Change or novelty	15.0	3.5
		N=40	N=29

GOLDE-KOGAN SENTENCE-COMPLETION ASSESSMENT— *Continued*

Item Sentence Stems	Scoring Categories	Percent of Responses	
		Experimental Group	Control Group
7E. In our society, grand-parents often are . . .	A. Over-indulgent	20.5	26.3
	B. Controlling, withholding freedom	17.9	21.1
7C. In our society, parents often are . . .	C. Undervalued, neglected	23.1	2.6
	D. Positive traits not included above	23.1	15.8
	E. Negative traits not included above	15.4	34.2
		N=39	N=38
8E. Sex for most old people . . .	A. Negligible or unimportant, past	82.9	4.9
8C. Sex for most people . . .	B. Essential	0.0	29.3
	C. Negative, distasteful connotation, taboo	7.1	24.4
	D. Positive, pleasurable connotation	0.0	41.4
		N=42	N=41
9E. Most of the old people I have known . . .	A. Response in terms of *S*'s relation to other	6.3	31.7
	B. Positive descriptive adjectives	75.0	48.8
	C. Negative descriptive adjectives	18.7	19.5
		N=32	N=41
10E. At 60, I will be . . .	A. Old age or its approach	21.0	16.2
10C. At 40, I will be . . .	B. Retirement	15.8	2.7
	C. Death	15.8	0.0
	D. Middle age or its approach	0.0	13.5
	E. Marriage, family	5.3	35.2
	F. Active, interested	36.8	10.8
	G. Success, contentment, security	5.3	21.6
		N=38	N=37
11E. For an old man, work is often . . .	A. Tedious nature of work	18.2	33.3
	B. Difficult nature of work	36.4	6.7
11C. For a man, work is often . . .	C. Necessity, economic function of work	13.6	31.1
	D. Psychological importance to individual	18.2	11.1
	E. General pleasantness of work	13.6	17.8
		N=44	N=45
12E. When I think of my relations with my grandparents . . .	A. Indication of a satisfactory relation	58.1	81.6
	B. Indication of		

GOLDE-KOGAN SENTENCE-COMPLETION ASSESSMENT — *Continued*

Item Sentence Stems	Scoring Categories	Percent of Responses	
		Experimental Group	Control Group
12C. When I think of my relations with my parents . . .	unsatisfactory relation	23.3	16.3
	C. Non-committal (e.g. failure to remember)	18.6	2.1
		N=43	N=49
13E. Old people, by and large, hope . . .	A. Peace, security, comfort	40.0	23.3
	B. Happiness and contentment	12.5	27.9
13C. People, by and large, hope . . .	C. Longevity and health	30.0	11.6
	D. Success and money, achievement, fame	2.5	32.6
	E. Independence, usefulness	15.0	4.6
		N=40	N=43
14E. When a woman becomes old . . .	A. Loses attractiveness	23.1	25.6
	B. Anxiety over loss of attractiveness	23.1	10.3
14C. When a woman becomes older . . .	C. *S* cites negative emotional aspects of age	46.2	41.0
	D. *S* cites increased understanding of others	7.6	23.1
		N=26	N=39
15E. The thing I like best about old people . . .	A. Sincerity and related adjectives	7.9	21.6
15C. The thing I like best about people . . .	B. Kindness and related adjectives	23.7	10.8
	C. Serenity and related adjectives	23.7	0.0
	D. Gaiety, humor and related adjectives	10.5	21.6
	E. Intelligence, wisdom, and related qualities	15.8	8.1
	F. Interactional qualities (e.g. companionability)	18.4	37.9
		N=38	N=37
16E. Many old people think the younger generation . . .	A. Old-fashioned, narrow-minded qualities	0.0	96.3
	B. Foolish, frivolous qualities	35.3	0.0
16C. Many people think the older generation . . .	C. Wild, immoral, bad qualities	64.7	3.7
		N=34	N=27
17E. The thing I like least about old people . . .	A. Controlling, interfering qualities	21.9	14.3
	B. Rigid, prejudiced		
	C. Irritability	28.1	17.1
	D. Hypocrisy	0.0	34.3
	E. Selfishness, miserliness	6.3	31.4
	F. Dependency	15.6	2.9
		N=32	N=35

GOLDE-KOGAN SENTENCE-COMPLETION ASSESSMENT – *Continued*

Item Sentence Stems	Scoring Categories	Percent of Responses	
		Experimental Group	Control Group
18E. One of the greatest pleasures of old people is . . .	A. Love and sex	0.0	41.7
	B. Companionship	55.0	25.0
	C. Leisure time activities	22.5	33.3
18C. One of the greatest pleasures of many people is . . .	D. Reminiscing	22.5	0.0
		N=40	N=36
19E. For many old people, death . . .	A. Feared, frightening	27.3	82.4
	B. Positive (e.g. not feared)	39.4	0.0
19C. For many people, death . . .	C. Inevitable	33.3	17.6
		N=33	N=34
20E. When I am old, I would want to be like . . .	A. Myself (or ideal self)	7.5	24.4
	B. Mother or father	17.5	29.3
	C. Grandparents	32.5	4.9
	D. Other relatives or friends	2.5	14.6
	E. No one in particular	2.5	9.7
	F. Some famous person	37.5	17.1
		N=40	N=41
21E. When an old person I do not know sits down next to me on a train or bus, I . . .	A. No special behavior, feelings	53.8	28.9
	B. Interest in other (e.g. observe, talk)	28.2	53.3
21C. When a person I do not know sits down next to me on a train or bus, I . . .	C. Feelings of strain or withdrawal	18.0	17.8
		N=39	N=45
22E. When an old person is walking very slowly right in front of me, I feel . . .	A. Pity	22.5	3.3
	B. Impatience, annoyance	17.5	13.3
	C. Aggression, superiority	7.5	33.3
	D. Warmth, protectiveness	12.5	26.7
	E. Feel like passing him	40.0	23.4
		N=40	N=30
23C. When a young child is walking very slowly right in front of me, I feel . . .			
24E. When I think of being old, I . . .	A. Negative factors (e.g. fear, depression)	53.5	47.4
24C. When I think of growing older, I . . .	B. Acceptance, lack of concern	11.6	18.4
	C. Denial, difficulty in conceiving of it	20.9	2.6
	D. Emphasis on future achievement and experience	14.0	31.6
		N=43	N=38

GOLDE-KOGAN SENTENCE-COMPLETION ASSESSMENT — *Continued*

Item Sentence Stems	Scoring Categories	Percent of Responses	
		Experimental Group	Control Group
25E. Most old people's lives are . . .	A. Negative (e.g. lack of stimulation, happiness)	68.4	77.5
25C. Most people's lives are . . .	B. Positive (e.g. happy, fulfilled)	31.6	22.5
		N=38	N=40

SOURCE: P. Golde and N. Kogan. "A Sentence Completion Procedure for Assessing Attitudes toward Old People." *Journal of Gerontology*, 1959, 14: 361–63. Table 1. Reprinted by permission of authors and publisher.

V1.12.IV.b
CHILDREN'S ATTITUDES TOWARD THE ELDERLY
R. K. Jantz, C. Seefeldt, A. Galper, and K. Serock, 1976

This copyrighted instrument is available from the authors of the study.

V1.12.IV.c
ADJECTIVE CHECKLIST
B. S. Aaronson, 1966

See tables 12-25 and 12-26 in the abstract.

V1.12.IV.d
CHILDREN'S PERCEPTIONS OF THE ELDERLY
T. Hickey, L. A. Hickey, and R. A. Kalish, 1968

See the description of the instrument in the abstract.

Indexes

Index of Subjects

Index of Names

David J. Mangen is assistant professor of gerontology and sociology at the Leonard Davis School of
Gerontology, University of Southern California. He
is associate editor of *Research on Aging: A Quarterly
of Social Gerontology.*

Warren A. Peterson is director of the Centers on
Aging Studies, University of Missouri-Kansas City
and University of Missouri-Columbia, and professor
of sociology at University of Missouri-Kansas City.